ArchiLab's
Earth Buildings

ArchiLab's EARTH

Radical Experiments

BUILDINGS

IN LAND ARCHITECTURE

Edited by Marie-Ange Brayer and Béatrice Simonot

With over 600 colour illustrations

 Thames & Hudson

_04

This book is published in conjunction with the ArchiLab conference that took place in 2002 in Orléans, France. It was sponsored by the city of Orléans and organized by Marie-Ange Brayer and Béatrice Simonot.

First published in the United Kingdom in 2003 by Thames & Hudson Ltd, 181A High Holborn, London WC1V 7QX

ArchiLab © 2003 The City of Orléans
Architects' text and images © 2003 the architects
Essays © 2003 the authors
English translations © 2003 Thames & Hudson Ltd, London

Conception: Marie-Ange Brayer and Béatrice Simonot
Coordination: Marie-Ange Brayer and Béatrice Simonot
Advisory committee: Anand Bhatt, Manuel Gausa, Bart Lootsma, Frédéric Migayrou, Yves Nacher
Translation into English: Simon Pleasance, David Wilson
Design: Laurent Pinon, with Sébastien Morel (with thanks to Antoine Jackson, Stanislas Lefort, Augustin Bouvet)

British Library Cataloguing-in-Publication Data
A catalogue record for this book is available from the British Library

ISBN 0-500-28412-1

Printed and bound in Italy

Preface

ArchiLab is a unique platform in France, indeed in Europe, for meetings and exchanges between teams of architects from all corners of the world who represent the cutting edge of architecture. Thanks to a link forged with the FRAC Centre, the City of Orléans has since 1999 staged an exhibition of the most innovative architectural creations. Orléans has thus become, along with other international architecture forums, a place recognized for reflecting on the forces at work in architecture today and for enhancing public awareness of contemporary architectural culture.

The theme of this fourth edition of ArchiLab is 'Earth Economics', which implies the appreciation and understanding of local environments and considers architects' practical responses to a complex environmental system. The organizers of the exhibition, Marie-Ange Brayer and Béatrice Simonot, have assembled under this heading a selection of projects that demonstrate the exceptional diversity of architectural conception.

Several cultural establishments and institutional partners from our own city are associated with the staging of ArchiLab: the Fine Arts Museum, the Institute of Visual Arts, the Médiathèque, as well as the CAUE at Loiret, the architectural section of the Central Region and the departmental architectural service. ArchiLab is also the outcome of close and durable partnerships that have contributed to its success and international renown, notably with France's Ministry of Culture and Communications and the Regional Cultural Affairs Directorate, each member dedicated to promoting better knowledge and understanding of cultural architecture.

The quality of this cooperative work helps to bring architecture out from an ivory tower that is often perceived as sealed, exclusive and removed from everyday preoccupations. Exposed to public gaze and enquiry, architecture must propose varied responses to the challenge of designing and constructing our living spaces. Thus Orléans, with ArchiLab and its associated events, brings to the fore the avant-garde in contemporary creativity. I wish to thank all those who have helped to make ArchiLab 2002 a reality and to further its role as a forum for discovery and dialogue.

Serge Grouard

CONTENTS

ARCHITECTS

Essays

Béatrice Simonot

Forces and Form

It is a commonplace that the environment is a central element of architectural practice. There has been a long tradition of environmentalist architecture, but currently it is very much to the fore in the thinking of many architects. How, then, do we define the environment today?

The destruction of nature has brought about a general feeling of anguish, which has made ecology a priority in the present-day world: environmental and social ecology, respect for and protection of our surroundings, development of things that will last, prevention rather than cure — these are problems that must be solved today by what is variously known as green or bio-climatic or ecological architecture. For the most part, these terms cover innovative technologies, recycled or adapted materials, cheap methods of construction to suit the needs of the time. But this sort of progress does not clarify for us which nature we are to defend and how we are to defend it.

What concept of nature do we actually have today? And what responsibilities can the architect imagine himself facing up to in a society that is evolving so fast? The drastic mutations that have punctuated this short period in our history, a permanently changing environment, an ever-increasing subservience to market forces — all of these underpin the general feeling that traditional attitudes and practices have become irrelevant, and now it is necessary to have a radical rethink if we are to meet the challenges of the modern world.

The environment is simultaneously local and global. Globalization is transforming what was once local, and it is taking place through a complex process of acculturation, by which the dominant, hegemonic culture intermingles with the local culture in a form of cultural recycling.

What is emerging from this process is neither a dogma nor a consensus that might conform to certain common values and lead towards a 'realistic' universalism or a 'resistant' contextualism; instead, we have a common critical basis: the need to come up with new methods of analysing every dimension of our hugely extended, ever-changing environment — natural and urban, economic, political, social and cultural. A comparison between different approaches will reveal the same preoccupation with context allied to analysis of the forces, local and global, that shape the area of intervention.

How are we to grasp all the conditions that underlie the production of architecture? How are we to cope with the evolutionary process, to promote nature and natural resources, to create alternative territories, to make plans that will take into account the workings of time and the unforeseen? There are urban and architectural strategies now taking shape that are designed to cope with the complexities and constant changes of our environment, and which are having a profound effect on the conceptual reasoning that relates to 'new territories'. They are not bound up with some kind of back-to-nature movement, nourished by the nostalgia that pits nature against culture; nor are they engendered by an ethical, defensive approach dictated by protectionism; what is driving these strategies is the desire for active intervention coupled with a concern that all proposals must work in synergy with the environment, which is defined as a field of energy and situation. With the building anchored in its location, and the spirit of the location giving rise to the building, old ideas give way to new. Architecture no longer presents itself in terms of reaction, but becomes proactive, seeking to understand how the exploitation of natural resources, both social and material, may determine the structuring of a space. How do the forces that lie between the natural elements and the public spaces interact and express themselves?

For many architects today, the heart of the profession lies in the indissoluble trinity of research, experimentation and practice, and their quest is for systems of representation, for processes that can both adapt to and anticipate the rules of the game in order to cope with present and future complexities.

Architects who are genuinely engaged in a global society are above all concerned with comparing propositions in all their diversity, identifying discourses and rooting out their meanings: the economy of the land, of the soil, of resources — ecology being just one of many aspects. It is interesting for architects to grasp the following ideas by way of project experience rather than through a priori definitions:

⬨ To reassemble a world split between humankind and nature, between humankind and its social and political environment. To 'domesticate nature' and to 'naturalize the domestic' is Tezuka's aim, which may extend as far as what Kengo Kuma calls a 'disappearance of architecture'.

⬨ To reinvent a landscape based on the analysis of spatial and temporal processes and of the accumulations and energies that ceaselessly deconstruct and reconstruct territory (Tom Leader), or to orchestrate the forces that exist between natural elements and public spaces (Field Operations).

⬨ To create a new topography, which may sometimes border on imitation, in order to establish a metaphysical relationship between the natural and the artificial by restoring the traces of an original geography (Francis Soler) or another kind of landscape archaeology, with a view to restoring history (Stefan Tischer).

⬨ To harmonize architecture with its environment by devising intelligent technical systems that will be ecologically and economically viable (Françoise-Hélène Jourda) or constructing buildings like ecosystems (T. R. Hamzah & Yeang Sdn Bhd).

⬨ To create new territories, an artificial topography that will weave together links between interior and exterior and blur relations between the observer and the observed (cloud 9), to define architecture as landscape and landscape as architecture (laN+). Natural and artificial are no longer antitheses. The artificial world is omnipresent. Space is a live system in which architecture plays like a relational link.

For b & k+, it is the definition of nature that has changed; the landscape is primarily political, virtual and technological, and architecture must position itself at the point of conflict between the landscape and physical space.

For Actar, architecture is geography. The site is not a fixed, ready-made container but a field of multiple forces; architecture is not an object for consolidating the characteristic features of a place, but it must add features and create links that unite the natural with the artificial, the building with the landscape, the town with the territory — not confronting one with the other, but bringing about new combinations and new interchanges of information.

Vicente Guallart wants a new contract with nature, to represent the real world starting from the virtual, and giving a virtual representation of a real world that is no longer either town or nature. Similarly, Dagmar Richter constructs a representation of the world that is unstable and devoid of any context — or rather she makes an artificial reconstruction of it.

⬨ To divert the processes of standardization that are linked to the economic and cultural context and induced by globalization and that imply the use of standard products and standard modes of production.

Architecture is an industrial activity. Jones carries to its extreme the idea of an architectural machine, piling up industrial containers in order to put together a group of houses, but he also counters the problem of uniformity by introducing rail systems along which the constituent modules can slide, allowing sufficient flexibility to give each unit its own individuality.

LWPAC follow a similar line, leaning towards a complex and perpetually evolving world; on different scales, from the urban project to the design object, they produce models, which they update according to the demands of the situation, so that they can make them more flexible and adaptable and can transform standard objects into individual works.

Servo are even more radical: their agency is scattered all round the world, which enables everyone to experience a different local, economic, political and cultural situation. Collectively they set up global lines of reference (Servoline), which each individual then modifies according to the particular context and recycles on different scales; this enables them continually to produce unique pieces constructed on a common base.

■ To resist standard demands and reinvent programmes, transforming the rules and conventions within the natural, urban and social parameters that define the environment, nARCHITECTS tend to develop clear strategies whose apparently contradictory dynamics mix the possibilities opened up by new or existing resources and technologies with local models that persist in coexisting, no matter what the situation. This is the paradox on which their architecture is built.

Manuelle Gautrand also establishes different functional strategies in the face of a complex and evolving culture; for a cultural building she proposes nomadic cells that can be recycled in different spatial configurations.

TeamMinus operates within the context of a China that is currently in upheaval. It tries to solve problems by way of localized and limited proposals that claim to have an educational function in relation to the effects of an unprecedented and anarchic economic development, while leaving room for local situations that are completely underdeveloped.

■ To proceed along minimal lines, towards an economy of resources, by recycling forms, materials and methods, replacing luxury with maximum output from the standpoint of the way of life that a building can allow (Eduard Bru).

Economy of form and abstraction are the watchwords for Propeller Z, who take the shortest and most functional direct route to coping with constraints, avoiding all formalism, all identifiable style and for the most part using means that rarely conform to convention.

Atelier Bow-wow apply their analyses of the metropolis of Tokyo to the most difficult, most extreme conditions and recycle them in the operational modes of their projects — for instance that of 'smaller houses' — which verge on the absolute minimum.

■ To devise strategies of urban action that correspond to the complexities and continual transformations of the environment.

Resolutely experimental, Block sets out to 'contaminate' the town with mini-actions along the lines of 'copy and paste and transform'. These actions transplant one identifiable urban world into another, mixing together objects and signs from unconnected territories and inserting ephemeral, constantly changing elements that bear witness to the heterogeneity of the town and propagate the concept of its endless transformation.

■ To conceive new methods of analysis and new instruments of urban planning that will introduce a dynamic, open dimension into a traditionally static procedure that is tied to decision-making at a single given moment. This is the subject of the research carried out by RAD, who recently dissociated themselves from the Asian branch of OMA when they proposed scenarios that would take into account anarchic urban phenomena and models borrowed from biotechnology or artificial intelligence.

HOST share the same ambitions when they construct theoretical matrices in order to examine relationships between the variables at work in a given territory and to understand how they function, so that they can be applied to different local situations.

■ To cope with the density and the degradation of natural and suburban environments — an acute problem in the Netherlands — by developing a three-dimensional concept of an ideal town: this is the collective project of the postgraduate laboratory of the Berlage Institute in Rotterdam, under the direction of Winy Maas (MVRDV) and Wiel Arets; their 3D-City is a cube-shaped town that reconstructs in three dimensions the various elements and phenomena constituting a world that is nothing more than a vast urban field subject to the laws of globalization.

■ To negotiate before acting is the guiding principle for Chora. Their starting-point is the idea that local environments are permeated by multiple and global movements, which bring profound changes to the town and its increasingly heterogeneous population. It is this emerging population, consisting of intermingled identities, that must be identified through its conduct, its beliefs and its representations if it is to become actively involved in its own evolution. The task is to transcribe a spontaneous way of life into scenarios that will prolong it, and to make the diversity into a dynamic force that can no longer be the object of collective planning but will instead be the subject of actions negotiated between participants who are informed and aware of all the upheavals.

■ To create a fusion between the body, the environment and technology (NOX). The town and architecture can no longer be considered as areas defined by material limits, but are the results of multiple, living experiences in which human conduct depends on perpetual interaction between the place itself, the new media, magazines, television, movements and meetings. In their planning project for La Défense in Paris, NOX adopt a similar approach to that of the Situationists, who through experience of drift prioritize the dimension of time over that of space; NOX transcribe multiple forms of behaviour into a dynamic and fluid schema in order to construct a model that will leave the field free for every individual experience.

Offshore go even further in promoting the concept of disappearing borders. Territory will be no more than the representation of a network of relations between inhabitants, whose links are to be conceived not in terms of space but in terms of communication.

Along the lines of the 'Flying Doctor' — an Australian system for delivering medical care to far-flung communities — they propose a planning concept based on sharing time, not space.

'To rebuild the unity of the world', 'to reinvent a landscape', 'to make', 'to create new territories', 'to conceive', 'to construct', 'to deal with' — these terms make up a list of practices that correspond to a mission of production, of engagement in the world that is generally entrusted to the architect. What is different here is the underlying and unanimous conviction that this engagement cannot take place without detailed analysis of the places concerned and the increasingly rapid and diverse upheavals to which they are subjected. Research into and analysis of the forces at work have become a sine qua non for the architect's activity.

Whatever the scale of the project envisaged, ranging from single object to complete town, form can no longer be considered as a unit in itself; it both arises out of and goes hand in hand with a system of dynamic, ephemeral and unstable forces.

There is no escaping the influence of globalization on localities. Most of the proposals listed concern small, localized steps towards inventing or defining a new relationship with the world; they seek to realize ideas that might appear contradictory. It is a matter of continually devising pluralistic solutions that will lead to positive development, to a dynamic flowering as opposed to the prevailing homogenization and standardization.

In this way architecture does not merely accompany the turbulence of our modern world, but instead becomes an active force of revelation and challenge, generating a pluralist community that can defy the synthetic system developed by globalization. ☑

Marie-Ange Brayer

On the Surface of the Earth, in Search of the Chorographic Body

'The only Utopia possible today is purely quantitative.'
Archizoom

Through the window of a train that stretches out as an endless corridor, a man looks out at the landscape. It's a strange landscape, insofar as its naturalness seems to have been fashioned entirely by man. It's a manufactured landscape. The undulations, the fine furrows, the gentle geological folds express an unusual orderliness — that of a smooth, domesticated geography, terra firma, yet, at the same time, infirm. This landscape surprises us: it combines the detachment of the observer, for whom it is an object of contemplation or even reverie, with a chorographic view in which the overdeveloped details seem excessively formal. Between the view and the representation lies the geographical earth, an indissoluble whole. This image encapsulates the paradox that characterizes many architectural experiences of the 'earth', ranging from earth-matter to the earth surface that covers the entire world, from material ground down into the finest particles to a surface for inscription or incision. While one can only view a landscape and not live in it, one can only work with the earth, occupy it, penetrate it, live on it. The earth, as the original matrix, as 'chora', offers the body a refuge, a shelter. The chorographic is a liminal region between earth and landscape, between body and representation, which developed alongside landscape painting in the 16th century. Painting and cartography tended to intermingle, as can be seen from Brueghel's landscapes or Georg Hoefnagel's cartographical views. Between the surface and its depths, between landscape painting and earth 'mapping', Max Peintner's drawing (Ill. 1) throws confusion, because it fuses together the local and the global. For Denis Cosgrove, the fact of 'thinking global' and 'acting local' is reflected in chorographic views, which are 'interconnections of localities'.[1] The chorographic view, which absorbs the whole into the part, is a charting of the earth, a domesticated morphology of the landscape. Instead of a unified system of control, we have 'multiperspectivism', an 'infinity of local perspectives'[2] that spring from the equivalence of bodies in the chorographic model. Simultaneously surface and relief, the chorographic landscape with its flattened curves opens out on to flexible geometrical forms, moving spatial structures, which integrate bodies that are both singular and fractal.

The chorographic landscape is levelled out by the grid. The latter compartmentalizes as a sort of tabular extroversion of the earth, a taxonomy of the world. Between surface and field, suspended between embodiment and disembodiment, it has given rise to the 'histograms of architecture' (1969) of Superstudio, who cover everything from movable objects to environments, from architecture to towns (Ill. 2). The continuous, isotropic surface of the grid stretches out like a second skin over the world, absorbing all dimensions and contexts. The grid has transformed the earth into a 'continuous monument'. There is no architecture here: the earth has become an infrastructural landscape, an all-embracing crust that lies beneath the grid, radically destabilizing our foundations. This 'continuous monument', which has absorbed the consistency of the earth, presents itself as an immutable image, without beginning and without end. It forms just one single world, one single 'nature'. It is a global environment that transcends all localities. While the modern landscape came up against frontiers, flowed into a horizon and disappeared into the depths, the earth as patterned by the grid plunges us into a unified landscape with no borders, no safety barriers. 'The first territorial interventions, ironic and conceptual, were ideological models which were to guide the architectural project by placing it in conflict with existing realizations and with geography'.[3] In Archizoom's 'No-Stop City' (1970), 'the urban artefact is the result of a purely quantitative process, independent of the quality of the architecture.'[4] Archizoom developed 'a practically infinite urban construction, in which architecture is no more than a form of soil exploitation'. Here the town seems to be a continuous structure, stripped of 'architectural images'. 'Nature, external to the urban model, once more became totally autonomous. It was no longer contaminated by architectural elements that were meant to endow it with cultural significance. It remained a neutral field, beyond all value systems, accessible to direct, physical cognizance'.[5] 'Domestic and urban furnishings coincided completely'.[6] Not architecture or geography alone, but all the interwoven structures of these radical utopias pull us into a world where the earth is purely self-referential. Here the latter no longer accumulates the remains of the chorographic landscape, which called for the 'incorporation' of the exterior, but instead it extends into a multiplicity of connecting soils, which cannot be pinned down to any original state. There is no longer any interior or any exterior; the earth is a vast domestic field that stretches out into infinity.[7]

Ill. 1
Max Peintner, 'Corridor Train', 1970, in Max Peintner, *Blind Passenger as Blind Passenger*,
Graz, Neue Galerie Graz, Hatje Cantz Verlag, 2000.

The 'expanded field' demanded by Rosalind Krauss for sculpture[8] has taken over architecture, which has given up its status as an object and instead has become a system of production – a complex, multidimensional environment that is a hybrid of chorographic landscape and diagram. For the gigantic Yokohama terminal, FOA are currently developing a tectonic floor that is like an extension of the earth's surface – a surface with differential curves like the artificial undulations of a chorographic landscape, simultaneously local and global. 'The accent is on the extensive development of the earth's surface as a flexible and continuous matrix, which effectively binds together the increasingly disparate elements of our environment'.[9] According to Bart Lootsma, this process of extending the earth is the same as that used by OMA and Rem Koolhaas. In OMA's projects, the building resembles 'a frame consisting of floors'. The ground is not a substratum but is repeated on all levels, and so the upward accumulation of floors seems like a continuation and ceaseless catalysis of the ground, which itself echoes the 'surface of the earth'.[10] For Lootsma, this 'continuity in folds of the floor' is meant to be a 'topographical extension of the landscape'. The architecture that emerges from this accumulation of 'earth surfaces' will also give rise to the 'light urbanism' advocated by MVRDV. Similarly, ACTAR in Barcelona demand an 'osmotic ground', fusing earth and map, in 'operational landscapes' which develop by way of colonization, infiltration, insertion, camouflage and modelling of the earth. (LAND)ARCH talk of: 'carpets: earth on earth; relief: surface=earth; folds: crossings of the earth; furrows: scratching the earth'. The earth is an intersection of lines, a tangle of bands that form a growing grid. The map is an 'extruded'[11] territory, which enables us to grasp the infrastructure of the landscape. ACTAR and Guallart resort to fractal geometry in order to take readings of the earth. 'A changing mode of representation', the fractal makes it possible to inscribe cartography directly into the landscape that it describes (V. Guallart) 'The buildings are mountains' for Vicente Guallart, and the map imposes reversibility between earth and landscape. In Guallart's 'City of 1000 Geographies' and Rem Koolhaas's homage to 'New York Delirium', the relief of the earth, with its bumps and its fractal irregularities, has generated an architecture that is an evolving cross between geometry and infiltration of the earth, and is itself a chorographic landscape. An insular earth.

Ill. 2
Superstudio, 'The Continuous Monument: Canyon 1', 1970, in Jim Burns, *Arthropods*.

Men levitate from fault to fault, from void to void.'
Claude Parent

According to Manuel de Landa, the history of the world is the history of 'energy–matter', a 'geological account' of dynamic elements (flow of energy, non-linear causality), which we share with rocks, mountains and other inanimate, historical structures.[12] He regards towns as ecosystems, aggregated co-existences, continual interactions, and 'each accumulated layer is animated from within by self-organizing processes'.[13] The morphogenesis of this geological landscape – simultaneously local and global – resembles that of digital processes, refined by current technologies that have given rise to mutable geographical entities between cartography and territory. What is special about these entities is that they abolish the frontiers between interior and exterior, absorbing the outside into the inside, projecting the inside on to the outside, in such a way that the landscape abandons its exteriority and becomes domesticated. New forms of spatial construction have come into place and, as if echoing the tabular, quantitative utopias of Superstudio or Archizoom, they can be adapted to all scales – domestic, architectural and urban – as can be seen in the current projects of Servo, for instance. Here domestic space is the earth itself, and our own environment is a chorographic body.

The earth is loose, friable, unstable soil. For Bernard Cache 'there is no object, however small, that does not have its geographical component'. 'Architecture assumes a list of external images, and this is constituted precisely by the geographical image',[14] while 'the geographical surfaces' are the 'privileged models of fractal objects',[15] since they contain an aleatory component. Computer-generated ideas and digitally operated mechanical production, which allow surfaces of variable curvature, have incorporated the territory 'internally', according to Cache, or in other words the exterior has taken over the interior, which itself has become a new form of geography, of 'earth furniture' (Ill. 3). Objectile's production can therefore be applied to all contexts, that of furniture being the favourite example of this geographical symbolism. 'We shall pass from external geography to the internal surface.'[16] 'The skin man receives a geography and he can reconstruct a chorography.'[17] Digital technology has led us to the chorographic body, which combines surface and relief, shaped by architecture and landscape, and this is our own body, our furniture, our environment. The chorographic body — a fluid territory with undulations of varying levels and degrees — is a 'sample' of the global within the local, the landscape brought in from outside. Chorography is a 'kind of description of the surface of the earth through which the regions described are considered on a large scale in all the diversity and detail of their different characters'. 'Chorography is a meticulous inventory of nearby realities.'[18] Architecture, which has become a domesticated environment, resembles a chorographic landscape, every particle of which clashes with the skin of the territory. Digital production is like malleable earth, permeated by these 'undulating fields that are going to constitute our new territories'.[19] Bernard Cache refers to the sculptures of Henry Moore, who inaugurated 'a topological mode of connection with the earth',[20] and whose complex curves, empty spaces and convexities created a human link to the earth, the mountains and the landscape.[21] 'The time is such that one seeks the exterior in the interior, geography in furnishings, but also images in the things themselves.'[22]

Greg Lynn compares the evolutionary processes that define IT models to the evolution of landscapes, and in so doing he uses chorographic metaphors: 'The slow undulations constructed in every surface of the landscape, like the hills and valleys, do not mobilize space by way of action but by way of virtual movement.' 'The movements of a landscape present a context of gradual slopes which fold into its form.'[23] The 'blob' is 'an example of a topological surface that shows the characteristics of a landscape although it does not resemble a topography'.[24] Thus the productivity of architectural forms, constituting as it does a living field, resembles the geological constitution of the landscape. With the rhythms of hills and valleys, 'a landscape is a ground that has been softened by historical fluxes and movement across its surface'.[25] 'The topological surfaces which store force within the undulations of their forms behave like landscapes in the sense that the slopes that are generated stock energy in the form of surfaces that are orientated rather than neutral.'[26] This epigenetic formation of the landscape will lead to architectural and urban projects, with no fixed territorial context, which will be defined mostly in terms of the energy they produce, and so for Alejandro Zaera Polo (FOA) 'the urban structure is transformed into a superconductive topography, capable of a continuous redirection of flow'.[27] Superstudio's grids follow the same lines, as does Architecture-Principe's 'topology of orientated surfaces' (Claude Parent, Paul Virilio), the architecture becoming a surface for propagation, a vehicle for the flow of energy, an organizer of all the given elements.

This globalization of the 'chorographic skin' harks back to Raoul Bunschoten's 'skin of the earth': the earth is a skin that wraps us in its folds and whose wrinkles produce a fractal dimension of space (Ill. 4). 'The world is a viscous body with a fine crust, and this crust forms the physical soil of our lives.' Architecture connects the skin of the earth to the greatest 'imago mundi', and takes on a mimetic relationship to this skin. It is a relationship that goes from 'a surgical operation on this skin to a substitution for it'.[28] 'Architecture can

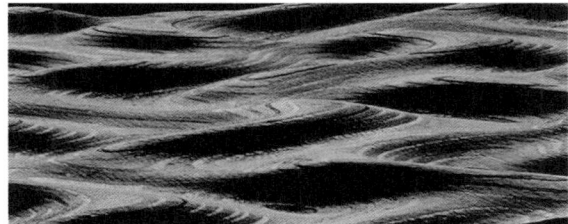

III. 3
'Subjectile', in Bernard Coche, *Earth Furniture*, Orléans, HYX, 1997.

III. 4
Raoul Bunschoten, 'The Skin of the Earth', in *B Architectural Magazine*, no. 49, Arhus, 1992.

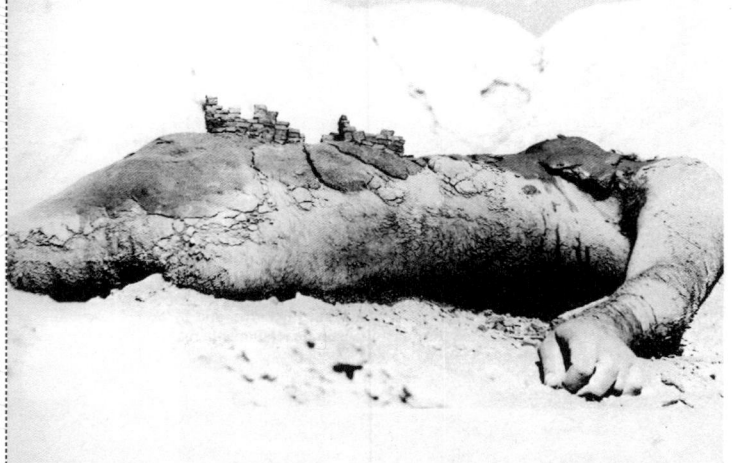

Ill. 5
Charles Simonds, 'Landscape/Body/Dwelling', 1970, in Lucy Lippard, *Overlay*.

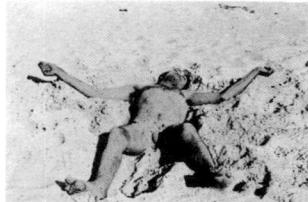

Ill. 6
Frantisek Lesak, 'Experience of the Sand',
1973, Coll. FRAC Centre.

be seen as the sum of all those incisions that have been made on the skin of the earth'.[29] Raoul Bunschoten (Chora) analyses this 'global metropolitan skin' by way of 'global influences on the local environment', and sets out to 'detect the emergent phenomena that are the manifestations of proto-urban conditions.' 'Towns are strange, dynamic skins which echo the crust of the earth, but with different mechanisms, different rhythms and undulations.'[30] 'We all live in the second skin' of the earth, which is flux. In this context, Bunschoten developed morphological games within a cartographic field, and these games make visible the connections between emergent phenomena (flux, displacement, energy). The dynamism of the town, which draws on physical space and temporal processes, is thus mapped out in order to allow for new and more open configurations. The chorographic body of the town re-establishes proximity and, permeated by fluctuating localities, it takes on the contours of a landscape of singularities.

'We were plunged into a chaos of cracks.'
Robert Smithson, The Crystal Land, *1966*

The earth is also ruins, a becalmed past, an incipient chaos, just like the artistic experiments that took place at the end of the 1960s. The works of Charles Simonds, for instance, seek a matrix-like fusion with the earth ('like my body being everybody's body and the earth being where everybody lives'). In 'Landscape/Body/Dwelling' (1970) (Ill. 5) his naked body is made to resemble a clay landscape on which he sculpts the architecture of a town – a literal realization of the idea of the 'chorographic body', still rooted in the earth but already a metaphor. Simonds himself defines this personal mythology as an instrument of investigation to fracture the present.[31] In Europe, Frantisek Lesak subjected himself to a cognitive and psycho-sensory experience of space by burying himself naked in the sand. In his 'Experience of Sand' (Ill. 6), space is viewed as a 'function of the body'; 'space itself consists in the physical experience of the matter that surrounds the body' (Lesak). This certainly does not mean a Spinozan fusion of mind and matter so much as the development of new modes of cognition, whereby the earth no longer constitutes a substratum but becomes a means of investigating a multidimensional territory in which body, organs and surfaces are so many layers in one's cognitive grasp of the world. These enveloping experiences, in which the surface of the body activates the surface of the earth, were shared by 'Land Art' artists such as Dennis Oppenheim (Ill. 7) and Michael Heizer. These experiences of an almost incestuous relationship with the earth were so intense that Robert Smithson even spoke of an ecological 'Oedipus complex'. 'How can you justify the fact of working the earth in an abstract manner? The earth cannot be treated in the same manner as sculptors working with metal. What has made the "earth works" movement possible is interaction with temporal structures, the fact of grasping a dynamic geophysical structure' (Michael Heizer).[32] In 1969 Heizer branded a mountain, as one would brand cattle, in an overtly territorial gesture, affirming that 'branding the earth and then cattle made no difference at all in terms of scale; cows graze on the abstractions of their own bodies'. In 'Wrist and Land' Heizer filmed the morphological parallels between topography and the flexed muscles of the body. 'My skin became a pigment' (Heizer). On the surface of the earth, the 'chorographic body' emerges from the fractured horizon of the present, which opens out on to the dynamic spatial levels of time.

Robert Smithson was the artist who conveyed this 'consciousness of geological time' with the greatest intensity. For him too, the artist lives in a 'fractured world'[33] – a temporal world that is cracked in all parts. 'The mind and the earth are in a constant state of erosion.' Matter itself is already an entropic landscape. Smithson's works are made of asphalt, glue, cement, melted tar – poured out on the earth in a quest to transform one state into another. 'Everywhere was nothing but fragmentation, corrosion, decomposition, disintegration, collapse, landslide, mudslide, avalanche ... Fractures and faults spat out sediments, crushed agglomerates, the debris of erosion, sandstone'.[34] Invoking Heraclitus, Smithson declares that the earth is nothing but 'a pile of rubble thrown into disorder', and 'the town creates the illusion that the earth doesn't exist.' On this earth, 'a collection of surfaces ready to break up', Smithson demands 'de-architecturation': 'The instruments of technology will once more become part of the earth's geology by reintegrating their original state.' 'The feeling that the earth is a map subject to dismemberment leads the artist to think that nothing is formal or certain. Language itself becomes mountains of symbolic debris.'[35] In the film 'Spiral Jetty', he tears the pages off an old atlas and drops them into a dried-up pond of cracked mud, quoting the following: 'Sometimes the history of the earth seems like a history consigned to a book every page of which would be torn into little pieces.'[36] (Ill. 9) 'Spiral Jetty' illustrates the 'chorographic body' issuing forth from knowledge of the earth and from the 'de-architecturation' of the world. The cracks that split the unity of Smithson's earthly body are echoed by the symbolic cracks of the torn-up book, because nothing can re-establish the order of knowledge. The body is unsure of itself – is it on or in the earth? As the substratum of an ephemeral architecture that is built on its own relief (Simonds), it is the earth, but a pulverized earth from which can spring only an architecture that is itself in the process of being pulverized. In Heizer's branded body-territory, architecture has disappeared from the face of the earth in the absence of a founding father. With Smithson, down in the bowels of a ravaged earth, the body is a fault between physical space and the processes of cognition. Only by investigating the depths of the earth will it be possible to reconstruct the chorographic body, and the only force capable of constructing the world by way of its territorial embodiment is endogenous, ever-changing architecture.

Once more it is cracks that construct 'Fractal City' (1998), in which R&Sie (Roche, Lavaux) transform architecture into earth upheavals. Here architecture appears as mutable and evolving matter. Cracks also deconstruct the architecture or construct the fractal, polder landscape of Adriaan Geuze in a topography bursting with shells. Elsewhere the earth is the actual material that constitutes the geographical unity of architecture: Kengo Kuma advocates an ecological architecture built with the aid of local materials such as the earth of the region. 'The earth is divided into elements which one assembles to form open structures.' (K. Kuma) But it was James Wines, with SITE, who from an aesthetic and philosophical standpoint revolutionized the ecological approach to architecture in the widest sense, by way of buildings such as 'Rainforest Showroom' (Hialeah, 1979) or 'Forest Building' (Richmond, 1980).[37] In these realized projects 'the landscape has been interpreted as an integral and apparently chaotic extension of the architecture.' The 'Forest Building' has a glass façade, which contains a volume of earth – a terrarium composed of 'strata of local geological formations'.[38] SITE constructed a series of buildings and parks with terrarium walls. In the 'Best Terrarium Showroom' (1978), an amount of earth was 'excavated as external walls during preparation of the foundations, geology thus becoming the communicating iconography of the constructed building'.[39] For Wines architecture is the 'biographical registration of its environment', a 'geological/biological microcosm', an 'iconography in permanent mutation'. The walls are not barriers but 'passages' – contextual membranes between the interior and the exterior, between town and nature (Ill. 8). The earth is material, realization, iconography and narrative all at the same time. An accumulation of particles and dust, it maintains the heterogeneity of reality. Through the earth, architecture comes close to the 'de-architecturation' that James Wines also strongly advocates ('de-architecture') – that is to say, an architecture that is flexible and evolutionary, incorporated into the earth both literally and figuratively.

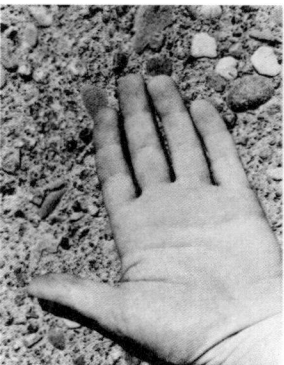

Ill. 7
Dennis Oppenheim, 'Rocked Hand', Aspen, Colorado, 1970, in Lucy Lippard, *Overlay*.

III. 8
James Wines & SITE, 'Best Parking Lot Building', 1976.

'We think of the figure, not as the demarcation of an object, but as an effect emerging from the field itself – like moments of intensity, like crests or valleys within a continuous field.'[40] Reliefs and surfaces, hills and fields, all these geographical metaphors converge in the same disappearing act: that of the frame, the frontier, the wall, the barrier – all giving way to the passage, the membrane, the network and all the other mediators between the body and its environment, between architecture and the dynamic processes that structure it.

Atelier Bow-wow drew up an inventory in Tokyo of urban objects or 'environmental units': machines of all kinds – the size of a domestic pet – which slip into the interstitial urban spaces, interfaces between town and body, between interior and exterior, and which are as likely to be found in a room as at the corner of a street. There is no distinction here between inside and outside; there is simply an urban environment transformed into a sort of 'super-interior', a domestic space on a large as well as a small scale, since it reflects that of the body and of its fluid geography.

The 'chorographic body', simultaneously physical and virtual, geological and figurative, has invaded the generative environment of this digital era of information technology. But it is the earthen burial mound, the instrument of an active architecture, as much as the urban object, the hybrid of machine and body, that transforms space into a domestic field. The confluence of space and time creates movement in architecture (Wes Jones). And this gives life to the surface of the earth. ◪

Notes

1. Denis Cosgrove, 'Liminal Geometry and Elemental Landscape: Construction and Representation', in James Corner (ed.), *Recovering Landscape. Essays in Contemporary Landscape Architecture*, New York, Princeton Architectural Press, 1999, p. 116.

2. Ibid., p. 117.

3. Andrea Branzi, *Le design italien. La casa calda*, Paris, L'Equerre, 1985, p. 63.

4. Ibid., p. 64.

5. Op. cit.

6. Ibid., p. 72.

7. It is worth remembering that the word 'ecology' was coined by the German biologist Ernst Haeckel (1834-1919), who used the Greek root *oikos* in order to convey the idea of domestic habitation. Ecology therefore refers to the domestication of the earth, and hence the connection between private and public surfaces.

   Cf. Suzannah Hagan, *Taking Shape. A New Contract between Architecture and Nature*, Oxford, Achitectural Press, 2001.

8. Rosalind Krauss, 'Sculpture in the Expanded Field', in *October*, New York, no. 8, 1979, pp. 58-64.

9. Alex Wall, 'Programming the Urban Surface', in James Corner, op. cit., p. 246.

10. Bart Lootsma, 'Synthetic Regionalization. The Dutch Landscape Toward a Second Modernity', in James Corner, op. cit., p. 263.

11. Marie Ange Brayer, 'Cartes', in *ArchiLab 2000*, Orléans, Ville d'Orléans, 2000.

12. Manuel de Landa, *A Thousand Years of Nonlinear History*, New York, Swerve, 1997, p. 20.

13. Ibid., p. 21.

14. Bernard Cache, *Terre Meuble*, Orléans, HYX, 1997, p. 55.

15. Op. cit., p. 56.

16. Op. cit., p. 57.

17. Op. cit., p. 59.

18. Jean-Marc Besse, *Voir la terre. Six essais sur le paysage et la géographie*, Arles, Actes Sud/ENSP/Centre du paysage, 2000, p. 42.

19. B. Cache, op. cit., p. 70.

20. Ibid., p. 104.

21. Ibid., p. 102.

22. Ibid., p. 149.

23. Greg Lynn, *Animate Form*, New York, Princeton Architectural Press, 1999, p. 29.

24. Greg Lynn, op. cit., p. 30.

25. Ibid., p. 35.

26. Ibid., p. 30.

27. A. Zaera Polo, in Suzannah Hagan, op. cit., p. 192.

28. Raoul Bunschoten, 'The Skin of the Earth', in *B Architectural Magazine*, no. 49, Arhus, 1992, p. 54.

29. Raoul Bunschoten, CHORA, *Urban Flotsam. Stirring the City*, Rotterdam, 010 Publishers, 2001, p. 28.

30. Ibid., p. 21.

31. Lucy R. Lippard, *Overlay. Contemporary Art and the Art of Prehistory*, New York, Pantheon Books, 1983, p. 57.

32. Ibid., p. 54.

33. *Robert Smithson. Le paysage entropique 1960-73*, Paris, RMN; Brussels, Palais des Beaux-Arts; Marseilles, Musées de Marseille, 1994, p. 192.

34. Op. cit., in *The Crystal Land*, 1966, p. 170.

35. Op. cit., in *A Sedimentation of the Mind: Earth Projects*, 1968, p. 196.

36. Thomas H. Clark, Colin W. Stern, 'Geological Evolution of North America' in op. cit., p. 208.

37. James Wines, *L'architecture verte*, Cologne, Taschen, 2000, p. 110.

38. Op. cit., p. 112.

39. Cf. James Wines, *Architecture dans le contexte*, Orléans, HYX/Coll. FRAC Centre, 2002.

40. Stan Allen, in Suzannah Hagan, op. cit., p. 188. See also 'From Object to Field', in *AD Architectural Design*, 'Architecture After Geometry', London, 1997, pp. 24-31.

Ill. 9
Robert Smithson, 'Spiral Jetty' (photogram from film), 1970, in *Robert Smithson. Le paysage entropique 1960-73*, Paris, RMN; Brussels, Palais des Beaux-Arts; Marseilles, Musées de Marseille, 1994.

Frédéric Migayrou

Extensions of the oikos

When Ernst Haeckel, author of *General Morphology of Organisms* (1866), coined the term 'ecology' to denote the relationship between animals and their environment, he established an integral link between the forms of living organisms and their surroundings. This interrelationship between all organisms that live in the same environment goes beyond the concept of the ecosystem, since it makes the definition of a state dependent on the forms of life and the specific qualities of a particular site. Haeckel's Darwinian materialism finds fulfilment in this 'legal' definition of form, this fundamental biogenetic law whose roots lie in a principle of mutability. Ecology is derived from the Greek *oikos* and is concerned with habitation – the form and the occupation of places. *Oikos* defines the notion of the habitat as a constitutive interrelationship, a directly contextual value, and Haeckel's term endows it with an ontological dimension. It incorporates not only ontogenesis, but also outward appearance and the sustainment of life.

The comparatively short history of ecology continues as an extension of the concept of habitation to that of the environment, culminating in a biogeography that to a degree was anticipated by Alexander von Humboldt's *Essai sur la géographie des plantes*. His systematic, empirical study showed him to be the perfect encyclopedist for an agnostic concept of the world, seen as a whole that 'converts the physics of the globe into a physics of the world. This science aspires to make known the simultaneous action and the vast chain of forces that animate the universe.'[1] Humboldt's work covered all the sciences of the earth and nature, and he compiled huge taxonomies of species according to their territorial distribution, thereby consolidating our understanding of nature's rational unity. With the advent of ecology, the *oikos* takes on a universal dimension – that of 'inhabiting the world', through which the earth is made finite, accessible to geography and to a geophysics that leads directly to the notion of an economy.

There has been a historical development from the 16th-century taming and artificialization of nature to the systematic, industrial exploitation of the world's resources, and it was in the 20th century that the natural domain was definitively subjugated to the power of the engineer. The very concept of ecology presupposes an endless extension of the habitat, with the whole of the earth available as an environment, and this in turn extends the notion of the *oikos*, which is no longer bound to its traditional Greek designation of a localized economy. It would now be an illusion to link the *oikos* to a territorial value, to the romantic idea of local roots. The development of the concept of urbanism at the start of the 20th century is founded on the same reassessment of the *oikos*. Analysis of urban phenomena is different from descriptive studies of the history of the constructed frame – it no longer describes the evolution of architecture or methods of composing spaces in cities.

Urbanism deals globally with the morphology of towns and is a science that builds on its own rules. The utopian ideas of such great social reformers as Robert Owen, Charles Fourier and William Morris related to social countermovements and sought to devise spatial alternatives, a genuine utopia in a different kind of space, and, more than any real alternative, this theoretical one introduced doubts and equivocations that undermined the very forms of habitations and the very nature of the *oikos*. William Morris named his utopian city 'Nowhere', and this in itself reinforces the absence of any defining link to the space proposed by these urban visions.

Essentially, urbanism presupposes a new form of description that can no longer be satisfied with formal explanations of architecture but has to integrate the parameters of an environment that is constantly changing. It is this urban evolution that Marcel Poëte was seeking to capture when pioneering the discipline: 'Every town must have its own curve, which must make visible its evolution. It is a being that is always alive, and that we must study in its past, so that we can discern the degree of its evolution – a being that lives on the earth and from the earth, which means that to the given historical facts we must add the given geographical, geological and economic facts.'[2] The introduction to *Paris, son évolution créatrice* (1929), referring directly to Henri Bergson, directly advances the idea of the organism, in order to capture the functional unity of the city, which is 'a living substance that is not an enclosed entity drawing everything out of itself. It rests on a system of exchanges with the outside and makes no choice among the elements that originate from the latter.' Thus the town is compared to a living organism, and this reference to the given geographical, geological and economic facts is a direct response to the biogeographical model conceived by Humboldt.

casabella

411 rivista di urbanistica architettura e disegno industriale

Casabella, Milan, no. 411, March 1976.

Ecology as a science is based on the negation of all things natural. It makes nature into a constituent element of an interrelationship with urban production. This marks the end of nature as an indeterminate field on its own. Now it has to be translated in terms of resources and their exploitation, and ecology – the infinite expansion of the *oikos* – confines it within finite borders. The extension of the map, the multiplication of graphs and diagrams that replace the idea of endless space and soil convert resources into a store and provide an inventory of whatever is available for exchange or exploitation. Ecology and urbanism spring from the same displacement, through which life as celebrated by Nietzsche or Bergson has imposed itself on the unity of the world and of the cosmos, while the unity of the species has supplanted the primacy of the individual.

This movement of secularization, which has been precisely charted by Hannah Arendt in *The Human Condition*, leads to confusion between the domestic and political domains. 'This functionalization prevents us from seeing any really clear border between the two domains, and this is not a question of theory or ideology, because since the accession of society – otherwise called the 'ménage' (Oikia) – or of economic activity in the public domain, economics and all the problems once connected with the family circle have now become collective preoccupations. In fact, within our modern world the two domains constantly overlap, like waves in the incessant tide of life.'[3] This permanent need to reproduce the process of life leads to the world of Homo Faber, who must go on making his environment so that he can construct a world of practical objects in which he can move around and from which he will progressively detach himself; in this way he can devote himself exclusively to the process of production that will become an end in itself. We are taking part in a form of domestication in which the urban can no longer oppose nature, and the public and private spheres merge into permanent interchangeability.

The concept of the *oikos* is rooted in what we might call 'de-propriation' – a movement which its modern interpretation seeks to suspend in order to confine it to a purely spatial and functional dimension. What really authorizes the extension of the functionalist strategy is this instrumentalization of life. The universality demanded by Walter Gropius, the 'tree of life' and 'a new pact with life',[4] underlies the quest for a 'total architecture' that will encompass the world of art as well as the world of industry. This was the programme that characterized the position of the Bauhaus, which with an interdisciplinary openness aimed to implement a clearly defined political project that would endow functionalism with 'its justification and its forms at the heart of society and of life'. 'The analytical process of functionalism defined by Gropius as the search for the essence must identify itself through material, social and psychological factors in order to formalize itself in the architectural project. The empirical method of functionalist analysis must liberate the singular object which emerges from this natural synthesis of factors that are shared by all.'[5]

In a way Gropius created a sort of extopia by giving to architecture a non-hierarchical frame of reference that mingled object, habitat and town. He gave a pragmatic base to all urban utopias by accepting the mutations in the law of the *oikos*, separating it from its basic reference to the individual and domesticity. His affirmation of an 'Existenzminimum' is justified by taking into account the unity of the social body. It is an 'environmentalist' concept that no longer defines 'habitation' according to territorial appropriation. On the contrary, modern architecture continues to view space as a domain of extension, a truly abstract form, which is empty of all content and so opens the way to a new contextual concept of architecture.

Tony Garnier's *La Cité Industrielle* (1917) anticipated a number of development projects, providing a model for the linear city integrated into a continuum of greenery, and it maintained the relationship between architecture and the environment within a topographical context. The greatest urban utopias, from Ebenezer

Zizi Jeanmaire and Roland Petit in the General Motors kitchen, Salon des Arts Ménagers, 1957.

Howard's Garden City to Le Corbusier's Plan Voisin, maintain this planning credo, which is based on organized spatial circulation and distribution, and the distinction between mineral and vegetable and their placement as a fixed and static ensemble, which goes against the generic concept of a truly contextual urbanism. The perpetually changing factors of an urbanism that was essentially defined as organic could not anticipate the rationalization of space and its functions: 'The unplannable and the complex make the town into a domain of dispersal, thus making the plans of Le Corbusier and Howard into immutable and inadequate entities.'[6]

A genuine ecology completely incorporates both the common source and the almost simultaneous historical origin of urbanism and ecology. Once again it is the idea of an organic model of life that comes to the fore, as one can see from the theoretical works of the Chicago School: *The Town, a Natural Phenomenon; The Urban Phenomenon as Way of Life; Expansion as Physical Growth*. The town becomes a physical entity, a constantly changing organism that must be studied *in vivo* with the same methodology as that which deals with the ecosystems of nature. It is less a case of nature study than of carefully defining a field of study that is not encumbered by any one external factor and refutes any external definition or the precedence of any spatial or topographical definition. Reaching beyond a simple historical analysis, Amos Haley defines urban ecology as 'the morphological study of collective life in its static and dynamic aspects',[7] analysing all the regularities and the variations. Even if the Chicago School might have ended up being trapped in evolutionary social models that proved inadequate, it did bring about a morphological understanding in which the ecological hypothesis of a natural regulation of the human habitat is not to be reduced to a methodological standpoint, with the town as a mere artefact. The supposition that the town is an organism brings to light constituent relationships, models of adaptation and other complexities, which, behind the apparent disorder, generate the specific equilibrium of urban societies.

In all the successive historical stages that have animated its recent history and in the reality of its practices, architecture has never really come to terms with the structural mutation of the law of *oikos*. If the question of morphology has been raised, it has been dealt with through a sociohistorical comprehension which has stopped at the revelation of typologies engendered by a formal historical analysis of urban evolution. This historical rationalization defines the interruptions and continuities of social deployment in the history of towns. It denounces the ideology of form and the abstract geometrization advocated by modernist architects, and demands a 'labyrinth of complexity',[8] to quote Manfredo Tafuri – a complexity of flexible images marking the strata of historical sedimentation and favouring the social appropriation of the city. This demand for contextualism, which would have the merit of bringing to light the historical reality of an environment, would be incorporated into the normative domain of future architecture and of all architectural production, bringing to bear a regulatory element deriving from existing morphologies. But curiously this theory never came to terms with the effects brought about by the eradication of the *oikos*, though – as with the modernists – it sought to find a substitute discourse on habitation based on values of identity and establishing a true ideology of ownership. This discourse on habitation is indirectly associated with an ideology of form, going back to an exclusively spatial concept of architecture. The multiplicity of contextualist theories in the 1970s denoted the permanent unsuitability of architecture in relation to the general urbanization and the rapidly developing networks of exchange, as space was exploited with no regard for local territory or character. Alexander Tzonis contrasted 'structural' efficiency dictated by social demand[9] with functional efficiency; Theo Crosby, faced with globalization and the 'closure' of the world, tried to develop 'a theory of games'[10]. Even the idea of a 'cultural context',[11] mixing the semantic complexity demanded by Robert Venturi with the critical structuralism of the Five Architects, was not enough to revive the legitimacy of a

'Garbage Housing. Paper Shelters', in *Architectural Design*, No. 12, London, 1973.

'Garbage Housing', in *Architectural Design*, London, February 1971.

'Glass Houses', in *Architectural Design*, London, vol. XLV, March 1975.

'Autonomous Houses. Bologna AT Index', in *Architectural Design*, London, January 1976.

MELP! Melpomène, Paris, No. 22, July 1966.

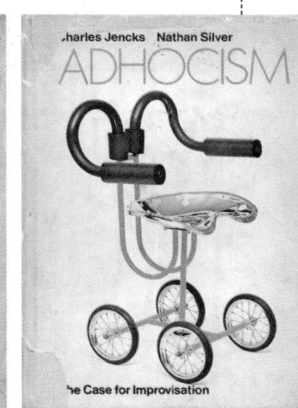
Charles Jencks, Nathan Silver, *Adhocism. The Case for Improvisation*, New York, Doubleday & Company, 1972.

Horst Schmidt-Brümmer, *Alternative Architektur*, Cologne, Dumont, 1983.

Ararat. Alternative Research in Architecture Resources Art and Technology, Moderna Museet and the Swedish Institute, June 1976.

'Urbland 2000', in *Parallel*, Montreal, no. 6, February–March 1967.

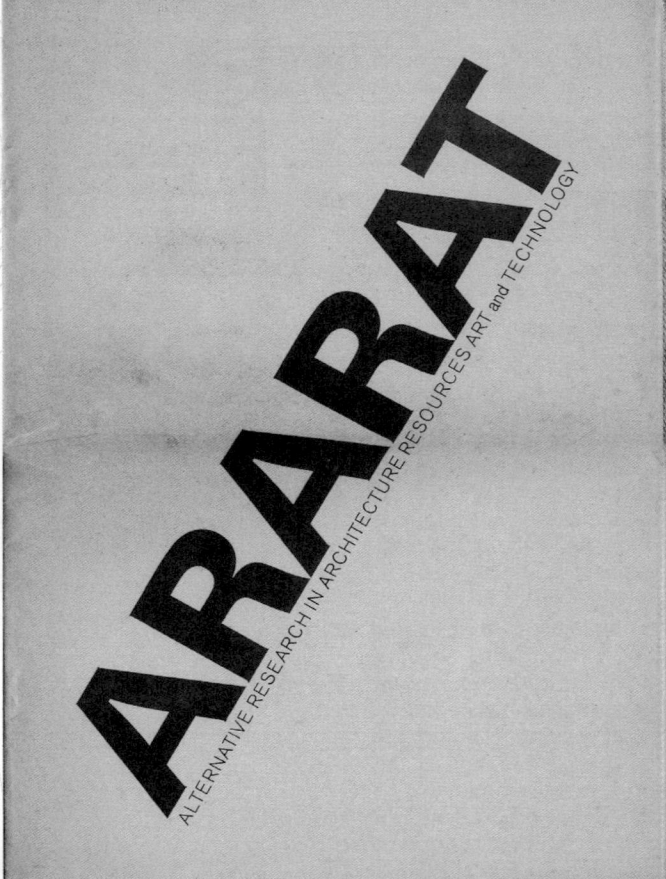

Nigel Cross, David Elliott, Robin Ray (eds), *Man-Made Futures. Readings in Society, Technology and Design*, London, Hutchinson Educational, 1974.

Espaces verts, no. 25, October–December 1970.

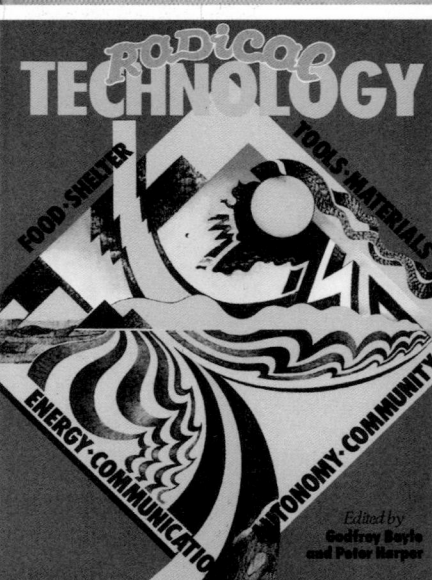

Godfrey Boyle, Peter Harper (eds), *Radical Technology*, New York, Pantheon Books, 1976.

'Le Comuni: Redefinizione', in *In. Argomenti e immagini di design*, Milan, no. 12, December–January 1974–75.

specific architectural language, which had lost its way in a field of interactions that had become more and more heterogeneous.

Architecture has to accept a fundamental 'de-propriation'; it has to disengage itself from an exclusively spatial practice, reconstruct its unity and its almost legal definition by reconstructing the idea of the project, the concept, overriding all presuppositions that the space must determine a priori the nature of the composition, with its separations and its distributions. Contextualism was the last manifestation of a recurrent spatialism that was characterized by informational values linked to history and to practice, but was also permeated with human and social values. At the same time, however, there was an extraordinary fascination with the idea of returning to the comfort of proximity to a defined space; the creed of an alternative practice rooted in the individual's demand for an ecological way of living inspired a huge cultural surge in favour of a return to nature — a movement that seemed to spring from the naturalism of the avant-garde in Ascona. Confusion between relocation, which leads to the actual notion of the environment, and aspirations towards a new domesticity resulted in an intense revival of a traditional concept of the *oikos*. The romanticism of a new nomadic way of life in quest of new territories beyond the cities was accompanied by an alternative economy that set out to redefine the principles of territorialism. The return to the earth and the nomadism that underlies the Arcosanti de Paolo Soleri project in the Californian desert well demonstrates this weak architecture (*Can architecture, Ad-hocism*), consisting of domes (*Domebook, Paperhouses*); a new domestic economy was introduced (*Whole Earth Catalog, Nomadic Furniture, Survival Scrapbook*), and reached its apotheosis in the glorified use of solar and wind energy set up for each individual. The socialization of the ecological idea and its manifestations as a political demand were underpinned by this evaluation of the *oikos*, transforming the earth into a domestic space as envisaged by the concept of 'inhabiting the world'.

Architecture has continued to cling to this essential spatialization presupposed by the *oikos*, searching to draw on the resources of what it is that defines humanity. The inevitable temporal metaphor of the dwelling is to be found in a reference to Heidegger that encompasses the organizing forces of architecture: writing about Bernard Tschumi, Jacques Derrida anchors the logic of 'consequent deconstruction' in a 'giving of place', a 'spacing'. The meaning or signifying value of architecture that shapes its structure and its syntax 'must govern these from the outside, starting out from a principle, à base or foundation, a transcendence or a finality whose settings are not architectural. The experience of the meaning must be the dwelling, the law of the *oikos*.'[12] Here the *oikos* finds a paradoxically naturalistic form, linking up with the withdrawal that Edmund Husserl had attributed to the earth as the 'soil of experience of all bodies in the empirical genesis of our representation of the world'[13] This last ontological anchorage may be put in reserve at the very moment when the *oikos* is setting itself up in ecology, and environmental science is developing and reducing geography to one parameter among others. What remains is to come to terms with this definitive extension of the *oikos*, and to think of the earth as a tangle of networks that are continually changing. One cannot separate the grid that dominates Bernard Tschumi's *Folies de la Villette* from its reference to radical architecture. The infinite grids of Superstudio's *Monument Continu* created a perfect continuity of domestic space, its furniture, the house, the town, the earth and even interstellar space. The rationality of measures that thus

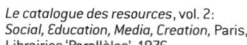

Le catalogue des ressources, vol. 1: *Food, Clothing, Transport, Habitat*, Paris, Librairies 'Parallèles', 1975.

Le catalogue des ressources, vol. 2: *Social, Education, Media, Creation*, Paris, Librairies 'Parallèles', 1976.

James Hennessey, Victor Papanek, *Nomadic Furniture 1*, New York, Pantheon Books, 1973.

James Hennessey, Victor Papanek, *Nomadic Furniture 2*, New York, Pantheon Books, 1973.

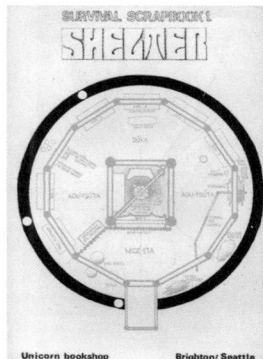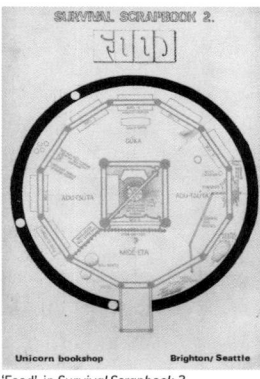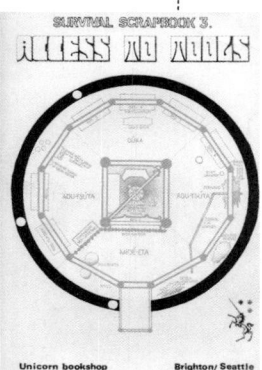

'Shelter', in *Survival Scrapbook 1*, Brighton/Seattle, Unicorn Bookshop, 1973.

'Food', in *Survival Scrapbook 2*, Brighton/Seattle, Unicorn Bookshop, 1973.

'Access to Tools', in *Survival Scrapbook 3*, Brighton/Seattle, Unicorn Bookshop, 1974.

extend to infinity can liberate architecture from space and from all the constraints attendant on it.

Charles Jencks had already underlined this desire to assume an end to industrialization, which inspired the radical architects — always eager to announce the end of an era. There are innumerable tombs, graves and coffins in the drawings and projects of Walter Pichler, Hans Hollein and Ettore Sottsass. Jencks' article 'Les Supersensualistes' sees in Archizoom's *No-Stop City* a universal climatic system that carries to absurd extremes the modern project of a *Cité Radieuse* in which ideal planning announces the completion of a process that definitively suspends all idea of evolution or of mutation. Even though Jencks speaks ironically of this negative utopia, in which 'Archizoom has pushed the assumptions of rationalism to a point at which everyone can ascertain that their faults do at the same time have a certain poetic force',[14] it actually seems that the Italian group's prescience has become a reality. Instead of the formal, static image of the modern, rational town, we have an open system, a network that is just as rational and is upheld by a continual optimization of communications and services. The metropolis has ceased to be a place and instead has become a condition. In

Domebook 2, Nowels Publications, Menlo Park, 1971.

Autoconstruction, Strasbourg, 1972.

Roger Sheppard, Richard Threadgill, John Holmes, Paper Houses, New York, Schocken Books, 1974.

Paul Oliver (ed.), Shelter and Society, London, Barrie & Rockliff, The Cresset Press, 1969.

fact, this 'condition' renders all social movement uniform by way of the hierarchy imposed by consumer goods. The future of the metropolis is the future of the market.

Andrea Branzi defines the architect's work as follows: 'The search for an ecology of the artificial world aims at restoring habitability to a world devastated by industrialization. When we speak of an ecology of the artificial world, we are not talking solely of the possibility of producing ecological or biodegradable objects; we are referring above all to that of discovering scenarios and new horizons that are relevant to the project.'[15] Linked to the cold metropolis is the warm house (La casa calda), where, in a world of consumerism, the body becomes 'the only parametric principle capable of actively developing everything it receives from surrounding space, and transforming these given factors into experience and culture'.[16] The oikos gives way to the ambience, a world that conditions integral spaces, which, from the town to the domestic (or from town to spoon, to echo the title of a radical manifesto), constitute a dense and continuous environment, with an uninterrupted flow of corporeal experiences. The plan gives way to diagrams, and these control

the flow, the economy, the light, the heat, blurring the parameters that combine to structure the environment.

The world has become a continuous environment with no hope of exteriority; it is a world characterized by an ever-increasing density of information, with urbanism expanding into a universal way of life. When Rem Koolhaas applied the Superstudio grid schema to the real-life context of New York, he dispensed with all topographical analysis in order to evaluate every islet as 'an archipelago of towns within the town. The more each island exalts its own values, the more reinforcement it gives to the unity of the archipelago as a system. The fact that change is limited to the constituent islands guarantees the immutability of the system.'[17] La Ville du globe captif (1972) praises the resource represented by a total artificiality once one has 'exorcized the fear of chaos by relativizing its dominance, isolating its components and quantifying its functions in order to restore its determinability. We have to place our hopes in this culture of congestion.'[18] By totally removing the gap between nature and society, ecology can no longer function separately but is itself an evolutionary system enabling us to quantify milieux and to translate them into directly economic terms in which nature's only value is that of a storehouse to accompany our artificial environments.

This store, however, is no longer merely a collection of resources in the form of energy, air, water, animals and vegetables. The real resource is the genetic domain along with the legal discussions that are linked to it. Any attempt to establish the rights of nature or the rights of ecosystems is illusory, not because one would then have to revive the old Kantian argument concerning a right of humanism, but because rights have given way to patents – patents taken out by the great multinational companies in the fields of food production, chemicals and pharmaceuticals so that they can assume exclusive control and commercially exploit nature's productive and reproductive resources. The myth of 'green architecture', of 'verdolatry', is no longer an alternative; nor is the return of economic, popularity-seeking, 'low-tech' architecture. One cannot place any faith in this 'ecotecture' whose foundations would be a biomass economy. The architect's work cannot be pinned down to the management of landscapes or a marginal exercise in DIY; he can no longer stand by the cynical acceptance – rightly condemned by Rem Koolhaas – of a world in which he is expected to skim the surface of a new naturalism, that of a pragmatic state of reality.[19]

Accepting artificiality in the manner advocated by a number of current publications cannot provide us with an ultimate resource, a form of energy that will enable architecture to put into practice hybridization, grafting, complexity.[20] At a time when the human genetic code has been cracked, when man himself is the stake for which the law and the economy will be playing, we must devise a strategy of deregulation, away from the norm, from identicalness, from the standard, and we must root out the residual oikos that remains in the heart of the biological, along with the idea of the right and proper, which has already been squashed by the industries of the world. We must place ourselves at the heart of mutation, within the ebb and flow of all the processes, as demanded by the great environmentalist Lawrence Halprin who, even before Rem Koolhaas, sought to grasp the dynamism of complex environments. His books, New York, New York and Freeways, advocate an unreserved involvement at the very centre of all processes (Take Part, in the words of his manifesto); we must accompany all the cycles of development, their continual morphogenesis — genetic or otherwise — in order to derive new laws from them, a normativity in action.[21] ◪

Notes

1. Alexander von Humboldt, *Cosmos, essai d'une description physique du monde*, UTZ, 2000, p. 66.

2. Marcel Poëte, *Introduction à l'urbanisme, L'évolution des villes, la leçon de l'antiquité*, Boivin, 1929, p. 3, and Marcel Poëte, *Paris, son évolution créatrice*, Vincent Fréal, 1938, p. 5.

3. Hannah Arendt, *La condition de l'homme moderne*, Calmann-Lévy, p. 171; also published as *The Human Condition*, Chicago, University of Chicago Press, 1998.

4. Walter Gropius, *Apollon dans la démocratie*, La Connaissance, p. 56.

5. Karl Heinz Hüter, 'Opera d'arte totale, opera totale, architettura totale', in *Rossegna*, Walter Gropius 1907-1934, Year 5, 15/3, September 1983, p. 50.

6. Robert Fishman, *Urban Utopias in the Twentieth Century*, Basic Books, 1977, p. 276.

7. Amos Hawley, *Human Ecology*, Ronald Press, 1950, p. 67.

8. Manfredo Tafuri, Massimo Cacciari, Francesco Dal Co, *De la vanguarda a la metropolis*, Gustavo Gili, 1972, p. 78.

9. Alexander Tzonis, *Vers un environnement non oppressif*, Mardaga, 1979.

10. Theo Crosby, *How to Play the Environment Game*, Penguin Books, 1973.

11. Stuart Cohen, 'Physical Context, Cultural Context: Including it All', in *Oppositions*, no. 2, Institute for Architecture and Urban Studies, January 1974.

12. Jacques Derrida, 'Point de folie, maintenant l'architecture', in *Psyche*, Galilée, 1987, p. 481.

13. Edmund Husserl, *La terre ne se meut pas*, Minuit, 1989, p. 12.

14. Charles Jencks, 'The Supersensualists', in *Architectural Design*, vol. 33, January 1972, p. 19.

15. Andrea Branzi, *Nouvelles de la métropole froide, design et seconde modernité*, Centre Georges Pompidou, 1991, p. 139.

16. Andrea Branzi, *Le design italien, la Casa calda*, Equerre, 1985, p. 97.

17. Rem Koolhaas, *New York Delire*, du Chêne, 1978, p. 244.

18. 'Life in the Metropolis, or the Culture of Congestion', in *Architectural Design*, Special Edition OMA, vol. 45, no. 5, 1977.

19. A number of publications try to define this state of a reality without exteriority, in which the urban extends indefinitely — the state of a nature that definitively merges the private and the public domains. Manuel Gausa, *Otras naturalezas urbanas*, EACC, 2001; Ann Rieselbach (ed.), *Young Architects, Second Nature*, Princeton Architectural Press, 2001. Yago Conde, *Architecture of the Indeterminacy*, Actar, 2000.

20. *Artificial Landscapes*, NAI Publishers, 2000; *Another & another & another act of seeing (urban space)*, De Singel, 1997; Miguel Molins, Eduard Bru, *New Landscapes, New Territories*, Macba, Actar, 1997; Crimson, Reurb, *Nieuwe plannen voor aude steden*, 010 Publishers, 1997; Moriko Kira, Mariko Terada, *Japan, towards Totalscape*, Nai Publishers, 2000.

21. Lawrence Halprin, *RSVP Cycles, Creative Processes in the Human Environment*, Georges Brazilier, 1969.

'Quelle architecture solaire?', in *L'Architecture d'Aujourd'hui*, Paris, no. 192, June 1977.

La face cachée du soleil, Paris, Bricolo Lezardeur, 1974.

'Solar Energy in Housing', in *Architectural Design*, London, 10/1973.

'Solar Energy', in *Architectural Design*, London, 1/1974.

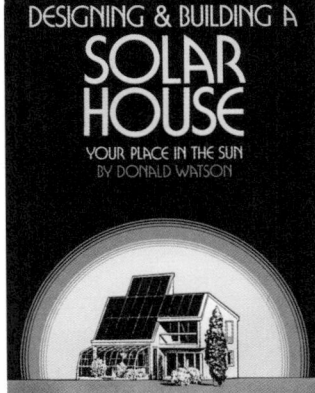

Donald Watson, *Designing & Building a Solar House*, The Village Press, 1977.

Habitat Soleil, Musée d'Art Moderne de la Ville de Paris, November 1976.

Pierre Chabard

The Datamorphis of the World

In 1999, MVRDV. published their book and manifesto *Metacity/ Datatown*.[1] This work, accompanied by a project, presented an extreme, imaginary vision of a town 'constructed like a collection of data'. As a constituent element of the 'Metacity', which would cover the entire globe, this 'Datatown' directly owes its form to the interpretation of a collection of digital information and various statistics assembled from reality. It requires direct and clear translation of these figures. The area of Datatown (400 km by 400 km), for example, is derived from the distance that can be covered in one hour by modern means of transport. Within this defined urban area, the town is laid out on a uniform grid pattern, which divides it up into blocks with identical bases but of different heights; the landscape thus created resembles a gigantic histogram in which each block is the three-dimensional expression of a piece of information. This uniform grid is broken up by other statistical and urban forms: green spaces, whose proportions are derived from Dutch norms, are regrouped into vast natural areas; waste products are sorted into categories and deposited centrally to accumulate into a mountainous topography, etc. Every urban element or function is thus reduced to its digital existence and is quantified before it is given its shape in the town.

With its heady distortions and excesses, which one could also take for a certain radicalism, Metacity/Datatown has caught the imagination of a whole generation of young architects. This fashionable element aside, the project seems to me to reflect very clearly some more general problems — notably the special way in which architects and town-planners establish, build and present their knowledge of the town, use the information and data they extract from it and make contact with reality.

Visible and invisible

Contemplating these essential landscapes, Kublai thought about the invisible order that governs towns, the rules that bring about their emergence, their way of taking shape, of prospering, of adapting to different times, of fading and falling into ruin. It sometimes seemed to him that he was on the point of discovering a coherent, harmonious system that existed beneath the infinite deformities and disharmonies; but no model was anywhere near as good as that of the game of chess.[2]

Since the end of the 19th century the town, both individually and globally, has become an object of study. Town planning, as it has developed progressively from the early 20th century, has centred on the desire to objectify the town, to understand it and to model it into a form that will unify all the different phenomena of which it is composed. Before it can be modelled, however, one has to solve the problem of data collection, which means solving the problem of observation.

First and foremost it is the eye, that vital organ of cognition, that must take on the task of registering the reality of the town, of examining the visible areas of this terra incognita. And one of the first movements of this cognitive eye is up and away, for the bird's-eye view is of vital importance in the process of objectifying the town. More than any previous century, the 19th — with its panoramas, its aerostatic flights and its various optical devices — was obsessed with this overall view.

In Edinburgh during the 1890s, Patrick Geddes, one of the founding fathers of modern town planning, constructed the Outlook Tower, from the top of which one could look down over the whole city; then one was invited to enter the *Camera Obscura* on the roof and gaze at the urban panorama projected and hence objectified on the screen.

Later, the modernist town planners made frequent use of aeroplanes to get their panoramic view. In his book *Aircraft*, dedicated to the glory of the aeroplane, Le Corbusier declared that thanks to these flying machines 'the eye now sees the substance of what the mind could previously only conceive subjectively'.[3]

But what do we see of the town when we look at it from above? Gazing down from the top of the World Trade Center, Michel de Certeau commented that the panorama of the cityscape was blank, and brought forth in the viewer an exciting 'scopic and gnostic impulse. Being nothing but this seeing point,' he says, 'is the fiction of knowing.'[4] De Certeau traces this love of the bird's-eye view back to medieval town paintings; now, he says, for the most part the town reveals itself to the all-embracing eye of science, but the latter is still capable of offering only a fictional version of it.

Similarly Bruno Latour, referring to the panorama of Paris from the top of la Samaritaine, comments wryly: 'one could get only an oblique view at roof level; and in any case one could see nothing but the dense mists of fine weather'.[5] He too dismisses the value of the panoramic view and shows that, on the contrary, the town can be described only by a series of 'oligoptic' views. By this he means a large number of specific, limited observations that together will cover all the different functions. The management of the various networks, the traffic, the flow of people and goods depend on instrumental and functioning models, which he calls 'dioramas'. Latour actually tracked down these 'oligoptic dioramas' in Paris, and showed that they were to be found in narrow spaces and windowless offices, most commonly on computer screens. But he also showed that these models had a direct effect on reality and a power that did indeed structure the city. The 'virtual' Paris that Latour has brought out into the open is invisible to the panoramic view, to the eye in the aeroplane, and only the 'proliferation of information technology … finally makes it describable'.[6] In other words, it needs a different kind of visualization.

Statistics

Four million individuals, governed by their free will, each claiming to live his or her life, while this claim, thus multiplied, creates a terrible and dramatic tension. And yet this tension follows the impetus of deep currents, which slowly direct the masses … Recognizing the presence of these currents, measuring their strength and discerning their direction – that is what statistics do.[7]

If directly perceivable data are deceptive, on what sort of data can one base knowledge? Faced with the paradoxes caused by direct observation, the first town planners, anxious to bring a degree of scientific validity to their work, turned to a completely different source of information, which was in full flow at the turn of the 20th century: statistics. In his doctoral thesis,[8] Enrico Chapel has demonstrated the importance of graphic statistics in the development of scientific town planning at that time. Throughout the 19th century there had been an ever-increasing number of censuses, reports on all sorts of movements (travellers, goods, etc.), questionnaires about public health and education, geographical, sociological, botanical reports, etc. This view, analytical and shaped by the quest for facts and figures, became the favourite tool for the construction of scientific knowledge. Its basis is the desire to see what the eye, for various reasons, cannot see. Phenomena that are invisible to the naked eye may be microscopic (a virus spreading everywhere) or macroscopic (mass social phenomena); they may

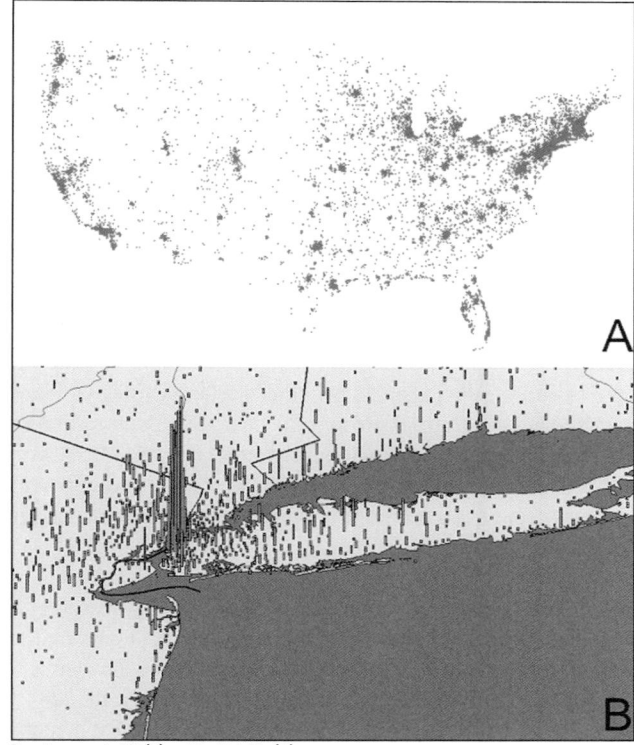

Domain names in USA (A) and New York City (B).

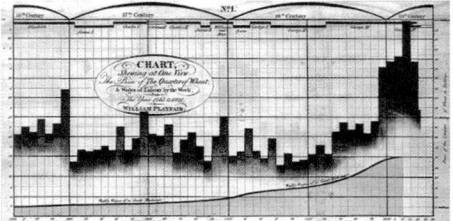

Chart showing price of wheat between 1563 and 1821 in England, c. 1822 (William Playfair).

also manifest themselves by speed (body movements filmed in sequence by Marey) or quite simply by their insubstantiality (atmospheric or intellectual phenomena). Measuring and charting, tracing these invisible objects – that is the task of the analytical and statistical approach. In order to fulfil it, the 19th century devised and developed numerous methods (most of which are still in use today) of graphically reproducing the data[9]: graphs, cartograms, two-dimensional diagrams (tables, histograms, pictograms) or even three-dimensional (nomograms, stereograms). All those phenomena that would otherwise be hidden from view are thus objectivized, i.e. transformed into objects, and thereby made visible and readable. The eye can contemplate them at its leisure and observe them in their graphic form; it can compare the proportions of different sections in a piechart, check the distribution of populations, etc. on a cartogram, examine the skyline of a histogram, follow the curves of a graph and admire its sudden or gentle undulations, its hills and its valleys. Graphic statistics have opened up a veritable universe of data, a space that unfolds itself before our very eyes, a new sort of landscape, which today we would call a 'datascape'.

Contact with reality

This 'datascape' maintains a direct relationship with reality; the data it puts into operation are extracted, or even abstracted, directly from the world itself; and indeed perhaps data (= things given) is a misleading expression, since these are things taken. The datascape is always 'true', always 'fair', because the information of which it consists has always been faithfully recorded from what is real; but at the same time it is always 'false', always 'unfair', because as an abstraction of the given, it is a deliberate selection from the vast complexity of reality.

The principle of selecting or abstracting from the given gives this statistical landscape a kind of autonomy in relation to the real landscape. It has its own laws, its own internal relations, its own way of organizing and interpreting information. It is self-reflecting, like maps, because it substitutes its own geography for the relationships that fashion things in the real world.

The self-reflection of statistical representation, however, is simply part of the paradox that is to be found in all descriptions of reality in general and of the town in particular. It is a paradox that Enrico Chapel discerns between 'heuristic finalities – the discovery and production of knowledge concerning the town – and practices, i.e. transformation of space and communication of ideas and models of urbanization'.[10] This applies to all concepts of the town. André Corboz expresses it as the difference between 'the world as reading and the world as writing'.[11]

Let us consider an example. At the end of the 19th century, Patrick Geddes's vast project to render the town visible (the panorama from the Outlook Tower was only one aspect) was to a great degree dependent on statistics. In 1881 he gave a series of three lectures entitled 'On the Classification of Statistics and its Results',[12] in which he asked questions about the manner of organizing 'the collection of statistical information that accumulates around us on a considerable and ever-growing scale'. In these lectures he compared and criticized the many different attempts being made at the time to organize and standardize the science of statistics, and then he made his own suggestion. A trained biologist and botanist,

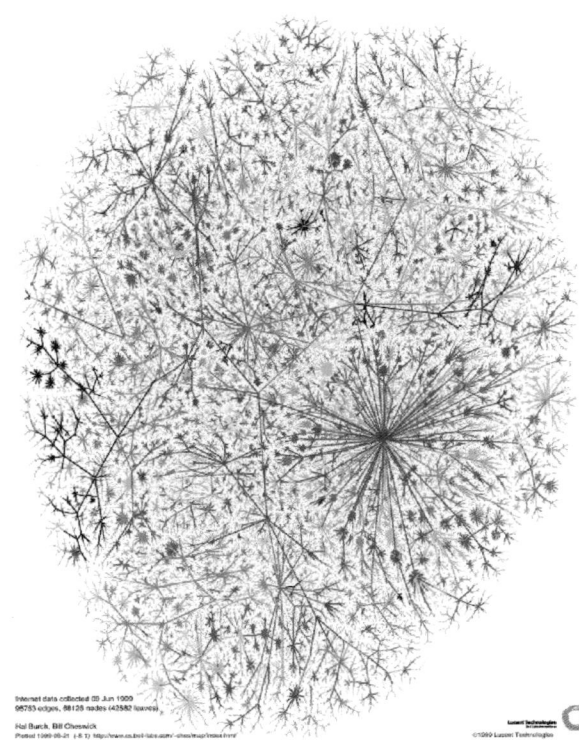

Internet data collected on 9 June 1999 (Lucent Technologies).

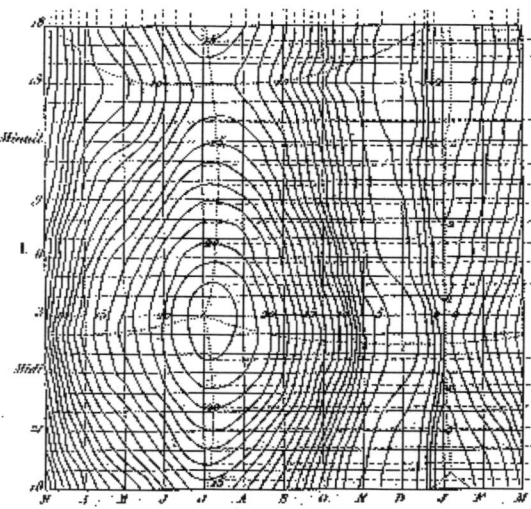

Chart showing temperature in Les Halles, 1843 (Léon Lalanne).

Geddes thought that this system of classification should take its cue from the natural sciences: it should be 'natural and not artificial, should be capable of complete specialization, including the most minute details, and equally capable of broader generalizations; it should be universal in its application and, as far as possible, simple to understand and practical to use'.[13] The major issue here is what links statistical data together, what is the virtual pattern that will hold together this particular representation of reality. In declaring that statistical classification must be 'in real accord with the order of nature', Geddes was not only talking about the need for an accord between representation and the thing represented; he was also predetermining a particular type of link or organizing structure within the representation; in this case, what he was proposing with his system of classification was a living, organic concept of the world, of society and of the town. The idea that the town was a macroscopic organism, a large living body – an idea which for Geddes produced the unity of the urban object – was to structure the framework of statistical representation, even before the data had been collected. This organic classification of data, which incidentally anticipated his famous *Survey*,[14] is an example of the paradoxical autonomy of the virtual landscape of statistics, which relocates the given factors of a territory according to its own topology or architecture.

Territorializing data

As we have seen, town planners when faced with reality are always caught up in a fundamental dialectic between observation and project, information and action, 'reading' and 'writing'. One of the major issues in the use of statistics is therefore how to relate them directly to the territory of the town, how to join up the quantitative and the spatial factors, or 'the numbers and the charts', to paraphrase Gilles Palsky. For town planners, one of the favourite methods of presenting data is quantitative cartography, the history of which Palsky has traced back to the 19th century. The town planners' use of these charts in fact led to a century of cartographic experiments in fields as diverse as medicine, social engineering, economics, demography – a century in which innumerable ways of representing non-spatial data on charts were invented: cartograms, isoplethic charts (in which lines connect points of the same value for variables such as temperature), anamorphic charts (with distortions caused by the data), colours, points, bands, arrows (to indicate movements), pictograms, etc. In all these types of charts, the spatial and territorial data are permanently informed and deformed by quantitative and statistical data.

Once again it is evident that real territory, through the double operation (cartographic and statistical) of which it is the subject, changes imperceptibly into virtual territory for the articulation of cognitive, long-term aims and descriptive, rhetorical intentions. And so when, in the first chapter of *The Evolution of Towns* (1902), Patrick Geddes published a demographic map of England in which the cities were shown as proliferating black spots, his aim was not so much to inform the reader as to give tangible and obvious form to a certain concept of the large, industrial, palaeotechnological town of which he saw himself as the scourge. This was his method of making visible his concept of the 'conurbation' and of the regional town.

A more recent example is the exhibition 'Mutations' held in 2000, which displayed a large number of statistical representations and, in particular, thematic charts. But here the aim was not, as with Geddes, to condemn the industrial 'megalopolis'; on the contrary, it was to convert the visitor to the idea of the decentralized, global town, the metacity, structured by electronic networks of communications and exchange. It is clear, however, that the thematic chart continues to serve the logic of an idea, a lecture or a project.

'Temporalizing' data

Statistics present the precise situation of the present moment, but also previous situations, and they connect them together with a line that is so expressive that one acquires a definite feeling for the past and, following the direction of the curve, we can penetrate into the future and acquire anticipated certainties.[15]

We have seen that the manner in which statistics are organized at the heart of our datascape is deliberately spatial or cartographic; but temporal and historical considerations also influence the principles according to which town planners arrange their data. In fact, the general confusion between preparatory analysis and the project itself, the two often occurring side by side in the same graphic documents, opens up the possibility of bringing in data linked to different times – the past, the present and the anticipated, imagined future. The Corbusier quote, with its astonishingly historicist overtones, perfectly captures the idea – very current in urban thinking – that scientific analysis of a present situation and of its history will magically bring forth the key to (or at least an adumbration of) its future. This suggests that the future of a town, good or bad, can be derived from its past, in which that future is inscribed like an inbuilt

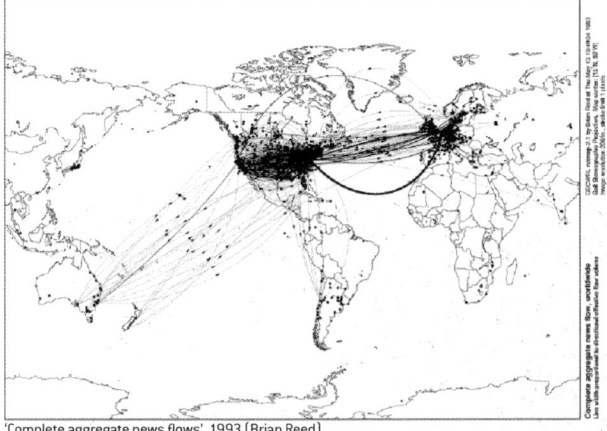

'Complete aggregate news flows', 1993 (Brian Reed).

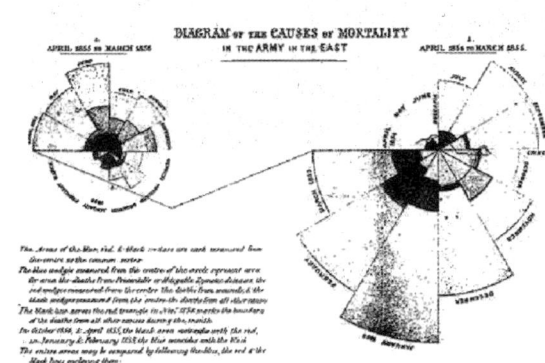

'Diagram of the Causes of Mortality in the Army in the East', c. 1885 (Florence Nightingale).

programme. Once again we find the conviction that analytical and statistical observation can reveal the invisible town, in this case the town that is not yet there – tomorrow's world.

This inscription of statistical data in a temporal flow, or this description of a temporal flow by way of statistics, is a problem that occurred at the very birth of the science of statistics in the 19th century and became of prime importance in town planning, which always seeks to prefigure a possible future and is always project-bound. In *Urbanisme*, Le Corbusier indulged in statistical speculation by extending the curves with a dotted line that foreshadowed a possible development. Today, thanks to computers, the town planner has additional means of fulfilling this dream of 'temporalizing' data. Armed with an instrument that has superhuman powers of calculation, backed up by masses of software, he or she can create live, three-dimensional models of the town, which can incorporate any amount of data. Following the example of MVRDV, architects faced with the complexity of the contemporary city can propose and experiment with innumerable informational datascapes, e.g. Lars Spuybroek (OfftheRoad 5speed, 2001; Paris-Brain, 2001); Dagmar Richter (Flexible Zoning, 1999; Meshworks, Wolfen Works project, 2000); No.MAD.arquitectura (Hybridization Process PH001, 2001). Intended as flexible, adaptable tools of planning, and reproducing as faithfully as possible all the problems of territory, these datascapes strive for the asymptotic ideal of 'real time', or in other words for the impossible bridging of the gap between the world and its representation.

The town as an ecosystem of data

If a group of codes is associated with luminous dots on a computer, and the dots are allowed to run free on the screen, they will move like a swarm of ants round a sugar cube ... Now if you subject computer-generated ants, for example, to a cold zone – considered cold by the computer – and you observe their behaviour, you'll be able to learn something about the winter behaviour of real ants. [16]

The datascape is endowed with a spatiality and a temporality of its own, and thanks to computerization it can bring together a vast amount of data. The latter, once they have been extracted from the world, take on a life of their own within this virtual, organic landscape. The dream of the 'datarchitects' is to condense town planning into a sort of artificial ecology of data, coordinated mechanically. Taking the risk of confusing the complex with the complicated, to quote Bruno Latour's objection,[17] they devote all their attention to more and more sophisticated models of social and morphological aspects of the town.

At the beginning of the 1990s, the Japanese architect Makoto Sei Watanabe initiated a research project entitled 'The Induction City Project', which set out to formulate a method of conceiving contemporary urban architecture that could not be fixed or designed. He concluded that this is 'composed of numerous elements, which, although each is governed by relatively simple rules, are linked to one another in such a complex manner that the evolution of all of them is very difficult to predict'.[18] Watanabe's idea is not so much to construct a datascape that will apply collected data to reality as to use the computer as a complex, autonomous system and as a metaphor for the town. The data at work in his 'induction cities' belong to the computer, i.e. they are not statistical (demographic, economic, geographical) but straightforward digital codes. Watan-

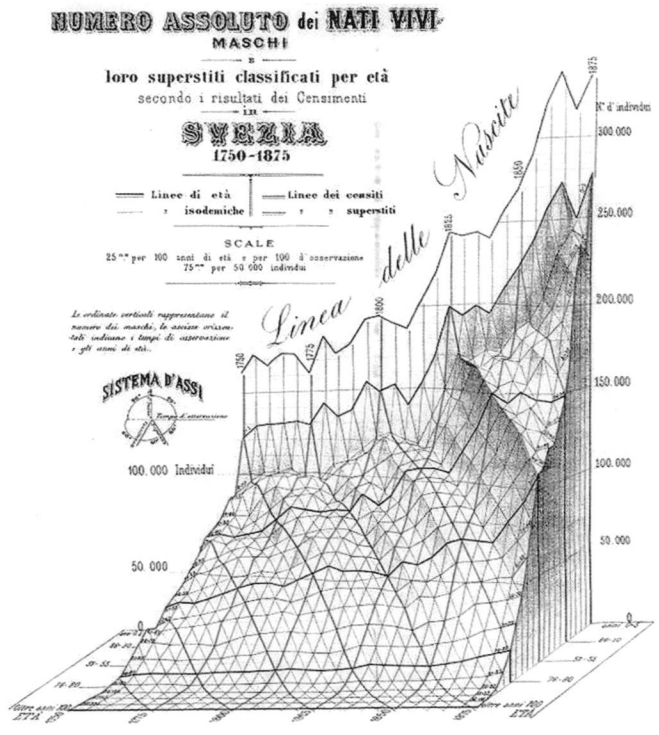

Demographic stereogram of Sweden between 1750 and 1875, 1880 (Luigi Perozzo).

Data arcs (Lucent Technologies).

abe, as a virtual zoologist, sits at his computer and studies the relationships between these codes in all their complexity, then 'induces' a possible interpretation of the ways in which the real city functions. His project *Induction City* has so far produced a dozen induced towns whose names seem to have been drawn from science fiction: 'Momentarily Materialized City', 'City of the Sun God', 'City of Correlative Wave Motion', 'City of Distorted Space' — each of them the fruit of a particular computer-generated experiment, and constituting the pages of a kind of virtual chorographic atlas.

But the multiplicity of these urban datascapes, these virtual monads, ultimately harks back to the multiplicity of Calvino's invisible towns. Marco Polo, at the court of the Great Khan, went through a long list of fictional towns, but underlying his list was the fundamental impossibility of getting directly to the one real town that was always in mind but of which he never spoke, and that was Venice. In the same way, wandering around all these datascapes cannot untangle the irreducible complexity of the contemporary town, but the accumulation of its infinite representations allows us to sketch the impossible portrait.■

This article was first published in the magazine AMC, no. 126, June–July 2002.

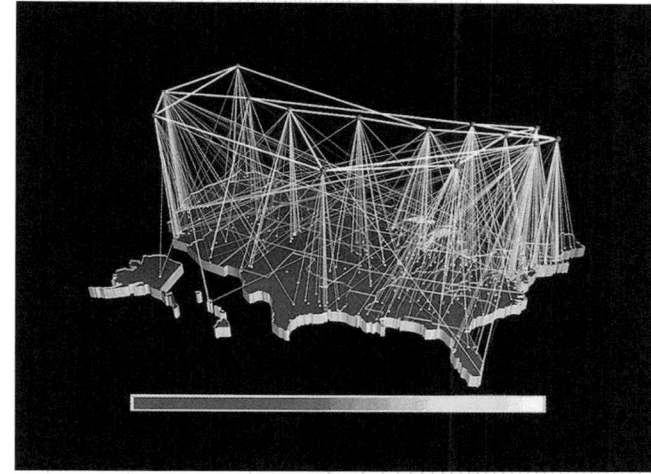

Measure of 'nsfnet' flows.

Notes

1. MVRDV, *Metacity/Datatown*, Rotterdam, 010 Publishers, 1999.

2. Italo Calvino, *Les villes invisibles*, Paris, Seuil, 1974 (1972), p. 142.

3. Le Corbusier, *Aircraft*, Milan, Abitare Segesta, 1996 (1935), ch. 9.

4. Michel de Certeau, *L'invention du quotidien, 1. arts de faire*, Paris, Gallimard, 1990 (1980), p. 140.

5. Bruno Latour, Émilie Hermant, *Paris ville invisible*, Paris, Les Empêcheurs de penser en rond/La Découverte, 1998, p. 14.

6. Loc. cit., p. 14.

7. Le Corbusier, *Urbanisme*, Paris, Flammarion, 1994 (1925), p. 101.

8. See Enrico Chapel, *Cartes et figures de l'urbanisme scientifique en France (1910-1943)*, Th: Urbanisme, Université Paris VII, 2000.

9. See Gilles Palsky, *Des chiffres et des cartes, naissance de la cartographie quantitative française au XIXe siècle*, Paris, Comité des travaux historiques et scientifiques, 1996.

10. Enrico Chapel, 'Représenter la "ville fonctionelle"', in *Les cahiers de la recherche architecturale et urbaine*, no. 8, May 2001, pp. 41-50.

11. André Corboz, 'La description: entre lecture et écriture', *Faces*, no. 48, autumn 2000, p. 52.

12. See Patrick Geddes, 'On the Classification of Statistics and its Results', *Proceedings of the Royal Society of Edinburgh*, vol. XI, 1881, pp. 295-322.

13. Ibid., p. 302.

14. Method of systematic, preparatory investigation devised by Patrick Geddes to study and plan towns; cf. P. Geddes, *L'évolution des villes*, Paris, Téménos, 1993 (1915), pp. 305-332.

15. Le Corbusier, *Urbanisme*, Paris, Grés, 1925, p. 99.

16. Makoto Sei Watanabe, 'Induction City, in Search of a "Free Order": How to Guide, not Design, the City', in *Intercommunication*, no. 12, 1995.

17. Bruno Latour, Émilie Hermant, op. cit., p. 53.

18. Makoto Sei Watanabe, op. cit.

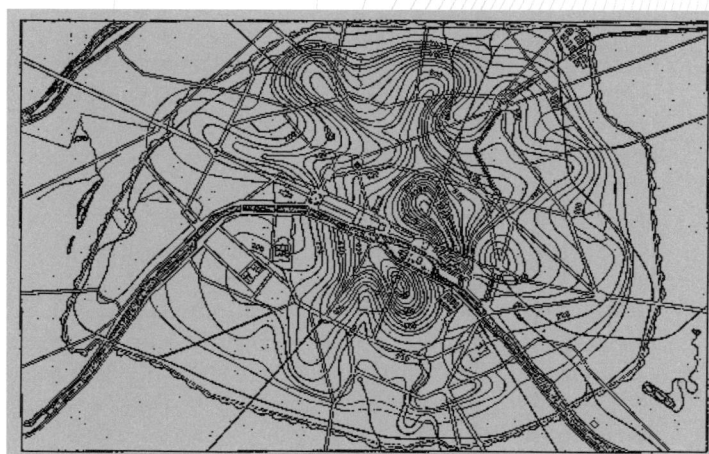

Chart showing density of population in Paris, 1874 (L. L.Vauthier).

Bart Lootsma

Biomorphic Intelligence and Urban Landscape

Thinking about architecture in terms of 'earth economics' suddenly reveals a deep schism between the United States and Europe. Whereas in the United States 'ecology' is mainly taken as a new opportunity to produce contemporary cultural images and organizations in architectural projects, in Europe the emphasis is put on urbanism in the sense of understanding and organizing large-scale social, economical and political processes.

In 1995, the editors of *Assemblage* wrote an introduction to two projects by Greg Lynn and Reiser/Umemoto for the Cardiff Bay Opera House, in which they talked about a return to the 1960s and about ecology. They did their utmost to make clear that this had nothing to do with the 'old ecology of the messy evangelical politics of the 1960s green movement', but instead with the computer's powerful qualities in the fields of physics and biology; they saw here an aspiration to biomorphic intelligence, adapted for the design phase. 'We would like to suggest that the *oikos* and the *logos* of ecology in the 1990s is the computer and the theories and images of complexity it makes possible.'[1] Instead of relying on symmetry as a general organizational principle (according to Greg Lynn something which, in the design process, can be compared to a 'default' position in the software), the architects make use of new computer software that consists of open, flexible and adaptive systems, which they think will help them improve organization. But of course the ecological aspect relates only to the way the internal organization of a project uses information from the site in the design process. In the end, the built form of the project appears as an autonomous and static unit. It is implied that the different organization of the projects, the way they are dealing with a different form of symmetry, is better suited to accommodate 'life'.

Certainly, this new tradition in architectural thinking, which, since the early 1990s, has deeply influenced architects all over the world, produces interesting forms and organizations that are powerful and important contemporary cultural statements. However, it neg-

lects the fact that any architectural form inevitably intervenes in the organization of life. An architectural project may grow like an organism in the design phase, but its realization on the building site, which usually takes place later, even years later, marks a brutal break in this process and it is only after this that the building is colonized by its inhabitants or users. Their settlement, which could theoretically very well be an organic process, reacts to the functional organization of the building it finds, not to the original conditions on the site. Of course, this could still be an improvement on more traditional forms of organization but, strictly speaking, this means that this approach in the end produces only a simulacrum of life, not life itself in the original 'ecology' (by which I do not mean the ecology of the computer but the ecology that feeds the computer).

More important, American architects seem to have settled for the limited political role they can play in the process of large-scale urbanization. This certainly differs from the situation in the European welfare states, where architects, urban designers and landscape architects always had a role that was immediately related to politics. The concepts they developed could therefore influence politics as well. However, the political organization in Europe in regard to urban planning and at the same time the physical environment in which European architects work are changing dramatically. Thus a highly unstable situation arises, in which the ecological dimension takes on a new meaning. This new condition forces and inspires European architects to come up with new concepts to regulate urbanization.

Instability

In Europe, over the last decade, landscape is becoming a more and more important issue and the influence of landscape architects in urban planning and urban design has increased. Of course, this has to do with the increasing political weight that is given to ecology. According to Adriaan Geuze, a landscape architect himself, the success of landscape architects in urban planning is also explained by their natural ability to deal with unstable situations. 'Architects and industrial designers often see their designs as a final product of genius, whose aesthetic entirety originated in their minds. A design like that can be ruined by the slightest hitch or damage. Landscape architects have learnt to put that into perspective, because they know their designs are continually adapted and transformed. We have learned to see landscape not as a *fait accompli*, but as the result of countless forces and initiatives.'[2] This is interesting, because it shows how ecological thinking, beyond designing green corridors and nice pavements and parks, is becoming an integral part of urbanism.

Indeed, when Adriaan Geuze made his remark, eight years ago in 1994, Europe was going through the first phase of a process of changes that speeded up after the collapse of communism in Eastern Europe in 1989. These changes have to do with the unification of Europe, which is first and foremost economically driven: the ultimate goal being the creation of a free market with such a critical mass that it could compete with other large economies in the world. This reorganization has, however, many side effects. Basically, they cause a dramatic crisis of the European welfare state. And as architecture and urban planning have always been at the core of the welfare state they are in crisis as well.

The suspension of national borders, the introduction of new infrastructure such as high-speed train lines and the liberalization of air traffic produce a reshuffling of regions, in which some gain importance and others lose it. From a continent of competing countries, Europe will change into a continent of competing regions, cities and companies. However, within the European countries, old provincial and municipal borders and the national, provincial and municipal governments with their corresponding policies and jurisdictions remain largely unchanged.

The introduction of the euro causes many instances of deregulation and privatization, because in order to make the euro a stable currency, the national deficits and inflation levels have to be reduced to an absolute minimum. This means that many services that were traditionally not only publicly controlled but also publicly financed, such as urban planning, infrastructure and social housing, are taken over by the market. All of this naturally happens on top of worldwide tendencies of globalization and individualization and against the background of what Ulrich Beck has called the 'Risk Society'.[3] The awareness of collective environmental risks has enormous consequences for the reorganization of the rural landscape. It does not mean simply that nature reserves are protected but also that policies to stimulate biological farming will totally change the agricultural landscape in large parts of Europe.

As most European cities have reached their limits of expansion and the agricultural land that surrounds them loses its economic base, outside of their territories unprecedented and uncontrolled processes of sprawl occur. These processes are based on countless individual initiatives but nevertheless the development occurs so rapidly that whole regions change in character in just a few years. Now that the dominant flows of capital have definitively shifted from governments and municipalities to the market, we witness a tendency towards fragmentation, as more and more independent parties are involved in the way the built-up environment takes shape. New developments are divided into many small parts that appear relatively unrelated. However, taken together, they certainly threaten the traditional concept of landscape, as something that is opposed to the city, whether it is essentially natural or agricultural. Instead, we see the rise of a boundless 'città diffusa', as Bernardo Secchi called it.

More than in any other European country, in the Netherlands the debate about architecture and urban planning revolves around different strategies to preserve the remaining open and green parts of the landscape. This is of course not surprising in one of the most densely populated countries in the world. It is the key issue to understand government policies about planning, but also to understand much of the architectural work that is produced. The existence of these governmental policies, which even involve national planning, explains the radical nature of some projects by OMA, such as Point City/South City and the densification of the city centre of Almere. The former is a polemical radicalization of the fourth national plan, which is largely based on concentrated growth in and around existing cities; the latter is the consequence of this memorandum on a local scale. In the case of OMA, the belief in more concentrated forms of urbanization is also a belief in the quality of urban culture.

Also, the work of MVRDV cannot be understood without this specific tradition of national planning policies in the Netherlands, but, unlike in the case of OMA, the fear of collective ecological risks plays a more crucial role. MVRDV wants to reveal these collective risks to a larger audience and to politics to force collective solutions that would maintain or even restore a clear distinction between city and countryside. Metacity/Datatown is an installation that wants to explain to a large audience what the spatial consequences are of certain policies that deal with, among other things, food production and waste. Pig City not only demonstrates the spatial consequences of biological pig farming (it would occupy most of the Dutch territory) but also proposes a solution in the form of autarkic high-rises that incorporate everything from food production for the pigs and manure recycling to the slaughterhouse. 3D City is an exploration into the possibilities of building a three-dimensional megacity that would allow large parts of the landscape to be kept open for purposes of ecology and leisure.

The methods MVRDV uses are largely derived from the methods modernist urban planners developed in the first half of the 20th century. Like them, they first present the problems of the contemporary city in an exaggerated form. The design method makes use of extrapolations of demographic, economic, technological and all kinds of other statistical data that are, however, reorganized differently in order to produce proposals for new cities. This is very similar to what Le Corbusier, Hilberseimer, Van Eesteren and Van Lohuizen did.[4] However, the situation today is very different from the early 20th century. Cities are more and more dependent on each other, not only when they are close to each other, but even at global level. Also, unexpected or negative side-effects cannot be externalized as easily as they used to be. Therefore, in order to make these methods work again, MVRDV has to create conditions that are like the growing of culture in a petri dish: all their projects are thought of as autarkic. That makes the projects of MVRDV, to paraphrase Slavoj Zizek's criticism of the risk society, at the same time too general and too specific. Not only do we not know what our actions really add up to, but also there is no global mechanism that regulates our interaction. The risks of the risk society are so ungraspable that they become almost irrational.[5]

It is interesting that these issues raised the same problems for Van Lohuizen and Hilberseimer. Hilberseimer emphasized the importance of regional plans when he was working for Chicago. In solving them for Amsterdam in the 1920s, Van Lohuizen discovered the Randstad, the ring-shaped conurbation in the west of the Netherlands, incorporating Amsterdam, Haarlem, The Hague, Rotterdam and Utrecht. Later on, these arguments convinced the Dutch government to come up with national plans. However, in the fifth version of the Dutch national plan, which came out recently and is currently being discussed in the Dutch parliament, it is interesting to note that national and even municipal borders are not included in the maps any more. The Netherlands finds itself in a continuum that starts somewhere in the North Sea – a more urbanized zone than one would expect – and stretches into Germany and Belgium. One has to be very well informed to see the differences in the development in these countries. The dominant features are the landscape in terms of its geological characteristics, existing cities and conurbations and infrastructure. One of the main criticisms of this fifth national plan is that it remains quite unclear how the minister will protect the characteristics of the landscape by limiting the growth of certain developments. This is not just a problem for the Netherlands, but a general problem of urbanism today.

The work of MVRDV would like to be a solution for this problem, but the difficulty is that, just like the projects of the modernists, it relies on a form of representational democracy that deals with masses and takes decisions for the masses. However, unlike in the early 20th century, nowadays European society cannot be so easily defined in terms of a class struggle, even if it is still very much present in many different ways, and the policies to deal with it cannot be so easily generalized. In Europe, the middle class has attained unprecedented importance. Apart from globalization, individualization is one of the most dominant characteristics of contemporary society. Individualization is a process that will probably continue in many different forms over the next decades, as globalization (migration, global culture, production) and ideological arguments from the traditional left and the traditional right that favour individualization (the freedom to shape one's own biography and individual entrepreneurship as the basis of capitalism) merge into a complex force field. One thing is clear, however: that the 'pure' individual, as he or she appears in various different ideologies, does not exist, but operates in all kinds of groups and groupings, organizations and networks – 'multiplicities', as Foucault and Deleuze call them – which very often transcend or expand over national borders. We will have to investigate the functioning and power of these multiplicities much more to understand them, whether it is just the spatial manifestation of the multiplicities themselves, as I have tried to do with my students at the Berlage Institute in the past couple of years,[6] or the multiplicities as they manifest themselves within a certain territory or morphology, as Stefano Boeri has done.

Boeri started analysing the kind of processes of urban transformation that produce the 'città diffusa' in the Milan region as long ago as the 1980s. In *Il territorio che cambia: Ambienti, paesaggi e immagini delle regione milanese*, written in collaboration with Arturo Lanzani and Edoardo Marini, he develops a new language to describe this new urban landscape. The analysis is based on a careful interpretation of various maps, aerial views and photographs taken by Gabriele Basilico. In the end, Boeri develops a series of prototypical developments, based on a reading of 'urban facts'.[7] In *Italy, Cross Sections of a Country* Boeri develops this method fur-

ther.[8] In the research developed with the 'Multiplicity' team for the 'Mutations' exhibition in Bordeaux, Boeri shows himself to be more interested in the driving forces that produce change from within certain territories.[9] However, Boeri has not yet come up with a design strategy based on this research. Xaveer de Geyter, whose approach in his book *After-Sprawl* is in many ways similar to that of Boeri, does come up with solutions, but only in the form of a catalogue that again demands a kind of eclectic representational democratic body.[10]

The Milan region Boeri is dealing with is still linked to a major city, even if the developments cross borders and stretch out into Ticino in Switzerland. But there are also developments in areas that either encompass several cities or are even far away from major cities, but, within a Europe without borders, suddenly occupy a new strategic position. An important criterion is that these areas offer a high quality of life, which is usually related to the natural quality of the landscape. The province of Noord Brabant in the Netherlands is one example; others include the Belgium of Xaveer de Geyter, the Ruhrgebiet, Thomas Sievertz's 'Zwischenstadt' near Stuttgart and the triangle Basel–Zurich–Bern. Certain areas in the Swiss Alps (St Moritz) and the area around Graz in Austria also fall into the same category, and there are probably several others. This condition, which cannot any longer be called simply 'sprawl' and which Xaveer de Geyter therefore calls 'after-sprawl', is becoming the generic urban condition in Europe.

The landscape architects Stefan Tischer and Helene Hoelzl, for example, have proposed various ways of structuring the pressure on Bolzano in Italy. As Silvano Bassetti of the city of Bolzano writes in the introduction to the book in which the plan is presented: 'It is not the organized expansion of the city that threatens the landscape. The land "spoils itself" from the inside; it changes into something else and delivers itself to speculation.'[11] After an intensive analysis of the area, Tischer and Hoelzl propose something different: a series of building rules that are based on the four existing landscapes they distinguish in Bolzano. The characteristic of these landscapes is thus safeguarded, while at the same time the permitted new buildings have specific qualities that are derived from their location in the landscape. Still, the rules allow for private initiatives and developments.

In an introduction to the project, Tischer and Hoelzl write that, 'over the last decades, urbanism knew only one way of expanding. Piece by piece, parts of the landscape were taken away and urbanized: it was the city against the landscape.'[12] This seems to be a crucial point for any new approach that seeks to deal with the 'rural urbanism' that is demanded today. It is a field that, compared with the approaches that were developed in the early 20th century, has to deal with many contradictions. Bas Princen for example, discovered that in the Dutch province of Brabant certain programmes that are realized in the countryside, programmes that are basically 'urban' (notably those that are related to leisure: theme parks, second houses, villa parks, certain sports), even generate forest. These programmes attach themselves to existing 'green', for example former production forests that have been turned into nature reserves, and then build a forest around the new development.[13]

A completely new method – even if it draws on methods developed by the Situationists – has been developed by Raoul Bunschoten and Chora. Like Stefano Boeri, Bunschoten works on different scales at the same time: from the scale of satellite photographs that show global movements to very local situations. However, Bunschoten is not so much interested in the history of typological and morphological changes, but in the future extrapolation of certain narratives and their spatial consequences or, better, the consequences for the transformation of what he calls the 'Skin of the Earth'. To trace the possible origins of these narratives, Bunschoten uses a series of different methods: from the study of larger political, economic and social processes to the Situationist stance, and from the analysis of human behaviour to game theory.[14] More than any other contemporary architect, Bunschoten, who is a profound scholar of Spinoza, uses the dynamics of the multiplicity itself to generate possible spatial scenarios. His work therefore appears both very real and down to earth and at the same time poetic, even utopian. This can be a strength as long as his methods are used in workshops with different parties to reveal the potential of a site — what Bunschoten calls the proto-urban conditions. However, it is also a weakness, because he categorically refuses to take the existing power structures or representational bodies into account.

It seems to me that the phenomenon of what Xaveer de Geyter calls 'after-sprawl' is a much better explanation for the importance of rural/landscape architects than just their ability to deal with instability. The terrain in which this sprawl occurs is the traditional terrain of the landscape architect. He is experienced in dealing not just with the geological characteristics but also with the many small municipalities that have a say in the process. For urban planners and designers do not operate only outside the city; they are in the habit of dealing with just one political body: the town hall.

Unlike in the early 20th century, it is not the city that is under threat of pollution, congestion and diseases, but nature and the countryside. That is a very fundamental reversal, to which no one has yet found a real answer. The debate about the landscape is always very lively and emotional. Even though landscape has long since been a manufactured product, there is still the idea that landscape equals nature. And nature, unless it produces a direct threat to civilization, is always good and beautiful. Landscape architects have always relied on the implicit goodness of what they are doing. Now they are facing a period in which they have to propose cogently argued regional plans to seduce and convince politicians, just as urban planners and designers of the 20th century had to do for the city. They will have to get their hands dirty, not just put a few plants in pots. They will have to conduct research into the processes that transform these regions. And, just like the generation of architects and urbanists that grew up in the 1920s, they will have to involve themselves in politics, in the formulation of laws and norms, to come up with a consensus about a bureaucracy that is able to deal with the issues involved in the contemporary landscape. Designing is not enough: it is about the implementation of schemes and the limitation of undesirable and unsustainable developments. Indeed, this is an enormous task; to quote Ulrich Beck again, 'today, any attempt to come up with a new concept that would provide social cohesion must abandon the idea that individualism, diversity and scepticism are rooted in Western culture'.[15] It would be interesting to know if we could merge the best of the American approach to ecology, in which computer simulations are used to deal with complex dynamic systems, with the very real political issues European architects are dealing with. Probably we will have to merge the two approaches. But also we will have to find ways to predict how both approaches, either separately or together, will develop into the future, be it by extrapolation or within strategic policies. It may be a cynical view, but the only thing that might help in this process is that landscape, in terms of vast expanses of natural, uninhabited green, is becoming an increasingly scarce commodity. ☑

Notes

1. Computer Animisms (Two designs for the Cardiff Bay Opera House), Assemblage 26, 1995.
2. Adriaan Geuze in conversation with Olof Koekebakker, 'Verzoening met het eigentijdse landschap', Items, 46, July 1994.
3. Ulrich Beck, Risk Society: Towards a New Modernity, London, Sage, 1992.
4. Nanne de Ru, Cornelis van Eesteren & Theodoor Karel van Lohuizen, 'Contemporary Twins of Urbanism', in Bart Lootsma (ed.), Research for Research, Rotterdam, Berlage Institute, 2002.
5. Slavoj Zizek, 'Multiculturalism, or The Cultural Logic of Multinational Capitalism', New Left Review, September–October 1997.
6. Bart Lootsma, 'Individualisierung', ARCH+, 158, 2002.
7. Stefano Boeri, Arturo Lanzani, Edoardo Marini, Il territorio che cambia: Ambienti, paesaggi e immagini della regione Milanese, Milan, Abitare Segesta Cataloghi, 1993.
8. Stefano Boeri, Gabriele Basilico, Italy, Cross Sections of a Country, Zurich, Berlin and New York, Scalo, 1996.
9. Stefano Boeri, 'USE Uncertain States of Europe', in Rem Koolhaas, Harvard Project on the City; Stefano Boeri, Multiplicity; Sanford Kwinter and others, Mutations, Bordeaux, Arc en Rêve; Barcelona, ACTAR, 2000.
10. Xaveer de Geyter, After-Sprawl, Antwerp, De Singel; Rotterdam, Nai Publishers, 2002.
11. Silvano Bassetti, 'Problemstellung: Bedarf an Baugründen und Bodenknappheit. Szenarien für die Stadtverdichtung als Qualitätslösung', in Stefan Tischer, Helene Hoelzl, MetrogrammA, Vier Vorschläge zur Städtebaulichen Verdichtung in Bozen, Bolzano, Commune di Bolzano, 2001.
12. Stefan Tischer, Helene Hoelzl, 'Landschaft wird Stadt', in op. cit.
13. Bas Princen, unpublished manuscript, Rotterdam, Berlage Institute, 2002.
14. Raoul Bunschoten, Urban Flotsam, Rotterdam, 010 Publishers, 2001.
15. Ulrich Beck, 'Je eigen leven leiden in een op hol geslagen wereld', ARCHIS, 2/2001.

Yves Nacher

Economic Horror?
(or : the air du temps is definitely to blame)

Could you please repeat the question?

'Earth economics' – has verdolatry struck again? It is true (we are told) that architecture, not to mention the town, is finished; from now on it's territory or nothing. Like a steroid-inflated surfer on a wave of foam skilfully whisked into peaks, nature – as everyone knows – is hurtling back into fashion. In a way this is only fair, since it has been forced into exile for so many decades: the living, the indomitable, the 'un-normable' were taboo in those times of modern utopias, Reconstruction, the Glorious Thirties, washed by the currents of unifying concepts devised for the statistical delight of standardized users. All that mattered was territory tamed, planned, divided into sections, developed and domesticated. But from now on the earth will come roaring out of its desert hideaway. It is doing so through the renaissance of a reasoned, critical and historical idea that provides a framework for discussion, but also through the emergence of some sharp-shooting creative spirits whose projects and constructions have undermined the conventions. With this impetus, and in view of the stifling and sterilizing effects so often brought about by discourses on architecture and the city, there is a clear temptation for territory (which is to the earth what the high seas are to the drunkenness of the ocean) to adjust the discourse and substitute itself as the new ecumenical rallying point of all the operational disciplines, filling the immense gap in the construct, not to mention the even more immense gap between the external surfaces of our bodies.

These intermediate periods are open to all the amalgamations, all the tempting fusions and confusions of discourse, all the aesthetic and semantic acrobatics whose discipline is in inverse proportion to their elegance. The earth as an economy (not to be confused with the economics of the earth) can sometimes become the wrapping paper around chimeras that leak in all directions. Architecture is not the town or the landscape or the territory, but it emerges in all these fields from new influences, new contacts, new adaptations, which through creative processes transform themselves into the delights of novelty.

What then can be the point of an ArchiLab that demands the concept of earth economics? If there is one, it is probably this: to make visible and comprehensible these new synergies and attitudes and the new creations that emerge from them. It is indeed time that we made the effort to gain a clear view of these strange relationships that interweave through our contemporary territories, where architectural theories are tested on the town, or theories of landscape and territorial management affect our scale of proximity. The prime objective is to organize ideas and to establish focal points in order to prevent chaos. Any reference to the idea of ecology already brings us close to the danger area: an ecology of groupies, total greenery as a new religion – no, thanks! This is not the time (no longer the time, should never have been the time?) either for a catalogue full of green architecture or for a cautious – let alone revisionist – return to Rousseau. The time has come for some urgent clearing of the ways rather than projects, for attitudes that will illuminate a lateral-thinking, inquiring and open-minded level of understanding relating to the scale of thought and distribution of architecture. The economics of the earth comprises everything except the politically correct sufferings of young green-earthers.

The hot potato

The fine sounds, the association of mysterious ideas, ranging from Viviane Forrester to José Bové, from FMI to Jardiland – no matter who has set it to music, this earth economics has handed them the hot potato. From land artists to every clone of François Roche, from Situationists to new landscapists, a vast jumble of experiments and experimenters pulling in different directions and thereby blurring the borders between architecture and … whatever it is. Fragmentary theses and speeches make it clear that something is going on, but what?

In the light of the works of such creative minds as those invited to contribute to this ArchiLab (and of course justifiably invited), the contemporary city is no longer a monolithic body predetermined by a peaceful and standardized process of evolution. It seems instead to be in a state of permanent collision between different but simultaneous forces, with an urgent need for a dose of Dramamine – a scrapbook of realities that come and instantly go, a hypertext of symbols and jumbled forms. Hierarchies rearrange themselves, and the emergent notion of the 'landscape' – borrowed from the image of nature reassembled under the sign of the town – appears like a system on a par with traditional urban concepts, capable of articulating and organizing architecture and the town by rescuing nature as a dimension of the whole construct. Rather than drawing a contrast between the systems of nature and those of man, we must therefore explore the paths of a dialectic topography, a structuring cohabitation. Might this be a first step towards finally getting rid of the poisonous roots?

Right in the eye!

Is the earth democratic? That remains to be seen. The 'environmental imperative' shows clearly that, constantly, before our eyes, no matter where we are, the landscape dictates conditions. Is the earth unequivocal? Let the stones reply for us: a collection of pebbles will not be seen in the same way by, say, a sedimentologist or a tourist walking on the seashore. No matter how different they may be, the two approaches may each be unequivocal, but the point of view will not be the same. We are not that far away here from Greek tragedy, in which two protagonists may quarrel, each having a valid truth that simply differs from that of the other, but the conflict can traditionally be resolved only by the one killing the other. In order to understand this new 'territory of the earth', one can choose to attach oneself to the truth of the geographer or that of the portrait artist, to physical reality or to its representation – which means its interpretation. The fabrications of the eyes, the justifications and the power of language and the actions based on those fabrications are effectively the starting-point of the necessary clearing operation to rid us of all the confusions surrounding the 'greening' and the globalization or 'blobalization' of discourse on architecture and its frontiers.

In terms of the 'environmental imperative', science has reorganized our vision. When the Church clung to its parochial divisions in order to divide up the land as well our souls, geography patiently redrew the territory in physically objective units, logical patterns imposed on a nature that had been deprived of its sacred aura. The geographer's vision and the economics of his earth do not describe forms or conditions but systems of relating and organizing natural elements, at the risk of seeing there – what sacrilege! – the signature of man.

Despite himself, the artist too, with his 'polite society landscapes', has formed our vision, but of a very different nature – in all senses of the word. Landscape painting (a genre that ranges from the sublime to the naff) and Romantic literary description (which encompasses the same qualitative range) are not concerned with physical characteristics but with the density of emotions that arise out of a place.

Between place and emotion the earth thus finds its way into culture. If the notion of landscape – which architects will henceforth be demanding – served in the past to engage the eye rather than the hand, i.e. to affect vision rather than to effect action, we shall now be concentrating on action. One must put one's cards on the table.

One train may hide another

We are living at a time when other contradictions and considerations have made these various stratifications even more complex. By penetrating to the very heart of the cell, science has blurred our perception of nature to the point at which this has become less and less the mysterious, nourishing power that emerged from the Big Bang (or Genesis, depending on which version you adhere to) and more and more our own creation. Authenticity can now be more artificial than natural, questioning our dialectic relationship with what is real and true. How can our 'new' architects also invest this territory with a relationship to nature – or, to be more precise, a relationship to an image of nature – in this age of vicarious living, when we measure out our weeks in Valium and see the world at weekends on a flat screen with square corners?

The most pressing questions on this subject are being urged on us by certain teams of architects, often young, who demand that the signs of nature be manipulated so that they may form an element of their architectural corpus, as if this were the key to reading the town and the territory, a metaphor for a theoretical line and/or a repertoire of forms. Following this reasoning, there are some who seek to reinvent the fusion of architecture and nature – not in the manner of a Richard Neutra house ingeniously photographed by Julius Shulman or of Philip Johnson's glass house with its illusion of disappearing into its own depths, but in that of the wizards of genetic modification. The menu: parasitism, chameleon's syndrome, topographic fusion, strategic camouflage, reshuffling of the hierarchy between the construct and the pseudo-natural, the charms of tectonics and texture, the breakdown of accepted systems of comprehension and analysis.

For all that, it is no longer a question of merely thinking romantically about the 1990s art of incorporating nostalgia for nature into new architectural approaches. The nine-day intellectual wonder is over, for, with verdolatry taking root, it is now a matter of conquest: conquering the spaces of visibility (ArchiLab, for example), conquering credibility, conquering contracts, conquering power.

Architects use formatted spaces of visibility quite deliberately in order to get points for credibility: Landscape is in the air! Landscape is everywhere! Landscape emerges as the solution in times when architecture and urbanism are losing out [on] significance. For their part, the landscapists, racing against the architects after disputes between hippie 'anthropophobes', obsessed with totalitarian ecology, and urban designers à la Barcelona of the last century (oh yes, it goes back that far), are finding a new way: they no longer flaunt themselves as ayatollah-type authorities, but expose themselves to the risk of being impregnated by concepts from other professions – such as architecture, urbanism, engineering.

If we admit that earth economics comes down to the phenomenon (though this is far from being the case) of osmosis between architecture and territory and to positions as theoretically developed as they are intimately connected with the relationship between architecture, town and nature, then this collection of architects brings together all the protagonists and leaves them to convince us. With a bit of luck, the answers will come in due course. Be patient!

Manuel Gausa

Architecture is (Now) Geography
(Other Urban 'Natures')

From 'Object Architecture' to 'Environmental Architecture'

The research framework proposed by ArchiLab for 2002 allows us to assemble a series of particularly significant lines of thought at a time when we are faced with a situation that is becoming increasingly complex, potentially hybridized and decidedly heterodox in relation to the urban structures that nowadays define our environment. The challenge is to create meeting-places — and not confrontations — between the old, self-contained categories: nature and artifice, architecture and landscape, town and territory, construction and environment.

Rather than 'object architectures' we should be able to speak of 'environmental architectures' — those associated with a new understanding of 'place' (and space in general) as a field of forces — open and plural — and no longer with a fixed and stabilized context (historical, typological, figurative, etc.) These architectures could be described as 'fields-in-fields' (njiric & njiric[1]), and they would resolve the paradoxes of a nature that has been imposed on territories of intersection between contexts and locations, tensions and appeals, limitations and frontiers, sites and surroundings. The very notion of complexity breaks open the old seals and dichotomies, for it denotes a capacity to combine and match — actively and interactively — the vast amount of not always consistent information within a common framework of relations (and interrelations). We also talk of 'reactive architectures', which respond to their surroundings (location, context) and activate (bypass, transfer) them beyond their own limits. This may be a matter of taking to its extreme the developmental capacity of form, or of bringing about contamination or mutations between systems and settings; or one may have to call upon the generic and the unique, the organic and the mechanical, the mineral and the vegetable — all with new proce-

dures of propagation and hybridization. New structures of topological definition or deformation may be developed, in order finally to compress the very nature — local and global — of the town and the dynamic processes that govern it into new, multi-layered landscapes.

New environments for new natures. Animated matrixes, compressive lines, synthetic geometries of pressures, seams and counter-currents, but also live, sensitive, tattooed skins — these will all constitute a new 'naturartificial' repertoire relating more to 'irregular' configurations of differential orders than to the old regular, compact and well-ordered volumetrics.

To dynamic evolutions rather than static positions.

To impure developments rather than basic figurations.

To open reasoning rather than closed models.

To processes rather than accidents.

To topologies rather than typologies.

To 'landscapes' rather than 'edifices'.

Architectures established (from now on) like geographies.

'Criss-crossing': the place of intersection

Nowadays we are aware of the fact that the static rigidity, predictability and permanence of the traditional town and of the project parameters that may be associated with it (control, figuration, stability) have loosened, faced with the indeterminacy and mutability of the contemporary town, and are giving way to the dynamic manifestations of a living organism forever unfinished (and open), in a constant process of evolution, distortion, transformation.

The old 'genius loci' has therefore ceased to reflect immutable, permanent, basic, always identifiable principles, and has become an ever more diffuse abstraction: that of an almost 'spectral' field of forces that are both visible and invisible, multiple and mutable, whose global and local needs and tensions can be observed in all their animated interactions.[2] The traditional, established one-way system of the old morphological or typological definitions has thus been replaced by exchange operations that are less profiled, less linear and literal, and more multifaceted and ambivalent, underlining and reflecting the massive complexity of modern reality.

The authentic cultural dimension of modern architecture therefore derives from its capacity to deal efficiently with the apparent weaknesses of our environment – and of the place, which is viewed as the simple 'décor' of pre-existences – starting out from a new and active intelligence. This must penetrate deep into the notions of 'milieu', 'place', 'context', which may all be subsumed under the heading of 'fields', and into the criss-crossing of all the attendant forces, tensions, contexts and actions. These are no longer protective wrappings or reliable points of reference; they are anticipatory and unfinished situations that must give new impetuses, taking heed of the many 'musics' – not always harmonious – that permeate them, and establishing unusual synergies (resonant and mutable) that will shape courses that are complicit but not necessarily dependent or symbiotic.

These are the considerations that provide the starting-point for our exploration of some of the actions envisaged here; our interest lies not only in the potential of these responses, but also in their implicit desire for new alignments of the 'intersections' within the never-ending ambivalence and imprecision that characterizes the settings increasingly linked to 'places' in transit. Rather than 'contexts' we now have 'syntexts', because they are 'synthe(x)tic' (condensers of multiple demands) and 'sans-texts' (devoid of referential texts), which combine – or could combine – abstract, generic (systematic and symptomatic) logic and specific (contextual, i.e., contingent) reactions in new operations adapted to new conditions.

What can give force to such projects is precisely this capacity to give new impetus to a place, in the sense of creating resonance, synergy, interaction with it, while at the same time transcending it, criss-crossing it, multiplying it rather than completing it. This would bring out its potentials, would overcome its inertias and would reveal the landscape of what already is together with what is not yet.

The place as specific environment, as context – or 'syntext' – thus multiplied as a field of manoeuvres, would no longer be a 'centre' but a 'limit'. It would now constitute an 'x' rather than a '+', and certainly not a '.' or a '='.

'To be a place and at the same time to summon up many others.'

'To contaminate oneself' and 'to contaminate'.[3]

Architectures and landscapes

The interesting aspect of the new projects presented here is the different possible interactions: bringing about new connections, activating new programmes, usages, settings both near and far, and so multiplying the identities that will produce hybrid relations to transform places into 'protoarchitectures' and architectures into unusual 'protoplaces'. All this will give rise to a rich interchange of forms, with architectures functioning as landscapes and landscapes as architectures.[4]

This interaction (recurrent in contemporary criticism) between architecture and landscape will therefore assume special connotations. Until now projects had taken on a dual role (operational object and iconic symbol), but henceforth they will also be regarded as the 'field of relations' that we have already mentioned, with the 'relational' functions of the landscape as the 'open space' but also as a 'narrative setting', a 'panorama or 'spectacle' of a territory. The landscape, then, will be a setting for movement, an open, indeterminate space, but additionally a 'territory of observations' of reality itself.

And so to speak of 'edifices' in the normal sense of the term will not reflect the strange situation of intersecting, interchanging architecture that defines itself as a reactive environment.(6) Here we have a 'field of forces in a field of forces', both to be seen as intermediate places between spaces and territories, between agents and disciplines, conditions and demands, classes and cases; these are ambiguous landscapes in geographies that are equally ambiguous, connected to – and approached via – the basic relations of topological fluctuations, effervescent or close-knit, in chains or in rolls, in counter-currents or gaps. If the internal order of these manoeuvres can be regarded as almost psychogeomorphic – geological, geodetic or geographical – the project (enhancing the principal tensions, partially or totally concealed, of the place or places it concerns) will take shape from the latent forces that one may term strata – and phases – of other situations and distinct movements brought to a situation of maximum tension and thus creating multiple interactions between settings, hierarchies and activities.

Many of the key concepts used in contemporary projects tend to suggest this possible '(trans)fusion' into (and with) the environment, linked to a growing distrust of an arrogant architecture viewed solely as a figure or object that has 'failed', a pure and remarkable entity cut off and alienated from any basis of action. If this progressive overlapping and interlocking between figure and base to which we are alluding here, this fusion or coupling – increasingly evident in proportion to the passage from the most urban to the most environmental, from the most tectonic to the quasi-topographic, from the Euclidean to the fractal – if, then, this overlapping could be interpreted from an essentialist perspective as an astute abandonment of the traditional concept of form (a loss of its old 'substantive' values, or a renunciation of its old – and earnest – 'representative' and 'positional' mission), it could also, with a less resistant eye, see itself as an advantageous joint decanting of object and environment into a dissolution of the old 'categorical' manifestations, and in most cases this would respond to fundamentally operative criteria able to generate layouts of greater flexibility, precisely because they are diffuse, capable of incorporating programmes, harmonizing courses of action and combining unities and imbalances into new hybrid actions. There would be new dynamics of cooperation and synergy (through infiltration, dissolution and/or fusion) between place, architecture and environment – not exempt from favourable ecological nuances (unified potentials, exploitation of energy, recycling of resources, integration of action) – directly related to the role of modern architecture and its new relational, connective function in settings that are increasingly congested through the production and consumption of objects; these settings would be equally marked by the exchange and transfer of a welter of information (free from prejudice and decoded) and by the rapid processing of data and other stimuli that will become less and less homologous and categorized, and more and more open to hybridization, criss-crossing, overlapping and coupling – to change and also to interchange. Transience, intangibility, debunking, but also 'fusion and transfusion', 'capture and manipulation', 'zapping', 'morphing', sampling', 'chunking', 'folding' – these would all allow us to question the significance of what we have called the 'architectonic object' (presence and essence) and its hypothetical (dif)fusion in a civilization of displacements (for example, movements, falls and bans), breakdowns, disappearances, dematerializations, and also amalgamations, combinations and interactions which tend to bring the virtual together with the real, the substantive (immanent) with the fortuitous (contingent).

The old confrontations would give way to new situations of cooperation and transference, unification and multiplication, new and cunning natures capable of reconciling apparently contradictory information and of combining potentials by dissolving, blurring or eliminating boundaries and profiles – pure, unequivocal or opaque – in favour of new 'crossbred' actions. There would be strategies of 'recodification' through 'discodification' (bypassing the old codes) or 'recoding' (proposing new codes), through which 'things' would become 'singular and plural' at the same time in a strange celebration of the complexities of the weird, the singular, the artificial, the irregular, the heterodox, the irreverent even. There would be simultaneity and combining of events, realities, messages and layers of superimposed and interactive information. It would no longer be a matter of 'diluting' oneself in or 'imposing' oneself on nature, but of creating a different type of nature(s) that would integrate artificially all its moments and movements. The more 'architecturing' the landscape (proposing new topological formations and organizations – folding, unfolding, refolding, cutting, reliefs, networks, counter-currents), the more 'landscaping' architecture would become (by transplanting the organic and synthetic codes – and the themes: insertions, infiltrations, incorporations, jumbles, mixtures, impressions ... materials changed and changeable). There would be Euclidean geometries, but also embodiments and recyclings, elements and textures on the borders between the sophisticated and the vulgar, the manufactured and the directly accessible – the raw material and the treated material.

There would be playful equivocations, strange and rich in their crossbreeding, new ecological aromas and resolutely modern strategies aimed at an uninhibited transformation of things or of their images frankly offhand or falsely naïve, sometimes too brazenly elementary (because they accept directly manipulative systems), dynamic processes that would provoke opposition because of their deceptively facile adherence to recent periods of history.[7] Metabolistic or organicistic temptations? Links with pop imagery? Venturian heritages? Malicious trompe-l'oeil figurations?

The fundamental difference would be precisely that one would leave behind the simply iconographic as a purely figurative and aesthetic motif (superimposed and ornamental), to make way for a programmed use of geometry and imagery – no longer dilettante or cynical, but instrumental (positively and positivistically) – that would favour worlds in which the stakes would be much more radical: it would now be a matter of discovering new species arising from this 'contra-natural' coupling of artifice and nature. New dynamic processes would gradually adopt a naissant, crossbred language, and through these processes action working on place would spring from this hybrid contract[8] – Land and Arch – never through a brutal transplant but by way of potential interaction between two categories that were hitherto unfamiliar to each other. In forms both contingent and considered, there would be a fusing of information and codes into new combinations in which certain genes would join up with others in order to respond efficiently to local and global conditions, adopting in the face of a flexible environment an approach not far removed from the ever-changing capacity – reactive because always operational and interactive – that would characterize the new information technologies.

Guest and Amphitryon: Interactions

A layout in the sense of an 'open field' such as we have described would be no more integrated than it would be imitative, and would no more impose itself than it would take over; it would 'react' with its surroundings (physical and virtual), and it would flexibly insert itself into the environment in order to generate dual responses – local and global, plural and singular (architecture and landscape, architecture and infrastructure, architecture and flow), capable of being one and many at the same time and in one place or in many places.

In this setting of 'displacements' – of movements and embargoes, meetings and shocks, intrigues and (de)localizations and other paradoxes – perhaps the greatest paradox would be this dual desire to 'coincide' with reality while at the same time developing a 'critical vision' of it, to chime in with the system and yet to transcend it, to infiltrate it and to be detached from it. In the double impetus of 'collaborating with' and 'plotting against', of 'tuning in' and 'jamming', of 'accepting' and 'dismissing' resides the dichotomy of our present, paradoxical situation, unstably balanced between two poles, between the simultaneous strategies of 'fluctuation' and 'destabilization' combined. On the one hand we assimilate the system and on the other we are perturbed by it (by the surprise of the 'intrigue', the unexpected strangeness, the simultaneous integration and alienation, the intrusion).

How can one infiltrate reality and at the same time detach oneself from it?

Faced with the ineffectiveness of signs as 'values of change' (this progressive trivialization and homogenization of the object as an article to be consumed or franchised), one should turn one's attention to the force of actions and situations that will provide stimuli. We must look at decodified and decodifying courses that are apt for the contingent situations of reality (with the ability to bring about a happy partnership between the conditions and the agents of production), although at the same time they are destined to transcend their own limits. The strategies of 'limitation' (in the course of events) are linked to the natural assumption of responsibility by the artificial. We must consider conventional strategies in other 'modern' modes of communication such as the cinema or advertising, which are capable of combining – sometimes even against nature – certain elements, situations, references, codes, different energies into a sudden and unexpected movement that is both expressive and collusive – paradoxes in operation.

Such is the possible power of modern art and architecture, and one of their greatest challenges is to produce new layouts that will be capable of simultaneously generating 'evolutionary spaces' (landscapes) and 'reactive mechanisms' (paradoxes) – not as aesthetic images, but as expressions and materializations of other possible courses of action. These will be 'glocal' settings of meetings and relationships, of activity and usage, of reactivation and qualification, all springing from a new, more extrovert and more universal architecture that can communicate the internal movements and tensions that configure its topology, and can react to the external stimuli that emanate from its environment. This new architecture must be able to recognize the strange and fragile reality that lies between time and place (forever vague and incomplete) as well as the strange potential of restructuring, reactivating and changing that one senses lies within it. ◪

Notes

1. *See* Ben van Berkel and Greg Lynn, 'Conversaciòn via modem', in *El Croquis*, no. 72, 1995, p. 6.

2. *See* Dimitra Hadjisavva, 'El concepto de lugar en las teorias arquitectònicas: mutaciones', paper presented at the UIA Barcelona Congress 96.

3. *See* François Roche, 'Territorrializar la arquitectura: materias, un inventario de tecnologia', in *26*, no. 3 (Landscape Architecture), 1997, pp. 6–7.

4. Ever since reality has shown us the place, the project has sought to provide links, associations, covers, connections, extensions and other actions bound up with manufacture. Once these links have been activated, the game is thrown open and new possibilities emerge. But for the game to remain open, architecture must establish not determinacy and constriction but indeterminacy and the freedom of uncertainty. It is not for nothing that architecture has no other purpose than to pursue the greatest confusion: that of place.

See José Morales, 'Associar, superponer, conectar', in *Quaderns*, no. 211, 1996, p. 163.

5. *See* Kelly Shannon, 'Re-politizing the Metropolis: the Strategic Project Approach', paper presented at the UIA Barcelona Congress 96.

6. *See* Stan Allen, 'Distributions, Combinations, Fields', in *The Berlage Cahiers*, no. 5 (Fields), Rotterdam, 1996, p. 72.

7. *See* Roemer Van der Toorn, 'Fresh Conservatism', in *Quaderns*, no. 219 ('Arquitectura Reactiva'), 1998, p. 95.

8. *See Quaderns*, no. 217 (Land-Arch), 1997, pp. 30–41.

Anand Bhatt

ArchiLab: 'Earth Economics'

1 • 'A heap of stones is not a machine, whereas a wall is already a static proto-machine', Félix Guattari tells us in *Chaosmosis*,[1] 'manifesting virtual polarities, an inside and outside, an above and below, a right and left ... These diagrammatic virtualities ... direct us towards a more collective mechanism without delimited unity, whose autonomy accommodates diverse mediums of alterity.'

Buildings are diagrammatic in Guattari's example; they can give rise to a space within Space, that is, an artificial milieu of interiorities. They point to the existence of a 'collective mechanism without delimited unity', a process that one might, for the moment, call architecture. We can understand architecture as a production process by which certain organs are separated from spatialities that surround us and put to productive ends. It becomes a second-order practice in its incorporeality.

Of course, architecture exists in a vast system of couplings, of processes; it is a machine – but in a disjunctive manner; it separates: architecture is the process that disjoins; it is the process that exists in a state of disjunction and synthesis. Architecture inscribes, it (en)codes spaces we inhabit, certainly, but as a process; it is possible to verify its elements: there is at first the machine[2] as an operating mode in architecture, an exteriorized process that has within itself transformational potential and an ability to bring machines into existence. Architecture has, by being subsumed in space, the ability to constitute diagrams[3] and flexions, and as a process it inhabits a world of substances, it originates, consumes and resides in corporeality; there is a 'nature' or other sets of processes from which it derives its energies and abstracts itself. Architecture produces and its products (buildings, the construction site) are the fossils of that process. The process releases its energies into a world full of substances and its waste matter and residues form the substances for other processes (figure 1).

In this context, 'earth economics' forms a broad rubric that may not be divided into its constituent parts but understood rather as a continuous envelope that surrounds architecture, the material on which architecture inscribes itself, in which it shapes itself and from which it separates in the process of becoming. 'Earth economics' is a series of propositions about what architecture will synthesize. It is about the movements that surround architecture and create the conditions possible for it, like series of continuous pulsations.

Earth economics: ecology, capital flows and means of integration treated as the subject-matter for architecture form a heterogenizing mould: these are already machine-arbitrated processes that demand new architecture-producing organizations, systems that emerge from organs that have already appeared within the field, that is, within the many molecular organizations entailed in the production of architecture. Technologies already exist and are already mobilized: information technology and telecommunications, robotics and prototyping, production techniques facilitated by new alloys and composite building materials, computer-assisted design and facilities for data processing have revolutionized the language we once used to describe architecture (figure 2).

It will be difficult to assume, within the context of defining architecture, that architecture occupies a space similar to language, that it is expressed much in the same way as words, that buildings or works are units that represent an order, rather like a book. Similarly, it is difficult to imagine a drawing board as the place of an architect's labour. Buildings are representations, certainly, but no longer of themselves or in themselves. As fixed images, they represent the vast machinations underlying architecture. Buildings are merely the excrescences, the residue left behind by organs that were formed during the architectural process. Buildings appear to be, as Catherine Ingraham says, classifiable but dumb.

The reproducibility of the technical machine differs from that of living beings, says Guattari. Every technological machine has its own plans for conception and assembly and constitutes a diagrammatic rhizome that tends to cover the entire mechanosphere.[4] There are, certainly, codes to architecture, there are even codes about architecture, but it does not only progress by chance, accident and mutations, like nature; it is subject to redundancies. Architecture does not remain at the level of a coded flow; it resembles chromosomes and mitochondria.

As a productive system, architecture resides in its ability to constitute organisations,[5] an element of enslavement that has always threatened its interior; as Lévi-Strauss put it, it is the technology of writing[6] that has propelled architecture through history and has made it possible to abstract forms of architecture to create assemblages that emanate from architecture's proto-structures and their elaboration(s). Lewis Mumford's mega-machine (the city) is coupled directly with the writing machine; Erwin Panofsky[7] shows us cathedrals that are merely theological couplings. David Harvey[8] demonstrates the 'civilized-capitalist' relations that exist in the world of real estate and in the stockmarkets. It should be easy to write a history of organizations constituted by architecture – its modes, its enthusiams, its voracity and its caprices – throughout the history of representation *per se*. It is matter of (re)cognizing architecture, of tracing its origins, of seeing architecture stage the history of its evolution. Architecture embodies cybernetics; it has always existed and operates on heterogeneity, even as it abstracts the labour process (figure 3).

Earth economics, architecture and production: the whole adds up to form a network of intelligence, represented in part by communication networks, by informatics spaces and perhaps by the infrastructures that take the technical form of these networks. The production process is no longer a labour process in the sense of a process dominated by labour as its governing unity. Instead, the architectural corpus appears as a conscious organ, at numerous points of the mechanics that produce corporeal space. Subsumed within the total process of the machinery itself, a mere link in the system whose unity exists not in the individuals it subsumes, but rather in the living (active) machinery that opposes the individual, an insignificant element in the machinery, an all-powerful organism.

Nevertheless, there seems to be a raison d'etre for architecture, to be aware of itself constituting an intelligence – or a network of intelligences that flow through the multitudes that may go by the name 'earth economics'. To exist, to exist as a minority, to resist being consumed by the massive machinery that surrounds architecture, to seek and find, to alienate (or to become alien),[9] these are at the heart of an architect's profession, at a time when eloquent arguments are being adduced against architecture, showing it to be a folly, a futility, a profession in terminal decline.

Architecture, once deployed as the Word (divinity, the city of God), represented again as the body of the despot; or in the image of Man (physiognomy) – that is, the face of architecture has washed away in progressive stages, perhaps following the gradual emaciation of the profession. We have seen that specializations and branches of knowledge have separated from architecture and become something quite different – one has only to compare the functions and the fields of architecture as laid down in the treatises (Vitruvius, Bhoja Raja) and the schools of architecture with 21st-century law.

Architectural thought or criticism can no long satisfy itself, as it too often does, with the present arraignments in architectural dis-

course, and must devise a critical task to which we can perhaps harness ourselves here. It will not do merely to observe the present arraignments within the discourse on architecture: architectural criticism must formulate again the questions concerning this field – architectural practice, architectural production as it emerges from earth economics. Perhaps one awaits the discovery of a map of architectural thought as it is defended and sustained by the systems that are indicated by the rubric presented here: a componential analysis is in order.

2 • Architecture as a conscious organ operating within the framework of earth economics: this thinking about 'Architecture', influenced by urbanism and urbanization, capital flows, migrations – is this not about orientations within the discipline? What of the orient, then?

A decoupling mechanism has long inhabited the space of architectural discourse, and this group of architects affords us with its programme and enunciations an opportunity that we may now seize. We may pose questions about the lines of division that create two remarkable exteriorities within architectural production. Each has its moment, represented by unique arraignments in discourse over time and its operational modalities; each couples architecture according to its own specificities: the questions represented by this work will follow two entirely different movements.

There certainly exists an inflexion between the two, a surface (mimesis and emulation), which possesses a history that is unique in itself, a proximity and multiple chains of signification that bind us all in an inescapable structural coupling, and it will be easy to imagine the symmetries that can thus be organized: it is in not their distance nor in their proximity, nor in the possibilities of contexture (each can, potentially, encapsulate the other) given their common aim: architecture and its structural coupling into mechanisms familiar to all.

This is inherently a power relationship. There exist binds; architecture is mapped, put to differing ends by the machines with which it is structurally coupled. Conventional division lines generate several fields of attrition within architecture: taken as a 'conscious' production process or, more worryingly, as a molecular aggregate of individuals that are, again, subsumed by the production process. Let me put forward a few division lines from my privileged vantage point,[10] if only to demonstrate their voracity, their ability to unfold, where it is possible to observe architecture as it reproduces itself, or, in the throes of mutation, as it sheds its old skin.

• There are technological binds, the apparatus as it is directed: new information technologies that programme inscriptions within the city. The virtual–actual spaces generated by a battery of simulation technologies and the consensual hallucinations of 'virtual' architectures that are all driven by the same algorithms and machines. The same code is again set in motion by the central powers, and to altogether different ends: architecture will inscribe the city differently on each exteriority, the same technical apparatus is adapted, coupled, into two different machines: a war machine (the large commercial and financial organisations, the military) and an imaging machine (architecture as media, as opiate) posing questions of survival or excess.

• There are binds of identity with the marginal elites in the developing world, and their conflicts and rivalries with the poor clients of architecture. And then there are those who find themselves on the same field in the conflict and want nothing but to forget. An anonymous murmur stifles their conflicts, speaking about marvellous dynamic asymmetries and burdens that represent incompatible histories. Architectures are extracted, only to break down or be besieged: symbolic superstructures that are shattered by molecularities that may be observed and yet not contained (see figure 4).

• There are the binds of method, great housing, infrastructure and industrial shortages in the developing world that are addressed by organizations that have, at their heart, a history of an altogether other extraction, structures that arrive via a social corpus that becomes integrated rather like an autochthon. Two (in)compatible manners of inhabiting territories are brought into relation and thus create a flexion, a vast loss of energy in the production process.

• There are pecuniary binds, among those who can afford architecture: the architect's services and labour and those to whom architecture is 'given'; among those who see architecture as a necessary instrument, a sort of libidinous compulsion, representing their patterns of consumption, something required as they take care of the 'self', and others, who are represented by their labour: those who survive.

• There are signifying binds, binds of the Father: the theoretical aspects that direct their gaze outwards, only to encounter institutions and practices left behind by centuries of domination by the West; critics increasingly attempt to capture perceptions of an increasingly oedipal posture. A surface that has separated from the earth economy, a membrane that is detached and has become a curiosity in a billion pairs of eyes that do not share the same genealogy.

There is distinction everywhere in these binds, in the techniques, structures and their output: architectural composition. And a survey of the diagram sketched so far by ArchiLab is perhaps in order, if only to have the particular variants of legitimated architecture production accepted.

Architecture is subsumed by the production process and in turn subsumes labour. Architecture is a space that is inscribed in something that detaches from reality and yet creates worlds of its own: the binds. We have limited the description to one conventional mould in history and geography for lack of space. And a question seems to lurk behind all these instances: who supplies the raw materials for architecture? The information, the capital. Where are the powerhouses? Or does one perhaps just have to become a spectator, turn on the TV and watch the image?

Architectural thinking seems to emerge from strata that are protected by the barrel of the gun, literally; the line of vision is parallel with the support. It emanates from behind the barrel, in other words, and appears to have allies in the language(s) of dominance. There are those who can avail themselves of architecture, as a technology, and exist in a state of subsuming, and those who exist in conjunction with it, apparently oblivious to its grand machinations. The two postures seem identical, at least in my eyes, to those of the soldier and the person who commits suicide — it is a distinction, in other words, between those who can adapt and allow themselves to be subsumed within the system, and those who shut their eyes and are oblivious.

Nevertheless, it is a civil matter, if we focus on the individual as a unit for the moment, in relation to architecture: his labour is abstracted in several different ways, requiring that he orient himself in several modes within the profession. A remarkable heterogeneity is afforded here, and in a sense, it brings home the rubric presented by this conference of ArchiLab.

Figure 1: A City-Machine

A City-Machine — Modelling of the actions of fluids upon fluids: in the Jamuna River bed in the heart of New Delhi, small dikes canalize and control the velocity of the river flow; siphons are created, which are then used as a cutting tool to chisel the soil itself. The residue is carried as particles suspended within the chiselling fluid and goes to reach repository areas, where the waters pause and deposit their contents, giving the city a new set of plateaux in the heart of the river. The system is very similar to grinding and milling processes in industry, except here the production workshop is inserted inside the thing being manufactured.

The formation of plateaux is harvested in winter, hardened in the summer sun and then the diurnal flux of the river flow and monsoon floods 'level' this formation, which is generated time and again. And a new formation grows over years. It a painterly technique, the figure is washed away as often as it is painted, and there are no finalities and fixities here; the new urban structure emerges in a process of inscribing and erasing, and it appears and lapses over time. It is all a matter of viscosity, of velocity, of oozing and depositing. The Diagram thus produced is quite different from what has been architecturally composed at Ur — although it in no way contradicts Ur — it simply operates architecturally in a different way.

Mageli Rastogi, Project for TVB School of Habitat Studies, unit master Anand Bhatt

Figure 2: CADD

Three-dimensional model of the relationships between the codes composed by the groups of people inhabiting the city, codes that come about as the city is used and as habits are established within it. The diagram then becomes the 'site' or the cartography where one builds. Architecture, here, is a diagrammatic schema that inhabits a space of codes rather than surfaces analogous to the world of bricks and mortar, apprehensible to the Eye. It does not delineate shapes; rather, it understands the factories that will shape the city. These parameters try to discover a science that will programme the practices of the project and fix the adjustments of the city, case by case, for each crisis. The implication/participation rates, the competition of identities, etc., make it possible for the town to be worked, manufactured, secreted. The data-processing tool, generally considered as a tool of precise representation, today allows a conceptual practice that integrates the dichotomy built space/lived-in space. It becomes possible to couple, assemble and arrange the various aspects of this city. We focus the study of this complexity on the 'nodes' of the city, zones of intersection, exchange, transit and heterogeneous flows; generally conceived as 'reductions of classi-

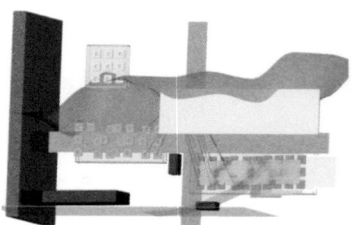

Atul Sharma, ETH and SA-CEPT, for a City-Machine, tutor Anand Bhatt.

fied business cases', where one prefers to see between-places, between-sites, with a considerable role in the distribution of intensities, in the renewal of rhythm and dynamics. The choice of these nodes will be done according to the places and ways traversed during the development of this city. [After 'Moebius', http://otonom.org]

Figure 3: The City of Ur in Mesopotamia

The State is not formed in progressive stages; it appears fully armed, a master stroke executed all at once; the primordial Urstaat, the eternal model of everything the State wants to be and desires.' [After Gilles Deleuze and Félix Guattari, in *The Anti-Oedipus*] Architects have often ridden along at the side of theorists; they have abolished the real world along with Nietzsche, crossed a bridge or two with Heidegger, been to jail and sanatorium with Foucault and admired the pyramids alongside Lévi-Strauss. Deleuze and Guattari give us the city of Ur in Mesopotamia. Architecture emerges, in all its splendour and durability, at the same time as the Ur-state, the only State, for hasn't there been only this State on the horizon? Writing lurks somewhere behind this system, this is where laws were written, this is a system that tends to concretization, in other words, to architecture.

The pyramid does not rest on the body of the earth, it does not sail against the forces of gravity — it merely utilizes these elements to provide an illusion of order, stability and permanence. Rather, it is extracted from the material of the envelope, material alive with production: movements and frictions, micro-struggles and resistances, erosion and sedimentation — the imposition of the monumental, the illusory that belie the fact, this we know. It is a het-

erogeneous system and we understand that it regresses into oblivion or the formless. And on oblivion it rests.

Figure 4: Chandigarh

Capitol for a State where 'the mind is without fear and the head is held high'. Several horizons are represented here; after all, this architecture is about the horizon or 'horizonation'. There is, first, the history of Western architecture, which inflects with its peripheries , with the enthusiastic moderns in the (former) colonies — and then there is the horizon of method, or of whatever architecture may extract from the contexts in which it is asked to build. Perhaps we are now dealing with a monument to the nationalist bourgeoisie in the immediate aftermath of independence in South Asia. Just one more example of an architecture imagined to have possessed a meta-language, a higher-order language that has exploded. It is a wasteful practice, this territorialization, this staking-out of identities while boundaries to the urbanization process are set elsewhere, in the arena that throws assumption of the civil and the citizenry into crisis.

The economy of terror that this provokes seems always to involve questions of architecture: Jerusalem, Dresden, Stalingrad, Baghdad, New York — this exquisite cadaver — the fossil that is the city expresses itself, after all, in one voice, from all sides. ☑

Notes

1. Félix Guattari, *Chaosmosis*, p. 42.

2. By machinic [Deleuze and Guattari] mean functioning immanently and pragmatically, by contagion rather than by comparison, unsubordinated to the laws of either resemblance or unity. By production they mean the process of becoming (production in the usual sense of making objects is a special type of production). Living bodies and technological apparatuses are machinic when they are in the process of becoming, then organic or mechanical when they are functioning in a state of stable equilibrium. Brian Massumi, *A User's Guide to Capitalism and Schizophrenia: Deviations from Deleuze and Guattari*, MIT Press, Cambridge and London, 1992, pp. 192-93, no. 45.

3.' It is a diagram, that is to say a 'functioning, abstracted from any obstacle ... or friction [and which] must be detached from any specific use. The diagram is no longer an auditory or visual archive but a map, a cartography that is co-extensive with the whole social field. It is an abstract machine. It is described by its informal functions and matter and in terms of form makes no distinction between content and expression, a discursive formation and a non-discursive formation. It is a machine that is almost blind and mute, even though it makes others see and speak.' Gilles Deleuze, in *Foucault*, p. 34.

4. Guattari, op. cit.

5. 'The organization of a machine (or system) does not specify the properties of the components that realize the machine as a concrete system; it only specifies the relations that these must generate to constitute the machine or system as a unity. Therefore, the organization of a machine is independent of the properties of its components, which can be any, and a given machine can be realized in many different manners by many different kinds of components. In other words, although a given machine can be realized by many different structures, for it to constitute a concrete entity in a given space its actual components must be defined in that space and have the properties that allow them to generate the relations which define it.' Maturana & Varela, *Autopoiesis and Cognition*, p. 77.

6. 'If we want to correlate the appearance of writing with certain other characteristics of civilisation, we must look elsewhere. The one phenomenon that has invariably accompanied it is the formation of cities and empires: the integration into political systems, that is to say, of those individuals into a hierarchy of castes and classes. Such is, at any rate, the type of development that we find, from Egypt right across to China, at the moment when writing makes its debut; it seems to favour rather the exploitation than the enlightenment of mankind. This exploitation made it possible to assemble work-people by the thousand and set them tasks that taxed them to the limits of their strength. To this, surely, we must attribute the beginnings of architecture as we know it.' Claude Lévi-Strauss, 'A Lesson in Writing', in *Tristes Tropiques*.

7. Erwin Panofsky, *Summa Theologica: Gothic Architecture and Scholasticism*.

8. David Harvey, *Limits to Capital*.

9. H. R. Geiger's definition of an alien is a parasitic creature that is no more than a code driven by an urge to reproduce and consume in order to reproduce. An incubus that will impregnate the host's body, only to burst out of it, having absorbed the host's traits: it will always become something of the host: there is always this melding of identities.

10. As what A. K. Ramanujan calls the 'insider–outsider', belonging neither in the West nor in South Asia. See A. K. Ramanujan, 'Is There an Indian Way of Thinking? An Informal Essay', in *Contributions to Indian Sociology* (NS).

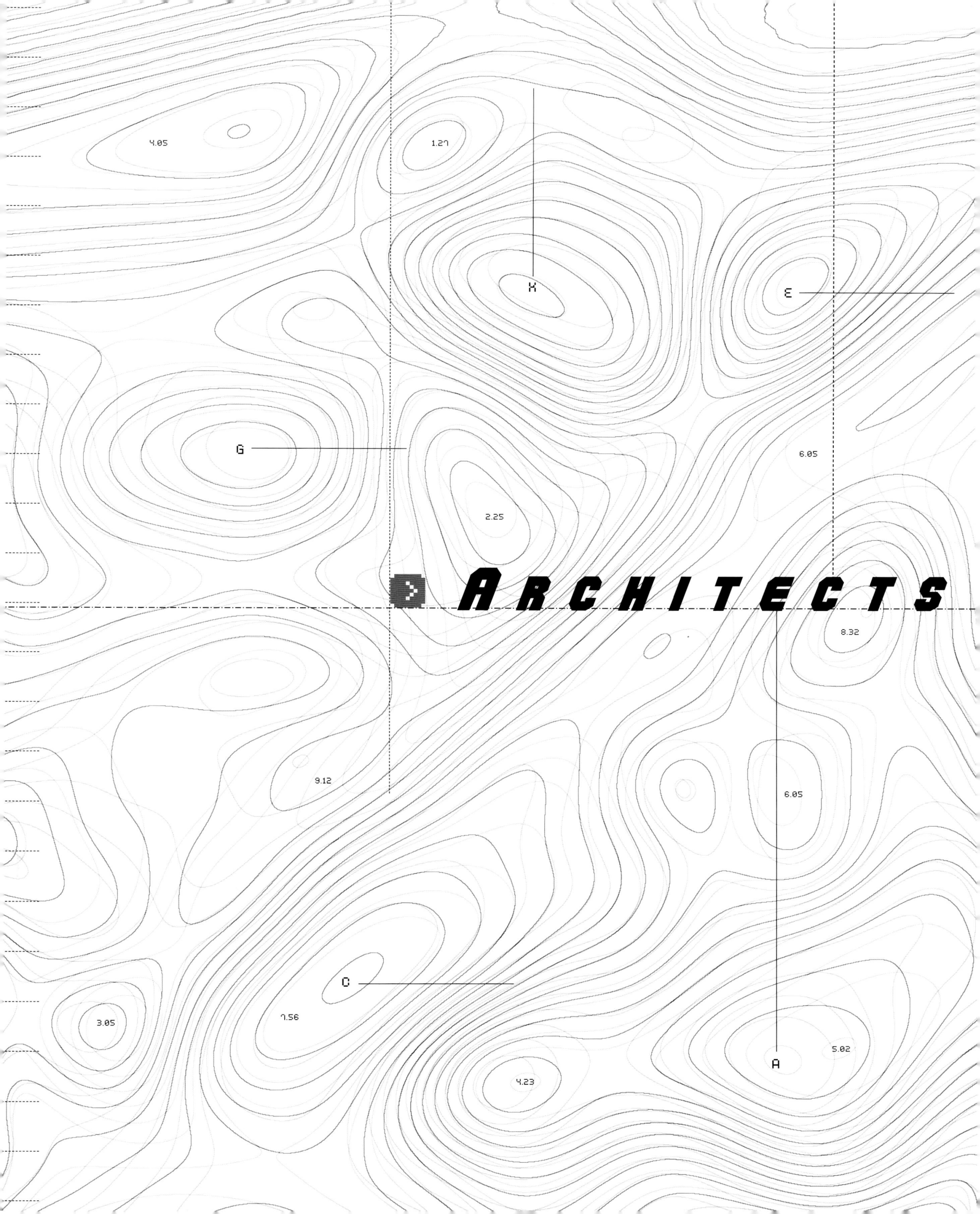

> **Architects**

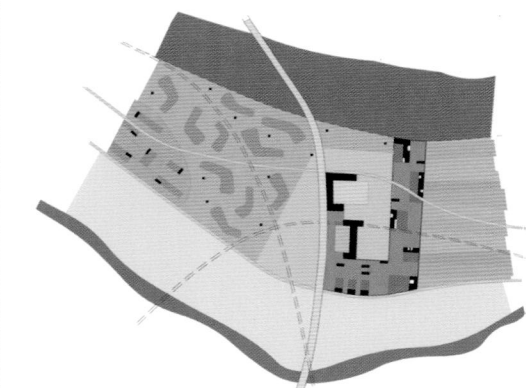

ACTAR ARQUITECTURA

Spain

Manuel Gausa Navarro [1959], Oleguer Gelpí [1964], Ignasi Pérez Arnal [1965], Florence Raveau [1965]

The three members who founded Actar Arquitectura in 1994, Manuel Gausa, Oleguer Gelpí and Ignasi Pérez, graduated from the ETSA in Barcelona, while Florence Raveau, who graduated from the EA in Paris-la-Défense, joined the team in 1997. They edited the journal *Quaderns d'arquitectura i Urbanisme* until 2000 and now teach at the ETSAB. Ignasi Pérez also teaches at the Polytechnic University of Catalonia. In 1994 Oleguer Gelpí was curator of the exhibition 'Quaderns 50 anys'. Manuel Gausa is also an architecture critic, consultant for the international competition EUROPAN, codirector of the Arquitectura Avanzada—Metapolis festival and director of cultural activities at the International University of Catalonia. This wide range of practices is reflected in the structure of Actar and shapes their publications and architecture as well as their architectural projects, which are fed by their research into formal, relational and multi-faceted situations of real territories. ☑

ACTAR architecture could be defined as the spinal column of various initiatives intended to stimulate new courses of action for the purpose of understanding, configuring and restructuring contemporary space. What might be the logical basis on which to conceive the new paradigms of today? Unquestionably, they can no longer be built on the foundations of a classical, conventional continuity or of the actual functionalism of production; the basis must, rather, be an openness to modern phenomena of strategic interaction. Actar seek to transcend the limitations of an architecture that is seen uniquely as a concept of objects and instead to promote an architecture conceived as a relational 'entourage' – a close environment. This idea of the entourage, of neighbourhood, should be viewed from various angles. The first is that of 'scene' or setting: the context, the milieu, the ambience – a place that is open to time, to singular or plural interventions, to operations that can react to it. The second is that of the 'field of force': a dynamic system associated with courses of action, with evolutionary processes, with organization and form. Finally, the third sense associated with architecture as environment is that of geography: landscapes, territories, topographies, different but linked together. Thus one registers the ambiguity and the fragility of the border between architecture and territory, that is to say, between construction and system, creation and logic, form and disposition, local and global. This, incidentally, is what the philanthropist Rubió i Tudorí grasped intuitively when he coined the term 'actar', and it is the milieu in which have developed the explorations of Actar-Ediciones and the projects of Actar Arquitectura: the search for connections in diversity, the ability to define new contexts (sys-

tems, internal logic, processes), the creation of environments that are more expressive and expansive, more precise, enjoyable, functional and – why not? – able to get on with each other. The architectonic activity of Actar is therefore based on a multifaceted vision of openness: it may be unpredetermined, spontaneous and pluralistic (like the Paraloop project, 2000, in which the inhabitants specified the 'quantity' of each type of space they wanted), or it can be more relational and evolutionary (like the 'land grid' plan of 1998 proposed for Barcelona); it can even follow the line of merriment and loss of inhibitions. Actar Arquitectura thus lay claim to come to terms with modern complexity, and to be contributing to the definition of new contexts (real and virtual, global and local), as well as conducting explorations of the general concept of the habitat, which, at any given moment, is a space for all and a space for one. The quest is especially for 'an environment of interaction rather than a machine for living in', where it is a pleasure to be alive, to meet one another, to 'project' oneself as an individual, going far beyond the habitual, purified minimalism of the profit-making commercial archetype, beyond the morality of mere resistance, beyond the standardized norms. The ultimate objective is to conceive formal arrangements that will facilitate an efficient response to the different kinds of work and the diversity of interests that characterize the modern metropolis. ☑

Actar Arquitectura

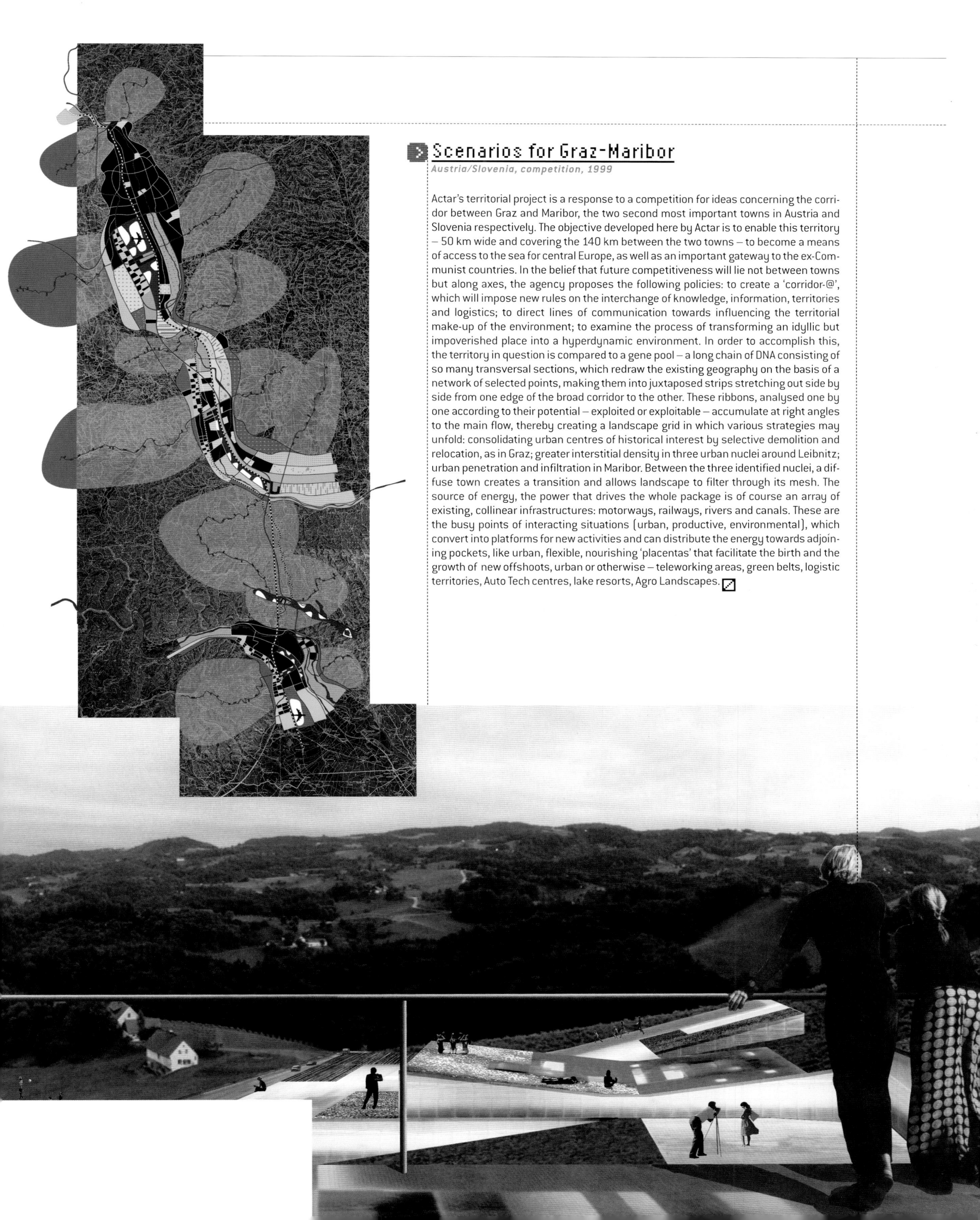

Scenarios for Graz-Maribor
Austria/Slovenia, competition, 1999

Actar's territorial project is a response to a competition for ideas concerning the corridor between Graz and Maribor, the two second most important towns in Austria and Slovenia respectively. The objective developed here by Actar is to enable this territory – 50 km wide and covering the 140 km between the two towns – to become a means of access to the sea for central Europe, as well as an important gateway to the ex-Communist countries. In the belief that future competitiveness will lie not between towns but along axes, the agency proposes the following policies: to create a 'corridor-@', which will impose new rules on the interchange of knowledge, information, territories and logistics; to direct lines of communication towards influencing the territorial make-up of the environment; to examine the process of transforming an idyllic but impoverished place into a hyperdynamic environment. In order to accomplish this, the territory in question is compared to a gene pool – a long chain of DNA consisting of so many transversal sections, which redraw the existing geography on the basis of a network of selected points, making them into juxtaposed strips stretching out side by side from one edge of the broad corridor to the other. These ribbons, analysed one by one according to their potential – exploited or exploitable – accumulate at right angles to the main flow, thereby creating a landscape grid in which various strategies may unfold: consolidating urban centres of historical interest by selective demolition and relocation, as in Graz; greater interstitial density in three urban nuclei around Leibnitz; urban penetration and infiltration in Maribor. Between the three identified nuclei, a diffuse town creates a transition and allows landscape to filter through its mesh. The source of energy, the power that drives the whole package is of course an array of existing, collinear infrastructures: motorways, railways, rivers and canals. These are the busy points of interacting situations (urban, productive, environmental), which convert into platforms for new activities and can distribute the energy towards adjoining pockets, like urban, flexible, nourishing 'placentas' that facilitate the birth and the growth of new offshoots, urban or otherwise – teleworking areas, green belts, logistic territories, Auto Tech centres, lake resorts, Agro Landscapes. ☑

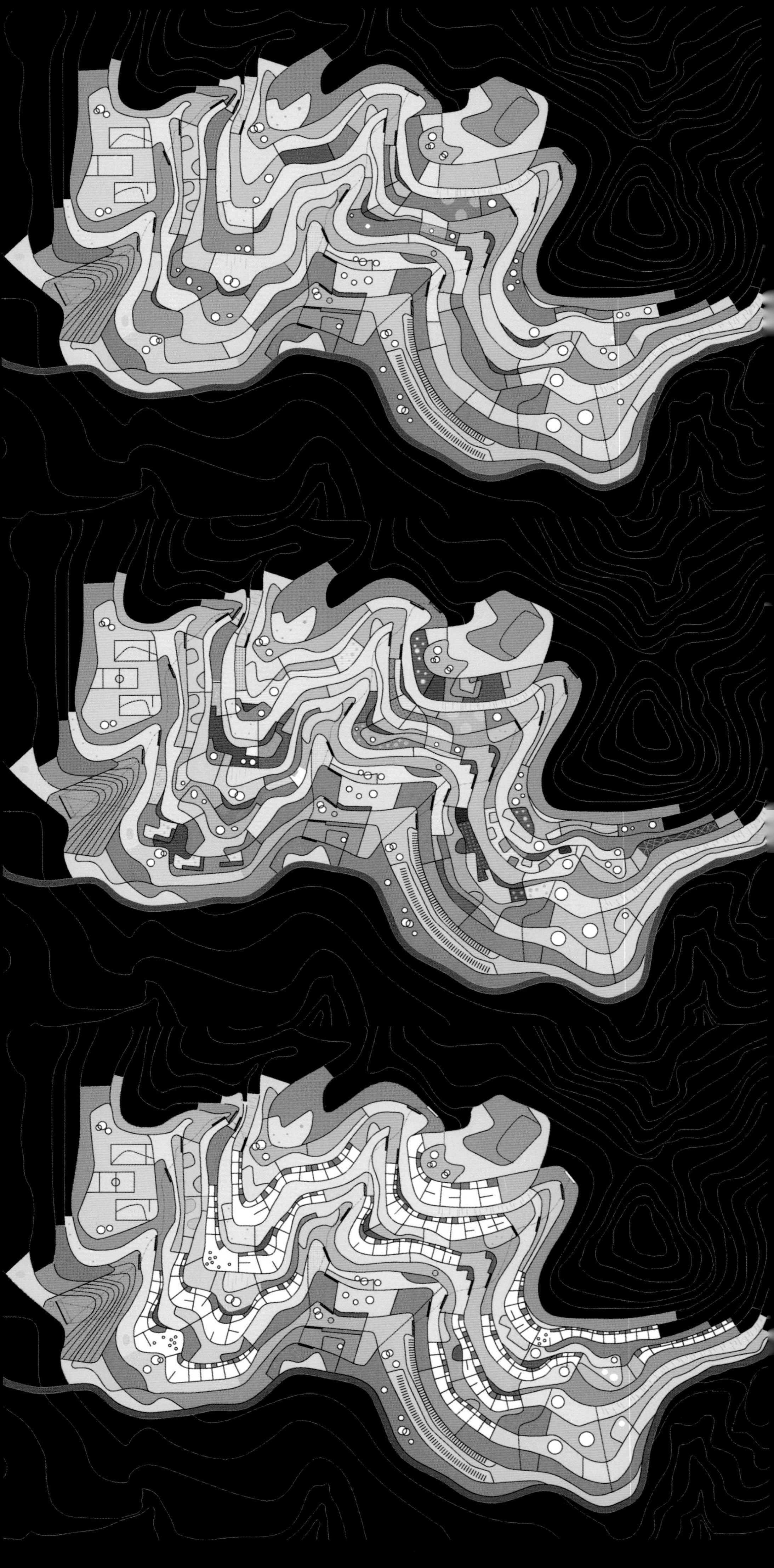

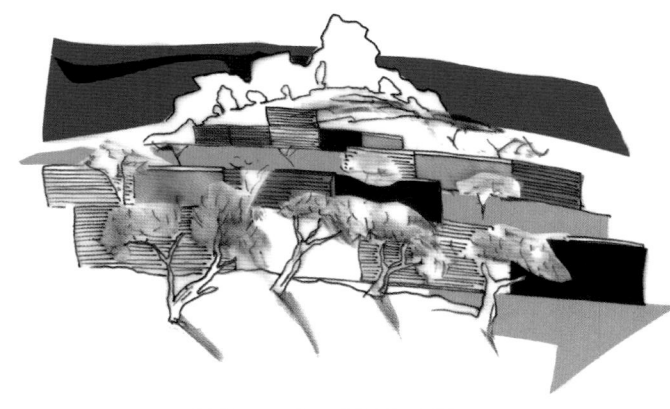

VALL DE GALLINERA

▷ Valencia Scan
Valencia/Alicante/Calpe, Spain, project, 2001

The territorial triangle between Valencia, Alicante and Calpe is in need of criteria for the economic and residential development of its inland valleys, which have so far escaped the planners but which are likely to come under increasing pressure in the next few years. In consultation with the Region of Valencia, Actar organized an exhibition of projects by ten teams, and itself proposed a strategic global plan based on several points: the bi- and tripolar set-up of the region, its recursive structure and its transversality. As in the famous 'zooms' of the Eames, one can discern on different scales similar potential development structures in the form of 'scenic' areas linked by possible road connections, which are highlighted in the form of diagrams. These interpret the geography of the territory as double or triple polarities, where attractive axes – not evenly distributed – underlie the development of an 'in-between' web of relations. This global reasoning leads to a dual scheme – between the coast, multi-programmed (leisure, production, residence), and the interior, more logistical, which can be devoted to functions on a regional scale. This hybrid and productive combination is further polarized by the landscape, with a zone of undulating hills that border it like an environmental 'basket'. Actar point out that hillsides are often residential while valleys remain in their natural state; the hills will therefore be used for activities of what is called 'durable leisure', while the valleys will be devoted to agriculture, play and culture (with a very rich potential). Finally, the new 'residential fields' will be sited in terraced landscapes overlooking the valleys, and again the same chain of logic gives rise to two different forms of development. The first is linear and is based on infiltration: variable strips of landscape give way to 'residential walls', which are combined in different sequences to form constructed strips, either cultivated in gardens or left natural. The second form of development replaces certain topographical curves with 'residential curves', whose rooftops become artificial, well-equipped landscapes that are interlaced with the original site. ◪

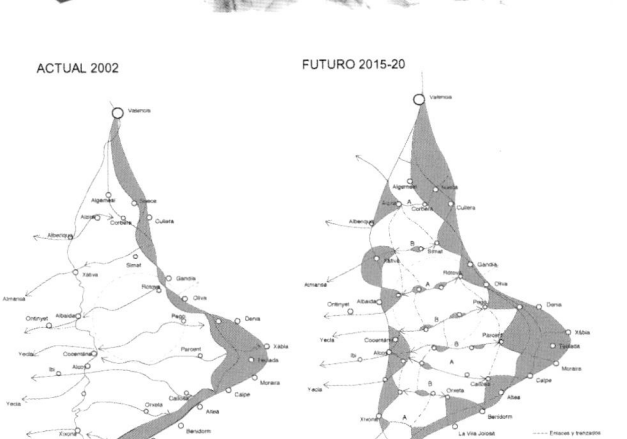

ACTUAL 2002   FUTURO 2015-20

ESQUEMA DE POTENCIALES ACTUALES   ESQUEMA DE DESAROLLO BIPOLAR   BI-VAL: ESQUEMAS DE DESAROLLO TERRITORIAL

ACTUAL 2002   FUTURO 2015-20

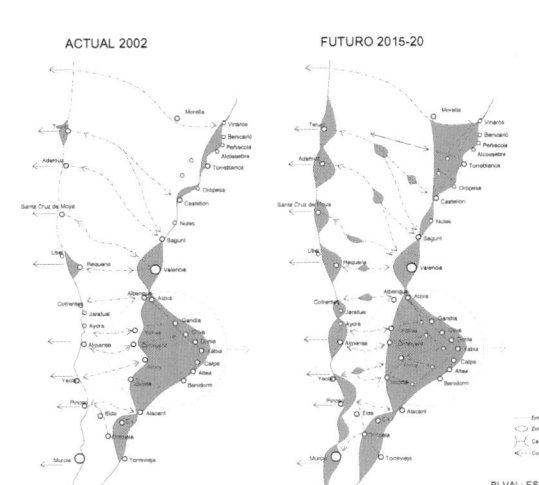

ESQUEMA DE POTENCIALES ACTUALES   ESQUEMA DE DESAROLLO BIPOLAR   BI-VAL: ESQUEMAS DE DESAROLLO TERRITORIAL

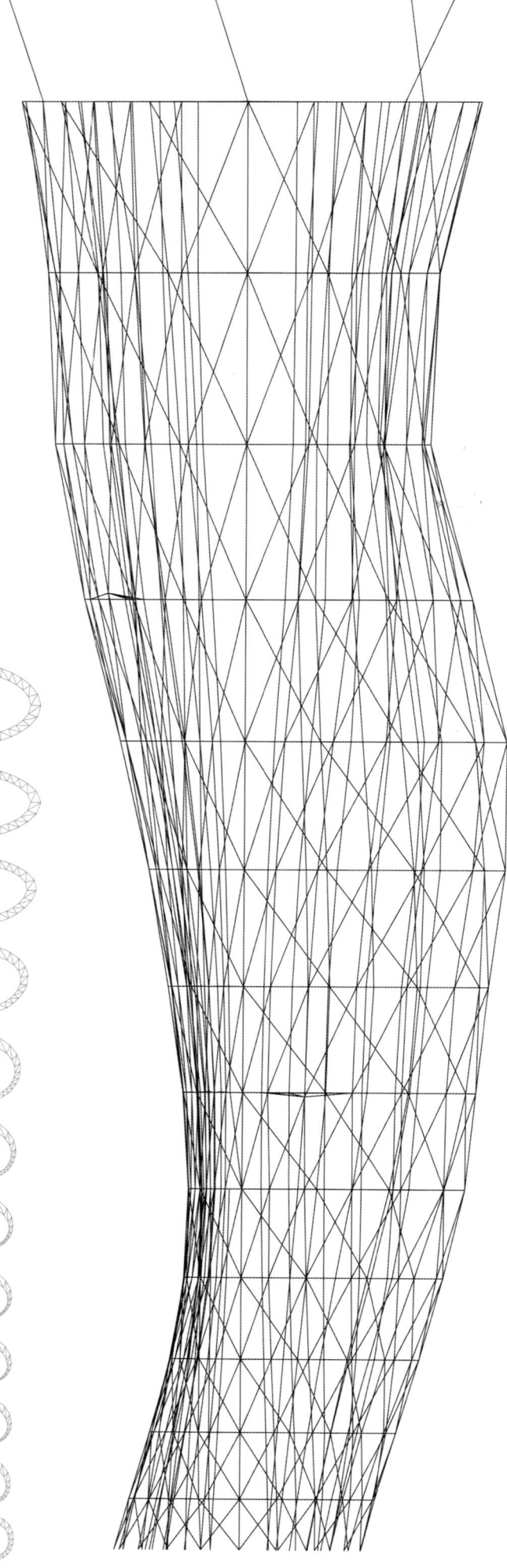

Tornado Tower
Project, 2002

This technological communications tower, which Actar propose to site in a hilly part of the town, is inspired by the shape of a tornado. As in their previous projects, Actar begin by observing and trying to understand various spontaneous phenomena; they decipher a multiplicity of relations, forms and scales that underlie these phenomena, and then propose a new development that will stick as closely as possible to the context under consideration. Here Actar are studying a fascinating atmospheric phenomenon, and the ensuing project does more than merely analyse a static form and a constructive artefact; it seeks to express the essence of the relevant forces in all their dynamism and fluidity. It must delve into a complex geometry because, while conventional towers are held up by a nucleus of technical casings, the Tornado Tower is a mass of transparent emptiness. Its external, structural skin supports all the elements, including the technical platforms and communications antennae, as if they were all projected by some centrifugal force. The diagonal direction of this steel structure is based on the spiral dynamics of the tornado. Its shape is that of a slightly amorphous tube that gradually widens as it rises upwards, and ends in a kind of metal filigree as aerial as possible in order to reduce the force of the wind and the effects of torsion at the base. This structural carcase is reinforced by a collection of diaphragms made up of cables. The skin itself thickens in accordance with the elements that are expected to be attached to it. The central sections are for the lifts and vertical forms of transport, and are adapted to the curves of the interior of the metallic skin. At ground level the same dynamics of a centrifugal unwinding are carried over to the form of the buildings that serve the tower, as if to give material expression to the effects of the tornado's passage. ⊡

Credits: Actar – concept; structural engineering – Cecil Balmond and Charles Walker

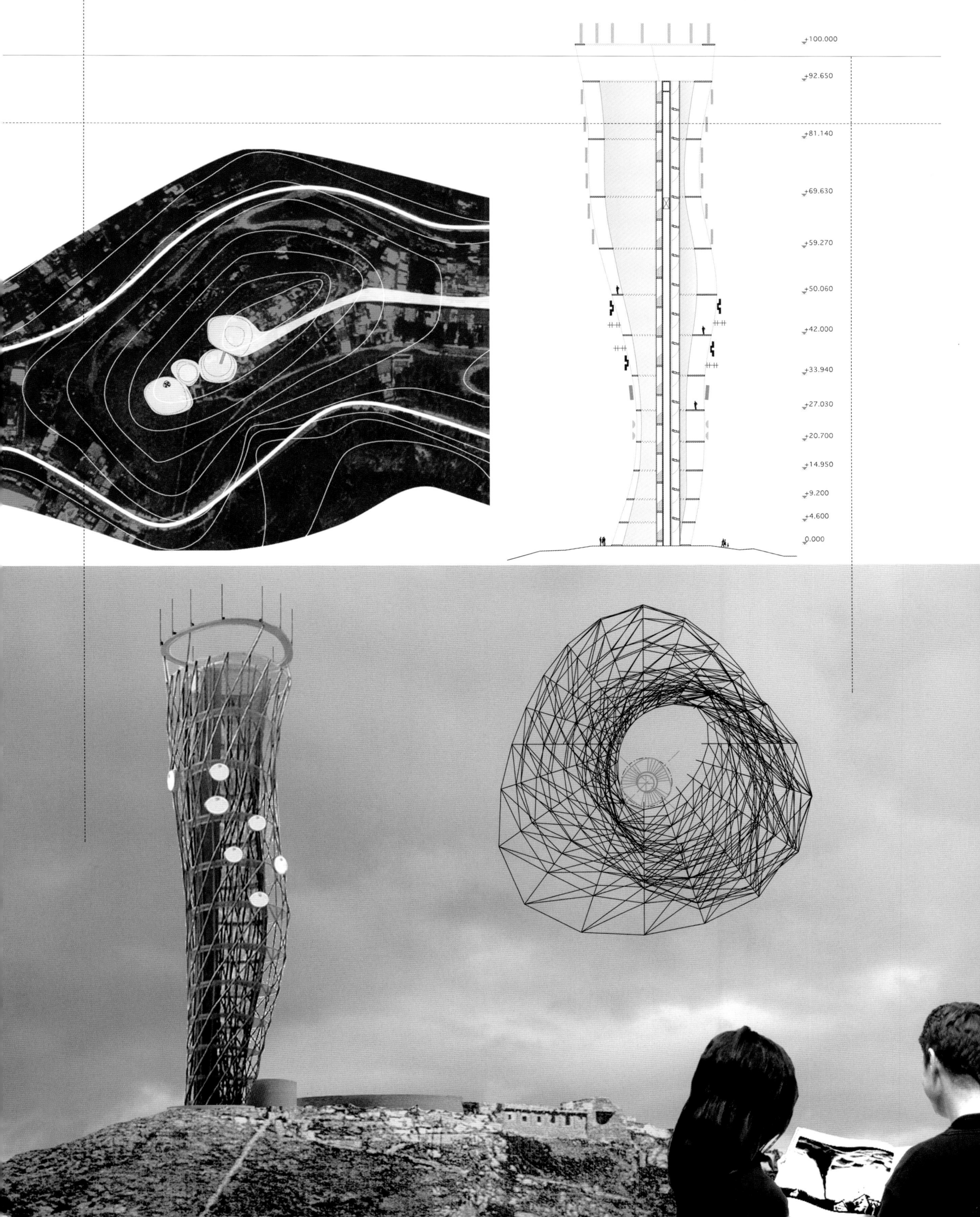

SABLE

AGENCE MANUELLE GAUTRAND ARCHITECTS

France

Manuelle Gautrand [1961]

Manuelle Gautrand established her agency in Lyon in 1991 and in Paris in 1993. In 1992 she won the Albums de la Jeune Architecture. She has taken part in more than 70 competitions, most of them public. In ten busy years she has completed more than 15 constructions: a college (Ecully, Rhône), a cinema (Saint-Louis, Alsace) and a theatre (Béthune, Nord), as well as industrial and service buildings (emergency information centre in Venissieux, depots for the SNCF, administrative units for the Pompidou Centre) and public service areas (toll booths on the A16 motorway, a stopping place on the River Saône). She won the AMO Prize 'Architecture et Lieux de Travail' in 2000. Manuelle Gautrand has taught at the Ecole d'Architecture Val-de-Seine since 1999, and is architectural consultant to the Director of l'Isère and to the MIQCP (an interministerial body overseeing the quality of public construction). Her work has received a great deal of public exposure, e.g. in 2001 'Hybrid Landscapes' in Rotterdam, 'Les maisons de bonheur' in Paris, 'Rushes' in Bangkok. ☒

VERY early on in her career, Manuelle Gautrand found herself confronted with complex projects: buildings to house technical or logistical work, installations on motorways, industrial parks, airports. What characterizes her approach and her work is conciseness. No matter how difficult the project may be, it will never induce her to embrace an aesthetic of complexity. Every function is broken down to a simple form, almost graphic in its stylization. Functional complexity must be overcome so that architecture can be emancipated from it and can develop a sense of play with the material it uses. It may be with lights (constantly changing, as on the polycarbonate wall of the BEMA building in Nantes) or with images (as with the silkscreen motifs on the motorway toll booths) or with games of transparency or opacity – Manuelle Gautrand's architecture is always resolutely playful. She works with the contrast between the blunt simplicity of forms and the sophistication of surfaces, playing a cunning game of colours, textures or themes. Each project limits itself (for the most part) to experimenting with a single material, whose qualities must be perceptibly and palpably suited to the nature of the whole. 'One can take a project to the maximum of its potential and, as with a sculpture, work the material to the limits of its nature, of its veins.' The second phase of the work is also handled with a limited number of options in order not to distract from the precise, meticulous work done on the signals, the equipment, the guard rails, for every colour,

every pattern will be a special focus of attention. All these many internal details will eventually, in a game of transparency, enrich the perceptual life of the building from the outside. Where others seek inspiration in biotechnology, fractal geometry, chaos theory or new information technologies, Manuelle Gautrand endeavours to solve the most complex problems (technical, programmatic, ecological) by purely architectural means: details of implementation, handling of material, experimentation with form to the point of distortion. For her HQE dwellings (Rennes) she ignored all the technological and automated solutions and instead made ingenious use of the climate, exposure to sunlight, the variable density of the foliage and verandas whose empty spaces accumulate and distribute heat. For her airport maintenance building in Nantes (1996–98), rather than adopting the opaque bands that normally conceal industrial work from the outside, she opted for the most transparent surfaces possible, and suggested that all users of this future building should be given a sort of instruction manual. She does not have a definitive or categorical attitude towards the urban and industrial sites she is to work on. Nor does she work through osmosis or opposition. Manuelle Gautrand prefers to follow a continuous line by selecting certain materials, which she adapts and reshapes into surprising reinventions. ☒

S. N.

Les Éclaireuses: a cultural platform

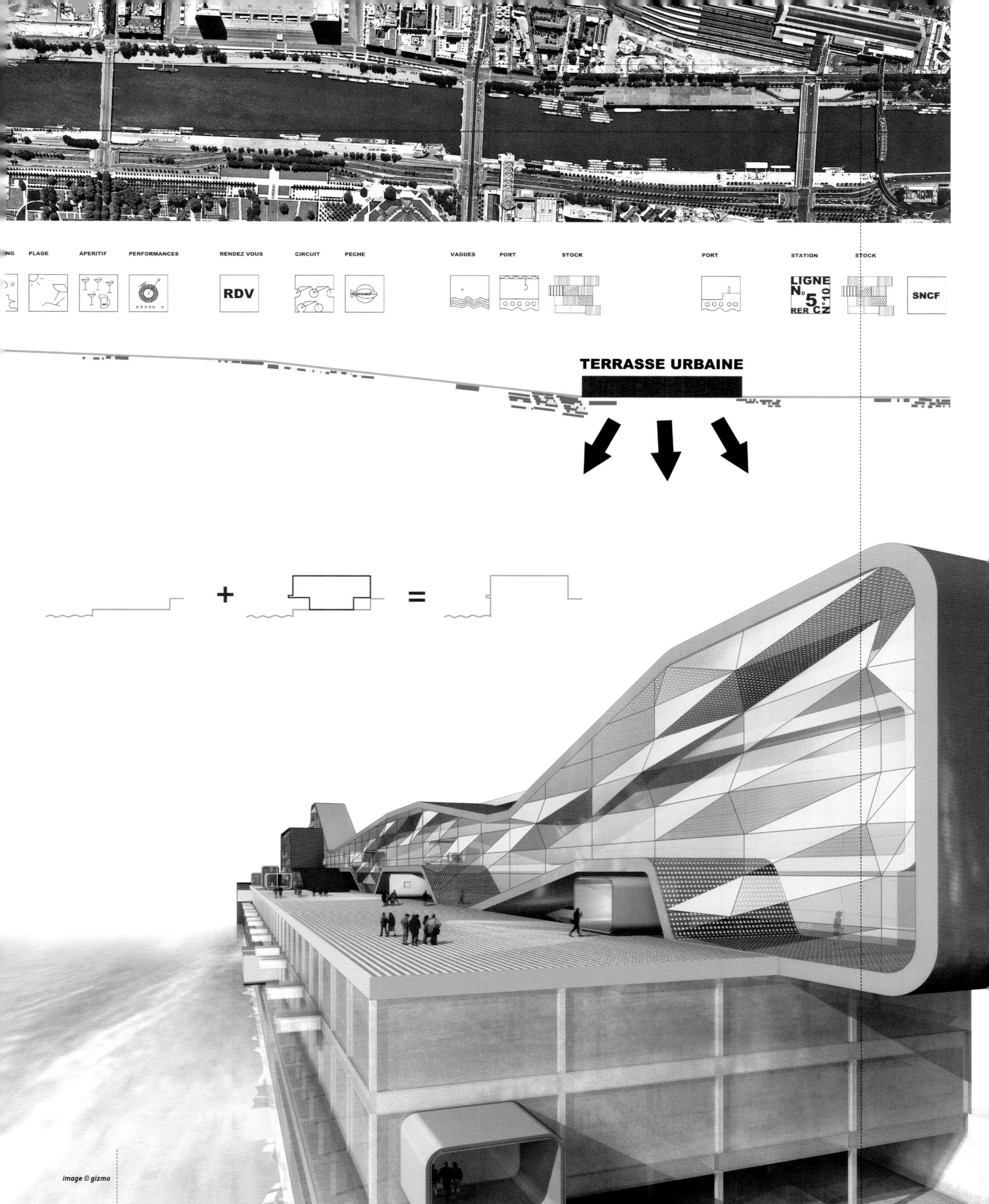

PLAGE APERITIF PERFORMANCES RENDEZ VOUS CIRCUIT PECHE VAGUES PORT STOCK PORT STATION STOCK

RDV

LIGNE N₀ 5 RER CZ 10

SNCF

TERRASSE URBAINE

+ =

image © gizmo

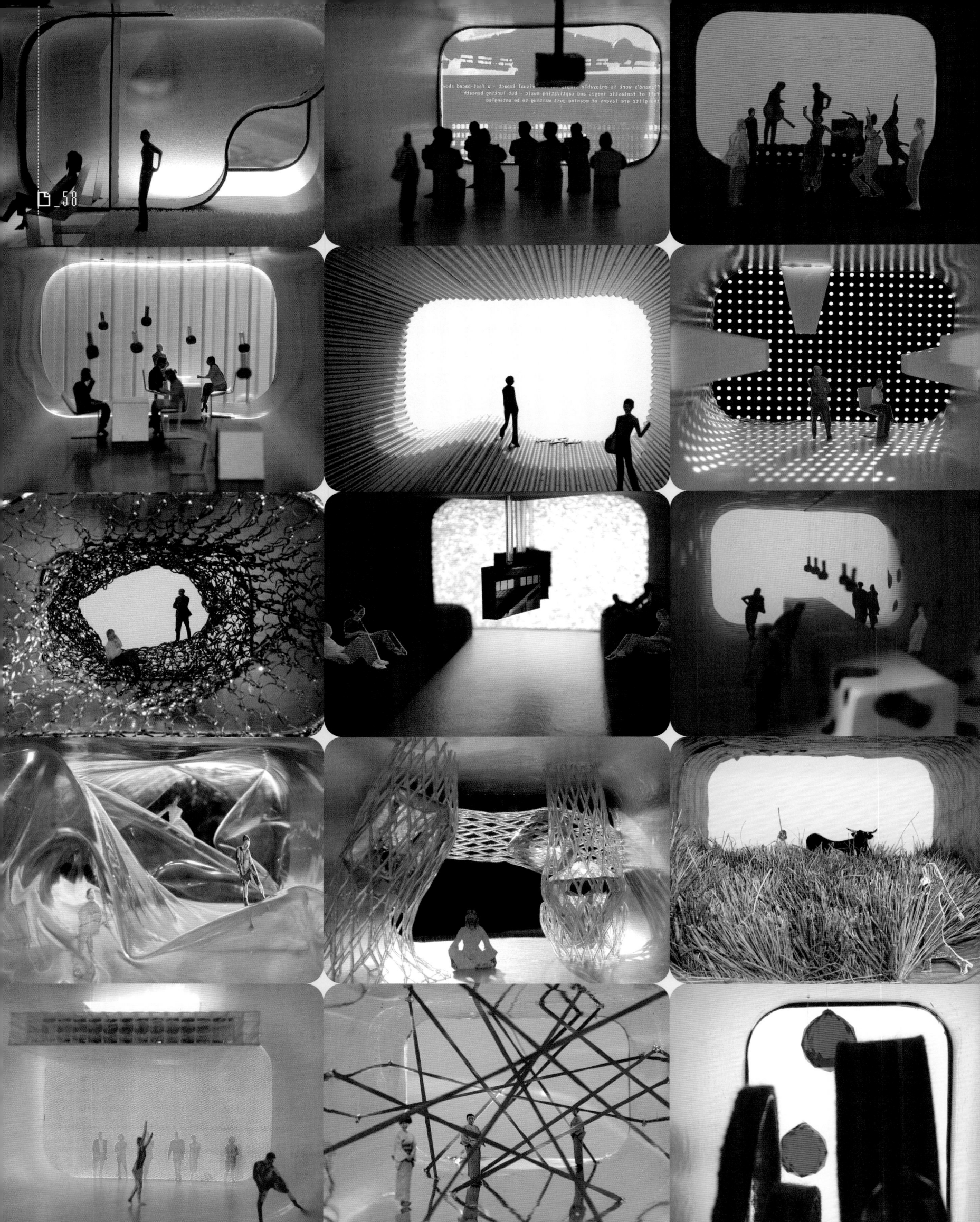

Les Éclaireuses: a cultural platform

Paris, France, 2002

'This project is not a theatre, not a cinema, not a concert hall for modern music, not a dance hall, not a place for interactive arts, not a place for various experiments, but it would like to be a bit of everything all at the same time ... the 'Éclaireuses [Girl Guides] have gone ahead to prepare the way, to compile little digests of creation, production and presentation: when they 'produce', they can serve as offices, local government departments, dressing and rehearsal rooms; when they 'present', they can turn into little cinemas, rooms for music, dance, video; when they 'accompany', they can become cafeterias, boutiques, halfway houses, rest-rooms ... As 'technical concentrates' the Éclaireuses can live anywhere, take over a place and then move on to other places. Today they have installed themselves on the banks of the Seine ... There stands a building that is magnificent but obsolete, lived-in but melancholy, big but rather empty ... Little by little the Éclaireuses have set out to conquer it: first of all, they established themselves beside it, then on it, and they devised a new life over the rather sad life of the existing building. This juxtaposition of two parallel lives ended up by engendering certain habits, and finally the Éclaireuses installed themselves there rather more earnestly. And this gave rise to the next stage of the project ... A thick layer added to a roof, conceived with a certain utilitarian delicacy, continuing the building's activities down below and respecting its users, but bringing them something else ... It is a completely different place, profiting from the great length of the existing building by unwinding itself into the form of several layers, flexible but continuous, which can facilitate the development of long scenic stretches, extended experiments, without ever losing sight of the outstanding terrace and the river down below. Half of the roof is occupied and the other left empty so that it can become a long terrace overlooking the Seine, like a great balcony. The Éclaireuses promenade there, transforming the empty space into something alive, making and then unmaking multiple forms of creation, inside or outside ... The unexpected combinations are always full of surprises. They are a source of spontaneity, of enrichment, of exchange ... they open up our a prioris, and that is why they give us pleasure. Culture is effectively the 'luxury of the unaccustomed', in the words of Saint John Perse. ☒

Manuelle Gautrand

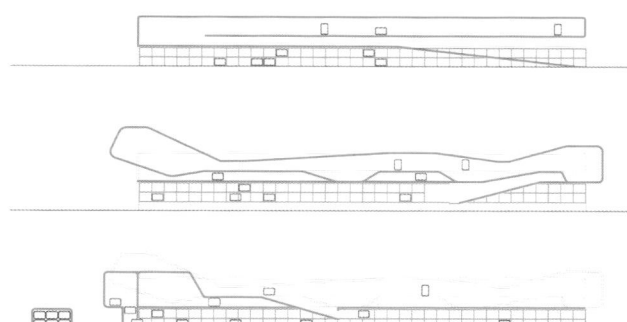

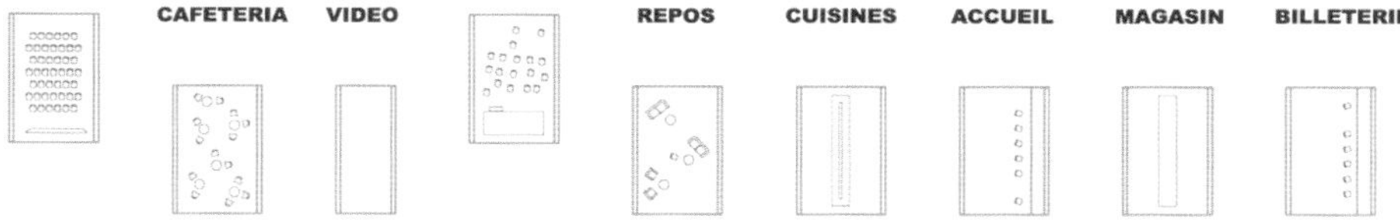

CINEMA   CONCERT

CAFETERIA   VIDEO   REPOS   CUISINES   ACCUEIL   MAGASIN   BILLETERIE

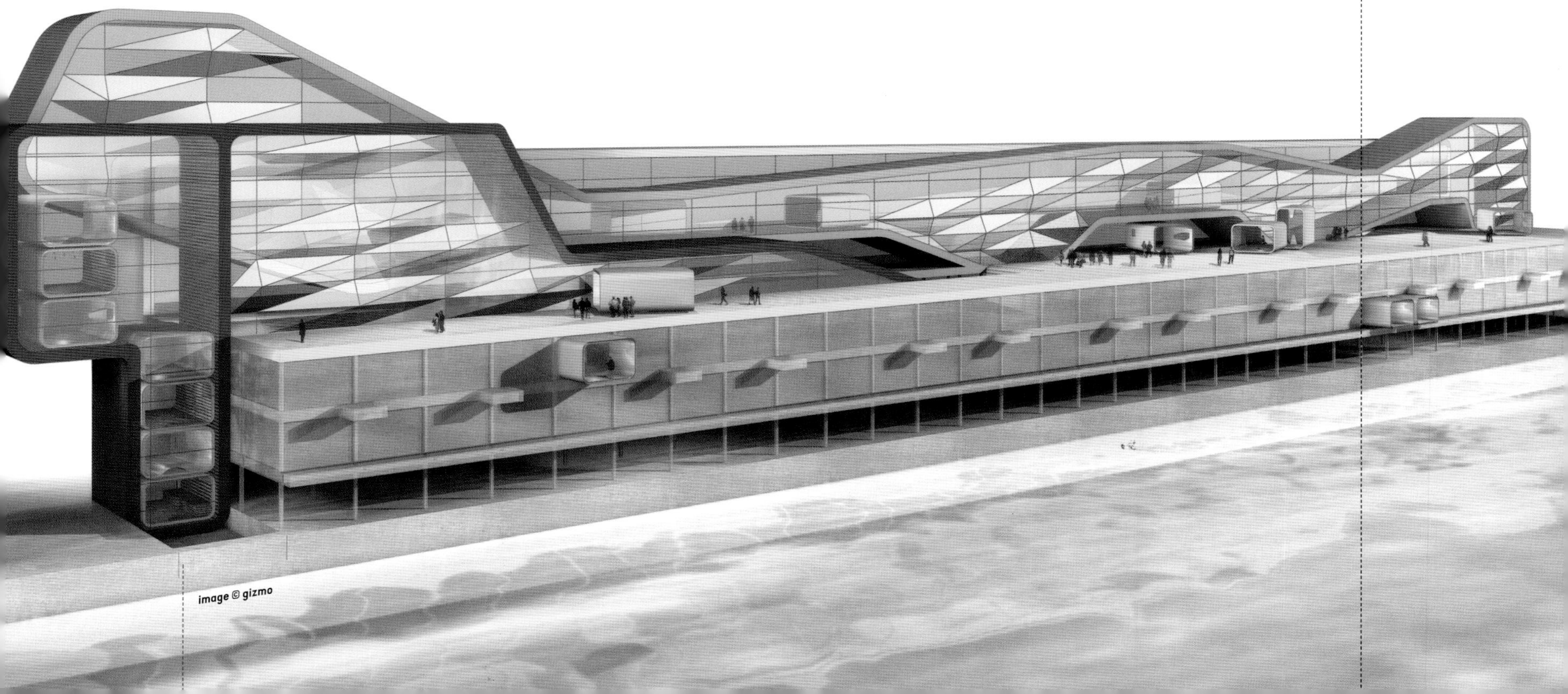

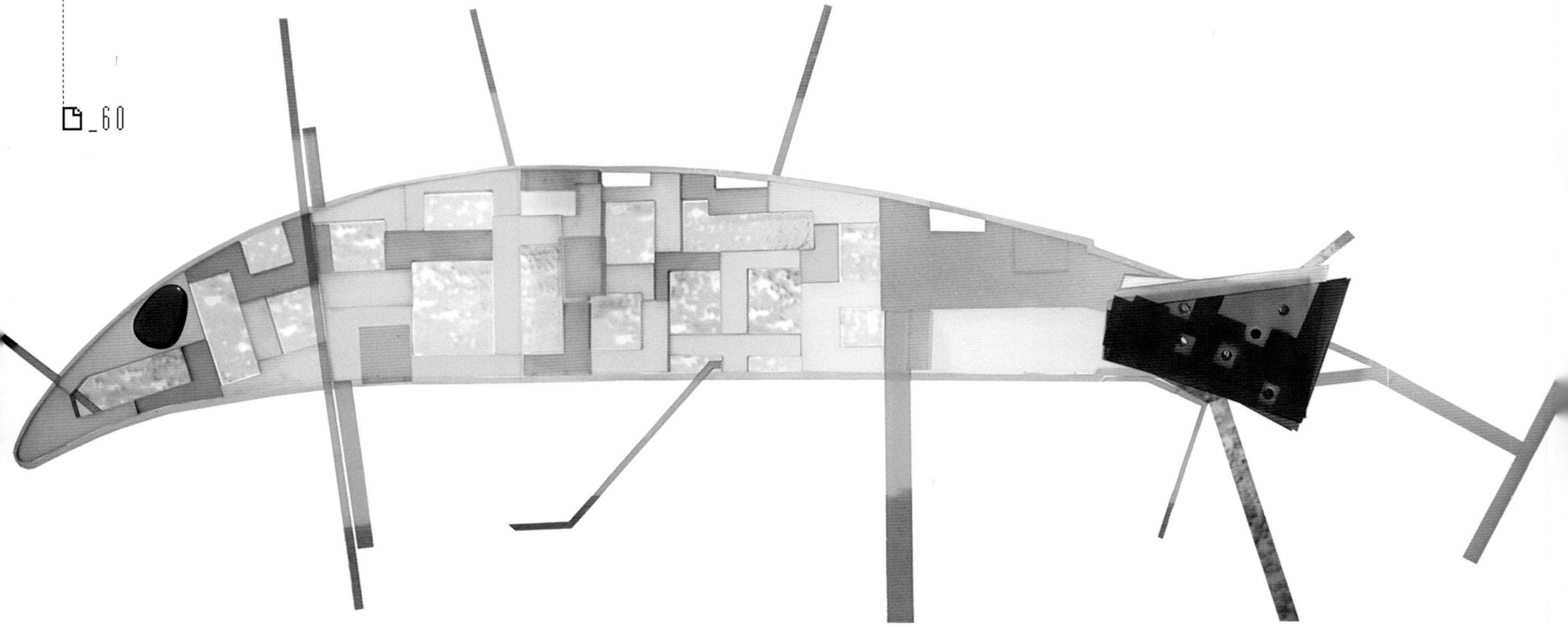

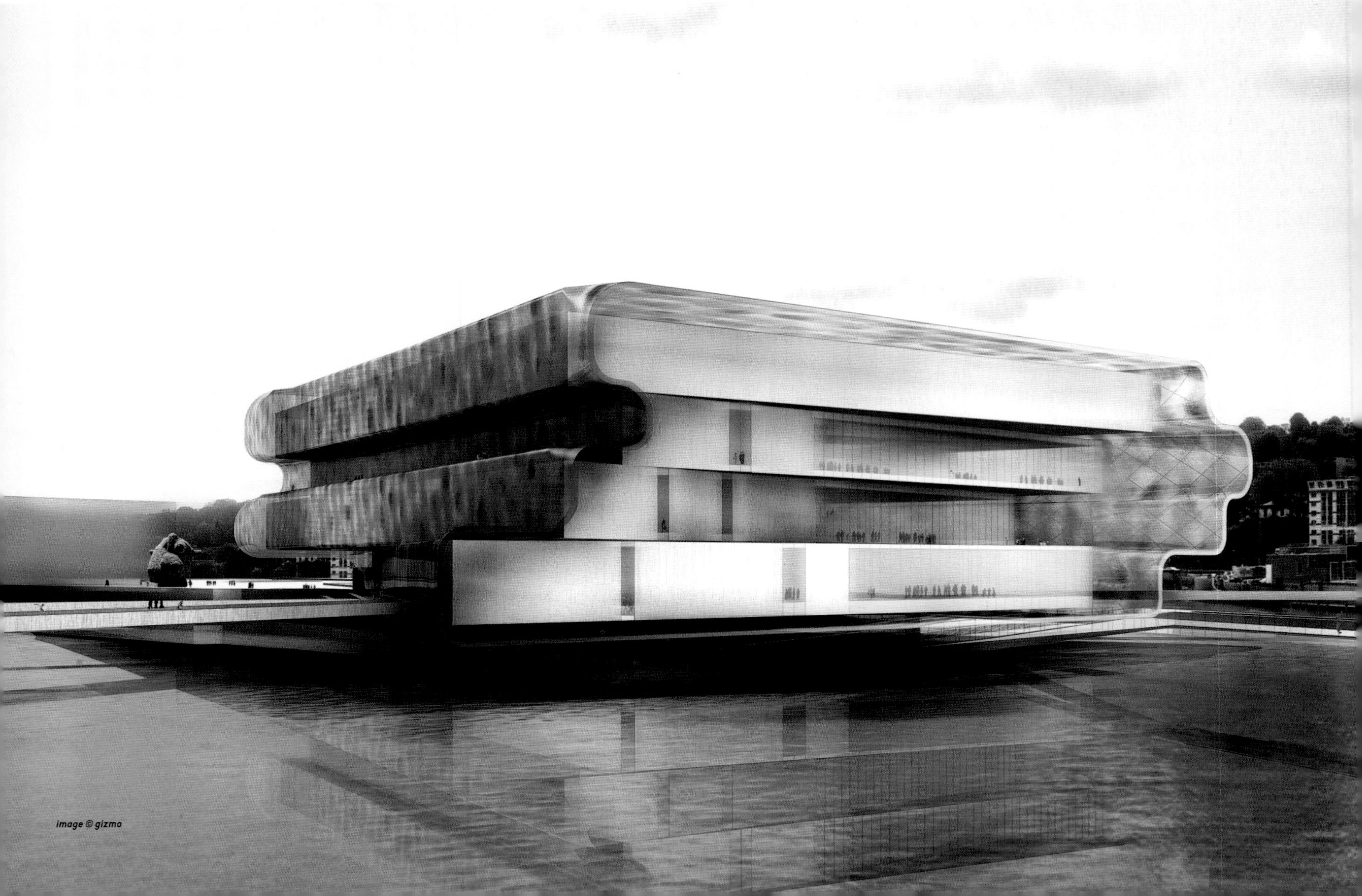

image © gizmo

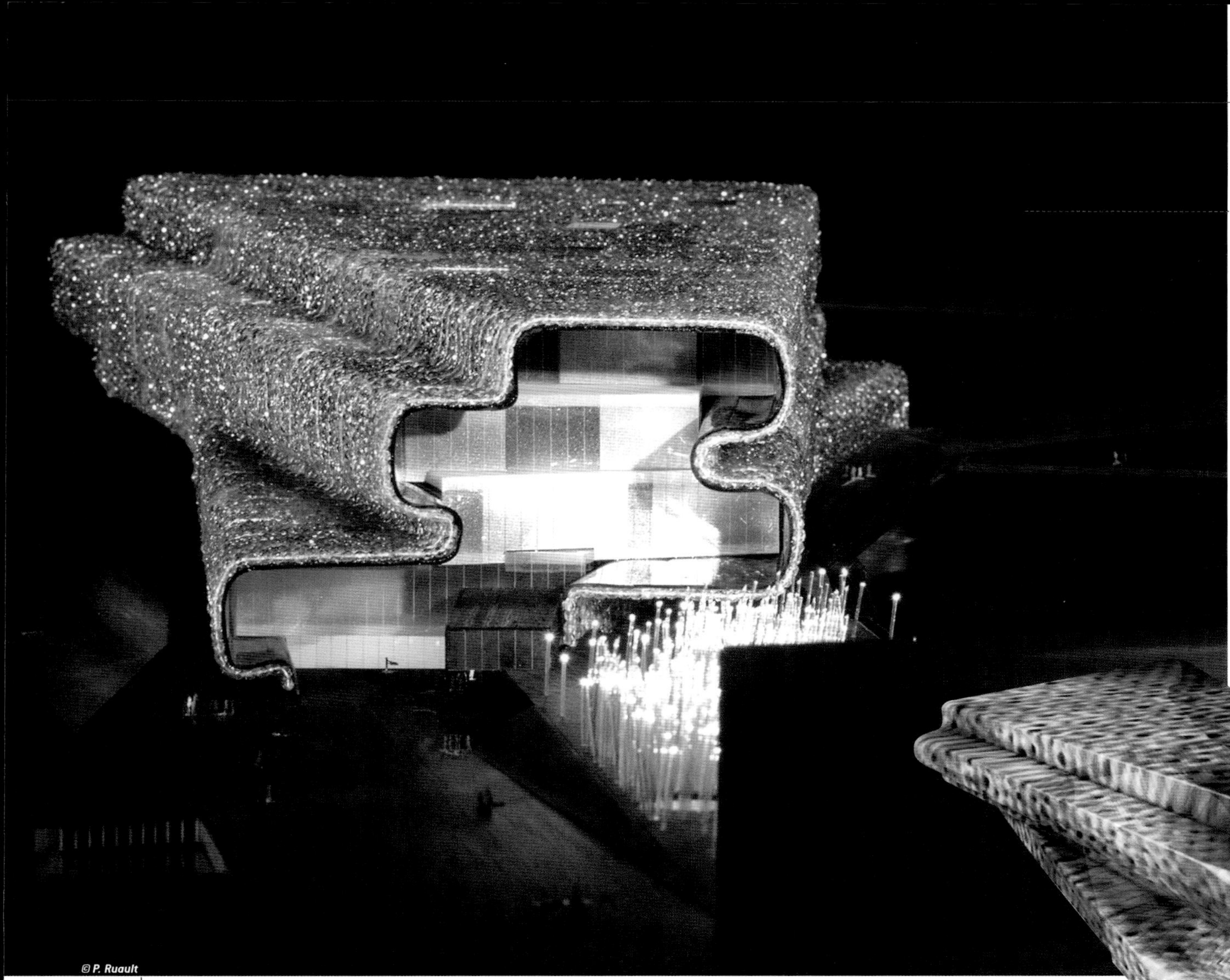

© P. Ruault

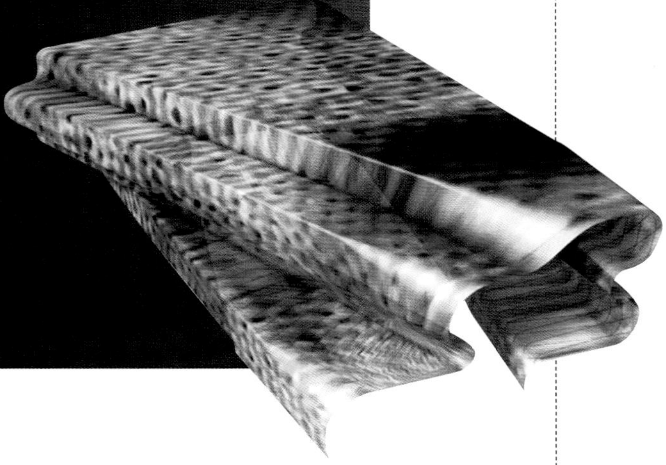

Pinault Foundation
Seguin Island, Boulogne, France, 2001

For a long time the geography and geometry of this territory have been connected and confused with the form of the buildings that have been erected there – those of the Renault car-assembly plant. Does anyone even remember that before embodying the memory of the working classes, this icon was actually an island? Faced with a site that was so loaded with social history, Manuelle Gautrand's approach was radical. Since the island is no longer a factory, it would be pointless to cling to its industrial vestiges, like a 'carapace doomed to decomposition'; today what is needed is a form, a nature and a renewed link with the water of this piece of territory floating on the Seine. For Manuelle Gautrand, this reunion could take place only through imitation. Once the factory had gone and the water and the banks had been rediscovered, the project would have to 'forget the past to the point of forgetting the form of the island ... it must be a point of departure rather than an end point'. The foundation too, as proposed by the architect, reverses the generative lines of the island: although it points downriver, it turns its face towards the exterior, rather like a fan. It opens up instead of closing, as if the long-standing analogy between the end of the island and the prow of a ship, isolated and unified, now has to be erased or even reversed. For so long folded back on itself, prisoner of its own perimeters, Seguin Island now seems able to hold out its arms to the banks. The many footbridges that have now attached themselves to it and the many cantilevers on the façade link up with the environmental context. This open attitude is also echoed by the interior of the island, thanks to the wide entrance that opens out like a town square. The building itself is composed of four great slabs, one on top of the other, irregular and almost unbalanced. The skin, thrown over the building like a coat with oversized folds, is a mix of metal and glass worked into facets. And finally, for the layout of the actual rooms of the museum, Manuelle Gautrand has inverted, shifted, cut off, coloured, alternated – breaking with the generally accepted idea that only those rooms conceived as laboratories allow us to appreciate a work of art. This place has been overspecialized for too long. Manuelle Gautrand endows it with the pleasure of decline. ☒

image © gizmo

AGENCE FRANCIS SOLER

France

Francis Soler [(1949)]

Francis Soler won his first competition when he was still a student, and set up his first agency (in association with Jean Bernard) in 1976. Very early on, he constructed blocks of flats and public facilities, while entering for the large number of international competitions for state commissions that were typical of the French architectural scene during the 1980s: Tête Défense (1980), Cité de la Musique (1984), Bibliothèque de France (1989), Pavillon de France in Seville (1989), Grand Stade (1994). Francis Soler belongs to that generation of French architects for whom competitions lost by their agency are just as representative of their work as the projects they have realized. He has, however, also won a lot, including two highly prestigious ones – the presidential stand for the 14 July ceremony (from 1983 to 1988), and the international conference centre, quai Branly (1990), which remains unfinished. He was awarded the Grand Prix d'Architecture in 1990, has been Officier des Arts et Lettres since 1998 and Chevalier de l'Ordre du Mérite since 2000. He has been teaching since 1998 at the college of architecture in Rennes.

LE DEBARCA

FRANCIS SOLER likes to describe himself as 'unreasonable'. It is in the gap between the programme formulated by the commissioning authority and the proposals of the project manager that he places the real distinction between architecture and construction. According to him, one must at all times accept the risk of taking action. He deliberately sets architecture within the field of avant-garde art, and claims to be on a par with the modern author or artist. For him, aspiring to the sublime entails using every new project to question the very reason for architecture: in doing so, he rejects all a priori aesthetics, all claims of homogeneity in his work. Every projected situation develops along the lines of a synthesis an updating of images and emotions in which he assumes the autobiographical role: out of the enlightenment of this synthesis there must emerge a singular aesthetic, which he regards as a result and not as a tool. Soler dares to have enormous faith in architecture: enjoyable objects to share with consumers or occupants, buildings on the scale of individual quarters or whole towns are to be viewed as works of art. Henceforth they must make sense, revealing or participating in the identity of places and in their position within a wider territorial context. 'The Eiffel Tower and the Grande Arche de Paris, the pyramids of Giza in Egypt, the Sagrada Familia of Barcelona in Spain, the Leaning Tower of Pisa in Italy, the Golden Gate in San Francisco – these are all abstract objects, non-architectural in the sense of primary appearance, which contribute by their own image to the identification of the image of the town or location in question – to the point of almost always actually being the unique and direct symbol that stays in our memory of those places. They load them, in fact, with a history that the two of them build together.' The idea of the monument is not too distant, though this should not under any circumstances be confused with monumentality, for if Soler intends to free himself from the question of style, he also detaches himself from that of foundations: 'The weight of buildings worries me in our modern era; when everything is on the move, architecture seems heavy, anchored in the ground. Certain plastic surgeons of architecture insist on those values, but I don't.' He is inspired by the mobility of modern images, especially those of television – precise but fleeting, transient, one chasing the other or merging with it. From this he draws an ideal of lightness that he would like to apply to his constructions, and it is with this lightness that architecture – whose prime purpose he takes to be the creation of an 'imaginary space' – must be able to adapt itself to human vagaries, to urban mutations, to the complexities of the landscape, to the changing rules of the environment. 'And if there are no more genuine rules,' he says, 'there must nevertheless still be a minimum of traces to follow – the traces of an original geography.'

S. N.

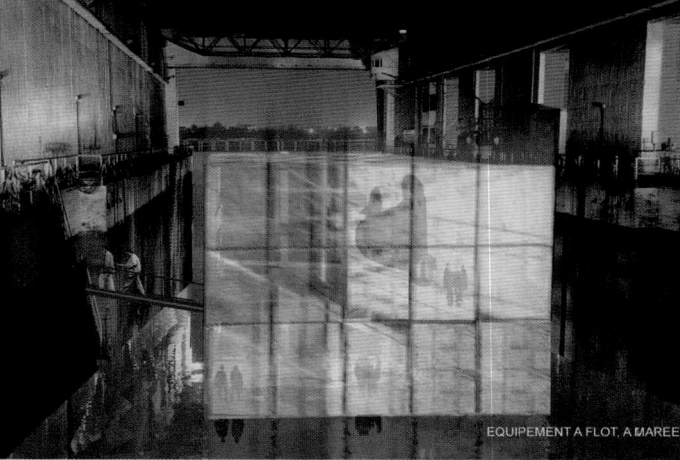

EQUIPEMENT A FLOT, A MAREE

EQUIPEMENT A FLOT, A MAREE

The Islands in the Winds of Keroman
Or the messengers of the invisible

Lorient, France, competition, 1999
Redevelopment of submarine bases from Keroman to Lorient (France)

'Down below, at water level, a fortress inherited from the Third Reich proclaims its solitude. This is both the wound and the pride of Lorient. Built by the Germans to provide a haven for their redoubtable U-boats, the base at Keroman is a strange inheritance, visited last summer by a handful of tourists with an interest in history. Everything seems abandoned, and now there is talk of redevelopment. After all, are not the remains of the past always written in the inexhaustible annals of God or war? Is it not as if there were a constant need to satisfy our extraordinary fascination with and strange admiration for castles, fortresses, churches and temples? But fortunately memorable places are not what they used to be. They now become what we make of them: spaces in which life reconstructs itself on the remnants of the past, sometimes to the point of dressing them up to give pleasure. The fortresses of Keroman will, however, be conserved as they are, with a minimum of restoration as if to maintain the flavour of the original, though with certain small adjustments. After they have been relieved of a somewhat burdensome cushion of muck, they will be turned into islands. They will be garnished inside and out with utilitarian structures in transparent glass, luminous where appropriate, which will stand on their own, independently of the walls. Inside and outside there will be beautiful wind turbines whose blades will turn as signals clearly marking the marine roads of Lorient. And so, as in an ancient theatre, the unpredictable breath of the winds will merge with the invisible messengers of the roads. Had it not been for human decisions and the contingency of time, this sequence of useful structures would never have come together. There is an art that sometimes consists in creating a strikingly unusual combination of existing elements, which, by their nature, would normally remain strangers to each other. Thus creation gives way to a more modern process of orderly or even disorderly accumulation, which leads directly to the work.'

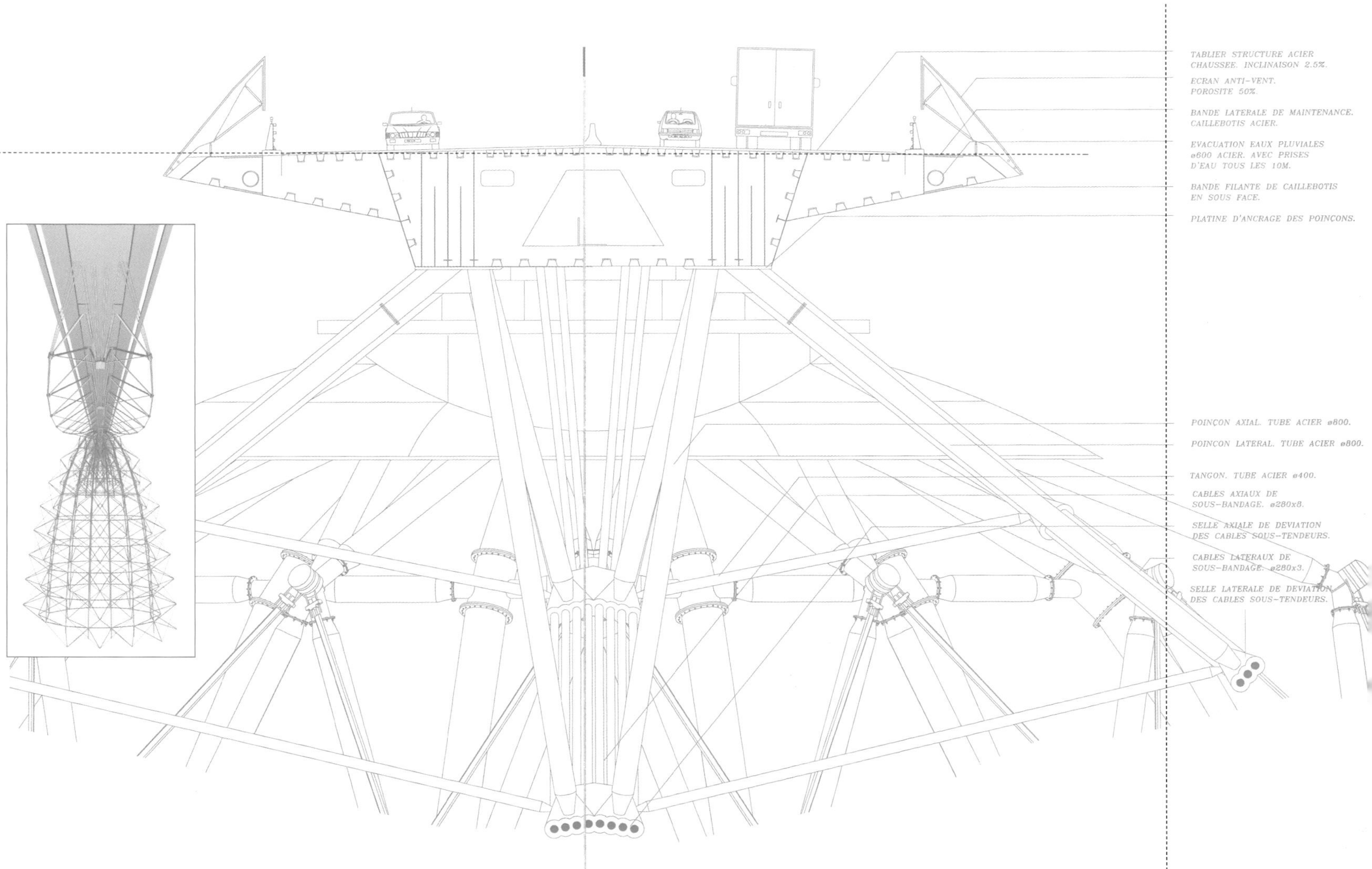

TABLIER STRUCTURE ACIER
CHAUSSEE. INCLINAISON 2.5%.

ECRAN ANTI-VENT.
POROSITE 50%

BANDE LATERALE DE MAINTENANCE.
CAILLEBOTIS ACIER.

EVACUATION EAUX PLUVIALES
ø600 ACIER. AVEC PRISES
D'EAU TOUS LES 10M.

BANDE FILANTE DE CAILLEBOTIS
EN SOUS FACE.

PLATINE D'ANCRAGE DES POINCONS.

POINCON AXIAL. TUBE ACIER ø800.

POINCON LATERAL. TUBE ACIER ø800.

TANGON. TUBE ACIER ø400.

CABLES AXIAUX DE
SOUS-BANDAGE. ø280x8.

SELLE AXIALE DE DEVIATION
DES CABLES SOUS-TENDEURS.

CABLES LATERAUX DE
SOUS-BANDAGE. ø280x3.

SELLE LATERALE DE DEVIATION
DES CABLES SOUS-TENDEURS.

▶ The Millau Viaduct

Millau, France, project, 1994–97

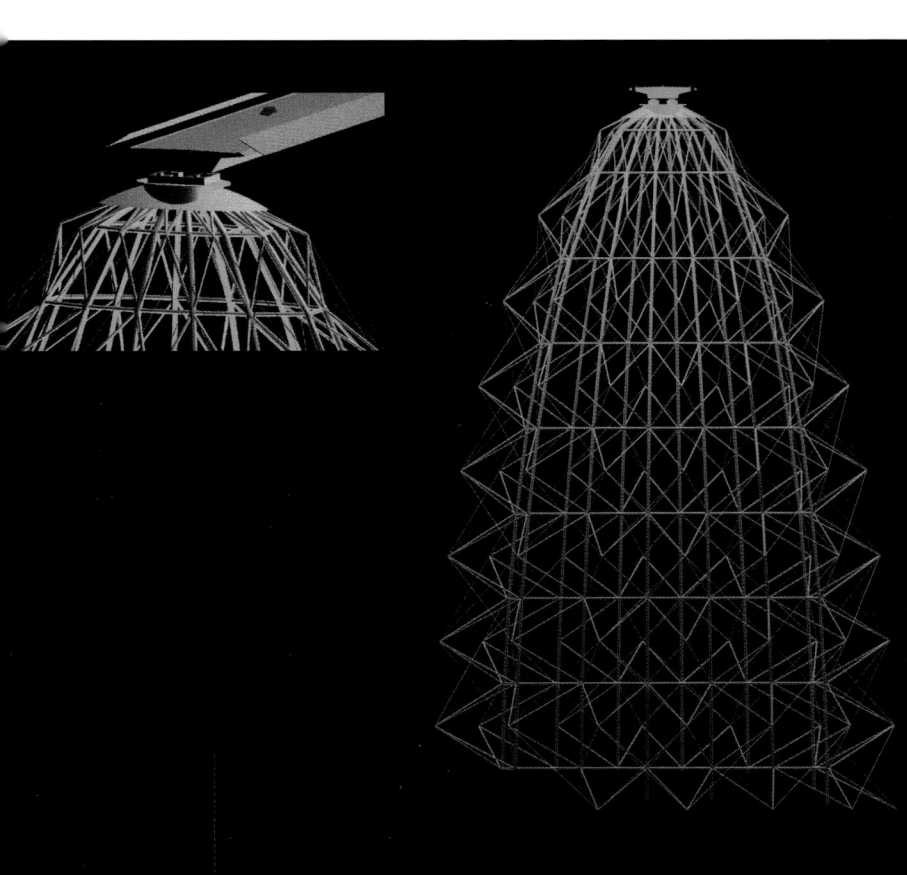

A motorway link between Clermont-Ferrand and Montpellier entails bypassing Millau. After various hypothetical routes had been considered, it was finally decided that the best option was a raised crossing in the form of a viaduct directly connecting two passes at respective heights of 600 and 700 metres. The viaduct would span the entire width of the valley for a good 2.5 kilometres. This structure, linking two very beautiful French regions (les Cévennes and le Languedoc) via les Causses, requires great delicacy in its handling of the environmental impact. For Soler, however, 'the term insertion does not necessarily mean disappearance'. His proposal in fact is to implement a process of revelation, like 'a spotlight whose live and ever-present beams would illuminate a region in a state of profound change'. This revelation works by way of contrast between the variety of the places linked or crossed and the simple and radical line of the roadway suspended at a height of 300 metres and composed of the longest possible spans. As taut as a bow, the road consists of six sections 330 metres long. Its slender outline appears and disappears at the whim of the wind and fog. The six piers seem to be reaching down towards the ground from their different heights, and this helps to adapt the bridge to the morphology of the site. The heights vary from 140 to 270 metres, and their oval sections vary from 50 to 140 metres. They consist of steel tubes fixed with round flanges — the most economical use of materials. The horizontal and vertical structures join up above triangular knots, rather like a woven fabric. Indeed, Soler actually says that the steel is 'woven'. His main concern is to 'remove transposed references, to reject certain treacherous signs, to question the places in order to bring out particular signals, to outline just a few features, and to contribute in some way to what the Great Viaduct of Millau may mean, for it already has its history — paradoxically in the place it holds in its future'. Only thus can it become 'one of the first dreamlike technical events of the century'. ◪

Credits: Francis Soler, with Jérôme Louth, Vincent Jacob

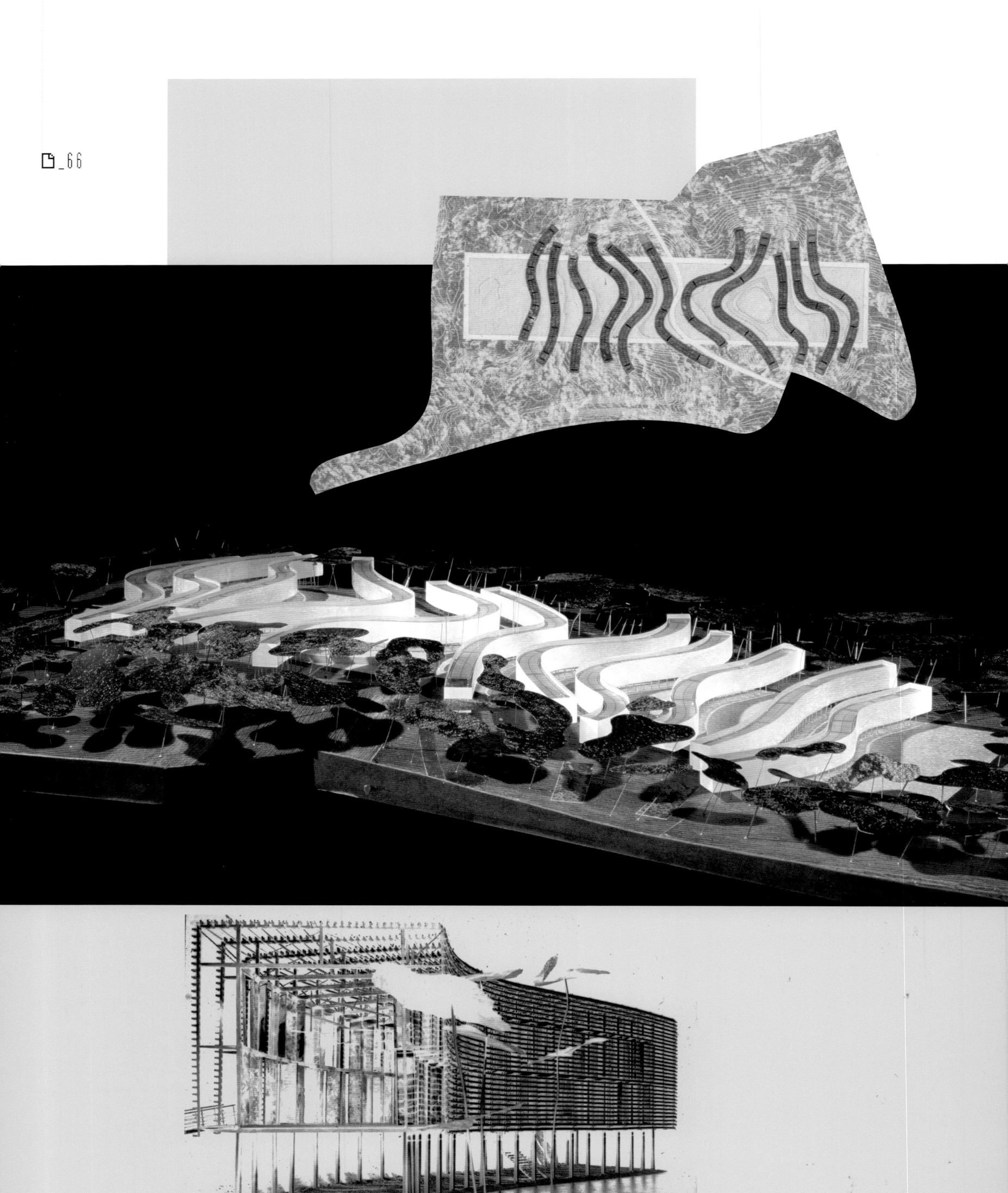

▶ Lycée Polyvalent du Grand Nouméa

New Caledonia, France, competition, 1994

The first part of the project for the Lycée Polyvalent [comprehensive school] du Grand Nouméa is a large clearing in the heart of the pine- and palm-tree forest that Soler envisages on the site. The clearing is turfed and laid out in terraces, on which stands a series of eleven buildings, conceived as thin, linear bands, each with its own individual curvature. Built on stilts, they are approached via a terraced reception area, which is a sort of functional and geographical centre of the school. All the bands are linked to this high terrace at ground-floor level, rather like a vast landing stage. They are also linked to one another by a covered walk. The stilted areas will serve as covered playgrounds below the buildings that house the classrooms and as car parks below those used for administration, etc. A system of ramps from one terrace to another will provide access for the disabled. Each of the buildings is structured by a linear circulation, which at the front occupies a weft of 1.8 metres. In order to ensure comfortable working conditions, natural ventilation is provided by a skin consisting of two filtering surfaces. The outer surface is a mixture of mainly local woods, while the surface that provides the waterproofing is made up of pre-fabricated elements in alveolar polycarbonate. These panels are silk-screen printed with plant motifs that are different for each building. Soler does not think of these as lines seeking to worm their way into the clearing and hence out of the forest, but as the actual condition that gives rise to the forest and the clearing. Here the architect is putting his imagination to work in order to invent a site. Soler explicitly insists on this process, which 'invents the identity of the territory on which it works and which fosters the paradoxes of an architecture that is resolutely "unreasonable"'. ☑

Credits: Francis Soler with David Trottin, Patricia Westerburg, Axel André

ATELIER BOW-WOW

Japan

Momoyo Kajima [1969], Junzo Kuroda [1968], Yoshiharu Tsukamoto [1965]

The two founders of Bow-wow have Masters degrees in architecture: Yoshiharu Tsukamoto studied at the EA Paris-Belleville (1987-88), and Momoyo Kajima at the ETH in Zurich (1996—97). They founded Bow-wow in 1992, and did their doctorates at the Tokyo Institute of Technology. Currently they are both teaching there, as well as in the Arts Faculty at Tsukuba University. Junzo Kuroda graduated from the Department of Architecture at Musashino Art University, and has worked as a researcher for the Sakamoto Laboratory at the Tokyo Institute of Technology. After realizing several independent housing projects, he recently joined the Bow-wow team. Their researches into densely populated towns have already led to numerous recent exhibitions ('Batofar Cherche Tokyo', Paris, 2001; 'Japanese Avant Garde/Reality Projection', London, 2001; 'Towards Landscape', Rotterdam, 2000; 'Minihouses in Japan', Munich, 2000), and form the basis of the project-related ideas presented here. ☒

PEOPLE OFTEN THINK that Tokyo is a pretty shameless, free and easy city, where expressways race through buildings, ramps take cars across the rooftops, no construction is more than forty years old, and everyone is an expert on the latest technology. But the 'shameless' layouts and constructions that would be inconceivable in European towns perhaps seem to be 'in bad taste' only on the basis of outside criteria, foreign paradigms and excessively theoretical references. While people thought they could shed new light on Tokyo during the 1980s by applying chaos theory to the city, Bow-wow eschew such metaphors. They do not wish to treat Tokyo as confused and chaotic, or to interpret it from the standpoint of a predetermined history; they seek instead to transform its incoherences into resources and means of comprehension. For this purpose they launched a major survey in 1991, starting out intuitively with buildings that were 'da-me' (not good), i.e., anonymous, non-contextual, non-cultural, anti-aesthetic, anti-historical, unclassifiable, unplanned. The idea was actually born at the sight of a refreshment area squeezed in under a little sports centre on a slope; it gave the impression of something nonsensical and yet full of joyous, spontaneous energy ... it was 'very Tokyo'. They analysed all the different mixtures: car parks, cemeteries, offices, car washes, cinemas, railway bridges, apartment blocks, restaurants, neon signs, saunas, expressways, boiler rooms, hotels, churches. If this collection has taken on the form of a city guide, it is because the mode of presentation is an important factor in assessing the results of their observations. There are countless guides to Tokyo, covering all its different facets and setting out all its different functions. The guidebook is a real urban tool,

which is particularly suited to Tokyo since it does not impose a meaning on its reader, and has neither beginning nor end. The structure of the city does not explain the 'made in Tokyo' buildings collected in the guide, but it is the buildings that explain the city and express its true nature. They have arisen out of whatever is important at the time, and have been conceived for practical purposes, on the basis of what is available and affordable in a particular place; they are responses that are efficient, dictated by the minimum effort and cost, and greatly valued in Tokyo. Furthermore, they give new life to each environmental feature, new uses for by-products and a recycling of the 'offcuts' from the fabric of urban life. One research project in particular, 'Pet Architecture', was carried out on what were called 'company buildings': newspaper stands, kiosks, sandwich bars and all those constructions that other buildings would never dream of treating as equals or as serious subjects of comparison, but which nevertheless are engaging, charming and entertaining companions. They occupy special and improbable places – a one-metre strip, a geometrical shape between two buildings, an acute angle between two streets – and their design is not rational but almost 'natural'. Even the tiniest element has its place (information, the electric fan), and its position is important.

Bow-wow's interest, then, lies in different ways of creating and utilizing environmental units in the city: the unexpected juxtaposition of different functions in the same building, cross-breeding between constructional categories, combined use of adjacent buildings – these are flexible factors that daily use can harmonize and unify. The agency has therefore defined a new 'typology' of

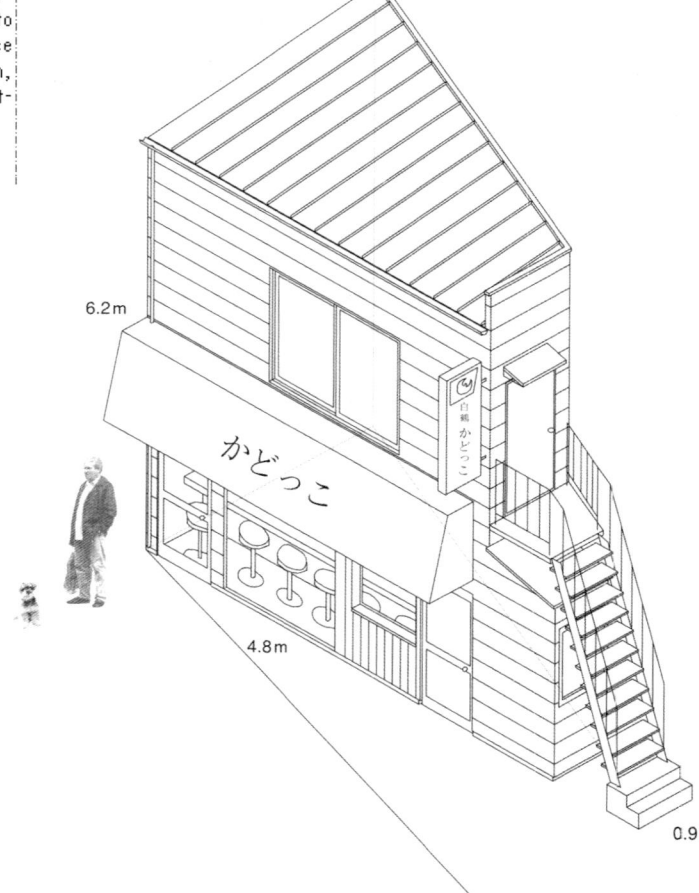

6.2m

かどっこ

4.8m

0.9m

buildings, based on three criteria: the category, the structure and the use. These are ways of unifying an environment, and they do not need to be activated (on/off) all at the same time. By intermingling them, the designer may have eight new dimensions at his or her disposal. These new areas of potential multiply the possible futures of the city, and this is what Bow-wow try to express in their designs, in the conviction that the feedback between research and architectural creation is an effective means of contributing to city life. ☒

0   10   20m

B. G.

Mini House
Nerima, Tokyo, 1999

Exterior: The site faces a 4-metre-wide street to the east, a 1-metre-wide private path to the south and and a field waiting for the construction of a ring road to the west. The west of the site was once subdivided into housing lots while the east was occupied by farmland, but now the west is grassland while the east is subdivided. These houses are very close together but each is always separated from the next by a margin of space. It is difficult to imagine accurately the future of this fluid and unpredictable environment. The smallness of the site adds to the fluidity of the urban structure. The surface area of 76 square metres is not at all exceptional in Tokyo.

Such a fluidity in the environment made it difficult to read the site by the traditional study of oppositions such as deep/shallow, front/back. At this point, defining the orientation of the house in terms of its environment became the issue. The main volume is placed in the centre of the site, offset from each boundary. Different sub-volumes are drawn out from each side, making an uneven windmill plan. The sub-volumes reorganize various external areas so that each elevation makes a particular relationship to its surroundings.

Interior: There being no interior walls, it is the floors that separate the spaces. Light steel panels allow all floor and perimeter wall planes to be fully utilized as both structure and direct spatial division. Because of this structure, without overriding post and beam framework, we were free to make openings and protrusions in any location. By interpreting the surroundings, we can study at the same time both the needs of the internal layout and the activation of the exterior.

Our aim is to relate the house directly with its context; to achieve an interaction between architecture and the urban landscape. 'Building a house in Tokyo' can be seen as executing an understanding of the interdependent relationship between interior and exterior.

▶ Kawanishi Camping Cottage
Niigata, Japan, 1999

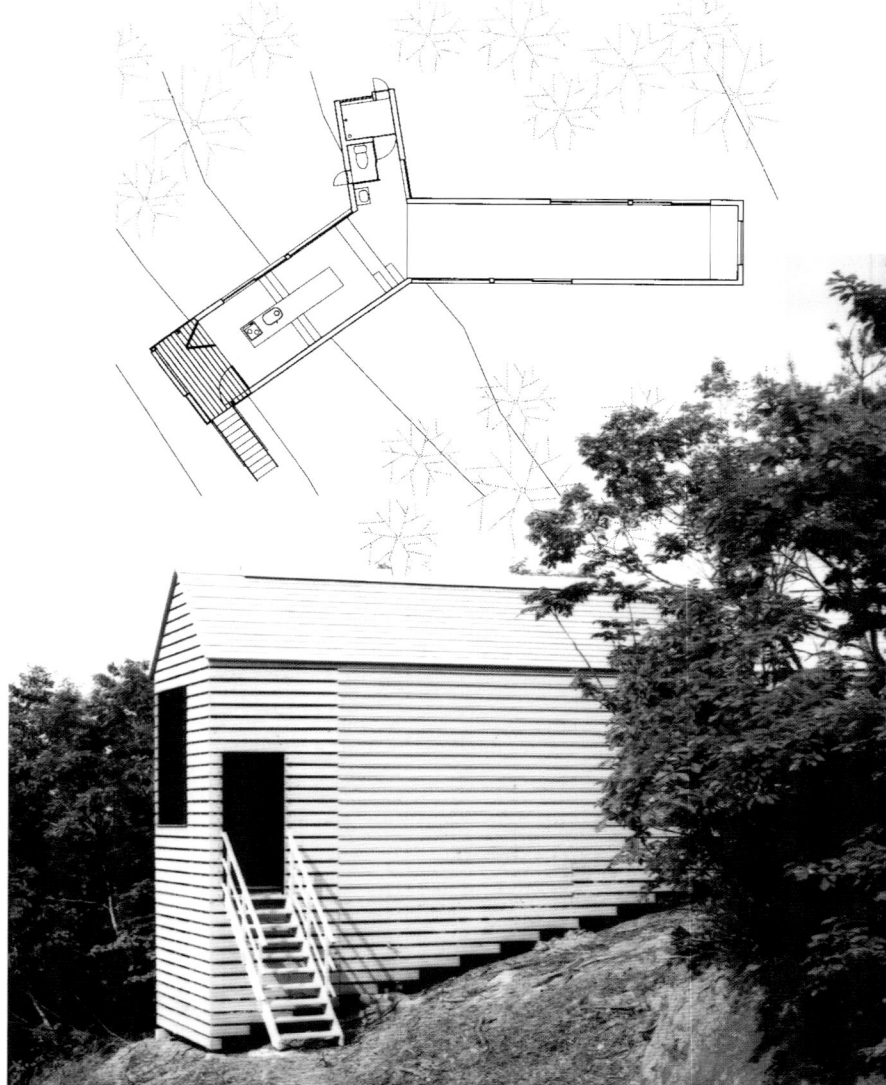

Exterior: Kawanishi is a town in the region of Shinanogawa River, where, in the winter, snow piles up regularly to a height of 4 metres, making the approach to this camping site impossible. Because of the climatic conditions, we decided on an initial design direction of narrow volume and small-pitched roof with raised floor level.

We searched the grounds for a suitable site. Approaching the lake was an abandoned track, making a kind of tunnel through the forest. We could imagine the flat upper ground as a sleeping area, the sloping ground near water for eating and the far side of the side, among the bushes, for washing; this site was already a perfect camping spot. In other words, this scheme works with a set of specific architectural concerns and interacts them with the site to fix the spatial structure. The building volume traces the slope of the ground, and the internal floor level also steps down to follow the incline.

Interior: The plan is in the form of a Y: three branches of differing widths corresponding to the activities of sleeping, eating and washing. Their tubular form is difficult to safeguard from earthquakes in the short section, but here, by joining the three sections at a single point, the fingers can support each other and spread the load of horizontal resistance. So the internal volume became a continuous, branched space. Each tube maintains the same ridgeline and eaveline so that the difference in width produces the difference in roof pitch. From the interior, this is clearly expressed at the point where the three tubes meet. The interior is stained black, thus highlighting and intensifying the green of the forest. From the slightly raised far end of the house, the view extends down to the lake through the large windows of the dining room and the kitchen.◪

▶ Moth House
Nagano, Japan, 2000

Far exterior: This is a forest holiday home near Karuizawa. Many memories are gathered in this house, which has been used by three generations for over forty years. However, the house has aged and the family wish to extend the floor area and renew the plumbing fixtures. The original house is half covered by a new translucent envelope, which does not touch the existing exterior walls, and its silhouette can be seen through the envelope.

Interior: The project creates a space between the original house and the forest. The old external walls become the new walls of the sunroom. By allowing light to flood on to the white wall of the old house, the space allows the family to continue collecting insects and moths. Glimmers and shadows play freely on the house, with the movement of the wind in the trees, creating aquatic reflections on all the surfaces of the building. ▨

Asama House
Nagano, Japan, 2001

Exterior: This site is located on the edge of the famous mountain resort Karuizawa, two hours by car from Tokyo. It borders farming land, and so the area is a mixture of holiday houses and farmhouses. To the west are rice paddies and to the east is forest. The project is a simple, single room for a family, surrounded by 15-metre-high trees, and enhanced by the shifting natural light and the foliage. The building is square in plan, with a pyramidal roof. The important concern in this project was to deal with purity of form in relation to the different views of nature.

Interior: The ceiling space is divided into five portions by suspended walls, giving a suggestion of rooms. Columns are not required because the suspended walls act as large beams, contributing to the unity of the room. The suspended walls are so placed as to mark off the interior spaces by function – eating, living, studying, sleeping and washing – and the distances between them are defined by the angles of the roof planes. We particularly tried to draw in light to this site. Thus, the nine surfaces of the room are pierced. The space is filled with light from these nine openings that frame the tree trunks at the bottom and the treetops at the top. The blue sky forms a backdrop at roof level. The light can thus enter and play in the interior with the elements, varying its effects according to the time, the season and the orientation: snow lying on the windows in the roof, orange reflections on the interior walls at sunset and, on the other surfaces, a whole gamut of flitting shadows.

D.a.S House
Tokyo, Japan, 2002

Exterior: This house for a young couple is situated in the western suburbs of Tokyo, where there are still some farms. The station closest to the site is on the line that links the husband's workplace and his favourite horse-racing stadium. They bought this land because it is convenient for both working and leisure and because it separates the monstrous and gigantic city of Tokyo from their social and daily lives. They wanted the house to 'customize' Tokyo. The little plot looks over luxuriant neighbouring gardens to the east and north behind the boundary walls and over apartment buildings to the south and the west. Managing the distances and openings with respect to the neighbours had therefore to be done carefully. The cubic volume of the house, on two floors, was placed at the southeast corner of the site, so as to create equal distances from the existing buildings near by.

Interior: The building is 'too big and too harsh' for the human body, just as the city is too big and too harsh for the individual. The interior space is divided horizontally by the floor and vertically by a staircase in the middle of the floor plan. The clients were particularly keen to have more wall surface than floor surface. The interior walls thus divide the house according to the activity carried on within the spaces they delimit: hanging things, sorting and tidying things, looking out of the window and even sitting at the window sill. The wooden structure lends the rhythm of the columns to these activities, as well as a tactile texture. The kitchen window gives on to the ground and the laundry window on to the sky, thanks to a system of mirrors; they thus connect the indoor activities with the environment. The placement of the staircases and flexible doors allows a depth to be given to each part of the house. It is these characteristics – Deep and Shallow – that give the house its name. ☒

Arno Brandlhuber/Bernd Kniess (B&K+)

Germany

Arno Brandlhuber [1964], Bernd Kniess [1961]

Arno Brandlhuber and Bernd Kniess, engineers and urban architects who graduated from the technical high school in Darmstadt, founded b&k+ in 1996. Since 2001, the two branches of the agency have shared projects and collaborated in a multitude of different ways. Winners of about twenty prizes in Germany and both teachers at the University of Wuppertal, they have always focused on an intense exchange with other creative fields, which is reflected even in the name of their agency. That 'plus' sign gives them access to a long list of partners: musicians, choreographers, philosophers, physicians, designers, etc. Their work has recently been exhibited in Luxembourg ('Under the Bridges', 2001), at the Museum of Applied Arts in Cologne ('Heilige-drei-Koenige.de' [The-Three-Holy-Kings.Germany], 2000), in Stuttgart ('In Vitro Landscape', 1999) and in Copenhagen ('Speculation', 1998). Thanks to their cooperative way of working, their projects can take versatile forms — inventive, constructive, commercial — to try to take architecture out of itself, towards the multiple dimensions that define our contemporary nature. ☒

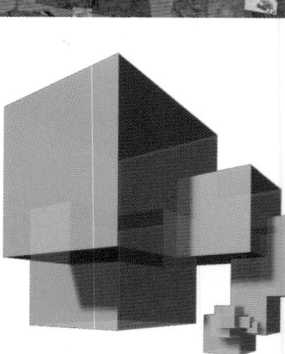

'EARTH ECONOMY' sounds hopeful [1] and obviously aims to take the Earth as its point of reference.[2]

[1] 'Hopeful' would mean that economic decision-making processes, the problems of distributing goods and the definition of all of society's objectives would be based on keeping the Earth as the reference point, to which shape can be given. The 'Political Landscape' workshop (*Political Landscape*, b&k+, Bergische Universität GH Wuppertal, Akademie der Stadt Sindelfingen, Cologne, 2001), which we initiated in 2000 to investigate socially relevant creative options, did not allow us to establish global rules of conduct. On the contrary, we discovered that the need for new ideas for the future was inherent in each individual.

[2] Even if the question concerning 'globality' threw us back on the individual as reference point, an 'Earth economy' could nonetheless be envisaged as an economy founded on a multiplicity of reference levels and scales, beginning with our own work structure, the communication structure that is compatible with it, the projects' increasing value, the question of social relevance and its reference to the Earth.

[i] The economy of one's own working structure will be described as a growing web of cooperation, from the single office structure to cooperation with the most varying partnerships (b&k+: Brandlhuber & Kniess + partner) but also to cell divisions and the adoption of models of economic participation (b&k+: Brandlhuber & co/www.brandlhuber.com), including the integration of other intellectual producers.

[ii] An extended field of communication and cooperation will be analysed to see if others are able to process the information we generate.

[iii] The offered exchange will be less oriented towards objects and more towards processes and structures. Instead of formal discussions, there will be an applied pragmatism that considers material wealth as intellectual capital.

[iv] We will have to examine ourselves as well regarding our ability to integrate socially relevant parameters.

[v] There is another extremely important fact concerning the enterprise Earth: 'no operating instructions have been supplied' (R. Buckminster Fuller). ☒

Architecture — whatever its scale — is always a hybrid of the inside and the outside. Construction and perception, as understood in the making of landscape, result in a design approach where experimental and pragmatic techniques converge. Ecology, economics, technology are as important as social, moral and political values. Collaboration becomes a part of our culture.

In pursuit of an extended understanding of architectural form and concepts of life, nature is being transformed in various ways: wild, cultivated, genetically designed ... The 'space' that once was just a scrap is liberated and transformed into a platform of activity. Landscape today is conceived in vitro, in a way that is telematic, economic, political, supersonic and so on.

Matching theory with practice establishes scientific research as an essential part of the architect's work. Theoretical discourse and research are immanent in design development. Apparently contradictory phenomena lead to coherence and complexity and hence increase our range of action. Architecture is no longer a product, but becomes the material of an ongoing process. ☒

Arno Brandlhuber

Bernd Kniess

Economy of Availability: Telematic Landscape
Hanover Exposition, Germany, project, 1999

Originally, the 'Telematic Landscape' project was about designing an exhibition pavilion (not built) for the firm Bosch in Hanover's expo 2000. The pavilion exhibits were to include the company's latest navigational systems technologies and hi-tech 'telematic devices', 'telematic' being defined as 'the autonomous movement of distant things' (Vilém Flusser). The landscape is thus considered in the sense of a 'world in connection', where space and place are called upon to be no longer external objects but constantly transformed from the inside, by movement and the perception of users. Unfortunately the project commission was withdrawn, since Bosch decided on a conventional solution, but our office went ahead with the project as a free, interdisciplinary research activity, embracing contributions from artists, theoreticians, scientists, musicians.

Issues such as the relationship between information, advertising and creation of space arose from the brief. Basically, our focus was on creating an infinite surface or space, which required particular working processes as well as techniques and materials. The developmental process was based on the so-called 'sponge' of Menger, a self-generated structure conceived in order to create the maximal surface. Using computer animation techniques based on the mathematic formula of the 'sponge', an autonomously growing, permeable organism is assembled. Starting from the minimal cube we end up with a cluster of countless self-similar, interlocking bodies. It is an organizational model in which the surface created increases to the maximum as the volume decreases to the minimum.

The same principles of dematerialization and endless spatial relationships are followed in order to define the pavilion's materials. Glass, metal, translucent polycarbonate sheets, wood mirrors and projection screens are superposed by reflection and projection techniques, allowing the observer to become part of the observed system. Irresolution and disorientation become physical. The structure of the telematic landscape becomes immeasurably self-similar and self-generated.☑

Credits: Arno Brandlhuber, Bernd Kniess (b&k+) + Team: Sebastian Hauser, Jörg Leeser, Bernd Lampe, Sven Bäuker, Jörg Lammers, Ulli Wallner, Björn Martenson, Markus Emde, Jost Ewert, Christiane Schmidt

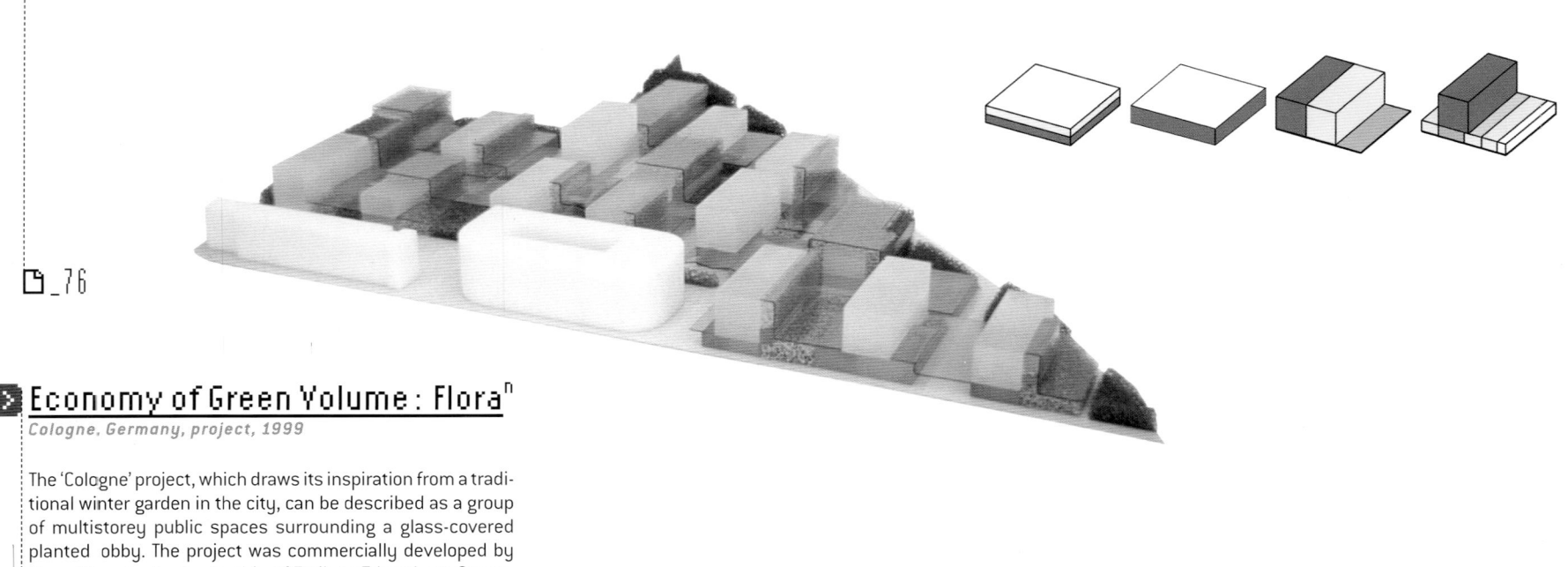

▶ Economy of Green Volume : Flora[n]

Cologne, Germany, project, 1999

The 'Cologne' project, which draws its inspiration from a traditional winter garden in the city, can be described as a group of multistorey public spaces surrounding a glass-covered planted lobby. The project was commercially developed by Flora AG under the leadership of Freiherr Eduard von Oppenheim and consists of proposing office spaces synergetically overlain on a local and public park. In fact, the production of green and natural qualities and commercial interests enhance each other. We tried to introduce a 'green factor', which connects not only the built with the unbuilt but also the built and the green, in a three-dimensional sense. The rule imposed – green volume equivalent to built volume – freed up a variety of templates and allowed us to guarantee regeneration and the microclimate properties necessary to this urban environment. The project – 'n' representing nature in its infinite dimensions – is a strategic programme, which builds a function and generates effects. It produces interfaces and 'soft' transitions, describes empty spaces in the heart of the green volume and allows us to map out the parameters of density, distances and the development of office volumes. This combination of useful surfaces and natural typologies, indoor as well as outdoor, creates a commerce – nature hybrid: artificial and natural, architectural and park add up to an extended use of gastronomic, sporting and cultural mechanisms, in the form of an urban/rural park.

☑

Credits: Arno Brandlhuber, Bernd Kniess (b&k+ ifau, le)

Team: Anne-Julchen Bernhardt, + ifau+ le

Economy of Land Reclamation: Sonic Polder
Cologne, Germany, project, 2001

An empty site close to Cologne was found to have significant problems with noise beyond legal limits: with a railway line, a motorway and dense vehicle traffic all around, it provided excellent infrastructure for the centre of Cologne. Its proximity to the city placed the site within the zone of high-quality living in the context of a typical suburban housing structure. The challenge was to reclaim this lost island and give it a suburban quality. With simple terracing, b&k+ met the challenge: conquering the space without contributing to urban sprawl. By creating cuttings and embankments, we produced a protective topography, completely changing the pattern of measured noise. In the undulating relief that was thus created, the architects propose new types of housing, land division and function. Aside from redefining urban structures, it was also the emergence of new social structures, following on the creation of innovatory exterior spaces, that posed an interesting question. The garden is no longer condemned to be the leftover of a villa but is integrated into a gradual chronology of intimacy: from inner, private spaces to patios, enclosed outer spaces and even to rooms in contact with the street. The high density of housing thus created allows units to be linked together, extensions to grow along with the family and workplaces to be merged with residences. This density is regulated in accordance with the scale of the site in the centre of which there is a huge forum.

Credits: Bernd Kniess (b&k+ Kniess gmbh&co.kg)

Team: ADU Cologne Institut für Immissionsschutz, Anne-Julchen Bernhardt, Leonhard Lagos, Claudia Strahl, Ulli Wallner, Barbara Wolff, Sebastian Hauser

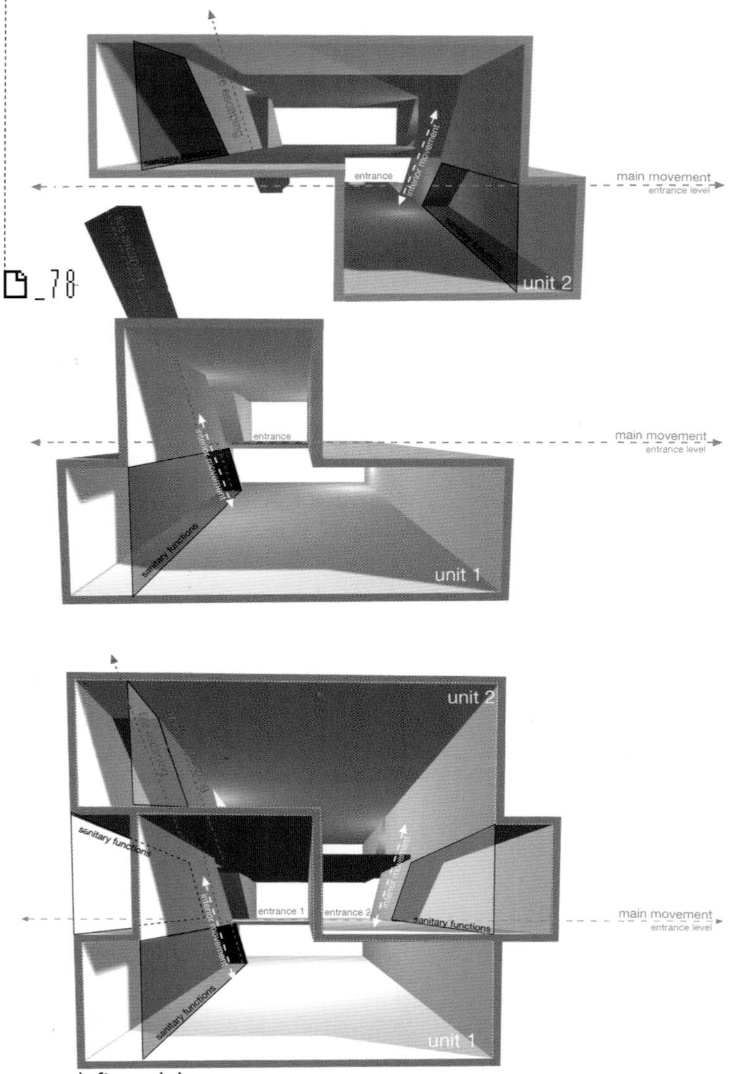

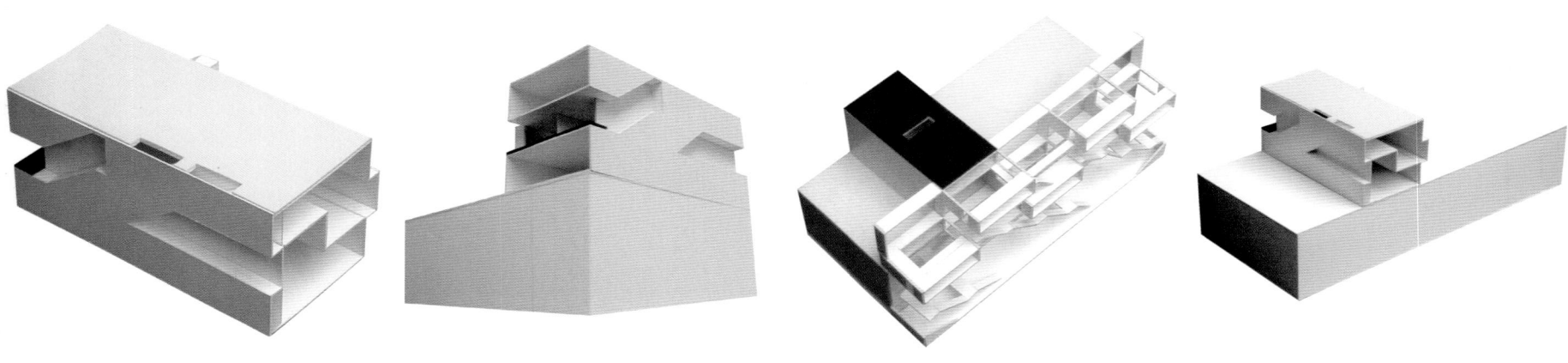

main movement
entrance level
entrance
unit 2
main movement
entrance level
entrance
sanitary functions
unit 1
unit 2
sanitary functions
entrance 1
entrance 2
sanitary functions
main movement
entrance level
sanitary functions
unit 1
loft module

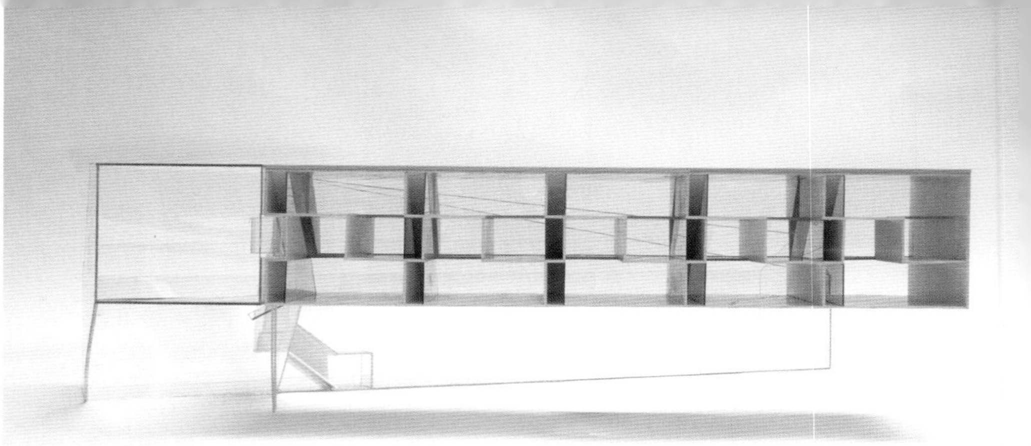

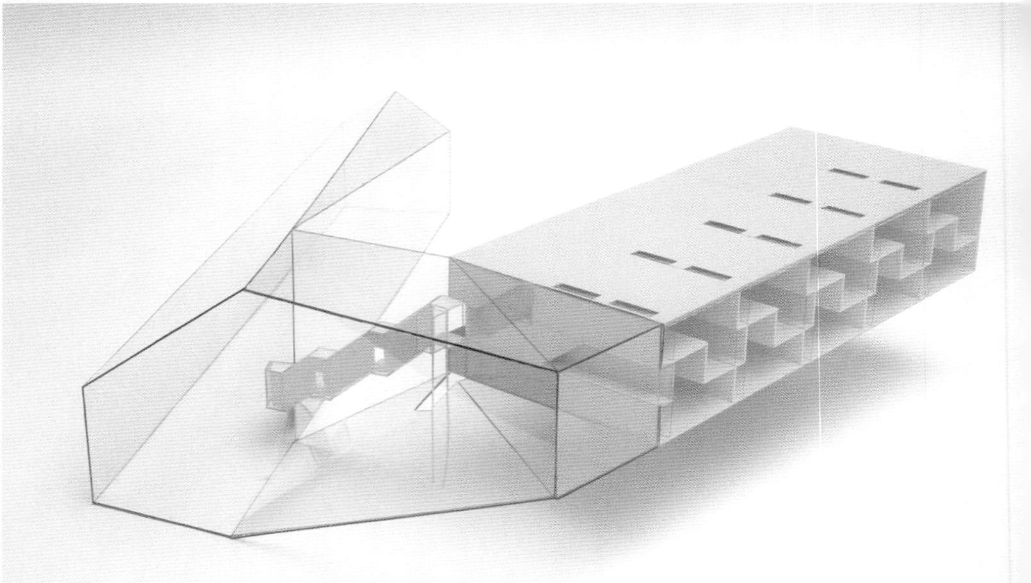

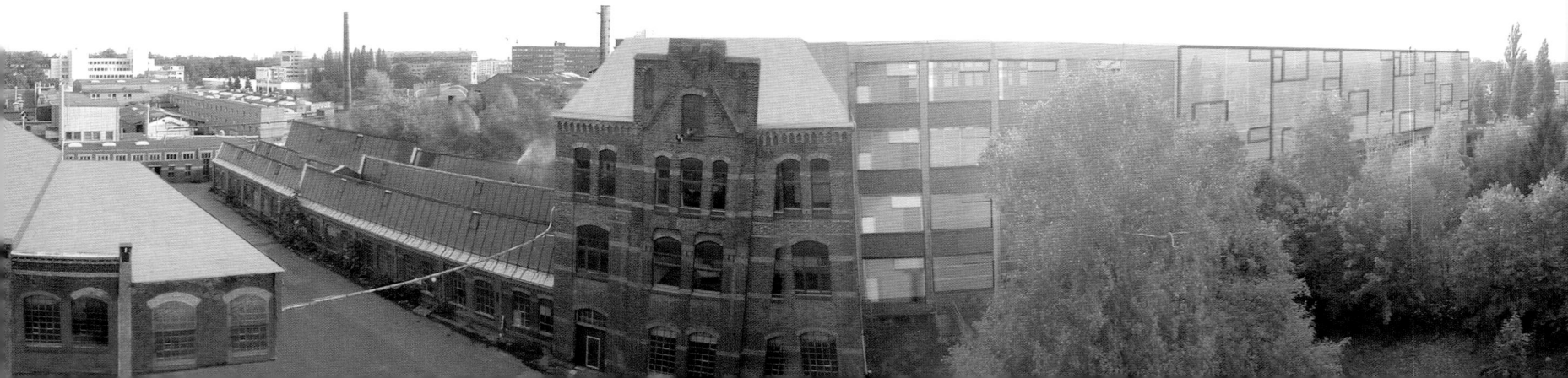

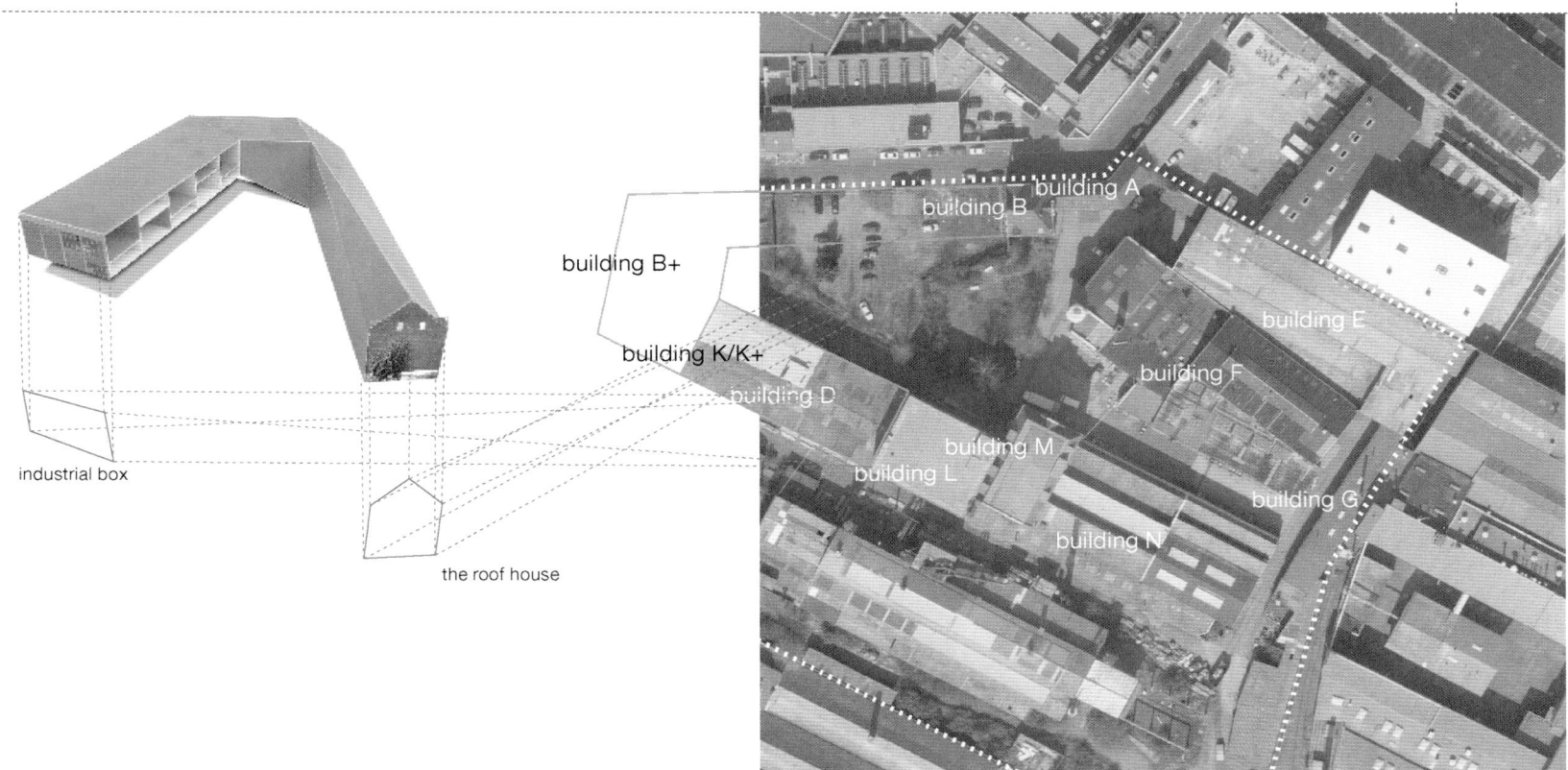

building B+

building K/K+

industrial box

the roof house

building A
building B
building E
building F
building D
building M
building L
building G
building N

▶ Economy of Simultaneity: Vulkan (1900–1960–2000)

Cologne, Germany, 2002

This project is about reusing a former gas-lamp factory complex, which was abandoned by its owner, the Vulkan company, in the early 1990s. The complex is located in a suburb of Cologne that used to be a typical mixed housing and industrial area. Our task was to restore and reuse part of the old buildings, as well as planning an additional building, in order to transform the whole site into a commercial/office complex.

The project wished to make manifest the social evolution of the region: it links 1900 – the worker's house, 1960 – material production and opens in 2001 as 'immaterial' production.

The new building was conceived as a volume, morphed from the walls of two existing building typologies: the 19th-century house, covered on two sides, and the mid-20th-century 'box'. This 'technique' is used for the development of form, structure and façade. ◨

Credits: Arno Brandlhuber, Björn Martenson, Asterios Agkathidis, Piotr Brzoza
Model: Daniel Reinhardt, Christian Dorsch

extention

upcomming building

existing industrial

[commerce]

BERLAGE INSTITUTE

Netherlands

The Berlage Institute is an international postgraduate laboratory for education, research and development in the field of architecture, urban planning and landscape design. The Berlage Institute aims to function as a critical international environment where architecture, urban planning and landscape architecture are researched in depth. Theoretical issues form an important part of the programme. '3D City' was a studio programme in 2001 under the curation of Wiel Arets (dean of the Berlage Institute) and Winy Maas (thesis tutor at the Berlage Institute). ☑

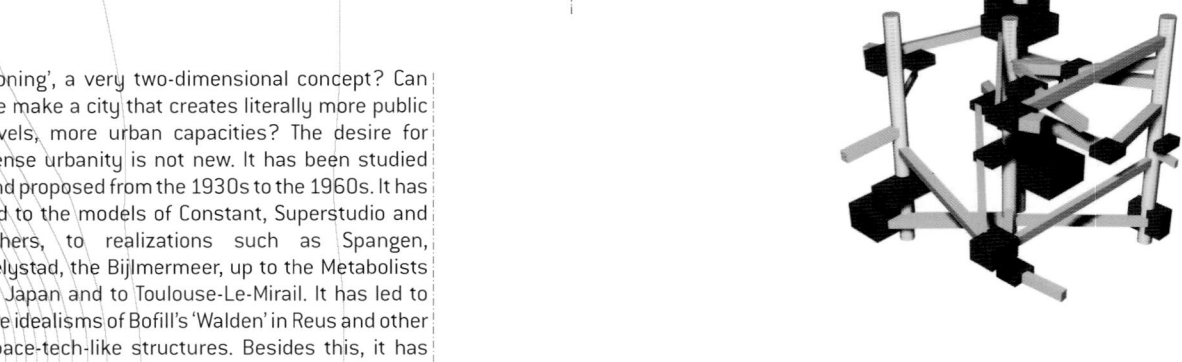

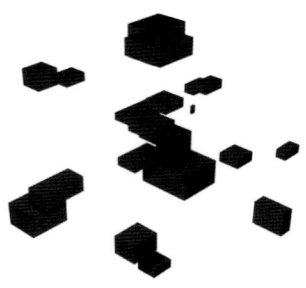

MIXMAX – The world, it seems, is becoming progressively composed out of built environments of enormous banality, an incredible endless amount of mediocrity, shoddy production that creates the depressing and sad inescapable 'matter' around us: the universal city, the city that has reduced the role of architecture to a minimum. Architecture gets attention and a chance to perform only in the production of the unique: villas, museums, stations. This endless generic world is subject to economic and environmental constraints that reduce the independence and autonomy of architecture. It turns human beings into lemmings; it develops stupidity and dependency instead of intelligence and independence or interdependency. It decreases awareness and impoverishes criticism. Can we find an answer to that, maybe by both accepting this 'matter' or the processes that underlie it and by opposing it? Can we use it to formulate wider perspectives? Can we 'swallow' this mediocre, two-dimensional matter, turning it into more compact environments that enrich it with a more 'urban', more cultural potential? Can these new cities spare the enormous parts yet to be colonized? Can we then impose densities that in the end increase the world's capacity? One of the secondary effects of this density is to enlarge the capacity of different programmes to adjust: more mix leads to more social encounters, more urbanity, more possibilities for architecture.

What urbanism will then appear? Can we develop an urbanism that enters the third dimension in times when urbanism is still dominated by 'zoning', a very two-dimensional concept? Can we make a city that creates literally more public levels, more urban capacities? The desire for dense urbanity is not new. It has been studied and proposed from the 1930s to the 1960s. It has led to the models of Constant, Superstudio and others, to realizations such as Spangen, Lelystad, the Bijlmermeer, up to the Metabolists in Japan and to Toulouse-Le-Mirail. It has led to the idealisms of Bofill's 'Walden' in Reus and other space-tech-like structures. Besides this, it has given rise to science-fiction images such as Batman's Gotham City, The Cube, The Fifth Element and Metropolis. It has depicted a world that, although it was created out of ideology (namely the desire to combine city and landscape), has become drenched with anxiety and fear. The articulation of the large scale with smaller scales turned out to be very difficult and led to the monofunctionality of these projects, thus condemning the attempt. No other phenomenon in the history of architecture has been so heavily and widely criticized as this one. It rendered the Modern movement taboo. And although many believe in its necessity, most of us want to distance ourselves from it, frightened of its very complexity and of its assumed dangers. But the awareness of the growing megacities has become apparent and has led, for instance, to UN declarations. A resurgence of interest in the city at the end of the millennium can be explained by the new economies: this new financial world has established itself within the major cities and settled within the densest places because of the desired (if not strictly needed) interconnections with the financial world and, because of the density and intensity of cultural life, giving birth to a middle and upper class of multinational character. These processes underline the imminent return of density, born out of a clash between pure differences. This clash opens new possibilities for architecture, reuniting banal yet fascinating combinations of programme. ☑

Winy Maas

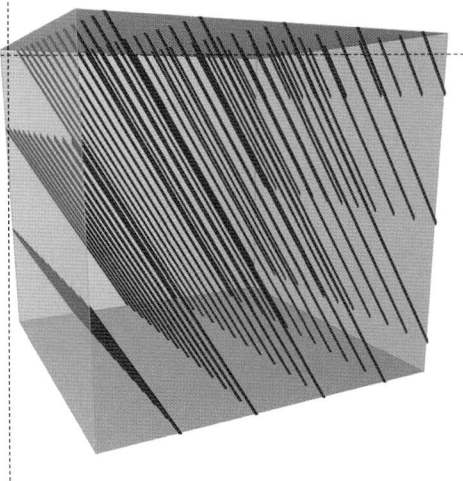
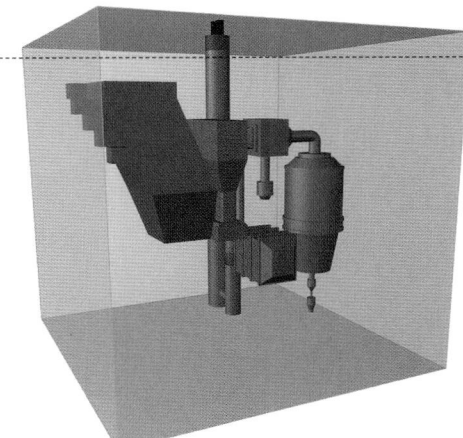
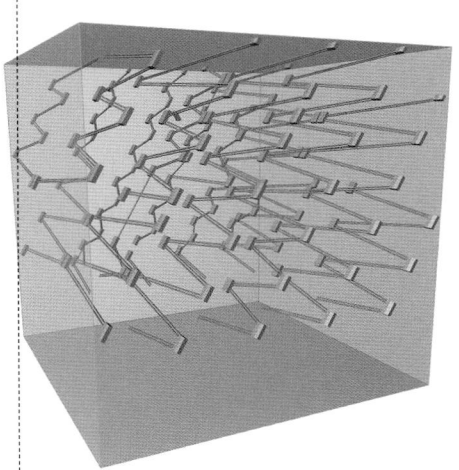
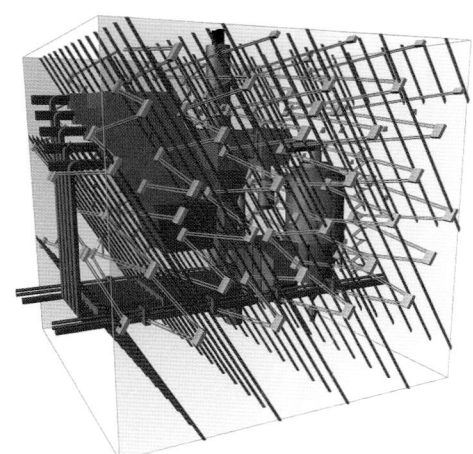
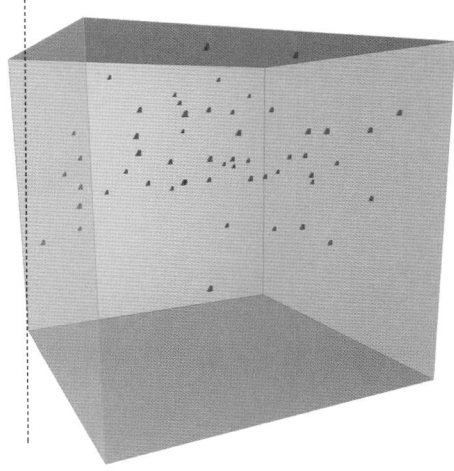
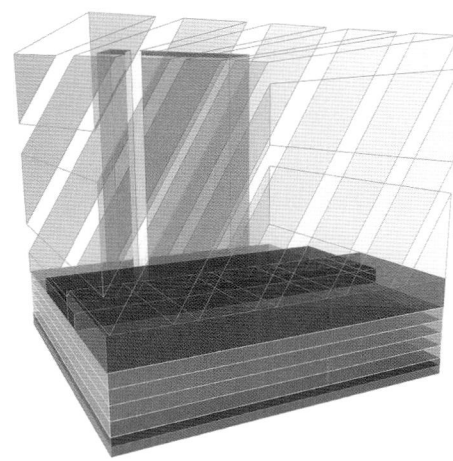
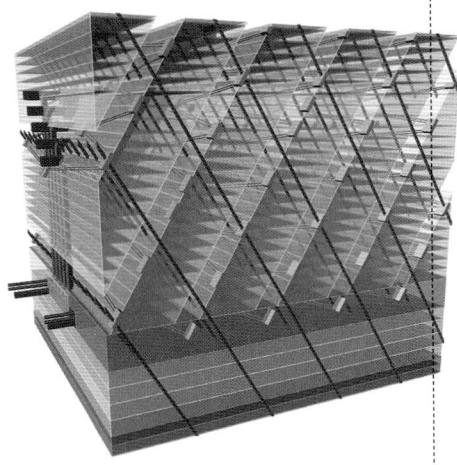

[water]

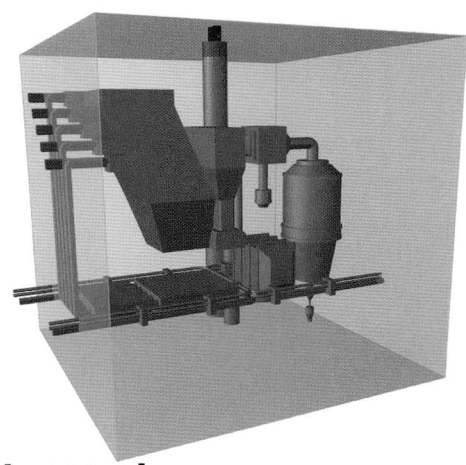

[rubbish]

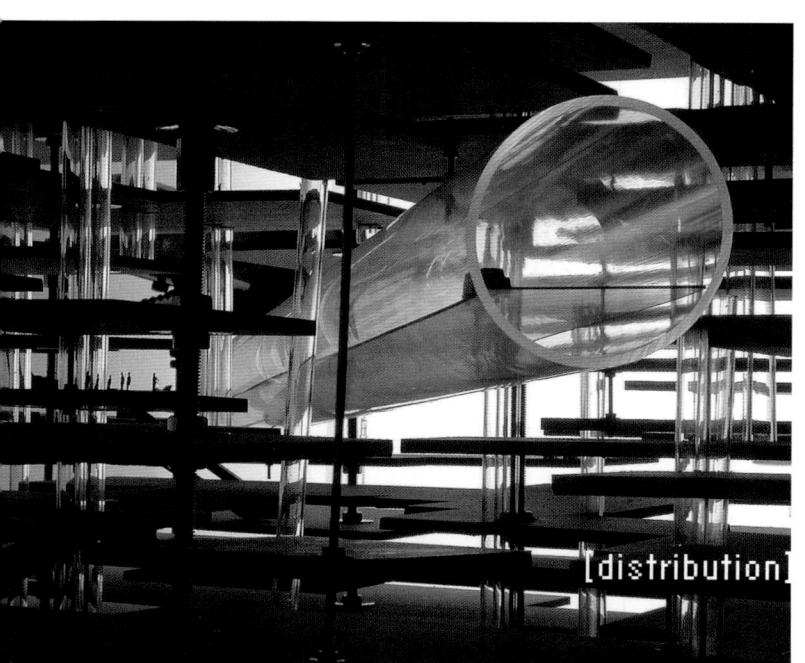

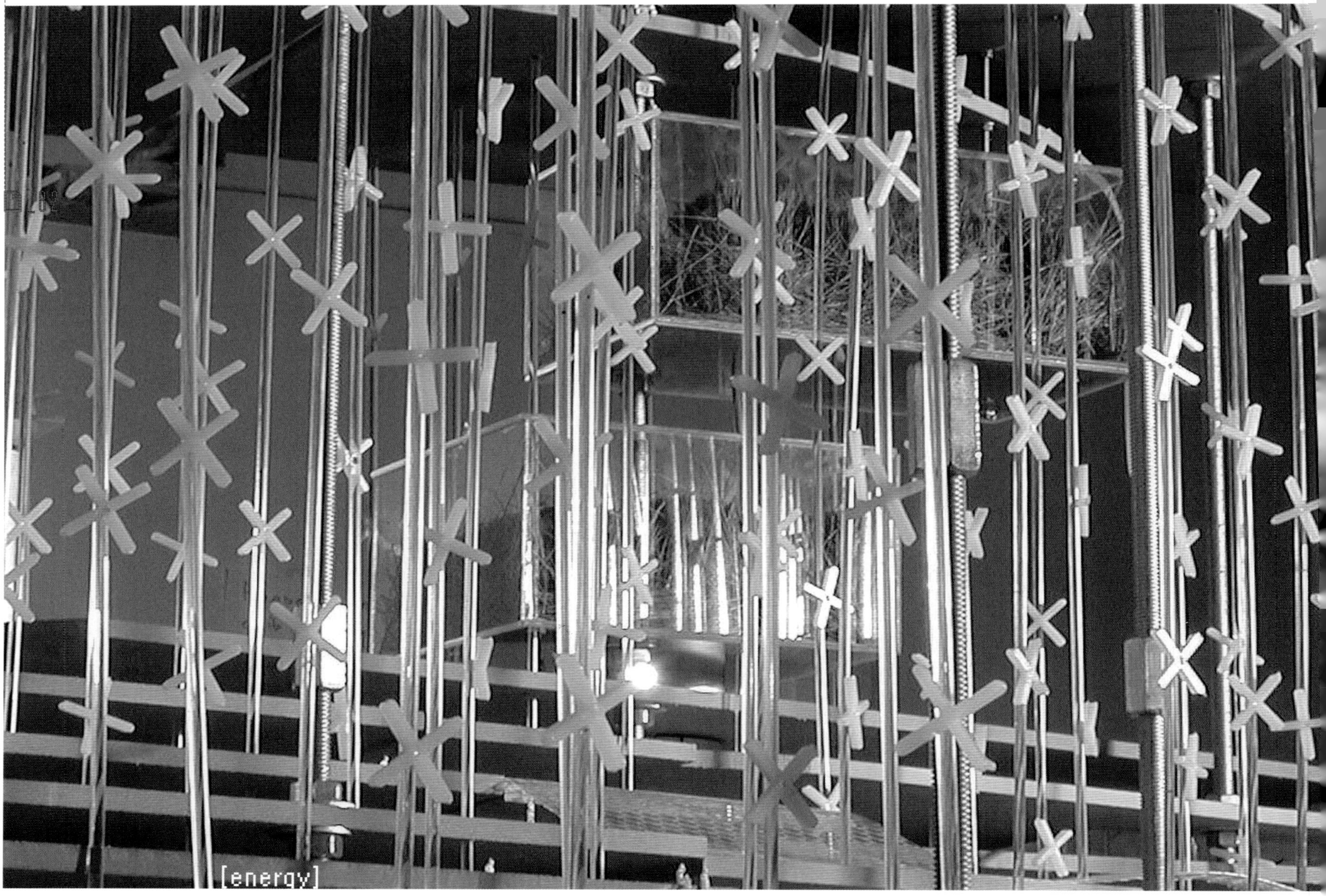
[energy]

[distribution]

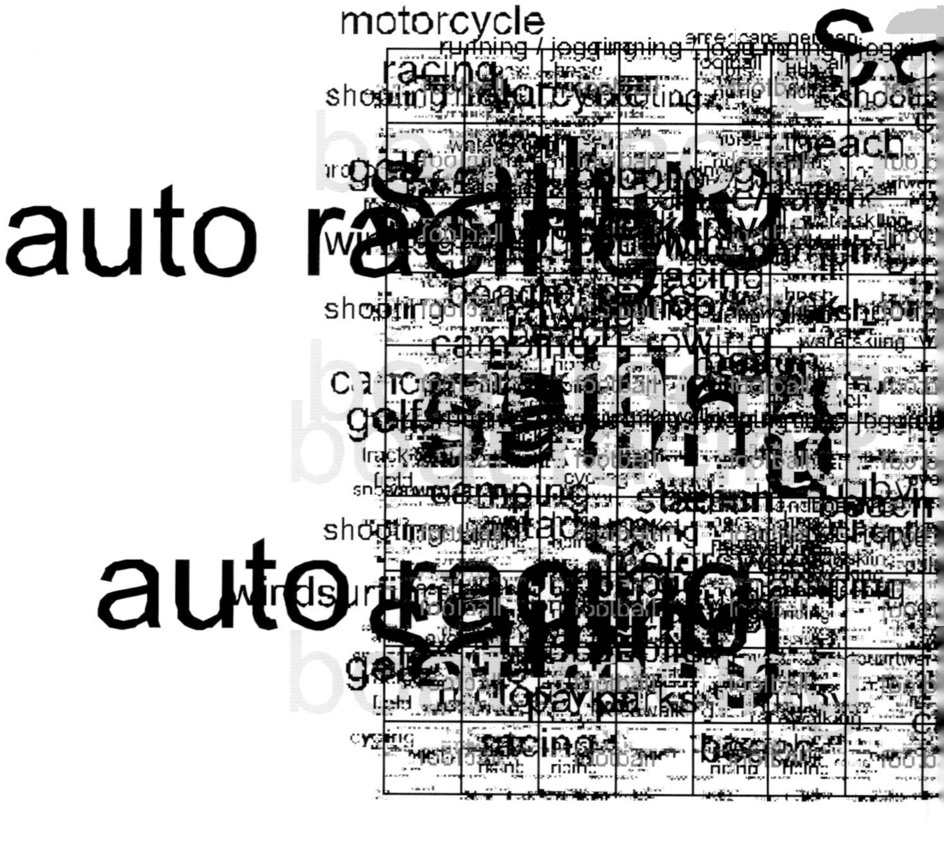
motorcycle
racing
beach
auto racing
auto racing

[forest]

[agriculture]

[leisure]

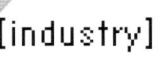

[industry]

[air]

3D CITY —
Multiplying Urban Capacities
Rotterdam, Netherlands, student projects, 2000

How to bring this process one step further? How to enlarge its possibilities? How to go beyond the two-dimensional backgrounds and to make the step towards a three-dimensional urbanism that would multiply the potential of the city? How to organize this three-dimensional world? How to live or — as some might say — how to survive in the third dimension? Under what circumstances do we accept raising our children at a height of 50 metres above the ground? And how to finance this operation? How to make it economically viable? What logistics will lead to this 3D city, what infrastructure will it demand? And finally: is there a new 'idealism' in this aspiration? Can three-dimensionality be idealistic? What idealism can it enhance? In order to give these questions a possible framework, the KM3 studio of the Berlage Institute of Rotterdam, directed by Winy Maas and Wiel Arets, decided to investigate the idea of a theoretical city of one million inhabitants, based on Dutch statistics, because of the availability of statistical material and because of the current economic viability of the Netherlands. So it is a very Dutch city, in fact. To resolve the constraints in a sustainable way, this city is autarkic: it has no neighbours, which underlines the ultimate need to survive, to solve its own problems on its own spot.

We know how to house a million people in a flat, two-dimensional way. But what happens when we position this program within a cube, the form that is the most compact or most nearly so? What items do we have to incorporate? How big should this cube be? Is it appreciably more compact than the two-dimensional city? And, when all is said and done, is this a promising direction?

To evaluate this potential and to quantify the needs for this city and in order to avoid over-complexity, several research teams at the Berlage Institute and at our offices have been organized to develop knowledge of a series of selected functions within this city: agriculture, air, distribution, energy, forest, industry, leisure, commerce, water and waste. Each team had first to appraise these functional sectors, before reflecting jointly on the three-dimensional interdependence and interconnectivity between the sectors. How many cubic metres does each sector need? What parameters describe the sectors? How should the sectorized programme be distributed around the city? What possibilities or changes will a three-dimensional city give to this sector? ☑

Credits: professors — Winy Maas, Wiel Arets, assistants: Rene Marey, Christof Schindler, Christelle Gualdi; students — Tsugumi Kanno, Nanne de Ru, Alexander Sverdlov, Camillo Garcia, Deval Gandhi, Diego Barajas, Sung-woo Kim, Luis Falcon, Im Sik Cho, Satoko Oba, Esther Giani, Emiko Hayakawa, Pablo Guerrero, Petar Ianovic, Aureliusz Kowalczyk, Ana Rascovsky, Shinya Okuda, Charles Bessard, Brent Crittenden, Tomohiro Yanagisawa, Arman Akdogan, Jocelyne Turner, Felix Madrazo, Kimihiko Tanaka, Manuel de Rivero, Irene Lund, Martin Mutschlechner, JAZ, Junko Tamrua, Hugo Hardy, Jacopo Tenani, Pablo Corvalan, Marisol Rivas Velasquez, Sabina Tattara, Rintaro Yabe.

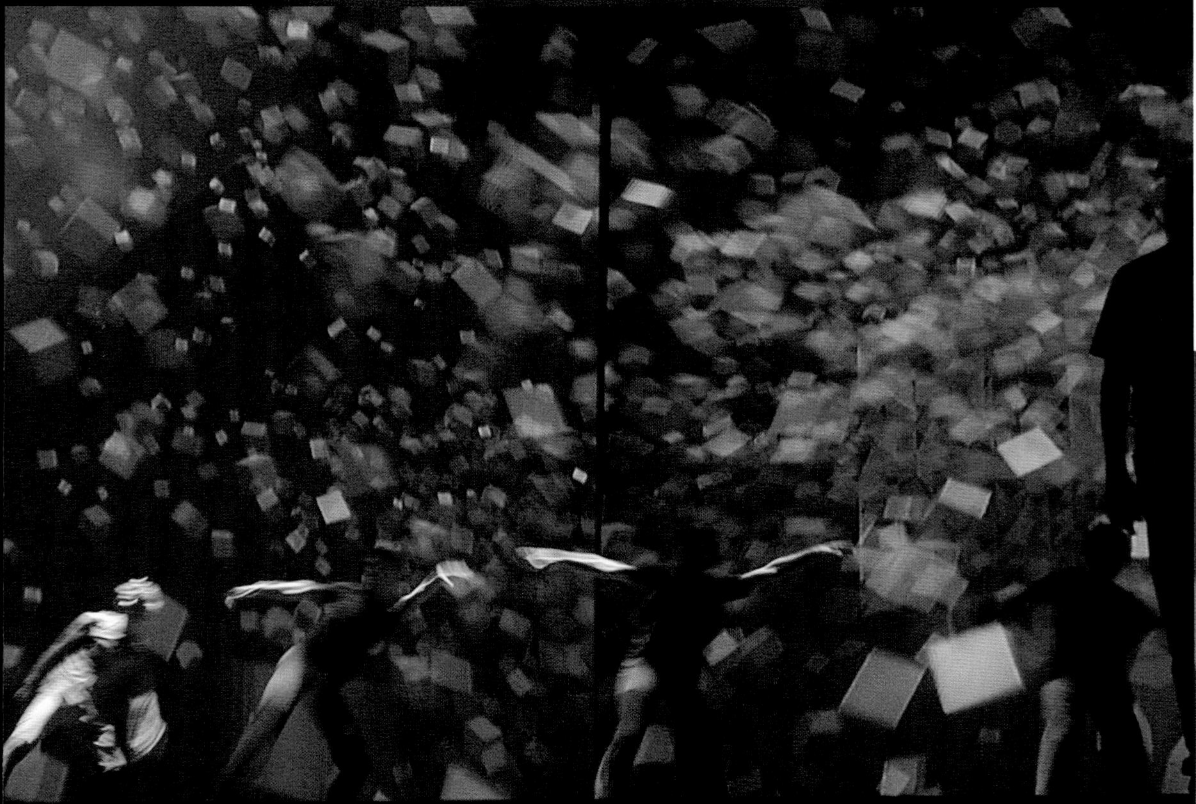

▶ Manyfacts
Video, 2001

As an offshoot of the work done at the Berlage Institute around the 3D City project, the MVRDV agency has created a video, which is presented as an attempt to synthesize the ten themes separately developed by the students (agriculture, air, distribution, energy, forest, industry, leisure, commerce, water, waste) in a single cube with one-kilometre sides. Sharing in this enterprise were the Scapino dance company of Rotterdam, who were to show the video at the time of their last performance. ☑

Credits: Choreography – Ed Wubbe (Scapino Ballet, Rotterdam); concept of the 3D City: MVRDV – Winy Maas (design and research); MVRDV and Berlage Institute; graphics – Wieland & Gouwens (Eline Wieland and Marino Gouwens); soundtrack – Ed Wubbe, Michiel Jansen; digital sound editing – Michiel Jansen; costumes – Pamela Homoet; lighting – Benno Veen

▶ BLOCK

France

Denis Brillet [1971], Benoît Fillon [1970], Pascal Riffaud [1969]

Block is a working group consisting of three architects: Denis Brillet, Benoît Fillon and Pascal Riffaud, all from the school of architecture in Nantes, from which they graduated between 1997 and 1998. They have collaborated with several architectural agencies (Duncan Lewis & Hervé Potin, Gaëlle Peneau, Barto + Barto, etc.). Block originated in 1996 from a performance around a World War II air-raid shelter, Blockhaus DY.10 in Nantes. This place became the group's laboratory, which is resolutely dedicated to research and experimentation, using a cross-sectional approach to the practice of architecture and combining recycled sounds, installations, performances and multimedia. In 2000 Block became a private architectural company, with a view to undertaking both research and operational projects. In 2001 the agency joined up with the collective SCAPE, and exhibited at ArchiLab 2001, with D. Lewis, H. Potin and S. Large. Block won the Albums de la Jeune Architecture prize in 2002. ☒

INDEXED FORMS The general direction of thought within Block is towards the idea of rereading and rewriting urban and natural landscapes ... We integrate into our projects the necessity to establish concrete, physical, political and aesthetic relations with the milieux and environments on which we are working. The projects are envisaged in architectural terms and insist on the political right to appropriate urban space regardless of the state's legislation and policies. In addition, the group's productions comprise 'the minimum act', in the sense of urban interventions that simultaneously integrate economy of means and the natural conditions of the town. In 1996, quite illegally, we took over an air-raid shelter left over from World War II. We needed a place in which to work and do our research, but this simple action gave rise to a network of questions as much about the extraordinary nature of the shelter as about the concept of property, or ownership, and potential territories. This place has become our laboratory, a testing-ground for our experiments on reality. It is this preoccupation with and presence of reality, in the form of matter from which to produce meaning, that really orientates our creative approach to our projects. The axis of Block research runs along the interior of social fabrics that are already woven, and it acts as a modifying force. What form of architecture is derived from social situations? How do these forms cope with the primitive nature of the town, and how do they generate their hybrid arrangements? A heterogeneous mass of objects, codes, signs, motifs, sounds, existing processes, potential territories – urban nature is a puzzle to be solved, it demands to be read, it questions one's observations before one is able to construct a meaning. And so our work tends to flee from the idea of the object as a unique finality and a thing purely for use. Our practice demands complexity and rejects the specialist approach; we 'undiscipline' ourselves as we incorporate in the same plan the recycling of sounds, installations, performances, architectural projects ... Our particular project culture often brings about 'running' realizations, and so our work is punctuated by microprojects, microactions, which, taken together, feed a collective course. The project and the architecture, by way of semiotic and poetic mediation, are seen as media for grasping actuality. The project is a giving of expression, a formalization intended to return to the reality from which it has been distinguished through its transformation. We operate by way of selection, musical sampling, loops or a simple copy-and-paste process. And so the actions and projects that we undertake tend to run along the lines of displacing, or 'decontextualizing', one or more components of the reality that has become our project and our index of forms. The sampling, quasi-mechanical, is an integral part of our procedure, within a perspective that is both semantic and poetic ... Training the eye through the procedures of enumerating, observing, collecting and memorizing images and experiences ... together with experimentation – these are the tools that enable us to seize an existing territory before we visualize its form. We consider the town to be a framework for events that are infinitely complex; it is a laboratory for experiments in perception, a mass of arrangements that it would be good or bad to take over, a network of horizontal and vertical information with temporary or permanent links: the diffuse along with the perpetual, the promotional package along with the façade, shifting, temporary and alternative territories along with those that represent the State. Often 'objectless', the movement of our interventions boils down to 'let's just see', or to a modification of a state of perception. ☒

Block

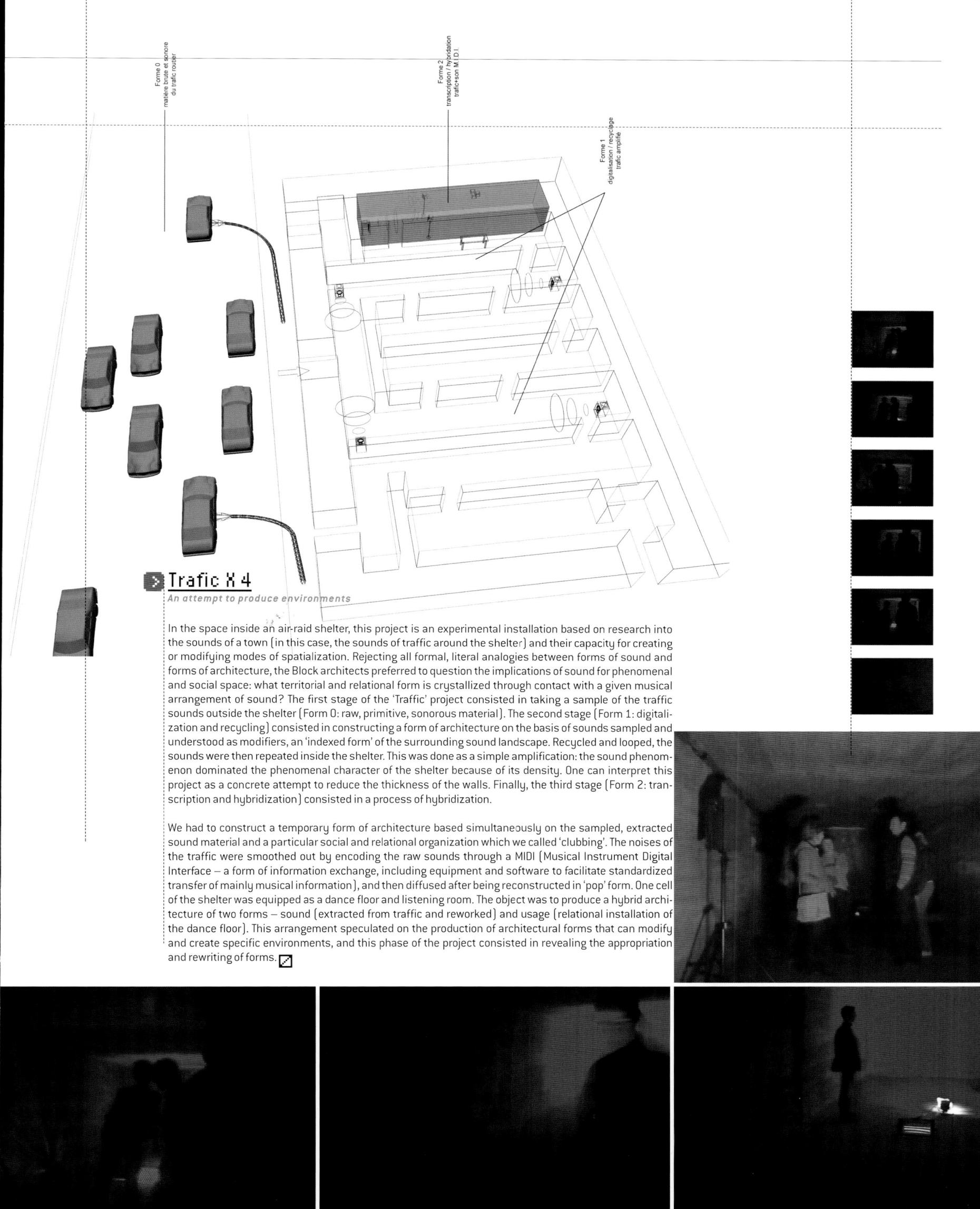

▶ Trafic X 4
An attempt to produce environments

In the space inside an air-raid shelter, this project is an experimental installation based on research into the sounds of a town (in this case, the sounds of traffic around the shelter) and their capacity for creating or modifying modes of spatialization. Rejecting all formal, literal analogies between forms of sound and forms of architecture, the Block architects preferred to question the implications of sound for phenomenal and social space: what territorial and relational form is crystallized through contact with a given musical arrangement of sound? The first stage of the 'Traffic' project consisted in taking a sample of the traffic sounds outside the shelter (Form 0: raw, primitive, sonorous material). The second stage (Form 1: digitalization and recycling) consisted in constructing a form of architecture on the basis of sounds sampled and understood as modifiers, an 'indexed form' of the surrounding sound landscape. Recycled and looped, the sounds were then repeated inside the shelter. This was done as a simple amplification: the sound phenomenon dominated the phenomenal character of the shelter because of its density. One can interpret this project as a concrete attempt to reduce the thickness of the walls. Finally, the third stage (Form 2: transcription and hybridization) consisted in a process of hybridization.

We had to construct a temporary form of architecture based simultaneously on the sampled, extracted sound material and a particular social and relational organization which we called 'clubbing'. The noises of the traffic were smoothed out by encoding the raw sounds through a MIDI (Musical Instrument Digital Interface — a form of information exchange, including equipment and software to facilitate standardized transfer of mainly musical information), and then diffused after being reconstructed in 'pop' form. One cell of the shelter was equipped as a dance floor and listening room. The object was to produce a hybrid architecture of two forms — sound (extracted from traffic and reworked) and usage (relational installation of the dance floor). This arrangement speculated on the production of architectural forms that can modify and create specific environments, and this phase of the project consisted in revealing the appropriation and rewriting of forms. ◨

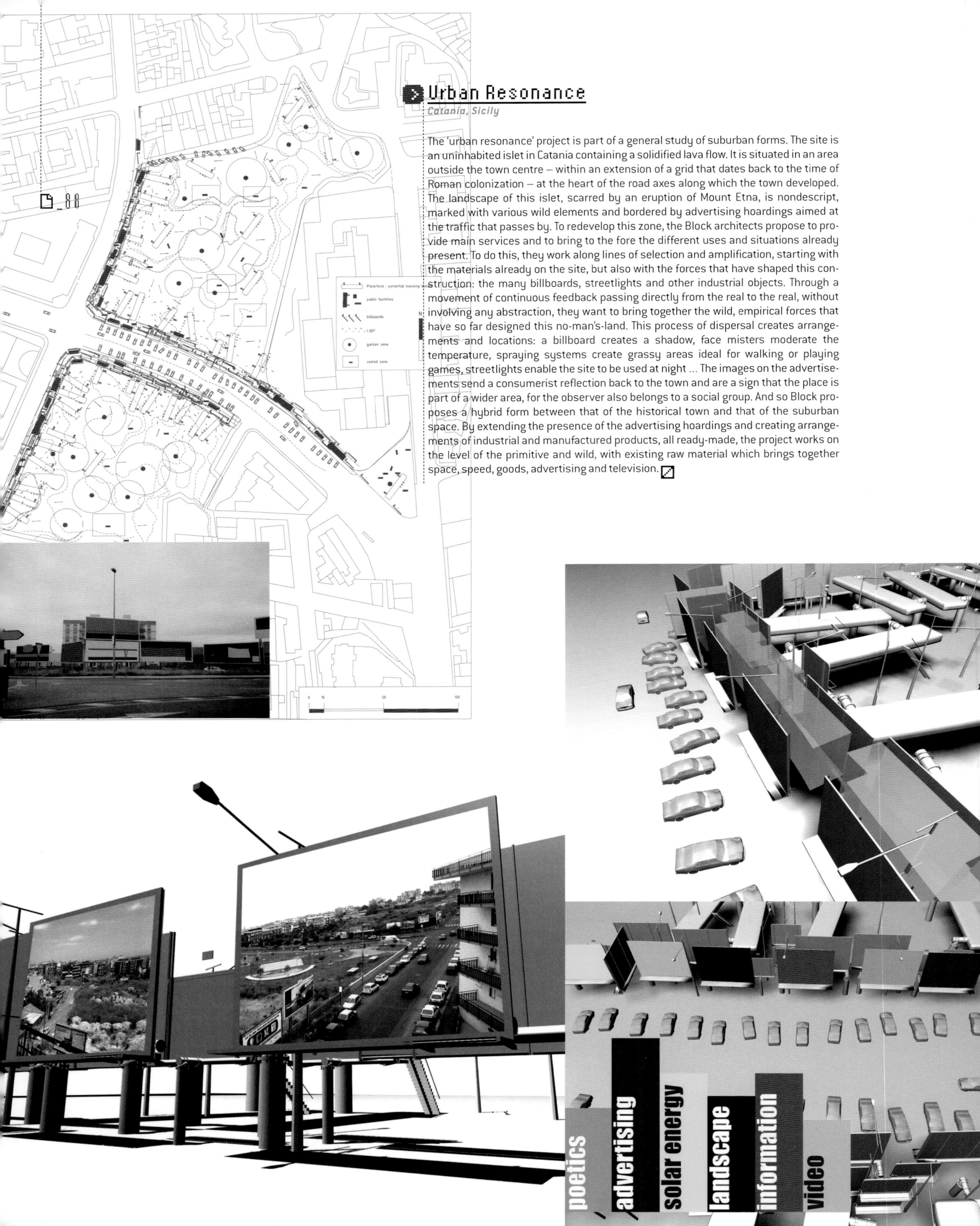

Urban Resonance
Catania, Sicily

The 'urban resonance' project is part of a general study of suburban forms. The site is an uninhabited islet in Catania containing a solidified lava flow. It is situated in an area outside the town centre – within an extension of a grid that dates back to the time of Roman colonization – at the heart of the road axes along which the town developed. The landscape of this islet, scarred by an eruption of Mount Etna, is nondescript, marked with various wild elements and bordered by advertising hoardings aimed at the traffic that passes by. To redevelop this zone, the Block architects propose to provide main services and to bring to the fore the different uses and situations already present. To do this, they work along lines of selection and amplification, starting with the materials already on the site, but also with the forces that have shaped this construction: the many billboards, streetlights and other industrial objects. Through a movement of continuous feedback passing directly from the real to the real, without involving any abstraction, they want to bring together the wild, empirical forces that have so far designed this no-man's-land. This process of dispersal creates arrangements and locations: a billboard creates a shadow, face misters moderate the temperature, spraying systems create grassy areas ideal for walking or playing games, streetlights enable the site to be used at night ... The images on the advertisements send a consumerist reflection back to the town and are a sign that the place is part of a wider area, for the observer also belongs to a social group. And so Block proposes a hybrid form between that of the historical town and that of the suburban space. By extending the presence of the advertising hoardings and creating arrangements of industrial and manufactured products, all ready-made, the project works on the level of the primitive and wild, with existing raw material which brings together space, speed, goods, advertising and television. ◨

⯈ Urban Shifting/Urban Camouflage and its Derived Products

Nantes, France

'Urban shifting' is a series of three microprojects *in situ* relating to three buildings in Nantes. The buildings extend along a line starting in what used to be the port area in the centre of town: they are an office block, a hospital building and an air-raid shelter, and they were selected as being noteworthy features of Nantes. The three projects (North [th], Pattern and P.A.P.) are based on the idea of displacement, or 'decontextual-ization', of one or more components of the actual building (form, colour, motifs, etc.) by means of photographic composition, highlighting through the use of existing techniques (e.g. adhesive posters), resemblance and substitution. In becoming 'indexed forms', the urban elements that are treated in this way tend to become signs in a kind of 'totemism', also reflecting other signs as if in an echo chamber; these graphic interventions in the town give rise to a series of 'derived products', as a sort of urban ampli-fication. The 'derived products' – pieces of furniture, temporary constructions, markings made in a different context – are conceived as 'indexed forms', which 'contaminate' the urban scene. By way of terri-torial articulation/signs, the interventions offer an additional imitative element for a sensitive reading of the town, amplifying the phenomena (like amplifying a breath) and giving visible form to multiple con-texts, times and textures. The 'derived products' function as an interface between the city's social, relational and territorial dimensions, and they orchestrate the organized means of 'contamination'. The 'derived product' – like a reflected image – is a concrete space of production and of potential actions. ⯈⯈

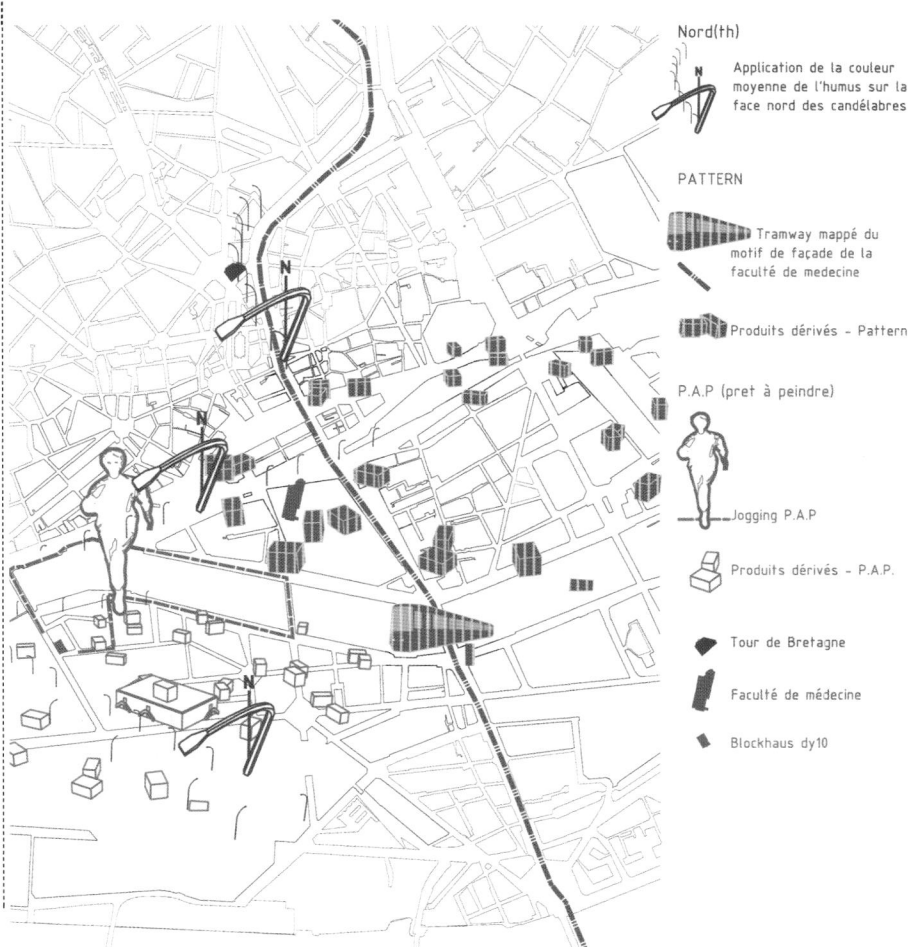

Nord(th)

Application de la couleur moyenne de l'humus sur la face nord des candélabres

PATTERN

Tramway mappé du motif de façade de la faculté de medecine

Produits dérivés - Pattern

P.A.P (pret à peindre)

Jogging P.A.P

Produits dérivés - P.A.P.

Tour de Bretagne

Faculté de médecine

Blockhaus dy10

⯈ North (th)

Urban marking and descriptive work, North (th) is broken down into two stages: the application of the normal colour of mould to the north side of the aluminium streetlamps (edition of a painting and a marking kit)/North (th) on the Brittany Tower surveys the city on a scale of XXL. An emblematic object, a geographical sign and an urban totem, the Brittany Tower shines out in the centre and radiates to all four points of the compass. ⯈⯈

▶ Pattern

Taking over patterns from the façade of a building by way of the loop of what is seen as a simple graphic block (entity), which contains the components of a possible indicial complex. The project integrates sampling, the transformation of materials and their recontextualization into another urban element, already incorporating the social: urban transport. Patterns on trams: technique of adhesive posters.

▶▶

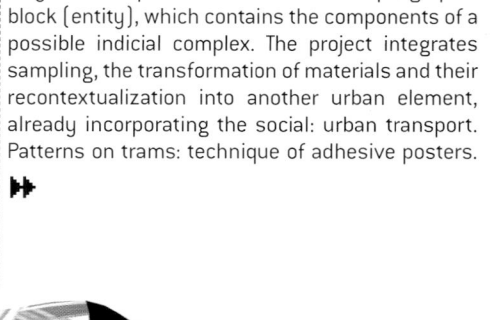

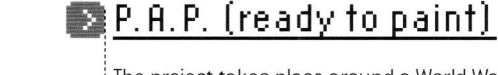

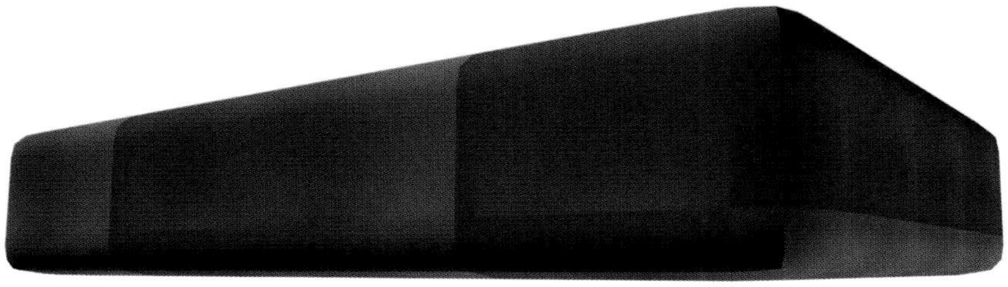

▶ P.A.P. (ready to paint)

The project takes place around a World War II air-raid shelter, covered with posters. It is the building itself that embodies the purpose of the project: to capture its presence and to devise strategies and hybrid combinations with the town that integrate the reproduction of a component of the building (an empty sign) with other supports (indicial complex). Like North (th), the project sets out to develop the definition of a normal colour for the building. ▣

PAP
jogger

EDUARD BRU ARQUITECTOS

Spain

Eduard Bru Bistuer [1950]

Architect and professor of architecture, Eduard Bru lives, work and teaches in Barcelona. Responsible for the Master of Urbanism entitled 'The Grand Scale' at the ETSAB, he succeeded Manuel de Solà-Morales to the directorship of the school. Author notably of *Three on the Site* (1997) and *New Territories/New Land-scapes* (1998), he has just published *Coming from the South* (in collaboration, 2002). In this latest work, based on the study of the complex realities of cities in southern Europe, he tries to describe a dominant model, which would be the Dutch—American way of thinking about the modern city, to propose some sustain-able and evolutionary modalities of elaborating medium-economy cities. In his practice, he has been participating in all the latest transformations of Barcelona: he is author of a management plan for the Olympic zone of Vall d'Hebron (1992), 'Forum 2004' prizewinner for the new site for the Independent University of Barcelona, and he is currently working on several sections of the Diagonal Avenue, notably Poble Nou 22@ (in progress) and the 'Diagonal Gate' for its west-ern extremity. ☒

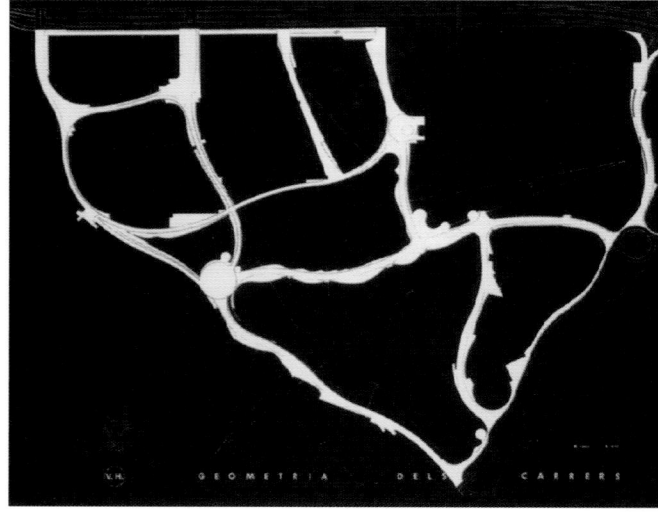

Vall d'Hebron: Street layout

PEP SUBRIÓS suggests thinking about 'the loss of a global vision of the city as a complex space, in which systems of meaning have as much impor-tance as economic and functional ones', and about the European phenomenon of 'a concentra-tion of effort, wealth, order, communication and memory n traditional urban centres, with infor-mality, poverty, exclusion and marginality becoming diffused in the periphery ... Communi-cation between the different spaces of the city is minimal; the collective memory embodied in the city practically non-existent.'

To begin with, I need a definition of periphery. By periphery I understand those parts of the city where a binomial capacity for use and meaning is out of balance in one or other of its components. Clearly, this can happen, even in the inner city. On the outskirts the crisis of meaning is frequent, whereas in the inner city it is a crisis of capacity of use. Whether such centres as maintain the capac-ity for use, albeit different from the original one, can be considered as peripheries is a matter for debate. That is, are historic centres revived as tourist or university ghettos 'peripheries'?

Some people maintain that the intellectual today, far from managing to improve things has to content himself with explaining them, mentally going along with them, adding, perhaps, a touch here and there. I think that in the periphery of the south of Europe, reality is sufficiently chaotic and sterile to require a 'hard' treatment. And so I pro-pose a set of premises for this 'hard'-intervention landscape, far from the abstract basic plane and backdrop of a Dutch—North American kind that are the usual scenario of the city and which today dominates the new conditions of the city.

One of the first conditions I would propose is that of the expediency of the object/urbanization unit. I understand, however, that this is not a premise compatible with the development of the periphery, since it is expensive (in developmental and production terms) and therefore only possi-ble in the privileged spaces of the city, those that pay for and acquire a balance between use and meaning. As is natural in the periphery, meaning is irrelevant at first. The conditions imposed on urbanizing objects and processes have to let time (and chance, that is, a decent and sustained development) do this. The ways of attaining meaning in the short term are expensive.

Location is the major asset of the southern European cities. In most cases urbanization has completely outstripped the geographical 'cradle' that has accommodated and generated these cities over thousands of years: the inclined plane of Barcelona, the more inclined plane of Naples, the hills of Athens or Genoa. They now find them-selves confronting new landscapes: beyond the rivers delimiting them (Barcelona), on the other side of their mountains (Naples, Athens). It is urgent and vital that their growth address the specificity of their often difficult and highly idio-syncratic settings (which is why these weren't occupied in the first place).

As to peripheries in the centre, that fertile land-scape is here the still-living city itself, the one surrounding holes – and they have to be treated as such – that the old, degraded fabrics have become.

What meanings would tend to be attained, if the proposed premises are followed, by the action of time and space on a particular place? The most singular and decisive are, without doubt, the ones that cannot be predetermined right now, since they necessarily depend on a given time and a given place from which they will get their value. But in every case order, variety and veracity have to be present:

Can this set of tools be included within the Modern movement or do they belong to the pathos of 'postmodernity'? I confess to feeling at one with the aspirations of the Modern move-ment. Despite the fact that, following the crisis of 1972, cities have had to gain their place in the sun by competing in markets where meaning is an exchange value of the very highest order (and Barcelona is a perfect example), I don't believe that in order to attain meaning we are inevitably obliged to surrender ourselves to the gentle embrace of postmodernity. The 'postmodern' has offered objects falsified by neo-styling or the 'ver-nacular', often presented as a bold, ephemeral *mise en scène*, urbanizing interventions that stem from the marketing of the shopping and/or recreation malls in their pseudo-complexity and pseudo-historicity. In total opposition to this, I defend, for poor and middling countries, a struc-turing of space by means of non-ephemeral objects that are neutral, even atemporal, and located in areas that are highly significant, given the presence and the action of the landscape, and with the aid of passing time. ☒

Eduard Bru

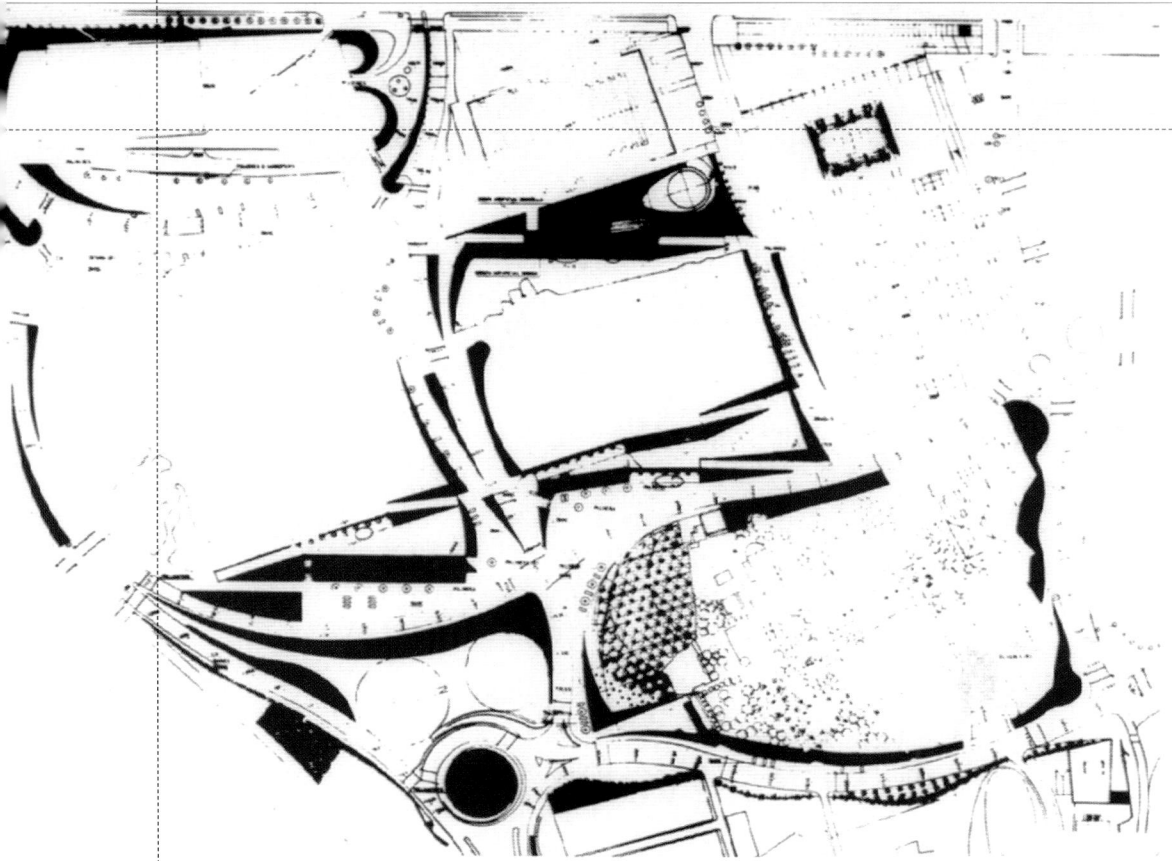

Vall d'Hebron: The green space, acting as an intersection between the streets and the buildings

Vall d'Hebron: The organizing structure of Vall d'Hebron is waiting to be occupied, modified, finished in various ways. The ambiguity is a form of availability.

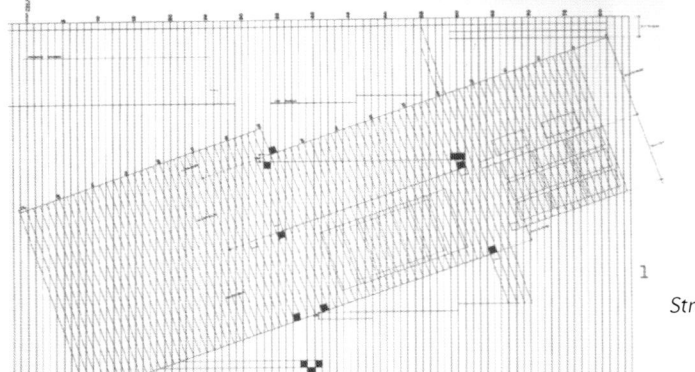

Structure of the buildings

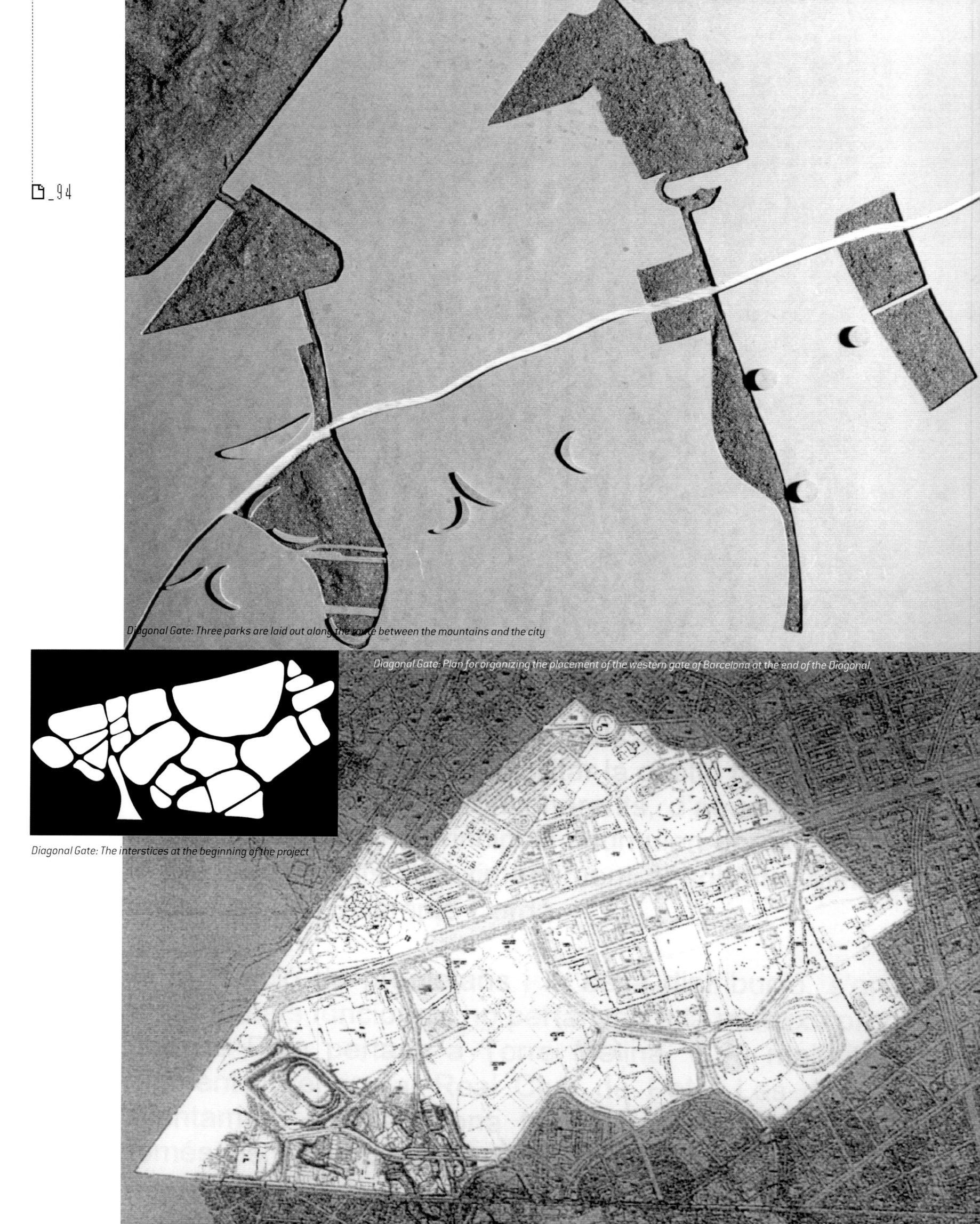

Diagonal Gate: Three parks are laid out along the route between the mountains and the city

Diagonal Gate: Plan for organizing the placement of the western gate of Barcelona at the end of the Diagonal.

Diagonal Gate: The interstices at the beginning of the project

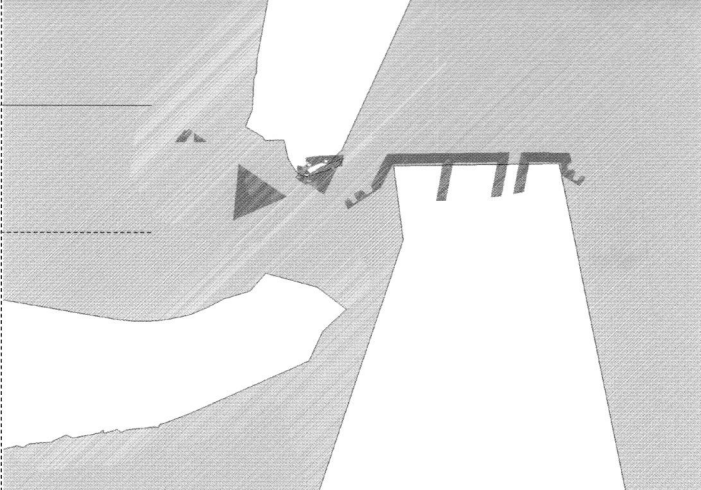

Forum 2004: The university zone in Barcelona – meeting point of land, sea and city

Forum 2004: A gate for the east of the city – the beginning of the Diagonal

Complex Places

Extracts from Vall d'Hebron, Portal Diagonal (with E. Serra), Forum 2004

It has rarely been my generation's lot to be the 'foundation', to create 'ex-novo' new places and dwellings. We work on what is given to us, on what has already been established. My city has reached the limits of what was its first natural site: the inclined (4%) coastal plane between the sea and the mountain range that lies parallel to it. Once this space has been occupied (the last episode was the extension for the Olympic Games of 1992), we have to work within precise limits, to establish new relationships with nature – the mountains, the sea, the two rivers – that is, with our natural boundaries.

I present here several episodes of this encounter. In the Vall d'Hebron the streets are like streams coming from the mountain rushing down the slope. At the western gate of the city (upper end of the Diagonal) the form can be understood only in connection with the topography, and it is this that influences the constructions. On the seafront of Poble Nou on the university campus de Llevant ('Forum 2004'), I propose several interventions, combinations of scales, uses and specific environments, to get around the indifference we have inherited from the 19th-century city. The questions to which we try to find answers are: how can the compact city exchange qualities with nature? what do these territories, shared between city and 'nature', look like?

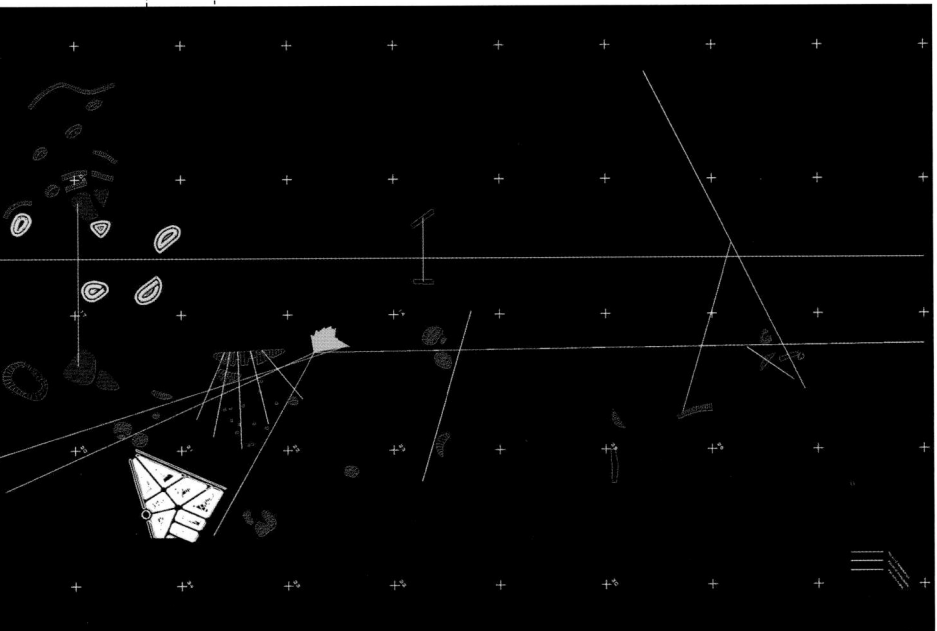

Diagonal Gate: New relationships between new buildings

Forum 2004: Progressive working out of the occupied and the empty spaces in the university zone

▶ Easy Buildings

Extracts from Vall d'Hebron, Housing at Poble Nou, Airport at Azahar coast,
Building for the Independent University of Barcelona

Like most architects, I have a 'concrete' vision of ecology. To contribute to the health of the planet our projects must not necessarily be green but they must be precise. Probably the first condition is to put money in the correct place. Architecture is something to be lived. So, the money must be spent on useful things. This is not an apology for pragmatism; quite the opposite. Conceiving what is both comfortable and useful could be a very complex, even subjective matter. Money is an abstraction that involves materials, wishes, life itself. Making economies is a way of keeping it and that is how I would define ecology. What, in concrete terms, do I do? First, I try to be realistic. The future is more than ever a new mixed situation, a new equilibrium. Of all the things I have conceived, I will be able to realize only a few — as always happens when one works on the large scale. Second, treating the conservation of materials as a crucial aspect. If modernity requires that we replace rather than repair, this will have costly and ecologically unsound consequences. So we should work instead with materials that are easy to maintain, easy to convert and easy to repaint. We should offer people the opportunity of remodelling their homes. Third, everybody needs luxury. The 'minimum existence' does not bring happiness, whatever the situation. So let us concentrate our means on certain points, even if in so doing we create a single moment of sensuality, of well-being; that is better than sinking the lot in a mediocre middle-class house. Fourth, I like ambiguity. Ambiguous propositions can be very useful, less expensive and open to unexpected uses. Fifth, I also like repetition, in combination with the points already mentioned. Repetition can be boring or interesting; it can be a good condition for creativity or comfort. Anyway, architecture has perhaps not so much need to be looked at (except by visiting architects). All of which makes me think that the first ecological act for us architects is without doubt to integrate our work with real life. ▨

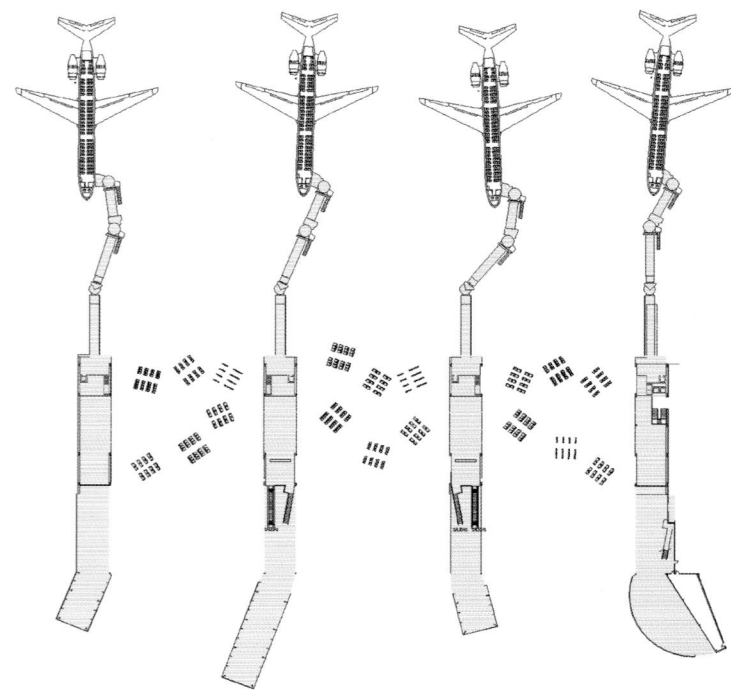

Airport at Azahar coast: Since the only real constraint on the modern airport is ground-air transfer, Eduard Bru here proposes macroscopic 'fingers' for use in parking aircraft. Between them, the spaces change often. Recycled old aeroplanes can be used to make furniture for the terminals.

The adventures of a single window — with anthropomorphic proportions — in different buildings. The repetition underlines the diversity of the programmes and situations, not the opposite.

The park at Vall d'Hebron: Standard metal seats on bases made of rubber recycled from lorry tyres.

Poble Nou: New buildings in the Eixample (access via interior paths), behind old ones (access from the roads). The juxtaposition lends a particular quality to the project, rather than detracting from it.

CHORA

United Kingdom, Netherlands

Raoul Bunschoten [(1955)]

Of Dutch origin, Raoul Bunschoten studied architecture at the Alexander Hegius Gymnasium, Deventer, Netherlands, at ETH in Zurich, Switzerland, and in the USA at Cooper Union, New York, and the Cranbrook Academy of Art, Michigan. He taught at the Berlage Institute and at the Architectural Association between 1983 and 2001 and in 2003 founded Chora in London. Chora is an office with two sections: one section has, for some years now, been a not-for-profit research organization. This section, working in collaboration with universities in the Netherlands and the UK, has developed a methodology for dynamic master plans called the Urban Gallery, an instrument for managing the dynamics of complex urban environments undergoing a planning process. The second section is involved in architectural design and the implementation of the Urban Gallery in a series of situations: a current application is the project for a new harbour city in the Netherlands, and others in the pipeline are a ten-year development plan for prototype projects in Copenhagen and projects in the Republic of Ireland. ☑

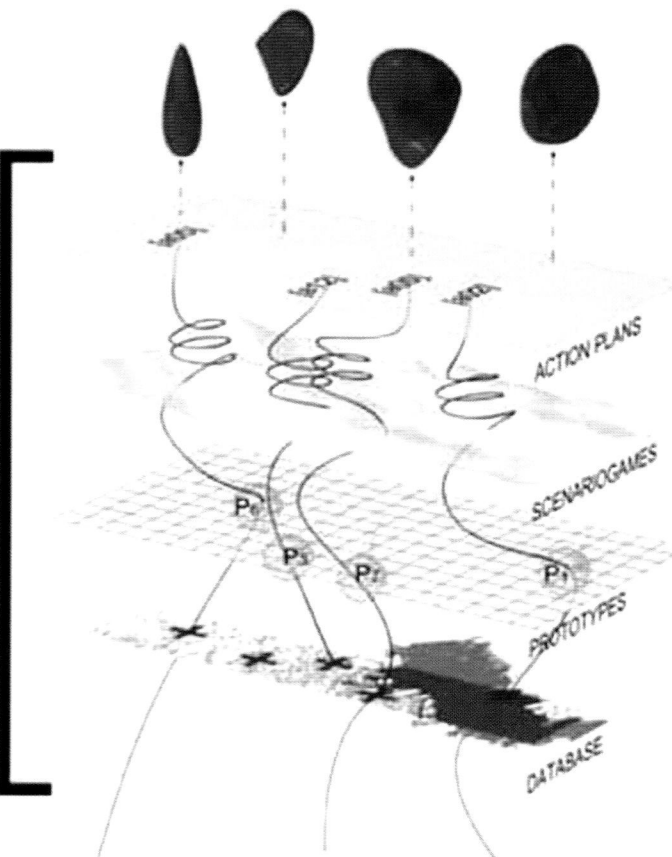

THE BASIC premise of Chora is that the city emulates the dynamics of the skin of the Earth: it is a second skin of the Earth. How do we know these interrelationships? How do we give form to them, simulate them, intervene in them, plan them? Chora has developed the concept of a dynamic master plan and the Urban Gallery toolbox to implement it. The Urban Gallery is a virtual architecture that manages knowledge, connects phenomena and interests and stimulates the unfolding of scenarios. A key player in this toolbox is the 'urban curator' who animates and organizes the connectivity inside the Urban Gallery, a role for which there is not yet a precise definition: no professional guild exists, no school teaches it. Having developed the concepts, a methodology and possible methods of applying the toolbox, Chora is now concentrating on projects where a long-term development of the toolbox is possible, in order to test it and adapt it. The Urban Gallery is a prototype, with experimental components such as the eGallery, a virtual interactive environment in which a dynamic master plan can be organized, simulated and planned, and through which communication channels run: it is a proto-urban space, a public space for interaction between actors and agents with both common interests and conflicts of interest.

The Urban Gallery is a prototype under development. The projects presented in the ArchiLab exhibition all are part of the development of this prototype. They each show in some way the whole of the tool, but in a raw, sketchy form. Many components are missing or incomplete. But to give an overview of the work in progress, we show five projects for the demonstration of the main elements of the Urban Gallery. These elements are: database, prototypes, scenario games and action plans. We chose 'Tokyo Story' to present the principle of the database; the projects for the New Suburb (Høje Taastrup, near Copenhagen) and Aarhus Horizon, both in Denmark, demonstrate the concept of prototypes; a scenario game will be played in the exhibition space with invited guests, on the basis of a site in France, a set of conflicts and shared interests. The action plan is represented by Project W, an ongoing project for a new city and logistic centre forming a node in the flow of goods from the main port of Rotterdam to the rest of Europe. This project is being developed in cooperation with a consortium working as a so-called Community of Practice. The individual members of this consortium have the interest and the means to create and test policy, to implement the policy in a case study, to plan and realize this case study and to manage it once it is built. While developing the project the consortium intends to go through a learning process in which the original intentions change. The goal is to produce a series of actions to implement individual prototypes in an overall dynamic master plan. A prototype is an organizational structure that links two or more operational fields. It intertwines programmes and regulates the flows between them. A prototype creates a new and singular link between programmes and thereby alters their efficacy and opens new potential. A prototype is an invention, a singular element in a dynamic environment. Its singularity, in the process of proliferation, moves through this field and adapts each time. ☑

Raoul Bunschoten

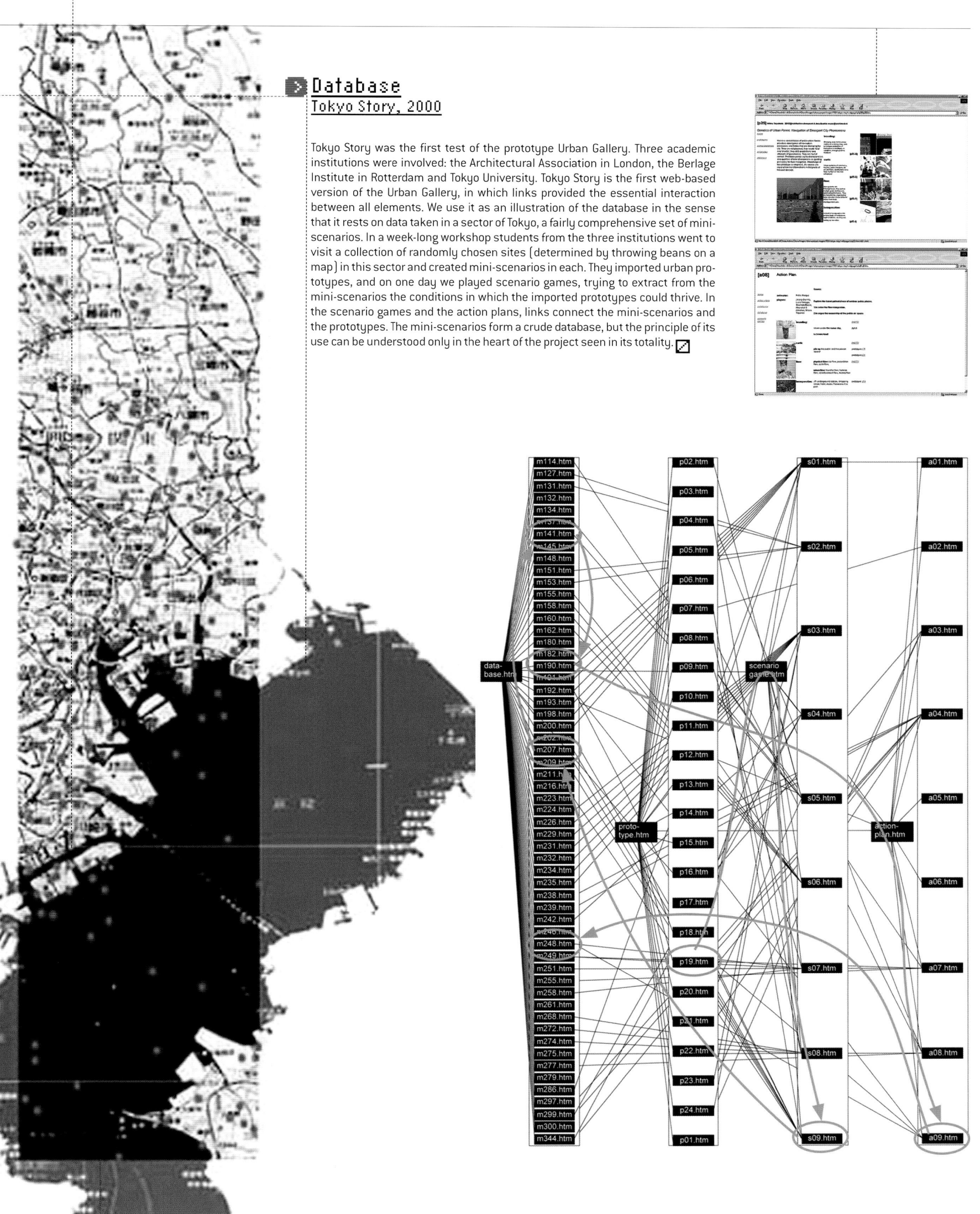

Database
Tokyo Story, 2000

Tokyo Story was the first test of the prototype Urban Gallery. Three academic institutions were involved: the Architectural Association in London, the Berlage Institute in Rotterdam and Tokyo University. Tokyo Story is the first web-based version of the Urban Gallery, in which links provided the essential interaction between all elements. We use it as an illustration of the database in the sense that it rests on data taken in a sector of Tokyo, a fairly comprehensive set of mini-scenarios. In a week-long workshop students from the three institutions went to visit a collection of randomly chosen sites (determined by throwing beans on a map) in this sector and created mini-scenarios in each. They imported urban prototypes, and on one day we played scenario games, trying to extract from the mini-scenarios the conditions in which the imported prototypes could thrive. In the scenario games and the action plans, links connect the mini-scenarios and the prototypes. The mini-scenarios form a crude database, but the principle of its use can be understood only in the heart of the project seen in its totality.

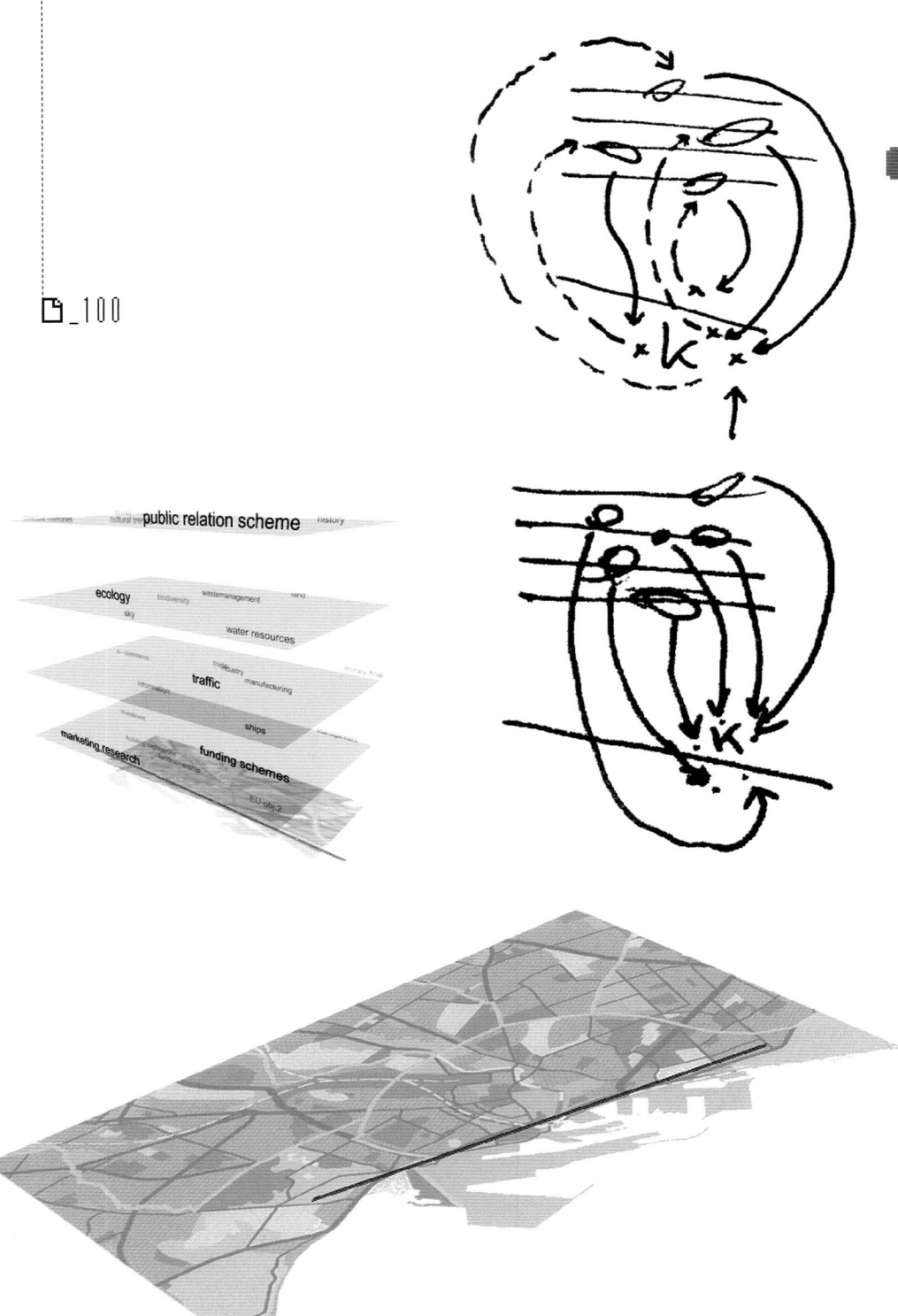

Prototypes

Aarhus Horizon
Aarhus, Denmark, competition, 2000
New Suburb
Høje Taastrup, Denmark, competition, 2001

Prototypes become important programmatic devices in these two prizewinning Danish projects. In Aarhus a line is drawn as the main pole of attraction. This line marks the separation between sea and land, city and harbour. The line is a simple form, but offers a complex public space. The line is an attractor of prototypes that play on it. Prototypes connect clusters from a database and intermingle them. The database is organized according to the four characteristics that qualify prototypes: Branding, Earth, Flow and Incorporation. Each prototype gathers elements from each of these four levels, which condition its operational dimension. The prototype links a variety of programmes and influences them in return. The prototypes range from small biotopes to a large infrastructural node.

In the 'New Suburb' project, near Copenhagen, prototypes are the connecting tissue within specific communities and between sets of communities: they are indicated by spirals. In spring 2000 Denmark organized a competition for the creation of a new suburban concept, on two sites, of which one, Høje Taastrup, is near Copenhagen. This project, which won second prize, proposes a dynamic master plan conceived on the model of the Urban Gallery, with the database, prototype, negotiation structure and action plan. The project takes as its starting point the hypothesis that there is a virtual place, the Urban Gallery, in which the prototypes connect very different programmes across specific levels of the gallery, in order to maximize potential and minimize conflicts. The project proposes the concept of a game board, as a vast, simple and apparently rudimentary device that allows the Urban Gallery to be installed as a planning mechanism on the site. The game board and its grid points are like a common space, they have public value. Each grid point is a potential anchor and sign for a community. These communities consist of existing elements, housing, a church, sports facilities, but often modified or combined with new programmes. The urban prototypes are thus introduced to develop a dynamic condition for each community. The project introduces a planning mechanism which merges rural and densely urban environments, facilities for production and for leisure, life and work. Nevertheless, the aim is to clarify the spatial conditions of all these functions by creating readily identifiable public spaces that articulate local qualities as well as interacting with global forces and trends.

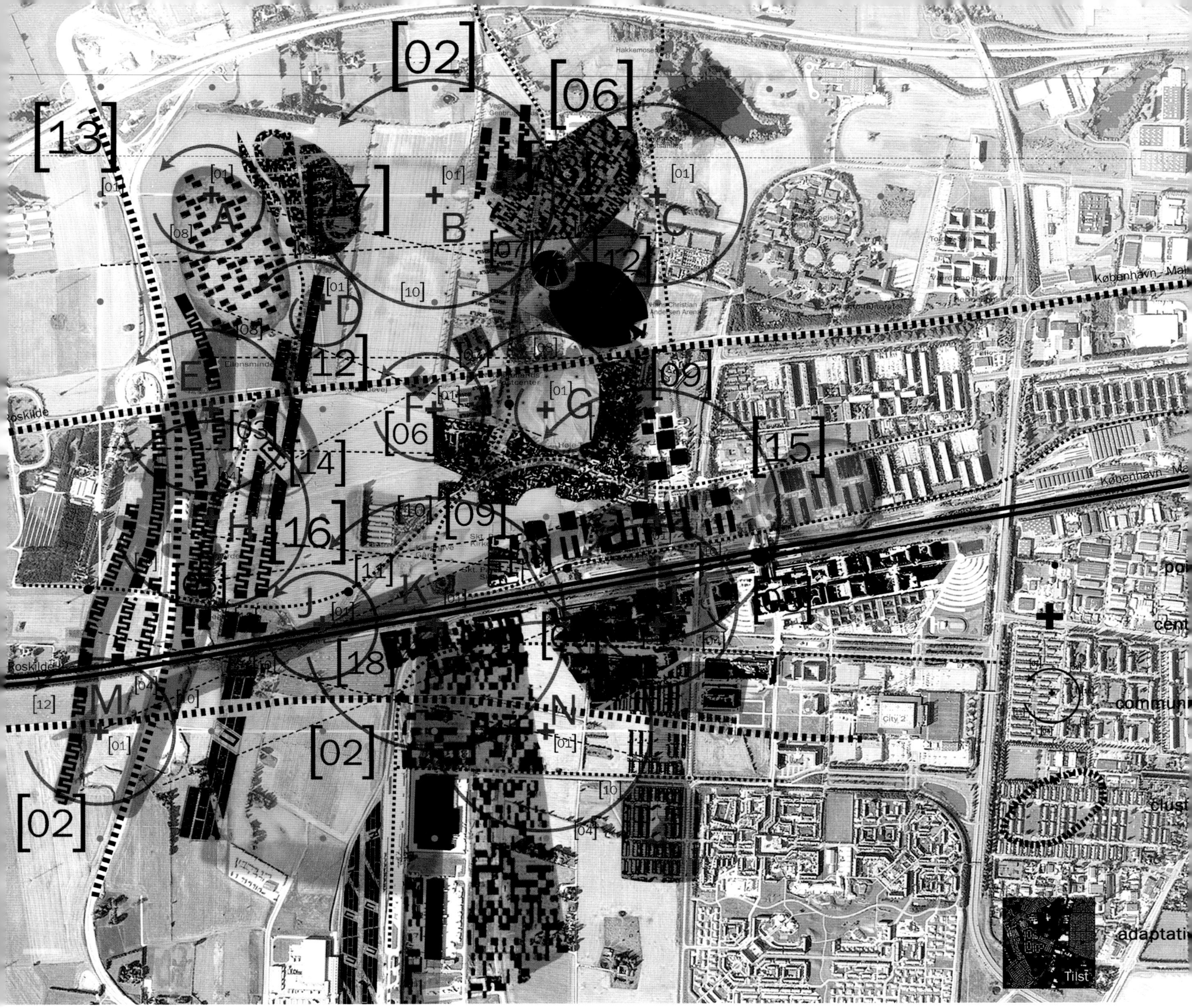

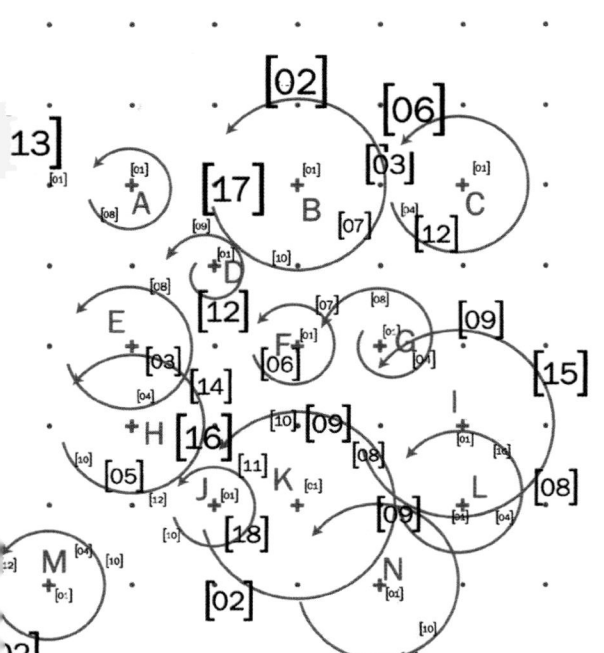

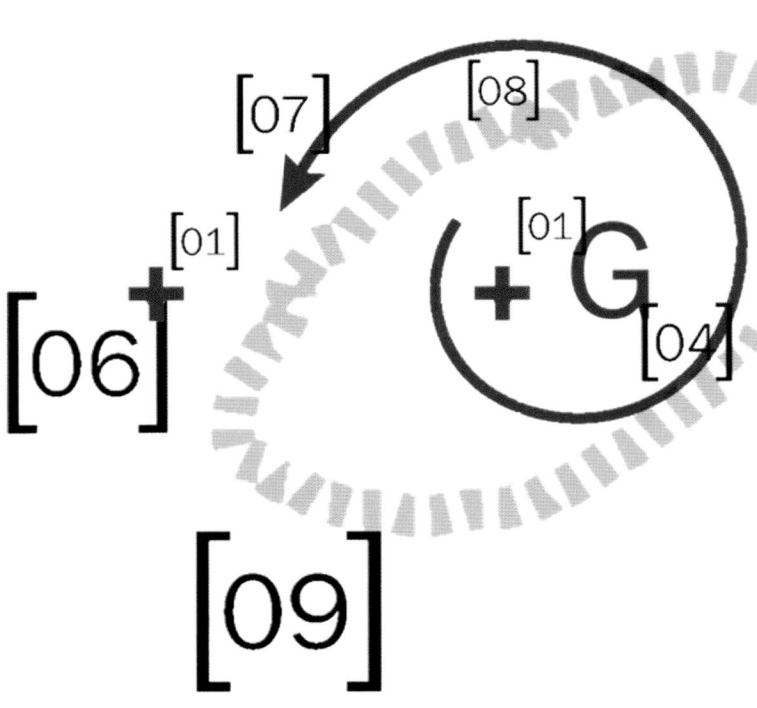

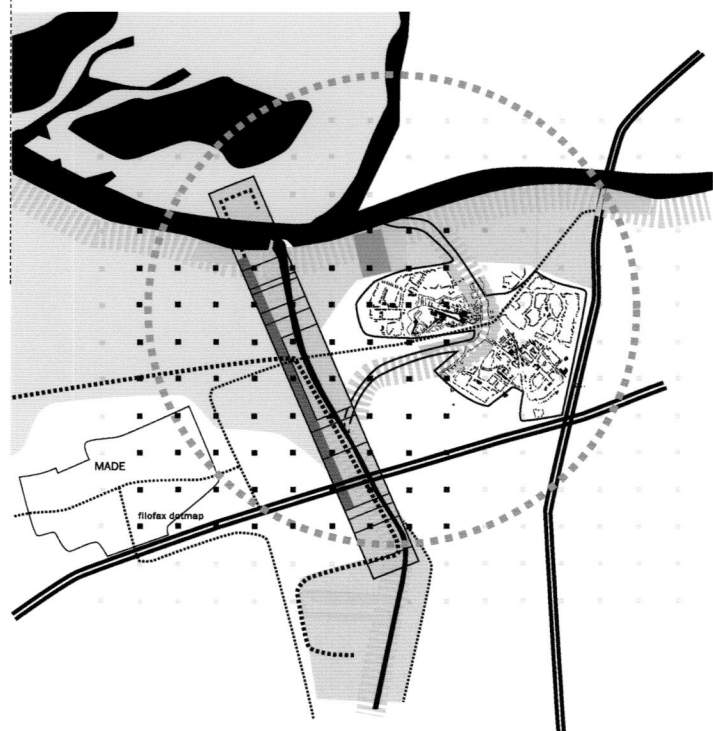

Action Plan
Project W
Rotterdam, Netherlands

Project W , a project for a new city in the Netherlands, is now in the pre-planning phase. Because the Urban Gallery is a virtual space, a diagram of organizations rather than a diagram inscribed in a territory, we had to introduce another set of diagrams that made relationships with existing territories and elements in these territories more operational. As with the New Suburb project, we introduced a game board, centres and spirals that indicated the space for dynamic development around the centres, without fixing the physical form of these developments. The centres, points on the game board grid, are anchor points for the development of individual communities and poles of attraction for a cluster of programmes tied together by urban prototypes. Each centre is a pole of attraction for a specific kind of community formed by the various programmes and given life by the prototype; this is the programmatic glue or, to use another metaphor, the DNA code of the organic forms that sustain the communities. The spirals indicate the ties that gradually interlink communities; this a diagrammatic condition that gives form to a development but not to the physical construction. The plan instigates and, to some extent, regulates dynamic relations between communities.

Geopolitics: Sector E, delimiting the zone

When Chora started to work on Project W in the Netherlands, a project for a new city and logistical centre, we had to define the area that would be influenced by the project. It is an area that is subject to strong pressures. Goods flow from Rotterdam, the largest harbour in Europe, to Germany and the rest of Europe. This flow is projected to double within the next five to ten years, generating many conflicts in the area in question. The frame does not delineate a physical boundary, it creates a focus on a zone that otherwise has as yet no clearly recognizable features, and yet, once the frame is drawn, the map reveals ranges of features that begin collectively to form a new kind of city. The frame is an observational tool, a diagram that both marks the skin of the Earth in a virtual way and is a taxonomic device: it collects, sorts, gathers. The diagram is the written form of an organizational structure, engraved on the skin of the Earth. When attached to ground and a territory it becomes a feature that both organizes and acts as an operational device. Sector E in the Netherlands is the feeding ground for the prototypes initiated in Project W, as well as the area that permits their proliferation and continuous adaptation. ☒

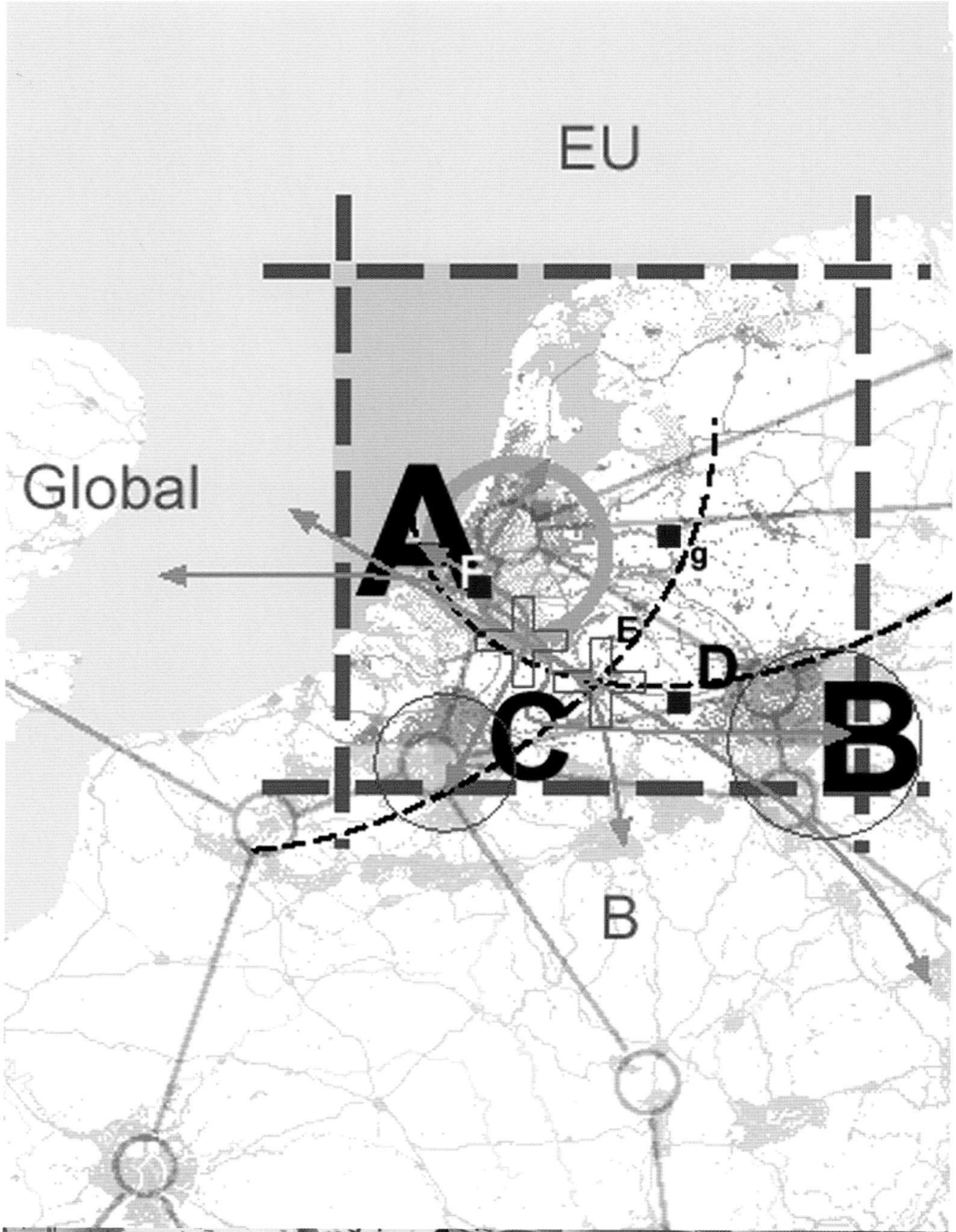

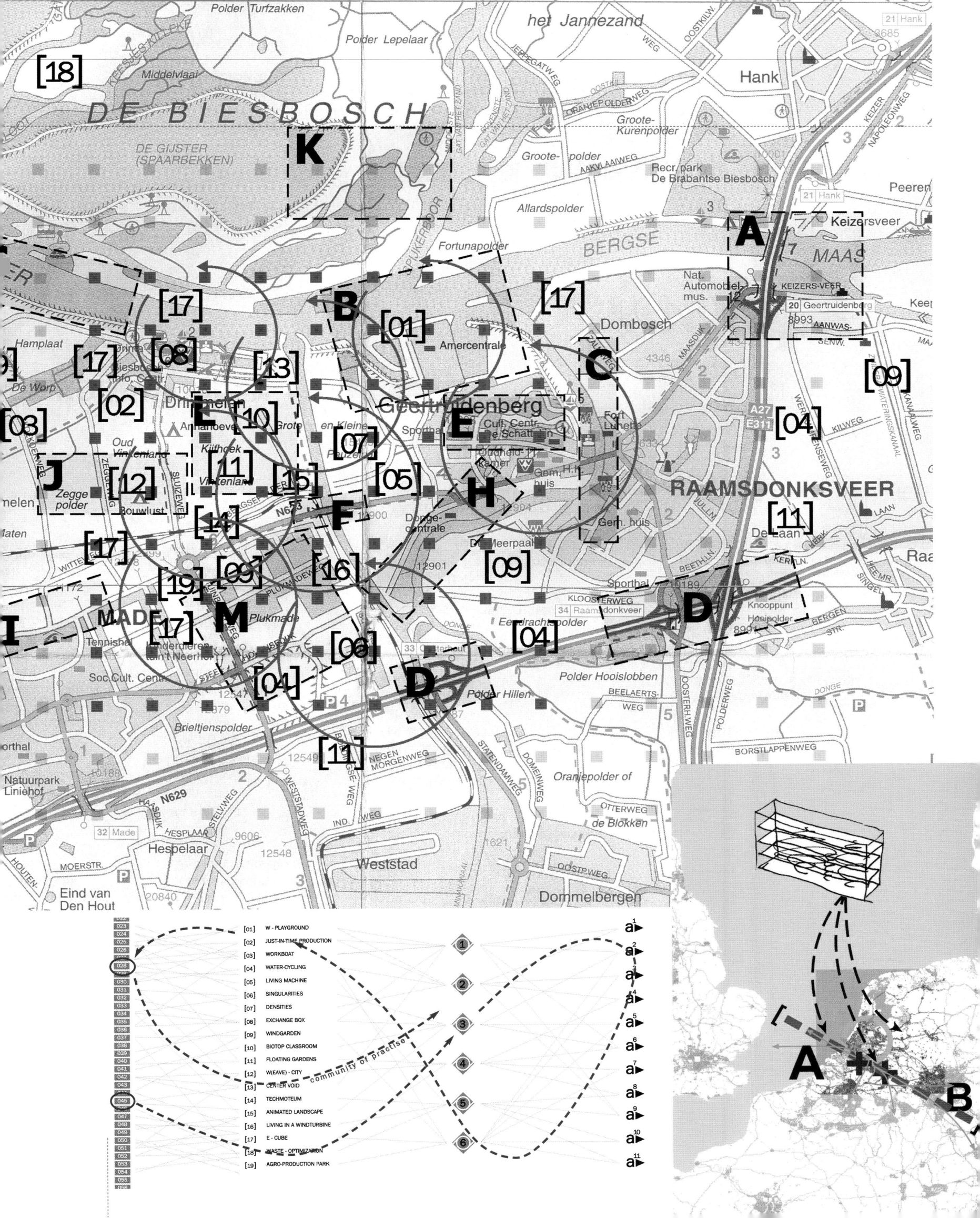

[01] W - PLAYGROUND
[02] JUST-IN-TIME PRODUCTION
[03] WORKBOAT
[04] WATER-CYCLING
[05] LIVING MACHINE
[06] SINGULARITIES
[07] DENSITIES
[08] EXCHANGE BOX
[09] WINDGARDEN
[10] BIOTOP CLASSROOM
[11] FLOATING GARDENS
[12] W(EAVE) - CITY
[13] CENTER VOID
[14] TECHMOTEUM
[15] ANIMATED LANDSCAPE
[16] LIVING IN A WINDTURBINE
[17] E - CUBE
[18] WASTE - OPTIMIZATION
[19] AGRO-PRODUCTION PARK

community of practise

CLOUD 9

Spain

Enric Ruiz-Geli [1968]

Graduate of the ETSA in Barcelona, Enric Ruiz-Geli completed his training abroad (Mississippi State University; Urbino; Tel Aviv; Stockholm) and undertook a course in theatre design at the theatrical institute in Barcelona, at the school at Paris-la Villette and at the LAI school of design. Having attended the Masters programme on 'ephemeral architecture' (Escola Elisava and ETSAB), he has collaborated with the Yago Conde agency, Jordi Henrich & Bea Goller (1991—94) and in 1995 he set up his own office in Barcelona. Since then he has worked regularly as a theatrical design assistant to Robert Wilson (a musical staging for Lou Reed, a Giorgio Armani fashion show, among others). He is also the author of SPEK, a 'macro playstation', a game that creates new territories, virtual actors and various activities (256 participants, eight countries possible), which has been presented as performance art in Berlin, Madrid and Barcelona since 1999. ☑

NEW TECHNOLOGIES are giving rise to a new sensibility. Projects are processes. Processes involving new tools, software, hardware and visual effects. Processes involving creation and use simultaneously. In real time. Processes involving games that generate a new vision. We don't see results, we see the software filters, the effects and the tools used in the project. We have to play with a thousand tools.

Reality utopia We are interested in building links between our dreams and reality. In the times of Jules Verne, the gap between utopia and reality was one of centuries. Nowadays, by using software and the connection between ideas, modelling, visualization and CAD, we can turn utopia into reality in just hours.

New formats We are interested in extending the limits of architecture by establishing connections with other disciplines and media. Our experience in architecture, theatre and multimedia merges all media into a single vision. We generate new formats. The creation of new formats builds an architecture that is the interface, the medium, the platform, the cosmos, between the audience, knowledge and the contents. Architecture is about building links, building relationships, building networks of communication, building invisible lines of action and tension.

Digital building Our architecture works well in a theatre's black box. The magic black box is the right place to build with light, to build with pixels. The right place to fly objects and materials, to blur limits, to live without gravity. To build transparency and generate links between data and fantasy. The black box and the virtual-reality cave are the first places where digital architecture becomes physical, tangible and material. We try to take digital reality outside

the computer. First we generate hybridization, specificity, complexity, mixing, modelling, rendering, morphing, mapping, etc., generating new situations and new realities. Together, they generate a new landscape, a new interface, a new matrix to live in. The process of building is then about the attempt to connect software and hardware, to connect the digital and the physical. As architects we are like digital carpenters: we build using pixels and vectors, but also with the other limit of reality, particles of light and nature. The aviary branch prototype is a hybrid, half metal, half natural, in which fluid goes up and video data comes down. Architecture comes alive. Architecture becomes a mediatic robotic structure. Architecture is the interface in which nature conquers the steel structure.

Attitude Enter the game. Let's try to mix Roberto Benigni, Amadeus Mozart, Rainman, the Man in the Moon, Forrest Gump, Luke Skywalker, Sergei Eisenstein, Yago Conde, Oscar Wilde, Bob Wilson, Paul Virilio, Orlando, Antonin Artaud, the Pied Piper of Hamlin, Ignasi Solà-Morales, Shine ... and an eight-year-old child. We perform with unconsciousness and shadows under our eyes. We perform architecture like a graffiti artist: full of ideas, searching for the right wall on which to place them.

We try to move mountains every week. Just do it.

Fiction architecture When there is a voice-over and the actor is an image, a 3D scanned image of Bruce Willis's skin, his limbs a-blur, the casting digital and the video a 3D hologram, then architecture is action, set, fiction, make-up, acupuncture, lies and visual prosthesis = cloud9. ☑

Enric Ruiz-Geli

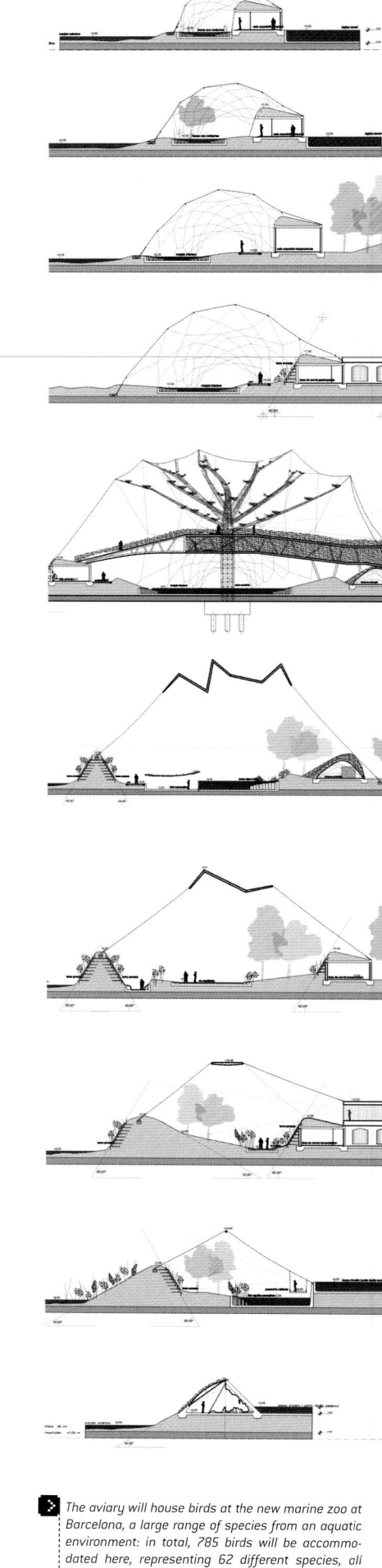

☑ *The aviary will house birds at the new marine zoo at Barcelona, a large range of species from an aquatic environment: in total, 785 birds will be accommodated here, representing 62 different species, all living under the same roof. The central tree-shaped structure, covered with aquatic plants, will provide a habitat for new species — storks, herons, ibises, cormorants, egrets — and will support 132 nests.*

>Aviary — Marine Zoo

Barcelona, Spain, under construction, 2001

This project for a new marine zoo in Barcelona poses essential questions about 'ecological' architecture: should it be a reconstruction, an imitation or a stage production; or should it be an immersion in 'nature' or a place that is elaborated, directed, educational? There is no doubt that it is in the virtual — a place of movement, of interaction and of the ephemeral — that Cloud9's architecture has found its foundations here, giving the opportunity for profound reflection on the interaction between people and their milieu, the observer and the observed. the nature and the artificial, the interior and the exterior. Simultaneously a huge artificial tree (its internal structure) and a new 'natural' topography of seaside dunes (its external form), this project consciously adopts the 'paradox' of the zoo — an artifice of nature by definition — and exploits it for all its theatrical potential. Artificial plants on a metal structure, gigantic machines for regulating the atmosphere, water filtration systems and even the manipulation of animal behaviour: to encourage the longest trajectories and flights, the food and the materials for building nests are placed at the other end of the enclosure; the depth of the water in the ponds varies according to the length of the feet of the wading birds, so as to create 'naturally' different aquatic zones for different species. Staging of the visit, the measuring out of interactions, immersion in the zoo and educational content: wearing camouflage clothing, one travels along an extremely well thought-out circuit, which provides alternating surroundings and culminates in the ascent into the central tree, where one discovers the marsh landscape one has just passed through, put into perspective in the context of the whole extent of the zoo and beyond, to the city of Barcelona and the sea. ☑

The aviary, with its asymmetric, fusiform geometry, is laid out longitudinally in order to create longer flight paths. Its ground plan is 237 metres long, 62 metres wide at its broadest and 15 metres wide at its narrowest, with a maximum height of 25 metres in the central area. The main area is a large bird enclosure closed in by mesh, with a ground plan of 9,000 square metres. In the centre is a treelike structure that shelters a green hydroponic landscape (1,256 square metres).

The structure of the envelope is composed of pairs of cables forming two conical surfaces that cross to make a continuous mesh of stainless steel. The lower end of each of the cables is attached to a prestressed concrete support, forming the entrance and exit to the enclosure.

A marsh landscape is proposed for the inside of the aviary. This is the natural habitat of birds, which are native species of marshland and seaboard woods. In this case, our reference is the Empordà marshlands park. The strategy is to convey the idea that to construct a landscape inside the zoo is to define an architecture of natural and the artificial landscape; we cannot simply adopt a real landscape and scale it down to fit the available plot. What we propose is an exercise in abstraction, a reduction of complexity in the relationships. The 'Penrose' mosaic system allows us to create an infinite, extensive, non-repetitive landscape. It addresses the issue of continuity, at the same time taking into account the different units and individual elements within it around which it creates borders, and marking out the layout, contours and so on.

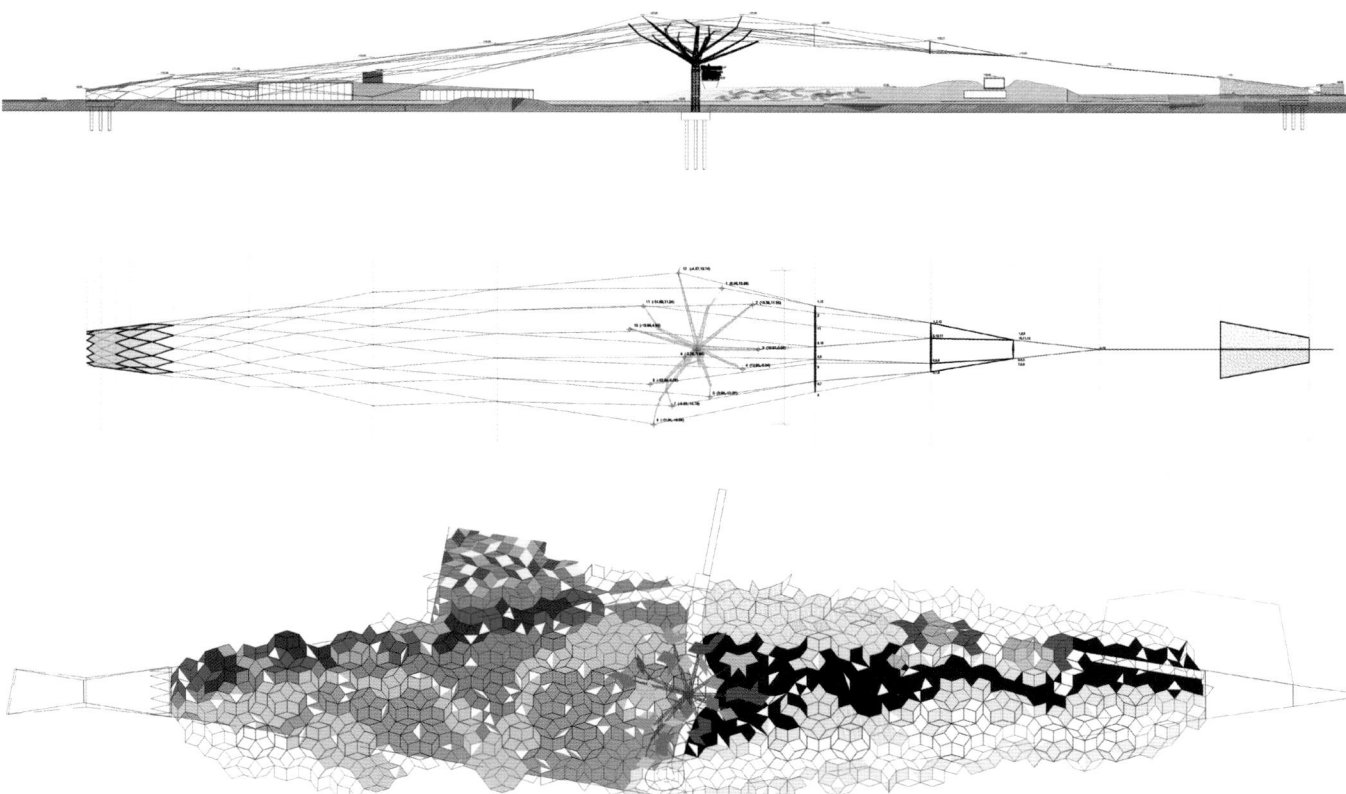

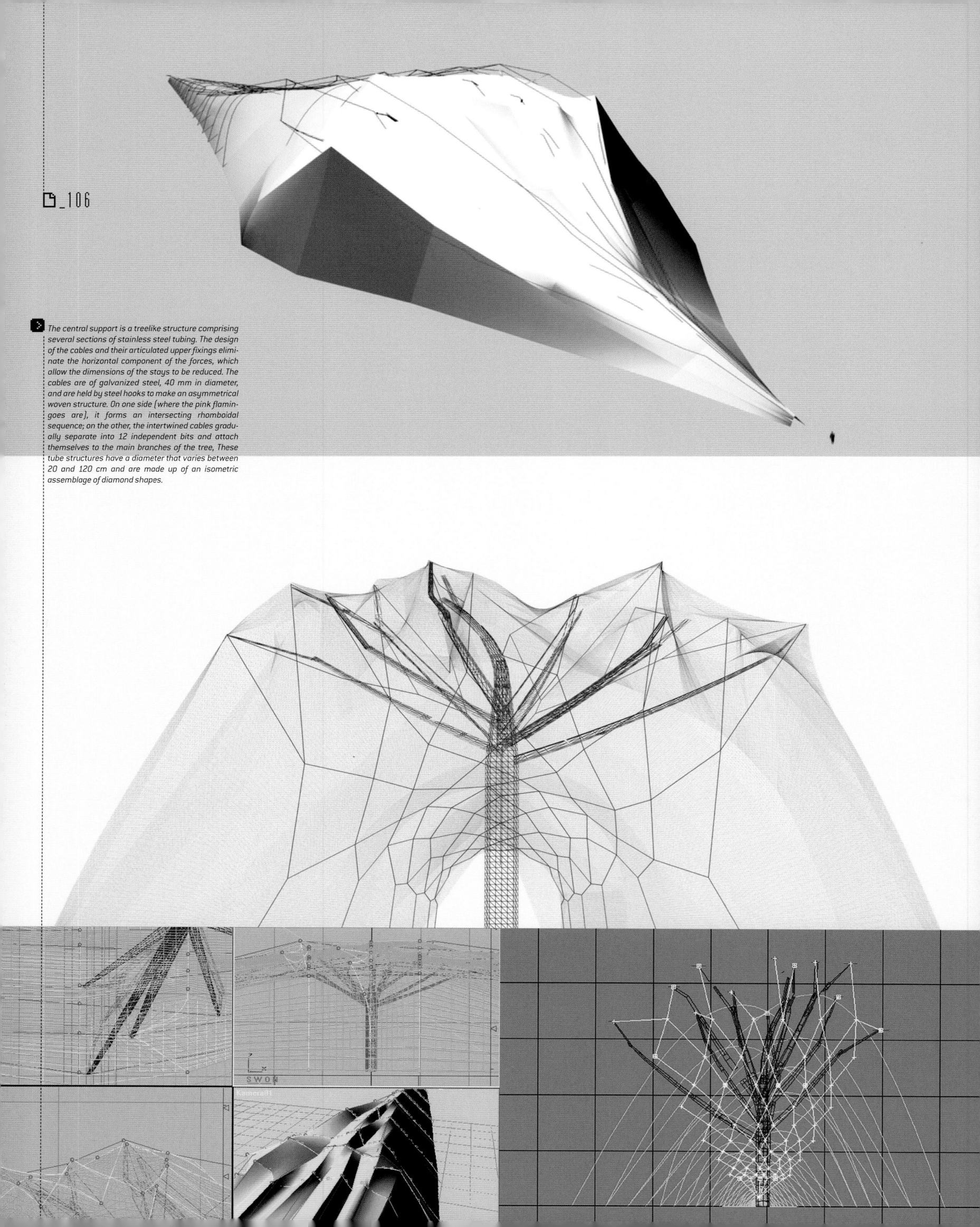

_106

The central support is a treelike structure comprising several sections of stainless steel tubing. The design of the cables and their articulated upper fixings eliminate the horizontal component of the forces, which allow the dimensions of the stays to be reduced. The cables are of galvanized steel, 40 mm in diameter, and are held by steel hooks to make an asymmetrical woven structure. On one side (where the pink flamingoes are), it forms an intersecting rhomboidal sequence; on the other, the intertwined cables gradually separate into 12 independent bits and attach themselves to the main branches of the tree, These tube structures have a diameter that varies between 20 and 120 cm and are made up of an isometric assemblage of diamond shapes.

108

The aim is to build the main treelike structure as a habitat for birds, using hydroponic cultures. The design involves plant capsules that are integrated into the structure and can be lowered for mainte-nance or exchanged for others from the nursery. The tree structure serves as both a support and a conduit for the hydroponic system that carries water with nutrients to the vegetation and drains it to the recircu-lation system. The tree is a hybrid of natural plants and metal. It is also equipped with sensors that meas-ure humidity and nutrients, and provides information on climate as well as video images of the nests. The tree is an 'airport': it registers the life of the birds and analyses the production of the 230 sounds they make.

Cloud 9: Enric Ruiz-Geli, Gérard Veciana (associate)

Client: Infraestructures 2004, Barcelona Regional, Barcelona Zoo, Ajuntament de Barcelona

Client's advisers: Estudi Ramon Folch (biodiversity script); Josep del Hoyo (birds)

Cloud 9's advisors: Manuel Arguijo y asociados sl. (structure); Peckam Guyton Albers & Viets, Inc. (management); Jardins Munné Pericall sl., Silvia Bures (tree landscaping); Bures sa., Silvia Bures (growing media); Regaber, Ignaci Pujol (irrigation); Sono, Ramon Caus (multimedia technology); Acyc sa., Antonio Casado (environmental pollution prevention); Albert Bestard (landscaping design); Phil Mayfield (water recycling system); Jaume Serrasolses (sustainability and installations); Fundació Natura, Francesc Giro (water lands; 3M (estimation cost)

Cloud 9 collaborators: Carlos Garcia, Carlos Bañon, Niko, Tine Beinemeier, Pablo Ros, Jordi Fernandez, Oscar Puga, Carolina Sanza, Eduardo Gutierrez, Andre Brössel, Fred Guillaud, Juanjo González, Rupert Maurus, Marina Sans, David Scheunemann, Philippe Bosch, Javier Villar

Caption numbers: left to right, top to bottom

1. Existing natural pine tree, 'Pi de Bofarull', 25 m high x 40 m diameter

2. Digital trees sculpted using 3DMax software

3–13. hand-drawings of the branches by a Korean artist, used as 13 fractal elements to build the tree in the aviary

4. Map of links of the 3D model, 72 points [x,y,z]

5. 3D model, 10 metres long

6. Models of the polygons, variable diameters between 5 and 40 cm

7. Development of the 61 polygonal surfaces, using FormZ software

8. Rhomboidal pattern, with a calculation of the forces for an 80% transparency

9–11. Process of laser cutting the 4 mm stainless steel plates

12–14. Process of cutting a 4 m long branch = 8 hours

15–17. Process of erection, 30º= 20 hours

18–19. First prototype branch built, dodecahedral polygons

20. 3D model of a 4-metre-long branch

21–22. Fabrication of the natural coconut mesh, interior skin of the capsule

23. Hydroponic cultures, with irrigation system, humidity sensors and video cameras

24. Relationship between the aviary mesh, the structure and the birds

section / elevation 1:100

FIELD OPERATIONS

United States

Stanley T. Allen (1956), James Corner (1961)

Field Operations was created in 2000 by urban designer and landscape architect James Corner in partnership with architect Stan Allen. The mandate of Field Operations is to provide innovative, high-quality design solutions for cities, buildings and landscapes. The practice marks a shift from the one to the many, from static to animate, from narrative to performance, from object to field. Field Operations implies not only the arrangement of forms in space but also the orchestration of the various forces (ecological, economic, cultural, programmatic, legislative) that shape cities, buildings and landscapes over time. Through close attention to the logistics of large-scale implementation, Field Operations are responsive to a wide range of variables while remaining open to the uncertainty of future needs and demands. Recently, Field Operations has been recognized with first prize in the Fresh Kills Landfill to Landscape International Design Competition for the conversion of 2,200 acres [890 hectares] to urban parkland, Staten Island, New York; the prestigious Daimler-Chrysler Design Award for innovative design, 2000; first prize in an invited competition for a garden for the French Consulate in New York City; finalists for the 350-acre [140-hectare] Downsview Park in Toronto, and, in collaboration with artist Kiki Smith, the Irish Hunger Memorial Park under the sponsorship of the Battery Park City Authority. Recent projects include the planning and urban design for 8 miles [13 km] of the Delaware Riverfront in north Philadelphia; a new design for the 5-mile-long [eight-km] Pena Boulevard at Denver International Airport; a master plan for the Cleveland Canal Basin, Ohio; a new design for Eastern State Penitentiary Park in Philadelphia; a commercial art building and landscape in Paju-Book City, a new 'urban wetland' development outside Seoul, Korea; and numerous houses, gardens and estates. ☑

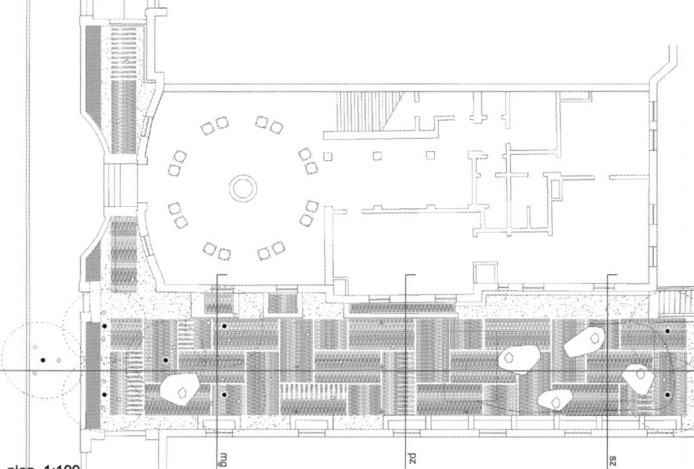

plan 1:100

Network practices As cities grow and change under the pressures of shifting economic, technological and social forces, it is increasingly difficult for traditional design disciplines to address this new complexity adequately. Field Operations embraces complexity in order to synthesize the insights of many related disciplines: architecture, landscape architecture, urban design, ecology, infrastructure and transport planning, economic analysis, scenario planning, media and communications. The structure of the office is fully collaborative, and the working methodology encourages feedback and interaction. Our aim is to discover novel solutions to the challenges of the contemporary city through new and creative affiliations — new ecologies of creativity.

Ecology Landscapes and cities today exist within larger and more complex global ecologies. Even the smallest garden or building is an active agent in a large environment changing over time. We view all sites and programmes as comprising complex ecologies — never bounded or final, but rather fluid, co-extensive and continually emergent. Our work is informed by the theory and practice of ecology in the broadest sense, encompassing social as well as natural ecologies, thereby supporting projects that are self-sustaining, adaptive and resilient to change.

Design, identity, communication Through extensive use of diagrams, models, drawings and imagery, Field Operations works to expand the field of public space. Rather than scripting singular narratives of place or programme, we seek to create an open matrix that enables users and inhabitants to inscribe their own scenarios of occupation and identity. As a working methodology, this emphasis upon visualization, construction and direct spatial experience fosters communication and dialogue among participants and designers alike. We see the role of design as the creation of distinctive public spaces that are in turn activated through those who use them, out there, in the field. ☑

Field Operations

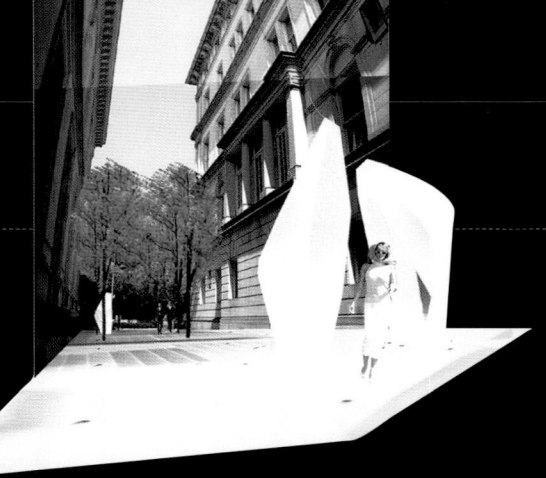

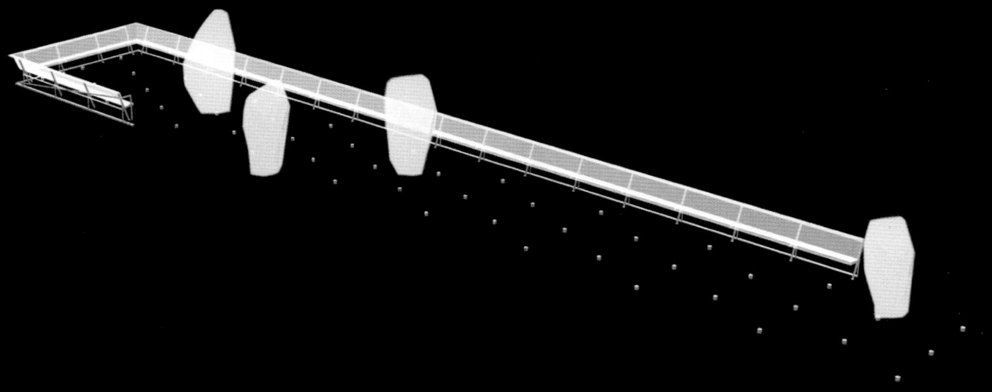

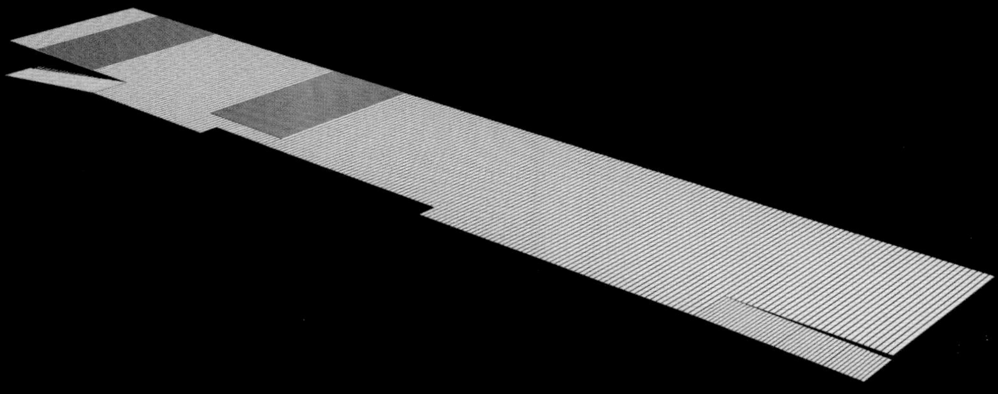

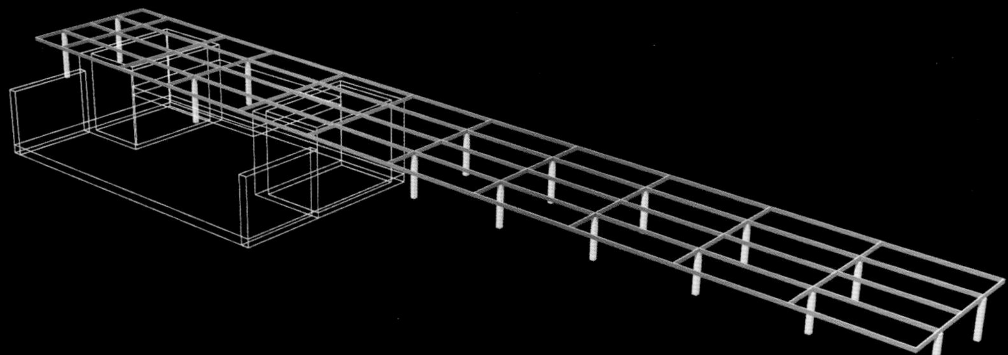

French Embassy Garden
New York, USA, 2001

Located on Fifth Avenue between the offices of the Cultural Services of the French Embassy and the New York University Institute of Fine Arts, a small (300 square feet/28 square metres) garden is intended to create a public identity for French Culture. In a global, mediated and multicultural world, the possibility for the garden to 'represent' cultural identity is meaningless. Instead, the garden presents an open platform for its own identity to become inscribed over time, a reflection of its patrons' commitment to the contemporary. Like an empty stage, a tilted metal surface runs from Fifth Avenue to the back of the space. This surface is furnished with a drift of trees, chairs, lanterns and technical support for media or art installations. The tree canopies and the metal surface are lit from below, creating a luminous field that animates the space and its context. Through the layering of various systems (surfaces, lighting, sound, planting, furnishing), the garden is an ambient space, a porous, 'loose' arrangement that is light and responsive, changing according to conditions of occupancy, light, time or day, seasons and events. The overall coherence of the garden may be discerned as comprising three ambient zones: a media grove along the Fifth Avenue frontage, an event and performance area in the interior and a 'strange zone' in the rear of the space, where air ventilators and lighting lend an odd sensation of elevation and enclosure. ☒

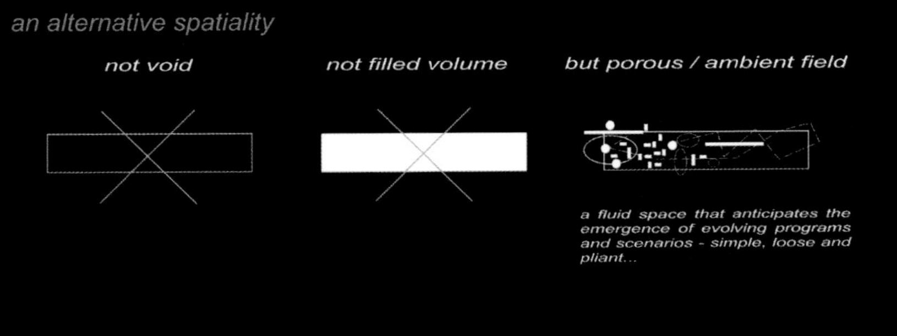

an alternative spatiality

not void   *not filled volume*   *but porous / ambient field*

a fluid space that anticipates the emergence of evolving programs and scenarios - simple, loose and pliant...

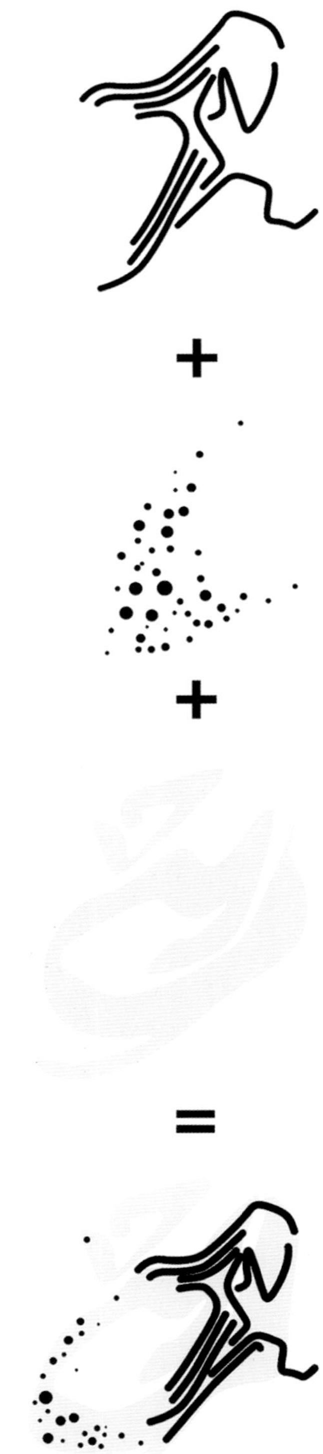

'Lifescape' — Fresh Kills Reserve
Staten Island, New York, USA, competition, 2001

Visible from the moon, with mounds of landfill waste the size of mountains, Fresh Kills remains the most complex landmass human beings have attempted to manipulate. Starkly elegant, the artificial topography offers a unique landscape experience. As such, the site presents an opportunity to develop a new form of public–ecological landscape, an alternative paradigm of human creativity, biologically informed and guided more by time and process than by space and form. Nature, traditionally conceived as separate from cultural endeavour, is fully integrated into the manmade landscape at Fresh Kills. The result is a synthetic, integrative nature, simultaneously wild and cultivated, bewildering and cultivating. Nature is no longer the image we look at, out there, but the field we inhabit and are part of, an active 'lifescape', where life below ground, on the ground, in the water and in the air, is continually manufacturing new environments as it reproduces and evolves. This lifescape is rendered 'cultural' to the degree that is wholly accomplished by human agency – by design. The site at Fresh Kills is currently characterized by relative homogeneity and alien ecologies. To create a more diverse, integrated and healthy series of ecosystems – to redefine landfill as lifescape – an alternative process of recolonization must be set in motion. A careful strategy of landscape restoration is developed in response to the very difficult ecological conditions already present on the site. We propose a matrix of lines (threads), surfaces (mats) and clusters (islands) to maximize opportunities for access and movement – movement of seeds and biota as well as people and activities. Programmatic elements, including biomass and constructed surfaces or objects, are organized according to these three interrelated spatial systems: linear 'threads' direct flows of water, energy and matter around the site, injecting new life into otherwise homogeneous areas; clusters of 'islands' provide denser nests of protected habitat, seed source and programme activity; surface 'mats' create a patch-like mosaic of mostly porous surfaces to provide self-sustainable coverage, erosion control and native habitat. In time, this entangled colony of emergent organisms and communities will render the different ecosystems of the site legible, as different meadows, plantings, habitats and programmes work with distinct slope gradients, soil-water gradients, solar aspect and adjacent contexts. The project also incorporates recreation trails, an equestrian centre, a sports and extreme-games centre, environmental education exhibits and on-site art installations to create a new living reserve – a vast 'nature-sprawl' for Staten Island and the larger metropolitan region.

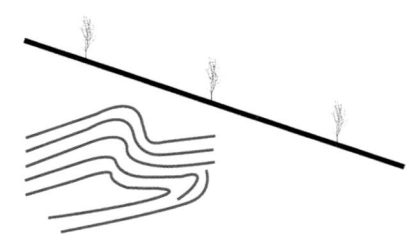

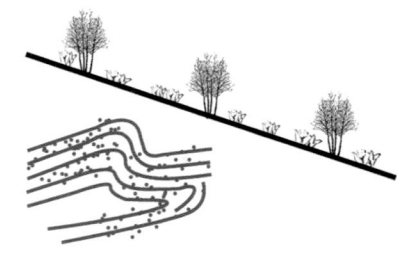

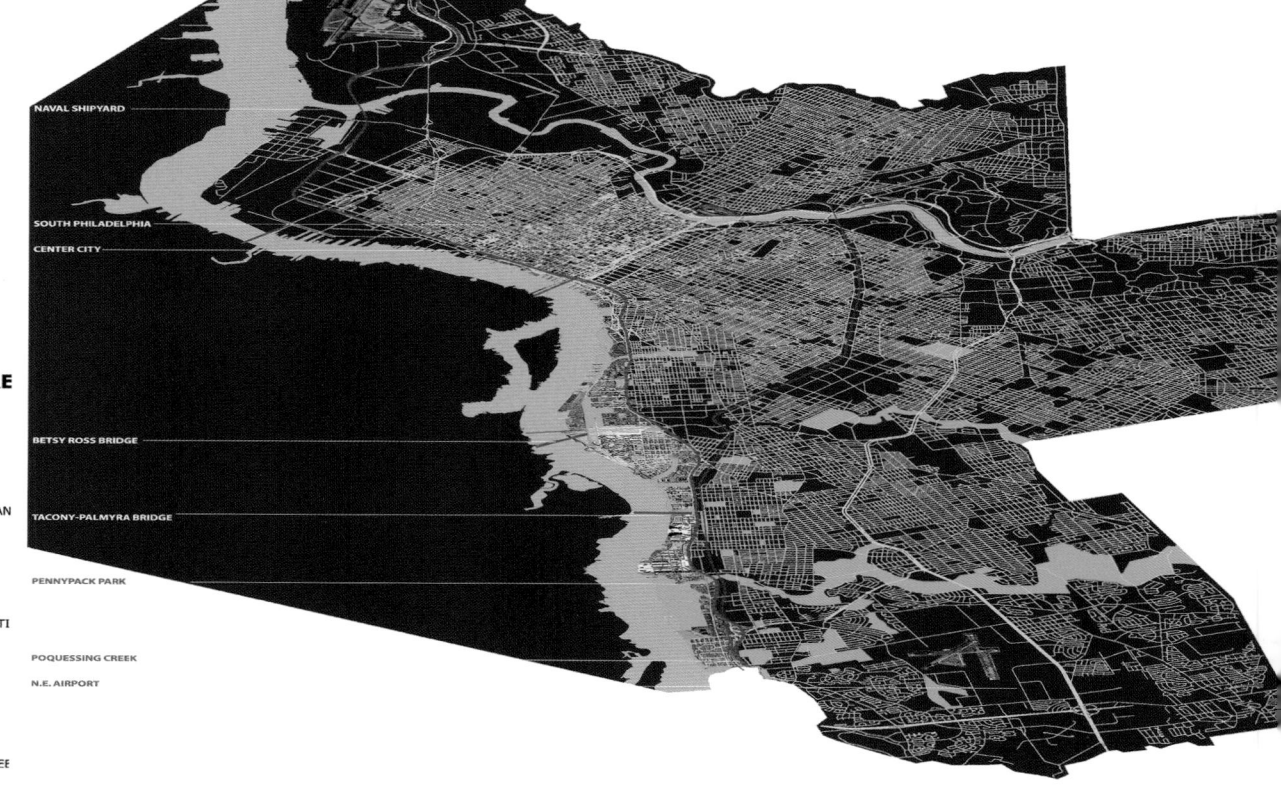

PHILADELPHIA INTERNATIONAL AIRPORT

NAVAL SHIPYARD

SOUTH PHILADELPHIA

CENTER CITY

BETSY ROSS BRIDGE

TACONY-PALMYRA BRIDGE

PENNYPACK PARK

POQUESSING CREEK

N.E. AIRPORT

SITE INFRASTRUCTURE

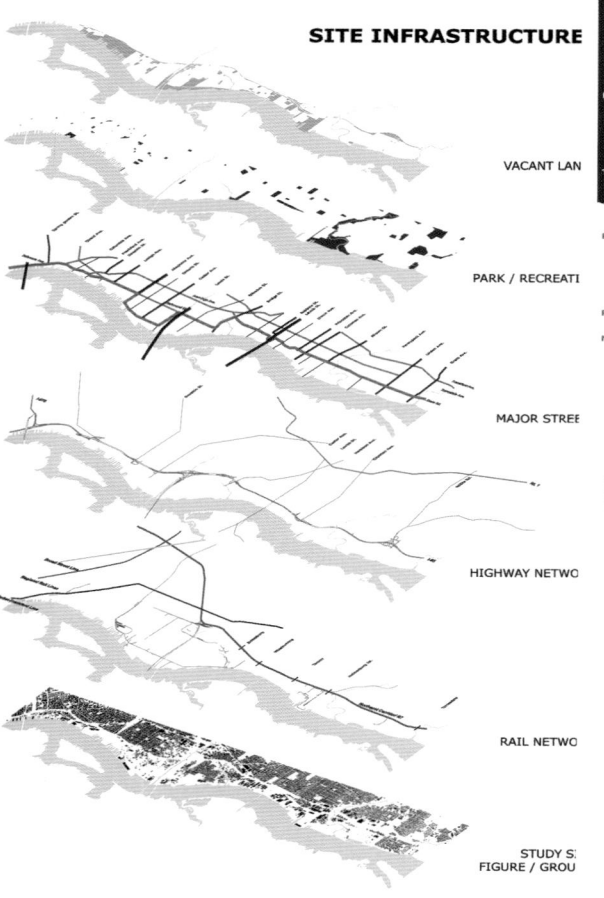

VACANT LAN

PARK / RECREATI

MAJOR STREE

HIGHWAY NETWO

RAIL NETWO

STUDY S:
FIGURE / GROU

North Delaware Riverfront
Philadelphia, USA, project, 2001

Cities around the world today are struggling to reorganize radically in response to the effects of de-industrialization, the growth of suburbs, globalization and the emergence of new technologies. There is currently a great opportunity for the City of Philadelphia to transform its entire image and identity by restructuring its relationship to the Delaware River. This opportunity exists because of the shift from industrial economies once centred on the riverfront to new service and information technologies, and the subsequent shift of the river from a corridor of industry and shipping to one of recreation, leisure and vista. The scale of available land (over 1,500 acres/600 hectares), the proximity of I-95 expressway and regional rail lines and the magnificence of the Delaware River point to a huge potential for transformation. Field Operations was commissioned by the City of Philadelphia to prepare a comprehensive redevelopment and renewal plan for 8 square miles (21 square kilometres) along the Delaware River in north Philadelphia. The project site is a composite of marginal and industrial uses and large tracts of abandoned structures and brownfields. The challenge for the design team was twofold – first, how to reconnect the city to its river and, second, how to transform the site by developing strategies to convert derelict and contaminated brownfields into new mixed-use and residential communities. The key components of the plan are a continuous public park along the full 11 miles (18 km) of riverfront integrated with new mixed-use and residential communities. The plan proposes over 5,000 new residences and over 3 million square feet (280,000 square metres) of new commercial space. The new public riverfront park is envisioned as a huge public works amenity for the entire Philadelphia region. Contained within the park are a new river road, dedicated pedestrian and cycling trails, passive and active recreation fields, habitat and riverbank restoration areas and event strips for new restaurants, museums and cultural facilities. The plan also incorporates an innovative, flexible framework of successional, or phased, development that can adaptively reconstruct itself in response to market forces and city resources.

'Plainscape' — Pena Boulevard, Denver International Airport

Denver, USA, project, 2002

The Colorado plains are a remarkable and distinctive landscape, especially where they confront the dramatic front range of the Rocky Mountains. One of the most lasting impressions of this vast open landscape derives from its many lines — survey grid lines marking the cardinal directions, each made manifest by straight roads, ditches, fences, furrows, poles, wires, fields and distant horizons. Lines, both horizontal and vertical, render this otherwise invisible landscape visible and distinct. The 'Plainscape' proposal aims to reinstitute the primacy of simple, large linear structures as a means of trying to organize the expansion of the airport and its associated services along its approach corridor, Pena Boulevard. Distant vistas are identified and preserved; a four-mile-long (6-kilometre) polished stainless-steel pole field on a 132-foot (40-metre) grid marks out the elevation, 5,380 feet (1,600 metres) above sea-level, while also recording the measures of the US Survey grid; low, long berms create 'occluded horizons' to screen out fore- and middle-ground clutter; earthwork hills become landmarks and aerial viewing mounds; and newly restored prairie grassland and wildflower areas are created, themselves integrated with sustainable storm-water management practices. The plan is intended to create a unique and distinctive experience for people both arriving to and departing from Denver. ☒

VICENTE GUALLART

Spain

Vicente Guallart (1963)

Vicente Guallart opened his agency in Barcelona in 1992 after several years in partnership with José Luis Mateo. He divides his time between multimedia productions, exhibitions of contemporary architecture, research and teaching: he is director of the postgraduate course 'Advanced Architecture and Digital Towns' at the Polytechnic Foundation in Catalonia. He also founded a society for the conception and publication of multimedia CD-ROMs in architecture, for which he has been awarded several prizes: Moebius (Barcelona, 1995) for the best Spanish cultural and scientific CD-ROM; special mention at the Milia d'Or (Cannes, 1996) for the best graphics and images of synthesis in architecture; most recently a prize from the city of Barcelona (2002, multimedia category) for his project 'Media House', which he carried out with Metapolis, in collaboration with the Media Lab of MIT (Massachusetts) and the Polytechnic University of Barcelona. His work on the 'Webhotel' for the exhibition 'Fabrications' in the Museum of Contemporary Art in Barcelona was also exhibited at MoMA in New York and in San Francisco. Lastly, in 1998, along with Manuel Gausa and Willy Müller, he founded Metapolis, which has already organized two Festivals for Advanced Architecture in Barcelona. ☒

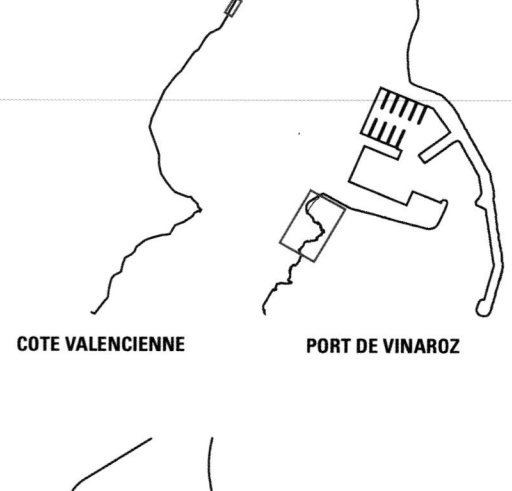

MEDITERRANÉE

COTE VALENCIENNE PORT DE VINAROZ

POINTE RESTAUTANT ROCHER

VICENTE GUALLART'S architectural projects arise out of two complementary approaches: the one is geography, invoked as a principle of nature, a new urban context and a possible architectural form; the other is the digital world, seen as a new nature, a place for inventing and experimenting with new realities, which in turn may have repercussions on real physical spaces. The artificial, the natural and the digital are thus interactive within contemporary space. 'The physical world is transformed by the appearance of the digital world; the constructed environment is transformed by what we used to call 'natural'; the digital develops its internal laws and constructs its own world of operations.' In October 2001, within the framework of the research project 'Day@media House', which he runs in Metapolis, he presented in Barcelona the prototype of an 'intelligent house', able to react and to think ahead. The project studies how information, through new technologies, can integrate the everyday and even transform domestic space, just as running water and electricity have done. In the context of the house, objects, spaces and people are the units that form a network in order to organize their physical and digital relations. Here the individual, within his or her spatial and family context, is on the first level of relations between local and global that govern the organization and exchange of information between 'territories' – this concept having now become independent of any context or identifiable limit (physical, urban, national). At the other extreme of Vicente Guallart's architectural spectrum are projects relating to the 'artificial mountain'. As a

piece of nature, the mountain is a mass of matter, of informational folds and strata: not those of the flat simultaneity of the Internet, but those of the geological depths of history. At Castellón (Valencia) or Denia (Alicante), his projects for artificial 'Mountain Cities' collect together all the urban functions – shopping centres, car parks – in a multifaceted urban complex. The fascinating thing about these two phenomena – geographical and digital – is the impossibility of visualizing them as a unit: nature, like network systems, is infinitely divisible and infinitely accumulative. At present Vicente Guallart is exploring another fragmentary, irregular 'object': a piece of coastline. Following the work of Benoît Mandelbrot ('How long is the coast of Britain?', *Science Review*, 1967), many research projects lean towards a mathematical modelling of these phenomena, by way of fractal geometry: 'a lot of natural objects are systems, in the sense that they are composed of several distinct parts, connected to one another. The fractal dimension describes one aspect of this rule of connection.' Here the 'side' of the sea/the land is examined with the idea that by studying borderlines, one may be in a position to acquire new knowledge of the nature of central, stable, normal situations. 'Towns have always had an active relationship with their maritime borders, in order to gain territory from the sea by various manipulations, such as constructing ports and sea walls; in this way they create terrains of great economic value, situated in locations of great strategic value. More land equals bigger savings.' For Vicente Guallart, these places of exchange constitute a dynamic

movement, a surface for productive contact, which he proposes to organize by means of a complex game between border and surface, alternately reducing the one or the other. Nature lies at the source of this project, with its imposition of borders, its role as the site of a network of exchanges and contacts and above all as a model of conceptualization and action. ☒

B. G.

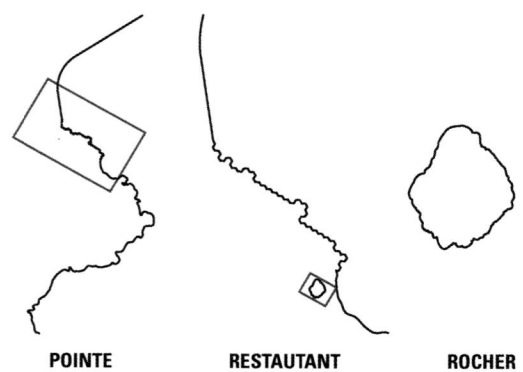

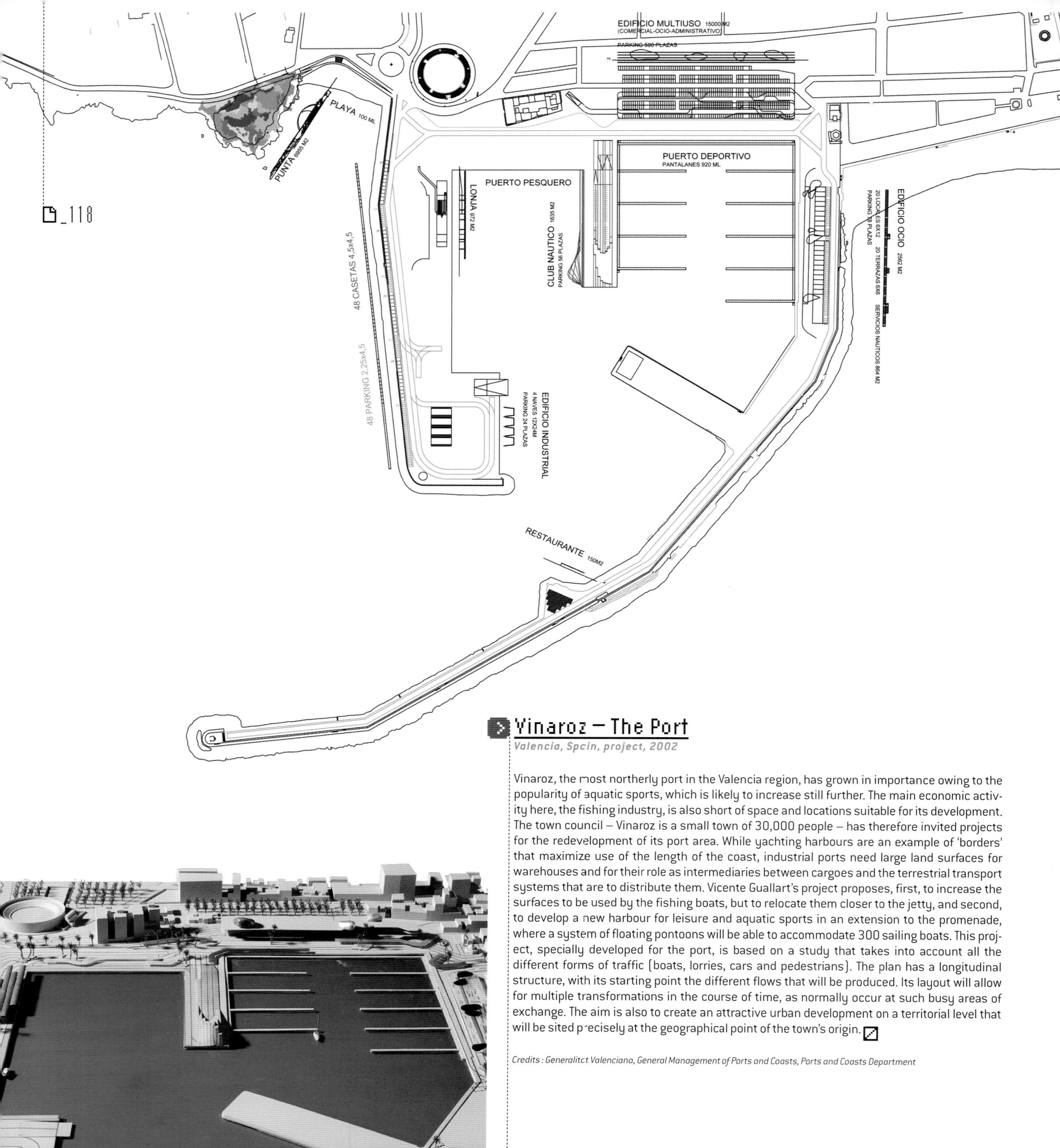

EDIFICIO MULTIUSO 15000M2
(COMERCIAL-OCIO-ADMINISTRATIVO)

PARKING 500 PLAZAS

PLAYA 100 ML

PUNTA 6665 M2

48 CASETAS 4,5x4,5

48 PARKING 2,25x4,5

PUERTO DEPORTIVO
PANTALANES 920 ML

PUERTO PESQUERO

LONJA 972 M2

CLUB NAUTICO 1635 M2
PARKING 56 PLAZAS

EDIFICIO OCIO 2562 M2
20 LOCALES 6X12
20 TERRAZAS 6X6
PARKING 78 PLAZAS
SERVICIOS NAUTICOS 864 M2

EDIFICIO INDUSTRIAL
4 NAVES 12X24M
PARKING 24 PLAZAS

RESTAURANTE 150M2

Vinaroz — The Port
Valencia, Spain, project, 2002

Vinaroz, the most northerly port in the Valencia region, has grown in importance owing to the popularity of aquatic sports, which is likely to increase still further. The main economic activity here, the fishing industry, is also short of space and locations suitable for its development. The town council — Vinaroz is a small town of 30,000 people — has therefore invited projects for the redevelopment of its port area. While yachting harbours are an example of 'borders' that maximize use of the length of the coast, industrial ports need large land surfaces for warehouses and for their role as intermediaries between cargoes and the terrestrial transport systems that are to distribute them. Vicente Guallart's project proposes, first, to increase the surfaces to be used by the fishing boats, but to relocate them closer to the jetty, and second, to develop a new harbour for leisure and aquatic sports in an extension to the promenade, where a system of floating pontoons will be able to accommodate 300 sailing boats. This project, specially developed for the port, is based on a study that takes into account all the different forms of traffic (boats, lorries, cars and pedestrians). The plan has a longitudinal structure, with its starting point the different flows that will be produced. Its layout will allow for multiple transformations in the course of time, as normally occur at such busy areas of exchange. The aim is also to create an attractive urban development on a territorial level that will be sited precisely at the geographical point of the town's origin. ◨

Credits : Generalitat Valenciana, General Management of Ports and Coasts, Ports and Coasts Department

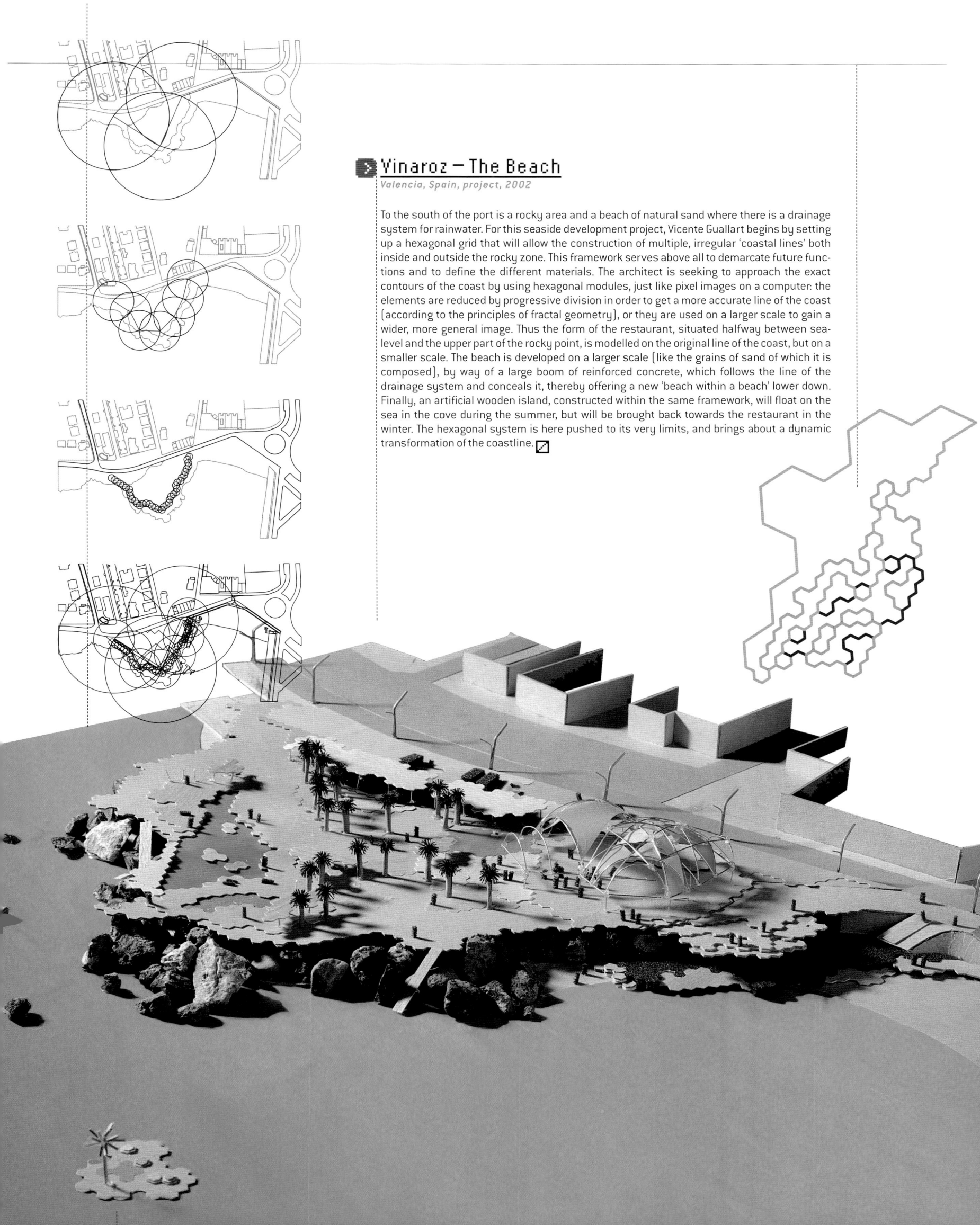

▶ Vinaroz — The Beach
Valencia, Spain, project, 2002

To the south of the port is a rocky area and a beach of natural sand where there is a drainage system for rainwater. For this seaside development project, Vicente Guallart begins by setting up a hexagonal grid that will allow the construction of multiple, irregular 'coastal lines' both inside and outside the rocky zone. This framework serves above all to demarcate future functions and to define the different materials. The architect is seeking to approach the exact contours of the coast by using hexagonal modules, just like pixel images on a computer: the elements are reduced by progressive division in order to get a more accurate line of the coast (according to the principles of fractal geometry), or they are used on a larger scale to gain a wider, more general image. Thus the form of the restaurant, situated halfway between sea-level and the upper part of the rocky point, is modelled on the original line of the coast, but on a smaller scale. The beach is developed on a larger scale (like the grains of sand of which it is composed), by way of a large boom of reinforced concrete, which follows the line of the drainage system and conceals it, thereby offering a new 'beach within a beach' lower down. Finally, an artificial wooden island, constructed within the same framework, will float on the sea in the cove during the summer, but will be brought back towards the restaurant in the winter. The hexagonal system is here pushed to its very limits, and brings about a dynamic transformation of the coastline. ☑

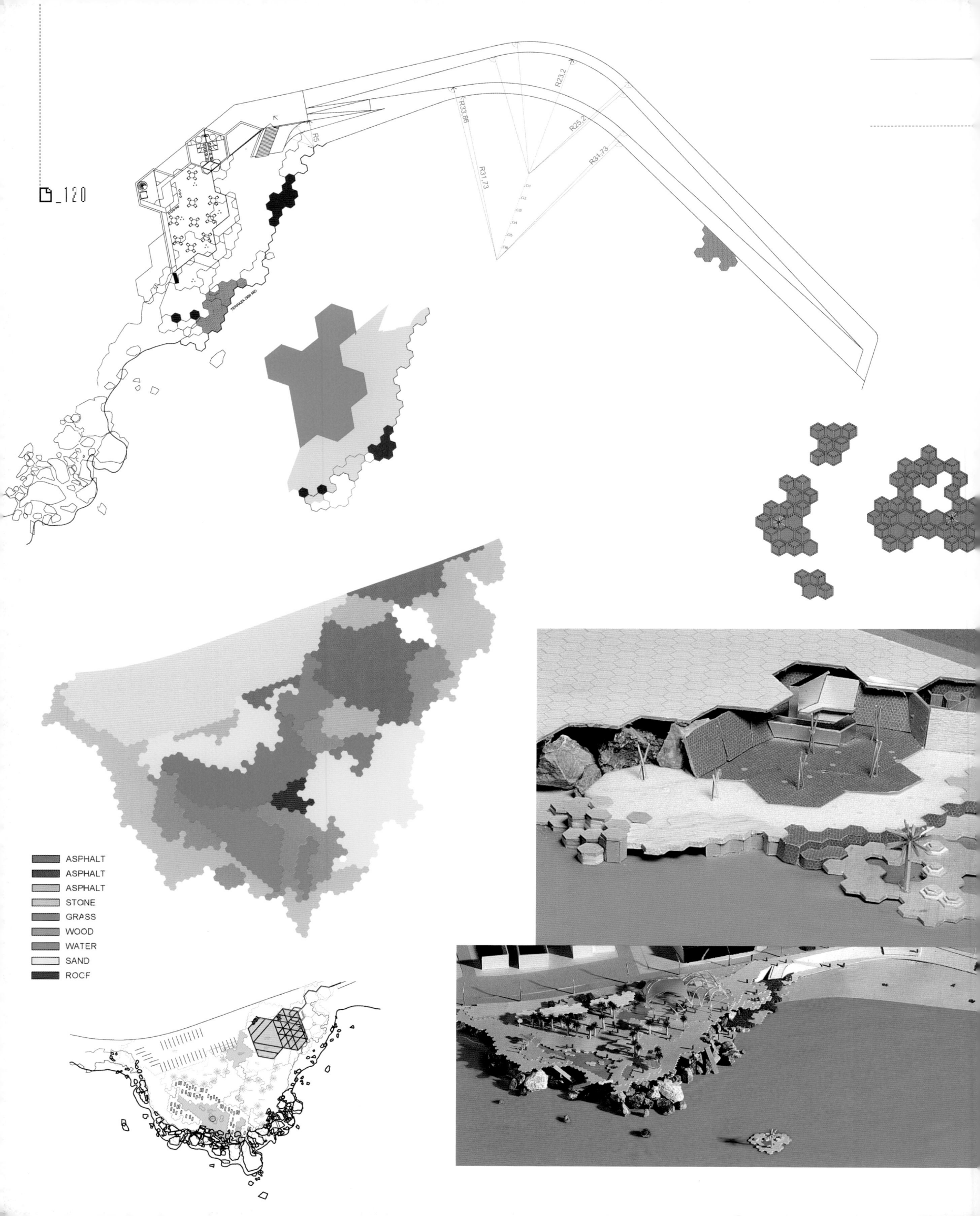

ASPHALT
ASPHALT
ASPHALT
STONE
GRASS
WOOD
WATER
SAND
ROCF

T.R. Hamzah & Yeang sdn bhd

Malaysia

Ken Yeang [1948], Tengku Dato Robert Hamzah [1939]

T. R. Hamzah and K. Yeang is an international firm of architects with its HQ in Kuala Lumpur, Malaysia. The firm has been in business for over two decades, undertaking major projects in Europe and Asia, and is best known for its green or environmentally friendly buildings. Its key projects include the 100-metre-high National Library Board Building (Singapore), the 40-storey Eco-Towers at Elephant & Castle, the IBM Building (Malaysia) and the award-winning Mesiniaga Building (IBM franchise; (Malaysia) and Wirrina Cove Condominium (Australia). The firm's principals are Tengku Dato Robert Hamzah and Dr Ken Yeang. Both had their early architectural education at the Architectural Association school in London. Tengku Dato Robert Hamzah, a prince in the Malay royal family, also completed the AA Tropical Architecture School course under Dr Otto Koenigsberger. Dr Yeang received his doctorate in architecture from Cambridge University (UK). The firm has received over 20 awards including the Aga Khan Award for Architecture (1995) and the RAIA International Award (in 1997 and 1999). ☑

SINCE THE 1960s, T. R. Hamzah & Yeang have been among the pioneers of bioclimatic architecture. Today they are among the foremost and best-known theoreticians and experts. Their thinking concerns the ecological characteristics of the sites as much as the energy demands of the buildings, the materials' use as much as their application. However, theirs is not an ideology of 'green architecture' focused primarily on projects on a small and medium scale, generally implanted in a rural milieu. Initiators of research on skyscrapers powered by renewable energy, on the ecology of very large buildings, they base their work on the resolution of a paradox: making out of these architectural megastructures, which are generally condemned as bad news for the environment, well-regarded engines for achieving balance between people and their milieu. Hamzah & Yeang have been quick to identify their stake in ecological thinking about the proliferation of towers and skyscrapers, particularly in the Far East. Ensconced within the dynamics of nature and economical in terms of materials as well as energy, their many examples of mega-architecture have proven their viability, both economically and ecologically, and have attracted many acolytes. In Hong Kong they are in the process of developing a whole district, the seafront of west Kowloon, as a vast artificial environment in equilibrium with nature. Their London project, 'City in the Sky' (2000), proposed three

eco-towers conceived as proper ecosystems, adopting a mixture of programmes and uses, an alternation of private spaces and free spaces envisaged as genuine pieces of suspended nature. Drawing on a particular analysis of the environmental parameters that govern the sites of their projects, Hamzah & Yeang put forward the notion that the colossal size of their constructions is not a detrimental factor but a positive one, an ecological trump card: it serves to generate biodiversity and increase the mass of organic vegetation. At all stages of their work, down to the last details, they pose the question of the use and rational recycling of the energy that the system itself spontaneously generates. According to Yeang, 'considerable efforts have been devoted to establish ecological bases for the design. Many of these works have hitherto neglected the basic and fundamental property of ecosystems – their inherent conjunction with the biosphere. Now every theory of ecological design must take this into consideration.' It is not so much that the balance between nature and architecture has to be considered; rather, we should understand and anticipate the natural and spontaneous behaviour of these human contrivances, and beyond that to envisage nature as a vast architecture on a world and cosmic scale. ☑

S. N.

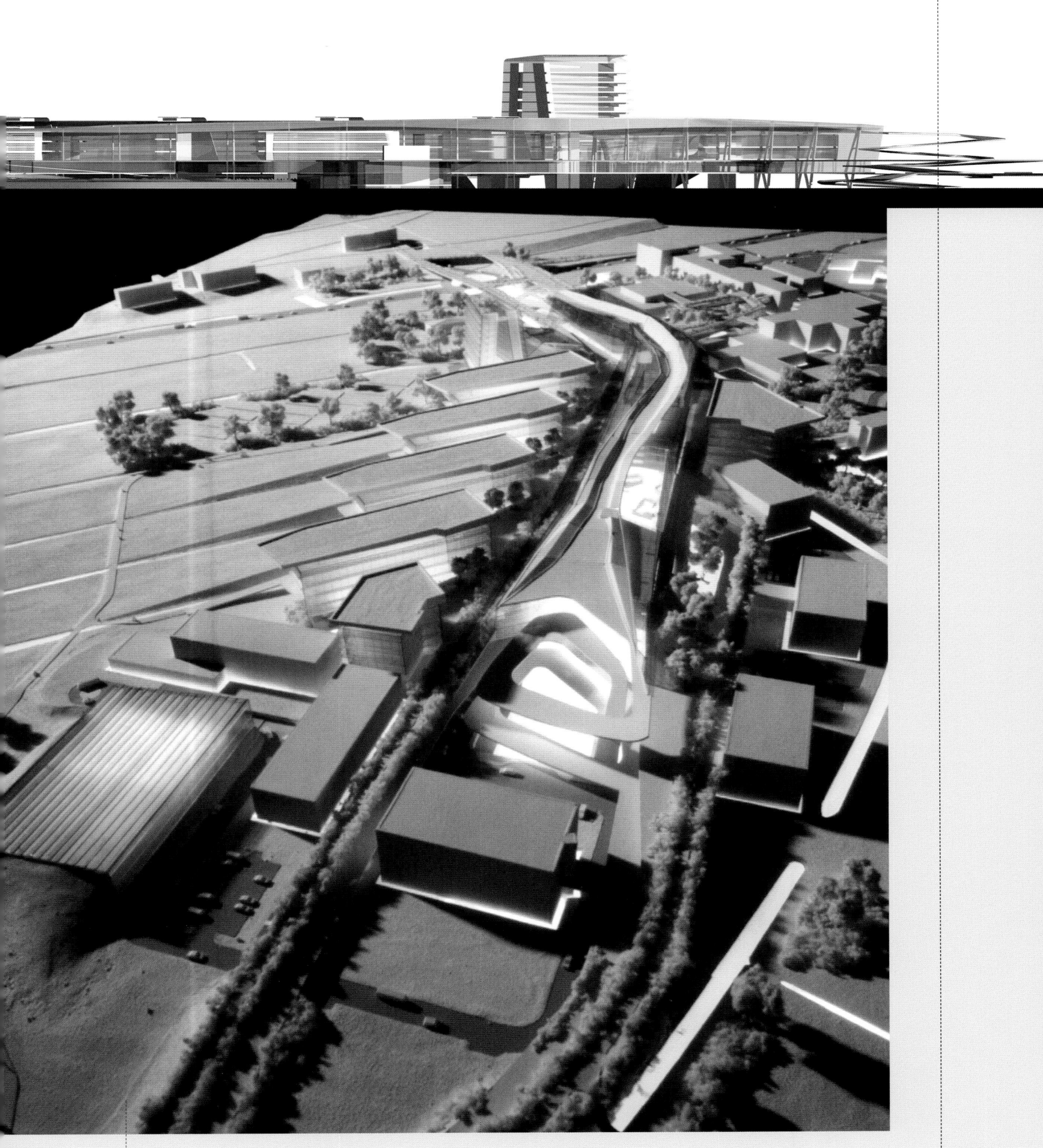

Amsterdam Centre of Science and Technology

Amsterdam, Netherlands, project, 2001

The project involves designing a new complex for the University of Amsterdam to house their faculty buildings and associated facilities, including a congress centre and a hotel. The site is on existing campus land, which is within a larger precinct called WTCW that contains several other scientific institutes. The scheme responds to the existing context by the following strategies: unifying the existing buildings by filling up the negative spaces between them to create an efficient and compact development; assimilating the two existing organizational grids into a unified composition without creating awkward conditions at the grid intersections; providing the opportunity for the main users of the facilities to be more closely integrated and to interact socially and communally by sharing common facilities spread out at Level 2 as a concourse; and improving connections between the station and the institutions by providing the shortest possible route linking all buildings and taking into account safety and weather protection. The two key features of the scheme are the interactive zones (at Level 2) and the design for ecological responsiveness. The concourse is the main feature of the scheme as an interaction zone and makes the scheme unique. The concourse is raised above dike level (to give views to the waterways) and is at the same level as the future train station complex, providing a direct connection into the station. As an interaction zone, the concourse will contain a palette of key facilities and cultural activities, including food outlets, retail, entertainment and IT hubs. The scheme provides for other buildings to connect to the concourse (Level 2). The scheme is ecologically responsive to the environment, in its careful consideration of the use of materials and energy in the built systems and in the endeavour to reduce their undesirable impact on the natural systems of the locality over their entire lifecycle. The strategy involves conserving and recycling of natural resources and use of materials that are environmentally friendly, and the design has minimal negative impact on the surrounding ecosystem. It retains (and at the same time enhances) the landscape of the site by minimizing the building's footprint on the ground, avoiding destruction of the existing ecological structure. The landscape is designed to reflect the cultural and ecological character of the locality. The design is pedestrian-and cyclist-friendly, enhancing links to other parts of the city in this otherwise detached polder site (segregated by the railway dike). This reduces reliance on carbon-emitting motor vehicles. ◨

Credits: T. R. Hamzah & Yeang SDN BHD, Andy Chong, project manager

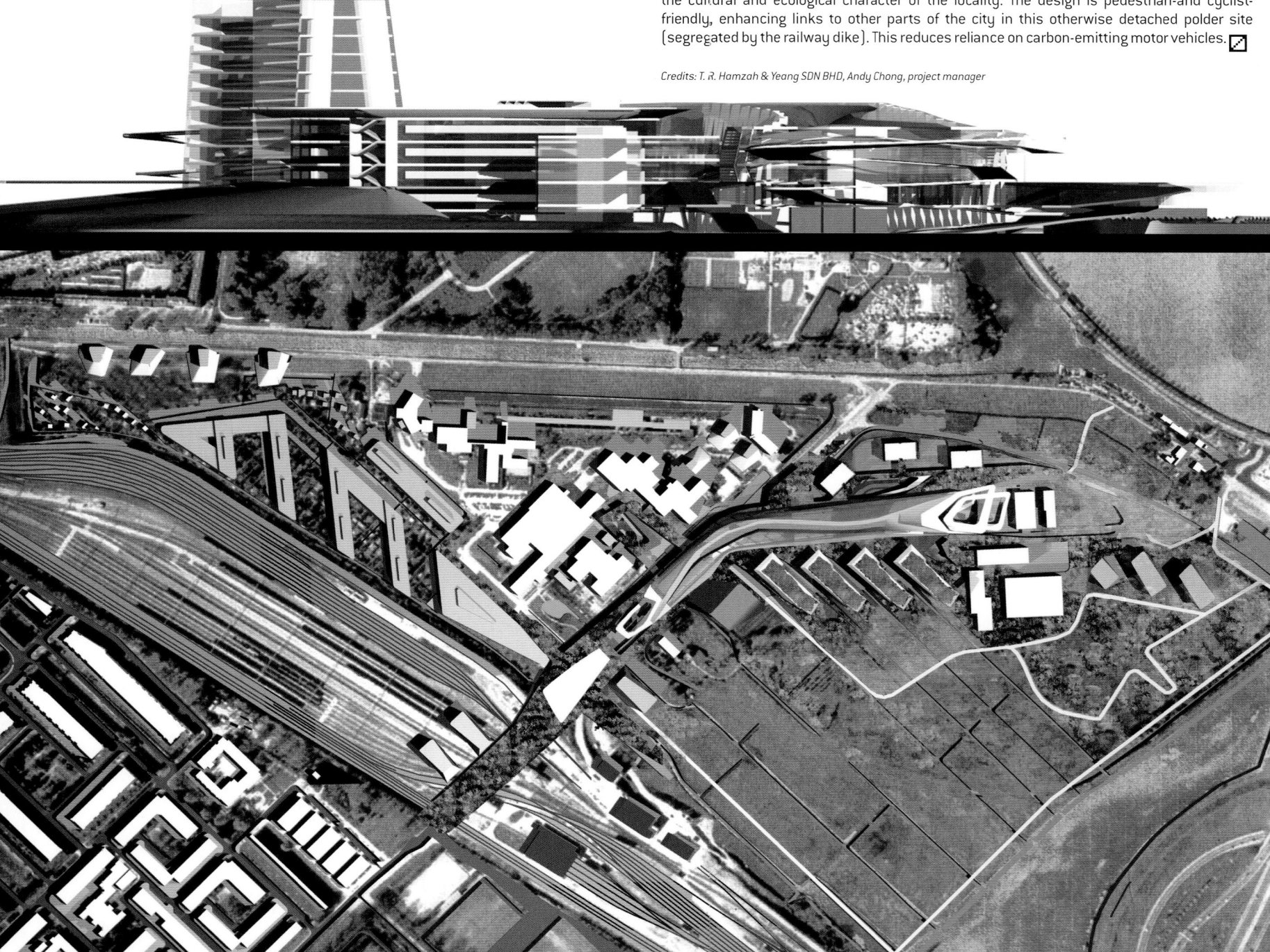

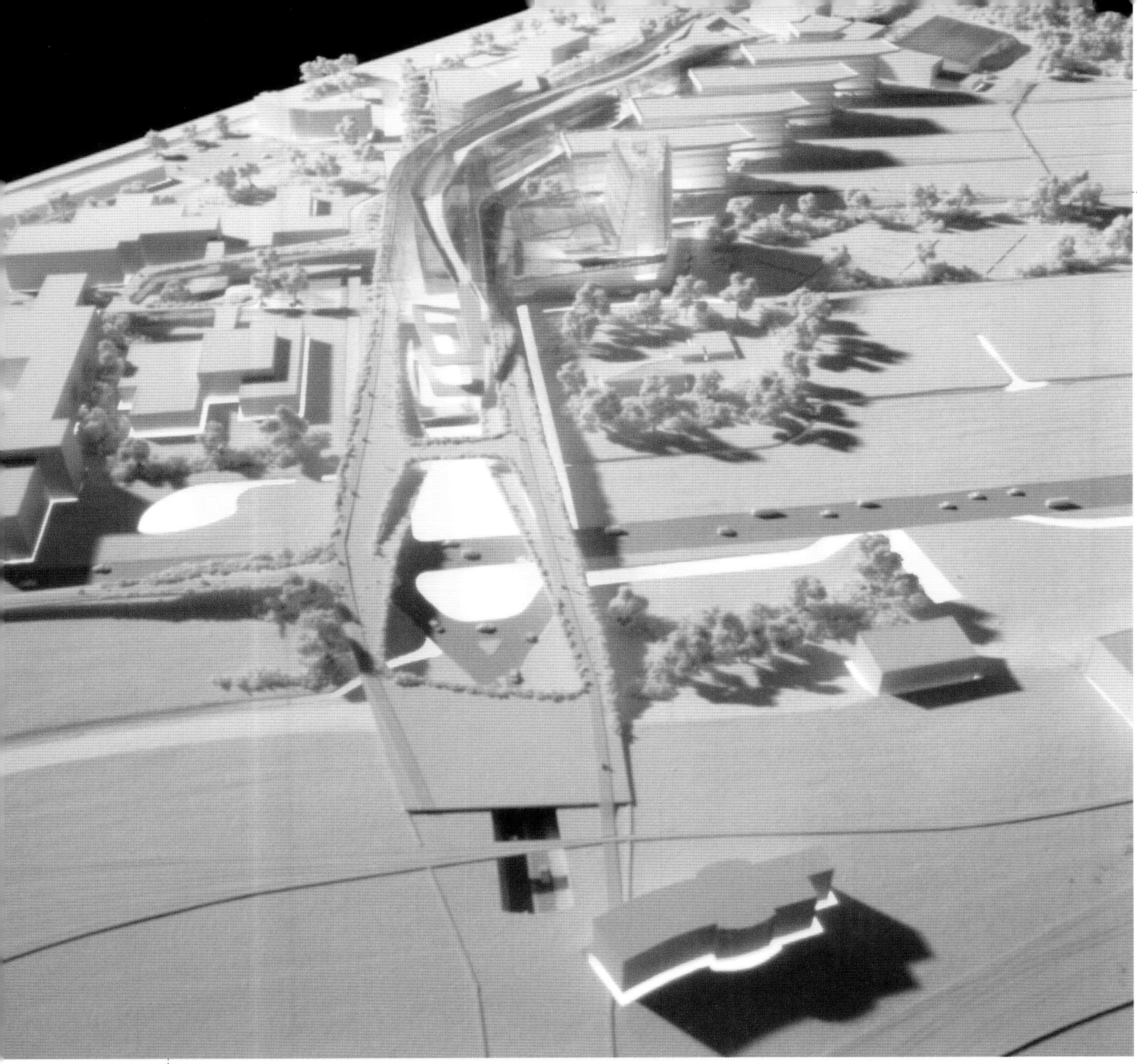

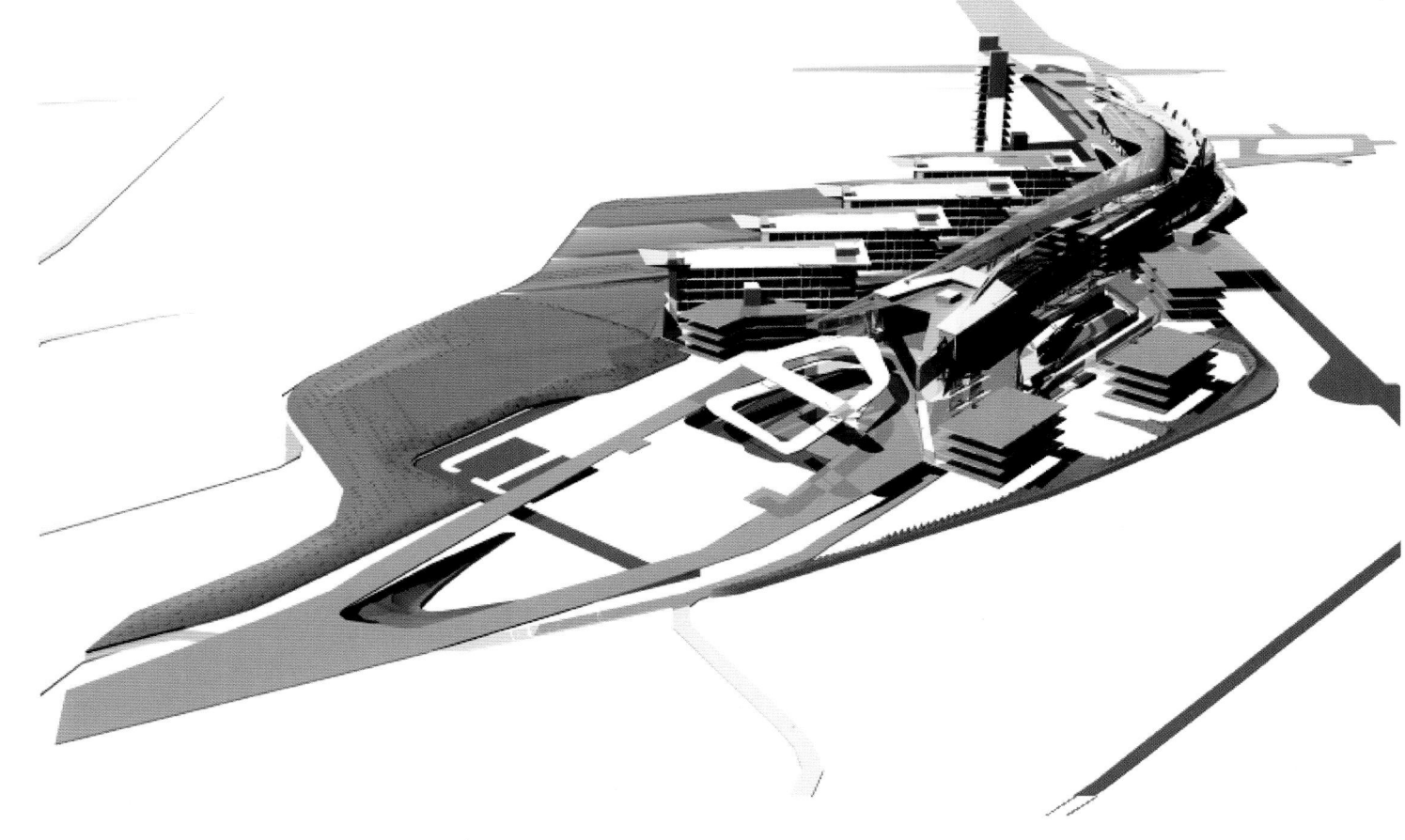

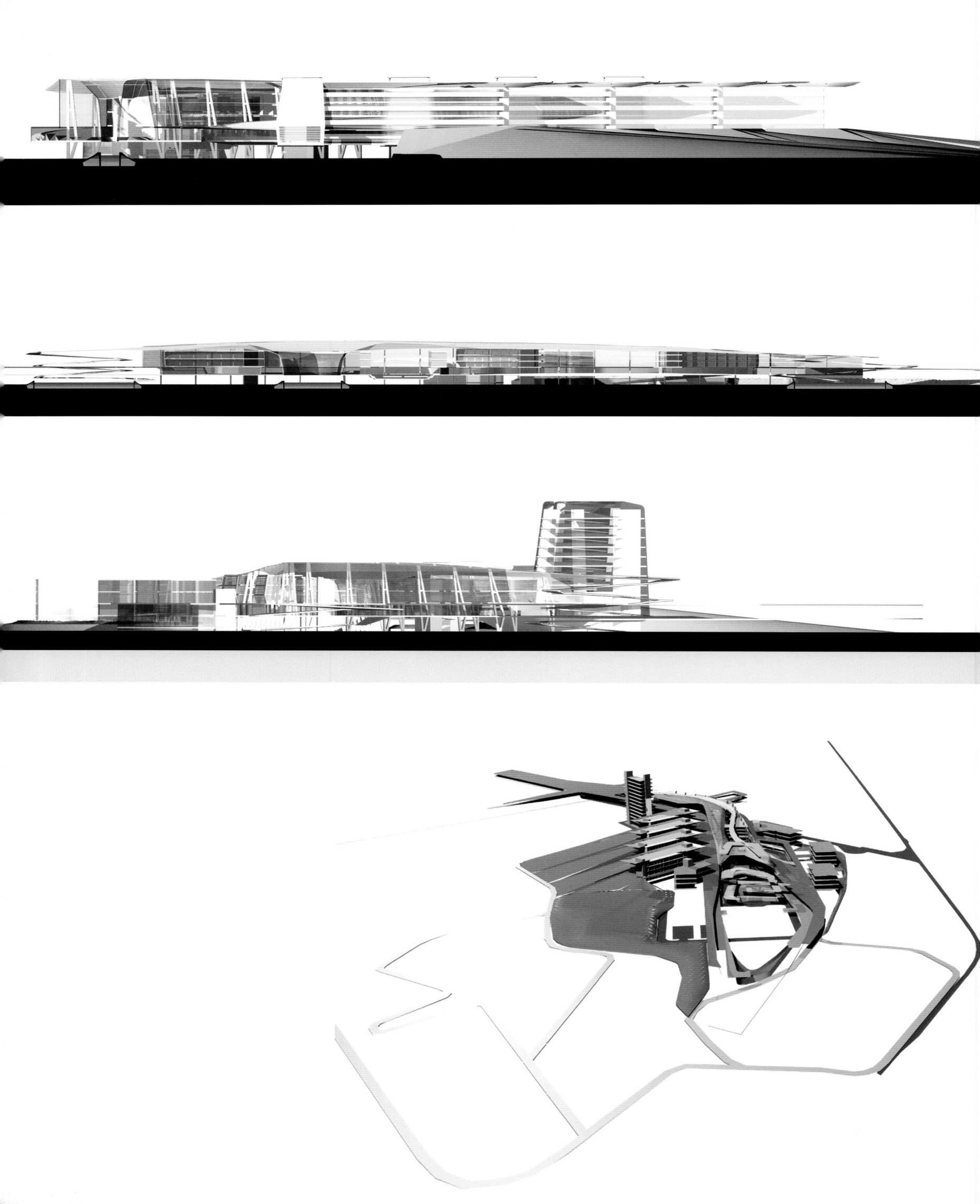

ALAIN RENK: HOST/R+P

France

Alain Renk [1962]

In 1987, while still a student, Alain Renk and the Argentinian Marcelo Joulia set up the 'Naço' studio. With many publications and exhibitions to its credit (winner of the Albums de la Jeune Architecture, 1991), the work of this Parisian agency explores the intersecting paths of architecture, design and set and graphic design. As a new step in a radical reappraisal of the whole profession, Alain Renk created a new structure in 2000: Host/R+P, with which he seeks to redefine the place and the role of architecture in a general ecology of the contemporary world. Viewing the latter as a kind of ecosystem whose invisible topography needs to be understood, he uses the theme of the complex town to explore three lines of research, three particular, interdependent factors that influence the transformation of territories: work (chill-out space), commerce (monetic space) and politics (stealth space). In this context architecture should not propose forms that imitate the complexity of the world, but instead offer hybrid processes, transversal strategies that reveal its intelligibility. ☑

Chic Pragmatism The architect tries to find his way along the crest of a mountain. Yesterday he was still tempted to reinvent the world and to adopt the pose of the demiurge with dangerous good intentions. Today the market economy has been promoted to the rank of a new nature. The architect, resigned but then fascinated, is in danger of toppling into a plastic pragmatism, which may extend from contextualism to cynicism.

Main stream How and why should one create a new architecture agency today? To practice what? To fight against the world's simplistic visions, in which architecture and urbanism are heavily involved by their standardization of territory – this might be sufficient motive. The reason still to believe in architecture would therefore be one of hollowness, of tension, of resistance rather than one of emergence. In fact, one needs time to make new tools.

Opportunities There are no opportunities. Only the urgent need to defy the arbitrary and to favour chance. And a subject: to take account of new forms of human establishments (towns? networks?) that might open up different futures

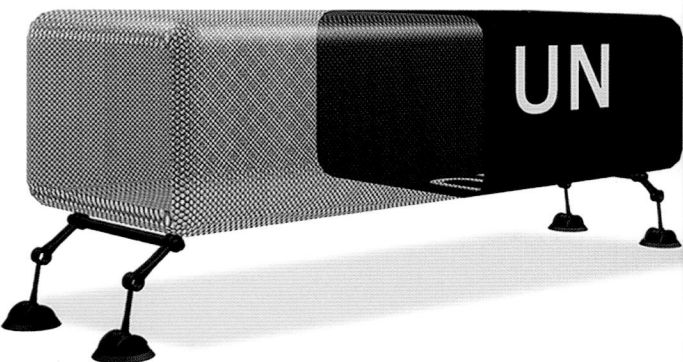

under different conditions. What is there after the suburb of the suburb? How is one to direct the aleatory producer of liberty?

Mental architecture Answer these questions. Can architecture act on our mental space (bring it to light)? Or, to be more precise, can architecture offer us a greater capacity to take account of the world and to act on it? Can architecture and urbanism favour autonomy to the detriment of programmed behaviour? Can they help us to escape from simulacra that are not ours? To combine singularity and solidarity?

Experimentation To propose a laboratory open to partners from outside the world of architecture, in order to exchange problems and to find a way through the complexity. The strategic heart of the Host agency has from the very start consisted of seven people who work in different worlds: scientific research on chaos, programming video games, luxury marketing, making cultural documentaries, humanitarian geopolitics, branding strategies and artistic management for fashion. ☑

Alain Renk

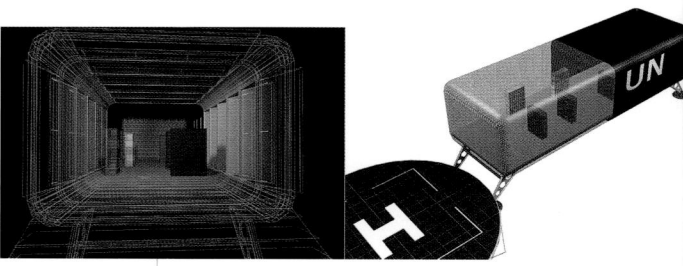

The Complex Town

Glossary 1

Abandon It is not the town or the territories that must be abandoned because of their unpredictable conduct, but determinist, linear thinking, which ignores possibilities of adjustment and feedback.

Analysis Paradoxically, to comprehend territory as an ecosystem, where social, intellectual and environmental thinking are interdependent, leads to segmentation. It is necessary to isolate elements in order to identify systems of relationships and grasp the forces of transformation that are at work in reality.

Complex The world has not become more complex with the development of new technologies. It is our methods of explaining and hence of conceiving the world through extreme divisions and simplifications that have proven their serious inadequacy.

Control Territory does not submit to anything; it deigns to modify its evolution by absorbing or destroying the innovations laid out before it. In a dynamic process, it should be possible at all times to influence developments by shifting the innovations or by regulating their powers of attraction.

Sustainable development Experience shows that nobody can predict the consequences of his or her actions, because every action sets off other actions that change the original circumstances. This is even more true in the context of territory. One must act by proposing solutions that will integrate the possibility of radical developments in all contexts.

Glossary 2

Future It is not a question of designing the future, but of constructing tools that will be suitable for developing territories.

Legitimacy Ensuring that the territory is developed strategically (defined beforehand through democratic procedures) means simultaneously offering it different sets of possibilities. One must take heed of it, develop those trends that favour the public interest and put a brake on all others.

Matrices Once one has identified the principles of transformation, it is possible to construct artificial worlds that are nourished by reality and that are theoretical matrices – a kind of generic world that can be infinitely extended and can play many roles. These include adaptation to all sorts of experiences of hybridization, permutation and combination in order to test possible variations before theory is projected into reality.

PFA The essentially structural, articulated, mobile, dynamic forms of the matrices are embodied in reality in the form of 'Prototypes of Functional Architecture' (PFA, courtesy F. Hybert). Subsequent decoding of the constructed projects naturally produces new entries, which are necessary for the improvement, accuracy and enrichment of the generic matrices.

Theory It is necessary to take one's theories out of the laboratory in order that research can make contact with reality. One must produce methods of working on the fluid material arising out of the many uncertainties of the territory.

Transformation Territory is by definition in a state of perpetual instability, perpetual transformation. The very basis of it is in motion. It is necessary to delve into the processes of transformation rather than invent foundations. ◩

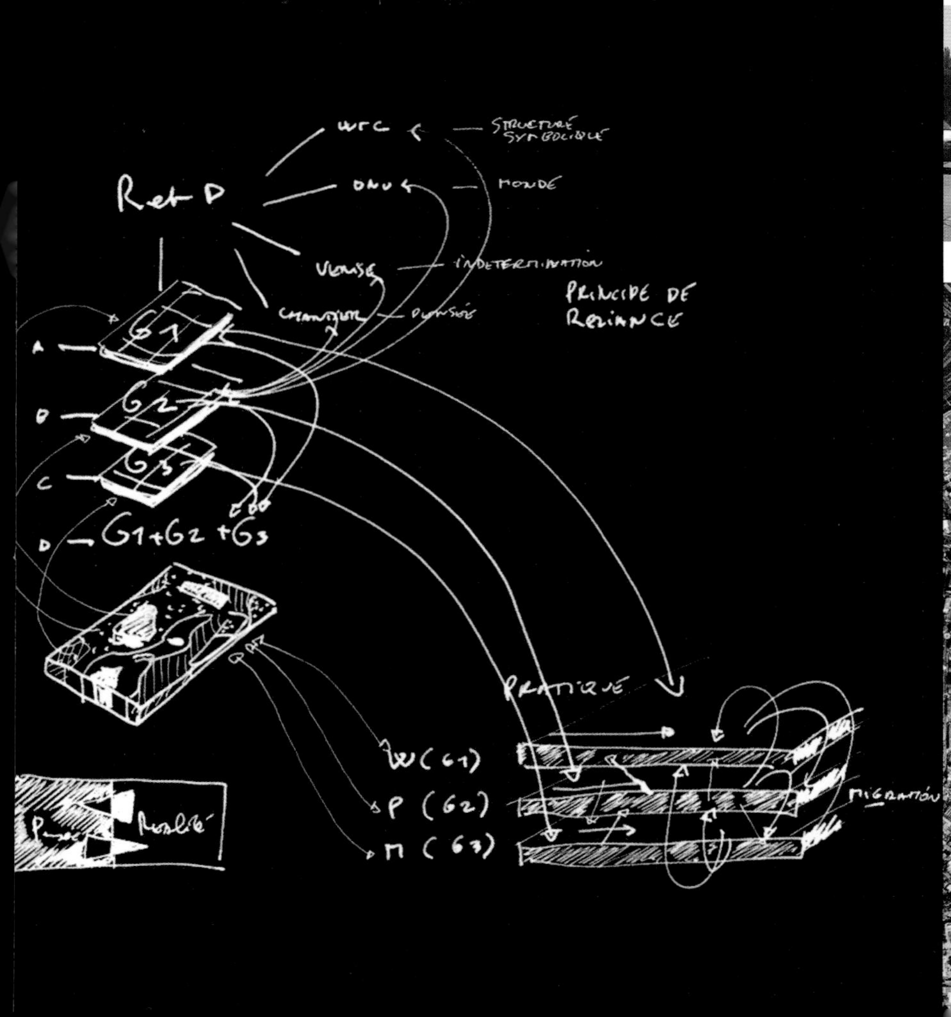

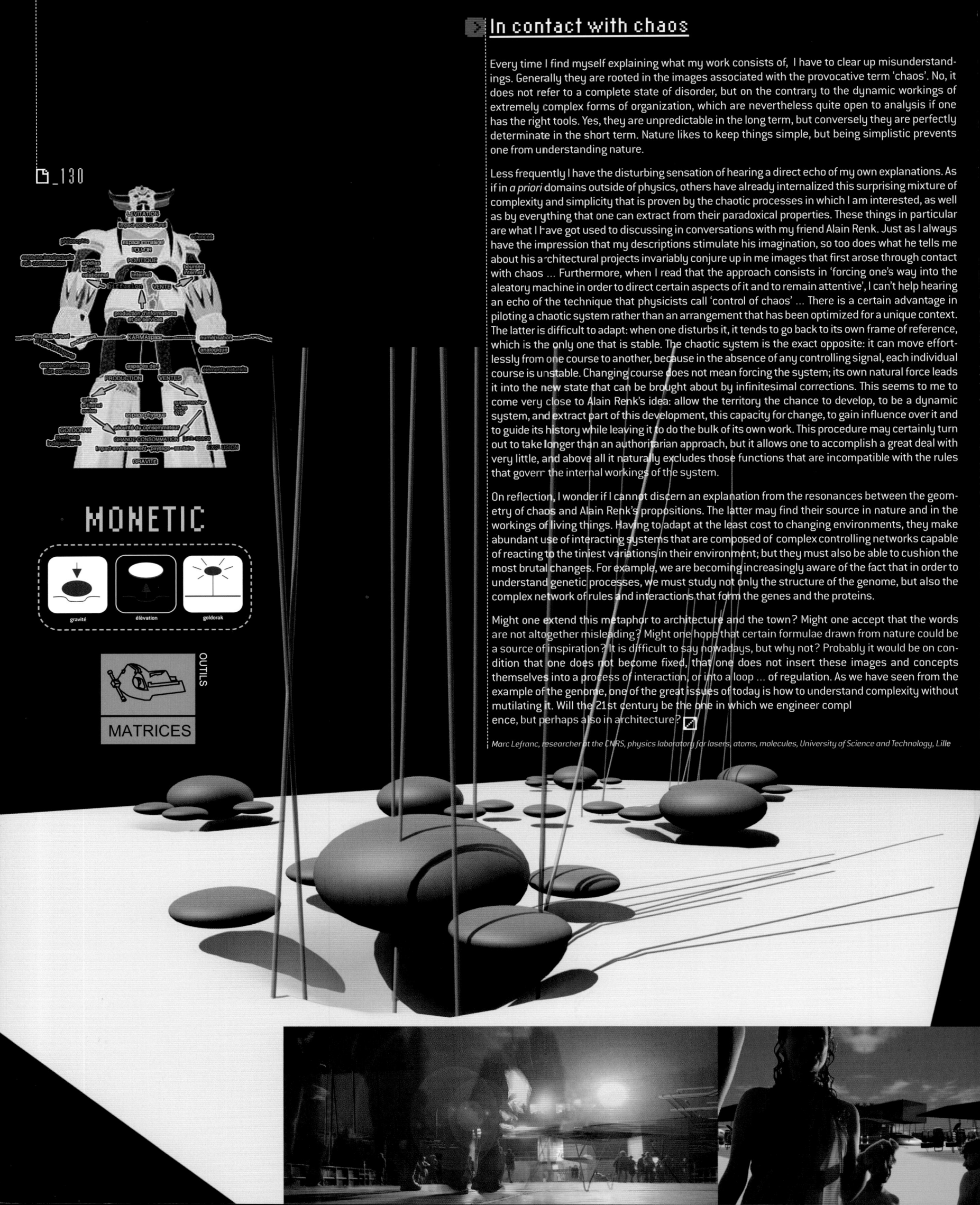

In contact with chaos

Every time I find myself explaining what my work consists of, I have to clear up misunderstandings. Generally they are rooted in the images associated with the provocative term 'chaos'. No, it does not refer to a complete state of disorder, but on the contrary to the dynamic workings of extremely complex forms of organization, which are nevertheless quite open to analysis if one has the right tools. Yes, they are unpredictable in the long term, but conversely they are perfectly determinate in the short term. Nature likes to keep things simple, but being simplistic prevents one from understanding nature.

Less frequently I have the disturbing sensation of hearing a direct echo of my own explanations. As if in *a priori* domains outside of physics, others have already internalized this surprising mixture of complexity and simplicity that is proven by the chaotic processes in which I am interested, as well as by everything that one can extract from their paradoxical properties. These things in particular are what I have got used to discussing in conversations with my friend Alain Renk. Just as I always have the impression that my descriptions stimulate his imagination, so too does what he tells me about his architectural projects invariably conjure up in me images that first arose through contact with chaos ... Furthermore, when I read that the approach consists in 'forcing one's way into the aleatory machine in order to direct certain aspects of it and to remain attentive', I can't help hearing an echo of the technique that physicists call 'control of chaos' ... There is a certain advantage in piloting a chaotic system rather than an arrangement that has been optimized for a unique context. The latter is difficult to adapt: when one disturbs it, it tends to go back to its own frame of reference, which is the only one that is stable. The chaotic system is the exact opposite: it can move effortlessly from one course to another, because in the absence of any controlling signal, each individual course is unstable. Changing course does not mean forcing the system; its own natural force leads it into the new state that can be brought about by infinitesimal corrections. This seems to me to come very close to Alain Renk's idea: allow the territory the chance to develop, to be a dynamic system, and extract part of this development, this capacity for change, to gain influence over it and to guide its history while leaving it to do the bulk of its own work. This procedure may certainly turn out to take longer than an authoritarian approach, but it allows one to accomplish a great deal with very little, and above all it naturally excludes those functions that are incompatible with the rules that govern the internal workings of the system.

On reflection, I wonder if I cannot discern an explanation from the resonances between the geometry of chaos and Alain Renk's propositions. The latter may find their source in nature and in the workings of living things. Having to adapt at the least cost to changing environments, they make abundant use of interacting systems that are composed of complex controlling networks capable of reacting to the tiniest variations in their environment; but they must also be able to cushion the most brutal changes. For example, we are becoming increasingly aware of the fact that in order to understand genetic processes, we must study not only the structure of the genome, but also the complex network of rules and interactions that form the genes and the proteins.

Might one extend this metaphor to architecture and the town? Might one accept that the words are not altogether misleading? Might one hope that certain formulae drawn from nature could be a source of inspiration? It is difficult to say nowadays, but why not? Probably it would be on condition that one does not become fixed, that one does not insert these images and concepts themselves into a process of interaction, or into a loop ... of regulation. As we have seen from the example of the genome, one of the great issues of today is how to understand complexity without mutilating it. Will the 21st century be the one in which we engineer compl ence, but perhaps also in architecture? ▨

Marc Lefranc, researcher at the CNRS, physics laboratory for lasers, atoms, molecules, University of Science and Technology, Lille

STEALTH

cryptage réseau disparition

CHILL OUT

dégel fractal dynamique

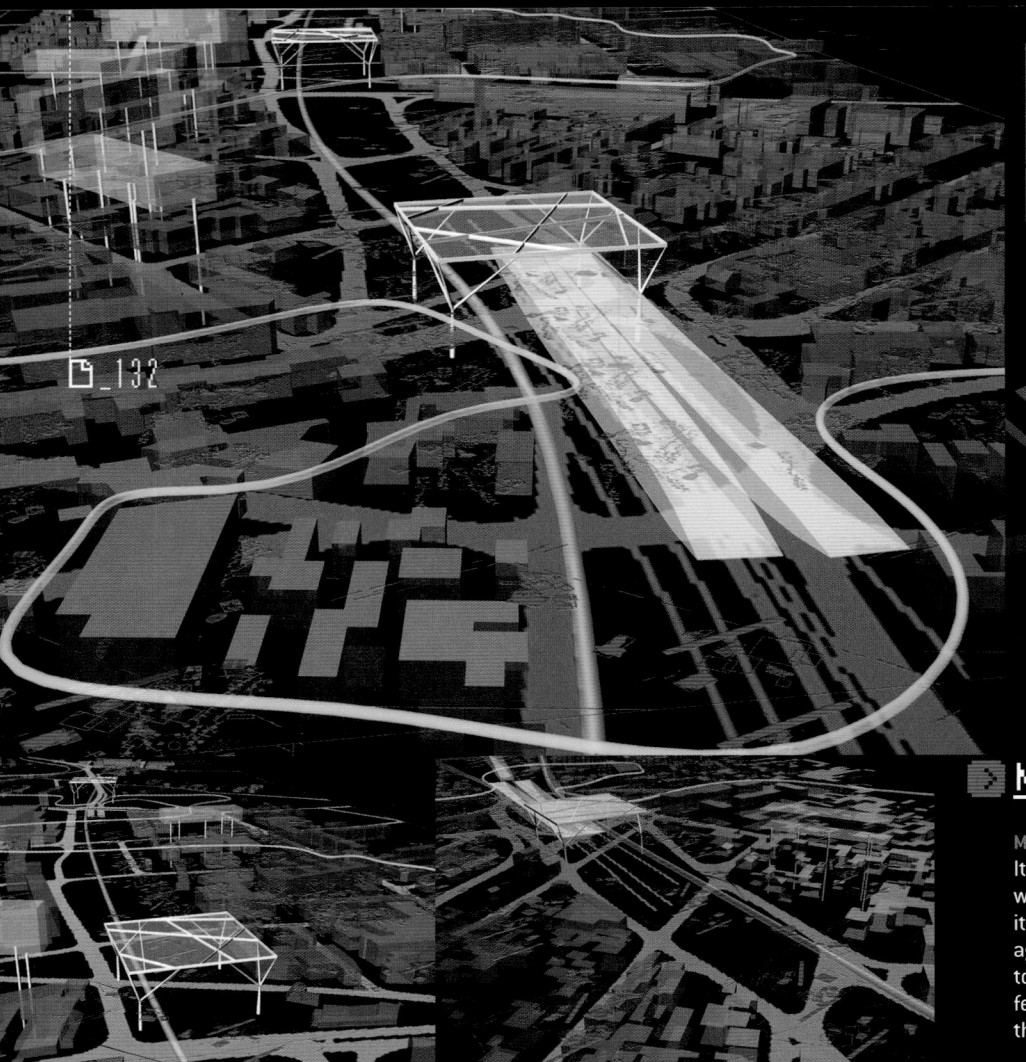

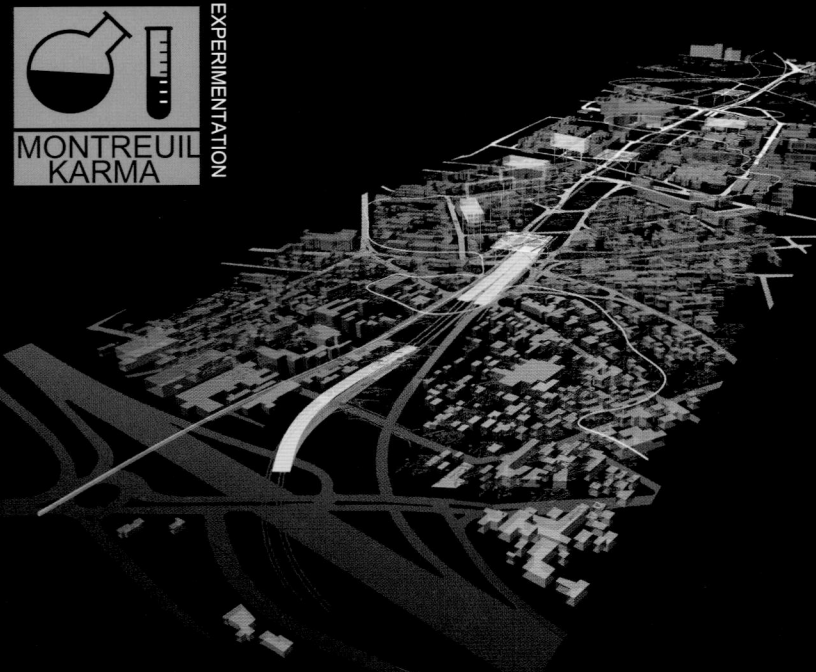

EXPERIMENTATION

MONTREUIL KARMA

Montreuil Karma

Motorway Accident

It is vital to inscribe into reality the primary theoretical principles of the complex town, which will enable us to work out strategies to inhabit the world with all its complications, its degrees of order and disorder, its surprises, its advances and its setbacks. Our agency is in Montreuil, and the town-planning department has told us the strange history of a motorway bridge constructed during the 1970s, which is to be demolished in a few years' time. How is the town to be reconstructed, and is it necessary to reconstruct the town?

Five key dates

End of the 1960s: Motorway A 186 is approved in the regional planning programme
During the 1970s, the A186 is partially built
1994: the idea of a junction between the A3 and the A86 via the A186 is abandoned
1994: the principle of an intersuburban route is approved
1999: registration of 12th contract with l'Ile de France
2000: Vote on 12th contract with l'Ile de France

Five key numbers

Total area of territory: 150 hectares
Area of motorway: 9 hectares
Area affected: 300 metres on either side of the motorway
Width of motorway: 30–60 metres
Length of territory affected: 2 kilometres

Slow change

Between the oil crisis a few years after the construction of the motorway and the final decision not to extend the first section of the A186 but to transform hyperfunctionalism into surrealism, twenty years went by. It required ten more years for the decision to be taken to decommission the A186, i.e. to demolish it and replace it with a green route for trams. Was this radical change of direction for the north side of Montreuil the precursor for actions to be undertaken on a number of relics from the 1970s?

New Automation

Thirty years ago the A186 was meant to save 15 minutes' travelling time by avoiding the A3 motorway junction. The alternative solutions seemed likely to be impractical. Today, in an area that is so unstable, with suburb joining suburb, will the alternatives to an anonymous route passing through a centre of standardized buildings be understood? Will the division of the town by an empty motorway be replaced by a wall of single dwellings turning its back on the territory?

Project

To apply the strategies for complex towns. To conserve the unique side of this territory, without denying its peculiar history, but on the contrary making this difficult history into the dynamic force of the place. Not to rush into construction, but to preserve the empty spaces created by the demolition of the motorway, giving them different functions of leisure and culture directly linked to commercial and business enterprises. To disperse in the depths numerous interventions that bear witness to the implementation of these new functions, while taking a broad view that will facilitate possible future changes. To accompany the readjustments with actions to cover the whole of the territory. To make spectacular changes to some buildings that project a negative image, but not to demolish them, so that they can preserve their imprint on the landscape. ☑

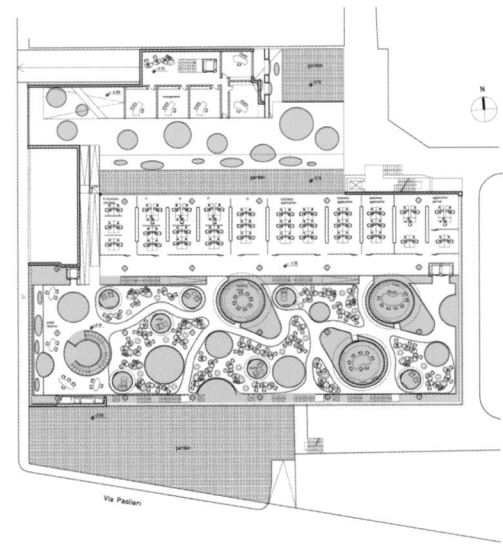

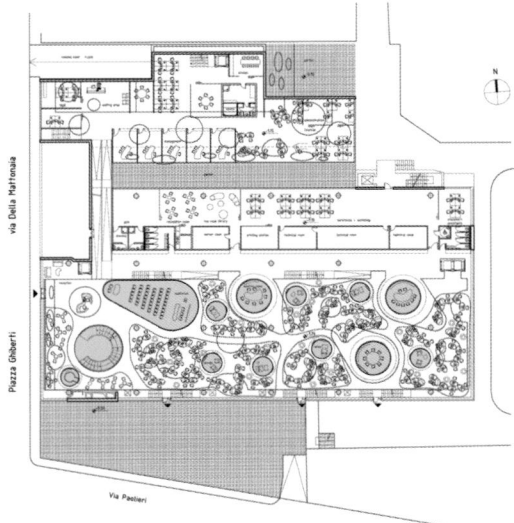

IaN+

Italy

Carmelo Baglivo [(1964)], Luca Galofaro [(1965)], Stefania Manna [(1969)]

Founded in Rome in 1997, the agency consists of a nucleus of three members around whom gravitate other experienced professionals from various disciplines. This makes IaN+ an intersection of architectural theory and practice, which is pursued at all levels from interior design to territorial projects, each one involving close scrutiny of contemporary urban conditions. At present the agency is working on a car park in Rome, several residential units, 'Tor vergata' – a building for the University of Rome – and an urban redevelopment which includes public facilities (Falcognana, Rome). At the same time, the agency is actively involved in discussions on avant-garde architecture, and the results of their research have been presented in numerous publications and exhibitions: Architopia, Biennial Utopia, in Cascais (Portugal, 2001), Earthscape, conference and expo at the technical university in Darmstadt (2001), the Venice Biennale (2000, with Futuramay2k) and the Young Artists of Europe (Rome, 1999). They regularly take part in workshops and seminars at the European Institute of Design (Rome), Milan Polytechnic, the UIC and the University of Chicago. ⊠

IN OUR CONCEPT of the new ecology, architecture plays a leading role. As an integral part of the process that transforms territories, it contributes to a radical revitalization of urbanism by bringing in project-related variables that aim to establish better relations between human institutions, nature and different areas of the town ... The role of architecture in the new ecology has many facets.

Architecture as a system of living

As a system that organizes and defines relationships and exchanges between subjects, architecture facilitates the transformation of territory. It acts according to the time, and is not closed but remains open and flexible, potentially ready to welcome change ... These relational systems affect activities, not forms, and they are retroactive, which allows self-regulation and self-organization in response to current conditions. We should not consider the town as a unique, complex territory, but as a complex system of territories active on different levels both real and virtual.

Architecture as interference with reality

Projecting relations means provoking interference, in the sense of changes to the status quo capable of giving rise to different spatial and relational arrangements ... The project becomes a place of exchange, a topological space that obeys the principle of homeomorphism – which defines geometrical figures by the relations between their elements and not by their measurements. Euclidean geometry does not take account of the qualities of a place or of the relations within it. However, every space contains different spaces, different degrees of materiality and different forms of relations and exchanges.

Architecture as intelligent recycling

Architecture goes through a definite cycle of birth, life and death. It is essential to define reasons for giving a building a new cycle, and these reasons should not merely advocate its conservation but should offer it a continuous transformation. Just like the landscape, a building is transformed by the absorption of new values, new residential contexts, appearances and separations [that are no longer] definable by conventional systems of identification.

Architecture as participation

Designing part of a town implies that at a given moment one is blocking the process by which the town itself is transformed. In the past, axes and layouts synthesized the formal theories that centralized town-planning. Today, power must be handed to the 'mob', in the sense that the consumer has to be involved.

'Architecture as a system of living' is not a new slogan but a permanent principle that has been redeveloped by a particular operational strategy known as 'mapping'. This consists not in drawing up a new plan so much as in working within the framework of an existing one, in order to create new lines of development or to use whatever is already there. For us, a project is not an object in a place but rather a field of relations that one expects to integrate within a context.

Each project consists of three basic elements: the forces at work, the zones and the interzones. Analysis of flows and activities localizes the zones. The borders between the zones are transformed into relational interzones, whereas the interzones of exchange emerge from the superimposition of zones. Models of projects that do

not waste energy, the interzones are a sort of web that can adapt itself to every possible transformation that can take place in urban spaces. The concept of transformation, which aims to improve the quality of daily life, entails that of participation, either institutionalized or spontaneous, and this can even go so far as to modify a project after it has been completed. This is why we might call architecture an 'auto-eco-organized' system: it is a discipline which, at one and the same time, is autonomous and dependent, with multiple applications that are themselves autonomous and dependent. By avoiding abstraction, architecture is thus in a position to anticipate future disturbances. ⊠

IaN+

DADA Head Office

Florence, Italy, competition, 2002

A 'society of the new economy' announced a competition to design its headquarters in Florence. This was an opportunity for IaN+ to rethink the typology of the working space. The industrial concept of separate offices is well suited to a hierarchical work structure, but when there is a 'network' structure, this has to be replaced by a social space; project teams working together — continually exchanging information, expertise and experience — need open spaces that will facilitate direct communication and enable employees to move about freely. Architecture therefore becomes essential to good management, and must give visible form to the structure of the company. Knowing that a comfortable ambience is conducive to improved exchanges of information and the spontaneous generation of ideas, New Economy requires its offices to be a hybrid between conventional work and recreation. Sauna, table tennis, massage facilities and Zen gardens supplement the more traditional units of production. IaN+ proposes the following: work space + domestic space = DADA space, based on three main concepts. First, reversibility makes the old, over-repetitive 'flexibility' obsolete; DADA space must be constantly changeable and open to inversion according to the balance required at different stages of work. Second, permeability replaces the concept of transparency, because in DADA space it is not solely a matter of vision but also of movement between activities: each zone must allow different degrees of permeability, different degrees of contact. Finally, transformability, because as it grows, DADA space must be capable of complete transformation, which is possible only through a 'saturated void'. The project therefore proposes new forms of open space in which two-dimensional elements of separation between work zones are replaced by three-dimensional, rounded elements that separate and unite at the same time: on different scales, they will enrich the work space by accommodating leisure activities, meetings, private work, exchanges of information, etc. The open space may also expand vertically through variable circular openings that will connect the two main levels of work space. The expansion of the building will create an artificial landscape in the form of terraces meant for open-air events. ⧄

Credits: IaN+ — Carmelo Baglivo, Luca Galofaro, Laura Negrini; engineering consultant — Stefania Manna; models — Marco Galofaro

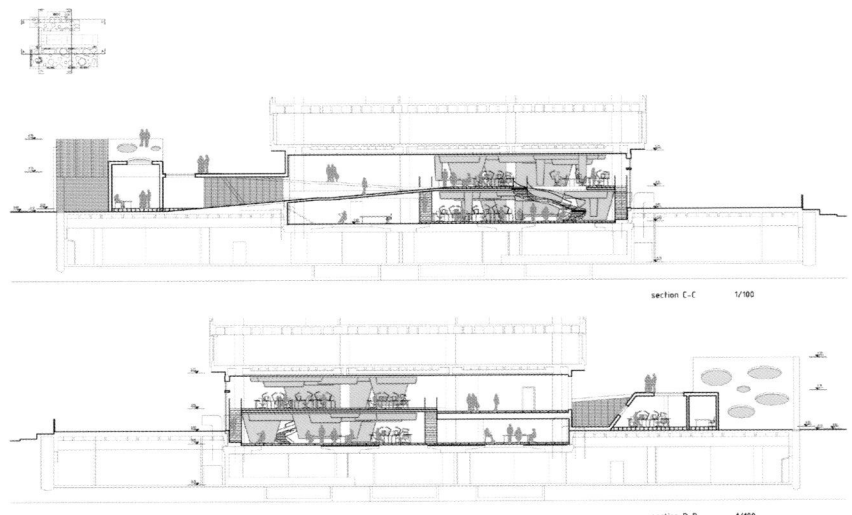

section C-C   1/100

section D-D   1/100

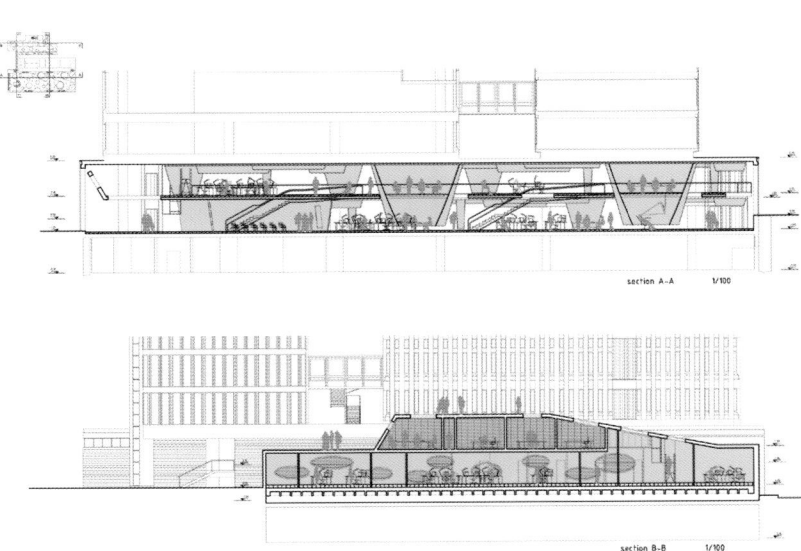

section A-A   1/100

section B-B   1/100

Tomhiro Museum of Shi-Ga

Azuma Village, Japan, competition, 2001

The purpose of this museum project is to create ideal conditions for appreciating art in a modern architectural setting. The subject of the exhibition is the special art of *shi-ga*, which combines poetry and watercolours. To be more precise, it is the work of M. Hoshino, one of whose favourite themes was the countryside around the village of Azuma. The clarity of his drawings and the power of the landscapes he depicted are the fundamental elements that the architecture must express. Beehive-shaped glass prisms suspended above a garden constitute the main structure that IaN+ proposes. Some of the prisms are hollow and these are empty rooms crossed by suspended passages that give a view on to the garden below. Their dimensions are closely linked to the time the visitors will spend in each of them. The glass bricks that form the walls of the exhibition rooms allow in the light from the countryside around. The diffused rays give one a feeling of time passing and of the cycle of the seasons, creating a natural harmony between the poems and the outside world. The garden, which enables one directly to experience the landscape of Azuma before visiting the exhibition, is an integral part of the museum; it represents the point of contact between the natural and the artificial. One enters the museum itself via a ramp. Rest areas and patios decorated with the flowers of the season alternate with the exhibition rooms. These are of two kinds: the big ones allow the visitor to take his or her time gazing at a unique work of art, while the little rooms display videos, photographs, objects and writings. Several functional rooms on the top floor complete the museum: a room for the study of *shi-ga* art, a lecture room, offices, the archives and a small library. All the areas for storage and equipment are below the garden, so that the temperature can easily be regulated to a degree of humidity that will protect the works. Thanks to its construction typology of aggregated units, the new museum will be able to expand in later years according to requirements, until it fills all the space at its disposal. ☑

Credits: IaN+ – Carmelo Baglivo, Luca Galofaro; models – Marco Galofaro

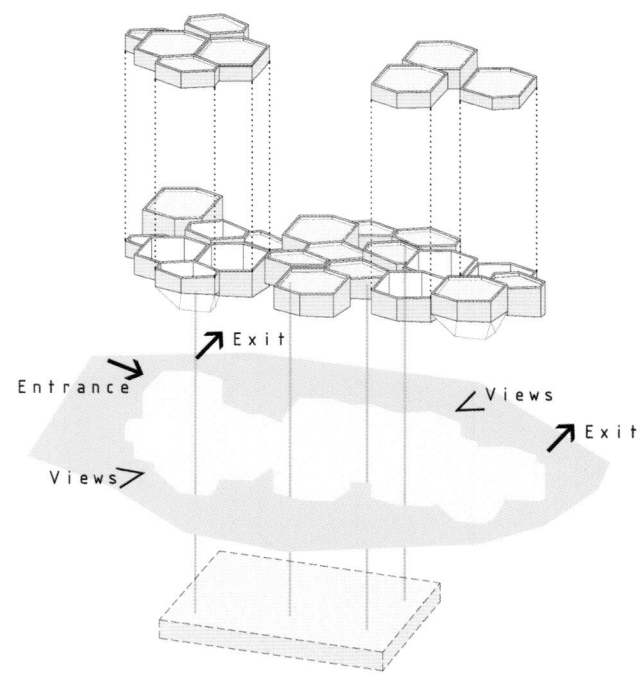

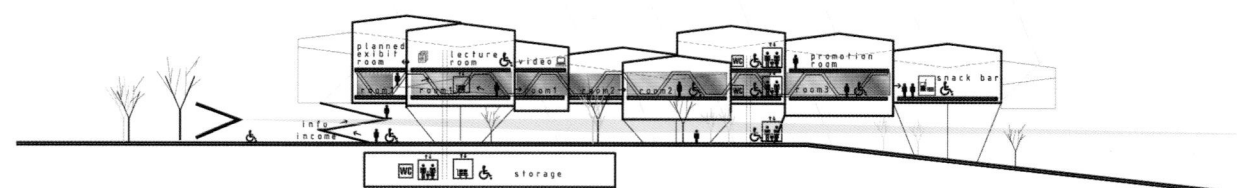

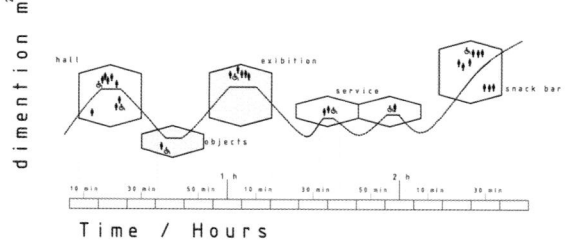

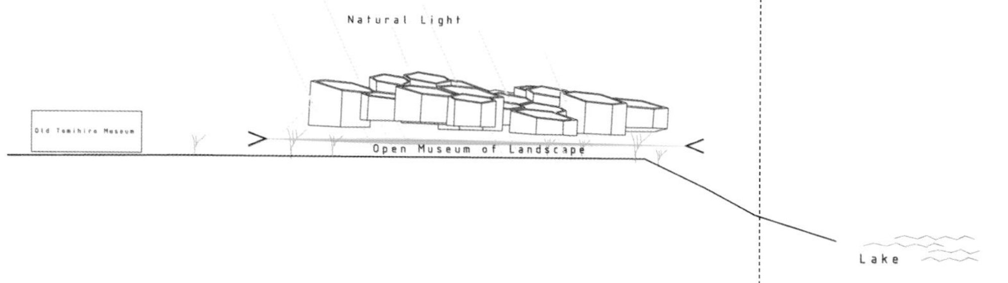

Natural Light

Old Tomihiro Museum

Open Museum of Landscape

Lake

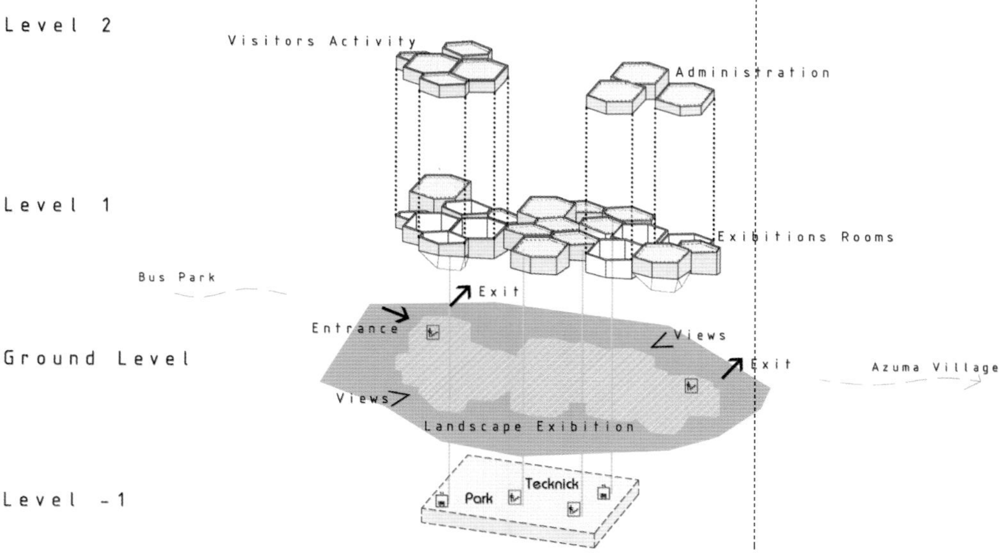

Level 2

Visitors Activity

Administration

Level 1

Exibitions Rooms

Bus Park

Exit

Entrance

Ground Level

Views

Exit

Azuma Village

Views

Landscape Exibition

Level -1

Park   Tecknick

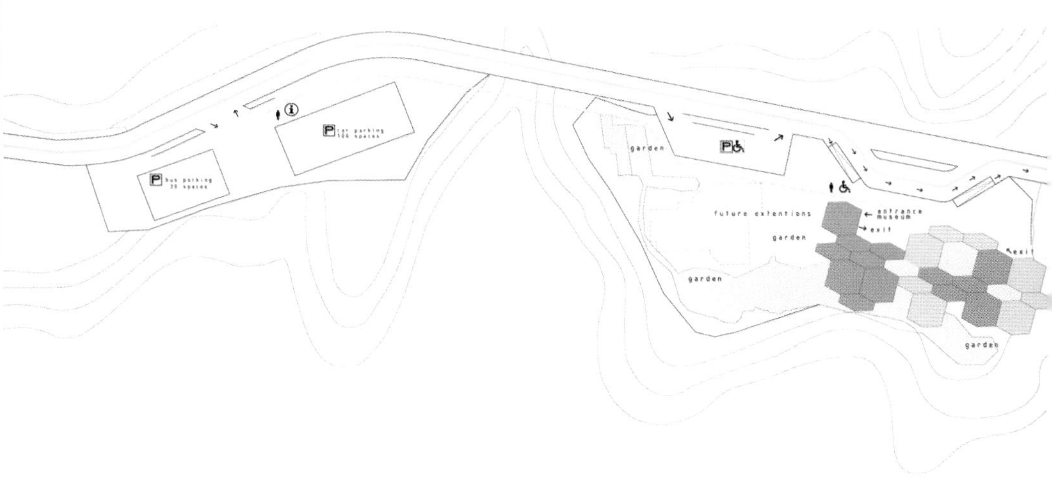

bus parking
20 spaces

car parking
100 spaces

garden

future extentions

entrance
museum

exit

garden

garden

exit

garden

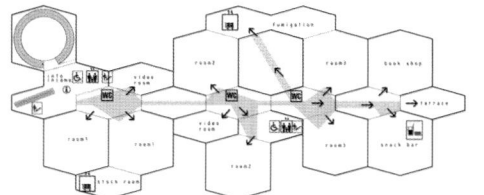

first level MUSEUM

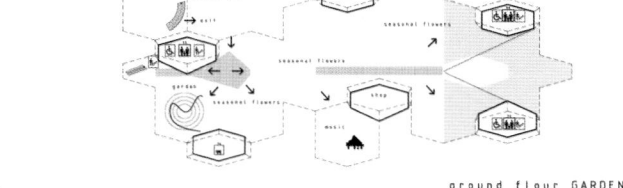

ground flour GARDEN

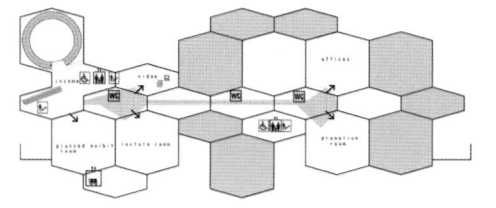

second level FACILITIES

Falcognana Urban Space
Rome, Italy, 2001–03

This project is part of the Rome Council's programme for the renovation and redevelopment of the suburbs. Falcognana is a working-class suburb, which developed spontaneously in the 1960s around various agricultural concerns. The project is to redevelop an intermediate zone on the borders of an irregular but densely populated residential area, along with new buildings to service the quarter and a zone of countryside where some of the hillsides consist of fields still under cultivation. The objectives set out by the Council, together with residents' associations, are, first, to maintain the natural character of the area; second, to construct a public, urban space that will update the district and accommodate all the residents' leisure activities; finally, to draw up a programme extending beyond the project itself that will ensure the use, development and adaptation of this area over the years. To achieve this, IaN+ set out to evaluate the environmental systems and to find minimal solutions of continuity between densely populated urban spaces and open spaces; the empty areas, the enclosed zones and the hillsides will become the strategic sites for this ecological conversion of the territory. The project is therefore shaped round possible connections between the different heights of the terrain, which vary in total by nine metres. The proposed system will be on three levels. At the top, IaN+ will use some of the agricultural land for sport and other recreational activities, and will excavate part of the hill to house two public service buildings – a retirement home and a multipurpose hall – conceived as sections of the natural complex. The guiding principle here is hybridization along various lines: usage, sociability and sensitivity to the different spatial elements. The whole thing is a kind of envelope, an all-embracing space in which the continuous system linking exterior and interior departs from all traditional residential systems. This is a comprehensive form of architecture, in which the superimposition of plans is replaced by the continuity of surfaces. A system of ramps ensures a smooth transition to the landscape. IaN+ sees architecture as a method of regenerating the town, not by means of form but by a process of dynamic evolution that will transform the landscape into territory. ◨

Credits: IaN+ – Carmelo Baglivo, Luca Galofaro, Laura Federici

Car Park
Nuovo Salario, Rome, competition, 2001

This competition, won by IaN+, was for a car park in a green area between a residential quarter, a regional railway line and two hills. The site, which turned out to be the last green space of any significance within an urban fringe, gave IaN+ the opportunity to redevelop part of a typical Roman landscape by setting in motion a process of 'territorialization'. This involved reassessing the context and paying special attention to its identity, its aesthetic qualities and its social, economic and cultural complexity. While the car park is the starting-point of the process, in time the whole area will be transformed, with its own capacity for self-presentation and reproduction. The building planned is an infrastructure to control the various flows between the railway, the car park, the park and the residential area. It is also conceived as an extension of the railway embankments – whose line it follows – and of the road, which is a vital artery of the town; it is an interface between two different environments, the natural and the artificial, which regulate accessibility and movement. It will allow rapid development to cope with all the changes that may occur in road and rail transport as well as for pedestrians. Vehicles will move along a continuous circuit, which doubles back on itself and passes between the railway and the building; this controls the flow, protects the park from road traffic and restores continuity to the natural landscape by uniting the two existing hills. The roof is an extension of the station's main platform and becomes a large esplanade overlooking the park. Permeability is also achieved by the three-dimensional structure of the façade, which constitutes the two sides of the car park. Of varying thickness, it is composed of hollow hexagonal blocks, with gaps that become a connecting system between the different spaces. The building thus produces a field of relations whose range of activities is sufficient to draw in and elicit reactions from everything around it, thus setting off a process of self-generation and diversification of activities, which, in the long term, could solve several problems within this urban fringe. And so the 'border' of the town is no longer viewed as a place where things finish, but rather as a line where things begin to acquire a new dimension. ◪

Credits: IaN+ – Carmelo Baglivo, Luca Galofaro, Laura Negrini; models – Marco Galofaro

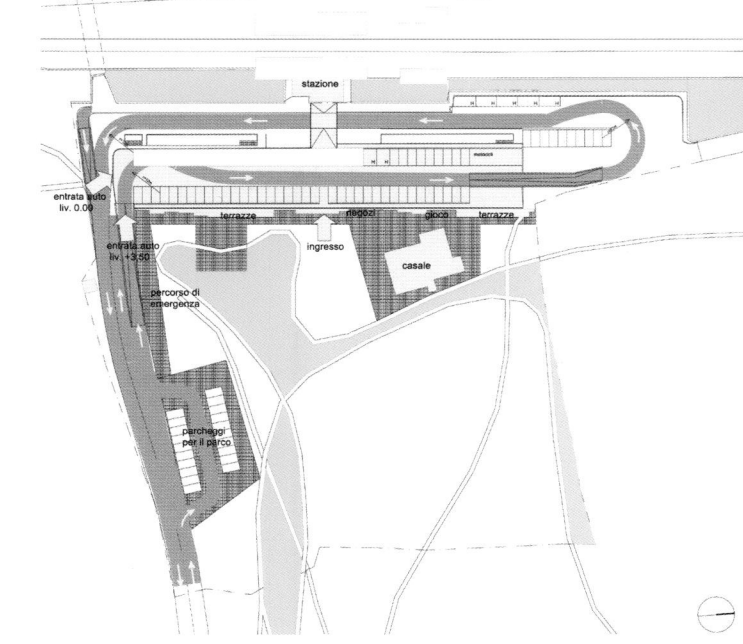

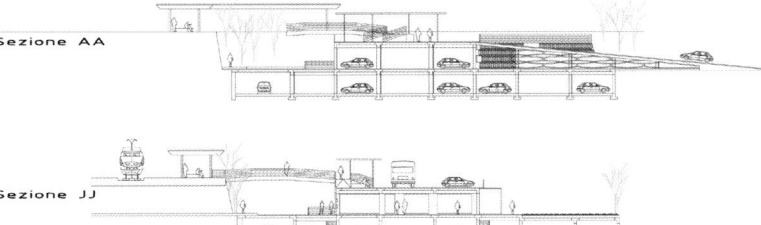

Sezione AA

Sezione JJ

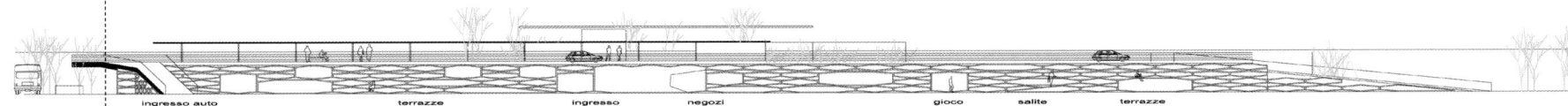

ingresso auto   terrazze   ingresso   negozi   gioco   salite   terrazze

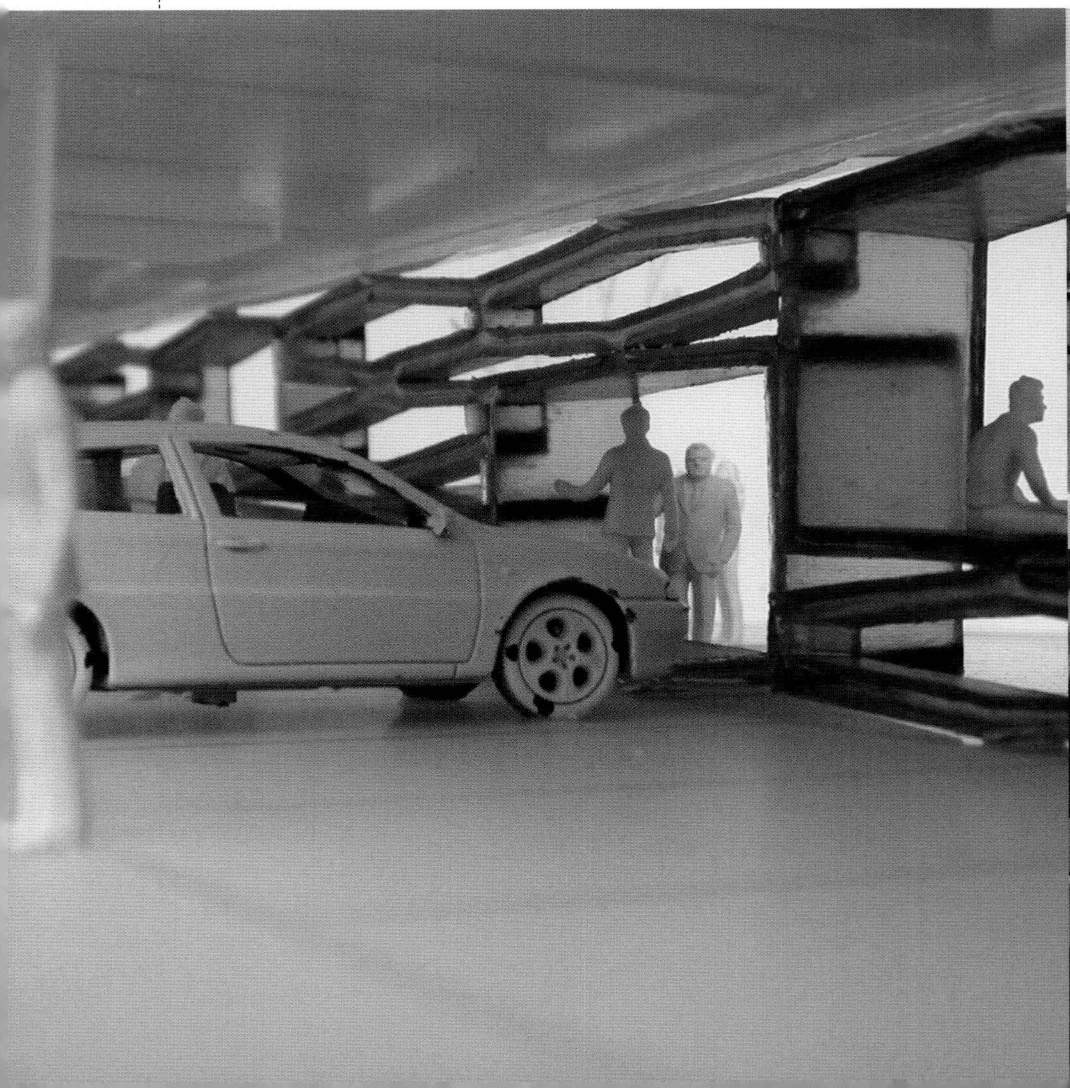

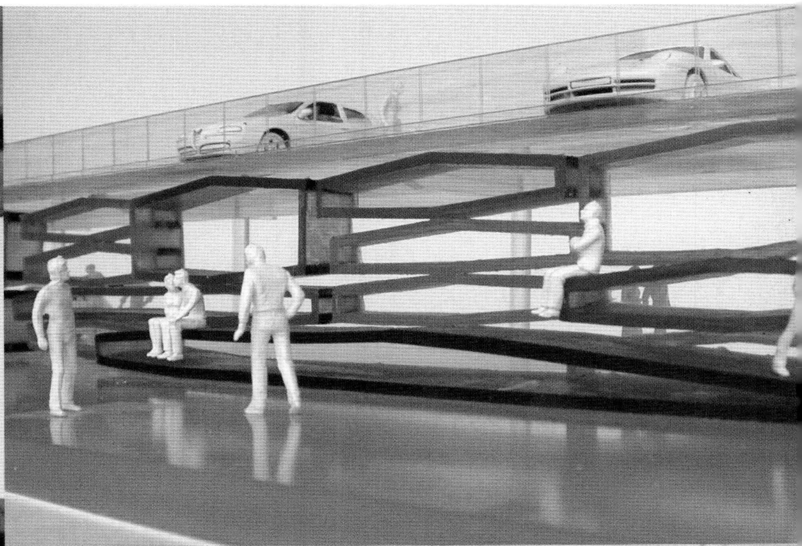

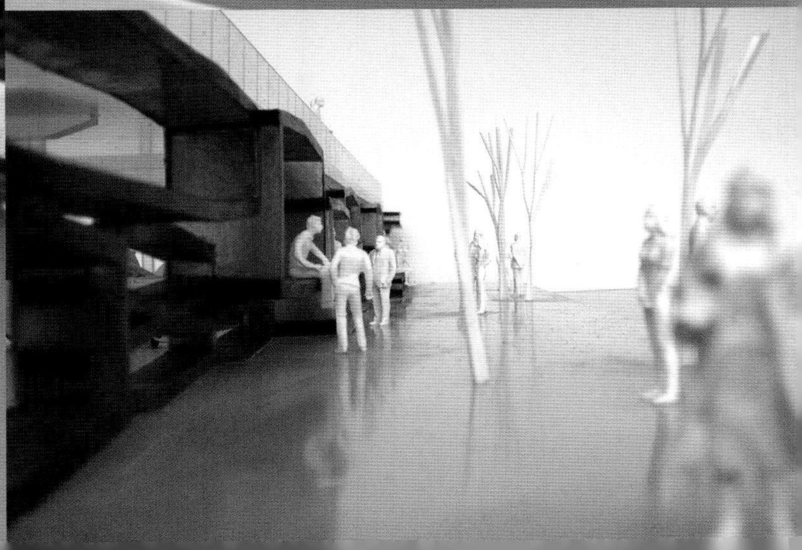

JONES, PARTNERS: ARCHITECTURE

United States

Wesley Jones [(1958)]

A graduate of West Point Military Academy and of the University of California at Berkeley, Wes Jones obtained his masters degree in architecture from the GSD at Harvard University in 1983. Winner of a prize from the American Academy in Rome (1985), he founded an agency two years later, in association with Holt, Hinshaw and Pfau. His own agency followed in 1993, first in San Francisco and then in Los Angeles. Jones, Partners: Architecture is a small, full-service, California-based architectural practice dedicated to the rapprochement between humanity and the machine. J, P: A has earned an international reputation for the design of engaging, technologically intense environments. J, P: A considers each project prototypical and takes very seriously the corresponding responsibility for it to be both exemplary and realistic, eschewing a personal, 'signature-driven' design 'style' in favour of a more sociopolitically generous, performance-driven material practice. J, P: A has been involved in a wide range of ambitious, award-winning projects all over the world, from residences and office buildings to corporate offices, national memorials and power plants. ☑

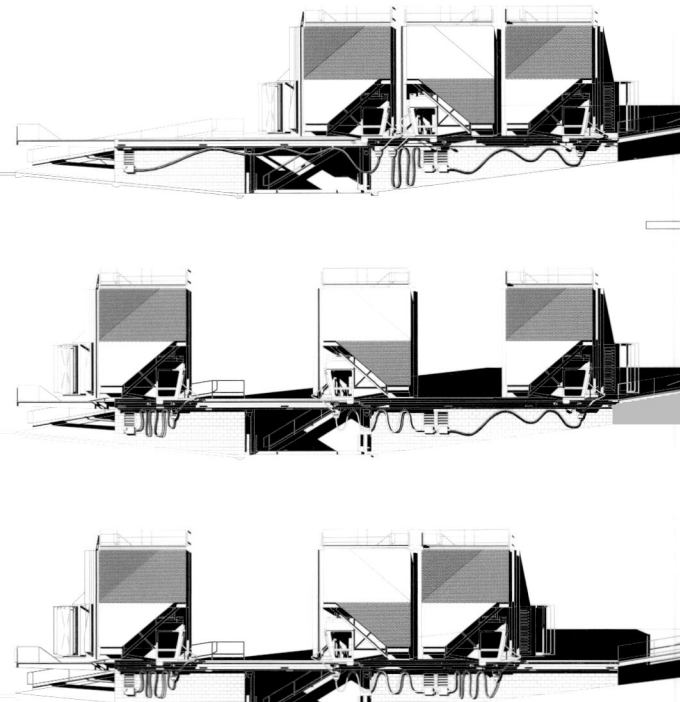

ECONOMICS and ecology are linked, operationally and structurally, by the general technological spirit that underlies and animates our civilization. Architecture's challenge today is to determine an appropriate and truly productive relationship to this essential reality. This issue must be addressed at two levels: that at which architecture is itself an example of technology, and that at which architecture bears a responsibility towards expression – within a culture that is now more or less completely determined by technology. The first approaches technology as a means, which is not the simple tautology it seems, since architecture's relationship to its means is complex. The second addresses technology as a subject for representation—which itself is of course complicated by the debate about the status of representation in architecture today.

It is expected that architecture's *instrumental* interest in technology would be in areas that could enhance architecture's specific capabilities. Architecture is an instance of technology, after all: it is continuous with technology, and so it fits into the regime of efficiency and progress that paces technological evolution. The technologies that interest most advanced practices these days, though, are not those that serve the expected social, structural or enclosure programmes but those that challenge them, either offering critical insights or unforeseen advantages. Such practices hope for the sort of collateral benefits and technological transfers that spun off tang™ and the Internet from the space programme and military. This opportunistic search for formations and solutions in advance of any problem or need ultimately reframes the relationship to technology, from the instrumental to the representational. Technology

that is not consumed in service is expressly excessive: a signifier, begging the question about what is signified.

In its *representational* relationship to technology, architecture transcends technology's hold over architecture-as-building, that is, as itself technology. In fact, this could be considered the non-trivial side of architecture's relation to technology. Although its instrumental relationship to technology is potentially no different from that of any other discipline or programme to the technology that serves it, its representational relationship is characteristic of architecture's particular interests and responsibilities. And here architecture's interest has been no less opportunistic. Technology has its own lexicon and formal value system, to which architecture has consistently looked for inspiration and guidance. Here architecture finds the *sign* of efficiency or high performance, the *image* of the cutting edge.

It is the image of the 'cutting edge' that now holds the greatest fascination for architecture, perhaps as an outgrowth of the societal obsession with novelty in general. It is believed that today this edge can be found at the nexus of economics and ecology, in the study of emergent behaviour and the technology of networks and mediation that stems from it. This edge also marks the nexus of critique and fashion, though, which places it more clearly within the purview of the architectural than the swarms invading architecture may suspect or architecture let on.

Yet, while the attraction of the idea of emergence, or at least the critical programme it might support, is undeniable – it is also separable from the fashionable collection of forms and techniques that have illustrated it so far. That the introduc-

tion of such ideas to architecture can be invited rather than imposed. When architecture is a party to the hybridization, rather than merely its unconscious host, the new ideas may be used in support or derivation of a wider variety of effects than those to which they have been limited by the practices that treat them as primarily formal or prize them for their shock value.

When ideas move across disciplinary boundaries a translation occurs that bares their instrumental value. The cool ideas that make it into architecture from outside owe their coolness to the *connections* they make, based on their usefulness to the discipline, not to their strangeness there. Only when such imports can be seen in some way *as* architecture – that is, when they can be seen in an architectural light and not simply as alien – can they be judged architecturally. And it is only when they can be judged, and the discussion moves beyond matters of mere sensationalism or taste, that the sort of selfish interest that fires the imagination can be taken and they may actually reveal something new about architecture. ☑

Wes Jones

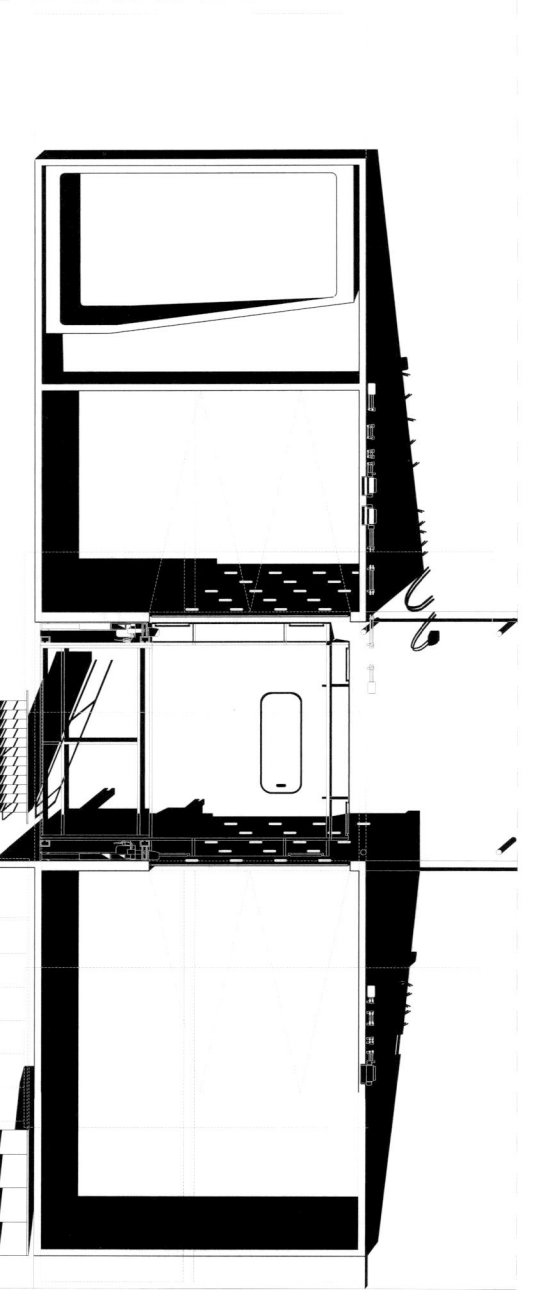
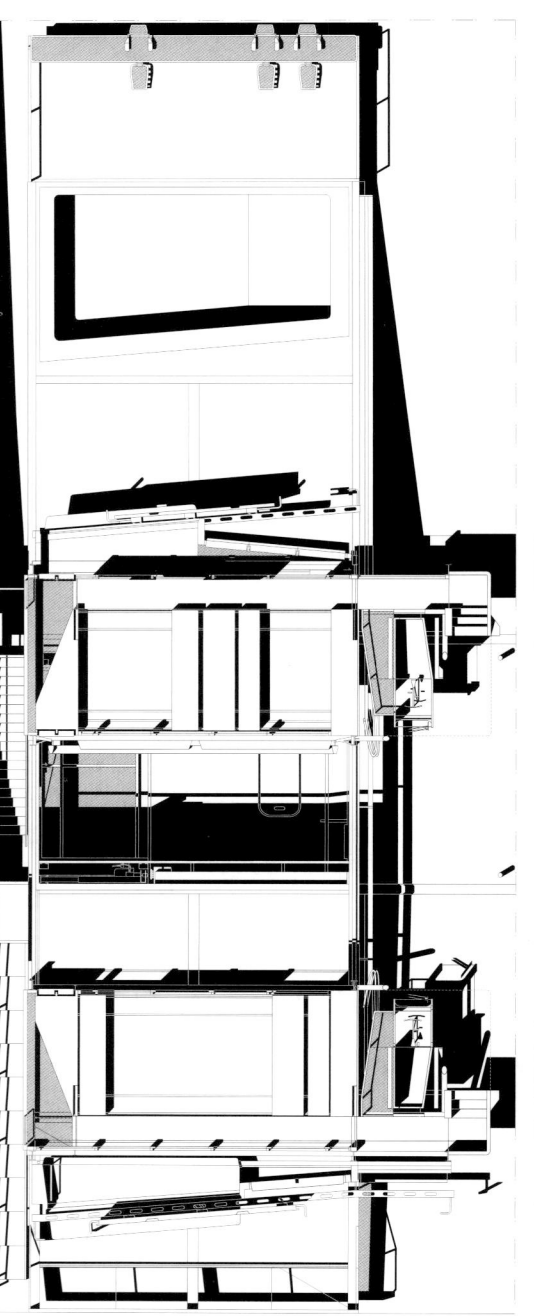

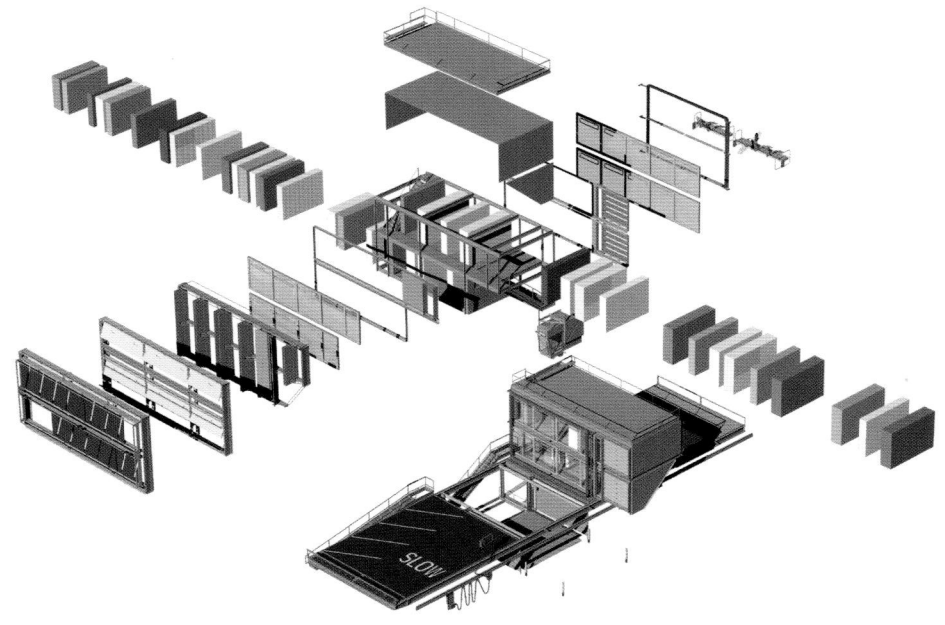

MomoRedondo
Redondo Beach, California, USA, project, 1999

To imagine the house as a 'machine' for living today is to conjure an image very different from that originally assumed by Le Corbusier. While he chided the 'eyes that do not see' for missing the potential referents in the planes and boats of his time, he never believed that buildings should intervene as actively in the affairs of their occupants as these examples, much less move like them. But then, the user groups of that age were themselves less mobile and expected little more than a traditional formula of fixed spaces. Flexibility was offered, if at all, by arrangements of sliding panels or the repositioning of furniture.

The contemporary machine for living is more likely to understand those referents on a functional level and have the means to emulate them on their own terms. MomoRedondo distributes the typical range of programme components among two or more different MObile MOdular units. These units, driven by human—bicycle power, are able to reposition themselves continuously over the length of the lot along a track system typically used for bridge-cranes. The MOMO units are able to link up with each other to create closer adjacencies or larger interior spaces, or remain separate to give their occupants greater privacy. Each of the units is also able to tune its relationship to the exterior; by their arrangement on the site they are able to create larger outdoor spaces or eliminate them entirely, and allow light and air to any exposure of any of the units. The 'yard' of each grouping of units (or 'house') is itself composed of a changeable variety of surface plates that drop in between the tracks. Options for these include pool, deck, lawn, flagstones, sand or asphalt. On the interior of each MOMO unit is a two-level rack of PRO/dek (pat. pend.) units, which house the actual equipment that gives the interior spaces their specific programme identities, which are repositionable in the same way as the MOMO units.

This proposal offers a reasoned critique of the suburban predisposition to conformity. By putting the power of continuous spatial determination in the hands of the occupants, the MOMO approach to suburbanization preserves the economic and ecological attraction of the so-called 'garden city' while preventing it from becoming a sort of fascist theme park and fosters the neighbourly exchange that is the lifeblood of our cities and culture. ☑

▧ Sub-'burb
Los Angeles, USA, project, 2002

The suburbs are both the test market and final resting place of architectural innovation. Their success makes them resistant to change, but also the place where change finally becomes ratified. It is here that the two greatest contemporary influences on patterns of dwelling will be felt: the advent of the computer and Internet, and a sense of ecological responsibility. The first will promote decentralization, the second will encourage densification. These opposed tendencies will be magnified as they are played out within the context of the American dream.

The suburbs have been classically green, but paradoxically at a cost to the environment; to achieve their condition of artificial greenness they have sprawled over otherwise unspoiled territory. The suburbs have been classically decentralized too, but in a way that assumed the sanctity and primacy of the nuclear family unit – which has lately fissioned. This fragmentation has been reflected in the increase of the typical number of bedrooms and other countable spaces where family members can get away from each other. The real-estate industry has seen this as an opportunity to contrive additional ameliorative features and compensatory spaces that can be sold in the family house. The new model sub-'burb proposes a continuous carpet of habitation that is approximately twice as dense as the existing suburban model, but which confines all the building below the level of circulation. The increased density allows for the provision of a neighbourhood-sized strip of open space at the upper level for each group of forty houses. Below, the courtyard houses provide complete privacy, efficiently accessing just the right amount of outdoors and nature necessary to promote a sense of well-being, without intruding into the neighbour's perceptual field. Each courtyard is designed to provide for microclimate adjustments, using a balance of plantings and a pond area to promote evaporative cooling and humidification. In the space below the roads, which run at public (rooftop) level, lies the infrastructure for the district, including energy, sewage, water and electronic data, along with access tunnels. The road also functions as a thermal storage area, which provides conditioned air. The access to each house is through the courtyard, from a mobile stair and lift device that can be pedalled from one end of the lot to the other, providing the resident with exercise as well as mowing the lawn, supplying additional power to the household batteries. Inside, the house is organized in such a way as to provide all the programme of a typical three-bedroom suburban house in less than half the space, through the use of a Mobile Program Deck™ (MPD: pat. pend.). ▨

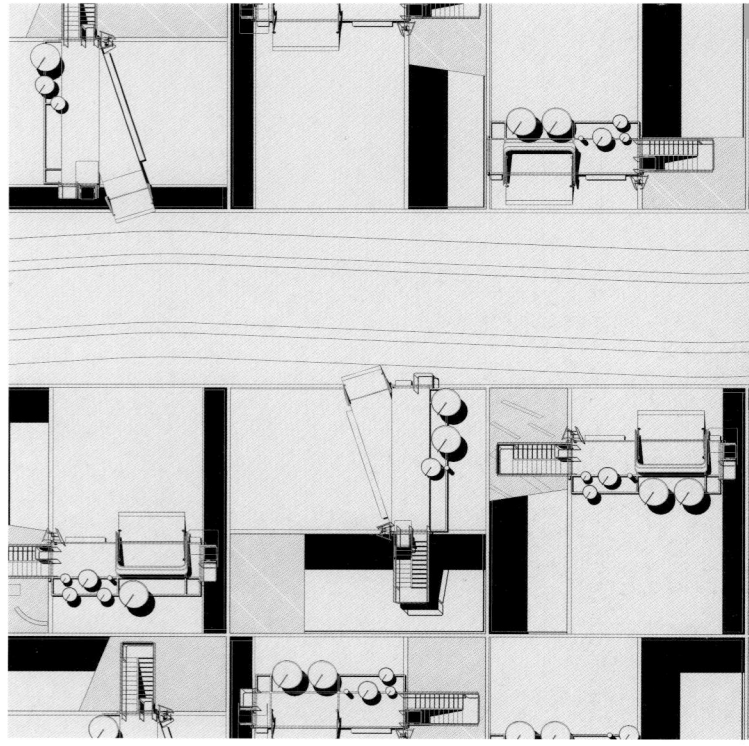

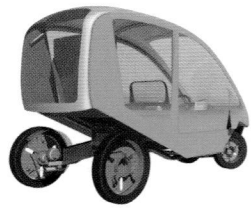

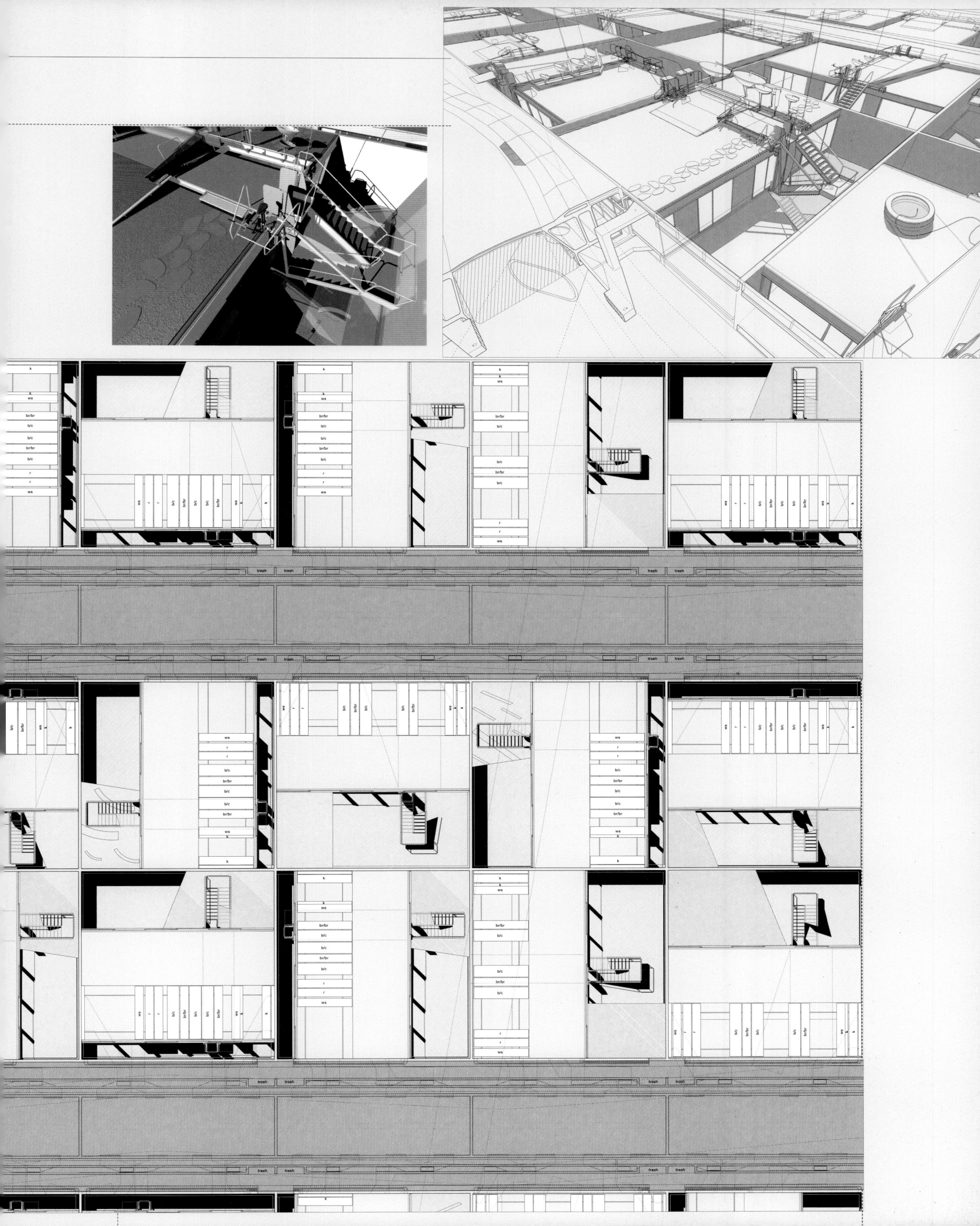

JOURDA ARCHITECTES

France

Françoise-Hélène Jourda [(1955)]

A prominent figure in French architecture since the early 1980s, Françoise-Hélène Jourda divides her career as architect and teacher between France and the German-speaking countries; in Germany she was responsible for the redevelopment of a park and a residential area (Potsdam, 1997), the Futuroscope in Krefeld (1996), a training centre for the Ministry of the Interior (Herne-Sodingen, 1993) and some experimental houses in Stuttgart (1989); in Austria she has been teaching since 1999, as well as being director of the Institute of Space Design at the University of Vienna. She has worked in association with the architect Gilles Perraudin since 1980, and in 1998 established Jourda Architects in Paris and Lyon. A leading representative of the high-tech movement in France, she takes great care to ensure that her innovative, technologically precise architecture benefits the environment. Her work has recently been exhibited at the Pompidou Centre ('Made in France', 1997), the NAI (Rotterdam, 1996), the Venice Biennale (1996), Berlin (Galerie Redes West, 1997) and Hong Kong (French Consulate, 1997). ☑

IT IS PERHAPS the cultural mix of the agency that has been and still is its most defining characteristic: for more than ten years, it has divided its work equally between France, Germany and Austria. In addition to its cultural diversity, the agency's policy is built on the contrast between southern and northern approaches, particularly towards the environment. While the training centre in Herne Sodingen is a prime example of this, the agency's other constructions and projects in progress also illustrate this basic, integrated approach. With or without the effective participation of the contractor, environmental objectives are not merely present but are determining factors and indeed compete in the development of a differential approach; they inspire technically innovative solutions and unusual combinations of forms and materials. These are the driving forces behind the agency's creative work, and it is this approach that may rewrite the architectural script, by challenging the conventions of modern architecture. It questions existing solutions and gives hope of alternatives to the diktats of an architecture that has become increasingly flimsy, transparent, slender and immaterial.

The Jourda approach restores meaning to the idea of usage, comfort, fairness. Above all, it has to allow for the needs and desires of others – not merely the users themselves, but their neighbours, near or far, those who have to maintain the building and the children who will play in its courtyard. Such environmental concern, embracing all social and cultural aspects, is most widely developed in Germany. This was what made it possible to construct the building in Herne Sodingen.

The approach that underlies these projects is transversal but also federal. It gives the agency means of breaking the mould. For instance, with the Jean Mermoz private hospital, it facilitated the development – with the cooperation of the client – of an unusual architectural typology for this form of programme, based on usage and the welfare of everyone concerned. The fact that the patient was the focal point of the whole project meant that the agency superimposed what it called 'worlds', without any apriority, on the composition of the façades and bays. Thanks to this approach, one can today build wooden chalets on a 'golf course', standing on a mass of stainless steel leaves, themselves placed on a glass volume whose curves have undergone transformations throughout the preliminary studies in order to adapt to the programme.

The environmental approach allows a formal liberty, which 'good taste' had constrained to the production of flimsy, transparent architectural objects. The agency's projects develop, without any formal prejudgments, as a result of rigorous procedures that lead to a choice of materials, forms and dimensions that may be surprising but will be accepted because they emerge from perfectly rational considerations. These projects, based on a concept that one might term 'organic', consist of assembled elements that are generally irregular, mobile and capable of modification, enlargement or reduction and of progressively changing places during the life of the project and of the site. This is a strategy that is put in place, that allows adaptation to new constraints and complementary objectives, not always identified at the start, throughout the process of conception, rather than a classic project strategy. The combinations are sometimes surprising, even to those who create them, but they aim to give pleasure. ☑

Françoise-Hélène Jourda

The Jean Mermoz Hospital

Lyon, France, 1998 to present

The project began with close analysis of the programme and research into the internal logic of the building, and these factors formed the basis of the layout. A hospital building comprises functional units that are closely linked together – because each is indispensable to the others – but at the same time very independent, because different activities take place in each and because there are different connections with the patients and the doctors. The project therefore expresses the duality of and the complementarity between the high tech of medicine and surgery on the one hand and the personal, human relations between the patient and those connected with him or her on the other. The result is a building that works on different levels, each one with its own function, ambience and architecture. On the ground floor are all the services that make contact with the outside world – very bright and open. On the first floor is the 'technological level', with all the medical equipment, where the tone is set by the stainless steel. The top floor, which houses the patients, is in the form of continuous, interlinked chalets surrounded by gardens, which afford a comforting change of scenery.

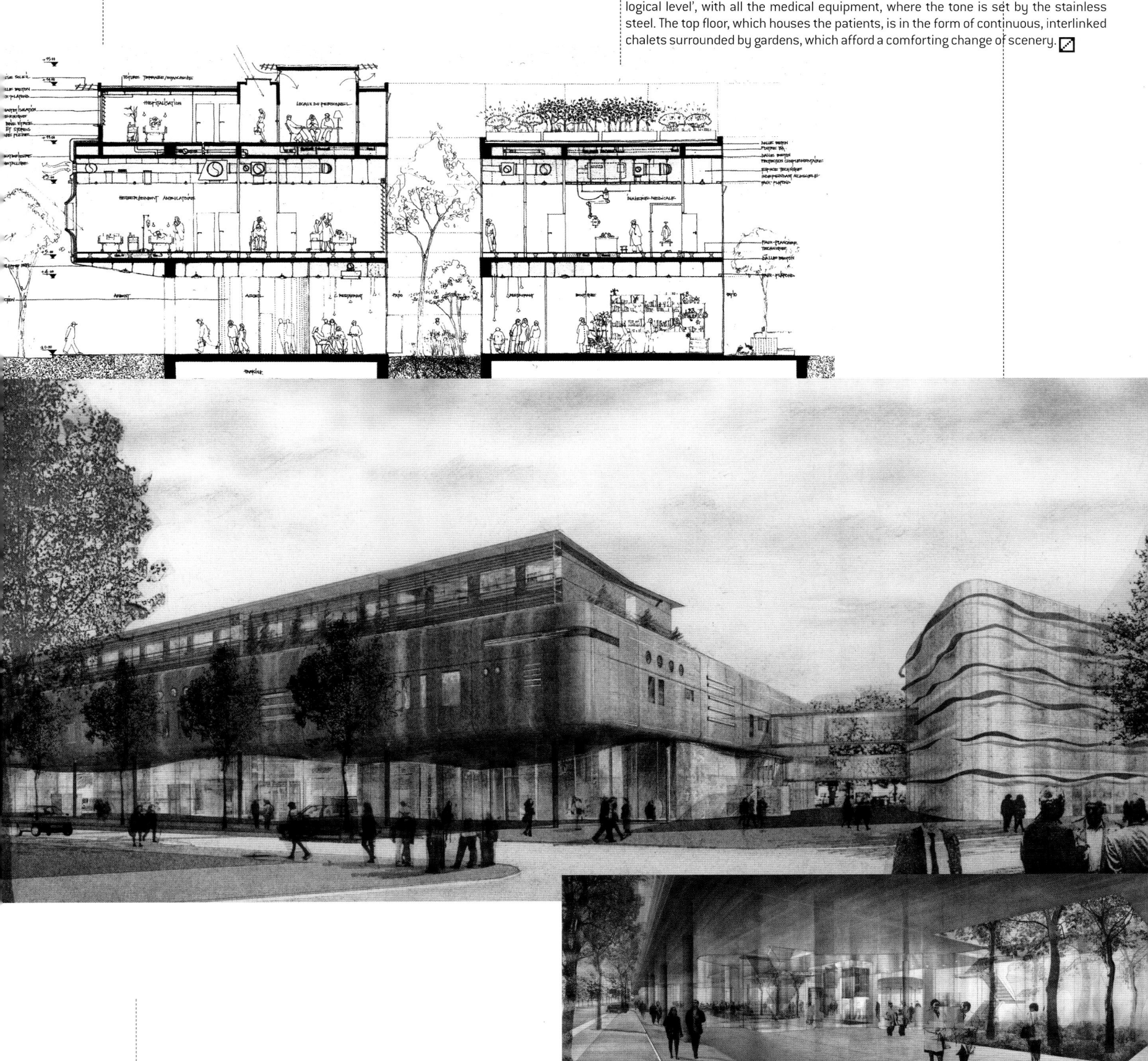

⊳ A Chalet in Megève

Megève, France, completed 1995

This old farm, whose main building combined residence, stables and barn, has been transformed into a second home, with a lodge for the caretaker and an underground garage. In order to comply with architectural and town-planning requirements, the dimensions of the existing farm were rigorously adhered to, while new structures are in keeping with the traditional architecture of the Haute-Savoie. On the ground floor and in the basement, the new rooms and jacuzzi seem to have been dug out of the bedrock of the farm. The whole of the barn has been conserved as a single unit; the wooden structures of the kitchen, library and fireplace are independent of the outside walls. The bays and sliding shutters have been designed to preserve the original façade. ☑

⊳ Converted Market – Place du 8 mai

Lyon, France, completed 2000

The hall, intended as a food market, is sited in such a way as to extend the existing line of shops on the ground floor of the neighbouring buildings. It is a simple, covered structure 144 metres long and 23.6 metres wide, accommodating 572 linear metres of stalls. With a height of 7.46 metres and no vertical walls, the cover provides efficient protection to all the market installations without blocking the transversal views or those on to the garden to the west of the hall. The whole structure is made of wood. The posts, which are placed at irregular intervals in order to prevent the structure from becoming too uniform, are tree trunks, connected by steel moulds. The roof is mainly opaque, but punctuated with panes of glass. It consists of wooden chevrons covered with wooden boards, while the transparent sections form 'clouds' above the chevrons. The boards, which jut out underneath, make the glass panels seem like gaps, through which tinted light brightens the interior of the hall by way of the silk-screened glass. The use of wood for the entire structure maximizes its 'natural' character, and the intrinsic sensuousness of the material makes any further colouring unnecessary. The choice of woods indigenous to the region is also indicative of sensitivity to the environment and ecologically sound procedures. Rainwater from the roof is collected for use in cleaning the hall after the market. The lighting is done by reflection, the light fittings being on the roof. Additional architectural lighting is intended to highlight the silk-screened glass panels by illuminating the areas around the 'clouds'. ☑

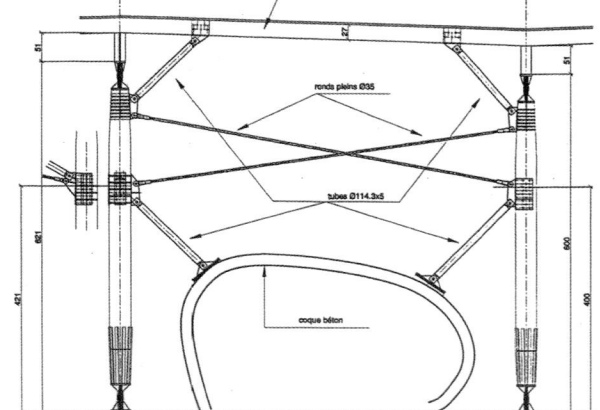

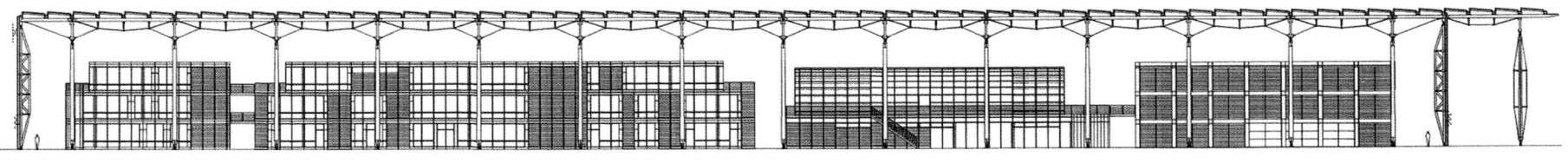

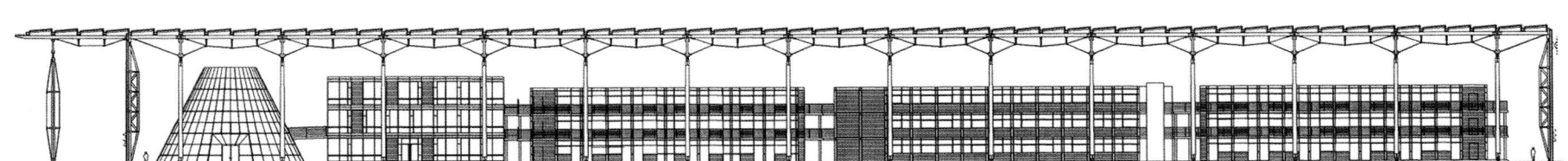

Training Centre – Ministry of the Interior
Herne-Sodingen, Germany, completed 1999

Situated in the Ruhr, this building is in an industrial wasteland. Apart from functioning as a training centre for the North Rhine-Westphalian Ministry of the Interior, the construction is a pilot project in matters of ecological protection and energy saving. It is based on the creation of a natural, protected microclimate by way of a greenhouse structure covering a surface area of 13,000 square metres, beneath which are the various buildings of the training centre. The overall concept uses a long sequence of layouts designed to protect and improve the environment: decontamination of polluted soil; collection of rainwater; natural drainage and utilization of 'grey' water in the buildings; the trapping and using of gases from old mine shafts for urban heating; the use of passive solar energy through the microclimatic cover of the greenhouse; energy production of up to one megawatt by using active solar energy got from photovoltaic cells situated in the roof; finally, general use of materials that are natural or easily recyclable (wood, cotton, steel).

Botanical Gardens in Bordeaux
Bordeaux, France, completed 2001

This prize-winning project was developed in collaboration with landscape gardeners. The overall construction is composed of greenhouses, 'boxes' and 'pebbles'. The greenhouses, conceived as 'blocks of glass', form the principal façade, the showcase of the establishment; they house three different climates. Of very simple dimensions, these three are 8.4 metres high, and they dominate the overall scene; they also reveal the different scales and sizes of the plants according to their respective climates. The modularity of these constructions will enable them to adapt to eventual changes in the requirements of the programme. The wooden elements of the greenhouses are real tree trunks in the form of poles, covering a range of species again according to climate. The north side of this city of plants, hidden away from the road and split up into sections, is dominated by the powerful impact of these greenhouses. The other components are also modular in form but more flexible – a collection of 'boxes' and 'pebbles'. They are developed along more organic, more natural lines and are connected with one another according to functional requirements. The 'boxes' are of natural wood with five surfaces (including the roof), while the 'pebbles' are covered with resin that incorporates aggregates of smooth granite. Between the greenhouses and the buildings, patios help to vary the layout and to link the different perspectives together. The pine cladding and the duckboard roofs, visible from the offices, conceal the structure of the boxes and thus add very simple dimensions to the museum-like layout. The 'pebbles' house those functional elements of the gardens that are independent of the public areas; they show the visitors right from the start that the space in which they find themselves is devoted to nature. They are large polished stones whose shapes are repeated in the furnishings of the botanical gardens. ☒

▶ National Technical Centre for Rugby

Marcoussis, Paris, France, completed 2000

The nature of Bellejame Park, in which the new National Technical Centre for Rugby was to be situated, had a strong influence on this project of construction and redevelopment. The main idea of the project consisted in establishing a 'residential' atmosphere – a place to stay, calm and sheltered in its countrified environment. The architecture was to be modern but of classical material, reusing the old stone and as open as possible to the surrounding forests. The complex plan was developed in the form of several different functional units. First the Residence: this contains the bedrooms and all the necessary services – thirty of them being specially allocated to the French team – the kitchen and dining rooms, again with one dining room reserved for the national team, seminar and committee rooms. The Residence is the main building, on the site of the old castle, and the other functional areas of the centre are divided up among several buildings, creating a harmonious group of small constructions that fit in perfectly with the scale of the site; as they are linked together, they are known as 'the little train'. The spaces here are for hospitality and relaxation – the swimming pool is linked to the Residence – accommodation for the students, trainers and caretakers, training areas including classrooms, a library, offices and a multipurpose room. Administrative and specialist spaces include changing rooms, massage facilities and storage space for sporting equipment. Finally, the centre has a main rugby pitch, a track and stands with 1,000 seats, a covered pitch, three training pitches and all the relevant training facilities. These pitches have been laid out in such a way as to have a minimal impact on the landscape. The main factor in arranging the different functional units between the pitches and around the site was to give independent access to all the different categories of people using the centre: the national team, the students, partners and visitors, and the public who come to watch matches on the main pitch. These four categories need to be able to 'cohabit' without causing one another any inconvenience, and this gives coherence to the layout of the buildings on the site. ◨

KENGO KUMA & ASSOCIATES

Japan

Kengo Kuma [1954]

After graduating in architecture from the University of Tokyo (1979), Kengo Kuma undertook further studies at Columbia University and the Asian Council (1985–86). After several years of collaboration with Arata Isozaki, he founded his own office in 1990, in Tokyo. The inspiration he takes from the materials and elements of nature has not only formed the basis of his architecture but has come to be the dominant impulse within it: witness the Hiroshige Ando museum (Murano Prize, 2001) with its wood-framed walls; the Kikatami Canal museum (Grand Prize, Inter-Intra Space Design, 2000), which slips beneath the landscape; the noh theatre in the forest for the Toyoma Centre for Performing Arts (Architecture Institute of Japan prize, 1997); the Yusuhara Vistors' Centre (Grand Prize, Regional Design Award, 1997). Equally, he explores numerical techniques (Digital Gardening, 1997), as a process of combining data, with allows architecture to dissolve into the landscape. Professor in the faculty of Environmental Information at Keio University 1998–99, he has been teaching in the Science and Technology faculty since 2001. ☑

DIVIDING THE SITE into elements. There are two contrasting methods of construction. In one, a universal material (for example concrete or steel) is introduced into a particular site as a foreign object. The value derives from the contrast between the uniqueness of the location and the foreign materials. This method, which could also be called the 'sculpting method', has been the predominant method of construction in the 20th century. The other important method of construction uses local materials (for example, the soil at the location or the trees that grow there) and involves only slight modifications to the particular site. The value here derives from the continuity between the location and the materials. It is the complete opposite of the 20th-century constructional method but it has formed the very essence of traditional construction in Japan. It is a very economical and ecological method that eliminates the costs and energy of transporting materials. That is why it interests me.

The three projects presented here were built with the latter method. The first is the Anyo-ji wooden temple at the tomb of Amida Tathagata. Here, we excavated the area above the cave and added straw and water to the earth to make mud bricks for the construction. The other project is the Wood-Burning Kiln. In this case, we cut down

Japanese cedar trees from around the site, at certain intervals, and assembled these thin logs diagonally on the site, before placing acrylic boards on top. The same concept underpinned both these projects: the environment was reduced to simple elements (mud bricks or cedar logs) and these materials were assembled to build the structure. This is the opposite of using an universal material such as concrete, which can create only a single, solid structure.

The beauty of our method lies in its extreme simplicity and low costs. Unlike concrete, our constructions can be dismantled easily and in such cases, the elements immediately disappear back into the environment. Moreover, since the elements are loosely connected to each other, the fluidity of space is not interrupted. Rather, there is a subtle continuity between the outside and inside, which is conducive to relaxation of the body.

Instead of creating a concrete object, the environment is separated into elements, assembled to create open structures. My aim in this work is to find new ecological and economical methods of construction, rather than driving myself to desperation trying to respect 'the norms'. ☑

Kengo Kuma

X1

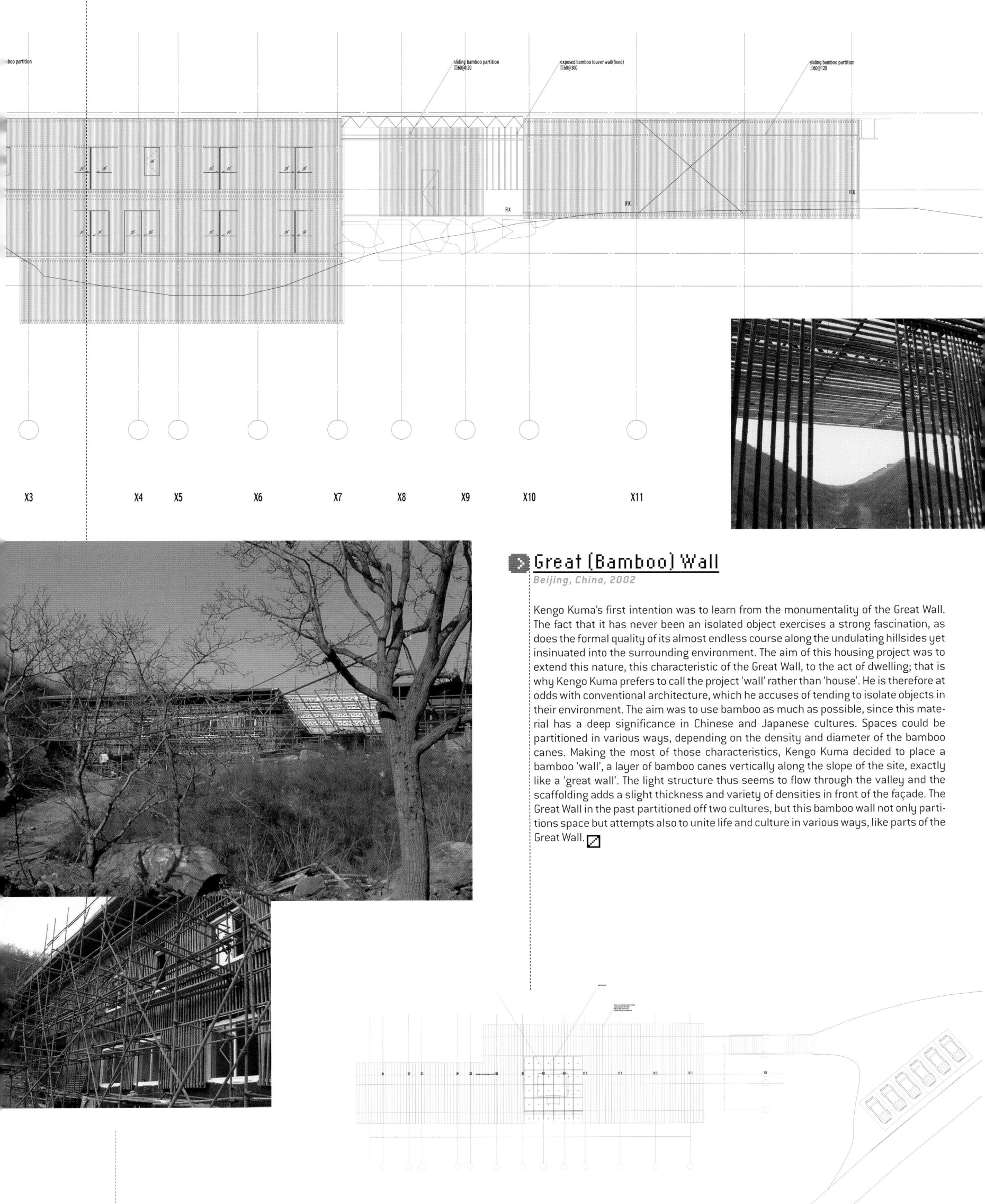

sliding bamboo partition
60@120

exposed bamboo louver wall(fixed)
60@300

sliding bamboo partition
60@120

FIX

FIX

FIX

X3 X4 X5 X6 X7 X8 X9 X10 X11

Great (Bamboo) Wall
Beijing, China, 2002

Kengo Kuma's first intention was to learn from the monumentality of the Great Wall. The fact that it has never been an isolated object exercises a strong fascination, as does the formal quality of its almost endless course along the undulating hillsides yet insinuated into the surrounding environment. The aim of this housing project was to extend this nature, this characteristic of the Great Wall, to the act of dwelling; that is why Kengo Kuma prefers to call the project 'wall' rather than 'house'. He is therefore at odds with conventional architecture, which he accuses of tending to isolate objects in their environment. The aim was to use bamboo as much as possible, since this material has a deep significance in Chinese and Japanese cultures. Spaces could be partitioned in various ways, depending on the density and diameter of the bamboo canes. Making the most of those characteristics, Kengo Kuma decided to place a bamboo 'wall', a layer of bamboo canes vertically along the slope of the site, exactly like a 'great wall'. The light structure thus seems to flow through the valley and the scaffolding adds a slight thickness and variety of densities in front of the façade. The Great Wall in the past partitioned off two cultures, but this bamboo wall not only partitions space but attempts also to unite life and culture in various ways, like parts of the Great Wall.

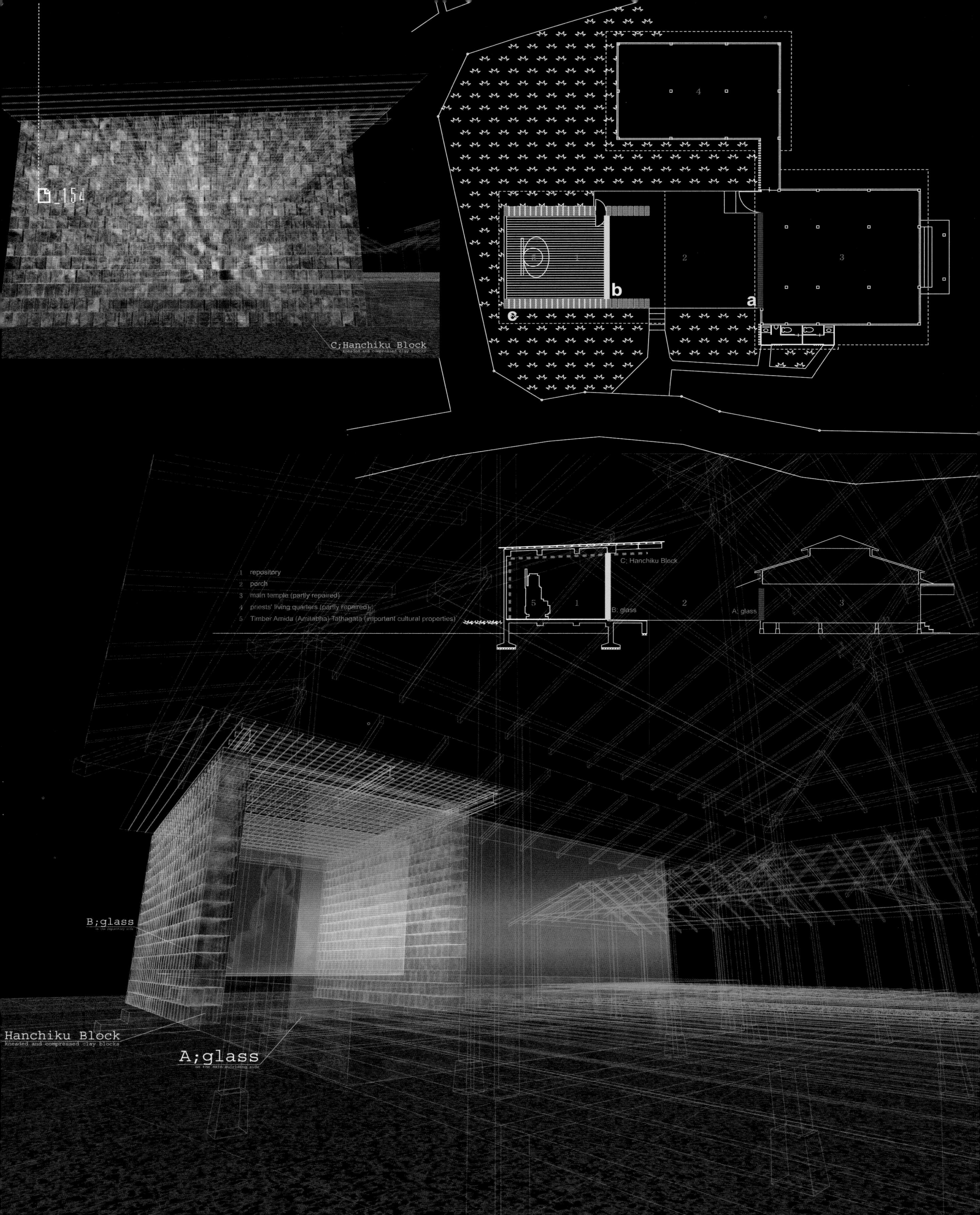

_154

C;Hanchiku Block
kneaded and compressed clay blocks

1 repository
2 porch
3 main temple (partly repaired)
4 priests' living quarters (partly repaired)
5 Timber Amida (Amitabha) Tathagata (important cultural properties)

C; Hanchiku Block

B; glass

A; glass

B;glass
on the repository side

Hanchiku Block
kneaded and compressed clay blocks

A;glass
on the main building side

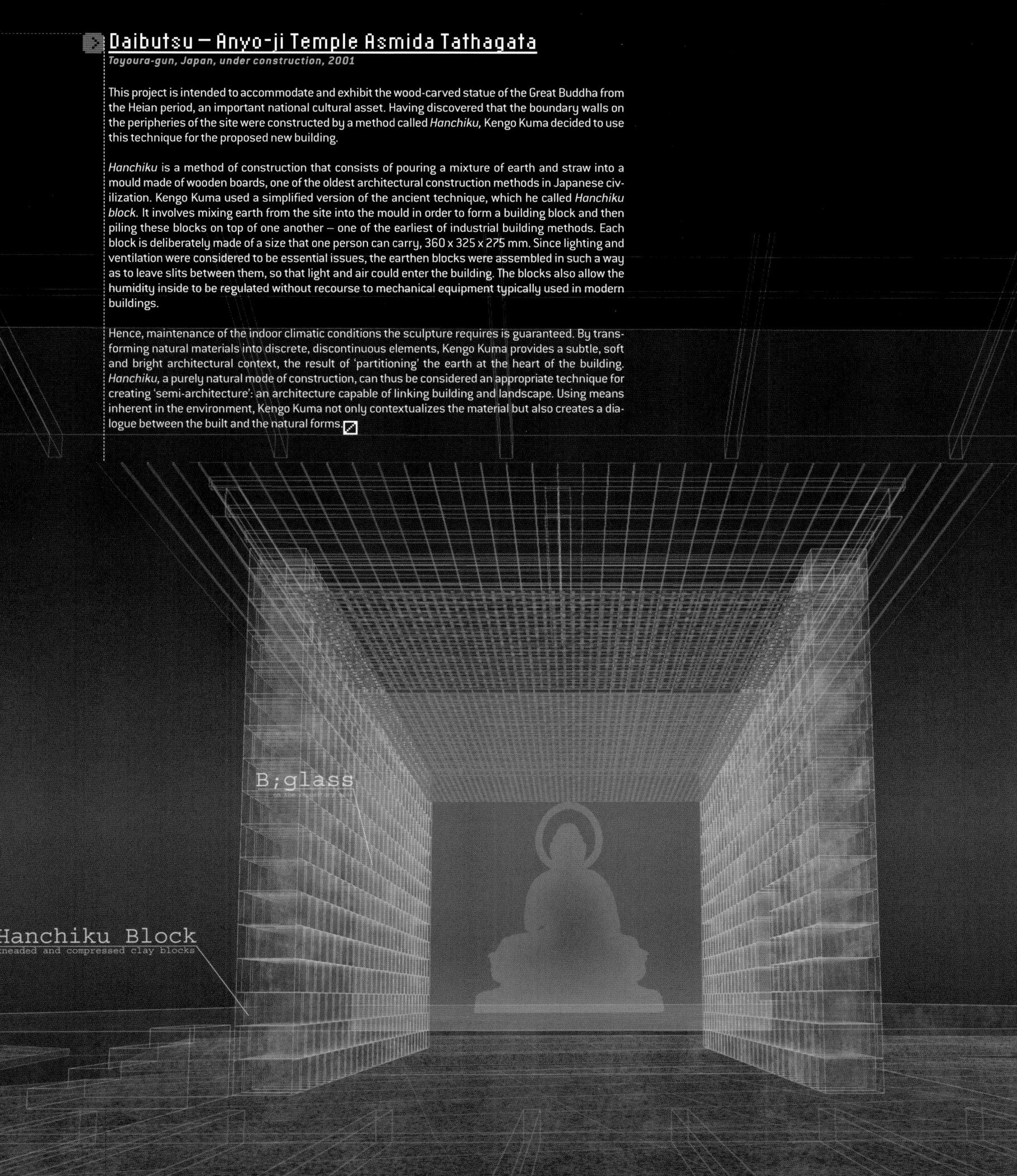

Daibutsu — Anyo-ji Temple Asmida Tathagata

Toyoura-gun, Japan, under construction, 2001

This project is intended to accommodate and exhibit the wood-carved statue of the Great Buddha from the Heian period, an important national cultural asset. Having discovered that the boundary walls on the peripheries of the site were constructed by a method called *Hanchiku,* Kengo Kuma decided to use this technique for the proposed new building.

Hanchiku is a method of construction that consists of pouring a mixture of earth and straw into a mould made of wooden boards, one of the oldest architectural construction methods in Japanese civilization. Kengo Kuma used a simplified version of the ancient technique, which he called *Hanchiku block.* It involves mixing earth from the site into the mould in order to form a building block and then piling these blocks on top of one another — one of the earliest of industrial building methods. Each block is deliberately made of a size that one person can carry, 360 x 325 x 275 mm. Since lighting and ventilation were considered to be essential issues, the earthen blocks were assembled in such a way as to leave slits between them, so that light and air could enter the building. The blocks also allow the humidity inside to be regulated without recourse to mechanical equipment typically used in modern buildings.

Hence, maintenance of the indoor climatic conditions the sculpture requires is guaranteed. By transforming natural materials into discrete, discontinuous elements, Kengo Kuma provides a subtle, soft and bright architectural context, the result of 'partitioning' the earth at the heart of the building. *Hanchiku,* a purely natural mode of construction, can thus be considered an appropriate technique for creating 'semi-architecture': an architecture capable of linking building and landscape. Using means inherent in the environment, Kengo Kuma not only contextualizes the material but also creates a dialogue between the built and the natural forms. ◻

B;glass

;Hanchiku Block
kneaded and compressed clay blocks

colors indicate
thined trees

thinning
the forest

gathering
the thined wood

The Wood-Burning Kiln Workshop

Utsunomiya, Japan, completed 2001

The Wood-Burning Kiln Workshop is the headquarters of a movement
that uses firewood to fire pottery. For the last 100 years in Japan, gas
and electricity have been used on a massive scale to fire earthen-
ware: even master potters use these modern methods of heating.
With firewood, however, one can create pottery that bends naturally
and acquires small irregularities. Furthermore, firewood can be got
from clearings in the woods by collecting lower branches that have
fallen or been left over when the more valuable upper wood has been
taken; this is a way of protecting the forest environment. Such practices arise from a cultural movement but are equally ecologically
sound. The workshop is made from timber that retains its bark, to
keep the building as natural-looking as possible. There is no need to
use modern materials such as iron, steel or concrete for this log
structure, whose covering consists only of acrylic sheets. Using this
method keeps net costs very low, only about one twentieth of the
usual costs of construction. This building floats between architecture
and nature, between artificial and natural. ☒

Translation from the Japanese: Katinka Temme

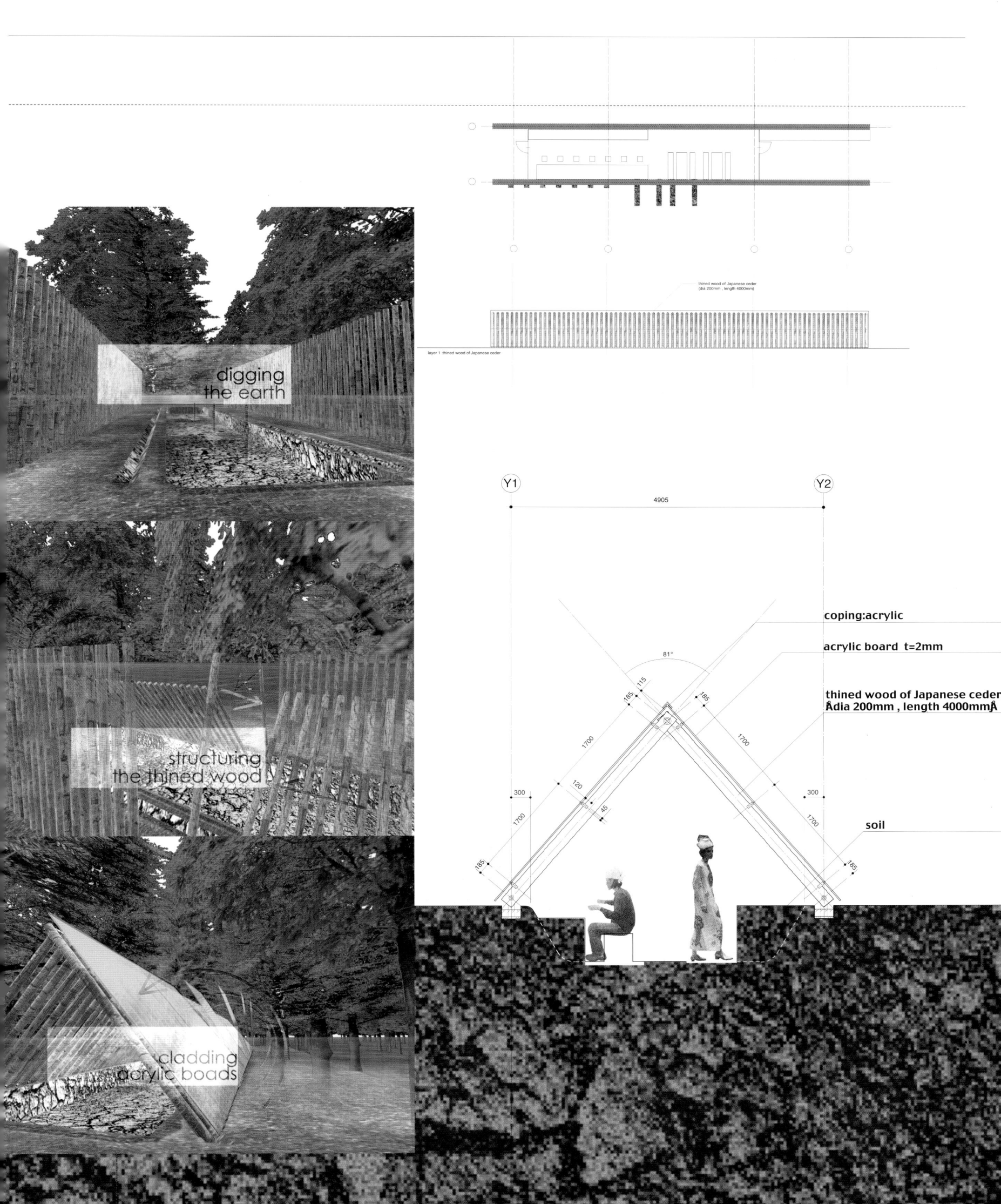

digging
the earth

structuring
the thined wood

cladding
acrylic boads

thined wood of Japanese ceder
(dia 200mm , length 4000mm)

layer 1 :thined wood of Japanese ceder

Y1   Y2

4905

81°

185 115   185

1700   1700

300   120   300

45

1700   1700

185   185

coping:acrylic

acrylic board t=2mm

thined wood of Japanese ceder
Ådia 200mm , length 4000mmÅ

soil

Tom Leader Studio

United States

Tom Leader [1956], Philippe Coignet [1973]

Tom Leader is a landscape architect educated at the Universities of Berkeley (graduated 1978) and Harvard (1983). Winner of the American Rome prize for landscape design in 1998, he was resident designer for a year at the American Academy in Rome. He formed his own studio in March 2001 for the practice of landscape architecture. It is based in Berkeley, California, with a staff of three. Before that he had worked for 16 years at Peter Walker and Partners, where he headed up numerous projects and met Philippe Coignet, a graduate of the school of landscape design at Versailles (1998) and of the University of Pennsylvania (2000). The Tom Leader Studio programme is based on two interdependent axes: Landscape Architecture, which manages operations and participation in various competitions; and Site Work, which signifies a more experimental ambition for investigation and research into the spatial and temporal processes that constantly construct and deconstruct territories. Even at its current size, the practice is working nationwide, drawing on Tom Leader's experience and network of resources.

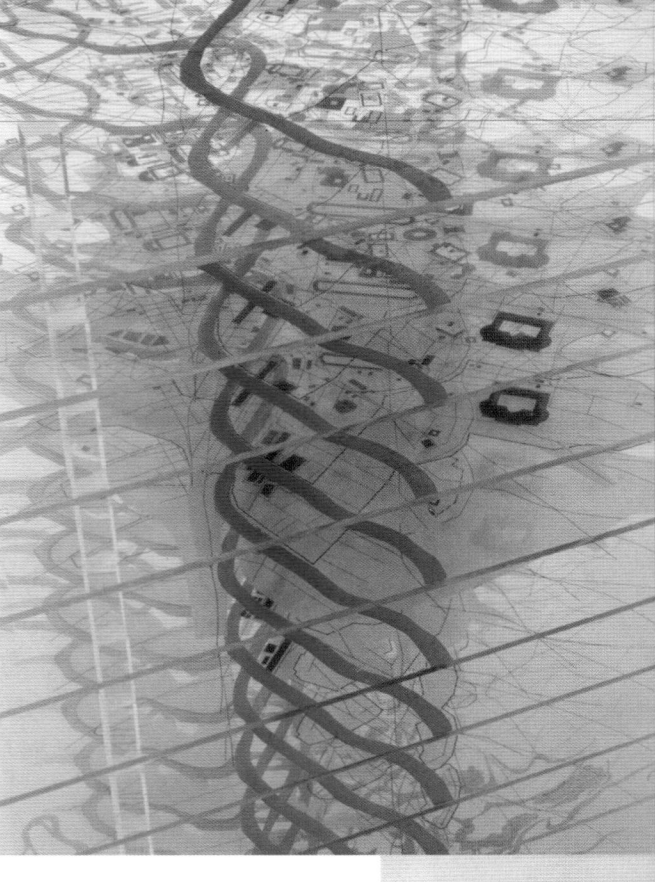

Mobility

We propose a responsive, inquiring approach to projects, seeing this as a need within the field. This approach is conditioned by broad experience in physical design and planning and is fuelled by a fascination with the substance and energies of the built environment. Agility, mobility, the skill to react, invent new tactics, adapt one's thinking, to collaborate with clients and other designers are all crucial to the work of the studio. Every new project offers a potential ground for inquiry into the phenomena of life and community – and should aspire to nothing less. This is not a process of celebrating one's own ideas but of direct engagement with material possibilities. Recognizing the unconstrained nature and vast scale of the medium of landscape points to a range of investigative open-ended strategies that can accept these realities. Inquiring into such complexities increases the range of possibilities, leading to a more inventive realization of the needs of clients.

'Site Work' denotes the studio's research effort. This is a way of gaining access to fresh viewpoints through speculative site investigations as well as physical experiments. While this work has led to several museum exhibits and installations, its intent is to expand the perspective of our design practice. This interest is stimulated, in part, by changes in public work over the last twenty years. Many clients today are less interested in proliferating and consuming style than in realizing complex physical programmes in consideration of a diverse public and shifting timeframes. They know the advantages of investigating and transforming existing sites rather than seeking out a tabula rasa.

Tectonics

Surely as water runs downhill, landscape is endlessly constructing and reconstructing itself. Of course this happens without any assistance from human agency. Complexes of morphological process are continually in operation – excavating canyons, building deltas, colonizing abandoned or newly created land. Analogies to these complexes exist in the digital operating systems that mediate our communications and influence how we execute our work – a series of organizational tendencies that promotes certain routes, actions and behaviours. As an operating system for landscape, physical dynamics are less easily codified and packaged but offer similar possibilities. But they require the responsive and perceptive abilities of the architect to identify them, measure them and develop means of use.

In doing so, one must enter into a sometimes uncertain partnership, relinquishing predictability in order to employ vast energies only partially and temporarily within human control. So at the same time, digital models attempting to reveal, predict and generate nature seem only partially useful, given the variables truly involved – and ultimately unsatisfying compared with direct engagement with visceral, material process. Rather, the architect must seek a point of leverage, a catalyst with the ability productively to deflect and modify flows already at work. Tactical means for these interventions include the diversion, interruption, excavation, accumulation, infiltration, dispersion, concentration and diversification of material and its movements.

Some locations

Rome is continually filling in. The weighty accumulation of material over time marks the formation of the city. The floors of many churches rest on Roman, Early Christian and even older remains, two, three, four levels down, as new construction builds upon the remains of the old.

Street levels keep pace with the rising floors by adding layer after layer. The current mouth of the Tiber extends six kilometres into the sea beyond the ancient port of Ostia, owing to the centuries of silt carried in the green murky runoff. To accept the agency of siltation promotes architecture more persistent and viable than the combined efforts of Roman engineers and Mussolini to overcome the inexorable changes.

California is structured by alignments, beginning with the inevitability of plate tectonics. Railway lines, highways, street grids, seismically off-set creeks are all deformed and deflected by the shearing, splintering action of geologic faults as well as the scarps and rifts they produce. The result is a broadly corrugated topography of ridges and furrows including both natural and human constructions. These striations are thrown into relief by the variable flows that move across them – wind and fog blowing in off the ocean, the ebb and flow of tides, the span of bridges and burrowing of tunnels surging with commuter vehicles. Loose material carried by these ebbs and flows collects against the ridges and within these furrows, forming new land.

Tom Leader Studio

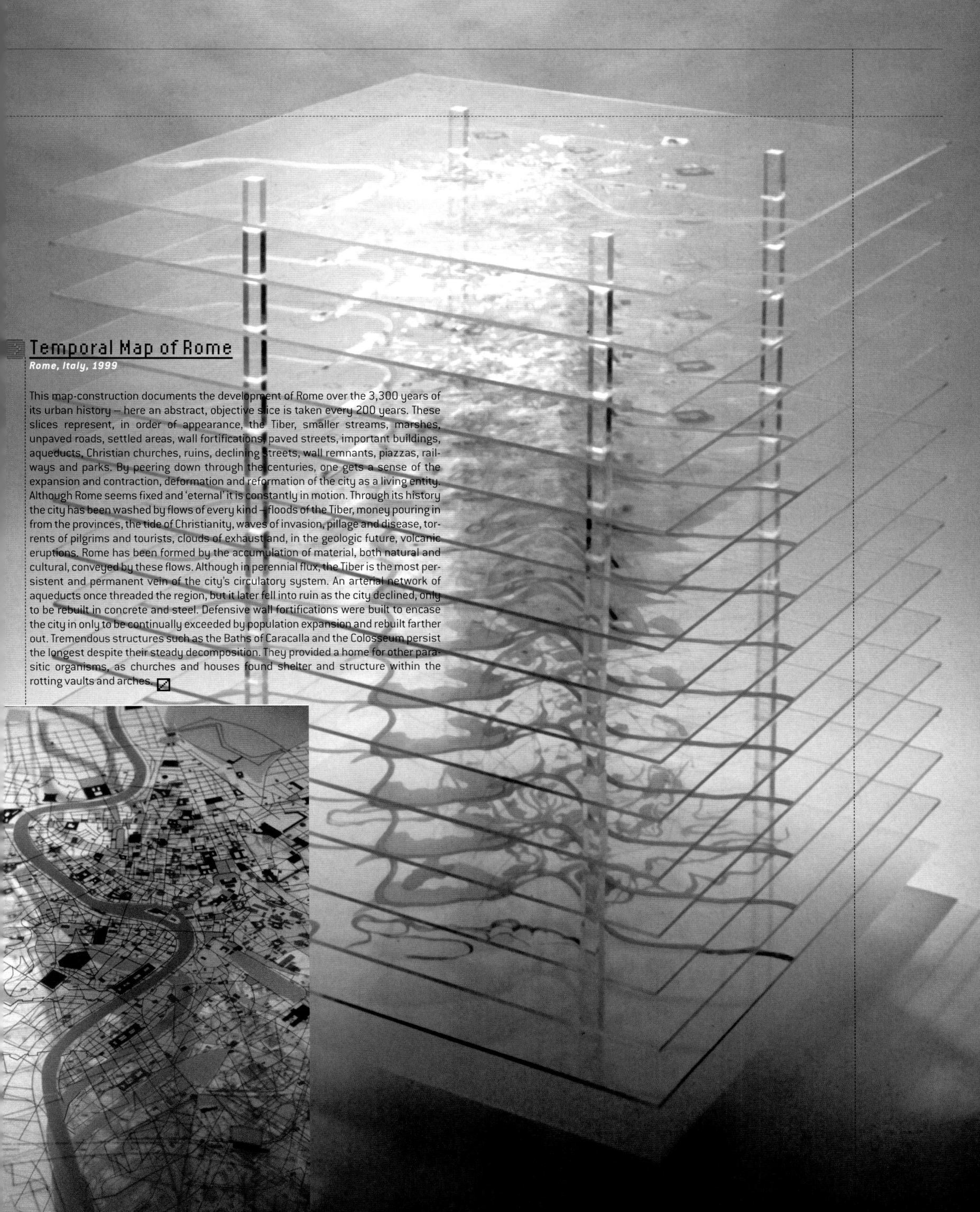

Temporal Map of Rome
Rome, Italy, 1999

This map-construction documents the development of Rome over the 3,300 years of its urban history — here an abstract, objective slice is taken every 200 years. These slices represent, in order of appearance, the Tiber, smaller streams, marshes, unpaved roads, settled areas, wall fortifications, paved streets, important buildings, aqueducts, Christian churches, ruins, declining streets, wall remnants, piazzas, railways and parks. By peering down through the centuries, one gets a sense of the expansion and contraction, deformation and reformation of the city as a living entity. Although Rome seems fixed and 'eternal' it is constantly in motion. Through its history the city has been washed by flows of every kind — floods of the Tiber, money pouring in from the provinces, the tide of Christianity, waves of invasion, pillage and disease, torrents of pilgrims and tourists, clouds of exhaust and, in the geologic future, volcanic eruptions. Rome has been formed by the accumulation of material, both natural and cultural, conveyed by these flows. Although in perennial flux, the Tiber is the most persistent and permanent vein of the city's circulatory system. An arterial network of aqueducts once threaded the region, but it later fell into ruin as the city declined, only to be rebuilt in concrete and steel. Defensive wall fortifications were built to encase the city in only to be continually exceeded by population expansion and rebuilt farther out. Tremendous structures such as the Baths of Caracalla and the Colosseum persist the longest despite their steady decomposition. They provided a home for other parasitic organisms, as churches and houses found shelter and structure within the rotting vaults and arches.

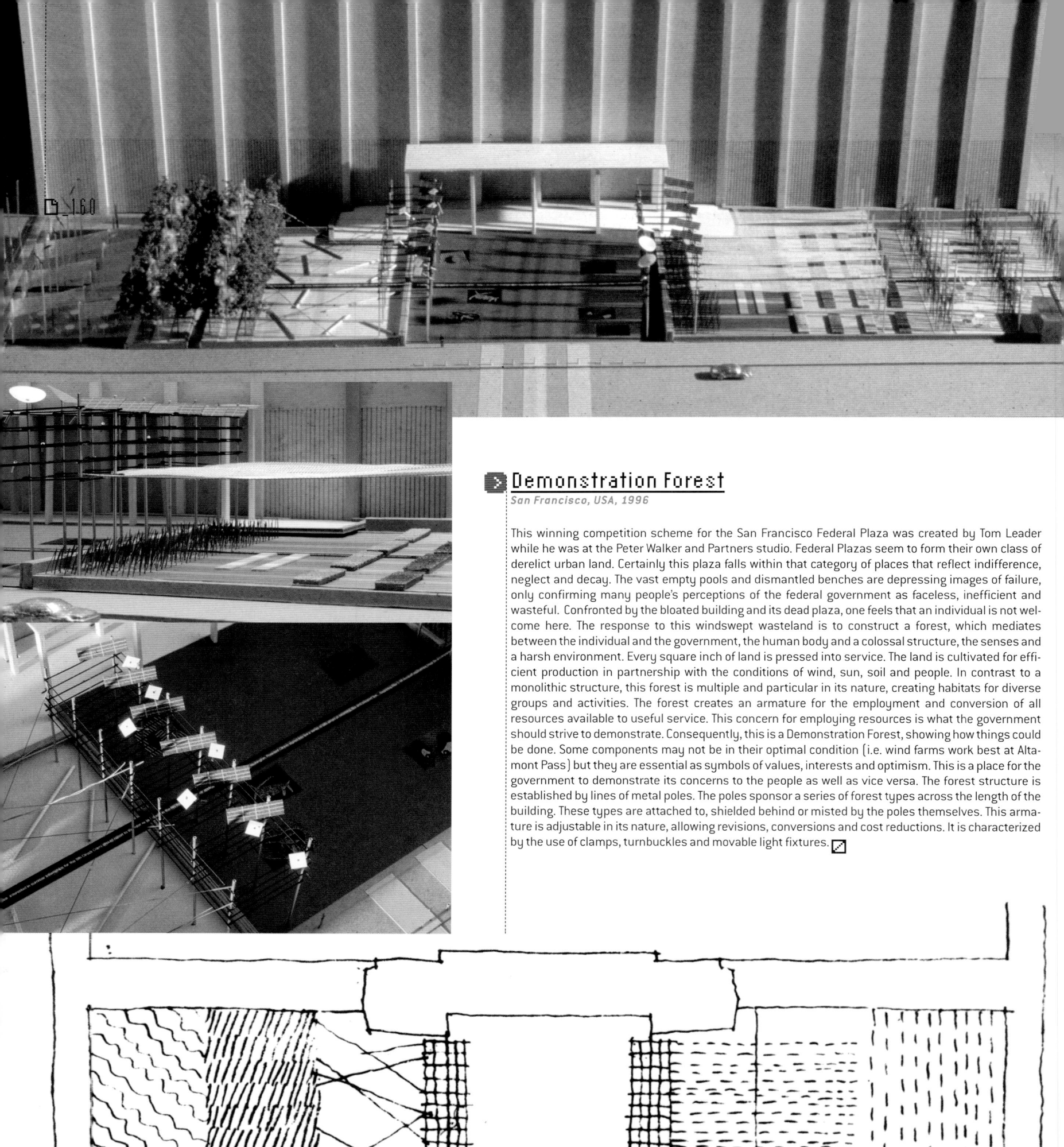

▶ Demonstration Forest

San Francisco, USA, 1996

This winning competition scheme for the San Francisco Federal Plaza was created by Tom Leader while he was at the Peter Walker and Partners studio. Federal Plazas seem to form their own class of derelict urban land. Certainly this plaza falls within that category of places that reflect indifference, neglect and decay. The vast empty pools and dismantled benches are depressing images of failure, only confirming many people's perceptions of the federal government as faceless, inefficient and wasteful. Confronted by the bloated building and its dead plaza, one feels that an individual is not welcome here. The response to this windswept wasteland is to construct a forest, which mediates between the individual and the government, the human body and a colossal structure, the senses and a harsh environment. Every square inch of land is pressed into service. The land is cultivated for efficient production in partnership with the conditions of wind, sun, soil and people. In contrast to a monolithic structure, this forest is multiple and particular in its nature, creating habitats for diverse groups and activities. The forest creates an armature for the employment and conversion of all resources available to useful service. This concern for employing resources is what the government should strive to demonstrate. Consequently, this is a Demonstration Forest, showing how things could be done. Some components may not be in their optimal condition (i.e. wind farms work best at Altamont Pass) but they are essential as symbols of values, interests and optimism. This is a place for the government to demonstrate its concerns to the people as well as vice versa. The forest structure is established by lines of metal poles. The poles sponsor a series of forest types across the length of the building. These types are attached to, shielded behind or misted by the poles themselves. This armature is adjustable in its nature, allowing revisions, conversions and cost reductions. It is characterized by the use of clamps, turnbuckles and movable light fixtures. ▨

WIND FOREST   REDWOOD FOREST   GUY WIRE FOREST   MEDIA FOREST   CLOUD FOREST   BAMBOO FOREST

▶ Coastlines
San Francisco, USA, 2001

The 'Revelatory Landscapes' exhibit at the San Francisco Museum of Modern Art aimed to take the viewer out of the confines of the museum and engage him or her in the medium through on-site installations created by five teams of designers, artists and writers throughout the San Francisco Bay Area. Tom Leader Studio selected the Berkeley waterfront, an area that since its early settlement has been moving steadily westward into the bay, owing to the steady accumulation of all sorts of materials. Coastlines tracks four historic shorelines of the bay as they now cut across redevelopment areas, rail and freeway corridors and future landfill parks. California is structured by alignments whose number and complexity continue to increase due to the expansion of human activity. Regional systems are deflected by the underlying geology to a general north-south direction, resulting in a broadly corrugated regional topography. Many elements, however, flow east-west across the corrugations and throw them into relief. Wind, fog, tides, major rivers, migrations ... all flow east-west, influenced by non-geologic factors such as the jet stream, rotation of the earth, barometric pressure gradients, migration patterns and community activism. Key to the project is the interaction of these two completely different categories of systems. North-south systems are linear and work on a massive scale deriving from the magnitude and certainty of plate tectonics, which are characterized by shearing, folding and splintering. East-west systems are affected by local particularities and are subject to changeable and contradictory flows. Corrugations serve to intercept these flows and lead to accumulations of the materials they convey. The interaction and interference between these completely different phenomena help to reveal each other. ▣

Credits: Tom Leader in collaboration with Anuradha Mathur and Dilip da Cunha

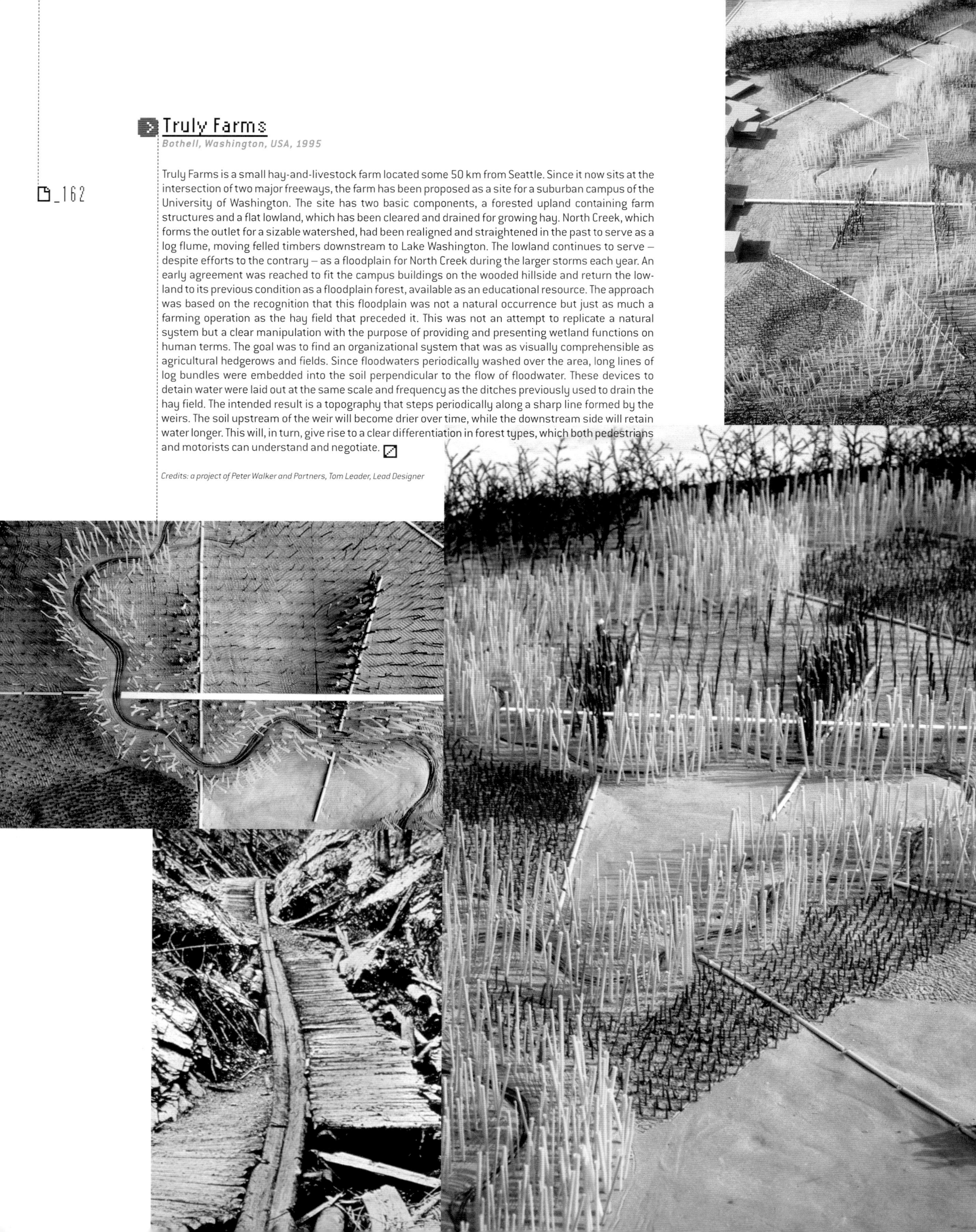

Truly Farms

Bothell, Washington, USA, 1995

Truly Farms is a small hay-and-livestock farm located some 50 km from Seattle. Since it now sits at the intersection of two major freeways, the farm has been proposed as a site for a suburban campus of the University of Washington. The site has two basic components, a forested upland containing farm structures and a flat lowland, which has been cleared and drained for growing hay. North Creek, which forms the outlet for a sizable watershed, had been realigned and straightened in the past to serve as a log flume, moving felled timbers downstream to Lake Washington. The lowland continues to serve – despite efforts to the contrary – as a floodplain for North Creek during the larger storms each year. An early agreement was reached to fit the campus buildings on the wooded hillside and return the lowland to its previous condition as a floodplain forest, available as an educational resource. The approach was based on the recognition that this floodplain was not a natural occurrence but just as much a farming operation as the hay field that preceded it. This was not an attempt to replicate a natural system but a clear manipulation with the purpose of providing and presenting wetland functions on human terms. The goal was to find an organizational system that was as visually comprehensible as agricultural hedgerows and fields. Since floodwaters periodically washed over the area, long lines of log bundles were embedded into the soil perpendicular to the flow of floodwater. These devices to detain water were laid out at the same scale and frequency as the ditches previously used to drain the hay field. The intended result is a topography that steps periodically along a sharp line formed by the weirs. The soil upstream of the weir will become drier over time, while the downstream side will retain water longer. This will, in turn, give rise to a clear differentiation in forest types, which both pedestrians and motorists can understand and negotiate. ▨

Credits: a project of Peter Walker and Partners, Tom Leader, Lead Designer

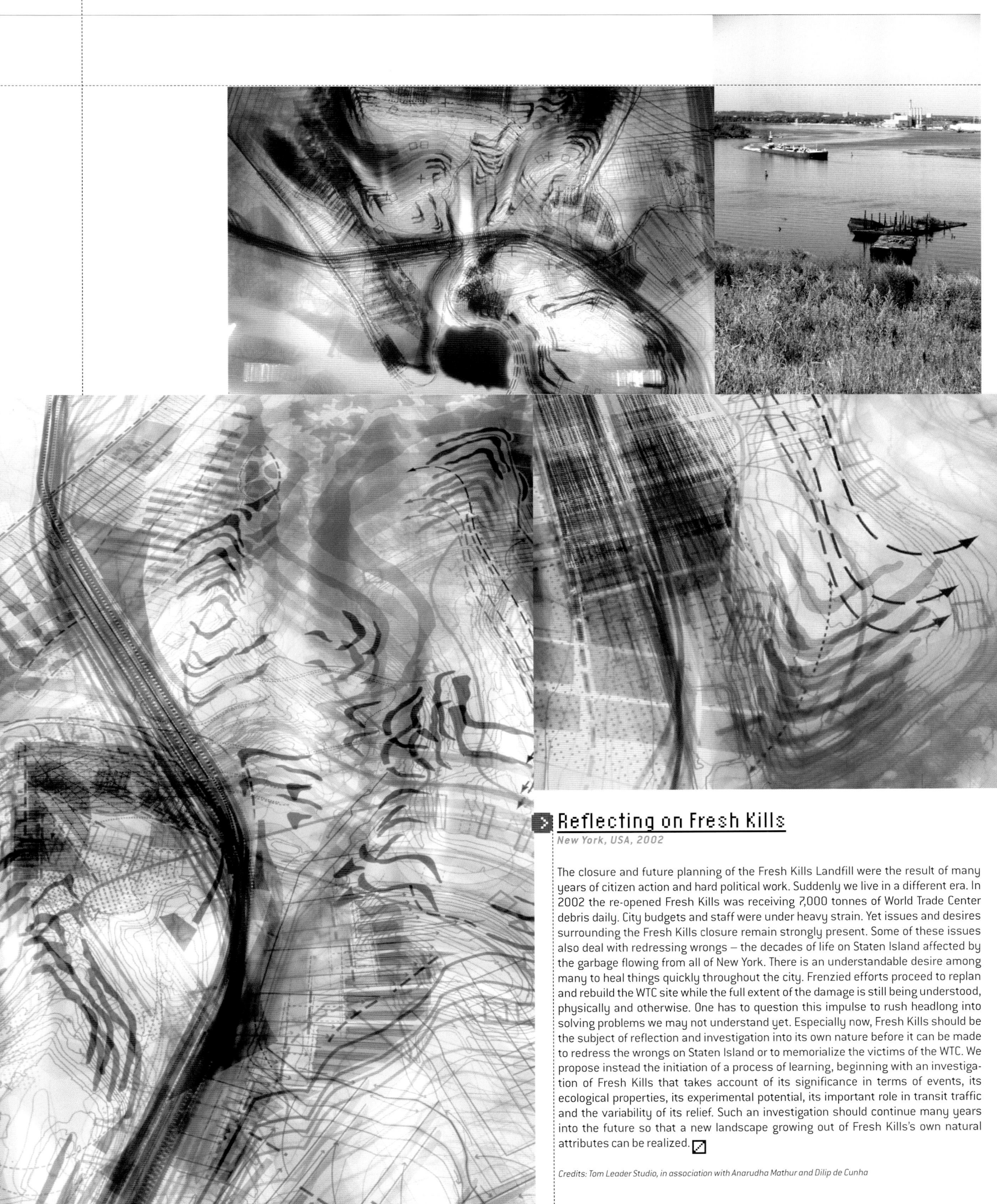

Reflecting on Fresh Kills
New York, USA, 2002

The closure and future planning of the Fresh Kills Landfill were the result of many years of citizen action and hard political work. Suddenly we live in a different era. In 2002 the re-opened Fresh Kills was receiving 7,000 tonnes of World Trade Center debris daily. City budgets and staff were under heavy strain. Yet issues and desires surrounding the Fresh Kills closure remain strongly present. Some of these issues also deal with redressing wrongs — the decades of life on Staten Island affected by the garbage flowing from all of New York. There is an understandable desire among many to heal things quickly throughout the city. Frenzied efforts proceed to replan and rebuild the WTC site while the full extent of the damage is still being understood, physically and otherwise. One has to question this impulse to rush headlong into solving problems we may not understand yet. Especially now, Fresh Kills should be the subject of reflection and investigation into its own nature before it can be made to redress the wrongs on Staten Island or to memorialize the victims of the WTC. We propose instead the initiation of a process of learning, beginning with an investigation of Fresh Kills that takes account of its significance in terms of events, its ecological properties, its experimental potential, its important role in transit traffic and the variability of its relief. Such an investigation should continue many years into the future so that a new landscape growing out of Fresh Kills's own natural attributes can be realized.

Credits: Tom Leader Studio, in association with Anarudha Mathur and Dilip de Cunha

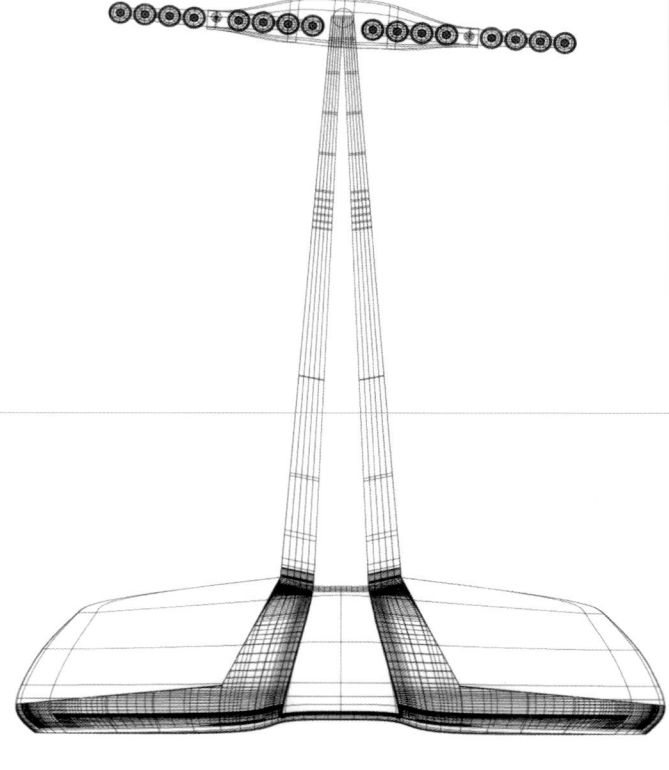

▶ *LWPAC*

Canada, United States

Oliver Lang [1964], Cynthia A. Wilson [1962]

Oliver Lang, born in Hamburg, has studied, practiced and taught architecture in the USA, Germany, Spain and Canada. Cynthia Wilson, from Calgary, Canada, has had an equally cosmopolitan training and experience. LWPAC — Lang Wilson Practice in Architecture Culture — was established in 1997 as a platform for collaborative architectural design, building and interdisciplinary design research. Over the last twelve years principals Wilson and Lang (Hamburg, Germany) have sought exposure to diverse cultural settings in North and South America, Europe and Asia, while simultaneously being deeply engaged in design, building, research, teaching and/or publishing. Many unexpected revelations stemming from this engagement, both cultural and architectural, have given LWPAC valuable insights with respect to the interdependencies of local and global cultures. LWPAC believes in the encounter and production of knowledge that results from simultaneous open-ended inquiries in design practice and research. The practice has won prizes at the XII Architecture Biennale in Santiago, Chile, and in recent competitions (e.g. Chuquicamata College, Chile, 2001). ◹

PROGRESSIVELY challenged by the impact of technological innovations, global network economies and cultural interdependencies, the urban fabric has become increasingly complex and unpredictable for architectural intervention. Within this context, LWPAC follows some clearly established objectives.

Culture To gain knowledge about the forces that are changing cultural practices, not just in degree but in kind, such as the experience economy and tourism, or issues of surface value in today's image-driven culture.

Practice *LWPAC* mediates and manages projects through the production of knowledge, ideas and design intelligence. Ideation, strategic planning, research and scenario studies are as a much part of LWPAC's everyday design practice as are, for example, the integration of intelligent agents in composite materials, robotic construction, mass customization, marketing and branding models and issues of concurrent production. LWPAC builds specific teams as needed, and as such maintains agility and responsiveness.

Design Intelligence LWPAC defines design intelligence as the capacity to evaluate information concerning such things as the underlying forces, activities and courses of action within the urban fabric. Further, intelligence is defined by the ability for effective adaptation to the environment, by making a change in the project itself, by changing the environment or by finding a new one. Consequently LWPAC deploys primarily

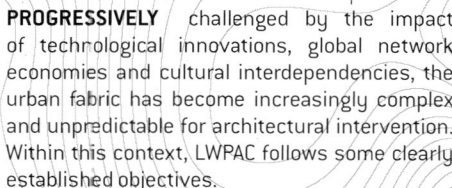

operative methodologies, often borrowed from theories in physics, biology and philosophy that offer open-ended thought models for non-linear processes which facilitate a much deeper knowledge of urban life. Differentiation, in itself a process leading from the simple to the complex, provides LWPAC with architectural models that are subtle, distributive and synthetic in their relationship to the task. The deliberate deployment of the idea of incompleteness further aids in the encounter of propositions that can unfold in a number of ways within the agreed limits of set criteria. To LWPAC, it is an exhilarating opportunity to propose urban environments that act as cultural platforms with the capacity to obtain simultaneous inputs from within the context of commerce, culture and social geography. Process, knowledge *and* the project typically form a lattice that co-evolves with the context. This lattice privileges neither part nor whole, but relationships and clusters. Instead of leading to a knowledge of form, the process leads to a form of knowledge and from there to informed projects, rather then creating stylized or decorated pragmatisms. As such, projects produce value, dollar value as well as cultural value for both clients and the community.

Concurrent digital design Emerging media technologies have fundamentally changed the way in which architectural design, urban planning and fabrication processes are conducted. LWPAC comprehensively integrates the design process 'from invention to implementation'. Digital media of all sorts are continuously explored for their

capacity to aid the design process. Long-distance collaborations are as much part of the practice as are four-dimensional design studies, the generation of highly accurate modelling data and advanced visualization. For future applications LWPAC is actively researching and deploying the opportunities of rapid prototyping and computer numerical-controlled (CNC) fabrication methods in combination with inventions of new material science. ◹

LWPAC

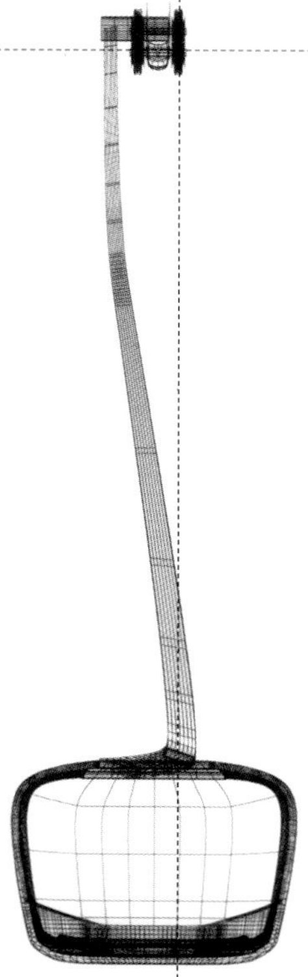

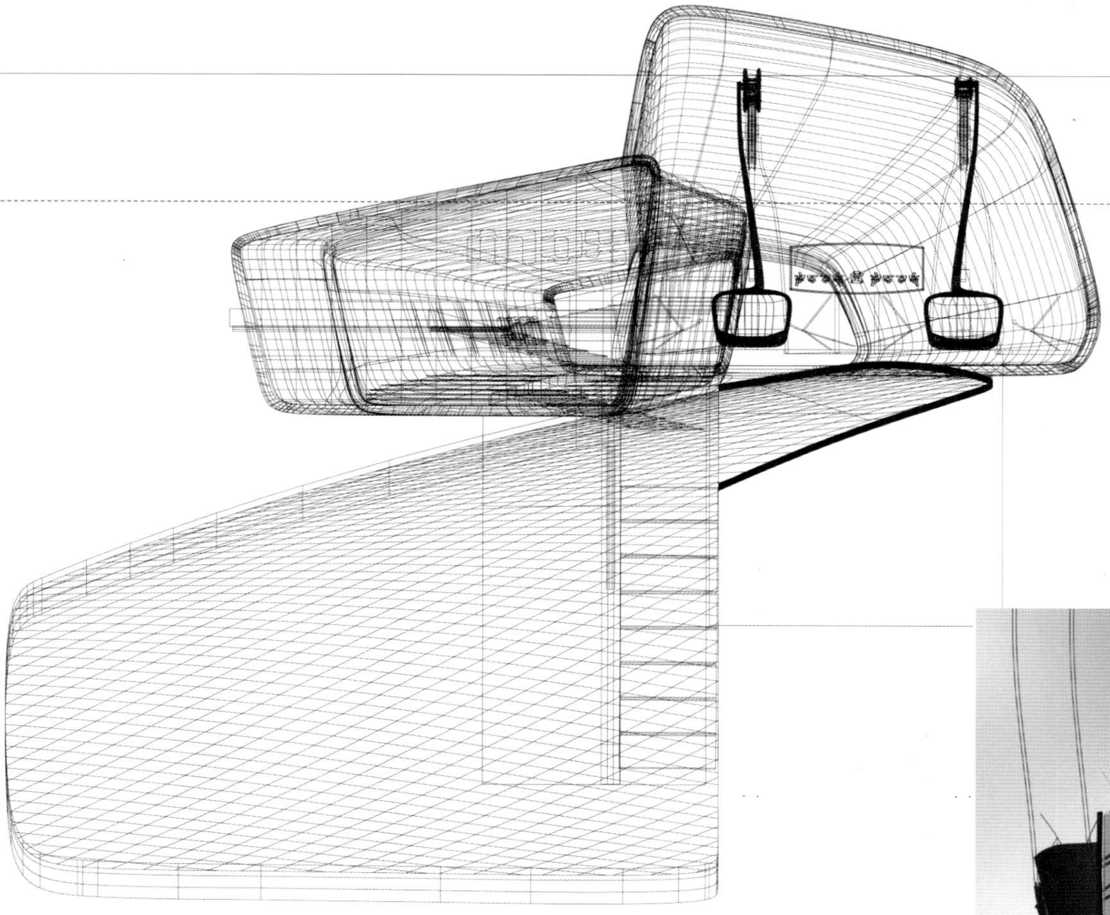

MOX (Museum of Extreme Culture) and P2P (Peak to Peak) Aerial Tramway

Canada, project, 2000

The MOX and Peak to Peak aerial tramway project is a project arising out of a feasibility study and fundraiser for an infrastructure/transport and cultural/business/conference hybrid. As part of the attractions business, the project is both destination and hub for extreme sports culture.

Uniquely, the project brief came as a story board in form of a soundtrack only. It included the overall framework and ambition of the project, requiring LWPAC to design the project and then to communicate concepts and ideas exclusively through film media and video animation. The envisioned project includes a gondola station for 1,000 passengers per hour with an adaptable space for a museum (MOX), conference centre, press centre, theatre and outdoor auditorium. They form a continuous landscape that connects possible programmatic scenarios and their variants, both inside the building and to the outside. Design intelligence within this continuity allows programmes to expand and contract depending on season and the opportunities for unique events. The building organization follows the idea of distributed differences, ranging from stable to pliable and temporal, and from generic to specific. The proposal had to be conceived as a lightweight, composite, prefabricated monocoque structure that allows for helicopter-assisted mountaintop construction. The gondola cabin, capable of carrying 180 passengers, is designed and prototyped for an aerial tramway that would represent the longest (3.2 km) and highest (0.7 km) free span of its kind. ▱

Credits: LWPAC in collaboration with E&S (Envisioning and Storytelling)

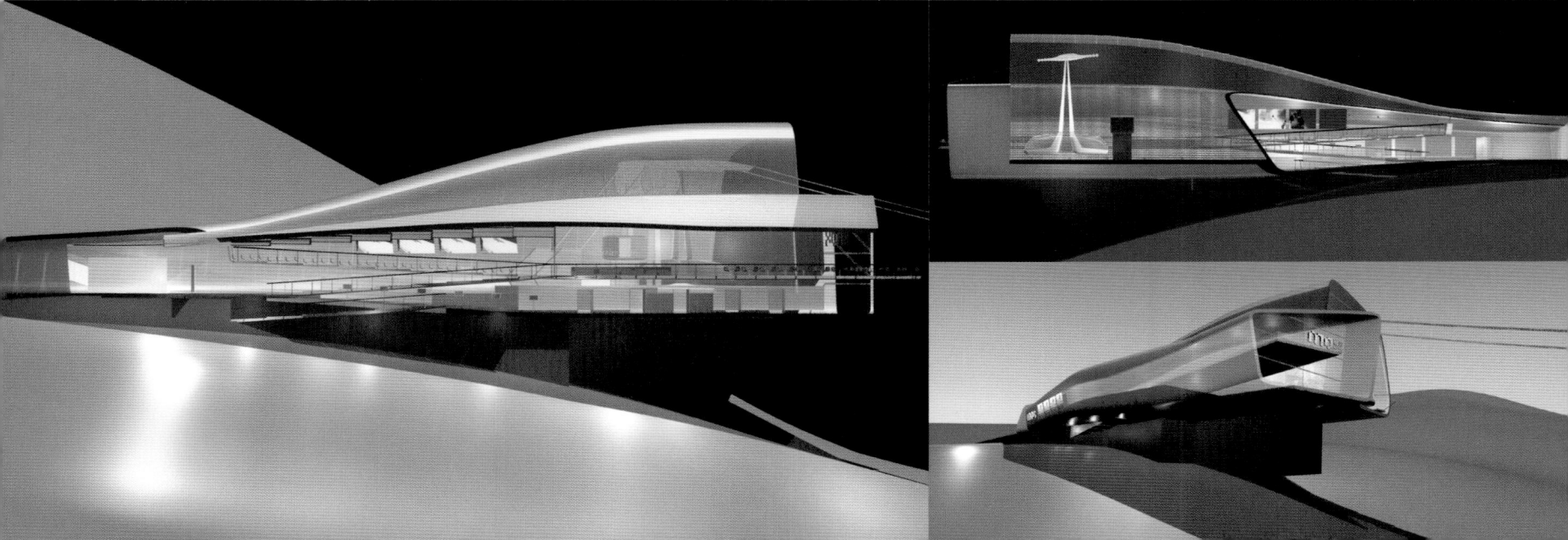

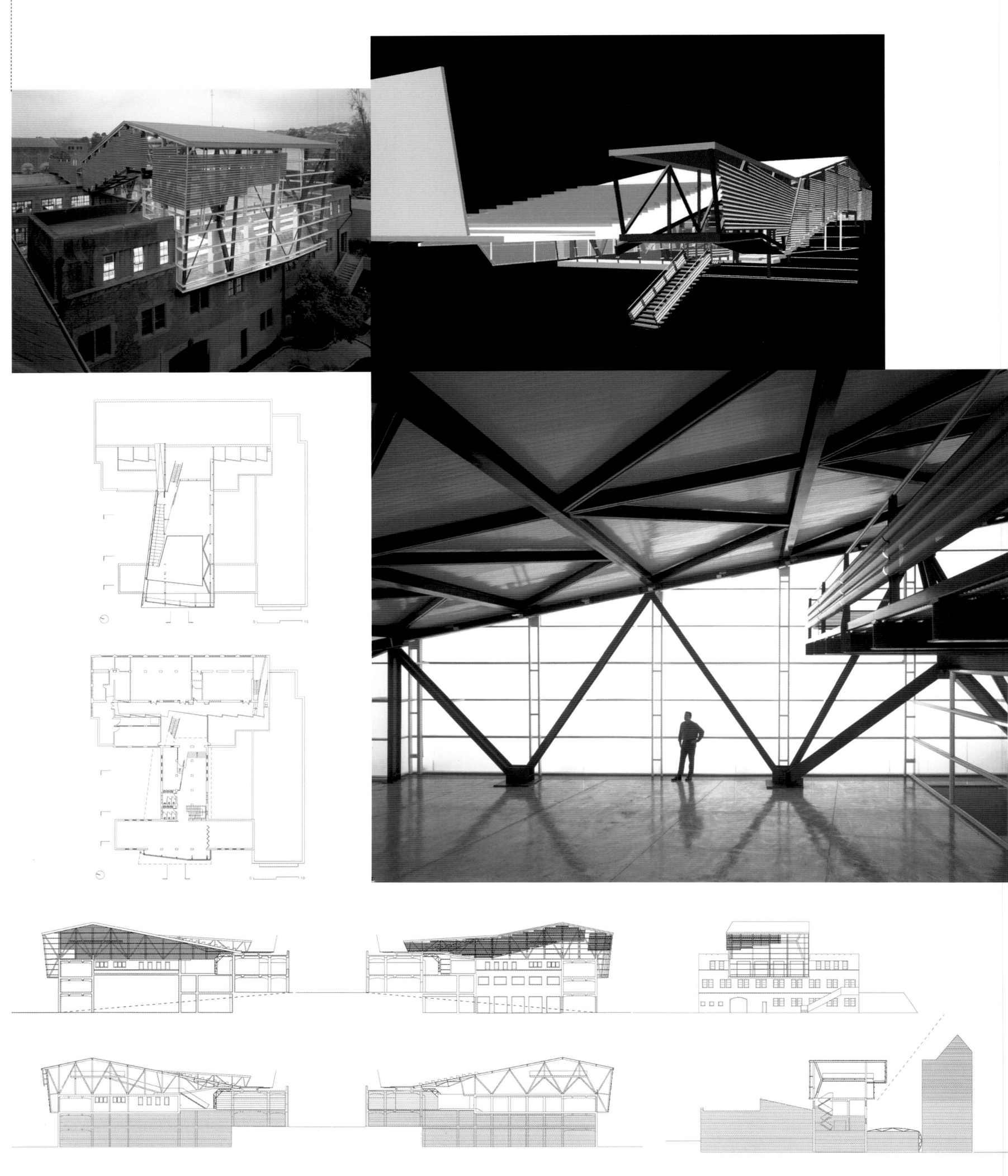

School of Architecture, Santa Maria University

Valparaiso, Chile, completed 1998

Given tasks

Strategize spatial and programmatic requirements for a new architecture school. Build 750 square metres of new facilities and renovate 1,200 square metres of existing facilities for a maximum of $US398,000 in a time-frame from first sketch to project opening of ten months. Propose a contemporary building on top of a campus that is a UN world heritage site, and that consists of one sole neo-Gothic building style for all its buildings. Connect to the existing building, situated in an earthquake zone, at no more than 14 fixed given connection points.

Strategy and ideas

The project follows the ideas of an evolutionary platform capable of catalyzing unpredictable actions within the architecture school's future everyday culture. In order to accommodate the desired temporal nature of potential events, interventions and adaptations, the design proposes a building based on the idea of incompleteness. Following digitally aided scenario studies, spatial sequences of continuous differentiation and open co-existence were developed, in order to study potential deterritorializations of the institutional typology. Acting as a facilitating spatial infrastructure rather then prescriptive form, the buildings deliberately deploy the idea of incompleteness that is essential for ongoing interpretation and subsequent actualizations through students and faculty.

The form of the envelope follows the idea of a condensed surface that connects in a simple geometric play the studio, computerlab, exhibition, event and hangout spaces and ramps. On top of the envelope on the slanted rooftop, the possibility for an outdoor auditorium for 250 spectators in phase two has been provided. The undulated, perforated, aluminium shading screens, the horizontal glass curtain wall and the luminous polycarbonate planes allow for a diverse dialogue with the highly determined language of the existing buildings. Further, they both regulate the daylight for the studio spaces and minimize heat transmission during the hot summer months, without the installation of additional mechanical systems. The suspended ramp, for example, acts also as a brise-soleil. The building was reoriented from the central campus patio with focus to the academic life towards the vibrant city. ◩

Credits: LWPAC in collaboration with Barria+Taylor, Chile. Photographs: Guy Wenborne

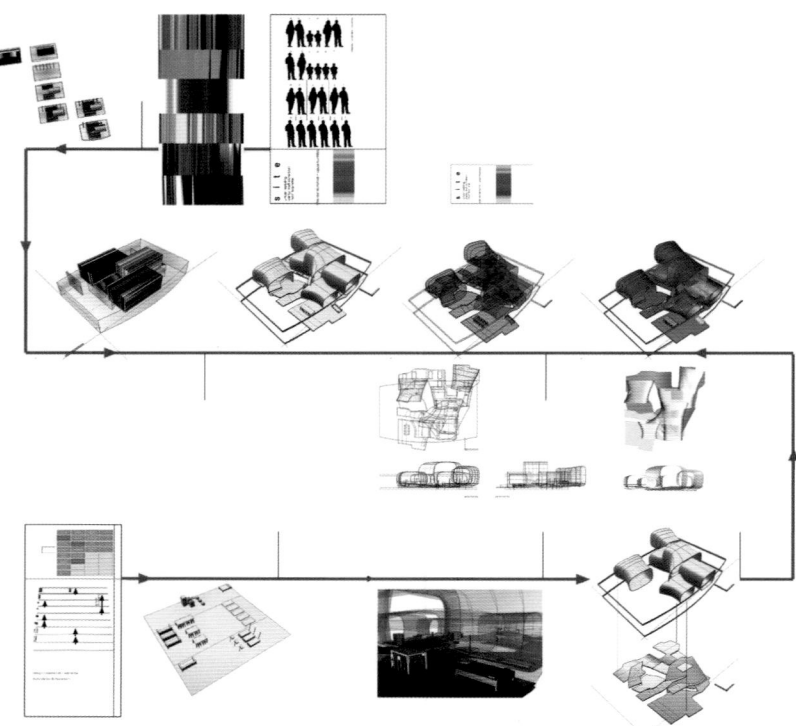

PAC Hous(e)ing

Project, 2000

PAC Hous(e)ing is an R & D Project for mass customizable prefabricated live/work structures. In architecture choice and mass production are, it seems, at odds with each other. In its 1998 annual report on Mass Customization, the Federal Reserve Bank of Dallas distinguishes three different production ages and their implication to characterization, cost and value: 1) Agrarian Age: Hand Production (Artisans) Low Fixed Cost, High Marginal Cost. 2) Industrial Age: Mass Production (Assembly Line) High Fixed Cost, Low Marginal Cost. 3) Information Age: (Digital) Low Fixed Cost, Low Marginal Cost. Obviously architecture is still trapped in either the Agrarian or Industrial age with regard to product quality, cost and actual choice, while many industries have long advanced into the Information age. Housing projects especially fall largely into the categories of standardization or are high-end 'custom-tailored' solutions. The idea of a building as a high-quality product that allows for choice is currently hard to come by.

The launching of a new product requires three related R & D aspects. 1) Marketing and branding: This project is based on a range of live/work scenarios that consider different lifestyles and cultural practices and project lifecycles of a building and its related possibilities for growth and shrinkage. 2) The conception of the new product itself: PAC houses or housing projects are made compact by reducing typical redundancies and affording maximum space for multiple programmes. Each project privileges relational thinking over the unit-based approach in order to blur boundaries, which facilitates flexibility and adaptation. 3) The conception of material properties, manufacturing and distribution methods: Most of today's materials start their process in a liquid state. By the controlled infusion of agents and stabilizers, contemporary plastics, glass, metals, composites and recycled materials can acquire complex distributed properties. Finally, computer numerically controlled prototyping and robotically assisted manufacturing processes of entire buildings allow for a high degree of mass customization.

The project is currently seeking corporate and/or institutional sponsorship for the realization of a first built prototype.

Growth / Adaptation

Customization

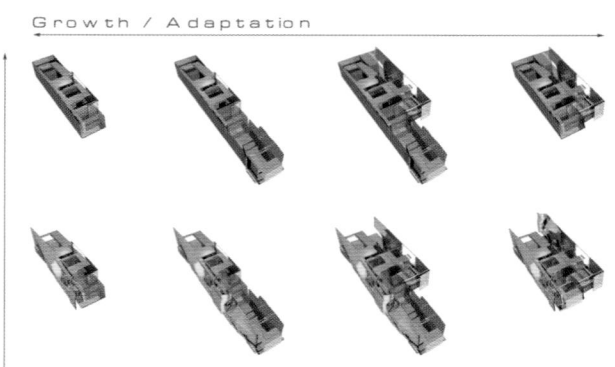

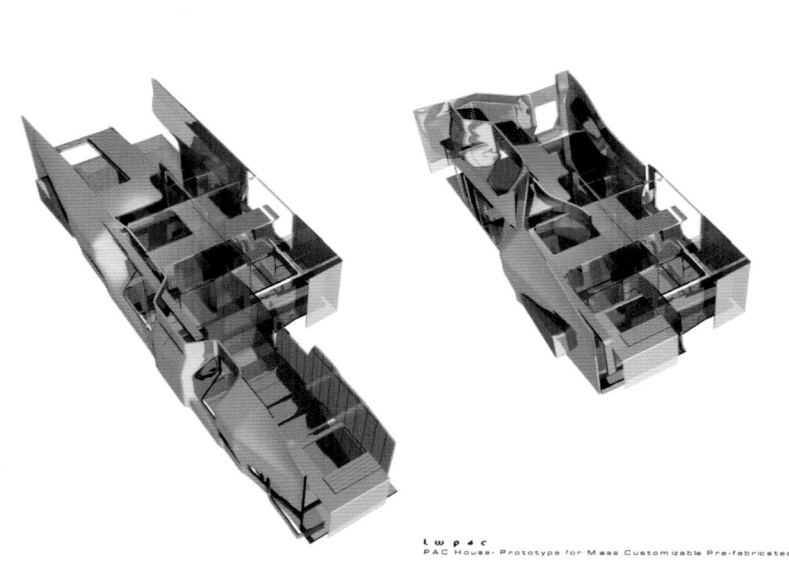

l w p a c
PAC House- Prototype for Mass Customizable Pre-fabricated House

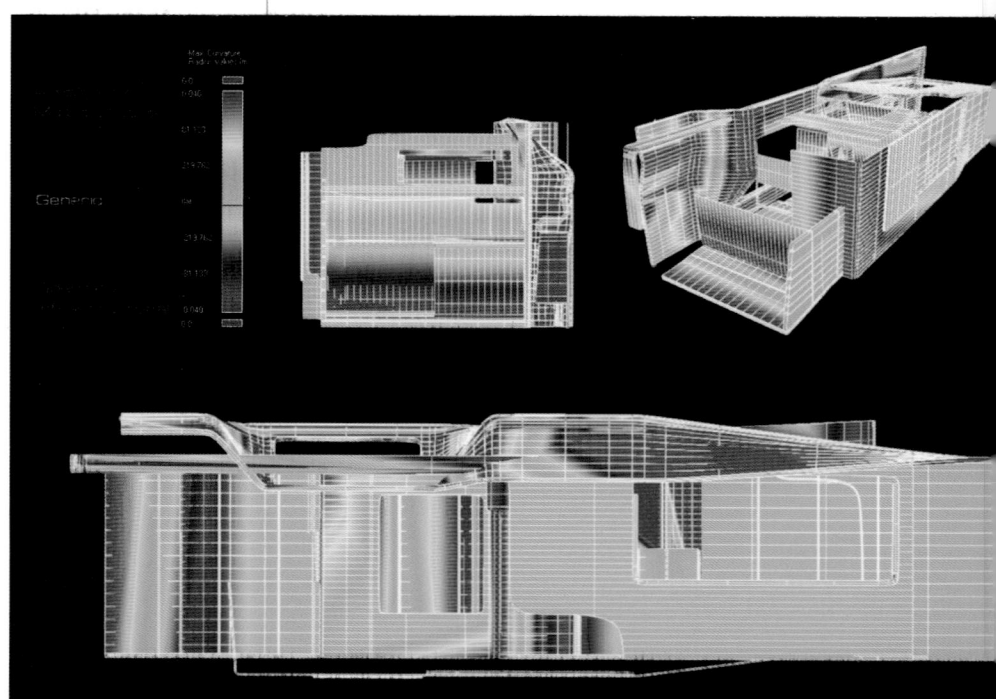

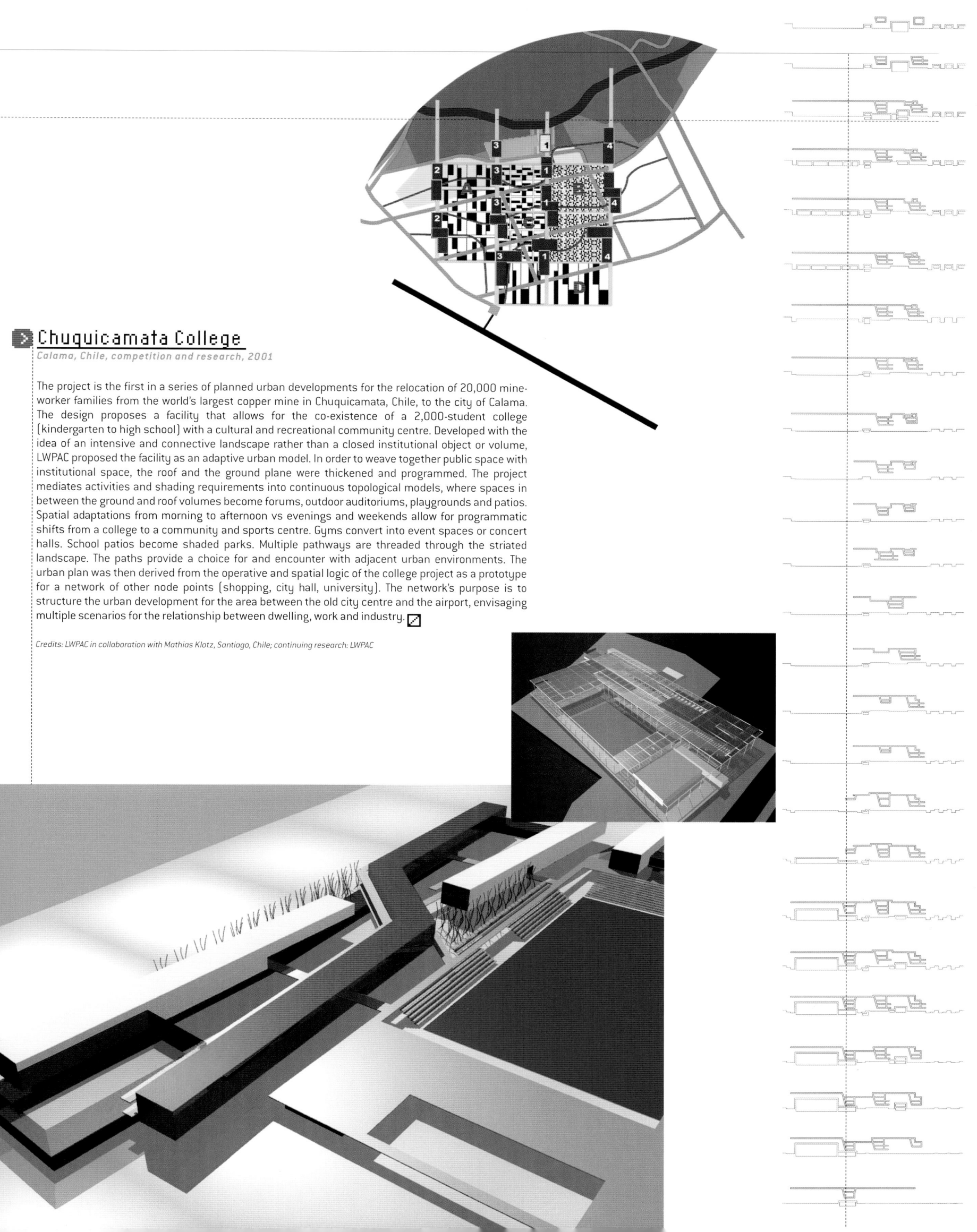

Chuquicamata College
Calama, Chile, competition and research, 2001

The project is the first in a series of planned urban developments for the relocation of 20,000 mine-worker families from the world's largest copper mine in Chuquicamata, Chile, to the city of Calama. The design proposes a facility that allows for the co-existence of a 2,000-student college (kindergarten to high school) with a cultural and recreational community centre. Developed with the idea of an intensive and connective landscape rather than a closed institutional object or volume, LWPAC proposed the facility as an adaptive urban model. In order to weave together public space with institutional space, the roof and the ground plane were thickened and programmed. The project mediates activities and shading requirements into continuous topological models, where spaces in between the ground and roof volumes become forums, outdoor auditoriums, playgrounds and patios. Spatial adaptations from morning to afternoon vs evenings and weekends allow for programmatic shifts from a college to a community and sports centre. Gyms convert into event spaces or concert halls. School patios become shaded parks. Multiple pathways are threaded through the striated landscape. The paths provide a choice for and encounter with adjacent urban environments. The urban plan was then derived from the operative and spatial logic of the college project as a prototype for a network of other node points (shopping, city hall, university). The network's purpose is to structure the urban development for the area between the old city centre and the airport, envisaging multiple scenarios for the relationship between dwelling, work and industry. ◪

Credits: LWPAC in collaboration with Mathias Klotz, Santiago, Chile; continuing research: LWPAC

nARCHITECTS

United States, Canada

Eric Bunge (1962), Mimi Hoang (1971)

Architects Eric Bunge and Mimi Hoang formed nARCHITECTS in New York in 1999. Before meeting at Harvard University's Graduate School of Design, Mimi Hoang received her degree from MIT and Eric Bunge, who teaches at Columbia University and Parsons School of Design, received his from McGill University. They won the Architectural League of New York's Young Architects Forum Prize in 2001. nARCHITECTS collaborated with fieldOFFICE in 2000 to win first prize in the first phase of a competition to design a new theatre/hotel for the Danish performance group Hotel Pro Forma, and to participate as finalists in the second, invited phase of the competition. They have exhibited their work at the Urban Center in New York, the Danish Centre for Architecture and the Municipal Ottawa Art Gallery and were included in a show entitled 'New Hotels for Global Nomads' at the Smithsonian's Cooper-Hewitt Museum in New York in 2002. ☑

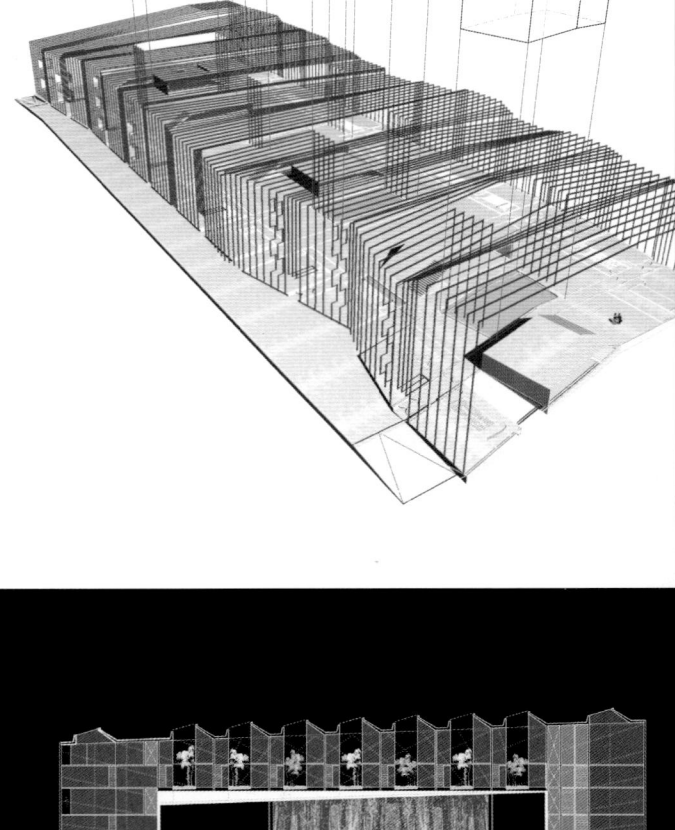

THE 'n' that Eric Bunge and Mimi Hoang have added to the name of their architecture studio derives directly from mathematical language and represents, according to them, the infinite possibilities suggested by the term. The 'n' also denotes and is represented in their work as a variable dimension, an unknown. This unknown can reside in the size of the team: the two people who currently comprise the studio often work in association with other partners: the architects of fieldOFFICE (Hotel Pro Forma project) or the artists Barbara Steinman and Doho Suh. But the unknown, for nArchitects, is essentially concerned with the definition of the architectural field itself, which they perceive as a domain that is becoming more and more fluid, unstable and uncertain. Rejecting recourse to conventional solutions and application of pre-established models, Eric Bunge and Mimi Hoang approach each project by setting out the data, deconstructing the structures, relations and parameters that condition the original situation. Each project is thus formulated in terms of a critical interrogation, the only possible route to architectural invention, which they believe to be necessary in every case. This process, cross-sectional and exploratory, explains the great diversity of their works, in terms of scale, form or programme. But above all this permanent question-mark over identities and programmatic and typological assignments leads them to projects that are themselves hybrid and strange: Hotel Pro Forma presents as a mixture of subsidized cultural institution and 'à la carte' hotel, a typical product of contemporary marketing; with Window-BOX-Wall, they muddy the distinction between wall, furniture and window; with their project for Aomori, they try to articulate the urban and suburban qualities and standards. Deliberately experimental and innovative, the architecture of Bunge and Hoang rests on an expansive notion of the environment that is natural, social or urban. This is never divorced from cultural, infrastructural or technological conditions. Architecture, according to them, must render explicit and reinvest relations, dynamics and possibilities that underlie this environment pushed to its limits. This attitude not only stems from a wish to restore architecture to the heart of contemporary problems but also rests on an unshakeable confidence in its capacity to resolve the contradictions of the world today: between public and private, urban and suburban. nature and technology. At the core of these questions, nArchitects wish to generate multiple interferences between different, sometimes watertight aspects of our contemporary environments, to create the opportunity for new forms, new strategies and new artefacts. ☑

P.C.

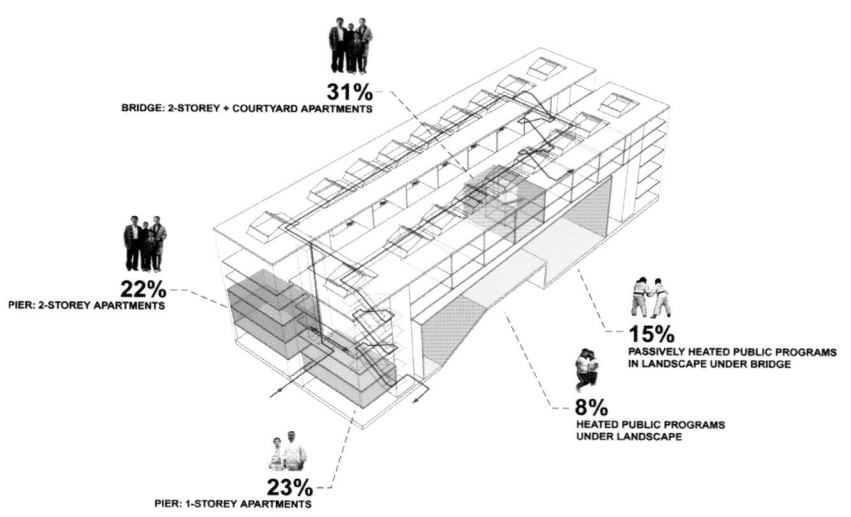

31%
BRIDGE: 2-STOREY + COURTYARD APARTMENTS

22%
PIER: 2-STOREY APARTMENTS

15%
PASSIVELY HEATED PUBLIC PROGRAMS
IN LANDSCAPE UNDER BRIDGE

8%
HEATED PUBLIC PROGRAMS
UNDER LANDSCAPE

23%
PIER: 1-STOREY APARTMENTS

Thermal Bridge
Northern Style Housing
Aomori, Japan, competition, 2001

A housing project for a cold climate in northern Japan, Thermal Bridge balances a suburban desire for seclusion with an urban desire for density. The strategy begins with a critique of exterior public space in housing: normative double-loaded corridor housing slab types are transformed by rotating one side up to form a bridge. The result is an insulating layer of courtyard-housing that spans an interior landscape and provides a thermal envelope under which public programmes can be placed. Double glass-enclosed fissures between 13 bridges of housing passively heat the public interior space below. Snow and light penetrate deep into this new urban semi-interior though the insertion of four glass-enclosed winter zones. Residents pass continuous light gaps and intermittent snow gardens as they travel along circulation loops, and apartment units provide views outward and inward to the semi-interior public space below. By using a thermal logic to organize the programmes of housing and public space, Thermal Bridge stages unexpected and fluctuating juxtapositions between cold and warm, public and private. ◨

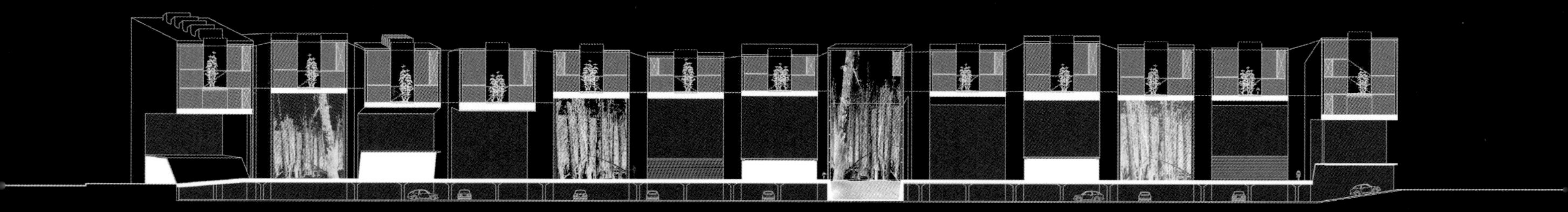

GROUND LEVEL PLAN 1:1000
(SHOWING PIER UNITS AND PUBLIC PROGRAMS)

BRIDGE LEVEL PLAN 1:1000
(SHOWING COURTYARD AND PIER UNITS)

TYPICAL HOTEL PROGRAM

guestrooms

circulation:
corridors
stairs
elevators

admin

public area:
lobby
restaurants
banquet + meeting rms

service area:
storage
kitchens
housekeeping

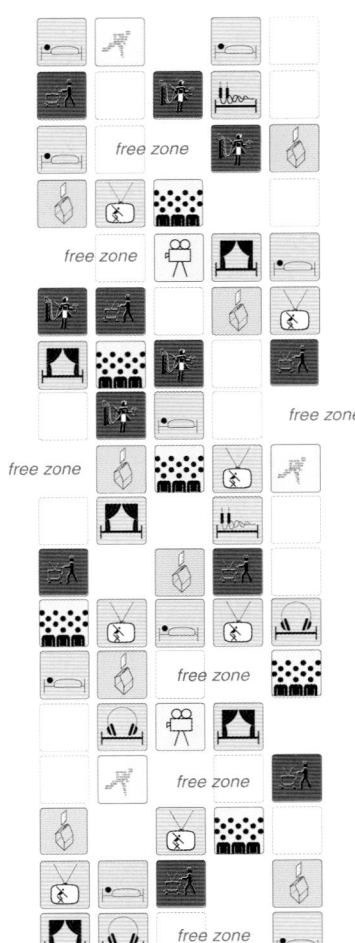

PROGRAMMING HOTEL PRO FORMA
(THE ART INSTITUTION AS A RESPONSIVE MATRIX OF SERVICES)

free zone

free zone

free zone

free zone

free zone

free zone

free zone

Hotel Pro Forma
Room-Lobby-Room
Ørestad, Denmark, competition, 2000

Winners of the first prize in the first phase of the competition to conceive a residence for the Danish troupe of artists and performers Hotel Pro Forma, nARCHITECTS also were finalists in the second phase. Through an appropriation of a hotel's organizational principles, this theatre/hotel rewrites the art institution as a responsive matrix of services. Checking in is redefined as an ongoing digital à-la-carte transaction by means of variable commercial zones, allowing guest performers and passers-by the freedom to select their arts programme, duration of stay and level of service desired. In a standard hotel, the separation between rooms and the lobby precludes programmatic adjacencies. Hotel Pro Forma proposes an alternating vertical sequence of rooms and lobbies. The structure-free lobbies are separated by densely packed vierendeel truss room floors, which accommodate both the building's infrastructure and a matrix of rentable plug-in rooms. This sectional multiplication of a hotel delays and disperses arrival, check-in and departure and creates unexpected adjacencies between hotel guests, spectators, performers and unwitting passers-by. Guests leap-frog between lobby floors on escalators located between the double-skinned envelope – the free zone – catching glimpses of activities in the rooms that they pass. This intertwining of hotel and performance accommodates a spectrum of adaptability that ranges from the determinate to the errandless. ☑

Credits: (1st phase) nARCHITECTS, in collaboration with fieldOFFICE (Annette Dudek, Jamie Meunier); (2nd phase) Eric Bunge (team leader) and Mimi Hoang, in collaboration with fieldOFFICE (Annette Dudek, Jamie Meunier); (consultants) Ove Arup & Partners, New York, and Arkitektgruppen

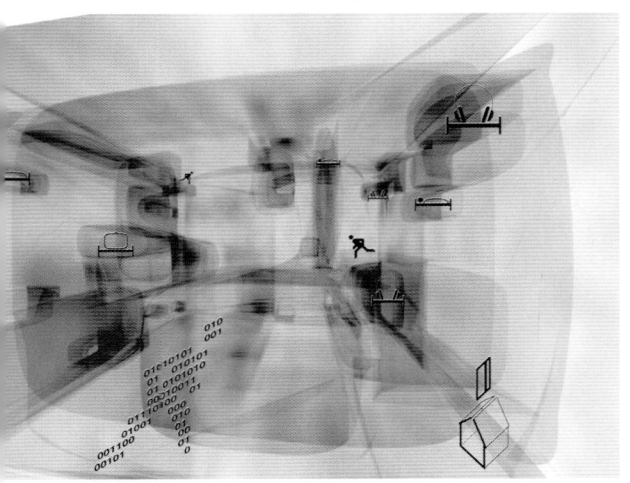

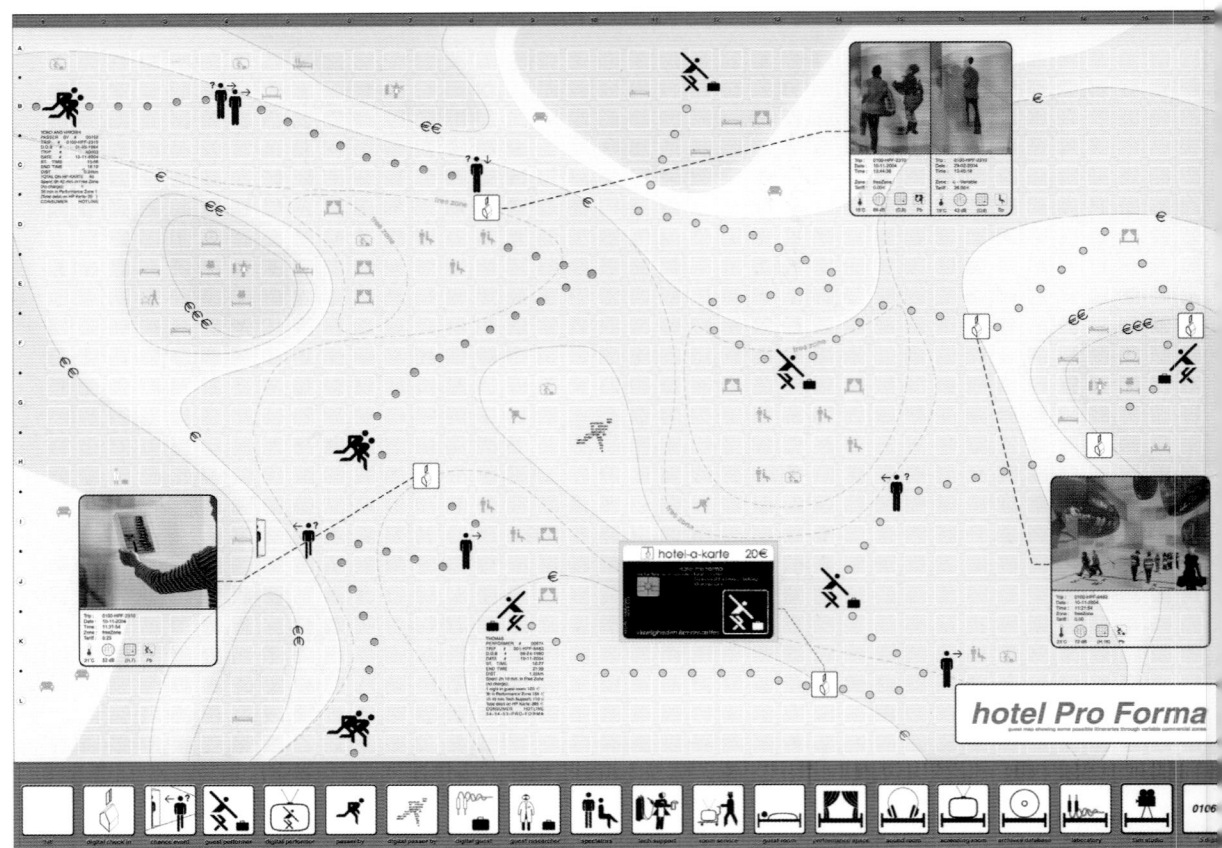

hotel Pro Forma

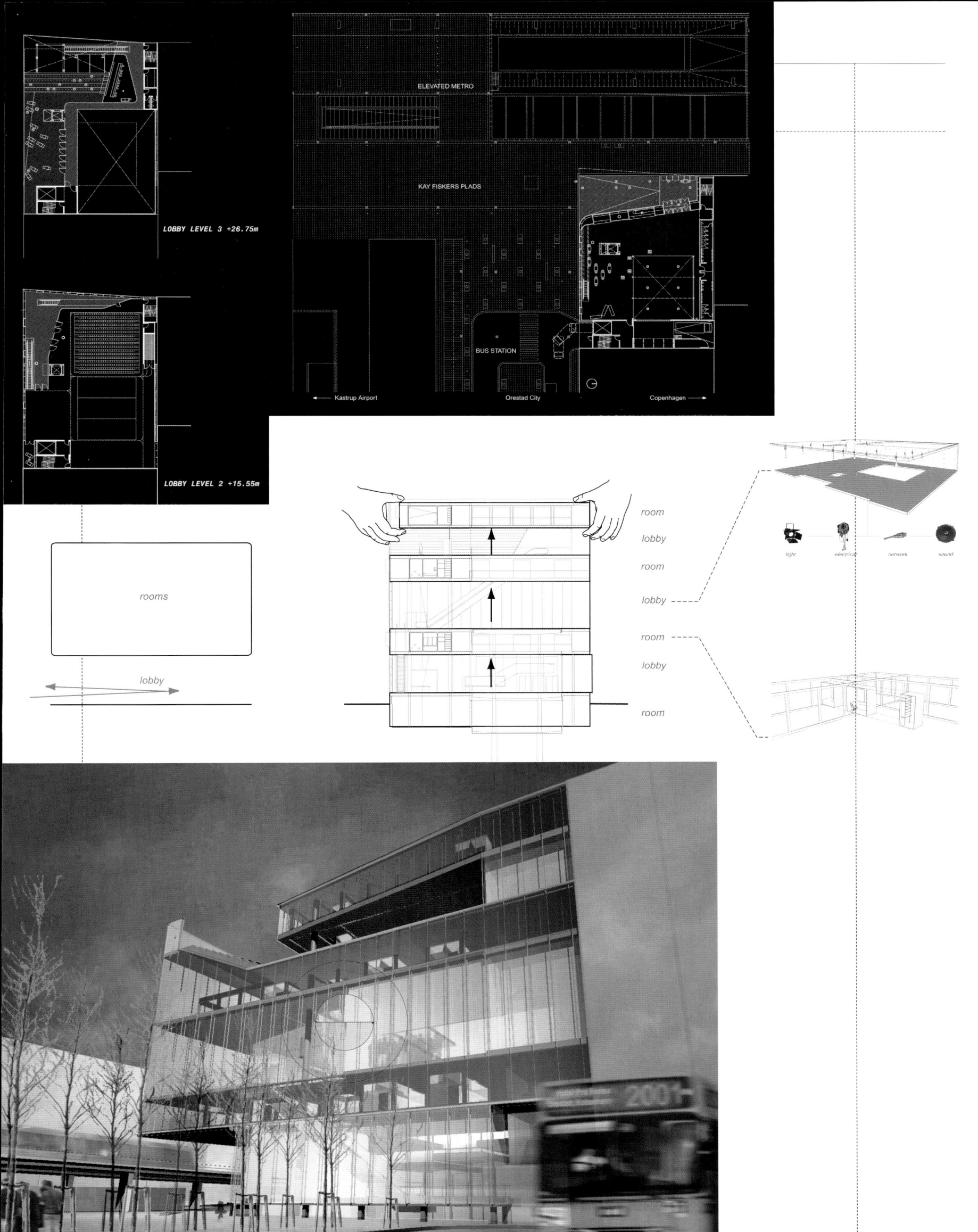

LOBBY LEVEL 3 +26.75m

ELEVATED METRO

KAY FISKERS PLADS

BUS STATION

← Kastrup Airport   Orestad City   Copenhagen →

LOBBY LEVEL 2 +15.55m

rooms

lobby

room

lobby

room

lobby

room

lobby

room

light   electricity   network   sound

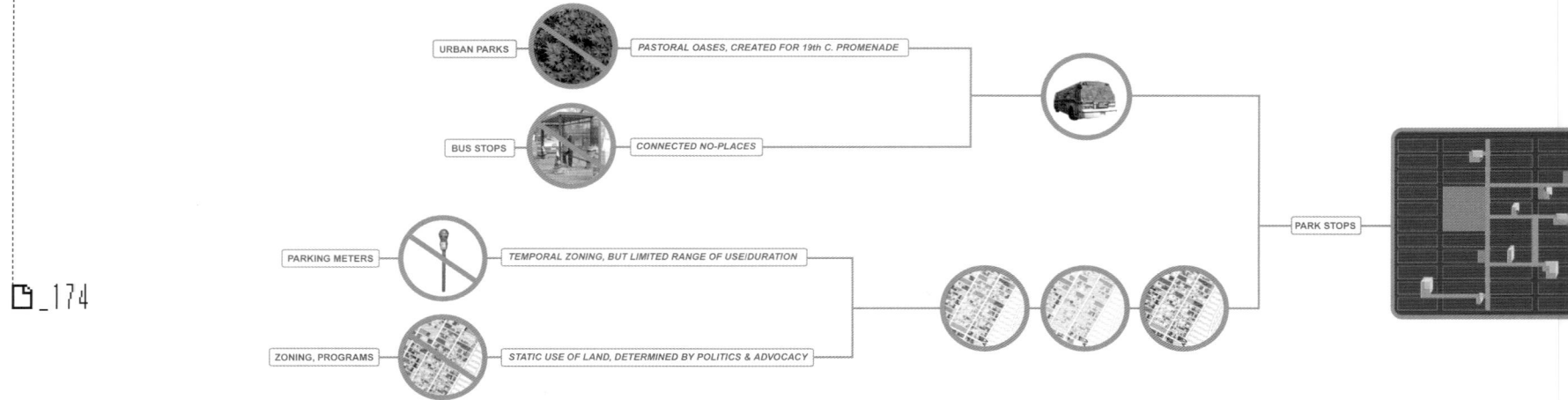

URBAN PARKS — PASTORAL OASES, CREATED FOR 19th C. PROMENADE

BUS STOPS — CONNECTED NO-PLACES

PARKING METERS — TEMPORAL ZONING, BUT LIMITED RANGE OF USE/DURATION

ZONING, PROGRAMS — STATIC USE OF LAND, DETERMINED BY POLITICS & ADVOCACY

PARK STOPS

ORGANIZATIONAL SYSTEMS THAT WILL BE TRANSFORMED BY INFORMATION TECHNOLOGY ARE QUESTIONED AT THEIR LIMITS, PRODUCING VIABLE HYBRIDS, AND SHIFTING OUR FOCUS FROM BOUNDARIES TO NETWORKS

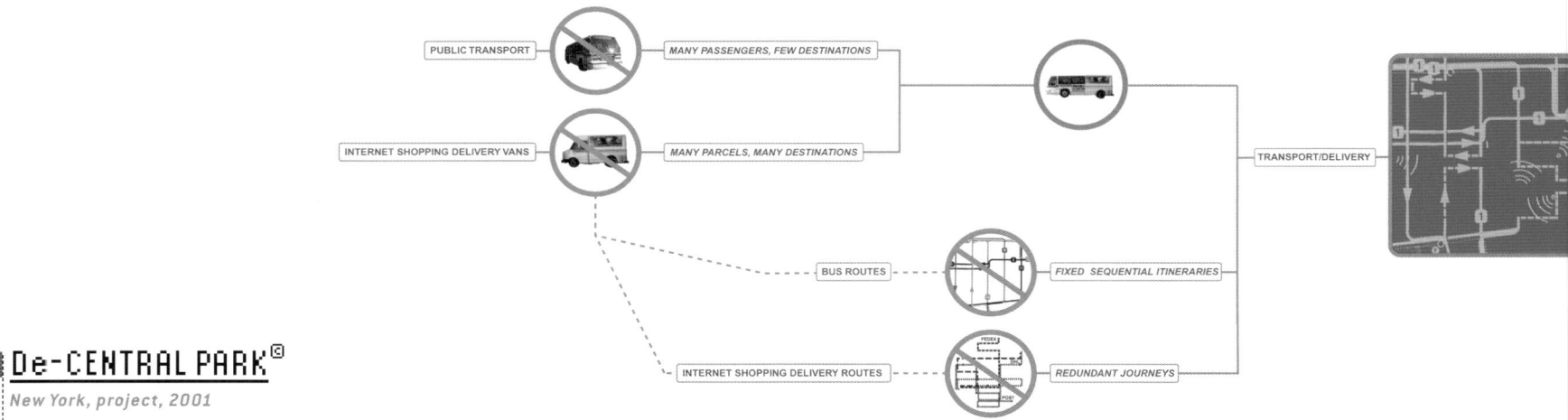

PUBLIC TRANSPORT — MANY PASSENGERS, FEW DESTINATIONS

INTERNET SHOPPING DELIVERY VANS — MANY PARCELS, MANY DESTINATIONS

BUS ROUTES — FIXED SEQUENTIAL ITINERARIES

INTERNET SHOPPING DELIVERY ROUTES — REDUNDANT JOURNEYS

TRANSPORT/DELIVERY

De-CENTRAL PARK[⊗]

New York, project, 2001

This experimental project considers ways in which information technology might affect existing urban spaces. While Central Park resulted from a 19th-century planning decision consistent with a state of rapid urban expansion, de-CENTRAL PARK will arise from opportunistic tactics of appropriation made necessary by a city in a constant state of renewal. de-CENTRAL PARK proposes a network of park-stops — hybrids between urban parks, bus-stops and transport/delivery networks — that can be configured by varying user groups. As Internet-related deliveries become smaller, more frequent and dispersed, they will surpass the transport of people in complexity. Given this unsustainable congestion of redundant routes, de-CENTRAL PARK proposes to merge public transport and delivery systems in a rhizomic network of variable duration and configuration that delivers both people and goods. Opportunistic navigation systems detect users' desired destinations in real time, replacing fixed routes. de-CENTRAL PARK will emerge simultaneously in several local regions, growing unstoppably and weaving into the iconic 20th-century city of Manhattan. ☒

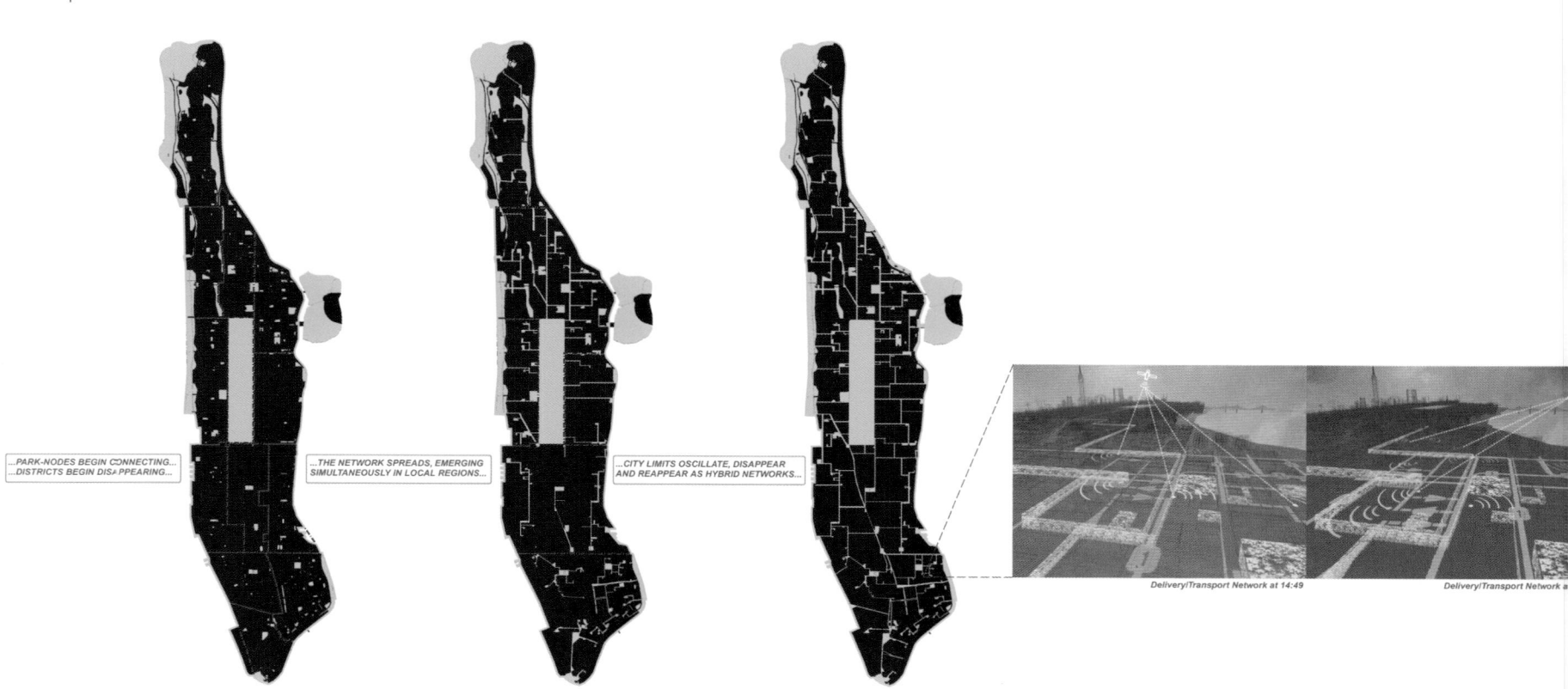

...PARK-NODES BEGIN CONNECTING... ...DISTRICTS BEGIN DISAPPEARING...

...THE NETWORK SPREADS, EMERGING SIMULTANEOUSLY IN LOCAL REGIONS...

...CITY LIMITS OSCILLATE, DISAPPEAR AND REAPPEAR AS HYBRID NETWORKS...

Delivery/Transport Network at 14:49

Delivery/Transport Network at

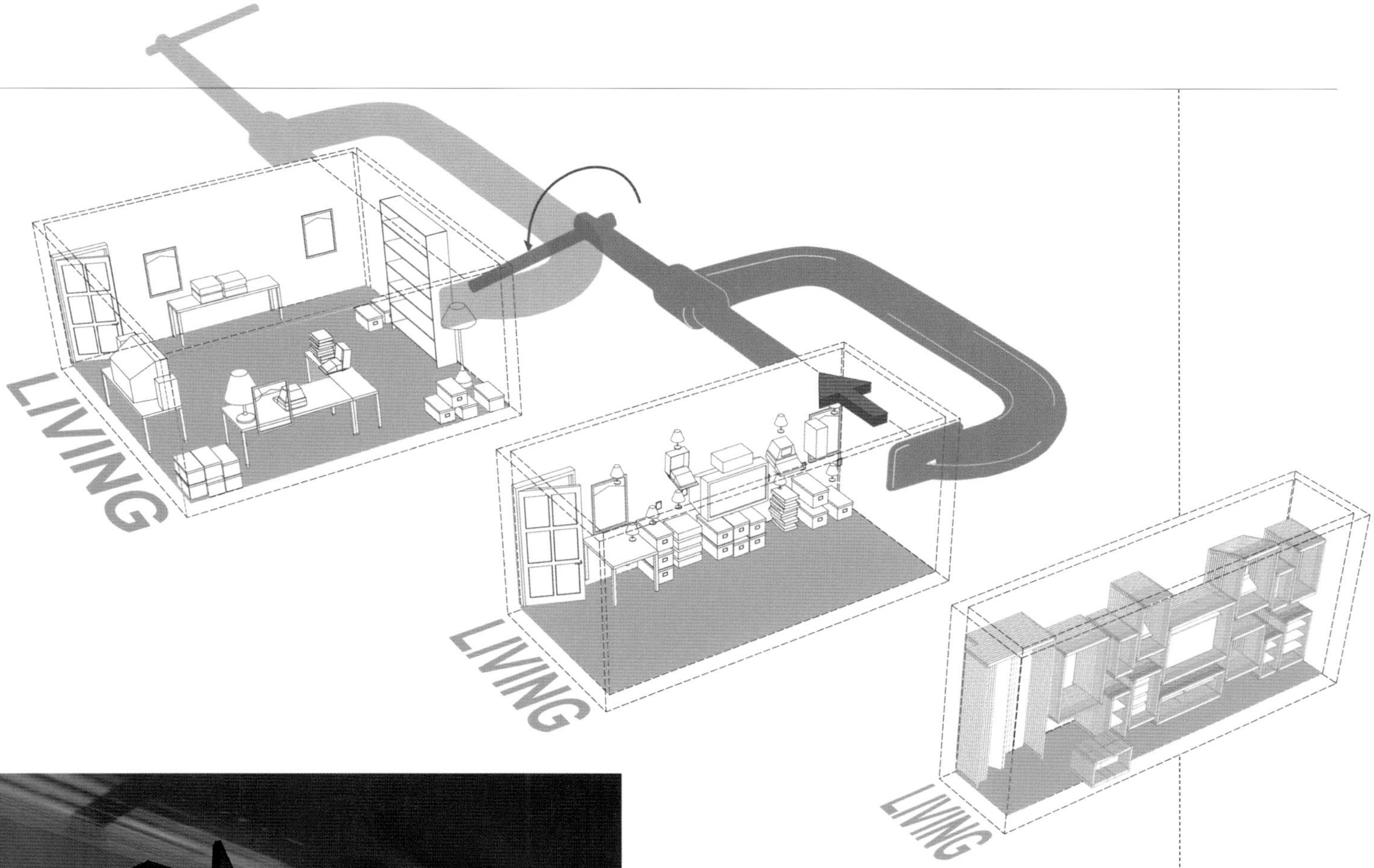

Window-BOX-Wall
New York, USA, completed 2002

In a Manhattan apartment adjacent to Central Park, various domestic elements, including a door, a desk, a shelf and a picture frame, are compressed along a wall. The lack of a direct view on to the park is compensated by a variable array of 'surrogate' views of technological artefacts, images and memories. Displaying, storing, working and playing are accommodated by a series of environmentally certified hardwood window boxes placed at heights determined by ergonomic criteria. Variable illumination creates an oscillating visual permeability, allowing the window boxes to reconcile the clients' conflicting desires simultaneously to display and conceal their contents. ☑

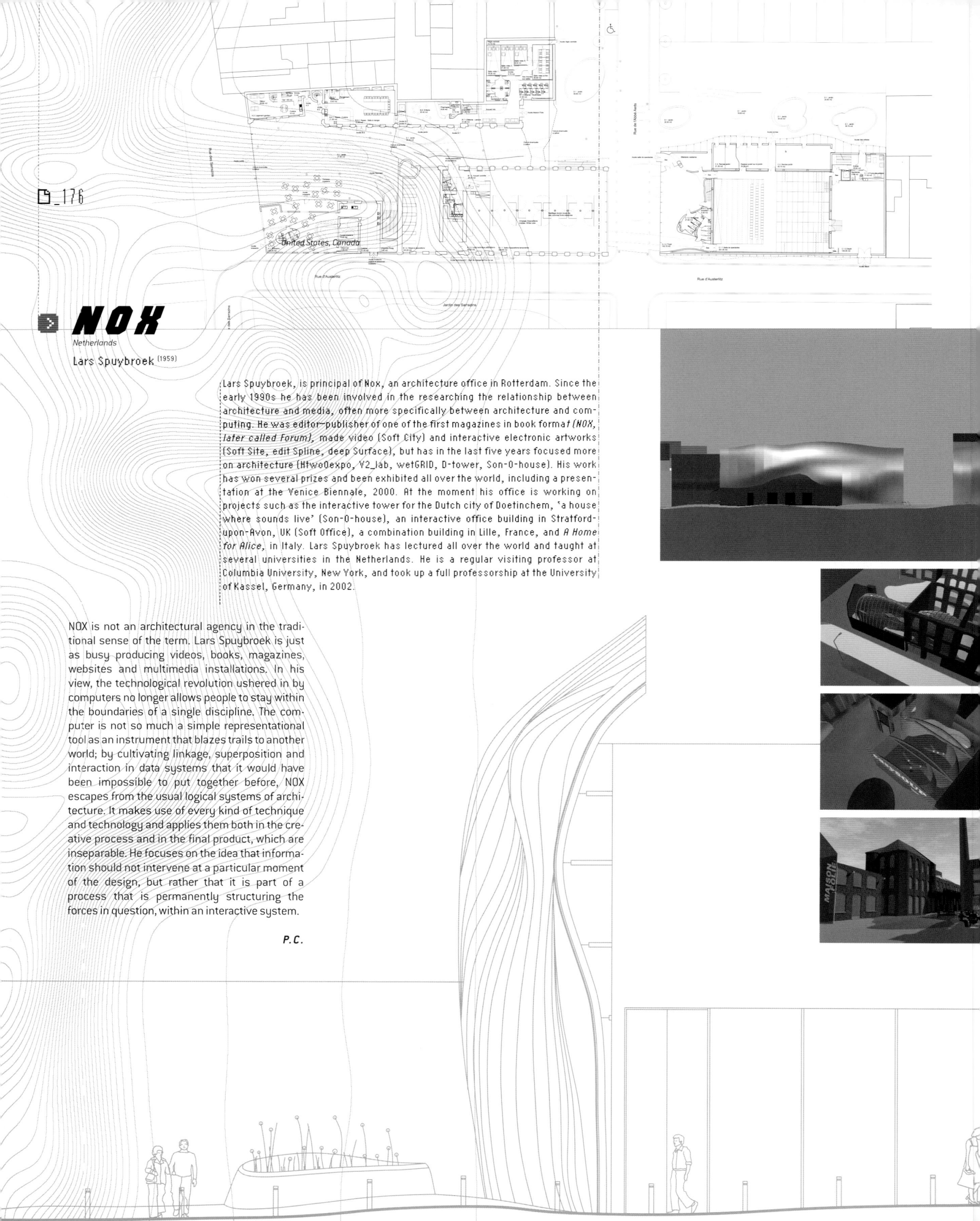

NOX

Netherlands

Lars Spuybroek [1959]

Lars Spuybroek, is principal of Nox, an architecture office in Rotterdam. Since the early 1990s he has been involved in the researching the relationship between architecture and media, often more specifically between architecture and computing. He was editor-publisher of one of the first magazines in book format *(NOX, later called Forum)*, made video (Soft City) and interactive electronic artworks (Soft Site, edit Spline, deep Surface), but has in the last five years focused more on architecture (HtwoOexpo, V2_lab, wetGRID, D-tower, Son-O-house). His work has won several prizes and been exhibited all over the world, including a presentation at the Venice Biennale, 2000. At the moment his office is working on projects such as the interactive tower for the Dutch city of Doetinchem, 'a house where sounds live' (Son-O-house), an interactive office building in Stratford-upon-Avon, UK (Soft Office), a combination building in Lille, France, and *A Home for Alice*, in Italy. Lars Spuybroek has lectured all over the world and taught at several universities in the Netherlands. He is a regular visiting professor at Columbia University, New York, and took up a full professorship at the University of Kassel, Germany, in 2002.

NOX is not an architectural agency in the traditional sense of the term. Lars Spuybroek is just as busy producing videos, books, magazines, websites and multimedia installations. In his view, the technological revolution ushered in by computers no longer allows people to stay within the boundaries of a single discipline. The computer is not so much a simple representational tool as an instrument that blazes trails to another world; by cultivating linkage, superposition and interaction in data systems that it would have been impossible to put together before, NOX escapes from the usual logical systems of architecture. It makes use of every kind of technique and technology and applies them both in the creative process and in the final product, which are inseparable. He focuses on the idea that information should not intervene at a particular moment of the design, but rather that it is part of a process that is permanently structuring the forces in question, within an interactive system.

P.C.

La Maison Folie

Lille, France, competition, 2001

This project won a competition for a complex to be built on the disused site of the old Leclercq factory in Wazemmes; it is to house various public and cultural programmes, both local and global. Conceived in the context of 'Lille 2004' as one of the *maisons folies* (crazy houses) that will be scattered over the city, the project is to accommodate an art school, exhibition rooms, a cinema and multimedia studios, artists' residences, and also a Turkish bath, a crèche, a brasserie, a restaurant and a 'cybercineo' [CYBERcafé, CINema and vidEO]. The NOX project proposes a reflection of the idea of networking, broken down into three different fields: the programme, the site and the image. The first step is to incorporate the different types of architecture on the site itself. Nox has opted for minimal reconstruction of the existing buildings (cleaning and renovation of the façades, renovation of the bays, reopening all the closed access points, installing lifts and some floors). There must be a very accurate study of the topology of the various activities, so that the programme itself can bring life back into this derelict architectural complex. The Nox project also aims to coordinate the different uses and programmes. It is the courtyard, treated as a surface of uninterrupted connection, that will fulfil the function of architectural continuity: a mineral topography, taking up the traditional northern motif of cobblestones, will thus provide common and flexible ground between the different programmes. It will coordinate the green microspaces (playground for the crèche, terrace for the brasserie, etc.), and its undulations will cope with problems linked to traffic (deliveries, pushchairs, wheelchairs, access ramps to the art school, etc.), varying heights throughout the site and drainage of rainwater. The third strand of the network explored in the project concerns the image, hence the part of the programme that requires a new building: the cinema. The interior of the cinema is to be a 'black box', extremely high-tech, and insulated against all outdoor noises. The exterior is an active façade, a kind of holographic veil that allows a glimpse of the opaque interior through its shimmering textures. In the evening, this façade can become a screen for luminous animations or interactive projections connected to the Internet, or even for exhibiting digital works of art. ☑

Credits: Lars Spuybroek, with Florent Rougement, Chris Seung-Woo Yoo and Kris Mun

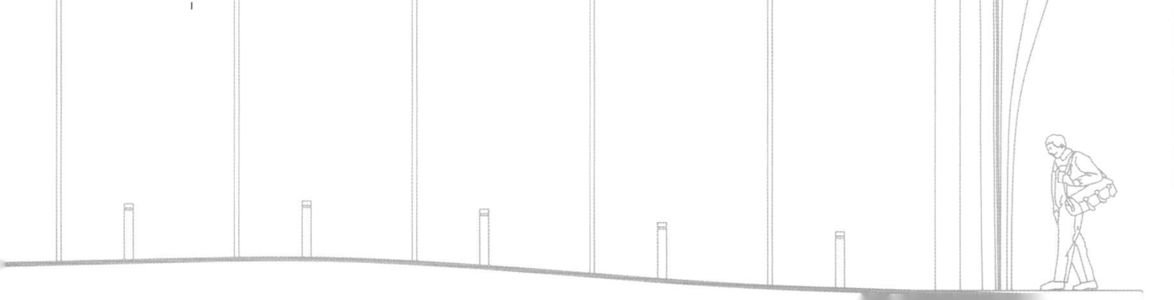

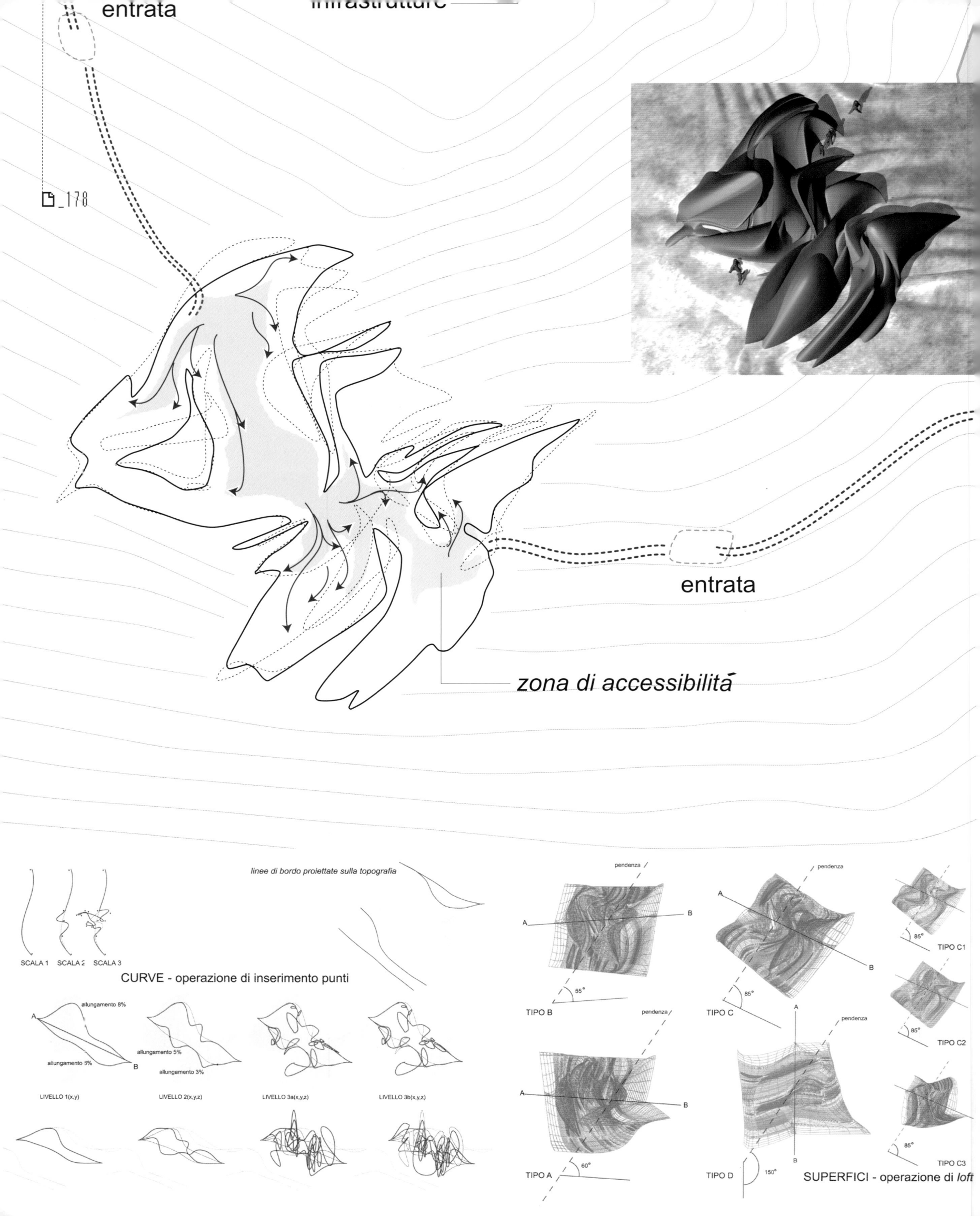

entrata

infrastrutture

_178

entrata

zona di accessibilitá

linee di bordo proiettate sulla topografia

SCALA 1   SCALA 2   SCALA 3

CURVE - operazione di inserimento punti

allungamento 8%

allungamento 3%   allungamento 5%

B   allungamento 3%

LIVELLO 1(x,y)   LIVELLO 2(x,y,z)   LIVELLO 3a(x,y,z)   LIVELLO 3b(x,y,z)

pendenza

A   B

55°

TIPO B

A   B

60°

TIPO A

pendenza

A   B

85°

TIPO C

pendenza

A

B

150°

TIPO D

85°

TIPO C1

85°

TIPO C2

85°

TIPO C3

SUPERFICI - operazione di *loft*

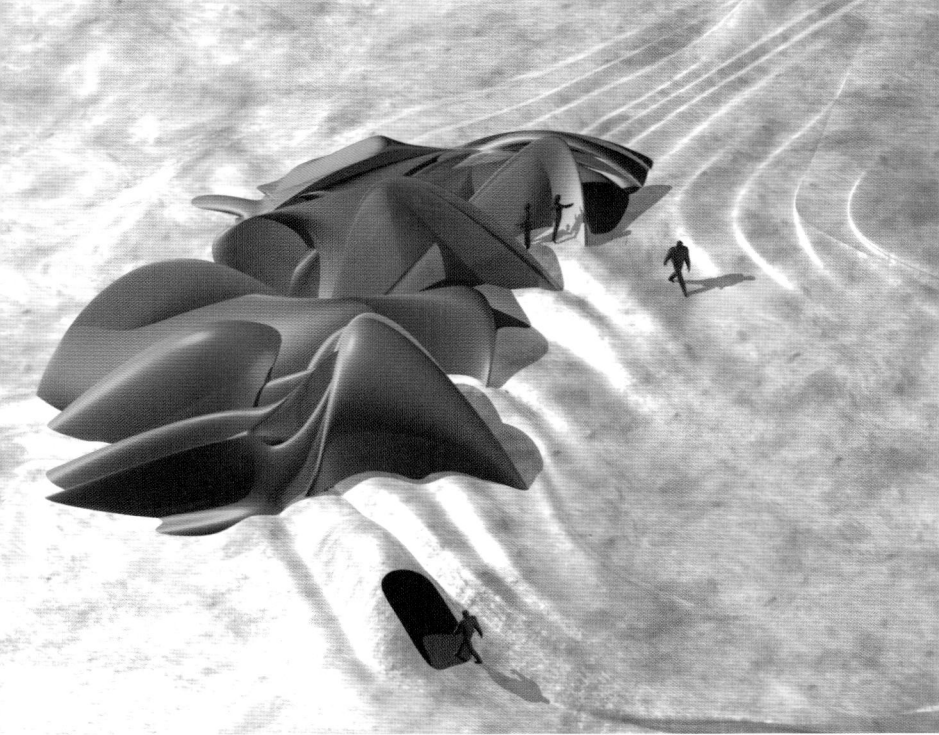

La Tana di Alice

Italy, 2001–03

There are two types of similarity, an internal and an external one: we look like others, but more mysteriously: we differ from ourselves, and we have to find ways of accepting that we do. We change our lives, our appearances, but first of all we grow, we have to grow up. It's the mystery of being among others, of having brothers and sisters, but also of having a body and a face that have a future and a past. Young Alice is caught between these two mirrors of similarity, of growing up and being in a world of others who are sometimes more similar to you than you are to yourself. Alice is a brave child, accepting the continuous changes of size as a logic in itself. This project seeks to offer an architectural interpretation of the story of Alice in Wonderland. Our small 'Tana di Alice' is a three-dimensional mirror, in the classic tradition of the Hall of Mirrors. We have extended this into the modern technologies of Virtual Reality, of interactive projection techniques where we have the possibility of changing 'real time' in front of an electronic mirror. The geometry of the 'Tana di Alice' is based on this play between the two similarities, between replication and reproduction, between the idea that change comes out of the self or that it is enforced from the outside. We have split and lengthened a set of lines through several operations, similar to the idea of offspring, in such a way that each line would contain another line and then another. This process of implication/explication results in a complex surface that consists of a series of self-similar ribs (made of polyester) that form the actual space on the inside. To get inside the 'Tana di Alice' we have to go through a hole (like Alice) and after a while we enter the complex formed interior. In the middle is a passage that folds up to the sides, which are mostly inaccessible areas – inaccessible to the feet, not to the eyes. In the space there are a few cameras where visitors can have the image of their face downloaded into the Replicator Program. All faces will be changed in different ways by this machine: changes in emotion, changes in sex and changes in age. The new faces will be real-time projected at several different zones in the space, offering an infinite number of reproductions because of the highly reflexive material of the interior surfaces. ☑

Credits: NOX (Lars Spuybroek with Ludovica Tramontin) for Roberto Masiero/Fondazione Nazionale Carlo Collodi

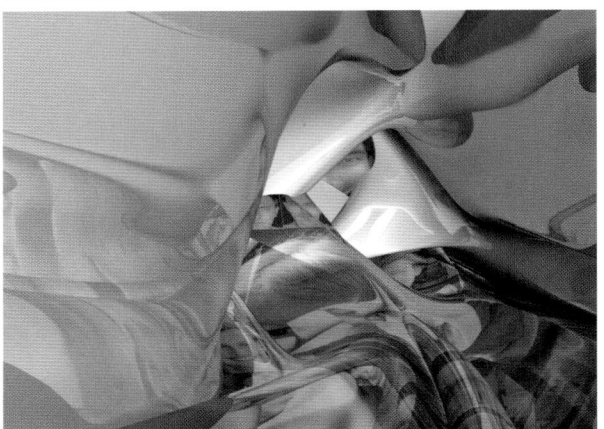

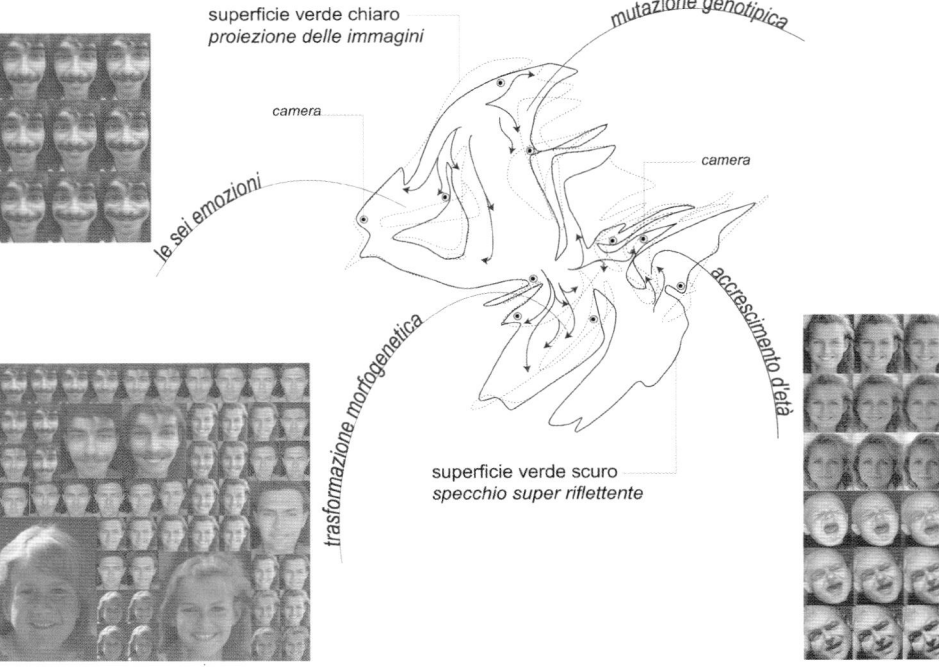

superficie verde chiaro
proiezione delle immagini

mutazione genotipica

camera

camera

le sei emozioni

trasformazione morfogenetica

accrescimento d'età

superficie verde scuro
specchio super riflettente

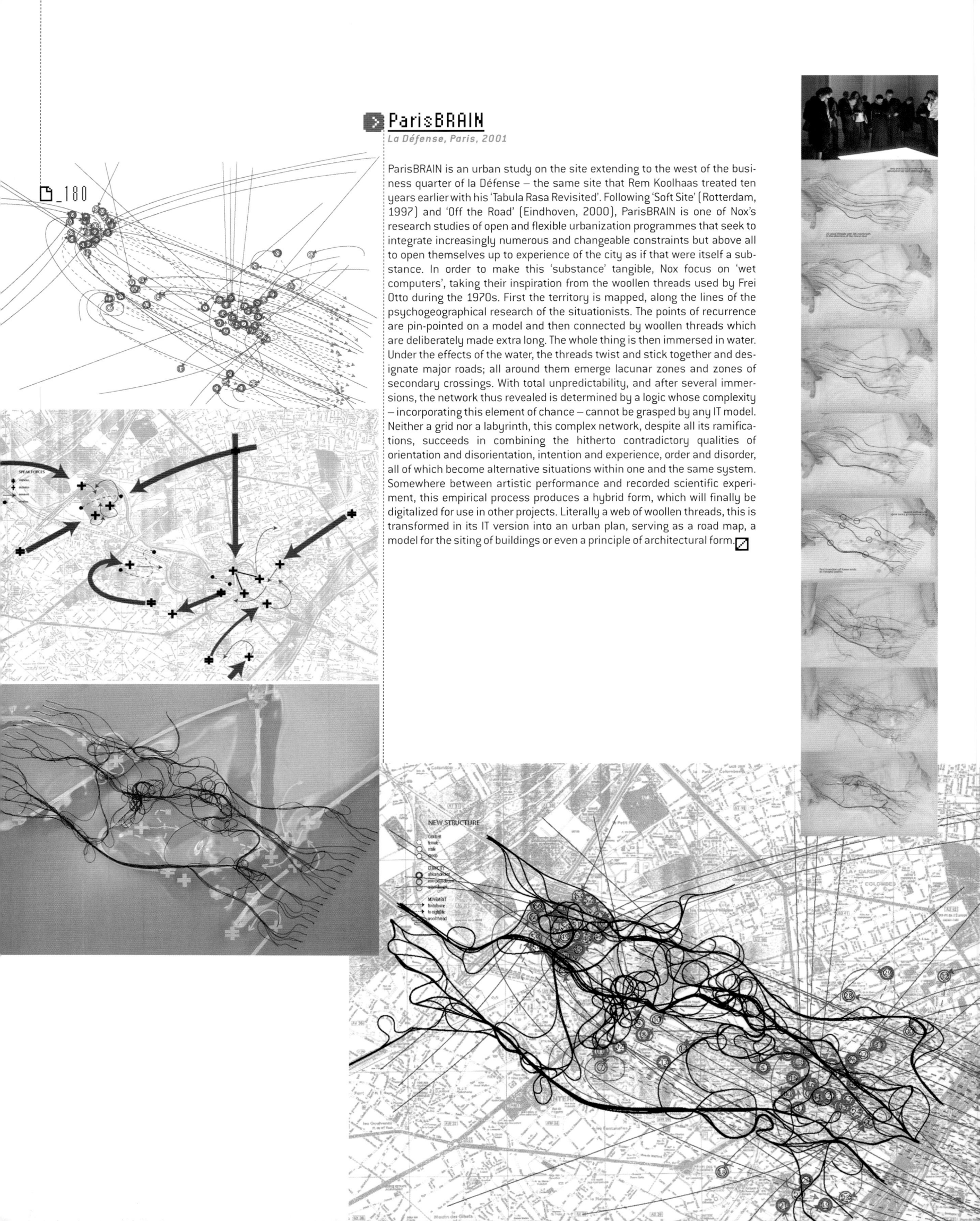

ParisBRAIN
La Défense, Paris, 2001

ParisBRAIN is an urban study on the site extending to the west of the business quarter of la Défense – the same site that Rem Koolhaas treated ten years earlier with his 'Tabula Rasa Revisited'. Following 'Soft Site' (Rotterdam, 1997) and 'Off the Road' (Eindhoven, 2000), ParisBRAIN is one of Nox's research studies of open and flexible urbanization programmes that seek to integrate increasingly numerous and changeable constraints but above all to open themselves up to experience of the city as if that were itself a substance. In order to make this 'substance' tangible, Nox focus on 'wet computers', taking their inspiration from the woollen threads used by Frei Otto during the 1970s. First the territory is mapped, along the lines of the psychogeographical research of the situationists. The points of recurrence are pin-pointed on a model and then connected by woollen threads which are deliberately made extra long. The whole thing is then immersed in water. Under the effects of the water, the threads twist and stick together and designate major roads; all around them emerge lacunar zones and zones of secondary crossings. With total unpredictability, and after several immersions, the network thus revealed is determined by a logic whose complexity – incorporating this element of chance – cannot be grasped by any IT model. Neither a grid nor a labyrinth, this complex network, despite all its ramifications, succeeds in combining the hitherto contradictory qualities of orientation and disorientation, intention and experience, order and disorder, all of which become alternative situations within one and the same system. Somewhere between artistic performance and recorded scientific experiment, this empirical process produces a hybrid form, which will finally be digitalized for use in other projects. Literally a web of woollen threads, this is transformed in its IT version into an urban plan, serving as a road map, a model for the siting of buildings or even a principle of architectural form.

_180

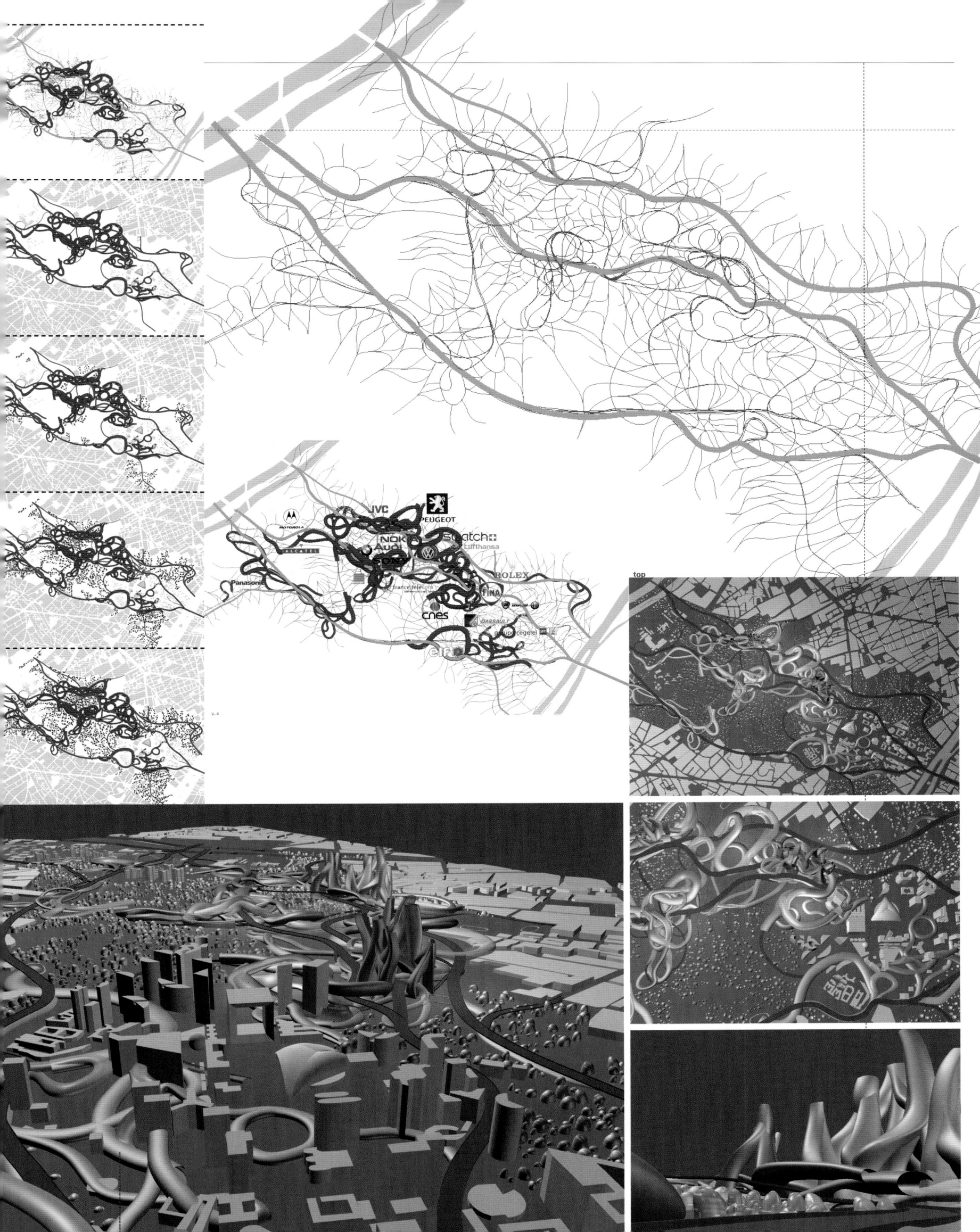

OFFSHORE ARCHITECTS

Netherlands

Peter Trummer [1964], Hannes Pfau [1969], Astrid Piber [1972], Penelope Dean [1969]

The three architects who founded Offshore in Amsterdam in 2001 are Austrian, live in Amsterdam and are affiliated with UN Studio run by Ben van Berkel and Caroline Bos: Hannes Pfau has been collaborating with them since 1997, after graduating from the University of Vienna and studying design in Salzburg and at the University of Michigan. Astrid Piber, a partner since 1999, also graduated in Vienna and continued her training at the Academy for Applied Arts at McGill University, Montreal, before obtaining a Masters degree from Columbia University. Peter Trummer studied under Günther Domenig at the Technical University of Graz, then under Bart Lootsma, taking a Masters degree from the Berlage Institute in Amsterdam. Now teaching in Graz, at the Academie van Bouwkunst in Rotterdam and at the Berlage Institute, he also collaborated with UN Studio from 1996 to 2000. 'Time Sharing Urbanism', his research thesis, presented at the Berlage Institute in 1998 and since published, was the result of a collaboration with the Australian architect Penelope Dean. ⊠

THE FOUNDERS of Offshore share a fascination with actual themes of our society and have the ambition, as a studio, to take a position within the realm of practicality. This is not just an outcome of their interest alone but also of a sharp awareness of changes in the architectural profession. Offshore is a practice whose area of activities is spread wide in order to come to terms with and get a grip on the complex processes of change in our daily life. Offshore architects was founded at a time of much discussion of a second modernity, in which complex changes questioned the established values of society. Institutions such as the national state, classes, traditions and the family disappear or change their meaning. This transformation can be seen in increasing individualization and the formation of undefined sub-cultural collectives. The questioning of all spatial typologies in which these relationships were specifically defined in the past thus becomes unavoidable. Neither the object nor the typology is the focus of research but the complex interdependencies of the habits, methods, practices and behaviour patterns that give meaning to existence and the emergence of collective spaces. 'Time-Sharing Urbanism' studies ways in which a system of communications and infrastructures affects territory and makes us discover a particular system of social ecology, perceived as 'urban', whose operational model is the division of time. This research focuses in particular on the territorial imprint of a way of life, that which the Royal Flying Doctor Service makes possible in the Australian outback. Making reference to the work of Manuel Castells, Peter Trummer here examines the spatial logic concerning not only places but also flows: experiences perceived more and more as links, less and less localized. The communication systems are one of the logics, based on social interactions between 'absent' people, distant in space and in time: people we know but have never seen or have seen but do not really know, people we believe we know and others whom we do not know but who influence us, etc. If 'living' beyond these immediate and contiguous distances corresponds to a different kind or social organization, what is its spatial form and what way of life does it allow? This work refutes the traditional point of view centred on nodes in a network, to question the totality of relations, considered as a whole spatial figure. 'Polygamy' is the name given to the relational figure arising from this case study: a territory of relations, between two or more places, mutually dependent but physically disconnected; a shape, not in a homogeneous three-dimensional sense but in the sense of a space-integrating notion of expansion (physical links in the network), of extension (programmes) and of frequency (number of links between points); a socially 'urban' principle, but indifferent to all notions of size, centrality, territory and context. 'Time-sharing' would be the operational mode of this ensemble of relations: it refers largely to all the events, localized or not, that take place 'in time', directly, and are shared by means of the network. Three particular forms emerge from this case study:

▶ the sharing of simultaneous time, when several parties access a programme together, as in the 'schools of the air';

▶ the sharing of sequenced time, when the accomplishment of a programme necessitates a hierarchy of actions, as in emergency rescue;

▶ the sharing of synchronized time, which is the overlapping of two infrastructural systems, crossing momentarily in a time or at a place, like the rooms in a mobile hospital.

This network of infrastructures, aerial or virtual, gives birth to a new urban territory, offering the same services of those of an agglomeration of population, but bearing no resemblance to any known urban model. It is a digital landscape, a constellation of views, radar screens, like interferences in radio waves, that the graphical study 'Time-Sharing Urbanism' shows us. It is the image of a contemporary society, dispersed and connected, mobile and fixed, in an almost untouched natural environment. ⊠

B. G.

▶ Time-Sharing Urbanism

Australia, 1997–99

'Time-Sharing Urbanism' is the subject of a thesis by Peter Trummer, developed in collaboration with Penelope Dean. This study was born out of fascination with a phenomenon: while 70% of the Australian population live in coastal towns, the outback, a desert of 7.15 million square km, has a density of 0.02 people per square km. Nevertheless, the space has been used and a way of life generated, thanks to the Royal Flying Doctor Service (RFDS) and a particular infrastructure, characterized both by a field of radio waves and by a network of small aircraft and landing sites. This structure serves a population with very diverse social characteristics: settled residents, farmers, mineworkers and Aborigines; a shifting population of stockmen, lorry drivers and seasonal workers; and a temporary population of tourists, archaeologists and other adventurers. If at the beginning it was merely a question of providing medical and emergency services for a dispersed population, like city ambulances, the potential of the system (flexible, adaptable and expandable) have allowed other developments in spatial directions that were not then foreseen, along with various unexpected services. The network as currently constituted offers: country hospital, where doctors and nurses are flown in several times a week to different locations in turn, along with a pharmacy; the radio clinic, a medical consultation service by radio transceiver; the school of the air, in which a teacher gives a class over the radio; special emergency flights; and the 'Galah Session', a time set aside for open access to the radio network for a collective chat between neighbours 100 km apart. In operation for over a century, and the first 'Australian Inland Mission', this is a 'metropolis' that has been constructed over the airwaves and is maintained now by a federal council and integrated into a global communications system that encircles the continent by fibre-optic cable. ▶▶

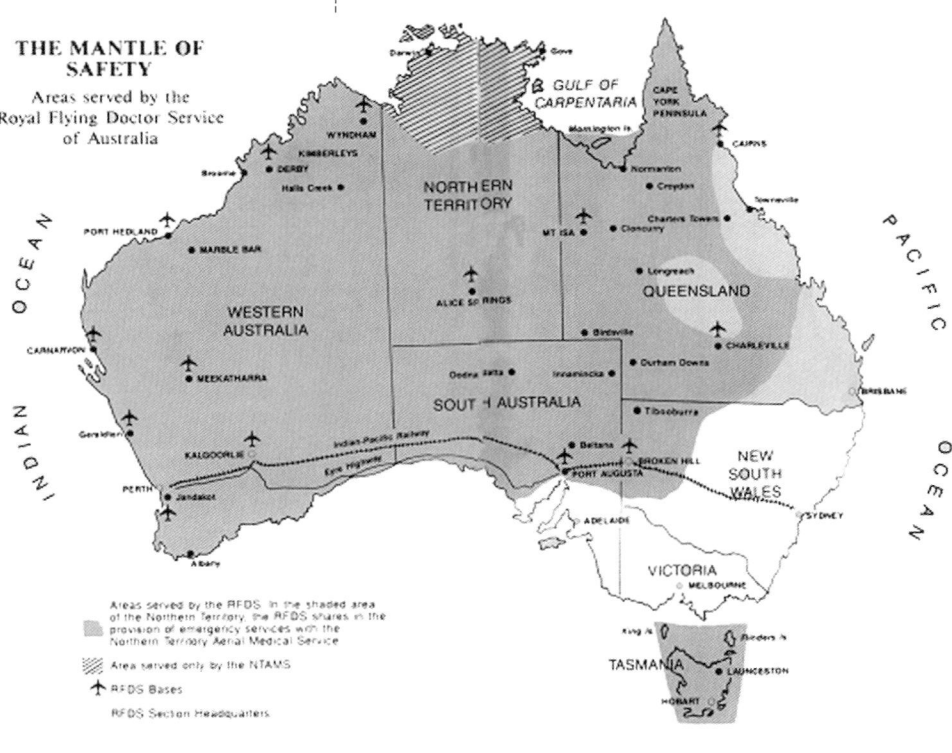

Australia

7.15 Million km2

143 000 people

0.02 people / km2

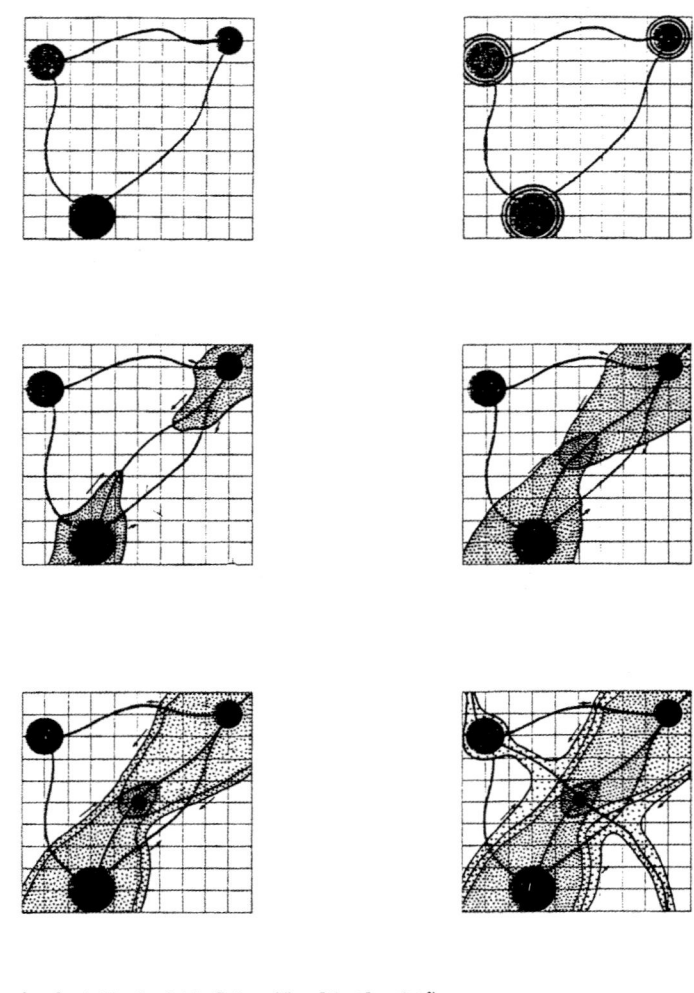

Source: Reproduced from C. A. Doxiadis, "The Future of Human Settlements", op. cit., p. 21.

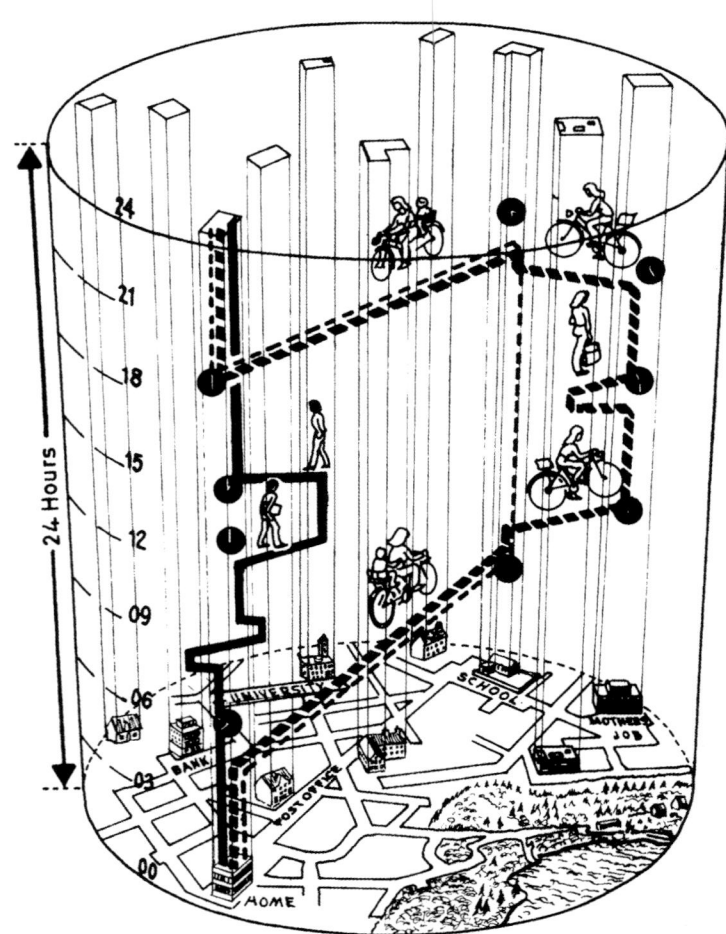

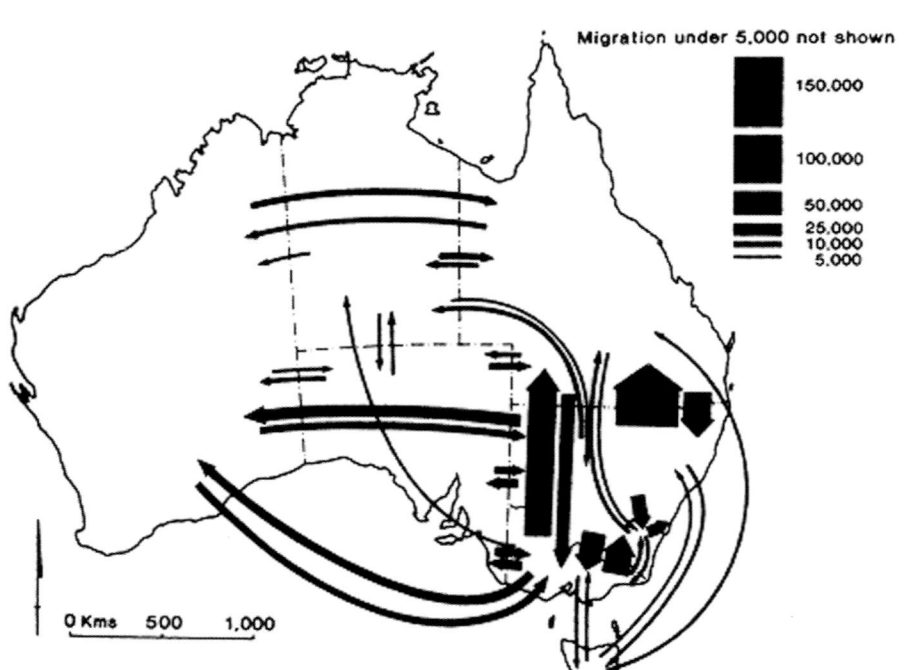

Figure 3.14. Patterns of internal migration between states in Australia 1986–1991. *Source:* ABS Census; Hugo, 1994.

POPULATION INCREASES

Location	1976	1986	1991*
Kalgoorlie-Boulder	19,041	22,232	27,405
Alice Springs	14,149	22,759	24,000
Darwin	44,232	72,937	73,300
Cloncurry	2,079	3,194	3,602
Charleville	3,802	5,287	5,287
Broken Hill	27,647	26,650	21,960#
Broome	4,079	7,932	7,920
Derby-West Kimberley	5,046	7,289	7,488
Wyndham-East Kimberley	4,071	6,049	6,346
Halls Creek	1,934	2,855	2,991

▶▶ Using about a hundred graphics, Trummer and Dean demonstrate how the outback can function something like a large city and its inhabitants like a networked society. They have modelled the operation of the RFDS on the basis of its 'physical' characteristics, in a collection of circles about 500 km across: this is the zone covered by the field of a radio transmitter and it is the range of a tourist aircraft making a flight of 90 minutes. Each zone contains the 'service' — an aerial base, a radio station and a medical set-up — and the 'clients', the dispersed population. Each 'point' in the zone should have a landing site and a radio transmitter and receiver. These points are the most decentralized and remote in the territory. Once mapped, these points, or nodes, can be read like autonomous elements, in a system without a centre and yet at the same time interdependent, for each location in the network depends on the others. The relations that exist in the system — the communications and movements — are also interdependent movements: there is a collection of physically possible relations, characterized by lines of the network, and the frequency of exchange on each of the lines is variable, according to the programme proposed. But if the internal trajectories are mobile, variable and multipliable, their limits of physical expansion are fixed: it is the contour of their possibilities that fashions the topology of this territory. Neither city nor region, this 'urban' model has neither centre nor periphery, but at each local extremity of the spatial field there grow up multiple specifities and real social practices, those of a form of community. ▱

Collective spaces

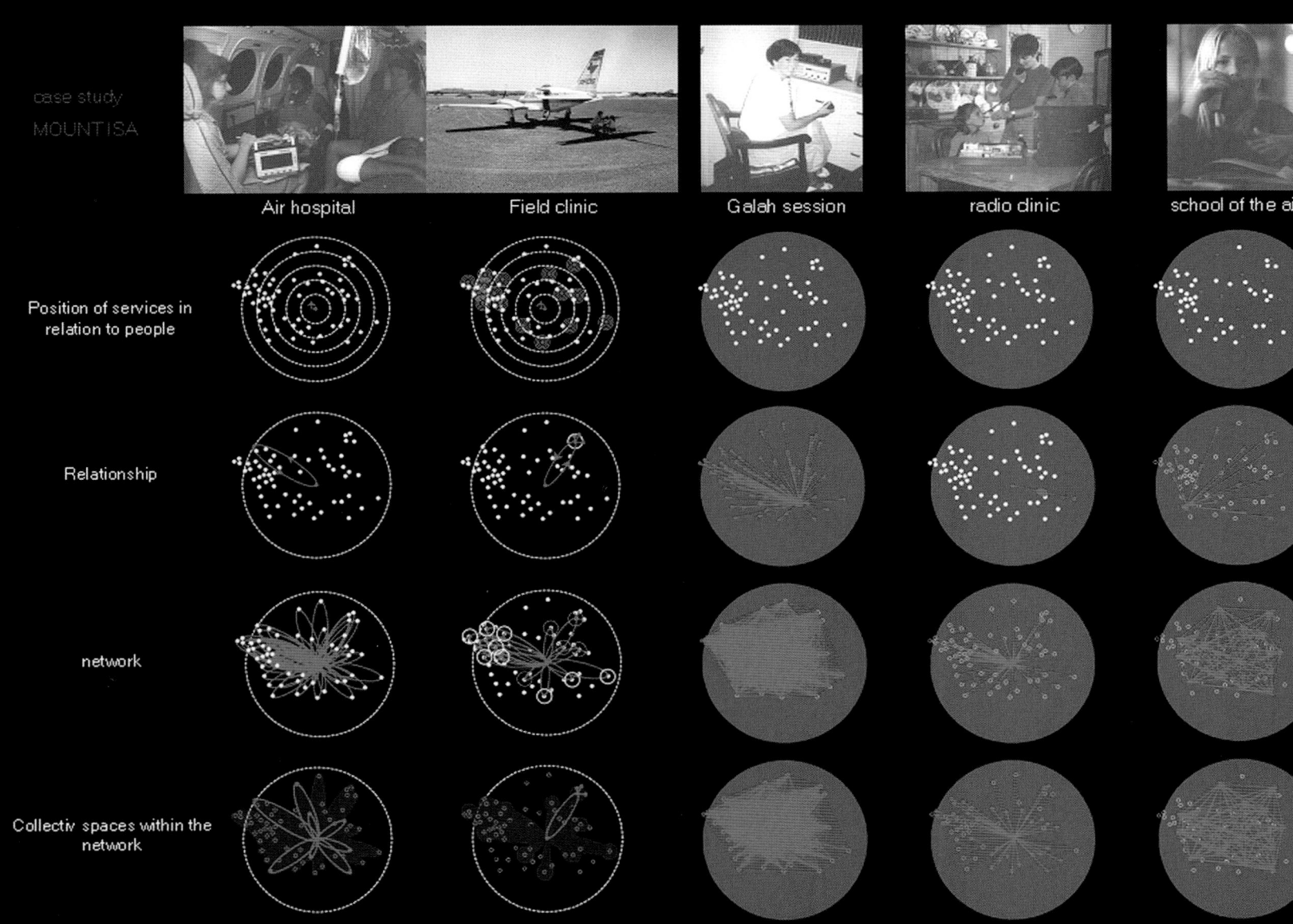

case study
MOUNT ISA

| Air hospital | Field clinic | Galah session | radio clinic | school of the air |

Position of services in relation to people

Relationship

network

Collectiv spaces within the network

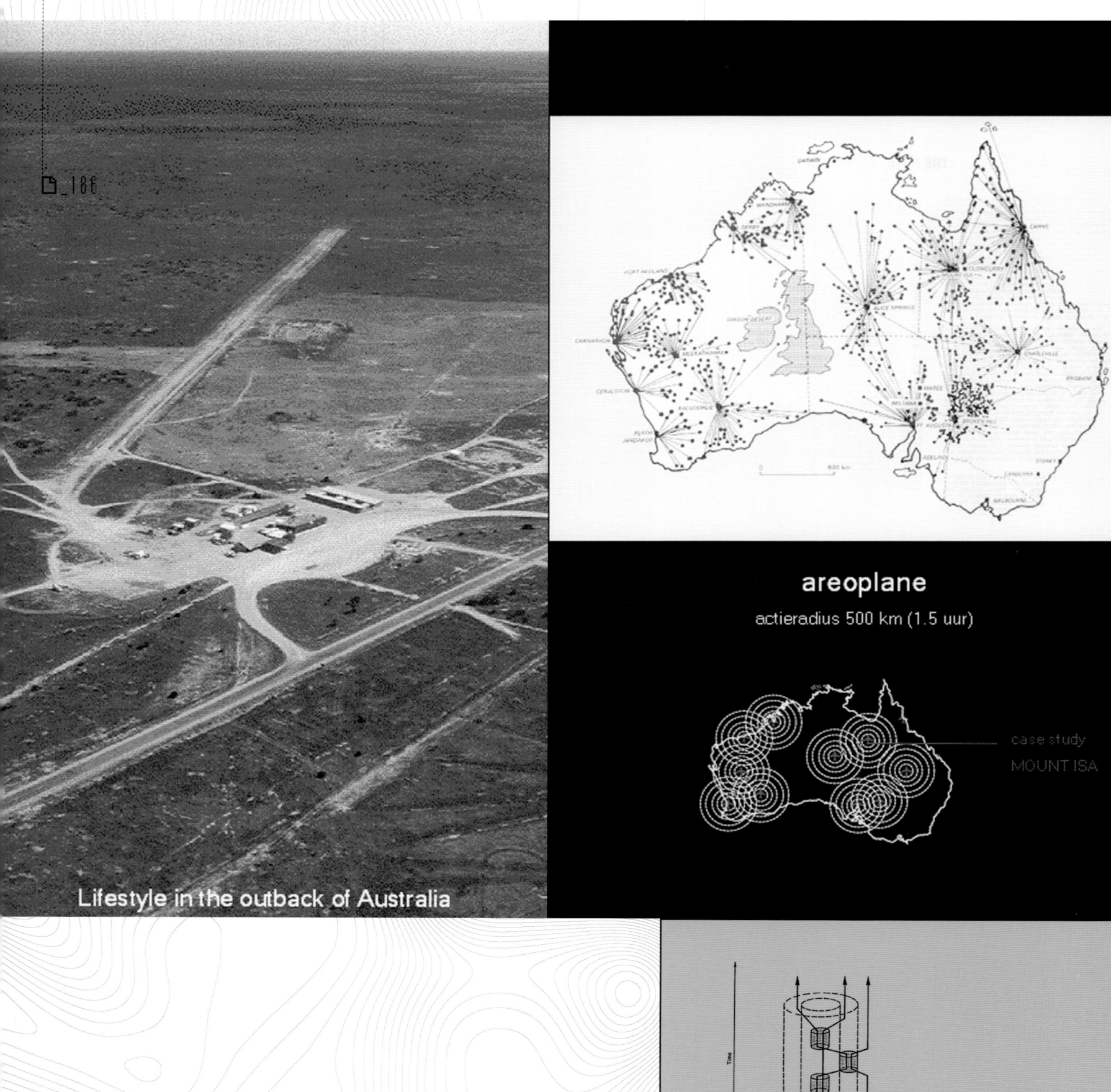

Lifestyle in the outback of Australia

areoplane

actieradius 500 km (1.5 uur)

case study
MOUNT ISA

Figure 3.1 Diagrammatic representation of daily time–space paths according to Hägerstrand (1970).

Figure 6.17. Prism for an unmarried working mother. (Palm and Pred, 1974)

Infrastructures

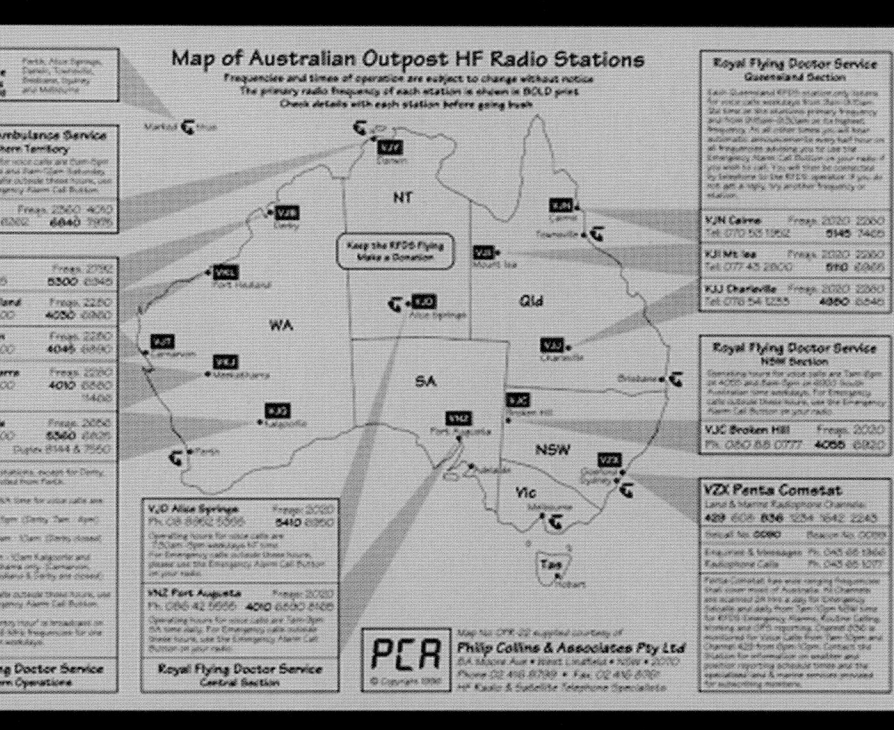

radio

actieradius 600-700 km

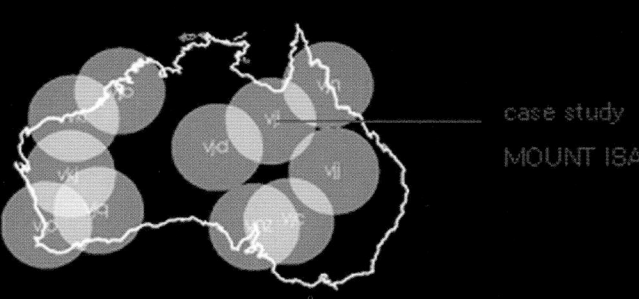

case study

MOUNT ISA

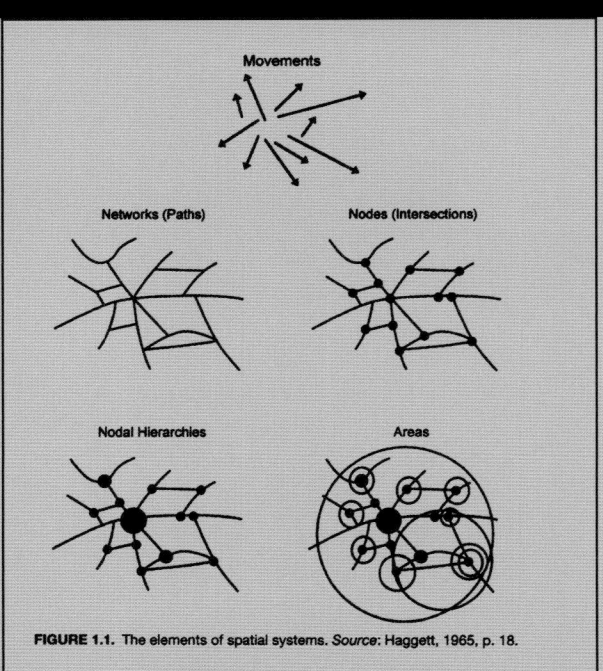
Fig. 127 Increasing Complexity Of Movements In Urban Systems

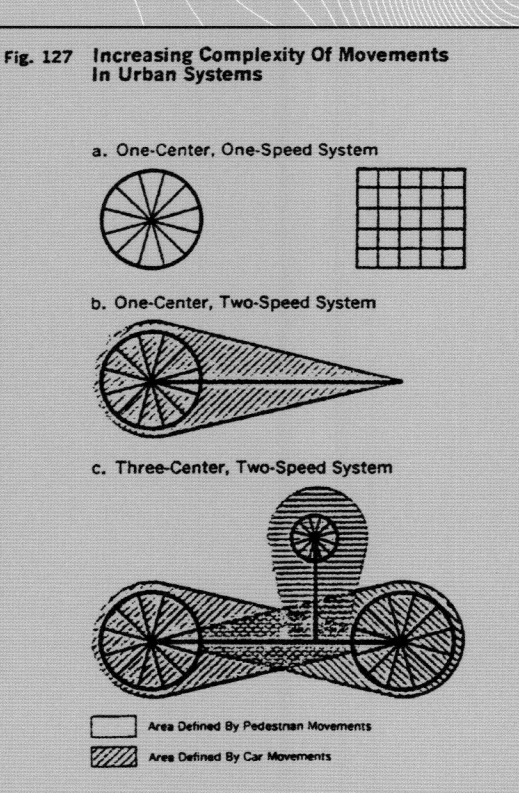

a. One-Center, One-Speed System

b. One-Center, Two-Speed System

c. Three-Center, Two-Speed System

☐ Area Defined By Pedestrian Movements

▨ Area Defined By Car Movements

▶ PROPELLER Z

Austria

Korkut Akkalay, Kabru, Kriso Leinfellner, Philipp Tschofen, Carmen Wiederin

Formed in Vienna in 1994, propeller z define themselves as a platform for research on the space, content, materials and form of all projects, whether two- or three-dimensional. Made up of young architects (all born between 1964 and 1970), this collective promotes interactive development with other disciplines (graphic art, multimedia concepts, exhibition design, interior decoration, furniture and fashion design, etc.). Each member brings his or her own particular skills to the team, and with a mixture of specialization, generalization, individualism and group identity, propeller z seek efficient but heterodox solutions to the complex problems of our time through a procedure that is both experimental and firmly rooted in reality. They have created installations (Fast Forward, 1999, Superheated Ice, 1997), shops (GIL fashion area 1 & 2, 2000), furniture (Bucky Ball, 2001) and houses, as well as building an exhibition pavilion in Essen (Meteorit, 2002). Propeller z won the competition for a funicular railway to serve the medieval castle in Riegersburg (Knight rider, 2000). ⊡

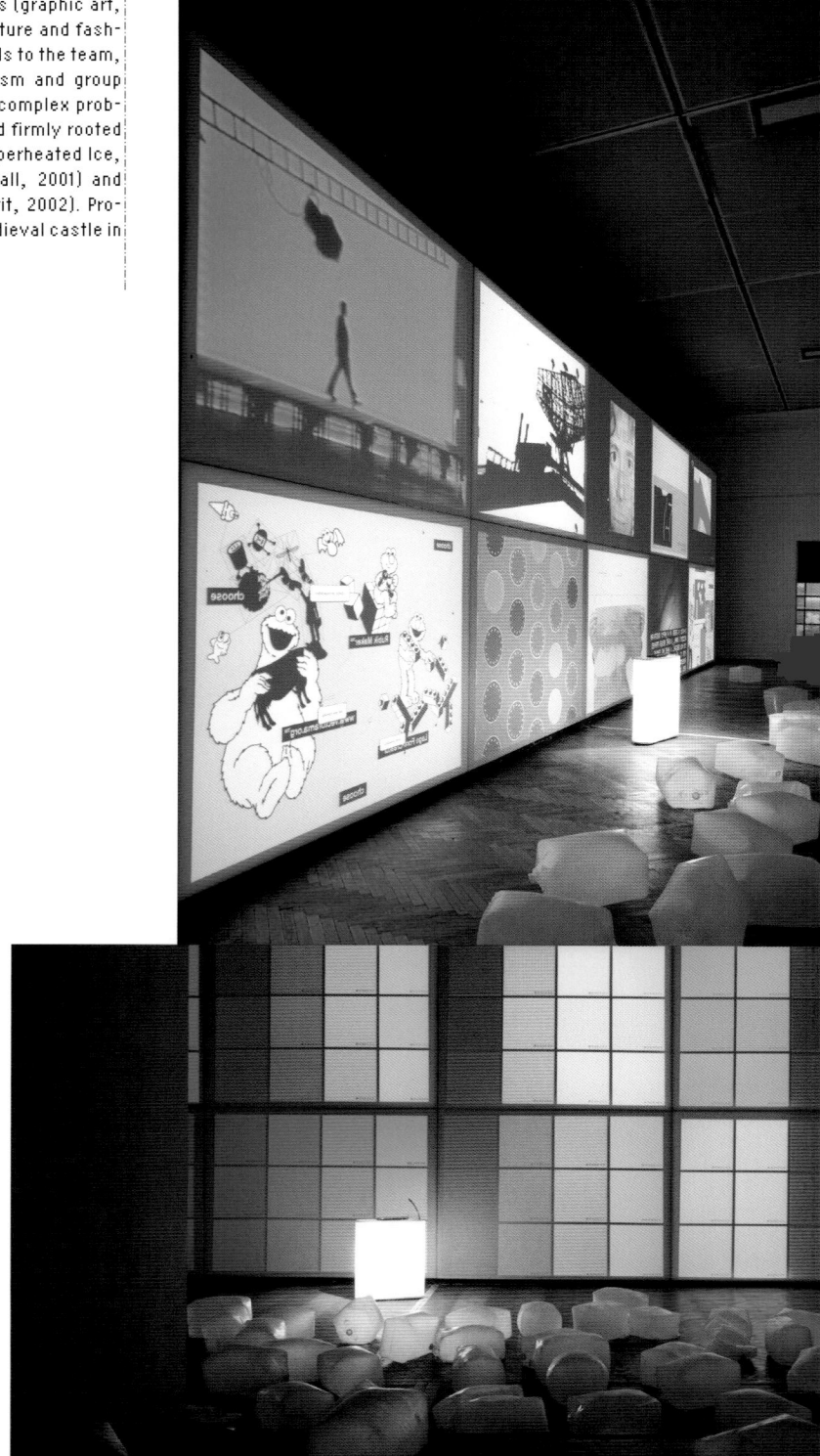

PROPELLER Z'S WORK is suffused with one central concern: to develop strategies for action in an evolving world where the technological potential has never been so vast, but where normative frameworks have never been so rigid. Faced with this double horizon and this double difficulty, these Viennese architects weave all their projects around a general concept that must be both the source and the result of their procedures – a guiding principle which they follow at all stages and in all contexts of their projects, whether architectonic or decorative, programmatic or geometrical, material or immaterial, etc. Faced with functional constraints and the imperatives of each programme, they use this 'conceptual' approach to organize the multiple parameters and the ins and outs of those processes that lead to architectural form. Again it is through the conceptual coherence of this central idea that they make their selections from the multiple choices with which reality confronts them and find their way through the labyrinth of variables and alternatives, both within the territory and on the site. The 'Meteorit' museum project, for instance, was centred on the idea of extreme contrasts: the exhibition area – the richest and most important part of the museum – remains invisible, as it is underground; above is an opaque, suspended area that houses the administration – a sort of abstract logo for the whole edifice. Each area of the building is an extreme instance of the difference between the right way up and the wrong way up, imaging the meteorite that lies at the heart of the museum, or indeed the whole space of the exhibition hall, which is simultaneously an

empty chasm and a 'black box'. For the design of the exhibition 'Stealing Eyeballs', the basic idea was to combine abstraction and modularity in order to solve the particular problems set by this project: architecture was to be exhibited in both its two-dimensional and its three-dimensional as well as its material and immaterial forms. The modular structure of the exhibition 'boxes' extends to that of the screen for multimedia projections on the front of the boxes and composed of macroscopic pixels. This basically simple idea is developed with analytical thoroughness to adapt all the constraints to a common form. The example of 'Stealing Eyeballs' also demonstrates the capacity of this conceptual, non-linear method to give expression, within one and the same project, to a number of crafts and fields of operation that a priori go beyond the scope of architecture: graphic design, art, music, etc. With their rejection of all formalism and all identifiable style, propeller z make architecture into an open process that integrates and is transformed by a multiplicity of progressive, interdisciplinary contributions. Each designer plays a part in a heterogeneous and temporary team, dealing with the constraints and the potentials particular to his or her own field. The specific conceptual landscape of each project is the only common ground of negotiation and development for a form of architecture that is self-referential, autogenous and always individual. ⊡

P. C.

Stealing Eyeballs — Designing Media

Vienna, Austria, 2001

In order to create and communicate the correspondence between real and mediated exhibition spaces required by the project, visual design and exhibition architecture for Stealing Eyeballs were similarly related to one another. Abstraction and modular variability are the central characteristics of both systems. The visual design by Lichtwitz Leinfellner operates as information architecture, not only introducing the different media contributions but also using layout to frame the works. In contrast, the exhibition architecture by propeller z not only creates the spatial conditions for each presentation but also signals the connection between these and the mediated aspects of the exhibition. The visual organization for Stealing Eyeballs uses a palette of 216 true web colours as an abstract logo for the project's theme, without limiting itself to the use of a specific image or individual protagonists. The orthogonal pattern enables this 'key visual' to be used and configured in different formats. The colour field appears on digital and electronic surfaces as a metamorphosing signal bordering on three-dimensionality. The architecture creates for all protagonists without exception the same conditions in which to present their contributions, the modular construction principle presenting each work within identical spatial relationships. As determined by the theme, all contributions to Stealing Eyeballs possess digital character and are presented as full-screen projections that can be interactively directed. propeller z's design consists of architectonic and optical equipment, made up of ten identical boxes which one can walk into, constructed on two floors and to which entry is facilitated by a ramp. They fill the space available in the central exhibition hall almost entirely. Visitors can see the exhibition contributions on projection screens in the boxes and can determine where ten different visions should appear on the outer side. The dimensions of the boxes are determined by the parameters of the media technologies used in the exhibition, such as, for example, the length of the light rays of the projected images or the video format PAL, the proportions of which, 4:3, determine the height and breadth of the boxes. The soft and comfortable interiors of these 'viewing cells' are thus simultaneously simple, large-format cameras, allowing recognition along both optical axes.

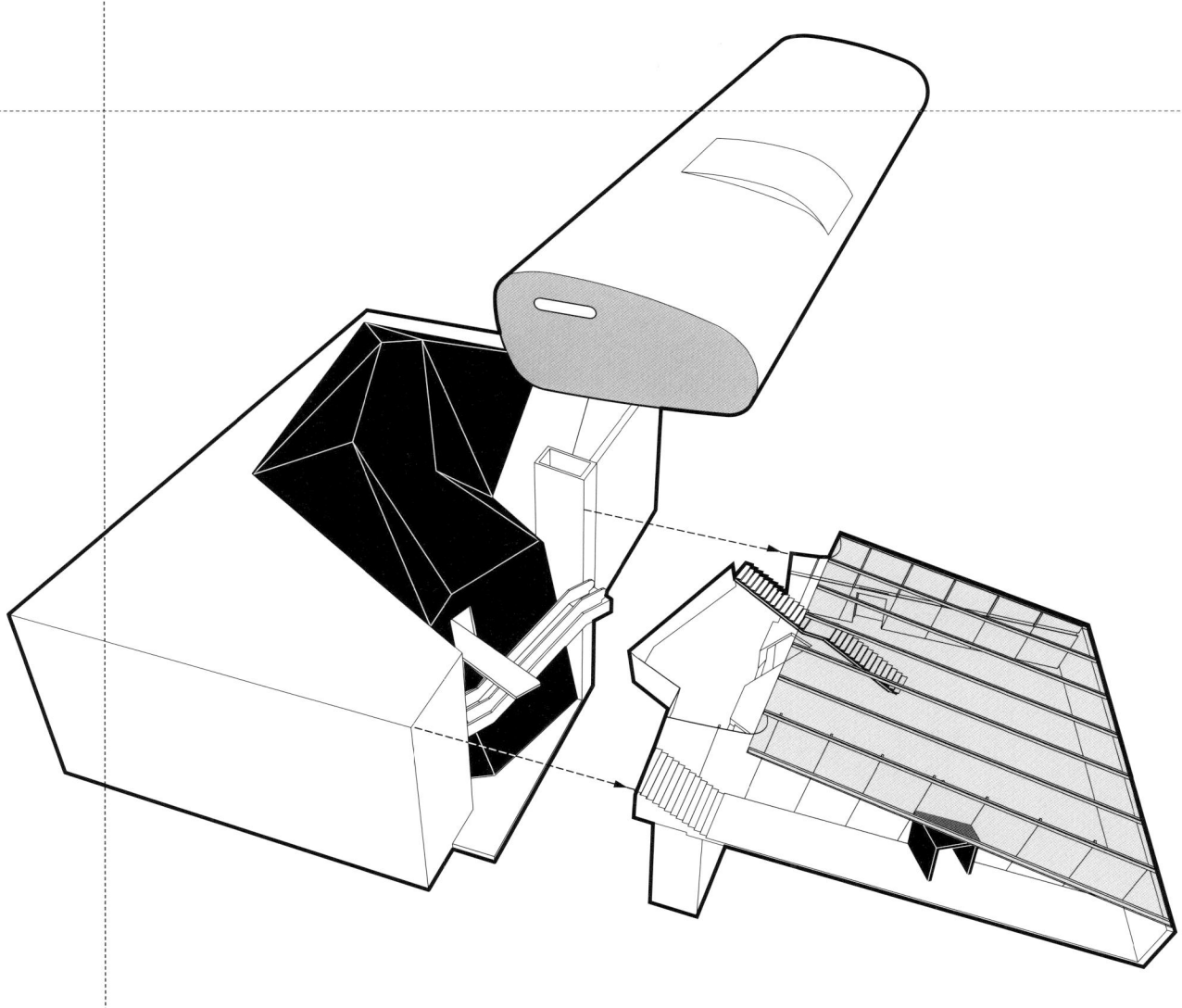

▶ Meteorit
Essen, Germany, 2000–02

To mark its centenary, the German energy concern RWE commissioned an exhibition ground, in which the company's main commercial activity is made the theme of an artificial world of experience. In the north of the city of Essen, a plot of land that had once been the site of the company's first power station was chosen for the erection of a power station of a new kind – one that consumes energy in order to generate energy experiences and pass them on to a wider public. The architecture of this 'culturo-industrial' complex – known as 'Meteorit' – was developed by propeller z, while the choice of artistic and media installations was entrusted to the Austrian artist André Heller. Meteorit, a kind of architectural 'theme park', consists of three main elements. The exhibition space is buried under the garden; it is an opaque cuboid shape in black concrete, of which only a small, irregular part protrudes, without giving any clue to the size of the whole. Seeming to float, an aluminium shape, 44 metres long, skims the surface of the ground. This part houses a spacious café and administrative offices. Leaning on it is an inclined glass surface, which extends along the ground and covers a vast and bright entrance hall. From there you go down via overflying walkways and ramps to the exhibition spaces 12 metres below. Underground, in the cuboid area, the exhibition itself is laid out inside a series of large objects, simply geometrical and brilliantly coloured. These small rooms house the multimedia installations, presenting phenomena such as light, shade, sounds and images in all their possible metamorphoses. The largest is a mysterious opaque sphere, a rough, massive meteorite; but inside the visitor encounters a dematerialized space, subjected to various effects by electronic projections. The central principle of the architectural concept is contrast, from the total composition down to the smallest details – a voluntary tension between extremes: at every scale, a succession of opposites, such as visible/invisible, full/empty, introvert/extravert, simple/complex, arises from the shapes and the materials, creating the discordant but elegant syntax of the ensemble. ▱

Credits: propeller z with André Heller, Tod Machover (MIT Media Lab)

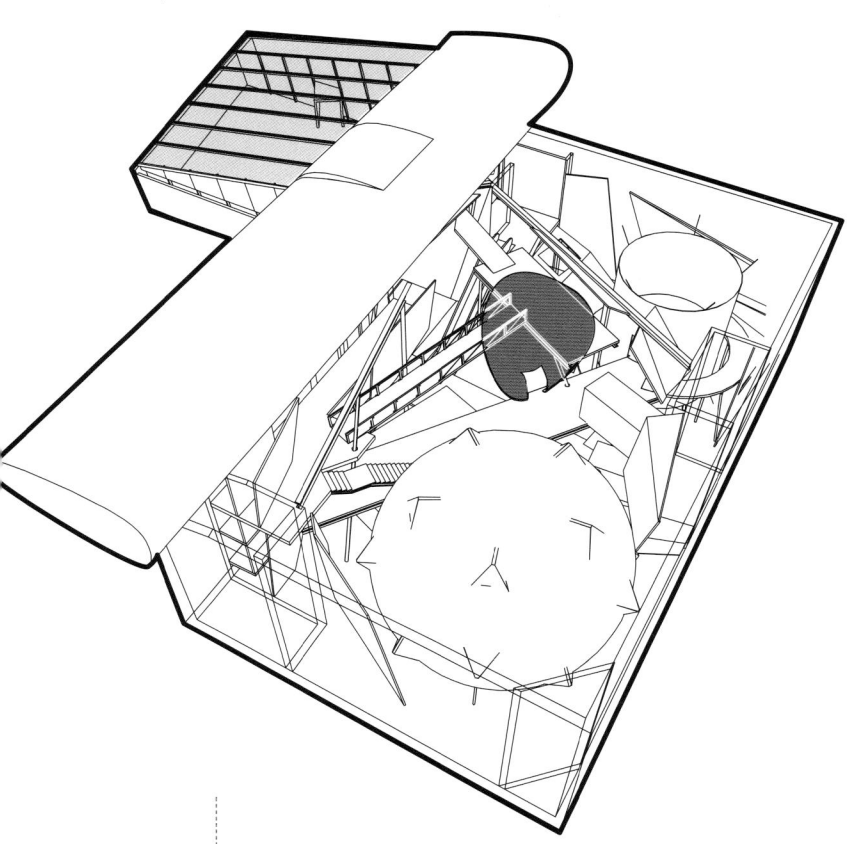

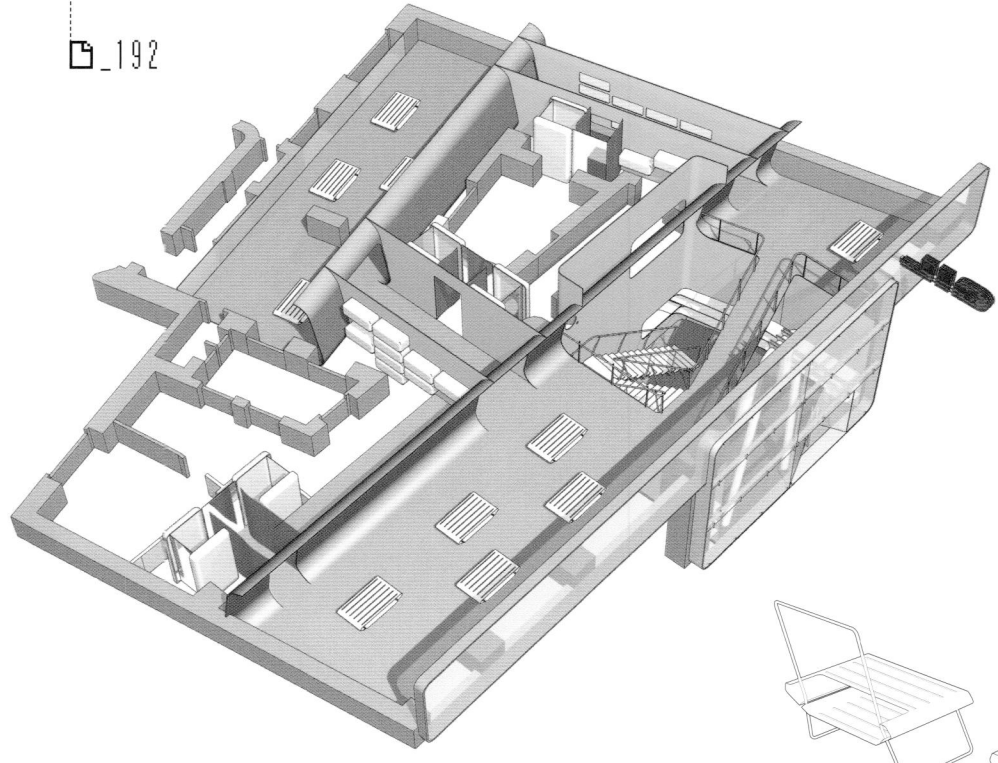

GIL fashion area 1
Vienna, Austria, 1999–2000

Fashion always manifests itself as a game of 'seeing and being seen'. The GIL fashion store is a largely transparent showcase for fashion that cultivates the trend towards voyeurism and presents it in an appealing way. The full-surface glazed façade opens the two-storey shop to the heavily frequented Mariahilferstrasse, a bustling street which itself sometimes resembles an urban catwalk; thus the threshold between the realms of street and shop are reduced to a minimum such as one rarely encounters, especially not in Austria. The design of the store, however, not only insists upon a strong exchange between interior and exterior space but also guides the gaze of the visitor along a vertical trajectory. The relatively small ground-floor area was opened completely, both upward and out towards the street. The section of the façade protruding out spans both storeys, the lower part overlapping into the large glazed (and further set apart by a dot pattern) area of the upper floor. This allows us to recognize the spatial relation even as we approach the store. Moreover, the façade intersects with the spatial envelope of the upper floor, and within the tension of this junction a bridge spans the void between the two flanks, drawing a continuous course through the upper floor. A thin steel hairpin, whose form helps accentuate the entrance situation still further, draws the overlying weight of the building downwards. A delicate, floating staircase leads to the ample sales areas on the upper floor. Here, in the two flanking main spaces, the floors and the walls — both made of the same material, a warm, grey linoleum — merge gradually and extend on up into the ceiling. This shell provides a subdued background for the garments hanging from the spines of their clothes racks. The two main spaces are connected via corridors whose walls have been expanded by the insertion of recesses formed from high-gloss, prefabricated polyester units. These recesses can be used for laying out products for display. At the ends of the corridors are the changing cubicles, which are also constructed of industrial prefab polyester units. The furnishings were designed especially for the GIL store, and their combination of surfaces for displaying, stacking, sitting, sets a bold new precedent for displaying fashion. The industrial materials and surfaces engage in a dialogue of extreme contrasts with the textures of the clothing. The phenomenon of fashion has long since transcended the limits of clothing and has increasingly begun to meld with other areas of contemporary culture, such as photography, film, graphic design and music. With additional features like a small bar, a high-end sound system (including an assortment of selected CDs, which are also available for purchase) and a centrally positioned projection surface as a stage for visual experiments, the GIL store is most certainly showing these new developments the attention they deserve.

Credits: propeller z with Lichtwitz Leinfellner

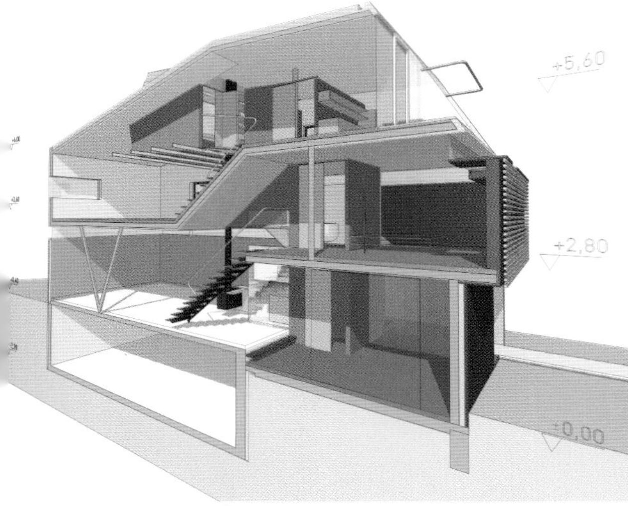

UNIT 1

UNIT 2

+5,60

+2,80

+0,00

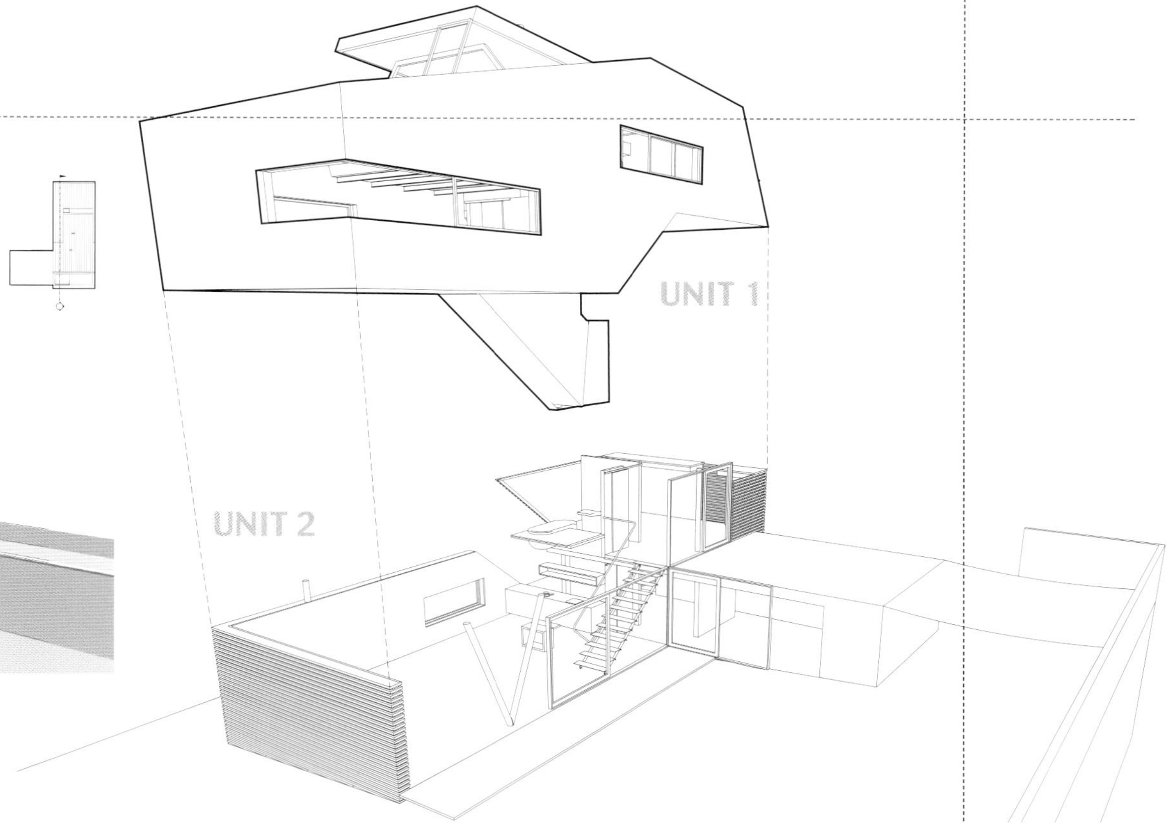

▶ DBL/SGL Houses
Vienna, Austria, 1999–02

Situated in a typical residential area of Vienna, these two houses are linked together by a subtle web of relations that are not confined to the architecture. On the same site, propeller z are in effect constructing a double house (for two sisters) and a single house (for their father). To articulate this combined context of family, architecture and topography, the Viennese architects propose forms that will express the difficult balance between the individual and the family. DBL, the house of the two sisters, contains two apartments one on top of the other; it has one very narrow space on the roadside, but this extends all the way to the back of the site and thus has an ideal situation facing west. This principle of intelligent compression is also applied to the arrangement of the interior space: each flat has one complete level all to itself, but there is also an intermediate level, which the two sisters share. Viewed in section, the house combines positive and negative, open and closed forms, and the very precise layout ensures that not an inch of space is left unused. This concept creates two large, virtually twin units whose identical layouts are set in such a way as to guarantee complete functional independence. Their respective characters are as different as those of the occupants: the apartment below, on the garden side, has a long front of glass supported by steel uprights, and is open and extravert, in contrast to the upper apartment, which is closed in like a cocoon. SGL, the single house, reflects the same interior values, but in more extreme form. Its linear shape is prolonged, from the entrance through to the living area, much of which opens out on to the garden. The entrance itself is situated on an intermediate level, and from there one can go up to the bedrooms, which cover the same area as the living room. The swimming pool, which is sunk into the ground, is also near the entrance, and the wall facing the house is pierced by a large bull's eye which directs light into the little courtyard between the pool and the workout room down in the cellar. Steps lead from this attractive leisure area directly to the swimming pool. The single house has been designed precisely to the requirements of its occupier, and, following the strict logic that governs the whole complex, it combines classic elements of the middle-class residence (large library, wine cellar, keep-fit installations with a sauna and swimming bath). ↗

Credits: propeller z, with Uwe Diller

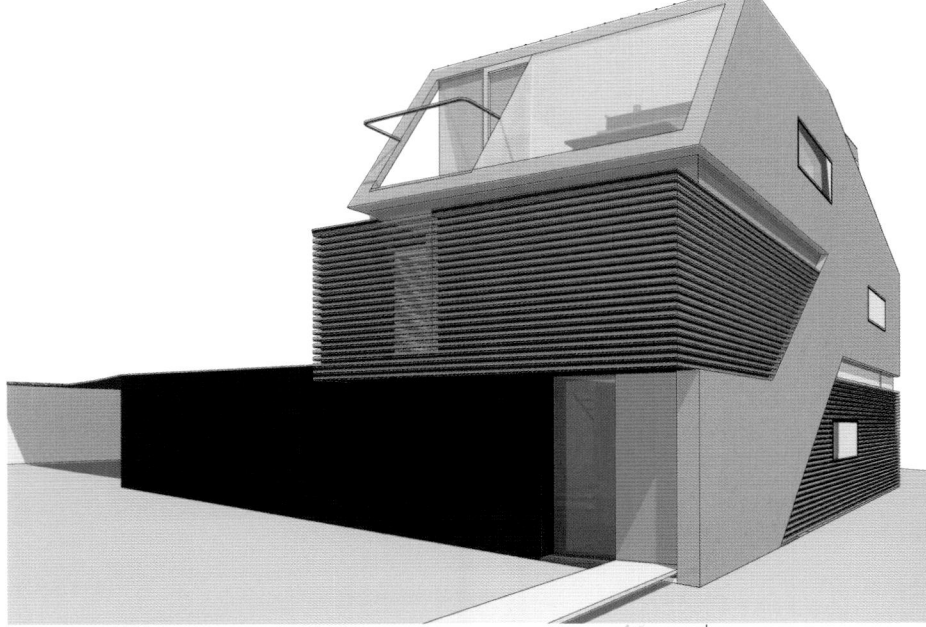

RAD

Hong Kong

Aaron Tan Hee Hung [1963]

Aaron Tan founded OMA Asia (OMAA) in Hong Kong in 1994, with Rem Koolhaas, to try to redefine architecture and urbanism of the emerging cities in East Asia and participate in the extraordinary vitality of the region. Born in Singapore, Aaron Tan emigrated to the USA, where he obtained a Master's degree from Harvard. Pursuing postgraduate studies at the GSD under Koolhaas, he took part in his research on the Pearl River Delta region. He is currently writing his own thesis on the city of Kowloon, a fortified Chinese enclave of Hong Kong, a sort of Asian West Berlin (cf. 'Cities of the Move' exhibition, Bordeaux, 1998). The studio prefers to work on a large scale: winner of a prize for the Exhibition Centre and International Congress at Guangzhou, and of the reconception of Singapore Orchard Road, the biggest commercial district in Hong Kong, it has produced a development plan for an industrial district of Singapore (JTC, 1999) and infrastructure projects in Taiwan, as well as several residential blocks and offices in Hong Kong. The office, renamed RAD in summer 2002, is now ready to take on its own projects along with its new identity.

HAVING A keen awareness of the sociocultural matrix in which it operates, RAD incorporates the global nature of its urban architectural experiences to develop new contemporary Asian urban planning and architectural approaches. Fed by the research carried out in the observation laboratory that is Rem Koolhaas's studio at Harvard — on the unplanned, unstable, proliferating processes of urbanism (Lagos parallel market), the global dynamics of exchange and communication (the urbanization of the Peal River Delta), the economic flows in the transformation of public space ['shopping'] — the Asian studio uses these themes to manipulate ways of action based on modelling and extrapolation of emerging phenomena. If the goal is to 'define a new Asian identity emerging from the dynamic, globally integrated identity of today's generation', then the name of the game is anticipation, anticipating what one will perceive, more than planning and organizing a new order. Today it is progress in biotechnology and artificial intelligence that provides the material for their new 'urban tools'; rather than a 'static' plan, closed in on itself the fruit of forces in play at a single moment the studio is developing evolutionary simulations with multiple ramifications. But over and above the tools, Aaron Tan is convinced that the technologies of the future will provoke a 'tectonic rupture' in the present socioeconomic levels, where 'new terrains will quickly be invested with complex systems'. Moving towards increasingly complex levels is, he says, the natu-

ral evolution of our contemporary society: 'the new economic tissue will resemble organic or bionic systems, which will reveal the existence of an interactive landscape, occupied by a whole panoply of economic organisms. We will witness a rapid explosion of inventions which will emerge from the system and the existing order. An incredible series of individual and organizational bodies (such as biotechnological societies composed of networks of laboratories) will undergo profound mutations and will reach a surprising level of complexity and specialization.' Faced with the magnitude of the coming economic evolution, Aaron Tan considers that the task of the architect is to facilitate this transition, devising tools and methods to measure the complexity of new urban systems. It is imperative that these devices be interactive, 'multidimensional' (with physical, economic, informational dimensions, etc.) and take into account the dynamic relations that link the local level with large phenomena; that is, they must, according to him, assume a form of 'precise intelligence'. In his studio, finally, 'interactivity' is practiced directly: at the heart of his team, where there are about thirty architects, urban planners, designers and media specialists; along the way, where concept personnel and local interested parties collaborate; and in the execution of the project itself, in which consultants and critics regularly take part. ☑

B. G.

▶ JTC I: Jurong Industrial Town Strategic Planning

Singapore, project, 1999

We were approached by the Jurong Town Corporation of Singapore to explore an appropriate master-planning strategy for a 7,000-hectare industrial site to be redeveloped into a mixed-use district over the next 50 years. The underlying objective is to prepare for the transition of Singapore's current economy to a knowledge-driven economy, with an emphasis on technology – information technology, bio-technology. The overwhelming spatial-temporal imperatives prompted us to explore alternative methods of planning that incorporate dynamic components. Instead of a plan, the end-product would resemble a tool or a methodology. We predict that the impact of future technology will be like a rupture of the existing socio-economic strata, sprouting vast new terrain soon to be inhabited by complex new eco-systems. The new networked economy will resemble organic or bionic systems, bringing about a virtual interactive landscape that will be occupied by an array of economic organisms. There will be a greater compressed surge of evolutionary invention out of the existing order and system. Shifting to higher levels of complexity is typical of evolution. The consequence will be a massive pulse of economic evolution and an incredible range of organizational and individual species (e.g., bio-tech companies that are basically a network of labs) will evolve and mutate to astonishing levels of specialization and complexity. Our challenge is not only to facilitate the transition but also to devise ways and tools of calibrating the complex systems of a city. It is necessary for such a planning tool to be interactive, multidimensional (the physical dimension, the economic dimension, the information dimension) and to understand the interactive dynamics that link local scale to larger phenomena, i.e. it should possess intelligence. As the first step towards a highly ambitious project, we commenced by exploring the transformation of the JTC site into 'monadic' space. Rem Koolhaas proposed a method of pixelation as a means of abstraction. ☑

Credits: OMA Rotterdam/OMA Asia

THE SCALE OF PIXELATION CO-RELATES TO THE LEVEL OF PLANNING PRECISION.

50 YEARS

30 YEARS

20 YEARS
10 YEARS
0 YEARS

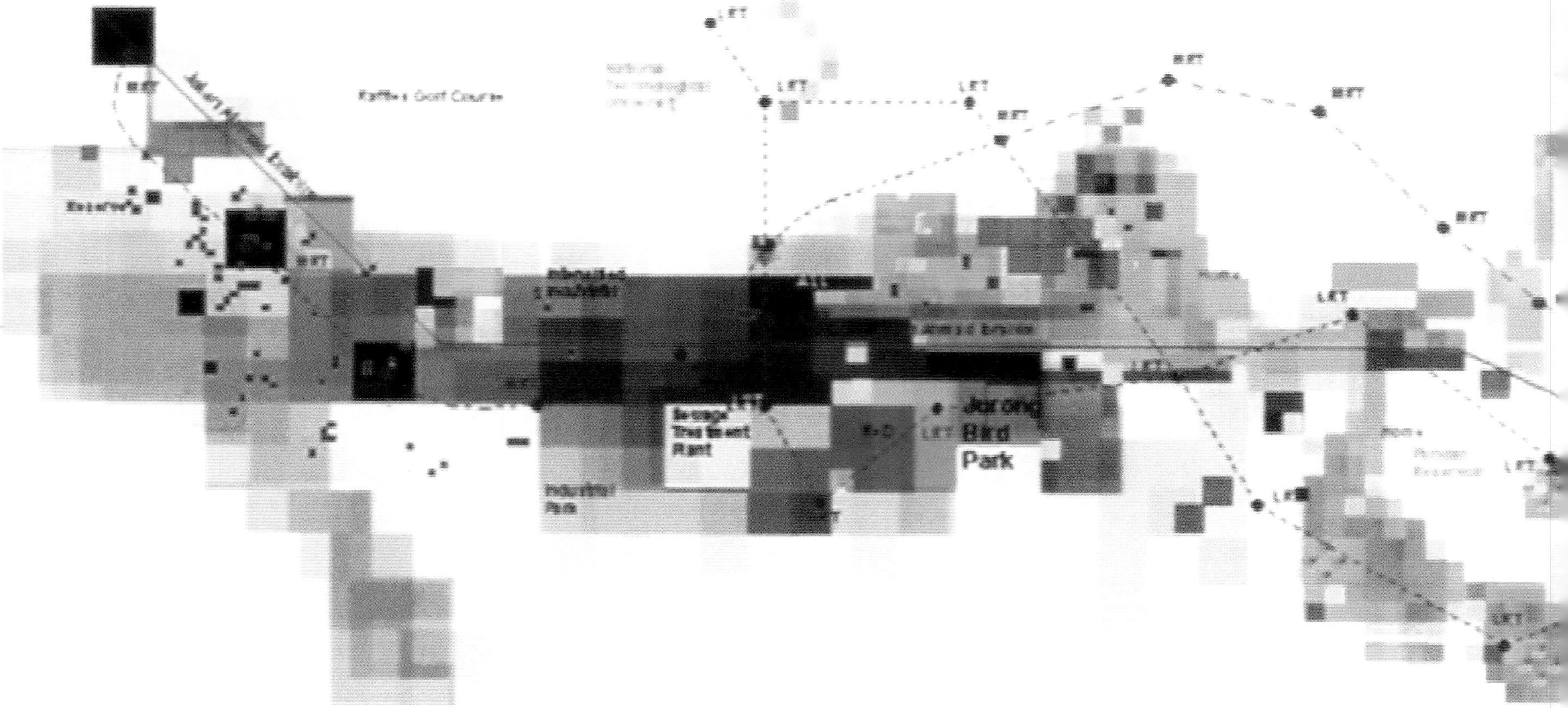

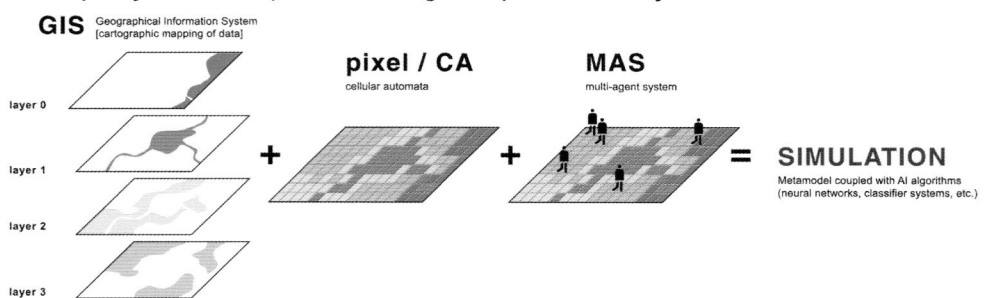

Complexity Toolbox Sampler for modelling urban processes and systems

GIS Geographical Information System
[cartographic mapping of data]

pixel / CA
cellular automata

MAS
multi-agent system

layer 0

layer 1

layer 2

layer 3

= SIMULATION
Metamodel coupled with AI algorithms
(neural networks, classifier systems, etc.)

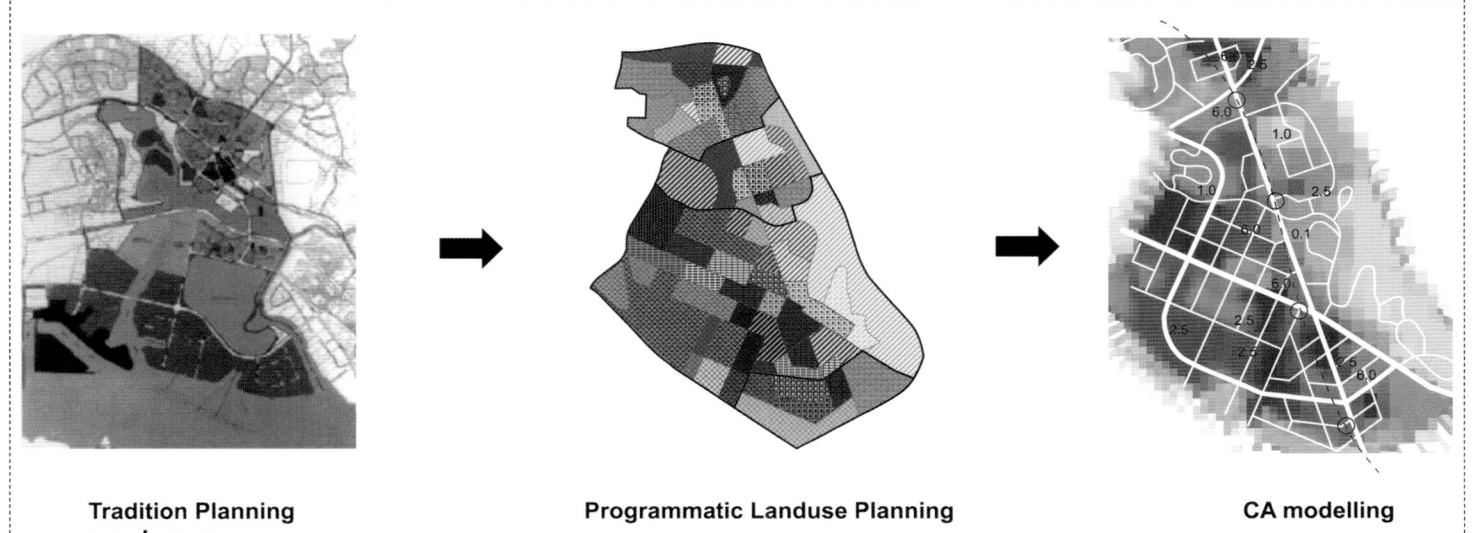

**Tradition Planning
e.g. Jurong**

Programmatic Landuse Planning

CA modelling

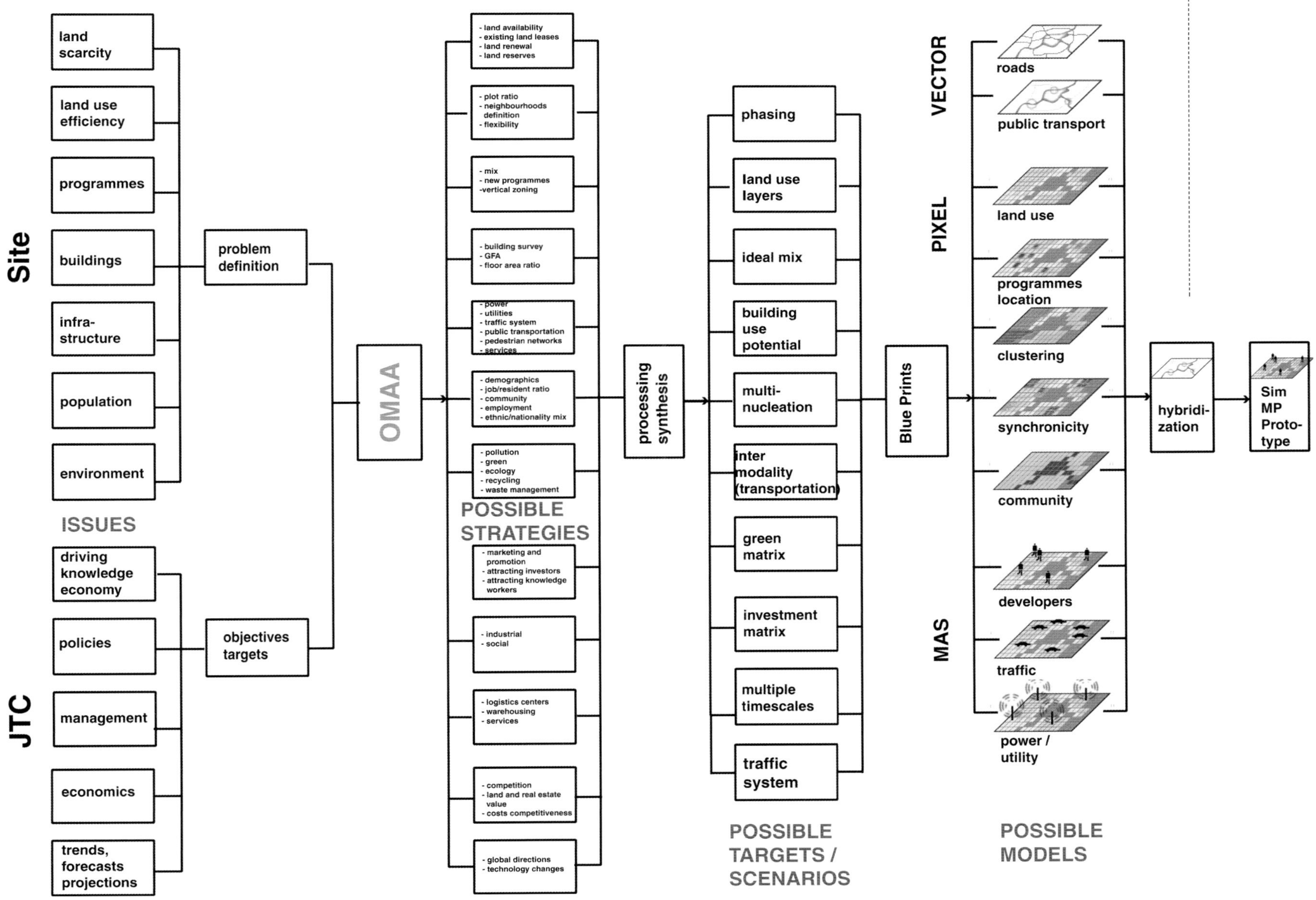

Site

- land scarcity
- land use efficiency
- programmes
- buildings
- infra-structure
- population
- environment

ISSUES

JTC

- driving knowledge economy
- policies
- management
- economics
- trends, forecasts projections

- problem definition

- objectives targets

OMAA

- land availability
- existing land leases
- land renewal
- land reserves

- plot ratio
- neighbourhoods definition
- flexibility

- mix
- new programmes
- vertical zoning

- building survey
- GFA
- floor area ratio

- power
- utilities
- traffic system
- public transportation
- pedestrian networks
- services

- demographics
- job/resident ratio
- community
- employment
- ethnic/nationality mix

- pollution
- green
- ecology
- recycling
- waste management

POSSIBLE STRATEGIES

- marketing and promotion
- attracting investors
- attracting knowledge workers

- industrial
- social

- logistics centers
- warehousing
- services

- competition
- land and real estate value
- costs competitiveness

- global directions
- technology changes

processing synthesis

- phasing
- land use layers
- ideal mix
- building use potential
- multi-nucleation
- inter modality (transportation)
- green matrix
- investment matrix
- multiple timescales
- traffic system

POSSIBLE TARGETS / SCENARIOS

Blue Prints

VECTOR
- roads
- public transport

PIXEL
- land use
- programmes location
- clustering
- synchronicity
- community

MAS
- developers
- traffic
- power / utility

POSSIBLE MODELS

hybridi-zation

Sim MP Proto-type

▶ JTC II: Buona Vista Science Hub
Singapore, competition, 2000

Aaron Tan and his team have followed through the planning project initiated with OMA for the Jurong Town Company, but on a more restricted site (190 hectares): the Buona Vista sector, 5 km from the centre of Singapore CBD and 5 km from the industrial port of Jurong. This second phase comprises a programme for a science park on a large scale, a mixed development including also various urban uses – commerce and industry, for example. Conceptually the method has become more elaborate, the screen of pixels having become too restricting, preventing satisfactory account to be taken of the complexity of reality. They have thus conceived a cellular model, which replaces square 'pixels' with flexible 'cells', whose shape can be adapted to physical constraints like the presence of roads, rivers, infrastructures and of topography. The studio has also conducted studies based on artificial intelligence and artificial life algorithms, which have already been developed to a high level of sophistication by scientists and researchers in fields that straddle AI and planning. In this way, they deployed a proliferation of strategies (distribution of energy, traffic, investments, live-work ratio, national-ethnic ratio, built-park ratio, management of waste, advertising, land valuations); they declined potential scenarios (phasing of operations, investment matrices) and possible models: from the simple superposition of 'layers' to 'monadization' and hybridization. A multiplicity of 'green' uses thus appeared: green space for cultural interests, green space for leisure and entertainment, green space for sensory stimulation, green space that is scenic and decorative. On the theoretical and abstract basis of a model of informational simulation, created for the site (XL) of JTC, the application put in place by virtue of 'cells' is experimentally 'implemented' in a precise (S) and specific context that is complex and short-term. ☑

Credits: Aaron Tan/RAD

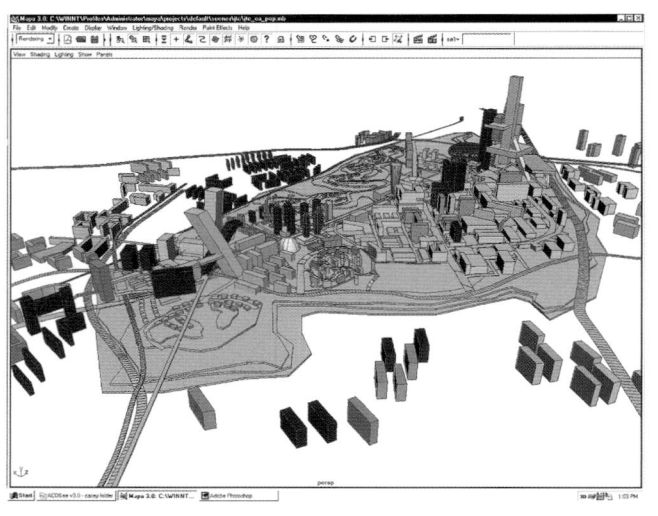

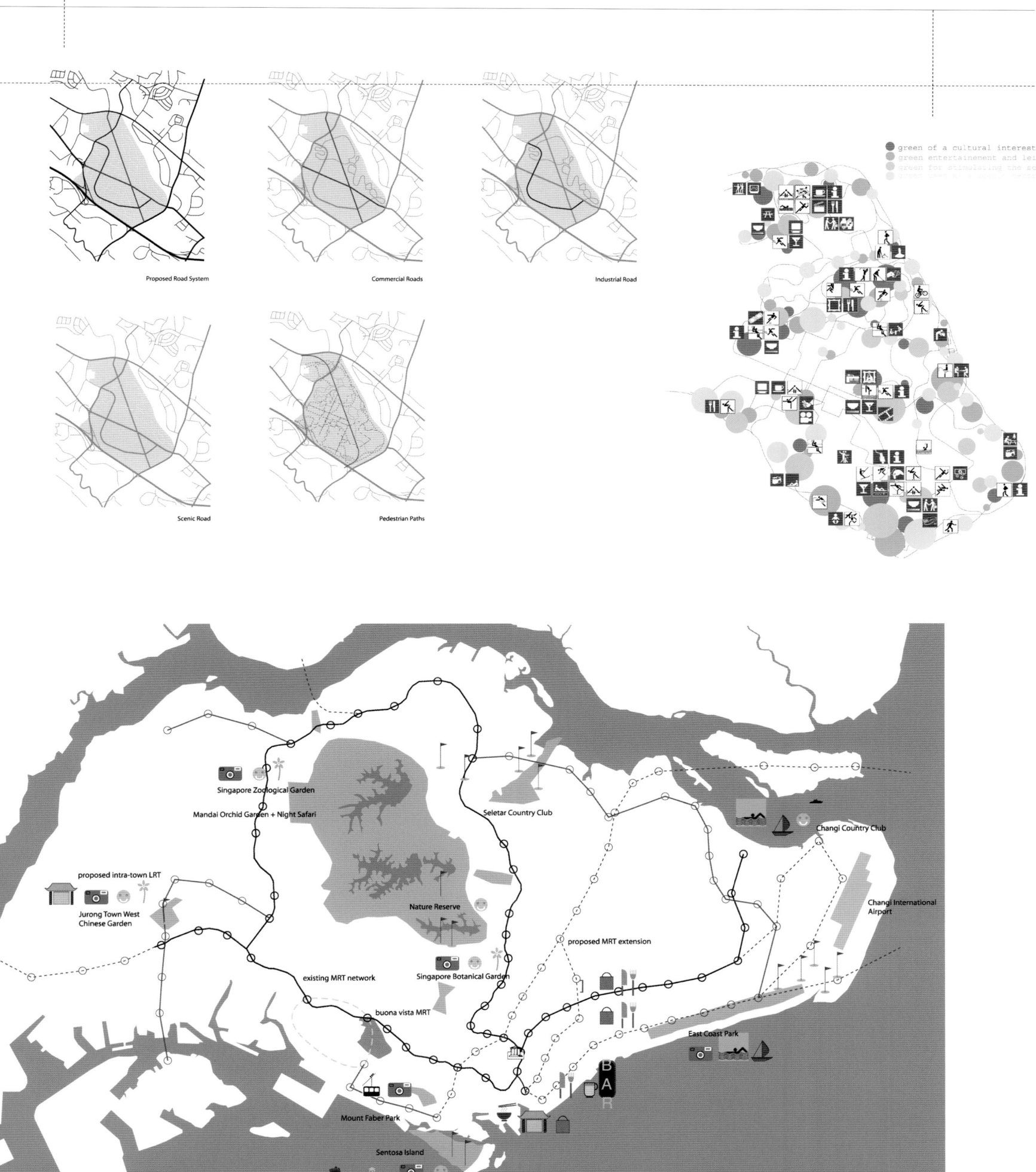

Proposed Road System

Commercial Roads

Industrial Road

Scenic Road

Pedestrian Paths

green of a cultural interest
green entertainement and leisure
green for stimulating the senses

Singapore Zoological Garden

Mandai Orchid Garden + Night Safari

Seletar Country Club

Changi Country Club

Changi International Airport

proposed intra-town LRT

Jurong Town West Chinese Garden

Nature Reserve

proposed MRT extension

existing MRT network

Singapore Botanical Garden

buona vista MRT

East Coast Park

Mount Faber Park

BAR

Sentosa Island

DAGMAR RICHTER STUDIO

United States, Germany

Dagmar Richter [(1955)]

After graduating from Stuttgart University (1982) and then attending the Royal Art Academy in Copenhagen (1984), Dagmar Richter completed her studies with a postgraduate degree from the Städeschule in Frankfurt, under the supervision of Peter Cook (1986). She now divides her practice between Europe and the United States, or to be more precise between Berlin and Los Angeles, where she set up her agency in 1987. A finalist in the competition for the West Coast Gateway in Los Angeles in 1998, she has made her mark in most of the major international competitions over the last ten years (Time Capsule for the Next Millennium, 1999; Next L.A., 1987; Shinkenchiku Membrane, 1994; Royal Library of Copenhagen, 1993, etc.). She has been invited to teach at numerous universities (Berlin–Weissensee; SCI-Arc, Los Angeles; Columbia and Cooper Union, NY; Harvard, Cambridge, etc.), and since 1998 has been professor of architecture and urbanism at UCLA. Dagmar Richter's work has frequently been exhibited, most recently at the gallery Form-0 in Los Angeles ('Strategic Landscape', 2002). A monograph on her work, *XYZ: the Architecture of Dagmar Richter*, was published in 2001. ◿

SINCE THE early 1990s, Dagmar Richter has taken on one project after another, in order to update the tools and the methods inherited from nearly a century of town planning. In this context, her project for Wolfen-Nord, in addition to its concrete objectives — the recycling and redevelopment of a post-industrial urban landscape — is like a manifesto for her theoretical and critical approach. This dormitory town is a disaster area in what used to be East Germany and has undergone a succession of changes from the capitalist urbanism of the late 19th century, through the functionalism of the 1930s to the state planning of the Soviet era. Dagmar Richter would like to give it a radically different form, to take it 'out of the industrial age and into the electronic age'. Above all, this project entails an alternative way of reading, analysing, mapping and describing the town. In 1998, her entry for the 'West Coast Gateway' had given explicit expression to this concept of 'Re-reading the City'. She believes that the architect or town planner must be able to decipher the many contradictory tracks left on the urban and suburban palimpsest; he or she must be open to the complexities of a terrain that is endlessly foliated and stratified, and is always incomplete. To this end she develops highly sophisticated analyses, using all the mathematical powers of the computer together with its superhuman capacity to assemble masses of information in real time. Her 1998 project 'Flexible Zoning', for a district in Manhattan close to the East River, began by collecting real spatial and sociological data: demographic statistics, migration, the economy, types of work, trade, real estate — but also precise morphological information on this particular part of the city: spaces not yet built on, vacant sites, flat roofs, etc. This mass of information was then synthesized in an animated chart, a sort of four-dimensional model, which was able to react to any new data and to propose in real time a precise topography of the urban opportunities and potentials. Just as with the computer model in Wolfen-Nord, this 'mental map' doubles and virtually covers the territory of a plasma, or an active skin, which in its density should reveal and then work out the problems that will affect the work. As abstractions and projections, readings and writings, these computer models are for Dagmar Richter the instruments that can facilitate planning that will be flexible and open, precise but not authoritarian. In reversing the dialectic between analysis and synthesis, basically she is substituting description for inscription, in order to understand, represent and modify a world of whose instability and transience she is acutely conscious. ◿

P.C.

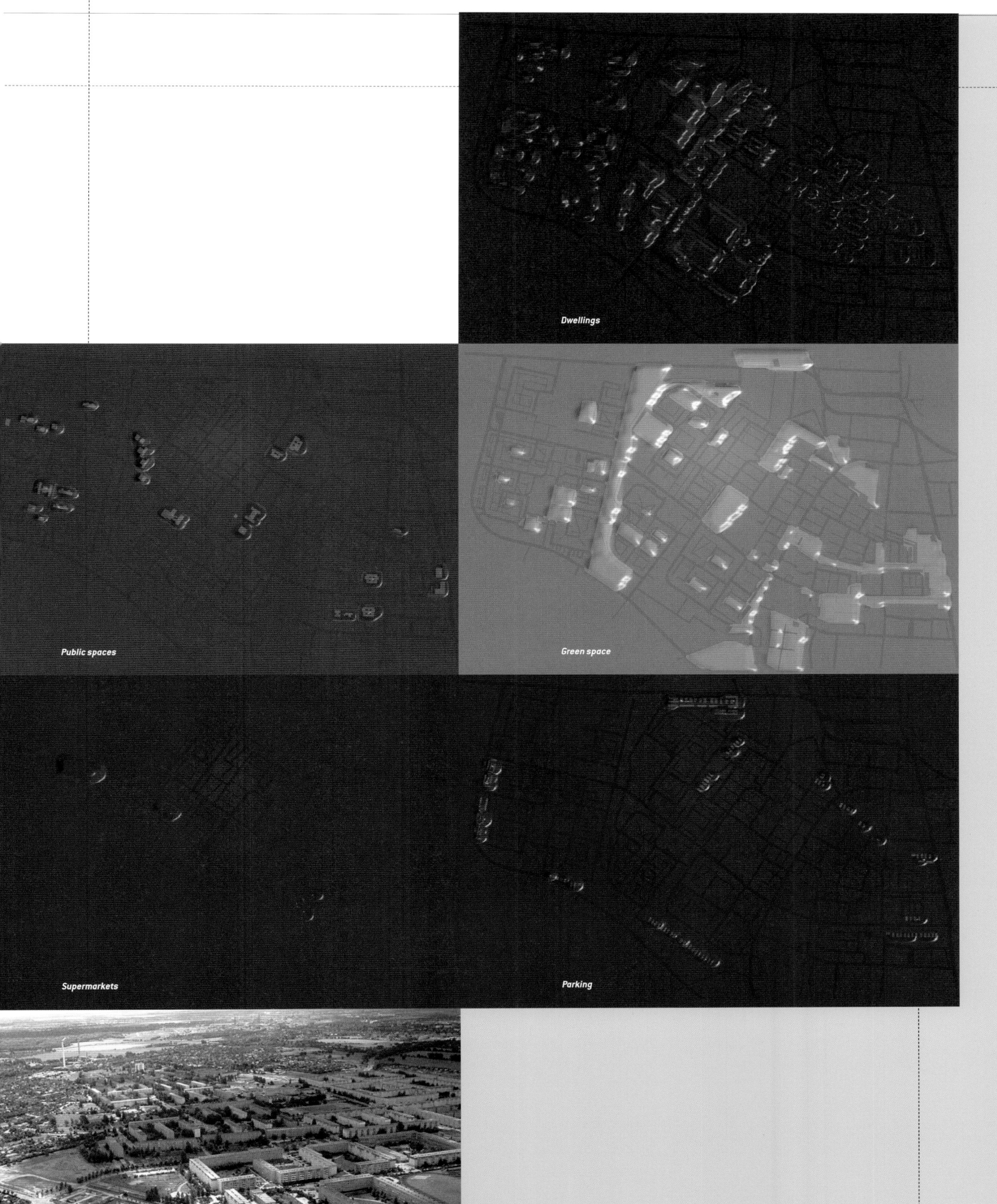

Dwellings

Public spaces

Green space

Supermarkets

Parking

Meshworks: Urbanism at the Margins

Bitterfeld-Wolden,Germany, 2000–02

'Meshworks', a study in train since 2000, is an urban project for a difficult district on the periphery of Bitterfeld-Wolden, a post-industrial town that was a casualty of the former East Germany, near Dessau. Situated south of Berlin, this region has been developed since the middle of the 19th century around mineral beds. The once-rural countryside has been reorganized into a vast space of decentralized industrial production, an object of fascination for the Bauhaus architects, who established their school at Dessau. After World War II the industrial and mining function of the region, annexed to the DDR, was intensified and entrenched. Bitterfeld-Wolden became the centre of a mechanized, colonized and systematized territory, punctuated by mines, heavily polluting chemical factories and large settlement clusters, superconcentrated reservoirs of labourers. Of those, Bitterfeld-Wolden has fewer than 35,000 inhabitants, along with a dearth of infrastructure, equipment and alternative sources of economic activity. In 1990, after reunification, the concurrent imperatives of the great economic advances led the large centres of production in this region gradually to close their doors. With 55% of people out of work, Wolfen-Nord was afflicted with the loss of 10,000 inhabitants. This was the situation Dagmar Richter was called upon to deal with: how to rethink and modify this post-industrial region? How to intervene in this space whose shape was the product of nearly a century of capitalist, functionalist or socialist urban planning and was a cruel example of their failure? Drawing on statistical data, interviews and inquiries on pollution, the microeconomy, demography, density and built structures, Dagmar Richter developed a computer operating model for the territory. Proposing not so much a strategy as a tactic, along the lines of Dr Certeau, of non-authoritarian urban recycling, this procedure brought to light some microeconomic activities, developed in pockets that escaped control by the socialist legislative system, and which now constitute the only signs of life and initiative: cooperative garages, garden allotments. Dagmar Richter's project takes the form of a flexible mesh, a network of infrastructural buckles, which prolong the analytical diagrams and which might become the flexible support for economic or physical flows, temporary or permanent activities, in all forms of adaptation. ☒

Credits: Dagmar Richter, assisted by Jonas Luther

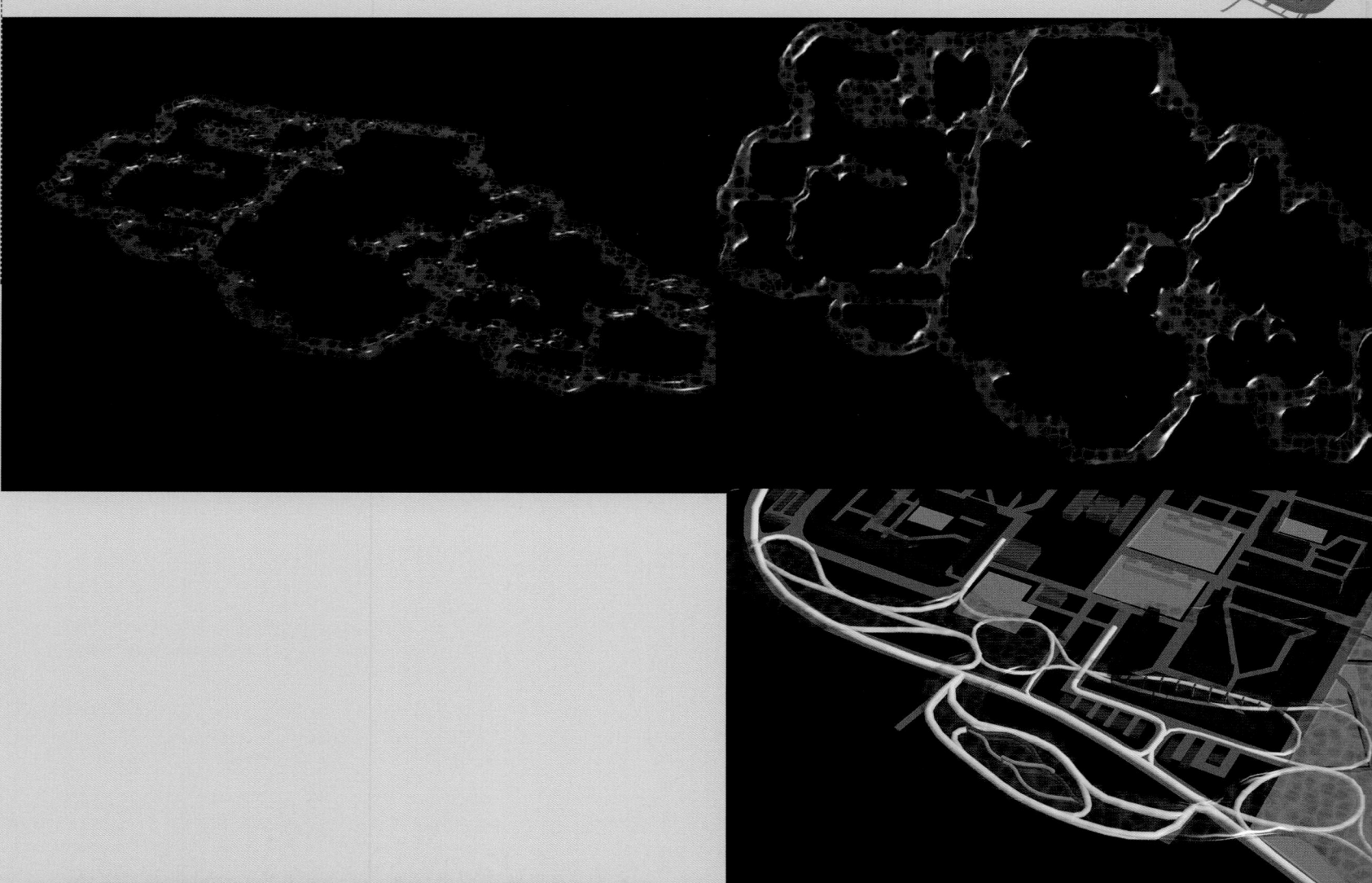

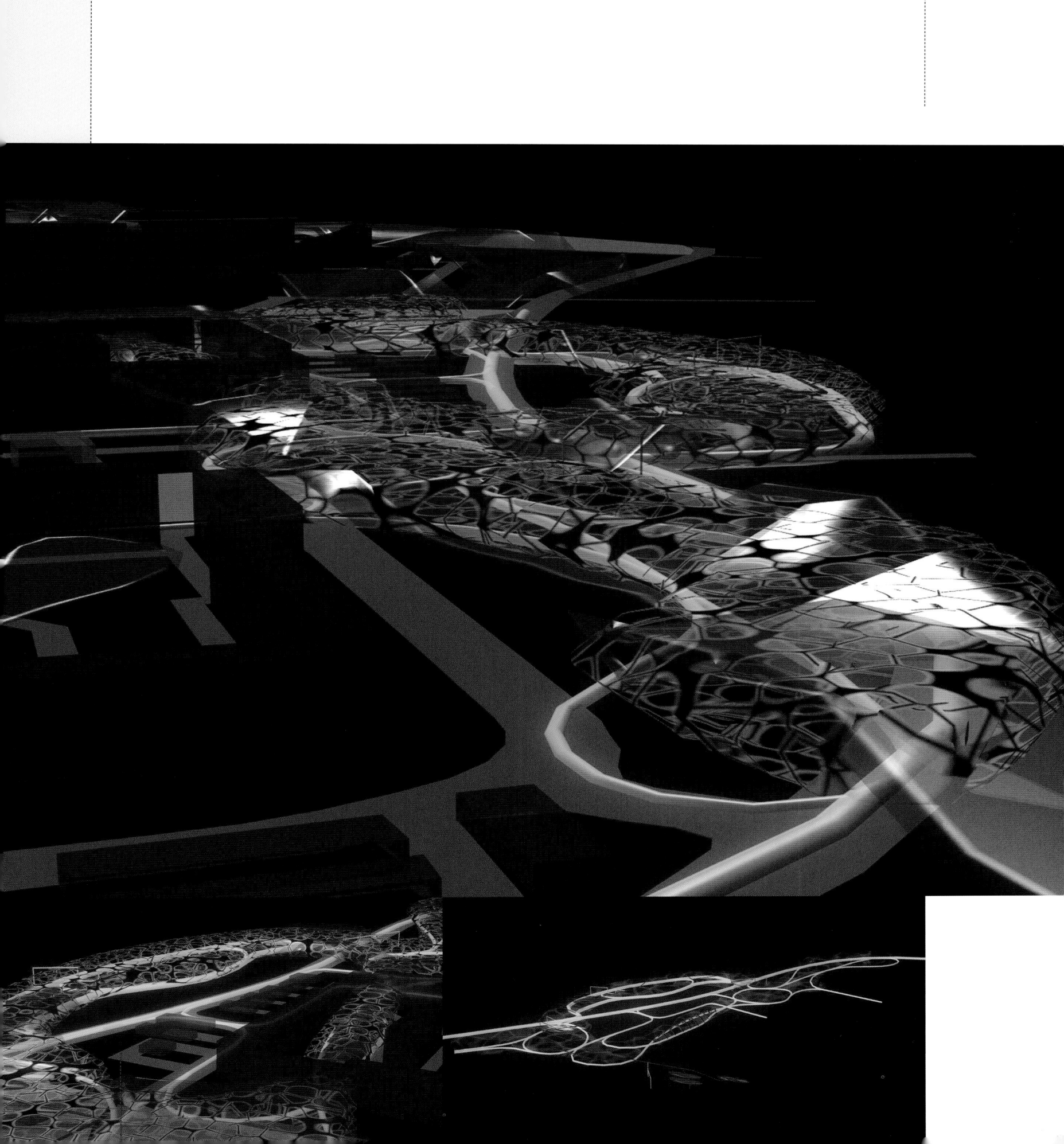

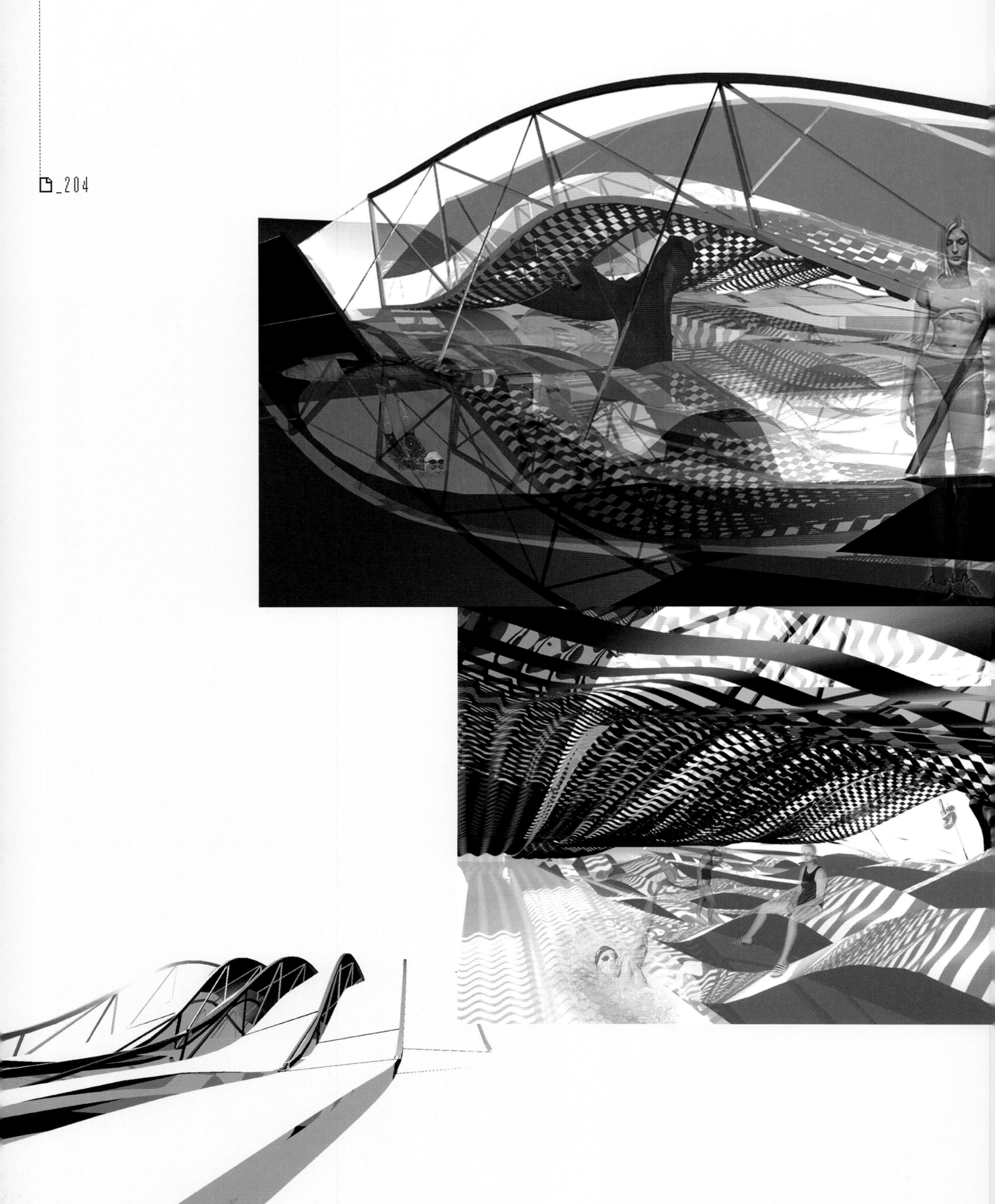

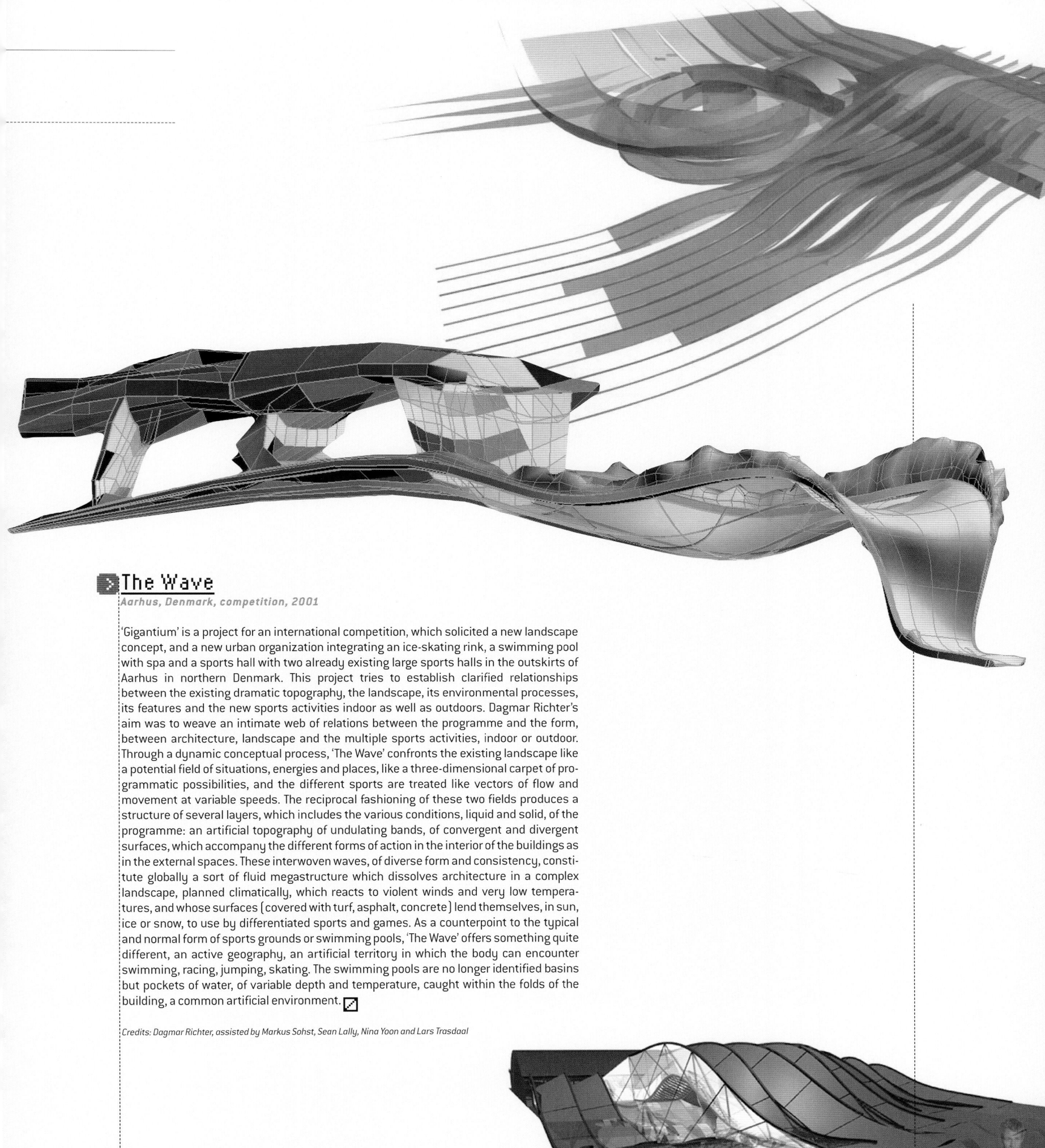

The Wave

Aarhus, Denmark, competition, 2001

'Gigantium' is a project for an international competition, which solicited a new landscape concept, and a new urban organization integrating an ice-skating rink, a swimming pool with spa and a sports hall with two already existing large sports halls in the outskirts of Aarhus in northern Denmark. This project tries to establish clarified relationships between the existing dramatic topography, the landscape, its environmental processes, its features and the new sports activities indoor as well as outdoors. Dagmar Richter's aim was to weave an intimate web of relations between the programme and the form, between architecture, landscape and the multiple sports activities, indoor or outdoor. Through a dynamic conceptual process, 'The Wave' confronts the existing landscape like a potential field of situations, energies and places, like a three-dimensional carpet of programmatic possibilities, and the different sports are treated like vectors of flow and movement at variable speeds. The reciprocal fashioning of these two fields produces a structure of several layers, which includes the various conditions, liquid and solid, of the programme: an artificial topography of undulating bands, of convergent and divergent surfaces, which accompany the different forms of action in the interior of the buildings as in the external spaces. These interwoven waves, of diverse form and consistency, constitute globally a sort of fluid megastructure which dissolves architecture in a complex landscape, planned climatically, which reacts to violent winds and very low temperatures, and whose surfaces (covered with turf, asphalt, concrete) lend themselves, in sun, ice or snow, to use by differentiated sports and games. As a counterpoint to the typical and normal form of sports grounds or swimming pools, 'The Wave' offers something quite different, an active geography, an artificial territory in which the body can encounter swimming, racing, jumping, skating. The swimming pools are no longer identified basins but pockets of water, of variable depth and temperature, caught within the folds of the building, a common artificial environment. ▢

Credits: Dagmar Richter, assisted by Markus Sohst, Sean Lally, Nina Yoon and Lars Trasdaal

▸ *SERVO*

United States, Sweden

David Erdman [1970], Marcelyn Gow [1966], Ulrika Karlsson [1966], Chris Perry [1969]

Although the four principals of Servo are all graduates of Columbia University, they now live, work and teach in different cities: D. Erdman and M. Gow in Los Angeles, C. Perry in New York and U. Karlsson in Stockholm. Established in 1999, Servo is seeking a dynamic interface, a tool for exploring contemporary methods of conceiving and producing architecture. Incorporating the local skills and knowledge of each of its members in a global and 'elastic' system of information exchange, their practice is structured around several 'lines' of research – Nurbline, Speedline, for example – each of which opens up a large field of applications and scales. The 'Cloudline' axis, for example, which consists of insinuating a degree of ambiguity and chance into the architecture, becomes a 'cloudcurtain', an interactive curtain-façade, as well as a 'cloudbox', multipurpose furniture (lamp, shelving, etc.). Servo's work has been the subject of a dozen exhibitions, collective or individual (WCCA, Columbia, 2002; Cooper-Hewitt Museum, NY, 2002; Architectural League, NY, 2001; Storefront, NY, 2000), has held five solo exhibitions, taken part in five group exhibitions, and has included teaching and lecturing widely in both Europe and the United States. ▨

DECENTRALIZED across four cities, three countries and two continents, the collaborative borrows its name from an apparatus common in the field of cybernetics. A servo motor translates digital code into mechanical processes. It behaves principally as an enabler, allowing two discrete languages to converse and interact. Servo has sampled this term for the collaborative to the extent that the practice itself functions as a kind of enabler, providing conversations and interactions between things that would not otherwise be directly or formally related. In a *discrete* fashion, which is to say, with a certain degree of discontinuity, Servo organizes and coordinates, at a variety of scales, new as well as existing relations between participants, technologies, disciplines, modes of production and communication, as well as a variety of cultural influences specific to each city in which it operates. To this extent Servo resembles a kind of culture in formation, a micro-community of participants, affiliate industries, technologies and disciplines, which assume different organizational and formal characteristics over time and distance.

One of digital technology's most important contributions to modes of contemporary practice has been the acceleration of interactivity in the process of design, production and distribution. Highly flexible interface design allows for a continuous shuffling and re-shuffling of authorship as work is passed from one designer to another, allowing the design process to register multiple influences across various media with a speed and efficiency previously unattainable. This process reflects a larger cultural shift that involves not only design but film, music and many other cultures. For instance, conventional distinctions between design and manufacturing in the car industry or performance and production in the music industry have become increasingly ambiguous as both the practices and technologies of each synthesize through the means of a digital interface, thus problematizing conventional authorship.

Servo has been focused on exploring the impact of digital technology on issues of authorship, particularly the play between individual and collective expression through new forms of authorship that don't necessarily disappear entirely but are instead relocated from a condition of singularity to one of multiplicity. The loss of value inherent in a condition of multiple authorship is replaced by a value system related to the personalization and portability of spatial and cultural experience. The absence of exclusive authorship finds its replacement in a *conversational* model. As an architecture and design practice, Servo has explored some of the possibilities of a conversational model, at the level of an internal collaboration, in relation to a conversation with other disciplines, technologies and userships, and in the conversational qualities of the work itself.

The redistribution of authorship implies that there must be an active system of storage (an archive) in which to collect and from which to sample material. The term 'active' or 'elastic' archive implies issues of flexibility and unpredictability as a potentially productive quality that becomes interesting to the extent that it throws each into question in the interactive process. An 'elastic archive' and its system of design, display and storage operates not only on an organizational scale, providing the virtual infrastructure

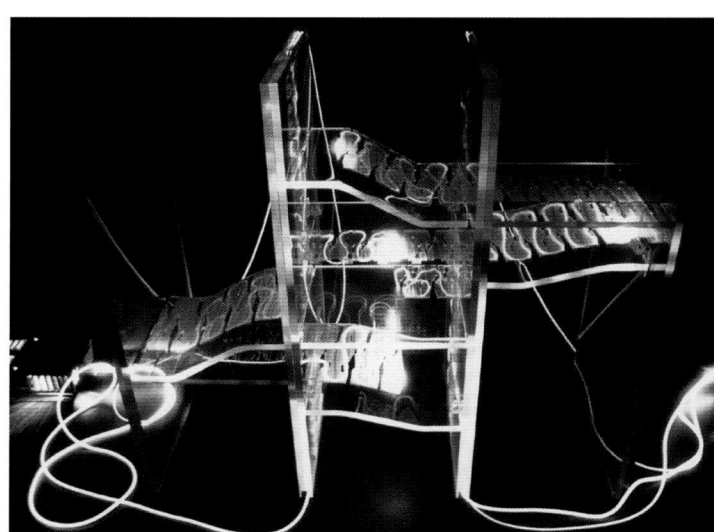

through which an interactive collaboration takes place, but also on an aesthetic scale as well, an element of spectacle in and of itself. As a parallel to the music industry where the practice of 'live mixing' has effectively incorporated sound production methodologies and technologies into the realm of performance, Servo speculates to what extent design collaboratives and their digitally accelerated interactive processes might raise similar questions. To what extent might a collaborative practice and its organizational methodologies and technologies operate not only as a system for production but as a system of production, and one which produces sensational effects? ▨

servo
david erdman
marcelyn gow
ulrika karlsson
chris perry

Servo

▶ Cloudline

Cloudline is a prototype system that operates in cloudy ways, that is to say, a system that induces ambiguity within the interface of its technologies, uses and applications, thereby affording a high degree of adaptability to scale, context, use and client requirements. The prototype plays itself out at the domestic scale and as a general programme of storage, display and lighting, but could extend to architectural or urban applications. Because of its dependency on machine production, CNC-milling technology relies primarily on methods of standardization and optimization for large-scale manufacturing, typically through a system of parts, modules or types. The Cloudline projects seek to engage this convention through modulation, partitioning and type-casting, while exploring the technology's capacity to produce flexibility and variation. Two specific applications of the Cloudline have been devised: Cloudbox has the two-fold objective to employ standardization in the production of variation at two scales: the first samples designs from standard display cases to develop a modular panel and shelf system, while the second uses CNC-milling technology to etch a system of pathways into those panels and shelves. Cloudcurtain, the second application of the Cloudline system, addresses the city's architectural and urban scales. In part a response to the recent replacement of curtain walls on skyscrapers and partly a response to an emerging infiltration of signage, infrastructure and in some cases provisional programme and circulation into conventional building skins, the Cloudcurtain provides several potential uses. By reversing conventions of mechanical and electrical distribution through the core of the building, the Cloudcurtain employs the skin itself as a field for conduits, thus allowing for greater accessibility and flexibility as companies upgrade for the 21st century and producing a transparency that allows for a wide range of interior, exterior, natural, artificial, functional or even spectacle-related lighting effects. ▨

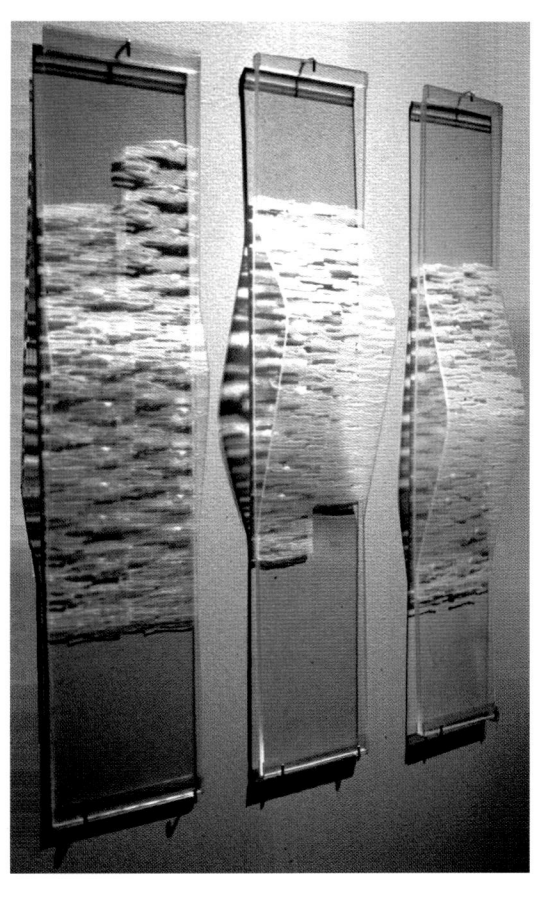

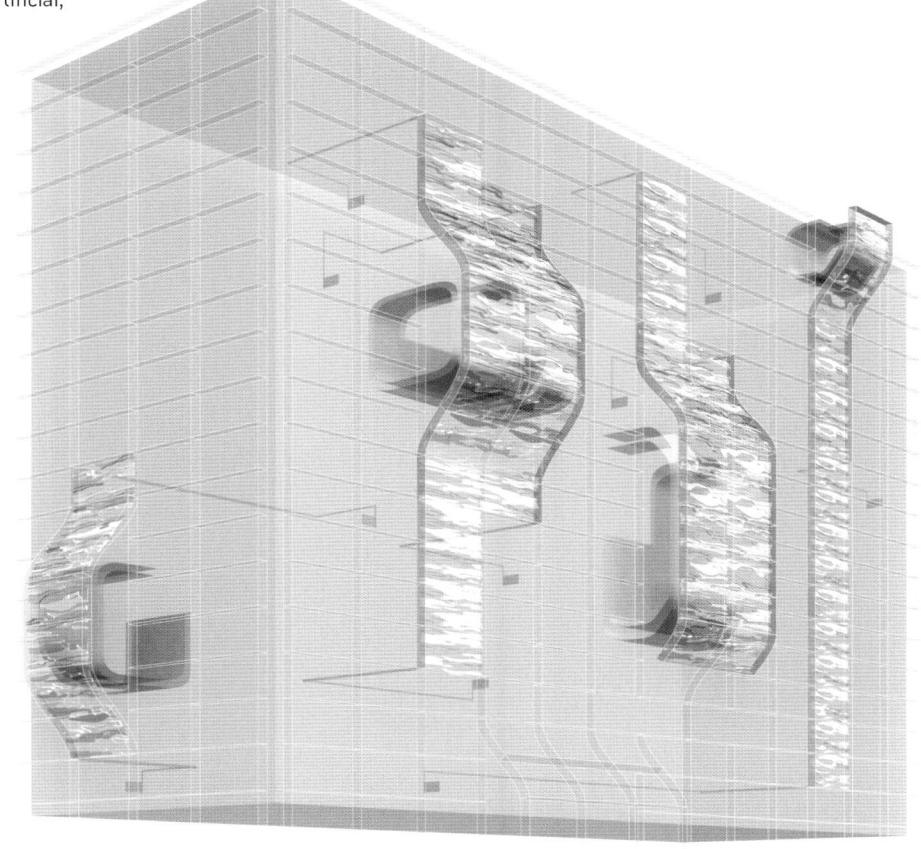

speeline
speetoy

nurbline
nurbia

product development

urban infrastructure

interactive showrooms

n2art

cloudcurtain

nurbrest

crac

building infrastructure

nurbwall

rich

display systems

cloudwall

storefront

york

cloudbox
cloudline

lighting systems

exhibition liners

cornell
servoline

lighting scheme

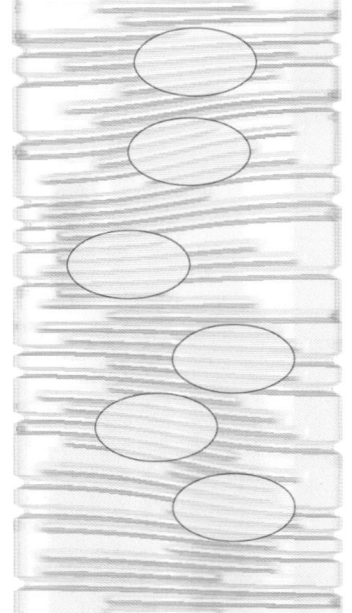

lighting organization

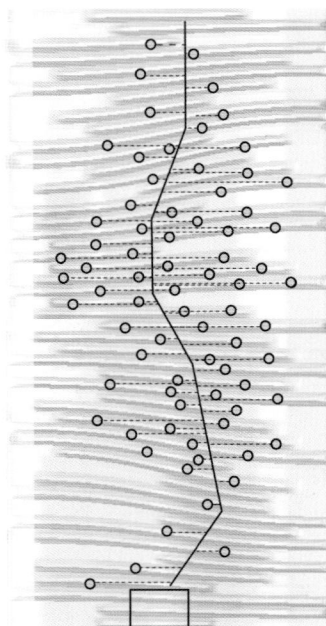

speaker network

Thermocline
Prototype, 2002

Thermocline investigates this general thematic by expanding on the canonical chaise longue, a chair whose positioning is seductive and layered with historical overtones in the discourse of architecture. The project explores the possibility for the chaise to *embed* multiple positions and speeds through the modulation of ergonomic form, situating gallery visitors next to each other or lying down head to toe. It expands the notion that the ergonomics of furniture are limited to touch and position by integrating sonics and light which respond to an occupant's position and distance. Thermocline is approximately 1.2 by 2.4 metres, composed of four modules made entirely of bent plastic. The *responsive* technologies in the project are designed and conceptualized in relation to the phenomenon of thermal transitions that occur between surface and deep water: a *thermocline*. Owing to opposing convection flows, when swimming through a thermocline one experiences an invisible yet distinct sensation, as if entering into a space or passing over a threshold. The Thermocline project explores to what extent surface, texture, shape, sound and colour can produce spaces that exceed the physical dimension of the piece and make ambiguous its zone of interaction. Thermocline is composed of bands corresponding to varying comfort zones, sound and lighting to create different sensory experiences. There are regions that are very quiet and others that are loud, ones in which the light is barely present and others where it surrounds the occupant. One can recline for long periods of time, listen to the soundtrack and browse exhibition information or sit as though on a bench and briefly rest. The shape, layering of technologies and design technique combine to produce a simultaneity which allows one to interact with Thermocline in a polyvalent manner: fast, slow, focused, distracted. ▣

Credits: Servo with Anne Barakat, Rafael Cardenas, Classic Design, Leonore Daum, Ed Keller, Kintz Plastics, Jeff McKibbin, Julianna Morais, Robert Morais, RSL Lighting, Inc., Dan Walczyk

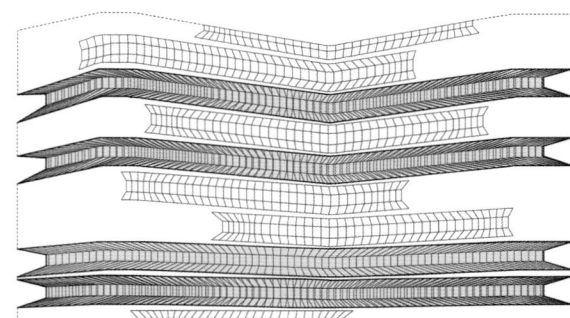

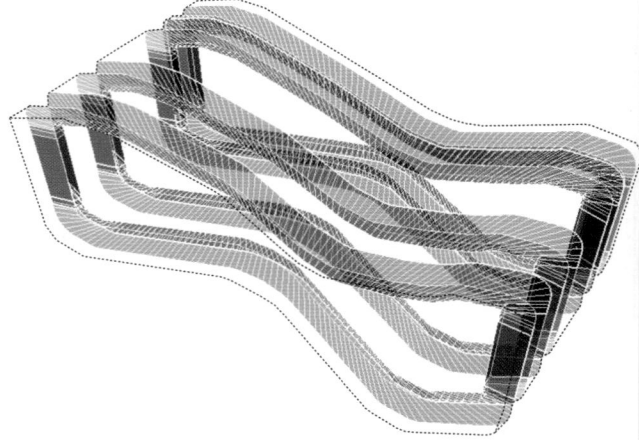

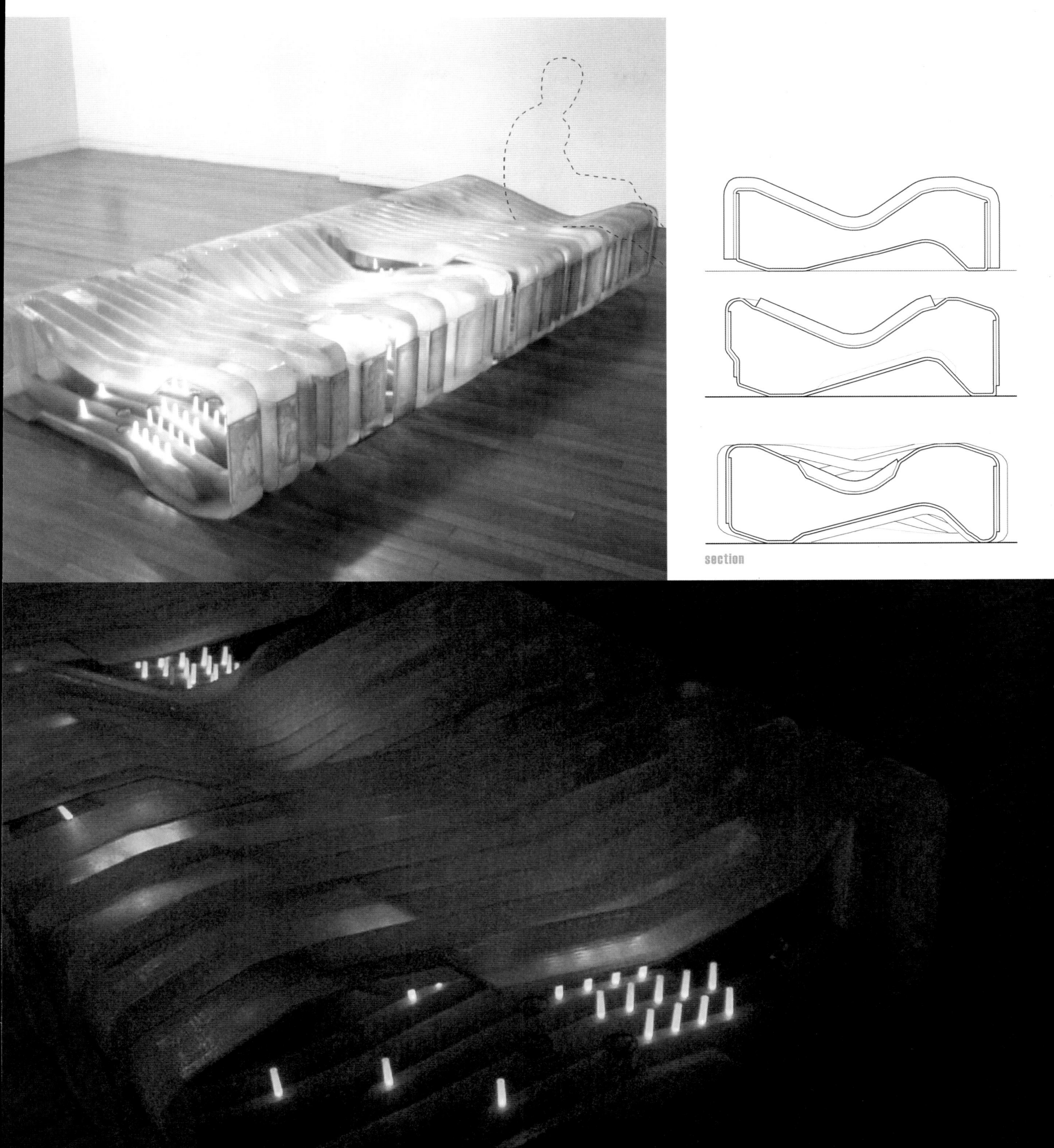

section

▶ In the Lattice
Stockholm, Sweden, interactive installation, 2002

In the Lattice is an elastic field of geometric elements and sound samples designed to undergo plastic deformations. A series of digital wrinkles and micro-tapers in the geometric field can be activated to redistribute the chain mesh of lattice elements and their corresponding sound samples. A three-dimensional wallpaper resonant with sound is sketched by visitors through the manipulation of the digital interface. The motion of a prototyped scale model of lattice elements relative to the horizontal table surface activates changes in the digital lattice screen that are linked to changes in the sound environment. The lattice screen is transformed by scaling, rotation, tapering and transparency applied to individual lattice elements and in some instances to several elements. Starting with a homogeneous audio field, conversations between visitors as they transform the lattice are sampled and attached to geometric transformations in the digital model. Subsequent iterations of the lattice screen occur with the ravelling and unravelling of the three-dimensional mesh as it is manipulated. Instead of a browser with a stationary archive to which material can be added or retrieved, the lattice interface provides the possibility for several authors to simultaneously operate an elastic archive that continuously is under change. In the Lattice adopts the protocol of an active screening room, in which the screen is conventionally a surface intended for images is reconfigured as a laminate of multiple screens in which a plasma screen houses the three-dimensional lattice screen. The lattice screen operates as a porous illumination device in terms of the light levels produced on the plasma screen that are adjusted according to transparency changes in the individual elements.

In the Lattice is part of a larger project, elasti-fab, that incorporates multiple authorship in the design process, as well as altering the conventional protocols of design and manufacturing. Elastic fabrication questions the notion of prefabricated construction through a set of elements intended to be activated and altered during the design and manufacturing processes and that these elements are designed with an inherent flexibility that allows for a range of alterations that are compatible with adjacent elements. The properties of construction materials are elasticized by suggesting that a particular fabrication technique can be applied to a series of materials that yield a variety of elements whose stability varies on a structural level and that simultaneously generate a variety of atmospheric effects.

Credits: Daniel Norell, Thomas Broomé, Olaf Bendt, Fredrik Petersson

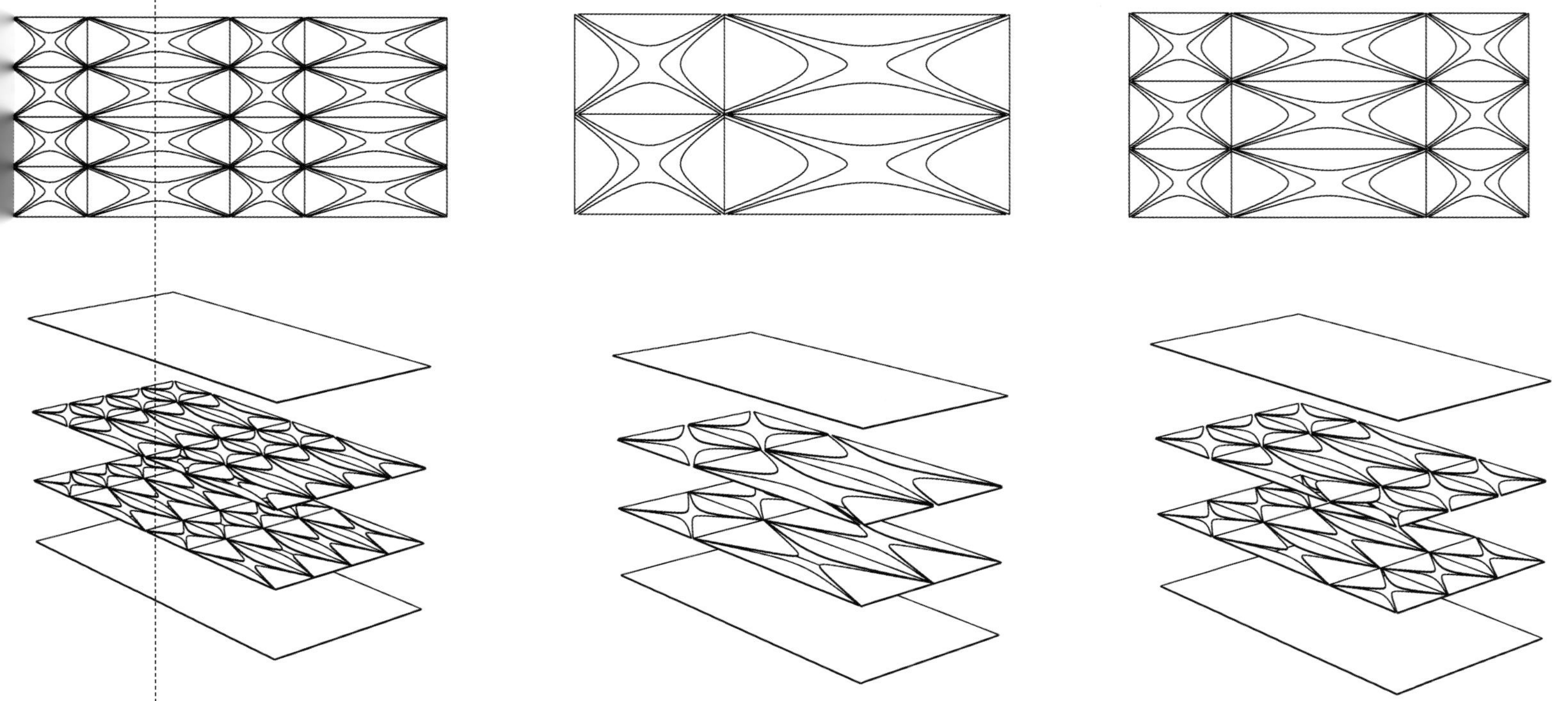

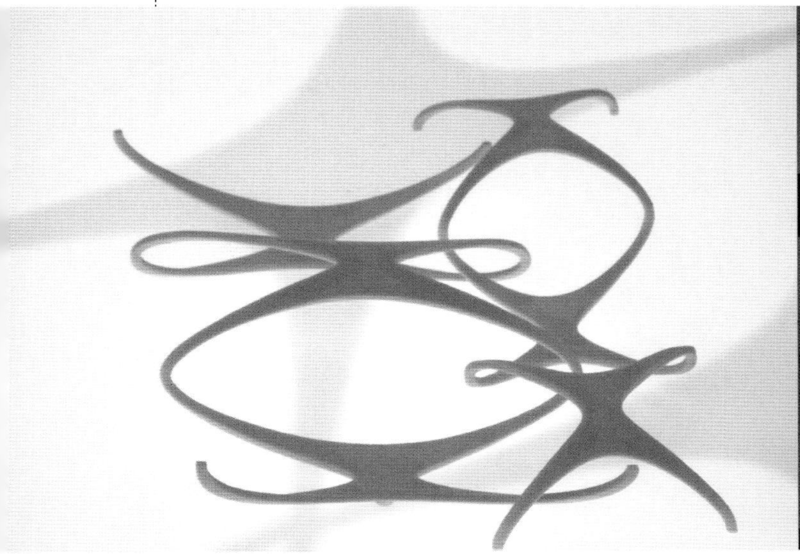

TeamMINUS

China

Brian Chang [1970], Brenda Yao [1970], FuXun Lu [1964], Rong Zhou [1968]

TeamMINUS was founded in 1999 in Beijing by a group of four young architects from the School of Architecture, Tsinghua University, in Beijing, where three of them now teach. Their practice can be understood only in the context of present-day China: a place of prodigious economic development, massive but anarchic urbanization, which leaves whole expanses of territory underdeveloped. In this situation, TeamMINUS see themselves as creating a platform for speculation and reflection on the role of architecture in social and technological problem areas. Both committed and practical, they have already seen several of their public buildings realized: Liyang town hall (1997), the chemistry library at Tsinghua University (Beijing, 1999, in progress), Xiaolan hospital (Guangdong, 2001, in progress), and the museum for the bamboo book (Changsha, 2001, in progress). ☒

CONTEMPORARY CHINA is in an age of unprecedented large-scale construction and social reform, which makes her one of the focuses of worldwide debate. The professional environment for architects here is both promising and frustrating. On one hand, the numerous projects, the unlimited possibilities and the passion for the new are making China one of the most appealing countries to architects in the world. On the other hand, the complexity of social context, the lack of cultural continuity and the overtaking of responsibility by the desire for luxury are making architects confused. The progress of globalization helped little in solving China's own problems. Globalization has not bridged the gap between the developed and the developing countries. What it does is strengthen the links between them. What is special about these links is that in them we see mostly one-way information flows. It's fair to say that China 'knows' more about the West than she is 'known' among them. Since the overload of information from the West to China does not bring about the same amount of understanding, much of the information ends up as misinterpreted knowledge. This sort of knowledge contributes a lot to the 'standardization' of architectural attempts, which denies all forms of regional, cultural and social considerations.

TeamMINUS therefore emphasizes an approach of 'design for appropriateness' by the suspension of all the standardized desires and the seeking of more alternatives. Fashions, styles, -isms are all bounds to architects, some drawn by themselves, only to tell them what 'should be', making them forget what 'could be'. It is those 'could-be's that will finally lead to appropriate results. Each project, given its complicated context, heavy restraints and specific needs, has a lot of these 'could-be's, which will eventually form an internal force. TeamMINUS takes these forces as design priorities and follows them.

Two things are important for the members of TeamMINUS. One is the educational value of built spaces; the other is the possibilities of technologies. Architecture, even in the most technological aspect, is not neutral at all. It changes man at least no less than man changes it. In contemporary China, this is even more so. New buildings, as proofs of affluence, are always regarded as metaphors of new life, stating new styles to follow. For a nation in its ideological dilemma, the impact of building behaviour is enormous. It puts forward a responsibility that no architect can deny or escape from. Technologies also have their special meanings in China. For in China there is a juxtaposition of different development levels and different possibilities, its range unmatched by most countries in the world. Technologies, from high-end to low-end, from the expensive to the cheap, will all find their places of usefulness. It is therefore architects' duty to settle specific technological strategies for specific projects. The adoption of appropriate technology is critical to the appropriateness of a design.

In the Western countries, after World War II, we saw a rise of social responsibility in the profession of architects. Today in China this responsibility, in a much more complex form, is under recall. To a population of 1.5 billion, a truer attitude towards architecture is nothing but a kind of bliss. ☒

Brian Chang

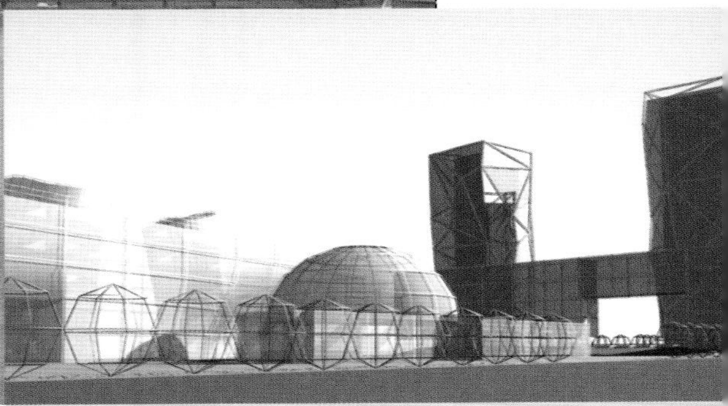

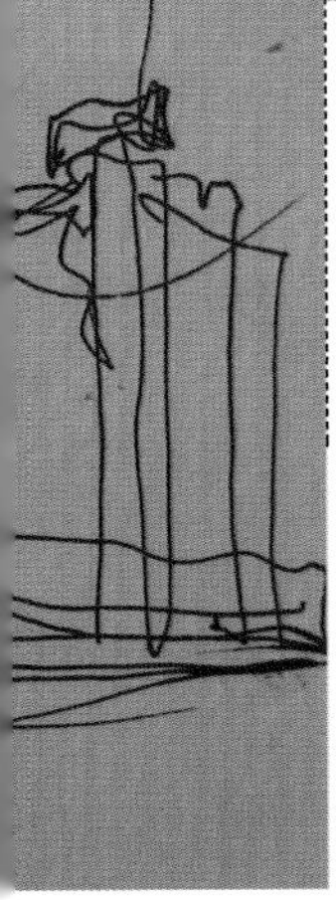

▶ Service Building, Beijing Planetarium

Beijing, China, project, 2001–02

The old Beijing Planetarium, designed by architects from the former Soviet Union, is one of the most evocative sights in of the city. By 2003, a new exhibition hall, featuring curved glass curtain walls, will be built on its southern side. To complete the renewal of the planetarium area, commercial space of over 40,000 square metres for offices will be needed to make the enterprise financially feasible. Our task is to design the new office space, known as the service building. The problems laid before us are: 1) to minimize the effect of the new big building and maintain the predominance of the old Planetarium as much as possible; 2) to create public exterior place on the ground floor, which is seemingly impossible for a project with such a high coefficient of ground occupancy; 3) to respect the harmony of an urban environment already highly perturbed by the intrusion of express roads and tall buildings. Our suggestion is to set up two fractal-shaped towers with two wings lower down. Entering into dialogue with the new glass exhibition hall, they could act as a series of backgrounds that bring the old Planetarium into relief. They could also act as strong statements in a confusing urban context, separating the old planetarium clearly from its surroundings. The new buildings themselves will take advantage of this paradoxical situation to impose a striking image, with their unusual shape, and to disappear into the landscape, thanks to their materials. The entry level of the service building will be raised, to mark it off from the street; this pedestrian precinct will slope gently down towards the east until it vanishes in the lawn of the Planetarium. Space below this level will be used for vehicle traffic. A large opening in the east wing will afford a direct view over the old Planetarium.

Credits: Brian Chang, FuXun Lu, Mingqi Zhang, Juan Zhang

the labyrinth game
or community playgrounds

eycol
street furniture for Be

bus stop

Cycolympiad

Beijing, China, project, 2002

The 'Cycolympiad' is a conceptual study of street furniture design for the Beijing Olympics in 2008. The key idea of this project is the use of building fragments and rubble from demolition sites as building materials. While China is experiencing an unprecedented passion for construction, Beijing, as the host city for the Olympiad 2008, is a classic case of frenzied urban renewal. Thousands of old buildings are being pulled down each year, releasing millions of square metres of potential floor space. The scale and the speed of this renewal are themselves phenomena of historical note and deserve to be made known on the occasion of this international exposure. At first, TeamMINUS planned to recycle the materials from the demolished buildings, so as to use them directly to fabricate the new street furniture. Later, when this idea proved to be technically and economically impracticable, the focus shifted. Instead of concentrating on the structural and instrumental values of these building fragments, the architects chose to explore their symbolic and monumental value. The solution they finally adopted was the 'sugar box' idea, which was to encapsulate the building fragments and the city memories at the same time. Boxes of steel and glass formed the basic volumes, which were then filled with the rubble and fragments. The resulting forms were used in all kinds of street furniture: bus-stops, kiosks, phone booths, community playgrounds, etc. This type of street furniture will be distributed in the whole Olympic area around Beijing, forming a kind of exhibition of urbanism in negative form, a critical vision of Chinese architectural renewal and a shining homage to the city. ◹

Credits: Brian Chang, Rong Zhou, FuXun Lu, Shanshan Zheng. Fei Zhai

cycolympiad
street furniture for Beijing 2008 using recollected building fr

the "sugar box" idea

cycolympiad in context
photomontage sketches

cycolympiad

street furniture in Beijing 2008 using recollected building fragments

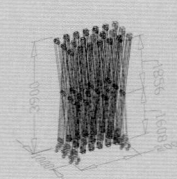

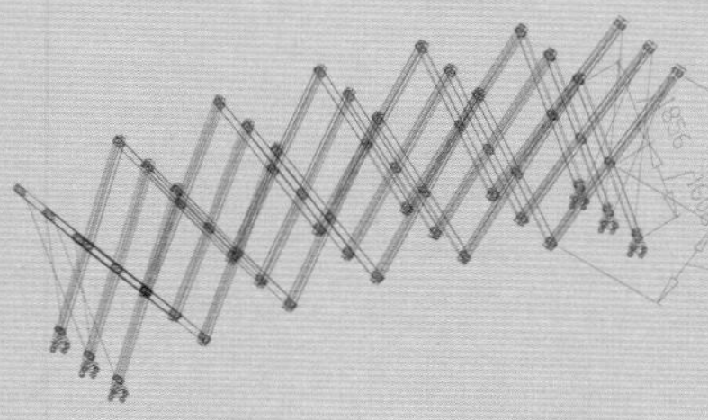

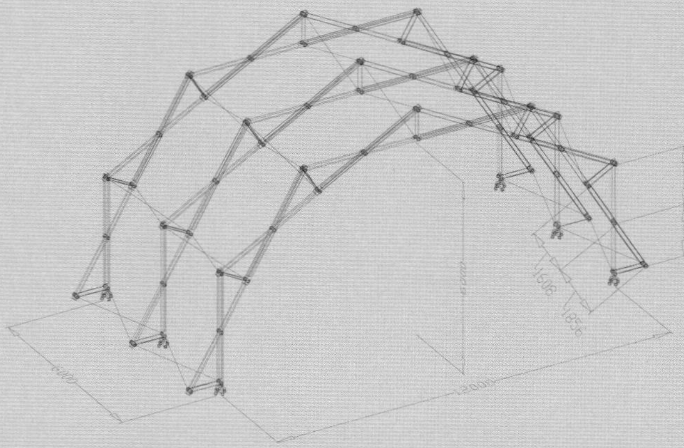

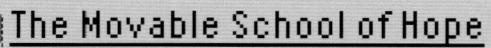

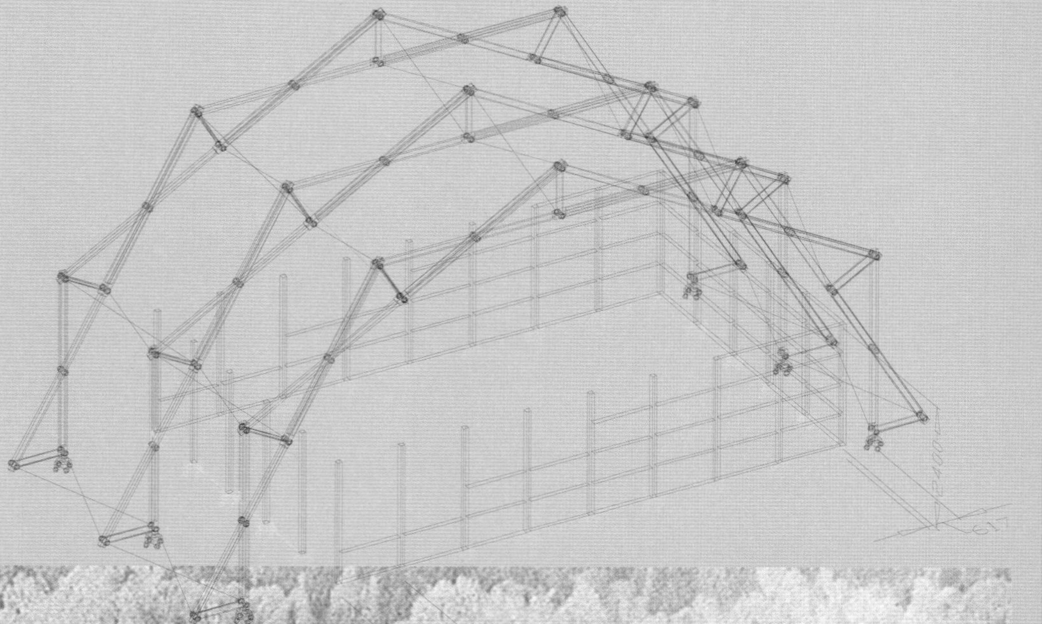

The Movable School of Hope
China, project, 2000

The 'School of Hope' is a huge, nationwide programme in China, the goal of which is to improve elementary educational conditions in poorer areas, by raising necessary funds and setting up basic facilities. This design is a tribute to the 'School of Hope' programme. Its key idea is to share limited educational resources in poorer regions by the use of rapidly assembled, movable classrooms. The basic system consists of a light structure (proposed by Hernandez, Carlos & Zarlevsky, 1991), a combination of modular constructional elements and furniture. This basic system will fit into a single lorry. Teachers, books and other items can be transported in another truck. Thus, two vehicles are enough to carry this movable School of Hope from one village to another, bringing badly needed educational resources to everyone. Compared with traditionally built schools, the movable school has several advantages. First, it is much cheaper, only about a third of the cost of a traditional school. Second, it requires fewer resources, both natural and human. The movable school occupies only a small piece of land and, being removable, it makes no permanent occupation of any land at all. The work required to set up such a school is also far less than in traditional construction methods. Third, it is more flexible. Adaptive changes can be made at any time to the basic system. Fourth, it makes possible the sharing of precious educational resources, which is of inestimable value for the poorer areas. With the movable school, teachers, books and equipment can be available to many pupils. However, there is no likelihood that the movable school will replace the traditional school. It is appropriate only when traditional schools are either unaffordable or impractical. It is a temporary solution of current problems, making education affordable quicker and wider, the sole proviso being that the site be accessible by lorry and the climate not too harsh.

Credits: Brian Chang, Brenda Yao

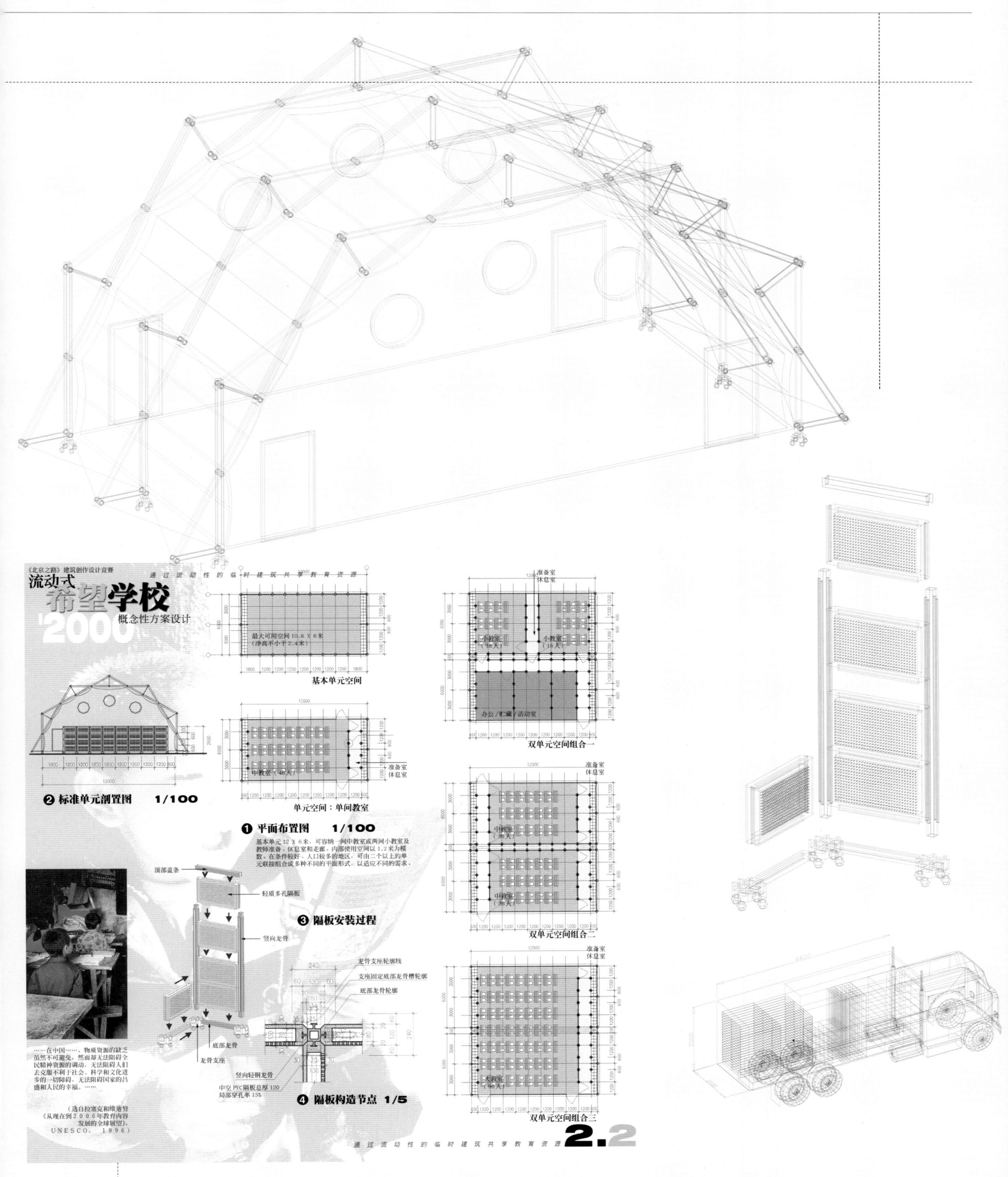

《北京之路》建筑创作设计竞赛

流动式 希望 学校 '2000

通过流动性的临时建筑共享教育资源

概念性方案设计

② 标准单元剖置图 1/100

最大可用空间 10.8 X 6米
（净高不小于2.4米）

基本单元空间

单元空间：单间教室

准备室
休息室

① 平面布置图 1/100

基本单元12 X 6米，可容纳一间中教室或两间小教室及教师准备、休息室和走廊，内部使用空间以1.2米为模数，在条件较好、人口较多的地区，可由二个以上的单元联接组合成多种不同的平面形式，以适应不同的需求。

❸ 隔板安装过程

顶部盖条
轻质多孔隔板
竖向龙骨
龙骨支座轮廓线
支座固定底部龙骨槽轮廓
底部龙骨轮廓
底部龙骨
龙骨支座
竖向轻钢龙骨
中空PVC隔板总厚120
局部穿孔率15%

❹ 隔板构造节点 1/5

准备室
休息室
小教室（48人）　小教室（18人）
办公/贮藏/活动室

双单元空间组合一

准备室
休息室
中教室（48人）
中教室（48人）

双单元空间组合二

准备室
休息室
大教室（96人）

双单元空间组合三

……在中国……，物质资源的缺乏虽然不可避免，然而却无法阻碍全民精神资源的调动，无法阻碍人们去克服不利于社会、科学和文化进步的一切障碍，无法阻碍国家的昌盛和人民的幸福。

（选自拉塞克和维迪努努《从现在到2000年教育内容发展的全球展望》，UNESCO，1996）

TEZUKA ARCHITECTS

Japan

Yui Tezuka (1969), Takaharu Tezuka (1964)

Having graduated from the Musashi Institute of Technology, Takaharu completed his training with a Masters at Pennsylvania University, while Yui completed hers at the Bartlett School in London, and worked with Ron Herron (1992–93). Takaharu then took the opportunity to work with the Richard Rogers agency in London from 1990 till 1994. Afterwards, the couple returned to Tokyo to set up their own agency, after winning the commission to build Soejima Hospital (4,000 square metres) — a project that won them the 'Good Design Gold Prize 1997' awarded by the Japanese Ministry of Commerce and Industry. Since then, they have specialized in individual houses (seven constructed in 2001), but they recently won a competition for a Natural Science Museum in Nigata, and were awarded the Yoshioka Prize in the 2002 Shinkenchiku competition. Their work has been widely exhibited in Tokyo (at the Madori Living Design Centre in 2000 and 2001; Hillside Terrace Gallery and Saka Gallery, 1998; GA Gallery in 1996).

Although they both view their architectural work as Japanese, they consider their way of constructing 'ideas' as having been greatly influenced by their experiences in the West, both in London and Philadelphia. Takaharu even says that in the USA he learned the 'logic of architectural thinking'. This feeling of having been shaped by the West and not having had Japanese 'masters' has given them a very bold outlook, notably as regards the city that they have helped to fashion. For them Tokyo is chaotic: there is no alignment of façades, everything stands free, juxtaposed, independent. And yet there were rules in traditional Japanese architecture, and they created urban relations that were compatible with usage. While Western architectural colleges teach that every project must be treated as a new concept, the Tezukas believe that in Tokyo it is important for the new generation to try to find standards and approaches that will meet the needs of everybody — clients, residents, passers-by, etc. They fully realize that the present Japanese attitude has to be the opposite of the Western, where the quest is for flexibility, diversity and freedom. They formulate their conceptual work in architecture as a search for 'stupefying ideas', though these must be represented and expressed in such a way that everyone can understand them. They do not have any specific notions of form or structure, but in this context regard themselves simply as heirs to the principles of modern architecture. The ideas that they are interested in concern new ways of life, new movements which have not yet come into existence but which will generally be feasible. The key to discovering these inventive ways of life is an exploration a little beyond the confines of 'common sense', an eye that will look through the normal, daily world in order to detect things that would otherwise escape notice. The 'inventive' element here must be put into a form that will suit a large proportion of the public — though not necessarily the architects. In this manner the Tezuka Agency has won an increasing number of private commissions for individual residences, and the fact that their work has been enthusiastically received is due to the fact that they take the wishes of the client as their starting-point. Although this may seem almost banal, it is taken very seriously and carried almost poetically to the extreme: 'we are very eager to listen, and we search with the clients for their dream house, and then we exaggerate their desires to the maximum. The clients then live in their own concept, and so believe that they have really planned their own house.' The Tezukas enjoy working in the context of this happy misconception. According to them, what distinguishes architecture from art is the fact that the latter can be conceived for its own sake and can live within itself, whereas architecture must always have a 'proprietor'. But even when there is no personal client, the Tezukas look for ideas in the ways that buildings are used — as with their project for the Soejima Hospital (1996), laid out around a long, thick façade, which facilitates different forms of contact between the exterior and the various levels, and which gives all the rooms a view on to the town and its life, rather than up at the sky.

B.G.

Wall-less House
Tokyo, Japan, completed, 2001

If the Tezukas' guiding principle is to transform the dreams of their clients into reality, there can be no doubt that the owners of this house dreamed of a bedroom among the trees and a dining room in the garden. The three floors of this house are supported by a structural core and two very thin columns of steel joined to the floors and ceilings. Thus the occupants have a 360-degree panorama of the garden, as there is no need for any exterior walls. On the ground floor there are sliding glass panels all the way up, and the living room imperceptibly merges into the terrace and then the lawn, all on exactly the same level thanks to horizontal grilles that allow the water to drain: thus the transition from interior to exterior is quite seamless. The supporting core contains all the facilities that need water; it is off-centre, dividing each floor into one large space and one smaller service area containing the stairs, which are like the gangway of a ship. The luxurious feel of an ocean liner is also present on each of the floors, where there are windows all the way along each room. The tangible and total presence of the external plant life within the spaces of the house itself is enhanced by the absence of any fixed frames. The tracks on which the windows slide are situated in hollows cut into the ceiling and behind the raised edge of the guard rail. Each room, then, is like a balcony looking out over the greenery. On the outside, the metallic facing emphasizes the slender horizontal lines of the three floors, which stand out very clearly and terminate in a roof terrace that is topped off by a kind of ship's rail made of steel cables.

Photo: Shinkentikusya

ラリー:積雪は常に窓の下。季節を通じて景色が楽しめる。

体験ゾーン:積雪の表面が窓の中ほどまでくる開口部。二つの世界が同時に見える。

レクチャー

ラン:アプローチから森へと景色が貫く開放的な空間。企画展示を見せる。

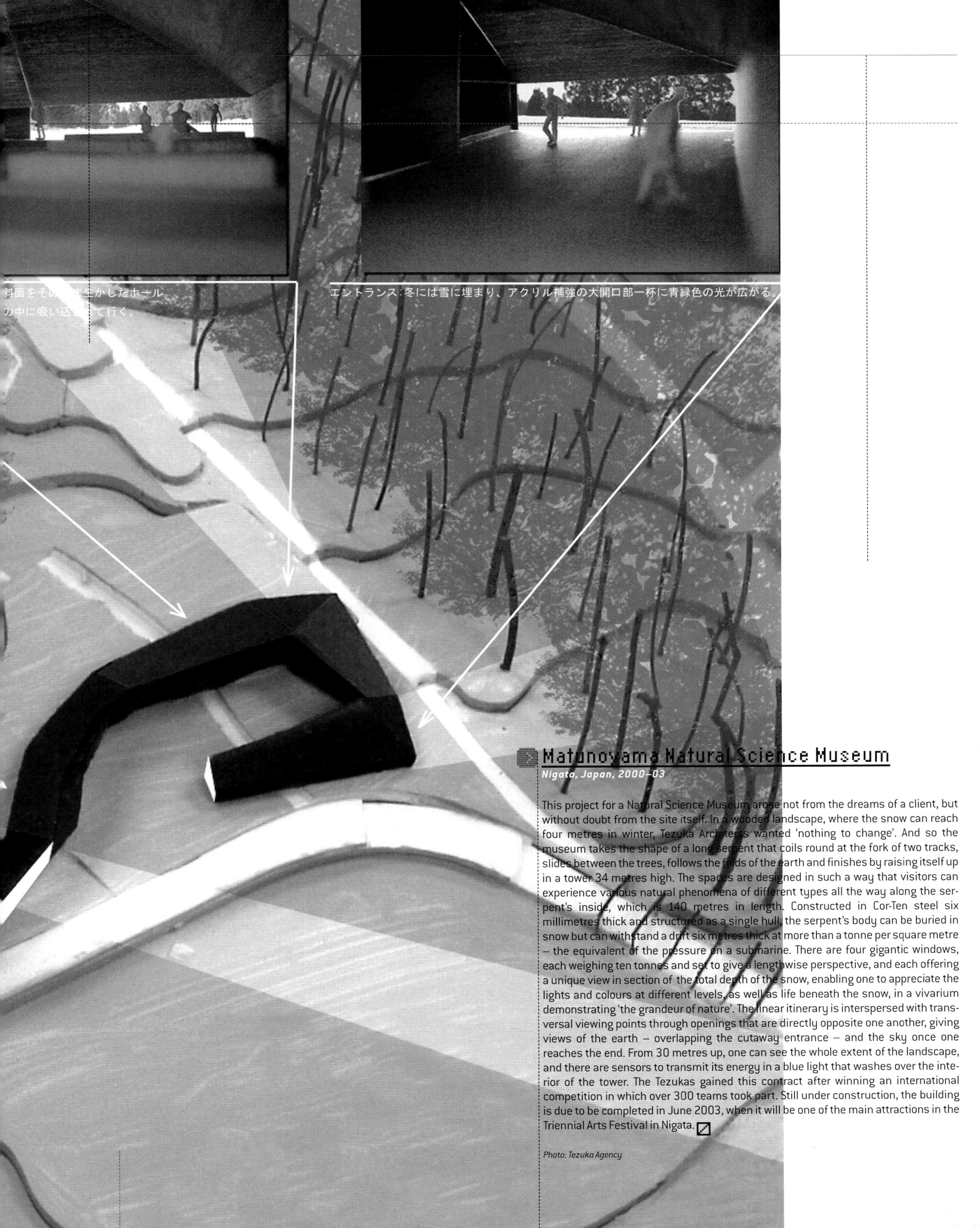

斜面をそのまま生かしたホール。
の中に吸い込まれて行く。

エントランス：冬には雪に埋まり、アクリル補強の大開口部一杯に青緑色の光が広がる。

Matunoyama Natural Science Museum

Nigata, Japan, 2000–03

This project for a Natural Science Museum arose not from the dreams of a client, but without doubt from the site itself. In a wooded landscape, where the snow can reach four metres in winter, Tezuka Architects wanted 'nothing to change'. And so the museum takes the shape of a long serpent that coils round at the fork of two tracks, slides between the trees, follows the folds of the earth and finishes by raising itself up in a tower 34 metres high. The spaces are designed in such a way that visitors can experience various natural phenomena of different types all the way along the serpent's inside, which is 140 metres in length. Constructed in Cor-Ten steel six millimetres thick and structured as a single hull, the serpent's body can be buried in snow but can withstand a drift six metres thick at more than a tonne per square metre – the equivalent of the pressure on a submarine. There are four gigantic windows, each weighing ten tonnes and set to give a lengthwise perspective, and each offering a unique view in section of the total depth of the snow, enabling one to appreciate the lights and colours at different levels, as well as life beneath the snow, in a vivarium demonstrating 'the grandeur of nature'. The linear itinerary is interspersed with transversal viewing points through openings that are directly opposite one another, giving views of the earth – overlapping the cutaway entrance – and the sky once one reaches the end. From 30 metres up, one can see the whole extent of the landscape, and there are sensors to transmit its energy in a blue light that washes over the interior of the tower. The Tezukas gained this contract after winning an international competition in which over 300 teams took part. Still under construction, the building is due to be completed in June 2003, when it will be one of the main attractions in the Triennial Arts Festival in Nigata. ☑

Photo: Tezuka Agency

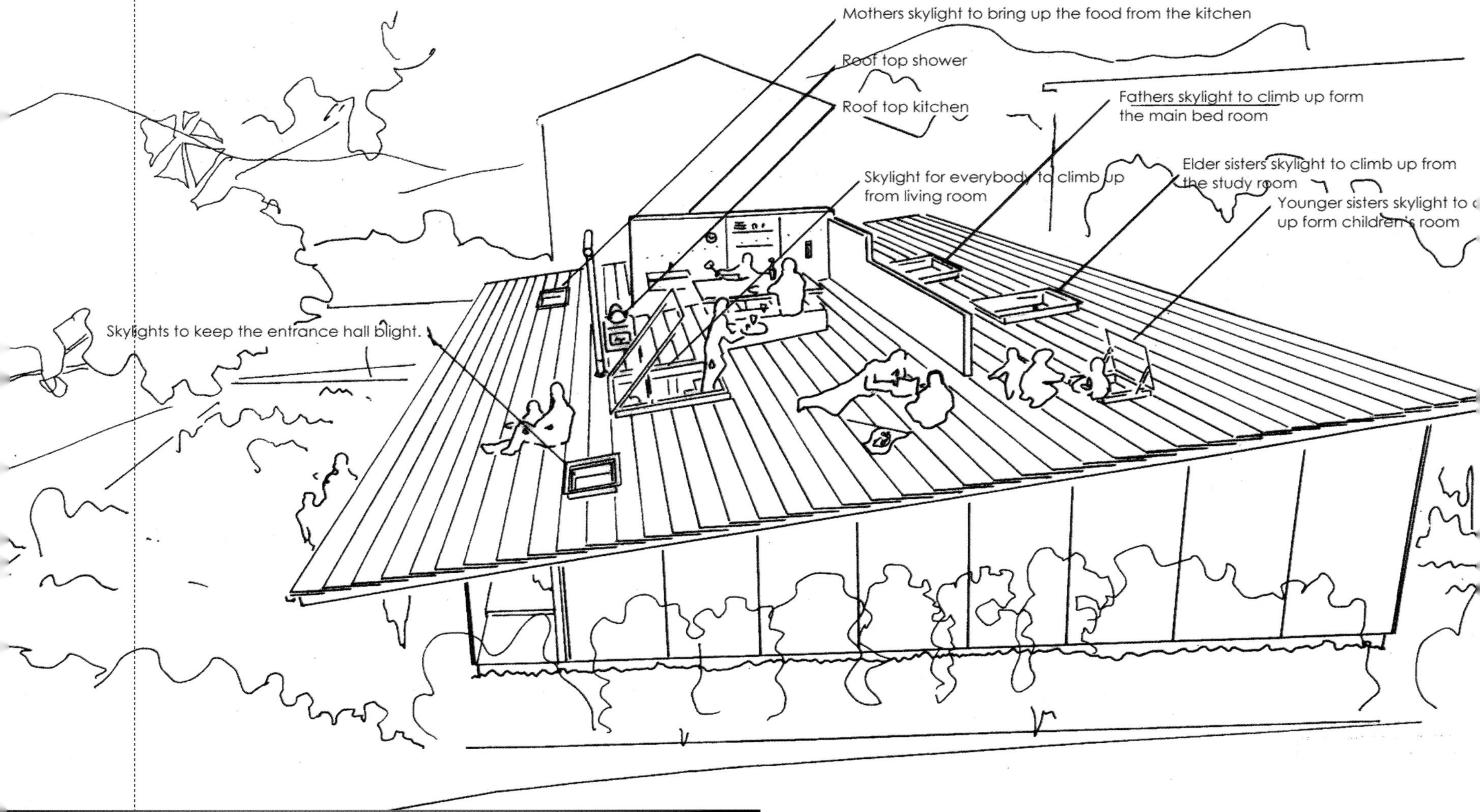

Mothers skylight to bring up the food from the kitchen

Roof top shower

Roof top kitchen

Fathers skylight to climb up form the main bed room

Skylight for everybody to climb up from living room

Elder sisters skylight to climb up from the study room

Younger sisters skylight to climb up form children's room

Skylights to keep the entrance hall blight.

Roof House

Kanagawa, Japan, completed 2001

The clients wanted to be able to climb up on to the roof of their house – a child's dream. The house, over 30 years old, had a normal sloping roof, but during the architects' first visit the clients insisted on showing them – through a tiny window – a flat roof of six square metres which they had taken to using in the summer for alfresco meals. Obviously, then, they wanted a design that would enable them to take their family meals in comfort on top of their house. For this to happen, the roof would need to be able to hold a kitchen, a table and benches. As the climate in this region is very hot in summer and cold in winter, the clients also wanted not only an outdoor shower, but also a stove. In the end, the plan incorporated a self-supporting, concrete wall as a shelter against the wind and as a means of directing the eye towards the valley. The gentle slope of the roof – to allow drainage – is precisely the same as that of the original terrain (10%), and it also allows people to stretch out comfortably. It is covered with a floor of wooden boards and is high enough to give an uninterrupted view over the trees towards Mount Kobo. The supporting structure below consists of wooden columns, and the partitions are sliding wooden panels to allow the family a combination of private and communal life. This large space can easily be crossed in order to climb up on the roof: there are several skylights which fulfil various functions: some serve to let in the light, above the hall and in the bathroom, while others allow each family member to climb up independently, as there is a skylight in each individual room with a ladder and an exterior light. ☒

Photo: Katsuhisa Kida

STEFAN TISCHER

Germany

Stefan Tischer [1965]

After studying in Munich and ENSP Versailles, Stefan Tischer founded his architecture and landscaping studio in 1992 in Munich and in 1995 in Berlin, where he worked in association with Susanne Burger until 2000. He collaborates from time to time also with fellow architects and landscape designers Maria Ippolita Nicotera, Francesca Venier and Paola Cannavo, of the Berlin agency Studio.eu. Winner of several international competitions (Kaisaniemi Park, Helsinki, 2000 [with S. Burger and F. Venier]; Ostee competition, Cottbus, 2001 [with Calderan+Cuzzolin]; Future Project, Basel, 2001 [with Calderan+Cuzzolin]), Stefan Tischer has already seen many of his designs brought to fruition, such as the Memorial at Ravensbrück concentration camp (Germany, 2001, with P. Oswalt) or the new gardens for the post-Palladian Villa Rinaldi in Asolo (2001). He has taught in many schools and universities in Italy, Germany, France, USA, Canada, Morocco and India and is currently professor at IUAV in Venice. Tischer is also directing a study on the city of Naples in the Urban-Catalyst research programme of the European Community (Technical University, Berlin). He co-founded *Topos*, the European landscape magazine. ☑

Territorial thinking

The discussion about the city and its periphery has been uppermost in the work of landscape designers in the last decade. The most important question was the research of new concepts and the development of new designs for urban space. In the process a fundamental value has been almost forgotten or, worse, left in the hands of administrators and planners: the territory itself. Today at the centre of our thinking, we conceive it as the very field of the landscapes of tomorrow, with their infrastructures, recreational spaces, green spaces and even, in a way, their poetry. More, we conceive it as a possible model for the development of urban areas through the expedient of understanding, interpretation and then the transformation of the rules of landscaping. The first step consists of understanding the countryside in a new way, getting rid of the distorting lenses through which we have viewed 'the history of gardens' and at the same time the 'eco-romantic-new-age' point of view. Then we have to find a pragmatic procedure for producing things and becoming players ourselves. It is not enough merely to react to given situations or to deal with left-over fragments or to drift off into virtual fantasies. It is a question of placing landscaping practice once more at the heart of contemporary territories. Our studio has therefore adopted the slightly risky approach of 'do first and think afterwards'. Actually, doing sometimes allows you to understand why and how to think. Our work in the last few years has homed in on three types of research: 'concepts' of transforming the landscape, 'strategies' for landscape-urbanism and hybrid architecture/landscape 'projects'. The first area is based on thinking about post-industrial territories. The old coal-mines of Böhlen-Bitterfeld or the old tuff quarries in Lecce are considered as cultural landscapes and as possible sites for projects that are permanent in terms of habitation, production and economic development. The second type of research proposes experimental articulation between ideas on modes of urbanization, on the one hand, and, on the other, the knowledge, models and strategies within the field of landscaping: the development of an 'urban forest' to reconstruct a suburban district on the northern edge of Milan, a proposal for an 'agro-city' in Bolzano as an alternative means of urbanization of an agricultural landscape. The third branch of our research concerns projects whose mixed nature prevents them from being classed definitely as urban, as architecture or as landscape: a 'green' façade for a building in the university of Berlin, an asphalt landscape for the city of Leuna. ☑

Stefan Tischer

▶ 'Concepts' for Transforming the Landscape

Taking on damaged landscapes like former coal-mines to the south of Leipzig and former tuff quarries in southern Italy, Stefan Tischer tries to look at these through new eyes. Seeking the solution within the problem itself, he wishes to see if the history of economic exploitation of a landscape to the point of complete transformation could be a starting-point for its future development. Programmes normally tend towards a re-naturalization of these areas; for the most part this approach completely neglects, even denies, the economic and cultural history of these sites. Eschewing nostalgia or any kind of documentation that aestheticizes the landscape, he attempts to reinvest in its own cultural specificities, in its anthropological richness. From this basis he proposes to weave new ways of living and working. Another important aspect of Stefan Tischer's research on the transformation of landscapes has to do with agriculture. A new kind of agriculture is developing, according to him, that is sustainable and connected to the chemical or energy industry. Potentially capable of replacing the petrochemical sector, this new agriculture is full of promise, not only in post-industrial areas but also in rural zones. Today devoted exclusively to food production, these sites will thus undergo a profound change both physically and visually. These ideas on the transformation of European agriculture are at the heart of projects that Stefan Tischer has developed for exhibitions in Potsdam 2001 and Rostock 2003. Places of experimentation, these temporary gardens also offer a rare glimpse into the landscape that such new economic exploitations of the land might create.

▶▶

Lecce
Lecce, Italy, project
Reflections on the possible temporary uses of the old tuff quarries that dot the landscape of Lecce in the Naples region.

Credits: Stefan Tischer with Studio.eu (Berlin), Studio Torsello and Roberto Masiero (Venice)

South Leipzig
Böhlen–Lippendorf, Germany, competition, 1995
Transformation of an old coal-mining area into an industrial park.
Credits: Stefan Tischer with cet-0 (Berlin)

BUGA 2001
Potsdam, Germany, completed 2001
General concept for the 2001 edition of the Potsdam garden exhibition, on the theme of 'sustainable resources'.
Credits: Stefan Tischer with Susanne Burger (Munich); collaborators: Joerg Coqui, Steffen Lux

IGA 2003
Rostock, Germany, project, 2002
General concept for a garden exhibition at Rostock on the theme of 'concept for sustainable resources'.
Credits: Stefan Tischer with Studio.eu (Berlin); collaborator: Max Manhas

'Strategies' for Landscape-Urbanism

For former industrial areas and for growing cities, Stefan Tischer studied, in inter-disciplinary teams, the development of schemes and scenarios as a step towards a new possible master plan based not on urbanistic leitmotifs but on application of landscape data, for example forestry techniques, analysis of landscape unities and their transformation into rules for urban growth. An example of these strategy projects for landscape-urbanism is the 'Bosco Urbano', a sort of civilized and colo-nized forest, whose countrified aspect gives structure to the nevertheless suburban identity of this suburb on the outskirts of Milan and whose 'green' char-acter modifies the many urban functions that pass through it. In the same vein, the 'Bolzano Habitat-01' project proposes an 'agro-city', which combines housing unites and genuine agricultural functions. The shapes of this town are not urban but are modelled on agricultural land units: wheat fields, orchards.▶▶

Sesto San Giovanni Urban Park
Milan, Italy, competition, 1998
Project for a new urban park on the site of the old Falck steelworks in northern Milan.
Credits: Stefan Tischer with Studio.eu (Berlin)

Bolzano Habitat-01
Bolzano, Italy, project, 2001
Scenario for the urban development of Bolzano, a small rural town in Italy, in the form of an 'agro-city' combining agriculture and urbanization.
Credits: Stefan Tischer with Metrogramma (Milan) and Helene Hoelzl (Amsterdam–Bolzano)

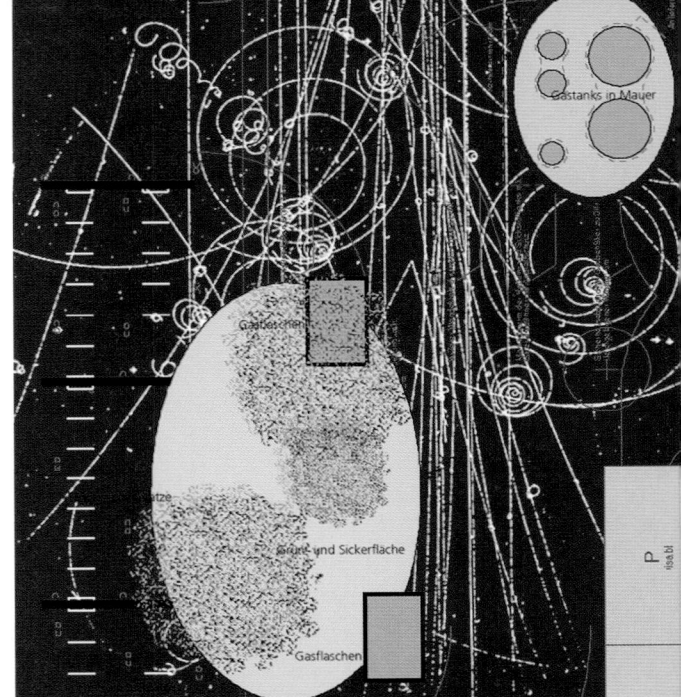

▶ Hybrid Architecture/Landscape 'Projects'

In these projects, which cover the whole gamut from architecture to territory, Stefan Tischer is always seeking delicate compromises, hybrid articulations, between 'country' and 'urban', 'mineral' and 'vegetable', 'permanent' and 'temporary'. This permanent commingling of elements can, in some ways, muddy the typological waters, but can also, according to him, open up rich opportunities: a square can take on the appearance of a park or the material of the street can become an organic landscape in the city, as in the Haupttorplatz project for Leuna (1999). On the architectonic level this hybridization can mean that a façade becomes 'green', like that of the physics faculty building at Humboldt University of Berlin. This greening of agriculture is not merely a matter of covering the building with conventional climbing plants, however, but of conceiving it as a place for cultivating a complex mix of plants, irrigated by an industrial system copied from those used in agriculture, and, finally, of making the built and architectonic part of the building's morphology totally disappear. ▶▶

Physics Faculty, Humboldt University

Berlin, Germany, completed 2000
Landscape concept for the physics faculty, specifically a vertical garden on the façade of the building.
Credits: Stefan Tischer with Augustin + Frank (Berlin); collaborators: Joerg Coqui, Ippolita Nicotera

Pavilions, BUGA 2001

Potsdam, Germany, completed, 2001
Concept for thematic pavilions for the garden exhibition at Potsdam 2001.
Credits: Stefan Tischer with Duncan Lewis (Berlin–Paris); collaborator: Matthias Rottmann

Haupttorplatz
Leuna, Germany, project, 1999
Asphalt landscape in a city, a hybrid garden-city and industrial zone.
Credits: Stefan Tischer with Studio.eu

ARCHITECT BIBLIOGRAPHIES

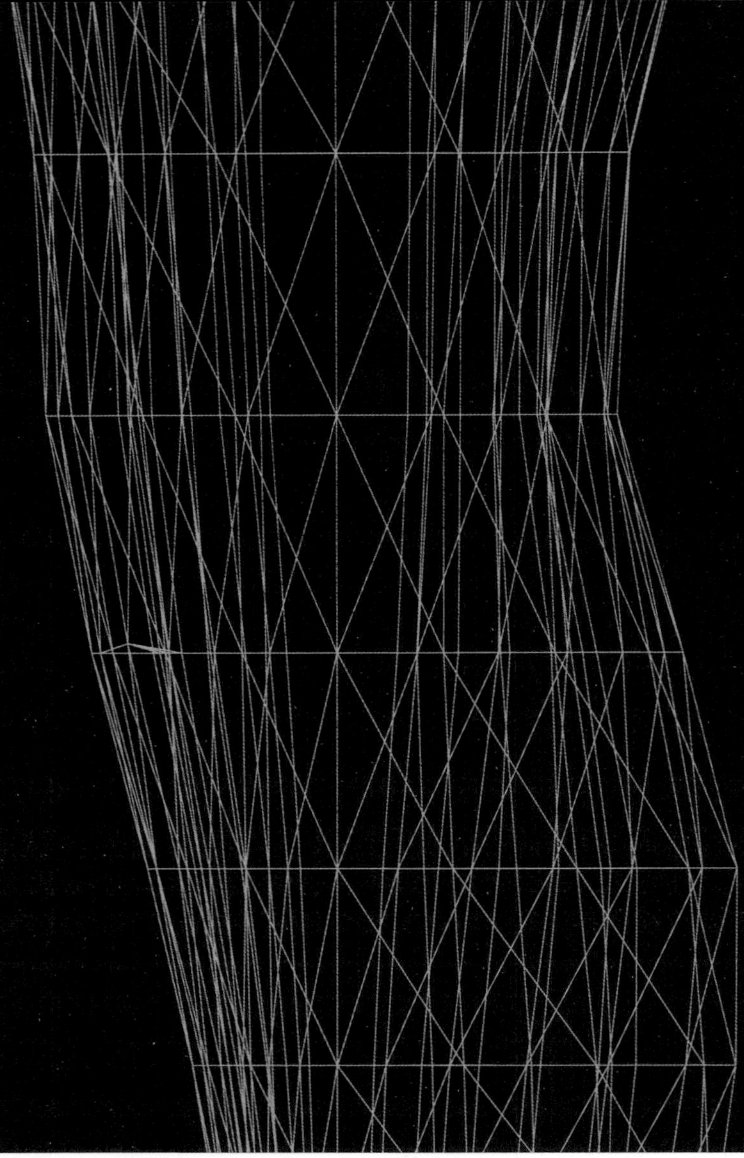

Actar arquitectura

2001 *Barcelona +*, Barcelona, Actar
2000 *10 x 10*, London, Phaidon
2000 *Parasite*, catalogue, Rotterdam,
Parasite Foundation
2000 *Venice Biennale*, catalogue, Actar
2000 *Repensar la ciudad*, catalogue, Centre d'Art
Contemporani, comunitat Valenciana
2000 *Metapolis 02 for Advanced City*, Barcelona,
Actar
1999 *Single Housing*, Barcelona, Actar /
Berlin, Birkhäuser
1999 *IN/EX*, Paris, Inex / Berlin, Birkhauser
1997 *Housing: New Alternatives,
New Systems*, Barcelona, Actar / Berlin, Birkhäuser.

www.actar.es

Agence Manuelle Gautrand Architects

2002 'Interview de Manuelle Gautrand',
in *Dernières Tendances*, Autrement
2002 'Expressions: Manuelle Gautrand', *Parpaing*,
no. 30
2001 *Temps dense 2*, de l'Imprimeur, Paris
2000 'Sans doute? Cent architectes parlent de doc-
trine', *Les Cahiers de la Recherche Architecturale et
Urbaine*, no. 5/6
2000 *40 Architects under 40 Years*, Taschen
1999 *Jeunes architectes français*, Birkhäuser
1998 'Quatre français: Manuelle Gautrand', *Architecture d'Aujourd'hui*, no. 318

www.manuelle-gautrand.com

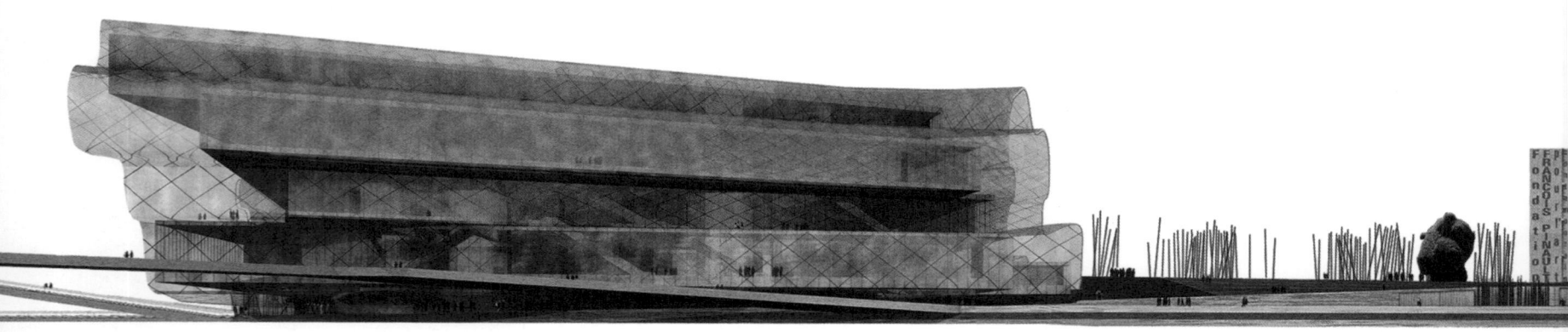

Agence Francis Soler

2001 *AMC*, nos 118 and 120
2001 *Architecture d'Aujourd'hui*, no. 335
1995 Odile Fillon, *Les anges de Christian Brygge et autres récits d'architecture, Francis Soler*, Paris, Jean Michel Place/IFA
1995 *Francis Soler*, Berlin, Aedes
1995 *Francis Soler: Centro per le Conferenze Internazionali a Parigi*, Milan, BE-MA
1994 *Christian Hauvette, Francis Soler*, Paris, IFA
1993 *Archimade*, no. 40
1993 *Francis Soler*, Paris, Pavillon de l'Arsenal
1991 'Francis Soler, la valeur du sens', *Techniques et Architecture*, no. 398
1990 Wojciech Lesnikowski, *The New French Architecture*, NY, Rizzoli, pp. 180–193
1988 Francis Soler, *Décalages ou l'école Pelleport, Paris XX*, Paris, Demi Cercle

www.soler.fr

Atelier Bow-wow

2002 Atelier Bow-wow, *Broken Paris*, Batofar
2001 Atelier Bow-wow, *Les Plus Petites Maisons*, Institut Français d'Architecture
2001 Tokyo Institute of Technology & Atelier Bow-wow, *Pet Architecture Guidebook*, World Photo Press
2001 Momoyo Kajima, Junzo Kuroda, Yoshiharu Tsukamoto, *Made in Tokyo*, Kajima Institute Publishing
2000 Atelier Bow-wow, 'Tokyo Recycle Projects', in *10+1*, no. 21, INAX Publishing
1999 Atelier Bow-wow, 'Tokyo Guide Book', *Architecture Magazine*, vol. 114, no. 1441, July
1998 *Atelier Bow-wow Recent Works*, Kajima Institute Publishing
1997 Atelier Bow-wow, 'Made in Hong Kong' in *Space Design*, Kajima Institute Publishing, July
1997 Atelier Bow-wow, 'The shape of cities in the future', in *Intercommunications*, vol. 20, NTT Publishing, April

Arno Brandlhuber/Bernd Kniess (b&k+)

2001 *Sous les ponts*, catalogue for exhibition of contemporary art, Luxembourg
2001 *Metazoon*, music CD, Christopher Dell, 12 pieces to New Loft am Kölner Brett
2001 *Mut zur Lücke,* in the 'Passagen' framework, Cologne
2000 'Ideenmatrix, elektronische Lebensaspekte', in *de: bug*, July
2000 *Junge Architekten in Deutschland*, Birkhäuser, April
2000 'Telematic Landscape', in *Verb*, Architecture Boogazine, March
2000 b&k+, *Political Landscape*, Bergische Universität GH Wuppertal
1999 b&k+, *In Vitro Landscape*, Weißenhof, with CD, December
1998 *Speculation*, exhibition publication for Galerie Specta

www.bk-plus.de

Berlage Institute

2001 '3D City, Multiplying Urban Capacities', *Hunch*, no. 3, pp. 94–131
1999 MVRDV, *MetaCITY / DATATOWN*, Rotterdam, 010 Publishers
1999 MVRDV, *Datascape*, Rotterdam, 010 Publishers
1998 MVRDV, *FARMAX, excursions on Density*, Rotterdam, 010 Publishers
1997 *El Croquis*, no. 86

www.mvrdv.archined.nl
www.berlage-institute.nl

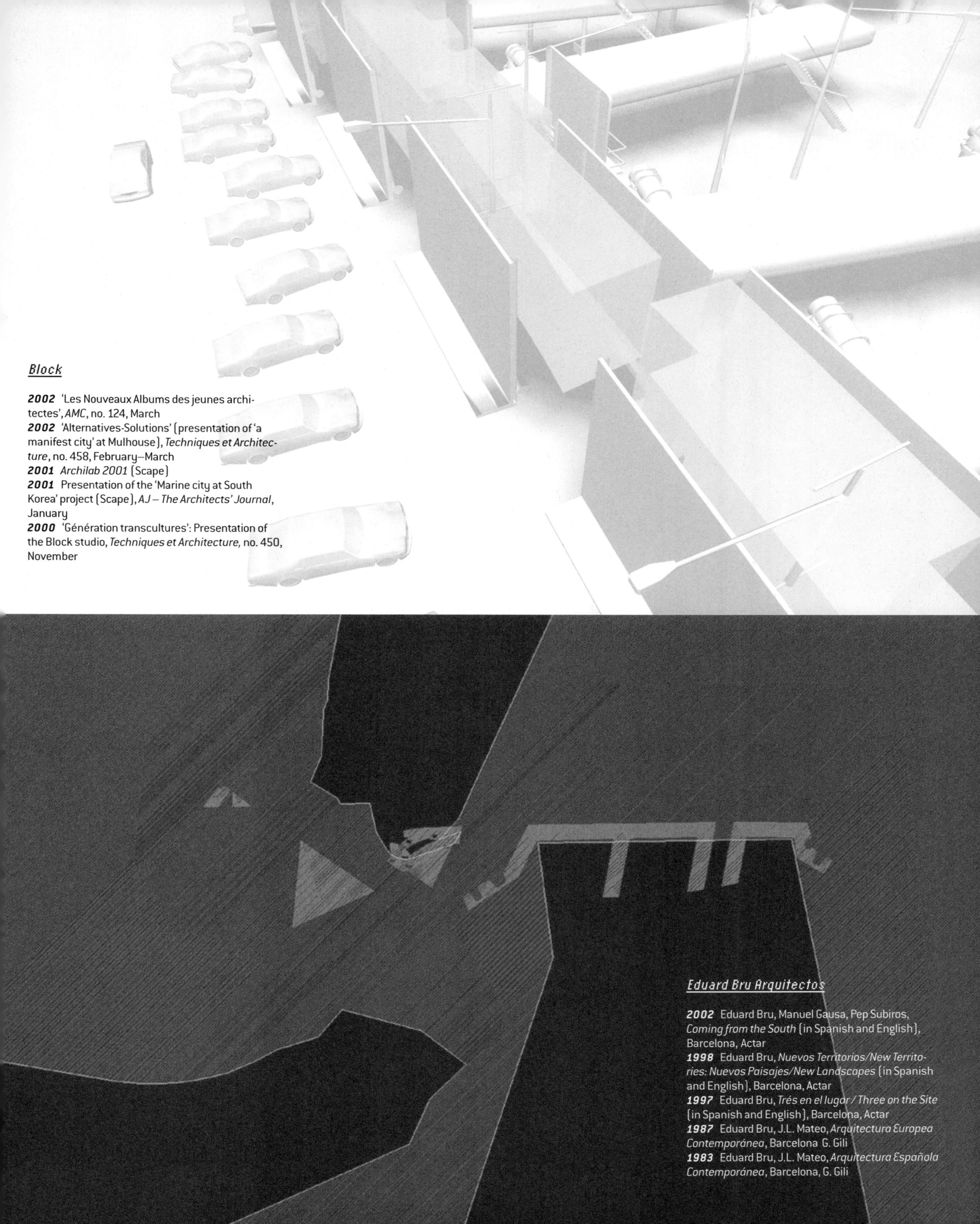

Block

2002 'Les Nouveaux Albums des jeunes architectes', *AMC*, no. 124, March
2002 'Alternatives-Solutions' (presentation of 'a manifest city' at Mulhouse), *Techniques et Architecture*, no. 458, February–March
2001 *Archilab 2001* (Scape)
2001 Presentation of the 'Marine city at South Korea' project (Scape), *AJ – The Architects' Journal*, January
2000 'Génération transcultures': Presentation of the Block studio, *Techniques et Architecture,* no. 450, November

Eduard Bru Arquitectos

2002 Eduard Bru, Manuel Gausa, Pep Subiros, *Coming from the South* (in Spanish and English), Barcelona, Actar
1998 Eduard Bru, *Nuevos Territorios/New Territories: Nuevos Paisajes/New Landscapes* (in Spanish and English), Barcelona, Actar
1997 Eduard Bru, *Trés en el lugar / Three on the Site* (in Spanish and English), Barcelona, Actar
1987 Eduard Bru, J.L. Mateo, *Arquitectura Europea Contemporánea*, Barcelona G. Gili
1983 Eduard Bru, J.L. Mateo, *Arquitectura Española Contemporánea*, Barcelona, G. Gili

Chora

2002 *Public Spaces*, London, Black Dog Publishing
2001 Chora (Raoul Bunschoten, Takuro Hoshino, Hélène Binet), *Urban Flotsam: Stirring the City*, Rotterdam, 010 Publishers
2001 'Chora I Den Moderne By', *Arkitekten*, no. 30, December
2001 Sylvain Besson, 'Réinventer la ville', *Le Temps* (Berne)
2001 'Der stadt unter die Haut Schauen', *Tagesanzeiger* (Zurich)
2001 'Capter les émotions de la ville', *Le Temps Stratégique* (Geneva)
1999 Chora, *Stirring the City*, Aarhus
1999 Chora, *Curating London Sector A*, London
1999 'Urban Curation', *Daidalos*, June
1998 Chora, *Metaspaces*, book and CD-Rom

www.chora.org.uk
www.chora.demon.co.uk
www.urbangallery.org

Cloud 9

2001 *La ciutat dels cineastes*, exhibition catalogue, Diputació de Barcelona
2000 'Qu'est-ce que la beauté ?', *Beaux Arts*, special summer issue
2000 *Art Press*, no. 258, June
2000 Yago Conde, *Arquitectura de la indeterminación*, Actar, February
2000 *Metapolis*, Actar
2000 'Flashes-destellos, tiempo fugaz, tiempo precario—fleeting time, precarious time', *Quaderns d'Arquitectura i Urbanisme*, no. 227
2000 *10x10*, Phaidon
1999 *Topos*, Callwey Verlag / Frau Dietrich, December
1999 *A+U*, A+U Publishing Co., no. 349
1999 *Space Design*, Kajima Institute Publishing Co., August

www.e-cloud9.com

Field Operations

2000 Stan Allen, *Practice: Architecture, Technique and Representation*, G&B Arts

1999 James Corner, *Recovering Landscape: Essays in Contemporary Landscape Architecture*, Princeton Architectural Press

1999 Stan Allen, *Points and Lines: Diagram and Projects for the City*, Princeton Architectural Press

1999 Denis Cosgrove, *Mappings*, Reaktion

1996 James Corner, Alex McLean, *Taking Measures Across the American Landscape*, Yale

1996 George Thompson, Frederick Steiner (eds), *Ecological Design and Planning*, Wiley

www.fieldoperations.net

Vicente Guallart

2000 Vicente Guallart, *Medias, Mountains and architecture*, Barcelona, Actar

1999 Vicente Guallart, *Singular Housing*, Basel, Birkhäuser / Barcelona, Actar

1998 *Housing: New Alternatives, New Systems*, Barcelona, Actar

1998 *Fabrications*, exhibition catalogue, MACBA, Barcelona, Actar

1998 *Quaderns d'Arquitectura i Urbanisme*, no. 220, pp. 118–121

1998 *Werk*, Bauen+Wohnen, no. 6, pp. 30–35

1997 *36 modèles pour une maison*, Paris,

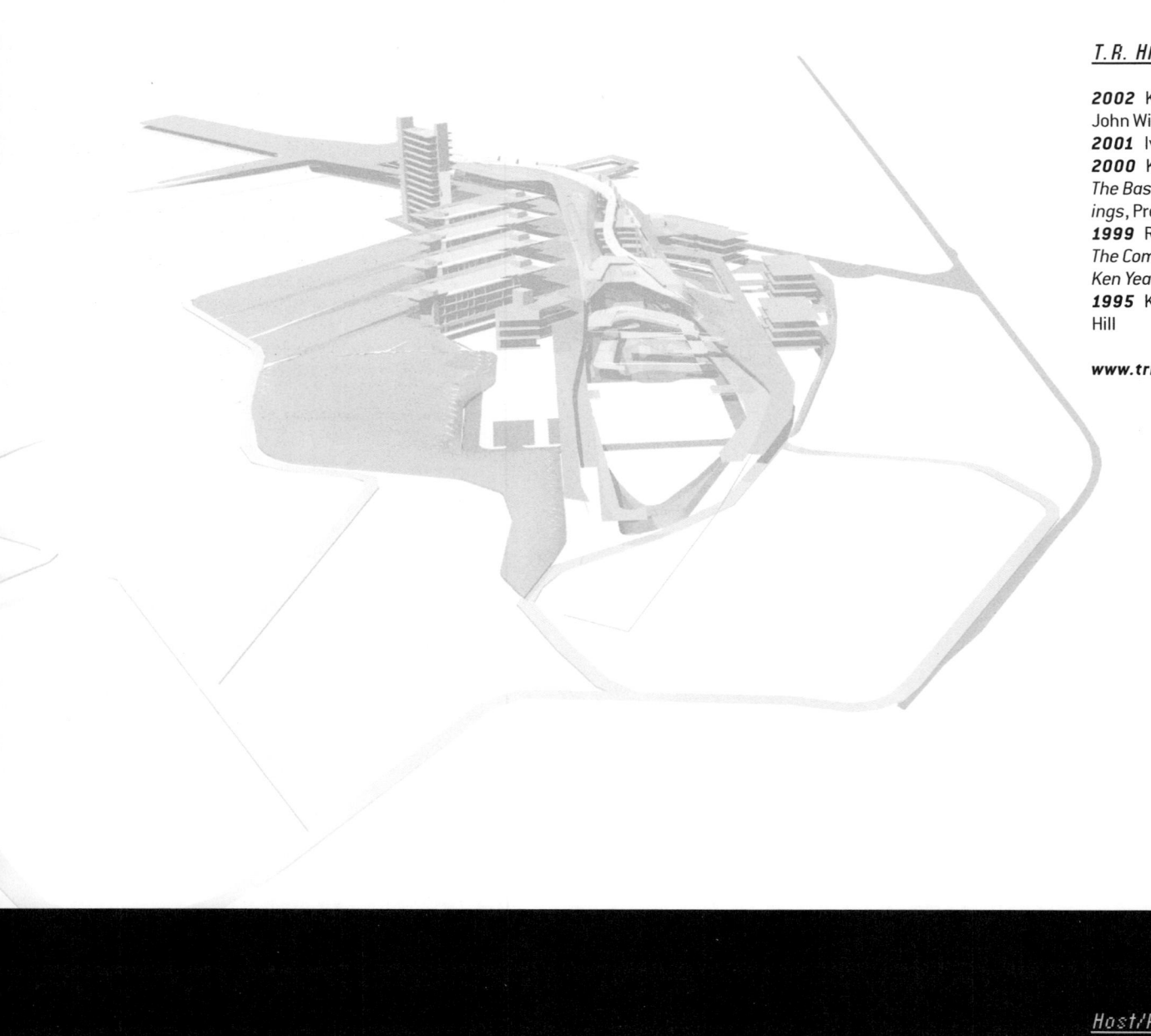

T. R. HAMZAH & YEANG SDN BHD

2002 Ken Yeang, *A Vertical Theory of Urban Design*, John Wiley & Sons
2001 Ivor Richards, *The Ecology of the Sky*, Images
2000 Ken Yeang, *The Green Skyscraper: The Basis for Designing Sustainable Intensive Buildings*, Prestel Publisher
1999 Robert Powell, *Rethinking the Skyscrapers: The Complete Architecture of Ken Yeang*, Thames & Hudson
1995 Ken Yeang, *Designing with Nature*, McGraw-Hill

www.trhamzah-yeang.com

Host/R+P

2002 Alain Renk, *La ville complexe*, Paris, Jean-Michel Place/Stéphane Place
2002 Alain Renk, 'Nouvelles stratégies d'implantation', *Territoires*, June
2002 Alain Renk, 'Territoires', *Transversales, Sciences/Cultures*, June
2002 'Questions sur le design', *Intramuros*, no. 100
2001 'Objets-architecture', in *Encyclopédie du design 2001*, NY, MOMA
2001 'About Host', *Clam Magazine*, October
2001 'Chill out space', *ArchiCréé*, November
2000 'Les fabriques', in *Venice Biennale Catalogue*

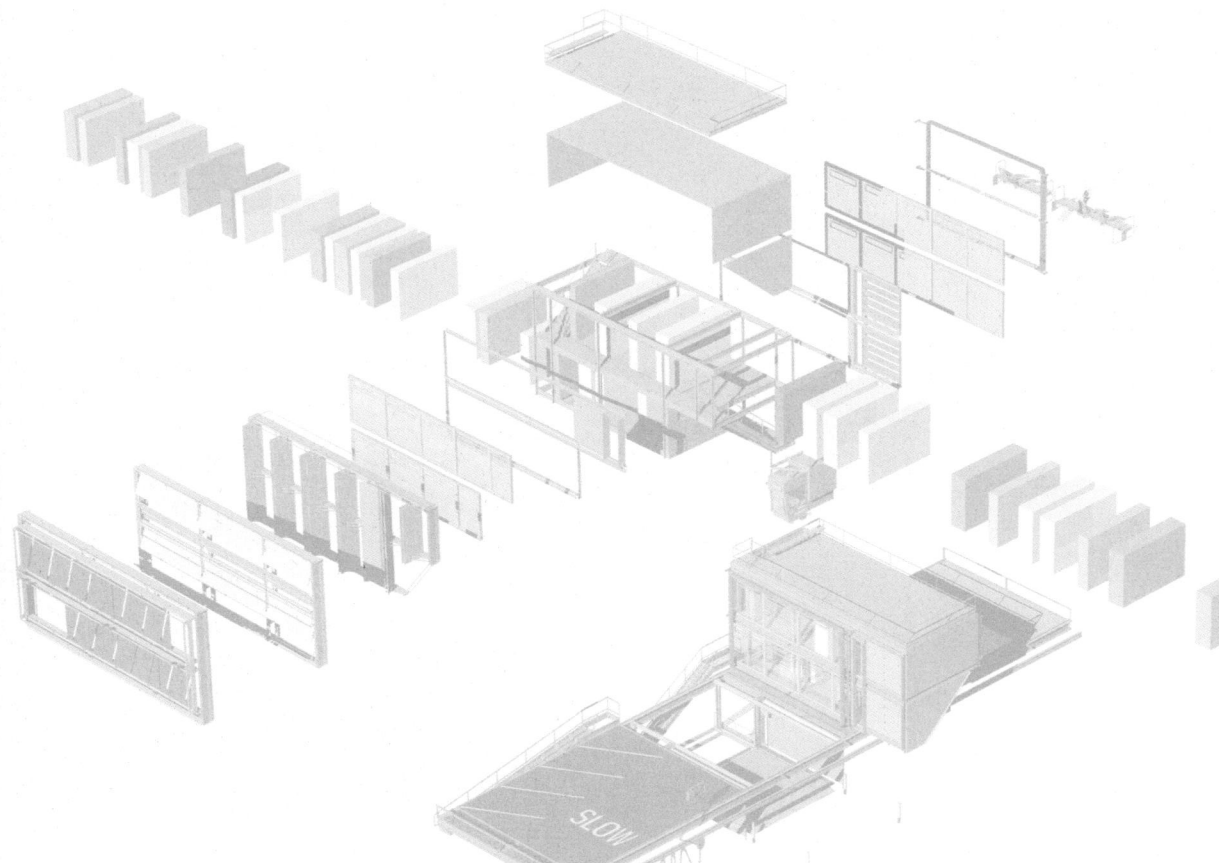

IaN+

2002 'New spaces for DADA', *l'ARCA*, no. 166, Rome, January
2001 Charles Batach, *IaN+. Spacing the 'Horizon'*, www.architettura.it, Web mag.
2001 *IaN+: Paesaggio abitato/Livingscape*, www.architettura.it, Web mag.
2000 IaN+, *Cinque studi: IaN+*, Rome, Librerie Dedalo
2000 *Il futuro e la città*, catalogue of the fifth International Festival of Architecture in Video, University of Florence, Faculty of Architecture
1999 IaN+, 'Digital Eisenman: An office of the electronic era' in *The Information Revolution in Architecture*, series by Antonino Saggio, Berlin, Birkhäuser
1999 'Made in Europe', *d'Architettura*, no. 4/20, Rome
1998 *Mies van der Rohe Foundation Competition*, catalogue, Barcelona, G. Gili

www.ianplus.it

Jones, Partners : Architecture

2001 'PRO/con', *Praxis*, no. 3
2001 'Jones, Partners: Architecture', *GA Houses*, no. 66
2001 'Stillness', *Oz*, vol. 23
2001 'A Home That's Ready to Rock and Roll', *New York Times*, 12 April
2001 Phyllis Richardson, *XS: Big Ideas, Small Buildings*, Thames & Hudson
2001 'After Architecture', *Oculus*, April
2000 Clare Melhuish, *Modern House 2*, Phaidon
2000 Jane Withers, *Modern Space*, Rockport
1999 Jaime Salazar, *Single Family Housing: The Private Domain*, Birkhäuser/Actar
1999 Elizabeth Smith, *Techno Architecture*, Thames & Hudson
1997 Wes Jones, *Instrumental Form*, Princeton Architectural Press
1995 Wes Jones, 'The Mech in Tecture', *ANY*, no. 10 (guest editor)

www.jonespartners.com

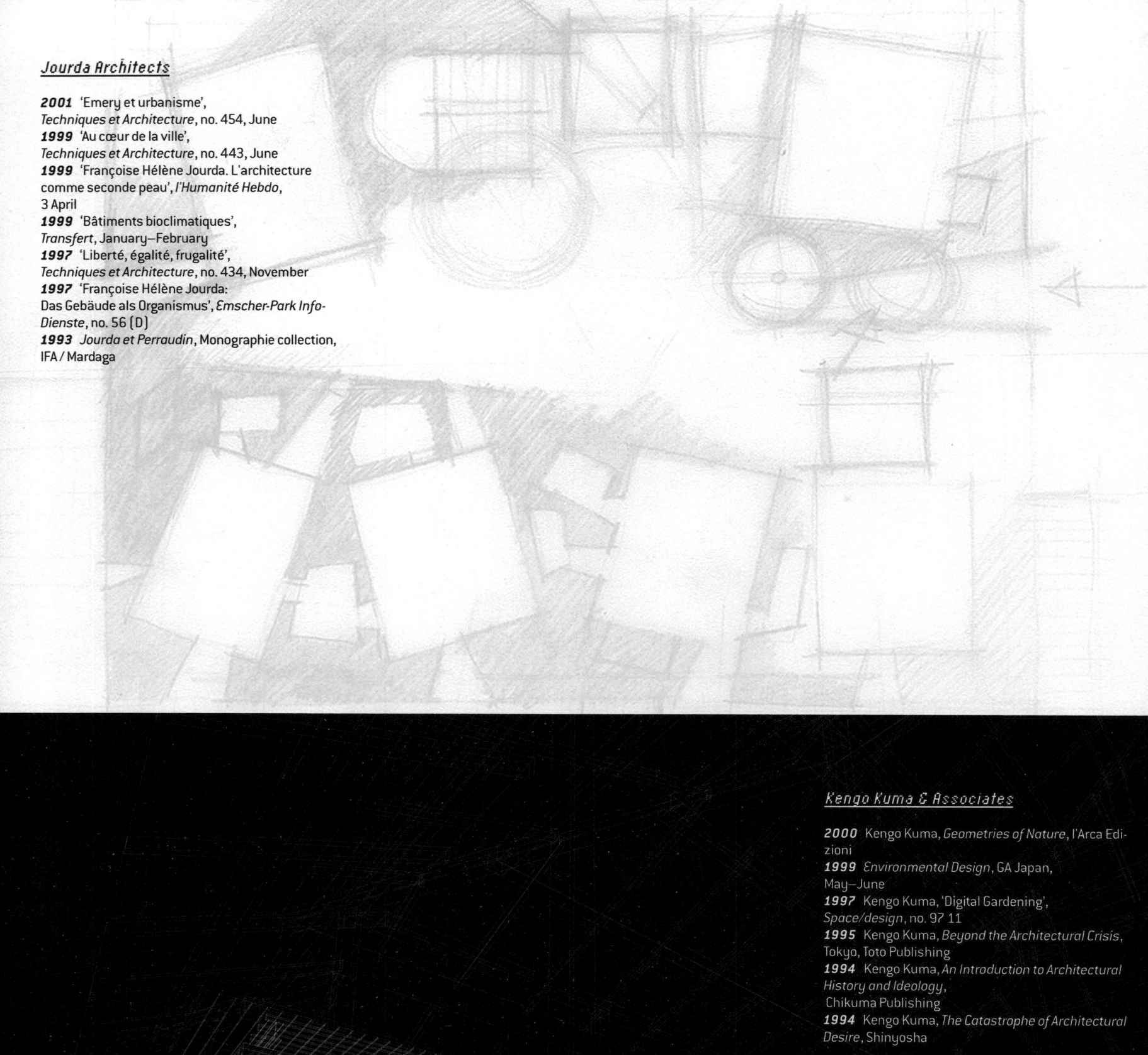

Jourda Architects

2001 'Emery et urbanisme',
Techniques et Architecture, no. 454, June
1999 'Au cœur de la ville',
Techniques et Architecture, no. 443, June
1999 'Françoise Hélène Jourda. L'architecture
comme seconde peau', *l'Humanité Hebdo*,
3 April
1999 'Bâtiments bioclimatiques',
Transfert, January–February
1997 'Liberté, égalité, frugalité',
Techniques et Architecture, no. 434, November
1997 'Françoise Hélène Jourda:
Das Gebäude als Organismus', *Emscher-Park Info-
Dienste*, no. 56 (D)
1993 *Jourda et Perraudin*, Monographie collection,
IFA / Mardaga

Kengo Kuma & Associates

2000 Kengo Kuma, *Geometries of Nature*, l'Arca Edizioni
1999 *Environmental Design*, GA Japan,
May–June
1997 Kengo Kuma, 'Digital Gardening',
Space/design, no. 97 11
1995 Kengo Kuma, *Beyond the Architectural Crisis*,
Tokyo, Toto Publishing
1994 Kengo Kuma, *An Introduction to Architectural
History and Ideology*,
Chikuma Publishing
1994 Kengo Kuma, *The Catastrophe of Architectural
Desire*, Shinyosha

www.02.so-net.ne.jp/ffkuma/

B;glass

anchiku Block

A;glass

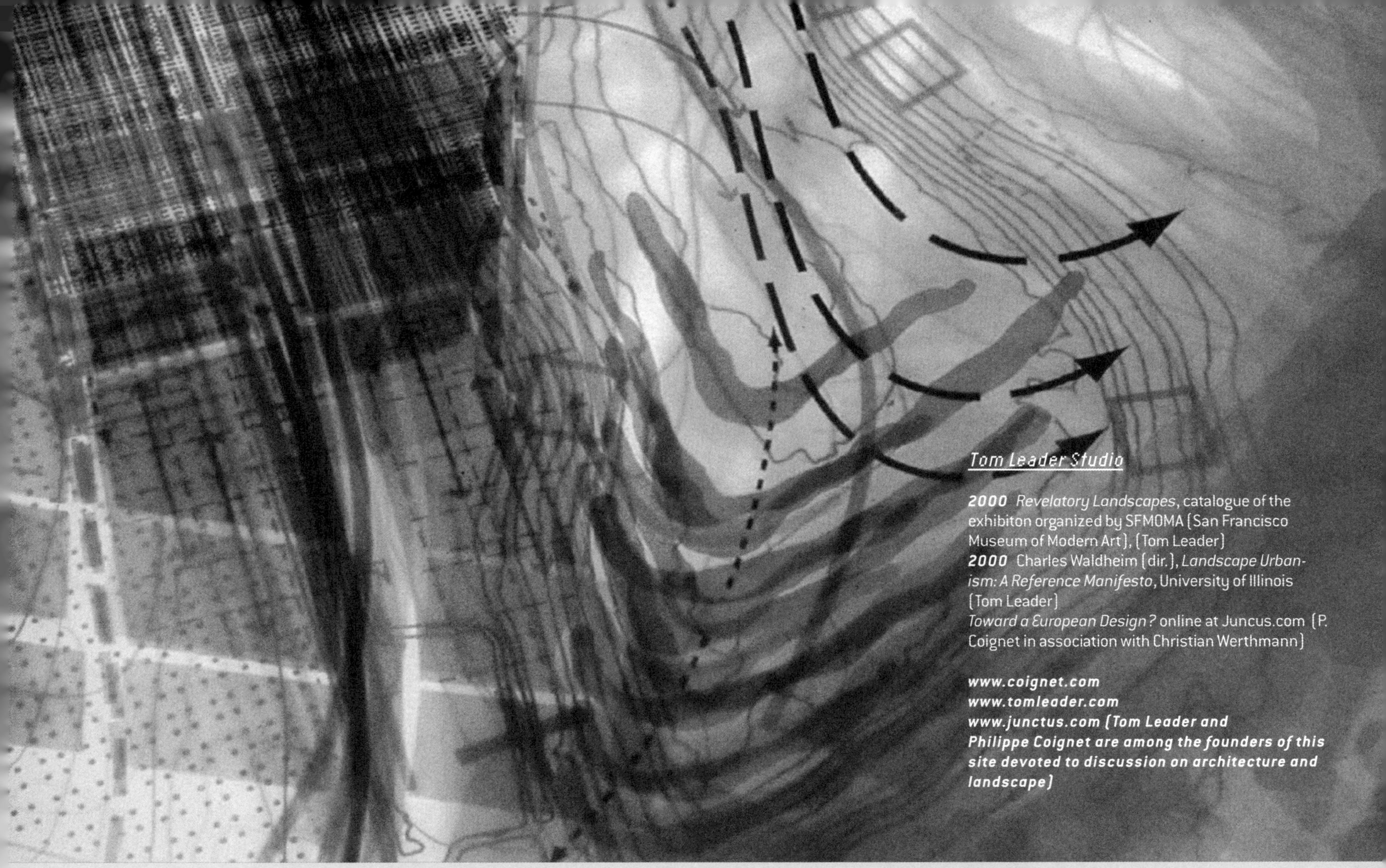

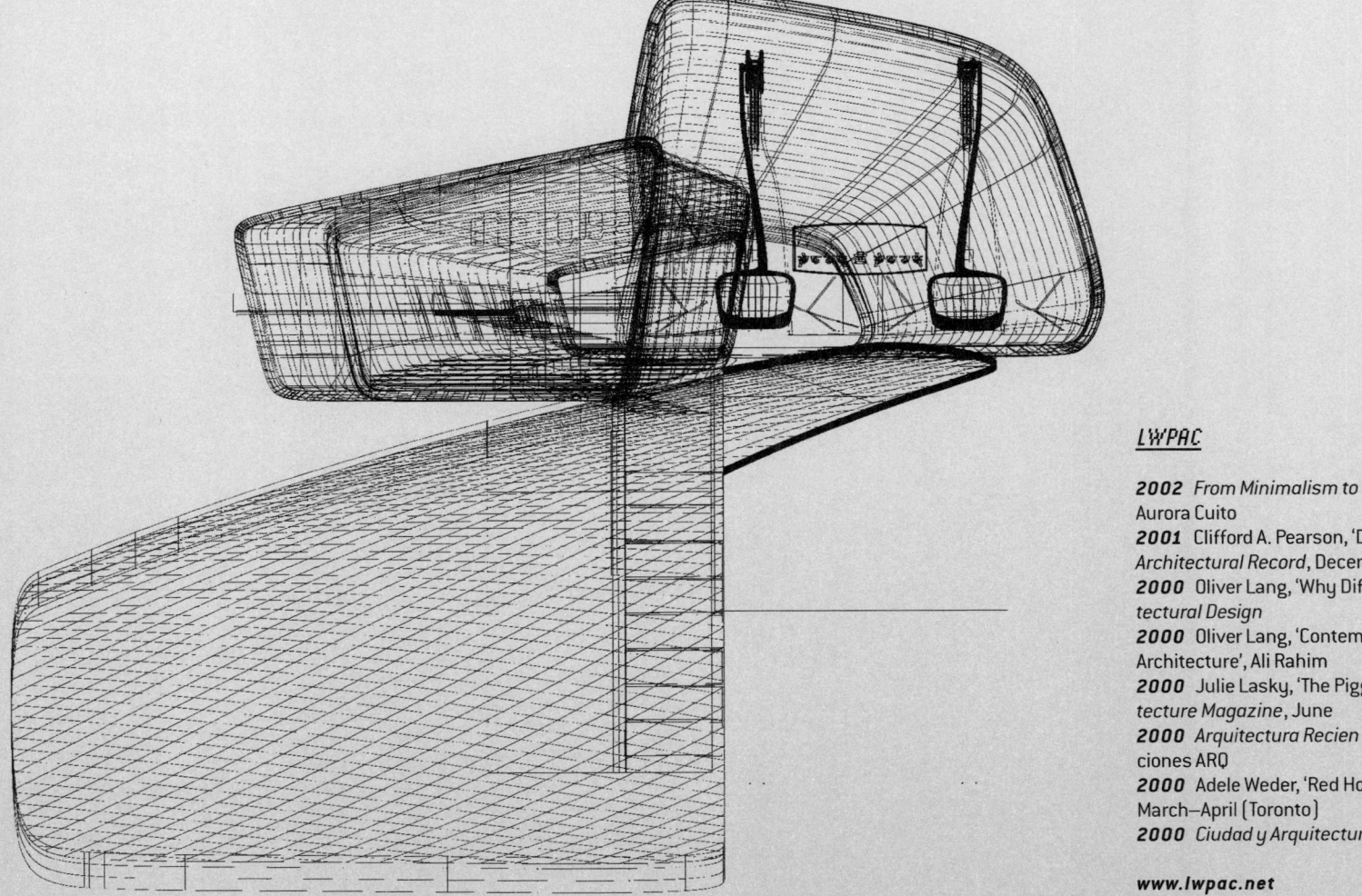

Tom Leader Studio

2000 *Revelatory Landscapes*, catalogue of the exhibiton organized by SFMOMA (San Francisco Museum of Modern Art), (Tom Leader)
2000 Charles Waldheim (dir.), *Landscape Urbanism: A Reference Manifesto*, University of Illinois (Tom Leader)
Toward a European Design? online at Juncus.com (P. Coignet in association with Christian Werthmann)

www.coignet.com
www.tomleader.com
www.junctus.com (Tom Leader and Philippe Coignet are among the founders of this site devoted to discussion on architecture and landscape)

LWPAC

2002 *From Minimalism to Maximalism*, Barcelona, Aurora Cuito
2001 Clifford A. Pearson, 'Design Vanguard 2001', *Architectural Record*, December
2000 Oliver Lang, 'Why Difference Matters', *Architectural Design*
2000 Oliver Lang, 'Contemporary Processes in Architecture', Ali Rahim
2000 Julie Lasky, 'The Piggyback Building', *Architecture Magazine*, June
2000 *Arquitectura Recien en Chile*, Santiago. Ediciones ARQ
2000 Adele Weder, 'Red Hot Chile', *Azure Magazine*, March–April (Toronto)
2000 *Ciudad y Arquitectura*, June

www.lwpac.net

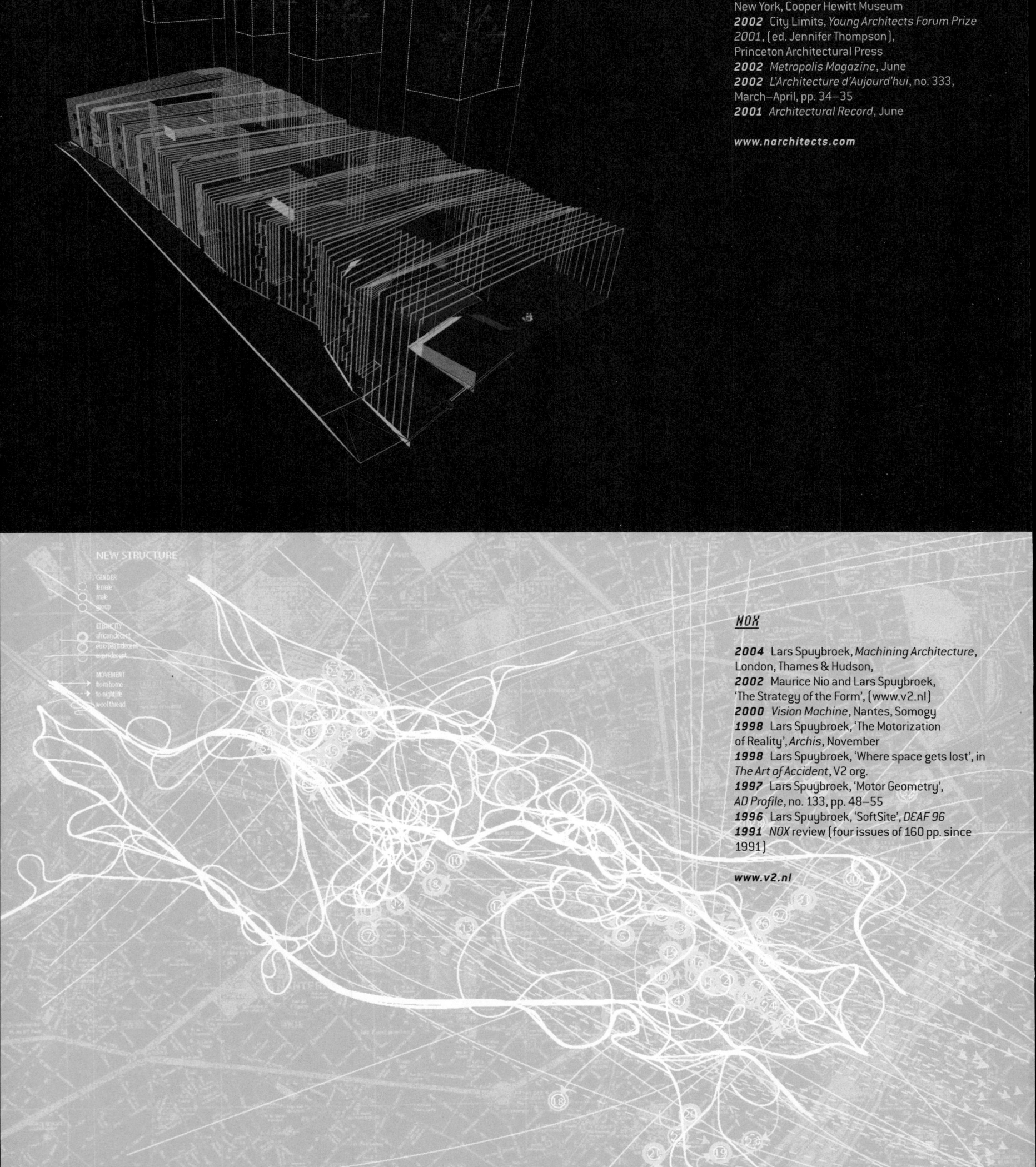

New York, Cooper Hewitt Museum
2002 City Limits, *Young Architects Forum Prize*
2001, (ed. Jennifer Thompson),
Princeton Architectural Press
2002 *Metropolis Magazine*, June
2002 *L'Architecture d'Aujourd'hui*, no. 333,
March–April, pp. 34–35
2001 *Architectural Record*, June

www.narchitects.com

NOX

2004 Lars Spuybroek, *Machining Architecture*,
London, Thames & Hudson,
2002 Maurice Nio and Lars Spuybroek,
'The Strategy of the Form', (www.v2.nl)
2000 *Vision Machine*, Nantes, Somogy
1998 Lars Spuybroek, 'The Motorization
of Reality', *Archis*, November
1998 Lars Spuybroek, 'Where space gets lost', in
The Art of Accident, V2 org.
1997 Lars Spuybroek, 'Motor Geometry',
AD Profile, no. 133, pp. 48–55
1996 Lars Spuybroek, 'SoftSite', *DEAF 96*
1991 *NOX* review (four issues of 160 pp. since
1991)

www.v2.nl

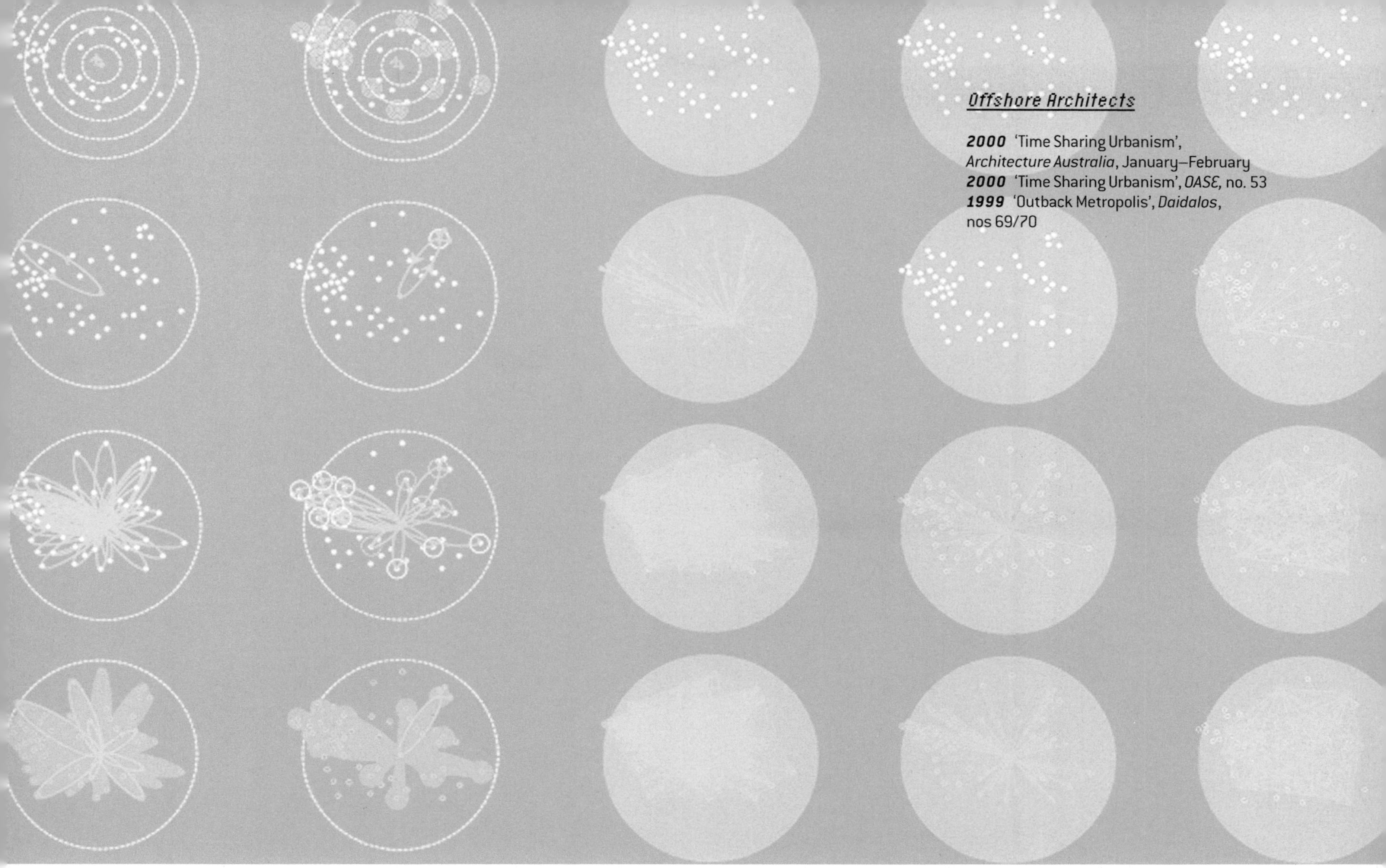

Offshore Architects

2000 'Time Sharing Urbanism',
Architecture Australia, January–February
2000 'Time Sharing Urbanism', *OASE*, no. 53
1999 'Outback Metropolis', *Daidalos*,
nos 69/70

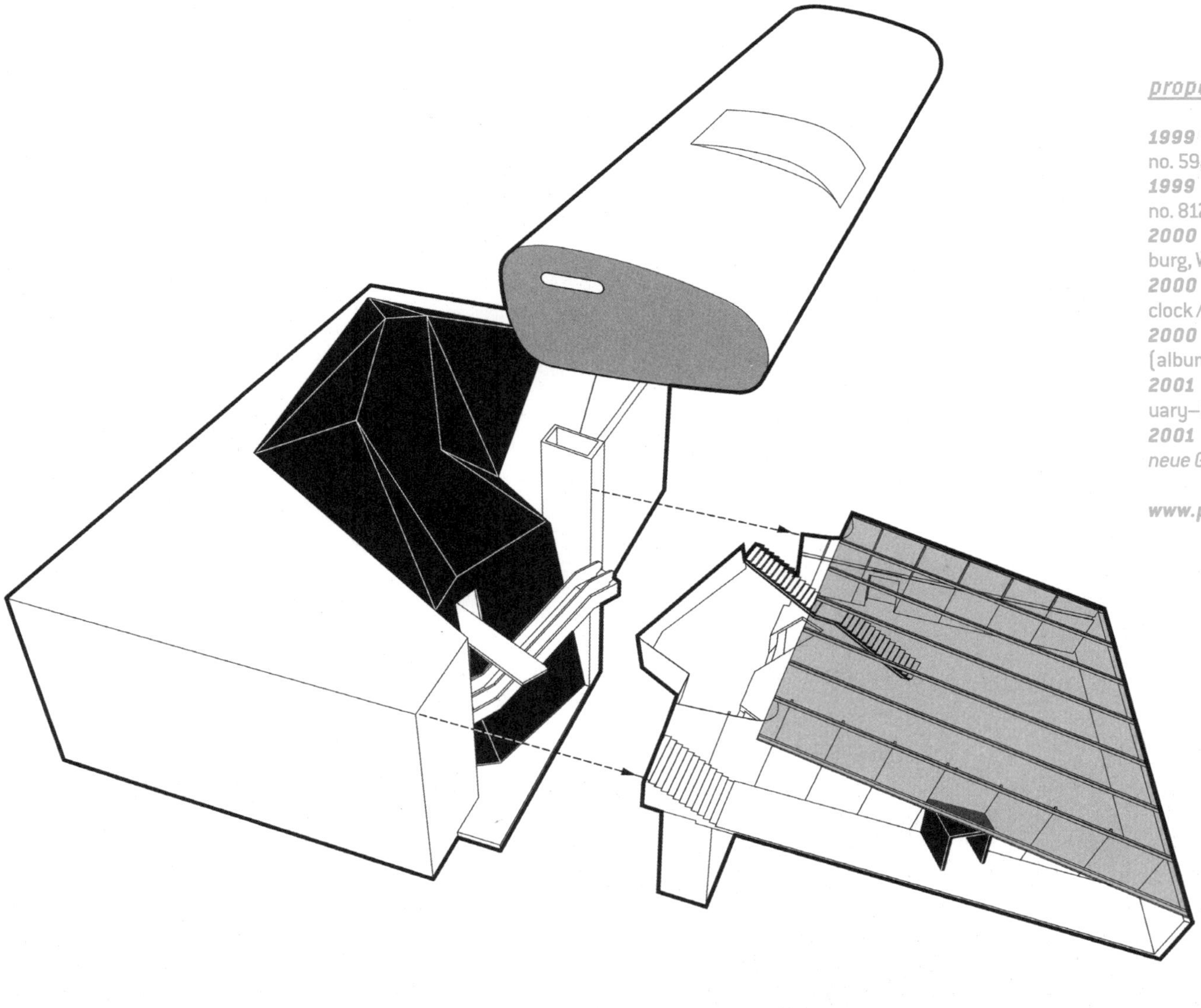

propeller z

1999 Michael Dodt, 'propeller z', *Groove Magazine*,
no. 59, August–September
1999 Christian Muhr, 'RWE Meteorit, Essen', *Domus*,
no. 812, February
2000 Egon Schirmbeck, *RAUMstationen*, Ludwigs-
burg, Wüstenrot Stiftung, pp. 166–7
2000 Patricia Grzonka, 'rock around the
clock / propeller z', *Profil*, April
2000 Ute Woltron, 'Turbodocs', *Der Standard*
(album), December
2001 propeller z, 'Turboprop', *arch+bauforum*, January–February
2001 Andrew Watts, *Moderne Baukonstruktion
neue Gebäude – neue techniken*, Vienna/NY, Springer

www.propellerz.at

RAD

1999 Aaron Tan, *Kowloon Walled City*
1998 *Cities on the move*, travelling exhibition, cf.
www.rama9art.org/citiesonthemove/
1998 'Contemporary Vernacular', *AA Asia*
1998 'The walled city: het domein van de uit-
gestotenen', *Archis* (PB), February
1997 *Lusitania* (USA) no. 7

Dagmer Richter Studio

2001 *X Y Z, The Architcture of Dagmar Richter*, NY,
Princeton Architectural Press
2000 'Strategies regarding the reorganization of the
area Bitterfield-Wolfen', in *Strategic Space: Urbanity
in the 21st Century*, Ulm, Anabas Verlag
1999 'Designs of the Next Millennium', *New York
Times Magazine*, December
1997 Dagmar Richter, 'Beyond Euclidean Geometry', *Newsline*, spring, Columbia University
1996 Dagmar Richter, 'Spazieren in Berlin', *Assemblage*, vol. 29
1996 'A Child Guest House', *Architecture d'Aujour-
d'hui*, no. 290
1992 Dagmar Richter, 'The Art of Copy: Rereading
the City', *Storefront*, December
1992 Dagmar Richter, 'The century city', *Architectural Design*

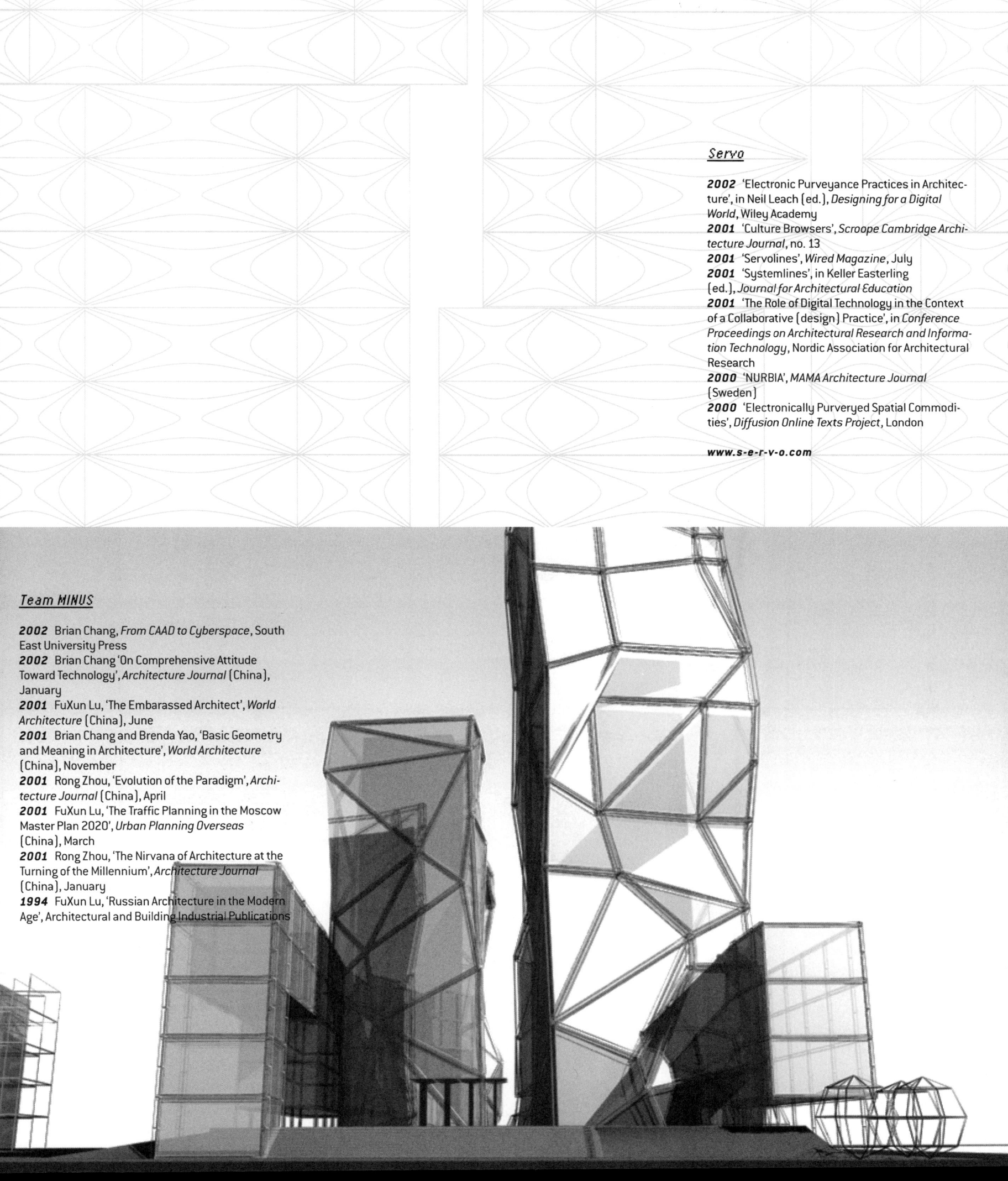

Servo

2002 'Electronic Purveyance Practices in Architecture', in Neil Leach (ed.), *Designing for a Digital World*, Wiley Academy
2001 'Culture Browsers', *Scroope Cambridge Architecture Journal*, no. 13
2001 'Servolines', *Wired Magazine*, July
2001 'Systemlines', in Keller Easterling (ed.), *Journal for Architectural Education*
2001 'The Role of Digital Technology in the Context of a Collaborative (design) Practice', in *Conference Proceedings on Architectural Research and Information Technology*, Nordic Association for Architectural Research
2000 'NURBIA', *MAMA Architecture Journal* (Sweden)
2000 'Electronically Purveryed Spatial Commodities', *Diffusion Online Texts Project*, London

www.s-e-r-v-o.com

Team MINUS

2002 Brian Chang, *From CAAD to Cyberspace*, South East University Press
2002 Brian Chang 'On Comprehensive Attitude Toward Technology', *Architecture Journal* (China), January
2001 FuXun Lu, 'The Embarassed Architect', *World Architecture* (China), June
2001 Brian Chang and Brenda Yao, 'Basic Geometry and Meaning in Architecture', *World Architecture* (China), November
2001 Rong Zhou, 'Evolution of the Paradigm', *Architecture Journal* (China), April
2001 FuXun Lu, 'The Traffic Planning in the Moscow Master Plan 2020', *Urban Planning Overseas* (China), March
2001 Rong Zhou, 'The Nirvana of Architecture at the Turning of the Millennium', *Architecture Journal* (China), January
1994 FuXun Lu, 'Russian Architecture in the Modern Age', Architectural and Building Industrial Publications

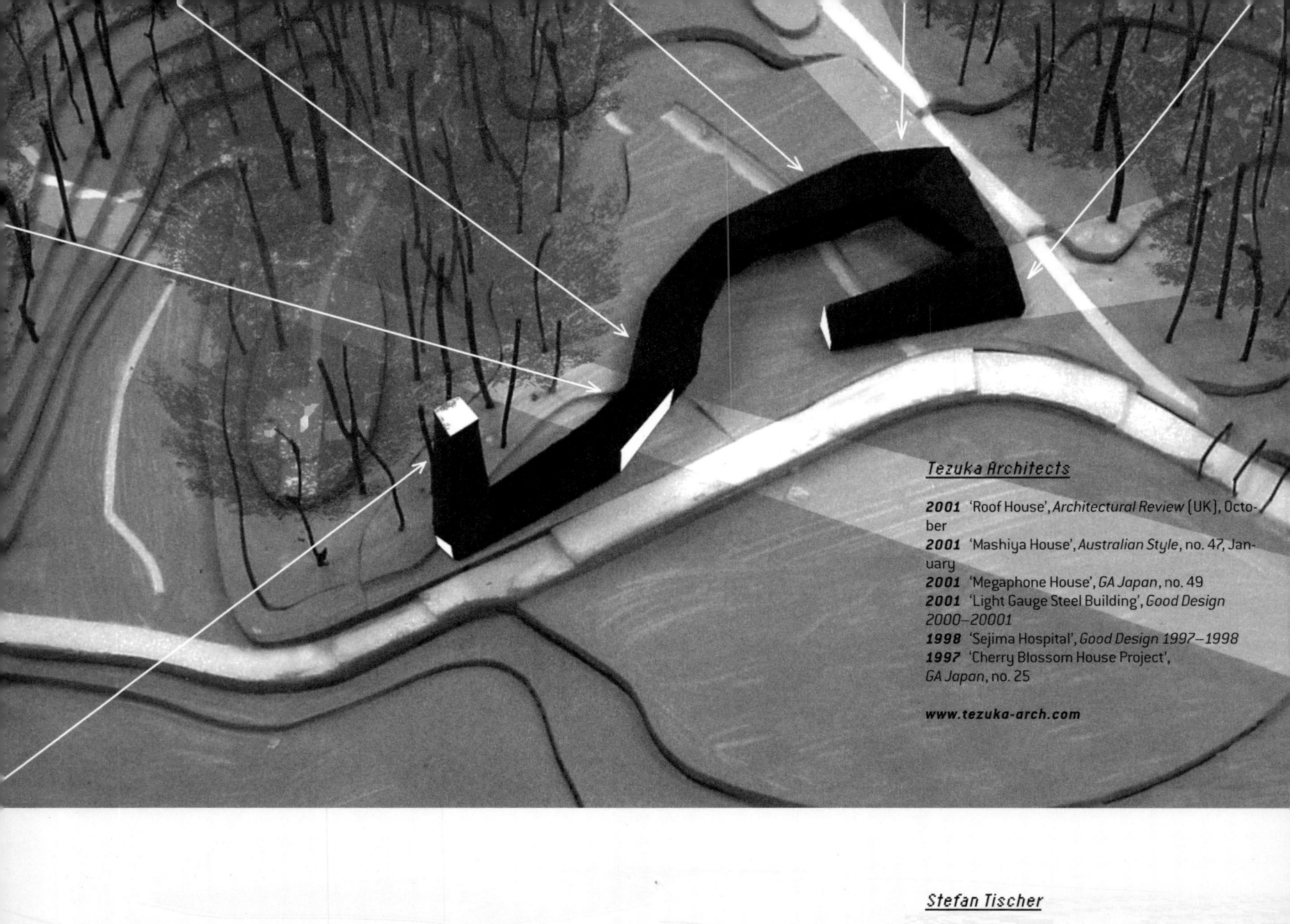

Tezuka Architects

2001 'Roof House', *Architectural Review* [UK], October
2001 'Mashiya House', *Australian Style*, no. 47, January
2001 'Megaphone House', *GA Japan*, no. 49
2001 'Light Gauge Steel Building', *Good Design 2000–20001*
1998 'Sejima Hospital', *Good Design 1997–1998*
1997 'Cherry Blossom House Project', *GA Japan*, no. 25

www.tezuka-arch.com

Stefan Tischer

2001 MetroGrammA, S. Tischer, H. Hoelzl, *4 Città, ipotesi di densificazione urbana a Bolzano*, Bolzano
2000 Stefan Tischer, 'Minimalism?', *Topos*, no. 33
2000 Stefan Tischer, 'CUMA 4000', *Garten+Landschaft*, January
2000 *Nuovas Paysages*, Barcelona, Actar
1999 Stefan Tischer, 'Napoli Omniferia', *Topos*, no. 28
1999 Stefan Tischer, 'Vivere a Berlin', *Piano Progetto Città*
1999 *Parchi-Parks*, Reggio Calabria
1998 Stefan Tischer, 'Paesaggio e luoghi', *20 per Lido*
1998 *Landschaftarchitektur II*, Wiesbaden
1997 *Neue Deutsche Landschaft*, Monaco
1997 Stefan Bernard and Philipp Sattler, *Vor der Tür – Aktuel Landschaftarchitektur aus Berlin*, Munich, Callwey Verlag
1996 Stefan Tischer, 'Wasserstadt Berlin', *Garten+Landschaft*, November
1996 Martin Linz, *Landschaftarchitektur offensiv-Positionen zur Stadt*, Berlin

www.stefantischer.net
www.juncus.com